MAGILL'S
LITERARY ANNUAL
1997

MAGILL'S LITERARY ANNUAL 1997

*Essay-Reviews of 200 Outstanding Books
Published in the United States during 1996*

With an Annotated Categories List

Volume One
A-L

Edited by
FRANK N. MAGILL

SALEM PRESS
Pasadena, California   Englewood Cliffs, New Jersey

∞ The paper used in these volumes conforms to the American National Standard for Permanence of Paper for Printed Library Materials, Z39.48_1984.

LIBRARY OF CONGRESS CATALOG CARD NO. 77-99209
ISBN 0-89356-297-1

FIRST PRINTING

PRINTED IN THE UNITED STATES OF AMERICA

PUBLISHER'S NOTE

Magill's Literary Annual, 1997, is the forty-second publication in a series that began in 1954. The philosophy behind the annual has been to evaluate critically each year a given number of major examples of serious literature published during the previous year. Our continuous effort is to provide coverage for works that are likely to be of more than passing general interest and that will stand up to the test of time. Individual critical articles for the first twenty-two years were collected and published in *Survey of Contemporary Literature* in 1977.

For the reader new to the Magill reference format, the following brief explanation should serve to facilitate the research process. The two hundred works represented in this year's annual are drawn from the following categories: fiction; poetry; literary criticism, literary history, and literary theory; essays; literary biography; autobiography, memoirs, diaries, and letters; biography; history; current affairs; science, history of science, and technology; economics; ethics and law; fine arts; media; nature, natural history, and the environment; philosophy and religion; psychology; sociology; travel; and women's issues. The articles are arranged alphabetically by book title in the two-volume set; a complete list of the titles included can be found at the beginning of volume 1. Following a list of titles are the titles arranged by category in an annotated listing. This list provides the reader with the title, author, page number, and a brief description of the particular work. The names of all contributing reviewers for the literary annual are listed alphabetically in the front of the book as well as at the end of their reviews. At the end of volume 2, there are four cumulative indexes covering works from the years 1977 to 1997: an index of Biographical Works by Subject, the Category Index, the Title Index, and the Author Index. The index of biographical works is arranged by subject rather than by author or title. Thus, readers will be able to locate easily a review of any biographical work published in the Magill annuals since 1977 (including memoirs, diaries, and letters—as well as biographies and autobiographies) by looking up the name of the person. Following the Category Index and the Title Index is the Author Index. Beneath each author's name appear the titles of all of his or her works reviewed in the Magill annuals since 1977. Next to each title, in parentheses, is the year of the annual in which the review appeared, followed by the page number. In all four indexes, titles which appeared in *Magill's History Annual*, 1983, and *Magill's Literary Annual, History and Biography*, 1984 and 1985, are indicated parenthetically by an "H" followed by the year of the annual in which the review appeared.

Each article begins with a block of top matter that indicates the title, author, publisher, and price of the work. When possible, the year of the author's birth is also provided. The top matter also includes the number of pages of the book, the type of work, and, when appropriate, the time period and locale represented in the text. Next, there is the same capsulized description of the work that appears in the annotated list of titles by category. When pertinent, a list of principal characters or of personages introduces the review.

The articles themselves are approximately two thousand words in length. They are original essay-reviews that analyze and present the focus, intent, and relative success of the author, as well as the makeup and point of view of the work under discussion. To assist the reader further, the articles are supplemented by a list of additional reviews for further study in a bibliographic format.

LIST OF TITLES

LIST OF TITLES

LIST OF TITLES

TITLES BY CATEGORY

ANNOTATED

TITLES BY CATEGORY

FICTION

page

TITLES BY CATEGORY

TITLES BY CATEGORY

TITLES BY CATEGORY

TITLES BY CATEGORY

TITLES BY CATEGORY

TITLES BY CATEGORY

AUTOBIOGRAPHY
MEMOIRS
DIARIES
LETTERS

TITLES BY CATEGORY

BIOGRAPHY

TITLES BY CATEGORY

HISTORY

TITLES BY CATEGORY

page

TITLES BY CATEGORY

ETHICS
page
LAW

FINE ARTS

TITLES BY CATEGORY

TITLES BY CATEGORY

CONTRIBUTING REVIEWERS FOR 1997 ANNUAL

Michael Adams
*City University of New York
Graduate School*

Thomas P. Adler
Purdue University

Andrew J. Angyal
Elon College

Stanley Archer
Texas A&M University

Edwin T. Arnold
Appalachian State University

Bryan Aubrey
Independent Scholar

Charles F. Bahmueller
Center for Civic Education

Barbara Bair
Duke University

Dan Barnett
*California State University,
Chico*

Robert A. Bascom
United Bible Societies

Charles Merrell Berg
University of Kansas

Mary G. Berg
Harvard University

Pegge Bochynski
Independent Scholar

Harold Branam
Savannah State University

Gerhard Brand
*California State University,
Los Angeles*

C. K. Breckenridge
Independent Scholar

Peter Brier
*California State University,
Los Angeles*

Wesley Britton
*Grayson County Community
College*

Jeffrey L. Buller
Georgia Southern University

Thomas J. Campbell
Pacific Lutheran University

John R. Carpenter
Independent Scholar

Ethan Casey
Independent Scholar

Thomas Cassidy
*South Carolina State
University*

Dolores L. Christie
Ursuline College

C. L. Chua
*California State University,
Fresno*

Richard Hauer Costa
Texas A&M University

Mary Virginia Davis
Independent Scholar

Frank Day
Clemson University

Bill Delaney
Independent Scholar

Francine Dempsey
The College of Saint Rose

Robert P. Ellis
Worcester State College

Thomas L. Erskine
Salisbury State University

Robert Faggen
Claremont McKenna College

Rebecca Hendrick
Flannagan
Francis Marion University

Roy C. Flannagan
Francis Marion University

Robert J. Forman
St. John's University, New York

Raymond Frey
Centenary College, New Jersey

Ann D. Garbett
Averett College

Leslie E. Gerber
Appalachian State University

Louise Grieco
Independent Scholar

Daniel L. Guillory
Millikin University

Christopher Hailey
Independent Scholar

Terry Heller
Coe College

Joseph W. Hinton
Independent Scholar

Theodore C. Humphrey
*California State Polytechnic
University, Pomona*

Philip K. Jason
United States Naval Academy

Shakuntala Jayaswal
University of New Haven

Jane Anderson Jones
*Manatee Community College,
South*

Cynthia Lee Katona
Ohlone College

Steven G. Kellman
*University of Texas at San
Antonio*

W. P. Kenney
Manhattan College

Lynn Kostoff
Frances Marion University

Kathy Krauss
Rogue Community College

James B. Lane
Indiana University Northwest

Eugene Larson
Los Angeles Pierce College

Leon Lewis
Appalachian State University

Elizabeth Johnston
Lipscomb
*Randolph-Macon Woman's
College*

R. C. Lutz
University of the Pacific

Janet McCann
Texas A&M University

Joanne McCarthy
Independent Scholar

Mark McCloskey
Independent Scholar

Philip McDermott
Independent Scholar

David W. Madden
*California State University,
Sacramento*

Paul D. Mageli
Independent Scholar

Maria Theresa Maggi
Independent Scholar

Lois Marchino
University of Texas at El Paso

Chogollah Maroufi
*California State University,
Los Angeles*

Charles E. May
*California State University,
Long Beach*

Laurence W. Mazzeno
Ursuline College

Kenneth W. Meadwell
*University of Winnipeg,
Manitoba, Canada*

Robert A. Morace
Daemen College

Gregory L. Morris
*Pennsylvania State University,
Erie, Behrend College*

Robert E. Morsberger
*California State Polytechnic
University, Pomona*

Daniel P. Murphy
Hanover College

John M. Muste
Ohio State University

Stella Nesanovich
McNeese State University

Lisa Paddock
Independent Scholar

Robert J. Paradowski
*Rochester Institute of
Technology*

David B. Parsell
Furman University

Thomas R. Peake
King College

David Peck
*California State University,
Long Beach*

Cliff Prewencki
Independent Scholar

Edna B. Quinn
Salisbury State University

Gregary J. Racz
Parsons School of Design

R. Kent Rasmussen
Independent Scholar

Rosemary M. Canfield
Reisman
*Charleston-Southern
University*

Bernard F. Rodgers, Jr.
Simon's Rock College of Bard

Carl Rollyson
*Baruch College of the City
University of New York*

Joseph Rosenblum
Independent Scholar

John K. Roth
Claremont McKenna College

Marc Rothenberg
Smithsonian Institution

Barbara Elman Schiffman
Independent Scholar

Barbara Kitt Seidman
Linfield College

T. A. Shippey
St. Louis University

Carroll Dale Short
Independent Scholar

R. Baird Shuman
*University of Illinois at
Urbana-Champaign*

Anne W. Sienkewicz
Independent Scholar

Thomas J. Sienkewicz
Monmouth College, Illinois

Ira Smolensky
Monmouth College, Illinois

Katherine R. Sopka
*Four Corners Analytic
Sciences*

Bradley Starr
*California State University,
Fullerton*

Gerald H. Strauss
Bloomsburg University

James Sullivan
*California State University,
Los Angeles*

Emily Teipe
Fullerton College

Jack E. Trotter
Francis Marion University

William Urban
Monmouth College, Illinois

Ronald G. Walker
Western Illinois University

Qun Wang
*California State University,
Monterey Bay*

Bruce Wiebe
Independent Scholar

Philip F. Williams
Arizona State University

John Wilson
Independent Scholar

Michael Witkoski
Independent Scholar

Robert E. Yahnke
University of Minnesota

MAGILL'S
LITERARY ANNUAL
1997

AN ACCIDENTAL AUTOBIOGRAPHY

Author: Barbara Grizzuti Harrison (1935-   )
Publisher: Houghton Mifflin (Boston). 396 pp. $24.95
Type of work: Autobiography
Time: The 1940's to the 1990's
Locale: Brooklyn and Manhattan; Libya, India, Italy, and Morocco

In a collection of "memories," Harrison examines the paraphernalia of her sensibility

Principal personages:
BARBARA GRIZZUTI HARRISON, an American writer
HER MOTHER
HER FATHER
ARNOLD HOROWITZ, her high-school English teacher
JAZZMAN, her African American lover
MR. HARRISON, her former husband
ANNA HARRISON, her daughter
JOSHUA HARRISON, her son

The facts about Barbara Grizzuti Harrison's life that one can glean from *An Accidental Autobiography* are these: She grew up in Brooklyn during the 1930's and 1940's; her father, a printer, was an Italian immigrant; her mother, a second-generation Italian, became a zealous Jehovah's Witness when Barbara was nine. Barbara became her mother's acolyte on Sunday door-to-door visits and served for three years as a housekeeper in the Jehovah's Witness headquarters and residence after she graduated from high school. Escaping her servitude, she moved to the East Village, had a love affair with an African American jazz musician (whose name she omits, referring to him throughout as Jazzman), and married a Mr. Harrison (Dale Harrison, an official with CARE, according to another source) with whom she had two children, Anna and Joshua. During her marriage, she lived in Libya and India; after her divorce, she became a freelance writer and passionate traveler. She has suffered throughout her adult life from panic attacks (a result of the childhood trauma of being caught between a sometimes abusive father and a disapproving mother) and in her later life from recurring lung infections: She is obsessed with the act of breathing.

It is with "Breathing Lessons," that Harrison begins her collection of memories, a collection she has organized alphabetically, rather than chronologically for, as she states in the "Introduction":

A linear biography would falsify, because it would cast things in a mold and present me with the temptation to find formal patterns where none exist. . . . I have no wish to be imprisoned in a frame of my own creation.
The path of memory is circular and coherent:

like a jazz symphony. Harrison's autobiography plays in a series of melodies, reprises, and riffs, allowing her to contemplate experiences from various angles, with different interpretations. Often she turns to a solo voice from outside to add color and depth to the mix.

Harrison revels in the sensual delights of life—not only sex and food but also the vistas and aromas of faraway places and New York streets, the color and texture of fabric scraps to be made into a collage, beautiful objects that she must possess, and the "soft and clear, cadenced and authoritative voice" of Red Barber's broadcasts that filled her childhood summer afternoons.

In the chapter entitled "Home Economics," she explores the contradictions of domesticity: the drudgery of housekeeping against the joy of serving her children "orichietti with porcini sauteed in truffle oil and sweet butter." Harrison's childhood and adolescence were filled with household tasks; while her mother was out preaching for the Witnesses, young Barbara was home washing dishes and ironing. At nineteen she moved into Bethel, the residence hall of the Witnesses and spent her days changing beds and scrubbing floors in the mansion built by Henry Ward Beecher. Her reflections on home economics are augmented with material from books on domestic science by the Beecher sisters and the nutritional philosophies of Adele Davis and Dr. Carlton Fredericks, with whom her mother was infatuated. Similarly in the chapter, "Food, Flesh and Fashion," Harrison at once delights in the pleasures of the body and bemoans its vulnerability to pain and deterioration—and fat.

The chapter begins with an examination of the fluctuating perceptions of the perfect female form according to fashionable dictates, moves on to a consideration of Anthelme Brillat-Savarin's nineteenth century *The Physiology of Taste*; an appreciation of the Italian contentment with food that makes each meal, not a test but a *festa*; an exploration into the cults of fasting, citing the work of medievalist Caroline Bynum, and concludes with her own dreams of having it all:

> I want everything—candlelight and music, soft fabric and strong hands caressing me, perfume and wine, love, sex, food, joy, the dance of the blood, and the unselfconsciousness that is the gift of angels. I want *always* and consistently to love my lovable body, which has given and received so much pleasure—and I don't know how. . . . I float above my body, regarding myself from a great height; I regard this body with pity, amusement, weariness, and love.

Harrison manages to collate a vast range of material into a coherent, if quirky, whole.

The "Men and God(s)," who are the recipients of Harrison's love, adoration, and dissection, include Dorothy Sayers' detective, Lord Peter Wimsey; the aforementioned sportscaster, Red Barber; her high-school English teacher, Arnold Horowitz; her lover Jazzman; and Federico Secundo, Emperor (*Stupor Mundi*, Wonder of the World, 1194-1250). Throughout this chapter she reveals, perhaps somewhat unwittingly, her genuine delight in a certain kind of male sensibility and her own inability to sustain a committed relationship. She envies the mutual affection and contentment present in the marriage of Lord Peter Wimsey and Harriet Vane; it presented a vivid contrast to her own marriage, which was beset by emotional seesaws and an underlying mutual dislike. The reader wonders if Harrison's discovery of *Gaudy Night* in a dusty Indian shop, shortly before the birth of her second child, contributed to or merely illuminated her marital discontent. Fantasy relationships can be dangerous. Harrison later found an embodiment of that fantasy, however, in the sixty-year marriage of Red and Lylah Barber. When she went to visit her childhood idol ("for me the living gods are men") in Tallahassee two or three years before his death, she was as enchanted with the mutual love and comfort displayed between husband and wife as she was with the memories Barber evoked. She comes to the realization that the two are probably interlinked. Barber's broadcasts of the Brooklyn Dodgers' games provided her childhood with a sunny, safe escape from her contentious and dangerous home—the love of life and happiness in his voice opened a gateway out from the rigid gloom of the Jehovah's Witnesses "into a world full of muddle and joy. And: no sweat. He made it sweet and easy."

The two other men who swung open that gateway were Arnold Horowitz and Jazzman. At New Utrecht High School in Bensonhurst, where Jewish girls were supposed to be smart and Italian girls were expected to get married, Barbara Grizzuti was singled out for her intelligence and talent by two English teachers: David Zeiger befriended her and Arnold Horowitz loved her. Both encouraged her to go to college, an option forbidden to her by her religion; Arnold cajoled her into taking the early entrance exam for the University of Chicago. She passed, but was not yet ready to forego her faith. She did, however, defy both her mother and the president of the Watch Tower Society, who forbade her to continue seeing Arnold—his was the only heart that spoke to hers. Although highly charged with passionate intensity, their relationship was never physically consummated, perhaps because of the diabetes which would claim Arnold's life shortly after Barbara married and moved abroad. Physical passion she found with Jazzman.

Having suffered a panic attack, Barbara left Bethel House, moved back home, and got a job at Macmillan. One night she went to Minton's with a girlfriend and fell in love with the nightclub's horn player. She bought him a drink, and he wooed her. The affair lasted three years, during which time Barbara moved into an East Village apartment, sat on Frank Sinatra's lap, was befriended by Billie Holiday, discovered that her lover was married, traveled to Kansas City and Indiana to meet his relatives, and became addicted to the sexual and spiritual pleasures that Jazzman shared with her. When he left her to return to his wife, Barbara married Mr. Harrison. Thirty-some years later, she telephoned Jazzman, and they once again became lovers. After a period of delirious renewed delight, their passion began to unravel. Jazzman did not want his children to see him with her; Barbara called Jazzman's wife and told her they were having an affair. Predictably, that was the end. The volatility of their personalities and circumstances prevented anything else. Despite Barbara Grizzuti Harrison's longing for the tranquil life and her stated envy of those who lead one, she seems temperamentally unsuited for it.

Her admiration for Federico Secundo underscores her own passionate sensibility. Harrison describes this Holy Roman Emperor who did battle with a succession of popes as "sentimental, affable, bold, friendly, dignified, mystical, pragmatic, rational, skeptical, irascible, messianic, tolerant, stubborn, pacific, profligate, virile, cunning, happy, gracious to people of all stations and classes, vivacious. . . . wounded as well as flawed." The litany of adjectives, many of which might be used to describe Harrison herself, reveals an exuberant personality that would be difficult to confine within a simple life.

The final four chapters of *An Accidental Autobiography* are constructed in two somewhat paradoxical pairs: "Notes from Abroad" with "Rooms: Signs and Symbols" and "Scars and Distinguishing Marks" with "Swimming." The vistas of foreign sojourns contrast with the often stifling enclosures of familiar rooms; the joys of casual friendships and chance encounters balance the heated claustrophobia of those forced to live together. Scarred by parental cruelties, Harrison discovered how to surrender her vulnerable body to water late in life. She was fifty years old before a friend taught her to swim after many earlier, failed attempts. In contrast to the paralyzing panic attacks to which she is accustomed, she experiences a blissful loss of self-consciousness and control in the water: "It closely resembles death." By the end of *An Accidental Autobiography*, the reader senses that Harrison, who continues to live "with great exuberance" (according to the book's dust jacket) has also come to terms with her own mortality.

Barbara Grizzuti Harrison's life has a quintessentially twentieth century American quality. Only in the United States could the daughter of Italian immigrants be baptized into the American melting pot over the radio by a sports commentator from Florida, be intellectually nurtured by a Jewish teacher, and be initiated into the pleasures of love and jazz by an African American musician. Growing up during World War II, Harrison experienced the worldwide spread of American influence as she traveled and lived abroad with a husband who was an official with an international aid agency. Divorced during the 1960's, she benefited from and contributed to the feminist movement that opened career doors and psychological closets. Although beloved by children and friends, she has had to face the necessity of growing old alone and self-sufficient. Harrison's dazzling kaleidoscopic imagery well befits the world she has inhabited and described.

Jane Anderson Jones

Sources for Further Study

Chicago Tribune. June 30, 1996, XIV, p. 2.
Commonweal. CXXIII, September 13, 1996, p. 31.
Library Journal. CXXI, April 1, 1996, p. 94.
Los Angeles Times Book Review. July 7, 1996, p. 6.
The Nation. CCLXII, June 24, 1996, p. 33.
The New York Times Book Review. CI, June 9, 1996, p. 9.
Publishers Weekly. CCXLIII, April 1, 1996, p. 60.
The Washington Post Book World. XXVI, July 7, 1996, p. 8.
Women's Review of Books. XIV, November, 1996, p. 20.

ACCORDION CRIMES

Author: E. Annie Proulx (1935-   )
Publisher: Scribner (New York). 381 pp. $25.00
Type of work: Novel
Time: The 1890's to the 1990's
Locale: Sicily; many areas of the United States, including Iowa, Texas, Louisiana, Illinois, Montana, Minnesota, and Mississippi

The story of an accordion and its various owners, who find in music a reminder of their roots and a sense of identity

> *Principal characters:*
> SILVANO, a Sicilian, son of the accordion maker
> HANS BEUTLE, a German immigrant
> ABELARDO RELÁMPAGO SALAZAR, a Texan of Mexican ancestry
> FÉLIDA SALAZAR, his daughter, a talented musician
> DOLOR GAGNON, an orphan of French extraction
> BUDDY MALEFOOT, a Louisiana Cajun
> OCTAVE, a black Louisiana fisherman
> JOEY NEWCOMER, a Polish musician
> FLORRY NEWCOMER, his daughter
> FAY MCGETTIGAN, a Montana ranch hand

The novels of E. Annie Proulx show life at its most heartbreaking. Her characters are frustrated, betrayed, and tormented; their hopes and their very survival are jeopardized by the forces of nature and by human malevolence. In *Postcards* (1992), Proulx shows how a family virtually destroys itself because the family members are incapable of forgetting old injuries; in *The Shipping News* (1993), she demonstrates how individuals are imperiled not only by human selfishness and irresponsibility but also by the unpredictable and unforgiving ocean on which these islanders must depend for their very existence. Although profound in their thematic implications, both of these earlier novels are limited in scope, the first, because though the action covers a fairly long period, it involves a single family, and the second, because it is the story of a brief period in the life of one protagonist, who lives in a small and close-knit community.

Accordion Crimes is very different from the author's earlier works. With its huge cast of characters, its dizzying changes in setting, and its hundred-year time span, it has the complexity, as well as the episodic quality, of an epic. There is no epic hero or heroine, however, to unify the work. The protagonist of *Accordion Crimes* is a green accordion, and each of the eight chapters in the book is presented as a separate installment in the accordion's adventuresome life.

Appropriately, the novel begins with the birth of the protagonist. That important event takes place in Sicily. Its creator is a man who is never named, but identified only as the accordion maker. When this craftsman and his son Silvano start on their way to New York, where they intend to settle, open a music store, and make their fortunes, the accordion accompanies them. Fate intervenes, however, as it does so often in this novel. On the train to Palermo, a stranger persuades the pair that New Orleans would be a better place for their venture. As a result of this conversation, the Sicilians alter their plans and take a ship for New Orleans. The consequences are far from happy. When an anti-Italian mob sweeps into a bar where the Sicilians sometimes stop to socialize and to play the music of their native country, the accordion maker is dragged out and beaten to death. Silvano survives, but as a diminished person. Blaming his father's death on his slowness in becoming assimilated, Silvano changes his own name to Bob Joe and sets about to forget his Sicilian heritage.

Although Silvano has no further interest in the accordion, fortunately it is rescued by Polio, an African American friend of the accordion maker who on occasion had borrowed the instrument to try out some of his own songs on it. Shortly after acquiring the accordion, however, Polio is killed by another blackman, whose only interest in the instrument is to make a profit by selling it. He takes the accordion up the Mississippi River, and it ends up as the property of Hans Beutle, a German immigrant, who has settled in Iowa but still recalls with nostalgia the beer-halls and the polkas of his homeland. After his death, the accordion passes into the hands of Abelardo Relámpago Salazar, a Texan. Salazar naïvely assumes that his sons will share his enthusiasm for the traditional music of his Mexican forebears. Unfortunately, they do not. Almost as if it were fated, one of them manages to lose the accordion.

The green accordion now appears in Maine, its owner a French Canadian, Dolor Gagnon. Its next home is with Buddy Malefoot, a Louisiana Cajun. Before long it has been taken to Chicago by an African American musician, Octave, who plans to heat up the frigid North with his Louisiana zydeco. Eventually the accordion becomes the property of two Polish musicians, Joey and Florry Newcomer. Later, in Montana, it warms the hearts of the Irish ranch hand Fay McGettigan and his Basque friend Javier.

Although by now it has outlasted a dozen owners, the green accordion is not immortal. It can live on only as long as some individual values it and cherishes it, and inevitably, there comes a time when no one can come to its rescue. The young children who spy it on a trash pile in Mississippi see no purpose for it except as something they can destroy. They pitch it onto the highway to watch it be crushed by an eighteen-wheeler.

In a world where it seems so much easier to destroy than to create, it is amazing that the green accordion lasted as long as it did. Certainly it fared much better than its owners. Beginning with the accordion maker himself, who thought he was making such a wise decision in changing his destination, Proulx's characters seem to rush toward disaster, as if driven by a malevolent fate. Hans Beutle survives all sorts of dangers, only to die of gangrene after having an operation to restore his virility. Salazar succumbs after being bitten in his own bed by a poisonous spider; Javier dies after being struck by a rattlesnake hiding under his prized accordion.

Even Javier's end, however, is not as ironic as that of Dolor Gagnon. Abandoned by both parents when he is quite young, Dolor grows up with almost no knowledge of his family or his heritage. Many years later, when he is able to verify the fact that he is French Canadian, for the first time in his life Dolor has some sense of his identity.

He begins to play French Canadian songs on his accordion, and when he realizes that very little effort is being made to preserve them, at last he has a purpose in life. Then Dolor is stricken by a disease the doctors cannot identify or cure, and he is confined to a wheelchair. At that point, a young woman of marriageable age decides to intervene. Convinced that she and St. Jude can provide the miracle which the young man so desperately needs, she takes Dolor to the shrine of the saint, and he is cured. As a matter of course, Dolor marries her, and it seems that fate has at last smiled upon him. After the wedding, however, his bride announces that in order to obtain the miracle, she promised St. Jude that Dolor would give up playing the accordion. Dolor feels he has no choice but to do so; he soon finds, however, that without his music life is unbearable, and he kills himself.

With fate seemingly so bent on frustrating the dreams and ending the lives of Proulx's characters, the novel could well be totally bleak, but it is not. After all, the protagonist endures for a century, and though all of its owners die, before they leave this earth a number of them have their share of happiness. Moreover, Proulx suggests that, despite the machinations of fate, human beings are not totally helpless. They have the power to make decisions about their lives, and, to some degree, their happiness or unhappiness will depend on the wisdom of those decisions.

One of the most difficult problems for immigrants to a new country is the degree to which they will put their old society and its traditions behind them. It is possible to break off all those connections, as Silvano does. Although he may not realize it, when he rejects his father and all that he loved, Silvano is really rejecting a part of himself. The story of Dolor Gagnon demonstrates how futile life can seem when it is stripped of its context and based solely on present pleasure. Even though it finally cost him his life, Dolor's appreciation of his heritage is clearly preferable to Joey Newcomer's cynical exploitation of his own. Like Silvano, Joey changed his name in order to signify his assimilation into his new country and his rejection of his heritage; since the only way Joey can earn his living, however, is by playing traditional music at Polish gatherings, he has ensured himself enduring discontent by refusing to admit who he is.

Most of those who play the green accordion, however, cherish their ties to the past. For Hans Beutle, music provides a break from the hard work of carving out a farm on the Iowa prairie; when he strikes up a polka, he is transported to a German beer-hall and the carefree days of his youth. Fay McGettigan has never seen the land of his ancestors; his Irish airs are important to him primarily because they bring him and his brother together and remind them both of the long-departed mother from whom they learned them. Painful though it may be to recall the sweetness of times which will never return, without those memories and those ties to the past one is not fully human or fully alive.

On the other hand, one can also pay a price for too slavish an adherence to the past. Thus Hans Beutle is never able to put his new country ahead of the old, and as a result, when war comes, he earns the distrust and dislike of his neighbors. Salazar's tradition-alism costs him even more. Among his people, Salazar insists, the accordion is considered a man's instrument. Therefore, even though his daughter Félida is the most talented of his offspring, he forbids her to touch the accordion which she can play almost as well as her father. When he discovers that she has been practicing on it, he strikes her and rails at her. During the night she runs away, leaving a knife in the accordion. Her father never sees her again. His adherence to tradition has cost Salazar his most promising child.

Such episodes suggest that there is some room for moral choice in a world which admittedly is beyond the control of any one individual. If it is possible to make wise decisions, particularly where tradition is concerned, then *Accordion Crimes* can end on a hopeful note, for its central theme is the future of the great American experiment, the attempt to forge a single nation out of peoples whose backgrounds are very different. It is only natural that each new immigrant should feel more at ease with his or her own people, and that tensions should result from these feelings of insecurity, as well as from long-standing national and ethnic enmities. Incidents such as the breakup of the Salazar family, however, show how disastrous ethnic isolation can be. At the same time, it would be a loss both for individuals and for the new nation if everyone took Silvano's course of action. In this context, it becomes apparent why Proulx chose the protagonist she did, for by lending itself to every tradition it encounters, the accordion not only survives but also provides a model for human behavior. There are moments in *Accordion Crimes* when people transcend their traditions, for example, when the Irish ranch hand offers the accordion to the Basque sheepherder, or when the Sicilian accordion maker is willing to listen to the music of the African American and later, when he entrusts the instrument to him. Like the accordion, the citizens of this nation may learn to move freely among cultures, adapting themselves to the fact of diversity and thus ensuring their survival.

Rosemary M. Canfield Reisman

Sources for Further Study

Booklist. XCII, April 15, 1996, p. 1395.
Chicago Tribune. June 9, 1996, XIV, p. 1.
Library Journal. CXXI, May 15, 1996, p. 85.
The Nation. CCLXII, June 24, 1996, p. 29.
The New Republic. CCXV, October 7, 1996, p. 44.
The New York Times Book Review. CI, June 23, 1996, p. 12.
Newsweek. CXXVII, June 10, 1996, p. 88.
Publishers Weekly. CCXLIII, April 15, 1996, p. 48.
Publishers Weekly. CCXLIII, June 3, 1996, p. 57.
Time. CXLVII, June 24, 1996, p. 76.
The Wall Street Journal. June 14, 1996, p. A12.

ACTIVE FAITH
How Christians Are Changing the Soul of American Politics

Author: Ralph Reed (1961-   )
Publisher: Free Press (New York). 311 pp. $25.00
Type of work: Current affairs

The leader of the Christian Coalition argues that his organization, far from being comprised of right-wing extremists with a hidden agenda, is actually comprised of middle-class Christian conservatives who seek to promote a pro-family agenda that they hope will save American culture from moral decline

The explosive growth of the Christian conservative movement is one of the most important developments of late twentieth century American politics. Ralph Reed, executive director of the Christian Coalition, claims that his organization has grown from fewer than five thousand members to more than 1.7 million in just seven years. This phenomenal growth has sparked much concern in the liberal media and political establishment. They have reacted to the growing political clout of religious conservatives with a mixture of puzzlement, anger, and mistrust, and have disdainfully referred to Reed's followers as "poor, uneducated, and easy to command."

In *Active Faith: How Christians Are Changing the Soul of American Politics*, Reed attempts to reshape the public perception of Christian conservatives by candidly presenting the motivations, methods, and goals of those he calls "people of faith." In this readable, informative book, he recounts his personal story, the history of religious influence in American social causes, the rise and fall of religious conservative political organizations during the 1980's, and the subsequent formation and development of the Christian Coalition. Finally, he proposes a "new theology of political activism for religious conservatives" that focuses not only on the hot-button issues of legalized abortion and homosexual rights but also on problems that affect the majority of Americans, such as balancing the national budget and offering tax relief to families.

As an experienced political activist, Reed is acutely sensitive to the unflattering redneck stereotype traditionally associated with the Religious Right. In an effort to abolish that image from the public consciousness, he offers himself as a prime example of the typical Christian conservative. Intelligent, polished, and well educated, Reed is a product of middle-class America. The son of a Miami eye surgeon, Reed was student-council president of his junior high school class, senior-class president and founder of a conservative club in high school, and executive director of the national College Republicans.

Although Reed earned a Ph.D. in American history from Emory University, his passion for politics led him away from academia into the world of political activism. When he experienced a religious awakening in 1983, Reed was an established Republican operative who enjoyed the rough-and-tumble game of hardball politics. He maintains that although his conversion to evangelical Christianity precipitated a change in his tactics, his "political philosophy was already well developed." Therefore, his newfound faith had little impact on his conservative views. When Reed met former presidential candidate and televangelist Pat Robertson at George Bush's inauguration in 1989, Robertson offered him the opportunity to launch a new conservative organization. This momentous meeting marked the birth of the Christian Coalition.

Traditionally, the American public has been suspicious of any group or organization which has attempted to wed religion with politics. Yet Reed's extensive background as a historian serves him well in demonstrating that, in the annals of American history, religion and politics are not such strange bedfellows. He persuasively argues that "Whether the issue was slavery and racism, the plight of labor and the poor, or the right to life for the unborn and aged, the faith community has always been the most vibrant and effective political force in the electorate." His painstaking analysis of the great social movements of the twentieth century—temperance reform, women's suffrage, the Social Gospel, the antiwar movement, the struggles of organized labor, and the Civil Rights movement—not only showcases his impressive historical knowledge but also shows how Christian activists' fight for justice has changed the face of American society. Reed's historical overview is more than an attempt to establish the important influence that religious conservatives have had on American politics. His survey examines the strengths and weaknesses of each movement in an attempt to discover which organizations were the most successful and why, to avoid repeating the mistakes made in the past by religious activists, and to apply his findings to the development of the Christian Coalition.

The Civil Rights movement led by Martin Luther King, Jr., provides Reed with a blueprint for success in merging religion, politics, and social reform. Beginning in the churches and gaining momentum at the grassroots level, the Civil Rights movement became a national power that transformed American culture. "Grassroots" is a word that is peppered throughout the pages of *Active Faith*. It is clear that Reed believes there is a great untapped political resource hidden within the suburbs and small towns of America. Enlisting people in the conservative cause at the grassroots level is a key tactic in furthering the growth and influence of the Christian Coalition, as well as a way to move Christian conservatives into mainstream American political life.

Reed's "fusionist" strategy is a new approach for Christian conservatives who have been typecast in the minds of the American public as fire-breathing religious zealots. In contrast, Reed adopts a conciliatory tone throughout his book in order to bridge the gap between conservatives and liberals. He castigates the Religious Right for promoting anti-Semitism, racism, gay-bashing, and anti-Catholicism and calls on them to right past wrongs. He even gives the liberals their due when he discusses their active role in causes relating to social concerns, such as the labor movement and the Civil Rights movement. He notes, "Liberals have been correct throughout history on issues of social injustice while we have been neglectful or derelict in applying the principles of our faith to establishing justice in a fallen world."

Apologizing for the past and present transgressions of religious conservatives is only part of Reed's strategy for "casting a wider net." His organization has allied itself with a number of ethnic and religious groups which Christian conservatives have formerly perceived as adversaries. For example, in an effort to close the rift between evangelicals and Jews, Reed tells of his repeated efforts to reach out to the Jewish community in an ongoing dialogue. In some areas of the country, the Christian Coalition has formed alliances with Catholic organizations to fight against pro-choice advocates. In another instance, when a bill was pending before the Virginia legislature to legalize riverboat gambling, the coalition joined with African Americans (who along with other minorities, Reed maintains, are most susceptible to the lure of gambling) to defeat the bill.

Reed's outreach efforts are not limited to past antagonists. He has also endeavored to find common ground with other political groups, most notably Ross Perot and his Reform Party. Because the coalition and the Reform Party share many of the same goals, such as balanced budgets, lower taxes, choice in education, term limits, and political reform, Reed views Perot's organization as a secular analog to the pro-family movement. His account of the spirited but friendly conversations with Perot is one of the most engaging narratives in the book and gives the reader a brief glimpse of two shrewd political bosses at work.

Reed also offers an insider's view of the backroom deals and compromises that are so much a part of the fabric of Washington politics. In a revealing account of the passage of the 1995 telecommunications bill, Reed tells of how the Christian Coalition fought for an amendment to restrict cyberporn on the Internet. House Speaker Newt Gingrich, usually a friend of the coalition, opposed the cyberporn restrictions. In an effort to avoid a confrontation with Gingrich and keep the cyberporn amendment in the bill, Reed worked out an eleventh-hour deal with one of Gingrich's allies. This is one of many examples that Reed offers of his willingness to make concessions in order to further the agenda of the coalition.

Reed's penchant for compromise is also evident in the way he and his followers choose to present their program to the American public. In Reed's view, "The pro-family movement has limited its effectiveness by concentrating disproportionately on issues such as abortion and homosexuality. . . . To win in the ballot box and in the court of public opinion, however, the pro-family movement must speak to the average voters." To this end, Reed promotes issues such as welfare reform and a balanced budget and, in the opinion of some pro-family advocates, allows his moderate agenda to eclipse causes conservatives hold dear.

Reed's decision to involve his organization in broad-based issues may make the conservative agenda more palatable to the liberal public, but Reed has provoked the ire of some of his well-known conservative compatriots. Reed's story about his conflict with James Dobson, founder of Focus on the Family, a Christian pro-life organization, is a case in point. When Reed declined to speak out against presidential hopeful Colin Powell for his pro-choice stance, Dobson accused Reed of hypocritically "skirting the great moral issues of the day." Reed replies that he did not publicly censure Powell because Powell would have viewed such an attack as a challenge and, as a result, might have decided to seek the nomination. Reed maintains that he did not want to sacrifice the long-term goals of the coalition by focusing on the position of a noncandidate.

In spite of Reed's willingness to take the heat from prominent Christian conserva-tives such as Dobson, and his repeated assertion that the Christian Coalition has no hidden agenda, his facile use of language often entraps him in political doublespeak that leaves the reader wondering about the ultimate goals of his fusionist strategy. In the last chapter, when Reed discusses the theology that drives the agenda of the coalition, he frequently contradicts himself thereby undermining his argument that people of faith are tolerant of views and lifestyles different from their own. For example, Reed claims that "The truth is that we eschew political power." Yet several pages earlier he says of the pro-family movement, "They must do more than 'send a message' to the elites and party leaders. They must win elections. They must govern. They must pull the levers of government and turn the wheels of the larger society for the good of the nation." Winning elections is certainly a way to boost the "effective-ness" and influence of religious conservatives, but to what end?

When Reed focuses on combustible issues such as homosexuality, he continues to contradict himself, but ironically, the contradictions that could muddy his message sometimes actually clarify it. For example, Reed eloquently and convincingly argues that the government should "tolerate" but not sanction homosexual behavior. He in no way sees his view as an attempt to "impose Judeo-Christian theology through the power of the state." Yet one of the goals of his "new theology of political activism for religious conservatives" is to "restore the culture's Judeo-Christian principles." Since, in the view of many religious conservatives, homosexuality is a sin, one wonders how homosexuals would fit into a society governed solely by Judeo-Christian principles.

Reed's primary objective in *Active Faith* is to demonstrate that the Christian Coalition is not a fringe political group seeking to impose its conservative religious convictions on society. His intent is to persuade the American public that the views of Christian conservatives are in line with those of mainstream America. When Reed discusses the history of religious activism in the United States, as well as the birth and growth of the coalition, he supports his thesis well. When he addresses abstract principles about the relationship between political power and religious belief, how-ever, the internal contradictions in his argument undermine his attempt to appear tolerant and moderate. Regardless of the weaknesses in *Active Faith*, it offers fasci-nating and compelling insight into one of the most dynamic forces in American politics.

Pegge Bochynski

Sources for Further Study

The Christian Century. CXIII, August 28, 1996, p. 812.
The Christian Science Monitor. August 19, 1996, p. 15.
Commentary. CII, July, 1996, p. 70.

Commonweal. CXXIII, September 27, 1996, p. 23.
Los Angeles Times. June 17, 1996, p. B5.
National Review. XLVIII, October 14, 1996, p. 85.
The New Republic. CCXV, July 8, 1996, p. 32.
The New York Times Book Review. CI, July 28, 1996, p. 14.
Vital Speeches. LXII, March 15, 1996, p. 329.

AFTER RAIN

Author: William Trevor (William Trevor Cox, 1928-   )
Publisher: Viking (New York). 213 pp. $22.95
Type of work: Short stories

A collection of twelve stories, most of them set in Ireland or England, by an Irish writer who sees clearly, in ordinary lives and relationships, states of the heart and mind that often lie hidden

William Trevor has been called the greatest living short-story writer in the language, and the evidence of *After Rain* suggests that such a view is not misplaced. The twelve stories in this collection are without exception marvelous, illuminating as they do the cracks and fissures in the emotional textures of a wide range of human relationships, in a variety of circumstances and settings. The stories reveal, often through a comment by the narrator coming with sudden force at the very end of the story, what has been endured, sacrificed, lost, compromised, or accepted in situations in which people interact with each other over long periods of time. Because of the absolute believability of all the characters and their actions, there is a sense of completeness and truth about these revelations, although many of them are subtle and unexpected.

Many of the stories focus on married couples. In Trevor's stories, couples tend not to get divorced. Instead they "work things out," often in an unconscious way, that leaves surface appearances intact but deeply shifts the subterranean landscape of their lives. In "A Day," for example, a woman lives with the knowledge, thanks to an intercepted letter seven years ago, that her husband of twenty years is having an affair, yet she has never confronted him with it. She spends part of her day imagining what the other woman is like, but she does this without animosity. She apparently has accepted that there has been an unacknowledged quid pro quo between herself and her husband: The marriage has been childless, and although he wished to adopt a child, she refused. An affair, then, is his rightful due, his payment for his acceptance without rancor of her childlessness.

The wife, however, has paid a price, of which a slow slide into closet alcoholism is probably the least. Her self-deceit is far more serious. She spends much of her day composing different scenarios that might happen in the future. Her favorite appears to be the belief that Elspeth, the lover, will become pregnant. The wife turns this to advantage, imagining that she and her husband will take the child and somehow contrive a happy ending from the long years of deception. The irony of her situation is that she remains fond of her husband, who is gentle and kind with her, and from the outside the marriage would look like a "good" one, but in truth it is nothing other than a long lie. Because of the knowledge she possesses, there can never be an honest exchange between them.

In "A Friendship," a wife who is bored with her successful but pompous lawyer husband allows herself to have an affair, encouraged by her best friend. Through the use of a few telling details, Trevor makes sure that the reader's sympathies are entirely with the wife. The husband is so preoccupied he does not go to say good-night to his two boys until they are already asleep (and if they are not, they pretend to be), and he is known among the wives and other women of their social circle as "Bad News," referring to the misfortune of being placed next to him at the dinner table.

The irony, however, is that the wife does love him, and when the affair, which has already ended, is discovered, she is filled with remorse. After a terrible quarrel—for the dialogue of which Trevor possesses perfect pitch—her husband forgives her. Nevertheless, he exacts a price for his forgiveness: She must never again see her friend who colluded in the deception. This price seems vindictive, until both the wife and the friend realize that "the forgiving of a wife was as much as there could be." A wronged husband could not forgive a treacherous friend as well. The wife accepts this, the friend knows, because of her feelings of guilt. She owes her husband a sacrifice, even though the loss of her best friend from childhood is a great one. Thus the trade is made for the "successful" marriage to continue: guilt is assuaged, honor satisfied, a friendship wrecked.

When Trevor does describe happy marriages, as in "Widows" and "Timothy's Birthday," he is merciless still, because even such ideal unions involve a price. In "Widows," a loved and loving husband dies. The wife's period of mourning is clouded by the appearance of a tradesman of dubious character who tells her that his bill for work done at their house had not been paid. Catherine distinctly remembers that her husband had withdrawn the exact amount from the bank to pay him. The tradesman insists he has no record of payment, and she cannot find a receipt. The mystery is never explained (a technique Trevor also uses in "Gilbert's Mother"), but the impression is left that the tradesman may be telling the truth, with the implication that there may be something about the dead man that the wife did not know.

Yet that is not the main point of the story, which is about the relationship between Catherine and her widowed sister, Alicia. Alicia had no happy memories of her marriage to a feckless philanderer. When Catherine's husband died, Alicia hoped that she and Catherine could return to the relationship they had had before they married, but it is not to be. This situation becomes apparent when Catherine agrees to pay the disputed bill; she does not want any bad publicity that might tarnish her husband's name and her happy memories of their marriage. This difference will always divide her from her sister, who has no such memories. The jealousy that this disparity arouses in Alicia will be the unspoken reality they will share from now on. Sisters are not sisters first, but widows. Past inequities are not to be easily rubbed out, and a happy marriage can spread a stain elsewhere.

A similar twist is contained in "Timothy's Birthday." An old Irish couple have been married for forty-two years, in which time they have scarcely been apart. Their fondness for one another, the narrator explains, was readily evident in how they spoke and acted.

The couple are seen preparing a meal in expectation that their son Timothy will visit them on his birthday, as he always does. This time, however, Timothy does not come. Instead, he sends a loutish young friend in his place to apologize and explain that Timothy is unwell. The mother soon guesses that this is not so, but she says nothing.

This husband and wife live stoically with their disappointments. The young man steals an ornament from them before leaving. By the end of the story, readers learn that the whole episode is a kind of vengeance exacted by the son, in part because his father had never accepted what appears to be Timothy's homosexual lifestyle, but more important, the vengeance is a result of "the jealousy their love of each other had bred in him, that had flourished into deviousness and cruelty." It is as if unhappiness has to squeeze in somewhere, and if it cannot do so in a marriage, it will find some other point of entry.

Trevor is not a political writer, but there is one story, "Last Ground," that sheds terrifying light on what Irish people call "the Troubles," the sectarian violence that has afflicted the six counties of Ulster since 1969. Milton Leeson, a Protestant boy in Northern Ireland, meets a strange woman in an orchard who says she is Saint Rosa. She plants a "holy" kiss upon him. He thinks she is not alive. Unfortunately, he lives in a family that is deeply proud of its Protestant traditions, symbolized each year when they take part in the July parade to commemorate the Protestant victory of William III in 1690.

Unable to forget the woman, Milton confides in his brother-in-law, a Protestant minister, who tells him not to tell his parents. The problem is that Saint Rosa is a Catholic saint. Milton secretly visits a Catholic priest, who is affronted that a saint has appeared to have visited a Protestant boy in an overwhelmingly Catholic neighborhood. Finally, Milton tells his mother and father. His father slaps his face twice.

Milton rides his bicycle to preach in nearby small towns, mentioning that Saint Rosa could forgive men on both sides for the violence they commit. His family is horrified. Milton has brought shame on them, and he is locked in his bedroom, a virtual prisoner. The word is put out that he is a bit touched in the head.

Finally, Milton is shot dead when he is alone in the house, by a man who is brought to the home by Garfield, Milton's brother, who lives in Belfast and is a friend of the "hard men," the Protestant paramilitaries. At the funeral, Hazel, a sister who had married and moved to England and only rarely returns to the family home, realizes the truth. Everyone knew what had happened: Milton's mother, his father, the clergyman, everyone in the neighborhood. The shame had been exorcised and silence agreed upon. The story illustrates the deep, irrational divisions that plague Ireland and their terrible consequences, better than any real-life account could do.

Perhaps the most moving story of the entire collection is the one that gives the volume its title. "After Rain" is in many ways an atypical Trevor story. Its protagonist is an unmarried woman; it is set in Italy rather than England or Ireland, and it ends with an astonishing moment of transcendence, quite unlike Trevor's typical ending, which focuses on the accumulated weight of the past, not the sudden release from it.

The protagonist is thirty-year-old Harriet, an Englishwoman who has just been dumped by her lover. They had been about to go on vacation together when the relationship ended, so to fill in the gap Harriet decides to spend the time at a plush hotel in Italy, where she went many times with her parents when she was a child. As she eats dinner and watches the crowded scene around her, she wonders about why she is able to win love but unable to keep it. Each time she finds love, it seems to exorcise the disappointment she felt at her parents' divorce, but sooner or later her romances always crumble into nothing.

She goes to a chapel to escape the heat and the rain and observes a painting of the Annunciation by an unknown artist. She notes all the details—the kneeling angel, the startled virgin, the background of arches, sky, and hills. The landscape is soft, as if no heat has ever touched it. Then she notes that the virgin's eyes express not alarm but wonderment.

When she leaves the church, Harriet finds the rain has stopped. The air is fresher. She strolls through the town, noticing that everything has been changed by the rain and emanates a cool fragrance that will not come again for weeks or months. Then she is hit by two revelations. The thought suddenly comes to her that she has cheated in her love affairs, although in what sense she does not know. Then she realizes that in the painting, the landscape has the same temporary quality that she is observing for herself now: It must have been after rain that the angel came.

Later, at dinner, her insight about herself is clarified. As long as she carries the expectation that present love can heal the past, it cannot do so: "He backed away, as others have, when she asked too much of love, when she tried to change the circumstances that are the past by imposing a brighter present, and constancy in the future above all else. She has been the victim of herself." This is a redemptive revelation, and she knows it, but she does not know how it came to her. All she knows, in the final, lovely line of the story, is that "Rain has sweetened the breathless air, the angel comes mysteriously also."

The religious images and the symbol of the cleansing rain combine to suggest that if our lives are a struggle to liberate ourselves from the binding tangle of our parents, such a thing might indeed be possible, beyond our striving, in an unfathomable moment of transcendence and grace.

Bryan Aubrey

Sources for Further Study

Boston Globe. September 29, 1996, p. N15.
Chicago Tribune. September 29, 1996, XIV, p. 1.
Library Journal. CXXI, September 15, 1996, p. 100.
Los Angeles Times Book Review. October 20, 1996, p. 2.
The New York Times Book Review. CI, October 20, 1996, p. 15.
Publishers Weekly. CCXLIII, July 29, 1996, p. 68.
The Spectator. CCLXXVII, October 5, 1996, p. 51.
The Times Literary Supplement. September 27, 1996, p. 23.

ALEKSANDER WAT
Life and Art of an Iconoclast

Author: Tomas Venclova (1937-   )
Publisher: Yale University Press (New Haven, Connecticut). 383 pp. $35.00
Type of work: Literary biography
Time: 1900-1967
Locale: Warsaw, Poland, and exile in Kazakhstan, U.S.S.R, Berkeley, California, and Paris, France

This study of Aleksander Wat concentrates on the writing of a man whose work documents the struggle for faith in the depths of this century's most inhuman totalitarian systems

> *Principal personages:*
> ALEKSANDER WAT, a Polish poet and writer
> PAULINA "OLA" WAT, his wife
> ANDRZEJ WAT, their son
> JOSEPH STALIN, the Soviet dictator who was the focus of much of Wat's thinking
> CZESŁAW MIŁOSZ, a Nobel Prize-winning Polish poet and champion of Wat in the United States

The Polish writer Aleksander Wat is best known to English readers for his memoir of imprisonment and exile in the Soviet Union, *Mój wiek: Pamiętnik mówieony* (1977; *My Century: The Odyssey of a Polish Intellectual*, 1988). Venclova's critical biography makes it clear just how much his ordeal in the Communist hell was a piece with the whole of the poet's life. It turns out that *My Century*, one of the great testaments to human endurance, was written by a tortured soul struggling constantly to escape the straitjacket of existence.

Wat was born on May 1, 1900, into a cultured Jewish family. His father, Mendel Chwat, was a noted expert on the Kabbalah, the main Jewish mystical tradition. Wat was not brought up in strict adherence to Judaism, however, and his Catholic nurse, who also taught the boy his first Polish, regularly took him with her to Mass. Under the circumstances, it was inevitable that Wat would never feel completely secure as a Pole or a Jew, but Venclova makes it clear the inner division went much deeper.

From the time he was a child, Wat was highly conscious of death and the fragility of identity. He characterized his life as a series of crises, which he sought to resolve through education and mysticism, both Jewish and Christian. This inner turmoil, perpetually creative, increasingly unbearable, underlies what Venclova terms Wat's "iconoclasm." In his discomfort, Wat could accept nothing at face value, not identity, not language. In Warsaw after World War I, Wat, nineteen and frightfully overeducated, led a wild, bohemian life, cutting an elegantly eccentric figure. With youthful—and uncharacteristic—self-confidence, he attacked old literary conventions with high spirits. In 1919, Wat and a friend introduced Futurism to Poland with a public reading in the tradition of the French Dadaists. They meant to cause a stir, and they did. For a while, Wat's literary allies engaged in more pranks aimed at shocking middle class complacency. Their activities were interrupted by the war between the Soviet Union and Poland, and once the Russians were defeated and pushed back, Wat gradually lost interest in such antics.

With Wat, iconoclasm was inherently connected with innovation, especially in literature. To capture the immediacy of experience, Wat felt he had to break free of the conventions of so-called rational language. Ready to use any means necessary, Wat replaced logic with connections of sound or position or similarity, skirting nonsense to break through to a new sense. His first major poetic work in this vein was *JA z jednej strony i JA z drugiej strony mego mopożelaznego piecyka* (1920; ME from one side and ME from the other side of my pug iron stove).

A long prose poem, composed partly by automatic writing, "Pug Iron Stove" is obscure, dense, and very personal. Similar to the writing of French poet Arthur Rimbaud, it depicts the search for the self through disintegration, but with Wat's distinctive blend of parody (often directed at himself). In the poem, Wat hopes the dissolution of the self (so much like what he would later experience in prison) can lead to a reintegration. Unfortunately, as will be the case time and again in his life and writing, Wat cannot make the final step to transcendence. Instead, there are proliferating images of disease and putrefaction while his identity is coopted by a double, a twin who turns into a nightmarish distortion (a role Wat would later project onto Joseph Stalin).

During the 1920's, Wat also experimented politically, becoming increasingly involved with the Polish Communist Party, like many futurists of the time. Wat insisted that he never actually joined the Party, but he wrote for its publications and even edited the most respected Communist literary magazine of the period, *The Literary Monthly*. For this, he landed in jail in 1931, branded a subversive.

Never really comfortable with Communist Party attacks on individual liberty, Wat repressed his misgivings out of a quasi-religious need for meaning. Yet he could not deny his nature, which marked his fiction with a nihilist and anarchic spirit. This attitude touched a nerve in the public, and he enjoyed great success with a collection of short stories called *Bezrobotny Lucyfer* (1927; *Lucifer Unemployed*, 1990).

These philosophical parables relying on parody and paradox attacked received opinions, especially ideas about progress, creating a profound impression with their irreverent and pseudoscientific posturing. Wat's was obviously not an orthodox Marxist outlook on scientific materialism, and the Party never trusted him.

Though considered dangerous by the government, Wat's ties with the Party steadily diminished throughout the 1930's, a result of mutual distrust and Wat's happy marriage. The beginning of World War II, however, forced him back into a very perilous association with the Party.

In 1939, Wat fled the Nazi army eastward to the town of Lwów, soon occupied by the Soviet army in accordance with the secret accord with Germany. What may have seemed at first like liberation became an authoritarian nightmare. A Polish Writers' Union was set up to promote Soviet interests, and Wat joined, either from cowardice or to protect his family. He later considered this collaboration the moral low point of his life, and it did him no good anyway.

In early 1940, he was arrested, and his wife and son were deported to the Kazakhstan Republic within the Soviet Union. Wat spent the better part of two years in Soviet prisons, including the most famous, Lubyanka. During that time, Wat endured an ordeal far worse than anything imagined in "Pug Iron Stove." The perpetual sense of crisis finally solidified into an actual crisis, and much to his surprise, he was not destroyed. He eventually emerged with his identity intact and stronger for the testing. At the utmost limits of his endurance, in horrible conditions in the prison at Saratov, he had a mystical experience that led to his conversion to Catholicism.

Wat would certainly have died if not for the German invasion of Russia. Suddenly, Poland was no longer a country divided between Stalin and Hitler, but a brave ally in Mother Russia's fight against the fascist invaders. Poland was recognized as a separate country, and most surviving Poles were released.

In November of 1941, Wat arrived in Kazakhstan, where the Soviets had set up a Polish enclave in exile. In the capital of Alma-Ata, he was reunited with his wife and son. Although his health never recovered from his years in jail, he was allowed a short period of relative happiness with his family. Soon, however, the Poles fell into Soviet disfavor once more.

Wat and his family were then sent deeper into exile to an isolated village where there was hardly food enough to eat. There he made the bravest stand of his life, organizing resistance to Party plans to issue everyone Soviet passports. He was briefly imprisoned, but retained his passport, which meant at war's end he remained officially a Pole, entitled to repatriation.

Despite all his troubles, Wat wrote some of his most famous verse during this time. "Willows in Alma-Ata," for example, circulated by word of mouth in Poland even before Wat's return. Its lyrical depiction of the sadness of the exile, which became a recurrent theme for Wat, served as a model for many young poets.

> Willows are willows everywhere
>
> Beautiful in rime and luster art thou, O willow of Alma-Ata.
> Yet if I forget thee, O dead willow from the Rozbrat street,
> let my hand forget her cunning!

From this opening onward, the deceptively simple poem employs many styles and themes from Polish literature and the Bible. Venclova shows how Wat's poetry of this period combines the abstract and the concrete, landscapes in particular, to achieve a calmness he would never quite manage to regain.

After the war, there was a brief flowering of Polish literature. A whole new generation of writers, such as Czesław Miłosz, did not deem Communism the enemy, at first. After returning to Warsaw in 1947, Wat himself turned a blind eye to much of what was happening in the country, hoping for the best despite the Stalinist occupation of Poland.

In 1949, however, in a scathing address to a literary gathering, Wat attacked Socialist Realism and ended his own hopes for publication. He supported himself with a little translating, but became increasingly ill. Many observers considered this condition psychosomatic, and even Venclova connects Wat's nervous ailment with the self-torturing he turned into art.

This anguish became more and more evident in poems where Wat compares himself to the walking dead or Hercules struggling to extricate himself from a poisoned cloak. Wat expresses this theme in his poem "In the Four Walls of My Pain":

> It grinds the living tissue,
> crushes the bone, squeezes the brain.
> To wring out with a bloody sweat
> words words words.

This poem, as restrictive in its structure as the fatal cloak, provides a good example of the way Wat matches style to content. This quality is what attracted the greatest comment and praise when Wat published a volume of poems in 1957 during the brief relaxation of tight Communist control in Poland.

Despite this success, Wat became more despondent. Deeply spiritual, he lacked sure faith. In 1953, Wat allowed himself to be baptized, but that did not quiet the spiritual restlessness. In fact, he became ever more aware of himself as a Jew. While retaining his Christian identity, he saw Christ as the archetypal suffering Jew.

Given the horrors of World War II, it is understandable that his attention turned to the mystery of evil's origin. He wrote a series of essays on Stalin, trying to understand the man's evil, which he considered fundamentally linguistic, a warping of the word that made moral behavior impossible. Wat also felt a personal complicity in evil. Not only had he edited a Party magazine and supported Communist governments during and after World War II, but he identified with Stalin: "the poet, master of signs and meanings" saw Stalin as his "opposite and twin, the Great Perverter and Depraver of signs."

Wat projected this guilt onto the world around him. In poems and essays, as well as an unfinished novel, Wat tried to come to terms with this evil, only to become more discouraged and depressed by his conclusions. He was increasingly aware of the divided impulse in his writing and the impossibility of resolving it. He wanted to grasp the secret of the universe while knowing it would always be multiform and open-ended. Venclova shows how the poetry, at its best, captures something of both the numinous and the actual. Writing about nature, for example, Wat creates a sensuous anthropomorphism, but it only made him more aware that he could not connect with the universal harmony. Worse, he saw in that harmony a parallel to the "harmony" promised by Stalin.

In constant distress, both emotionally and physically, Wat traveled overseas, primarily for medical treatments. He never felt comfortable as an exile and worried especially about the status of his son, but in 1959 he requested asylum in France since he could no longer publish in Poland. Unable to make a living even in the West because of his illness, he became increasingly depressed.

In 1963, he was persuaded to go to Berkeley, California, where Miłosz taught. For a brief time, Wat's health improved, but the pain soon returned, worse than ever. Unable to fulfill his duties at the University of California, he became more and more unhappy with himself. To help him get something on paper, a friend suggested he tape his memoirs in sessions with Miłosz. Wat covered only part of what he hoped to, but the transcribed and edited tapes of these interviews were later published as *My Century*.

Although it is one of the great prison memoirs, the book remains a mostly literary construct, as Venclova points out. Throughout this biography of Wat, Venclova provides many excellent close readings of Wat's poems. On the other hand, the biographical material provided by Venclova is often sketchy. Although the important details are here and Venclova certainly documents Wat's tortured existence, the reader will have to turn to *My Century* to glimpse something of the living man.

Still this is an excellent introduction to the life and work of a writer whose nature forced him to acknowledge the absurd when he sought the divine. Then history forced him to live the extremes of both. That something so frail as human consciousness could survive—and bear witness—gives Wat's poetry and memoirs an authority and power that assures their lasting significance. Unfortunately, Wat himself, riven by illness and depression, could not benefit from his own example. Deciding to end the long exile that he could no longer endure, Wat committed suicide on July 29, 1967.

Philip McDermott

Sources for Further Study

Choice. XXXIV, November, 1996, p. 466.
Library Journal. CXXI, May 1, 1996, p. 95.
New Criterion. XIV, May, 1996, p. 68.
The New York Review of Books. XLIII, November 28, 1996, p. 4.
The New York Times Book Review. CI, September 8, 1996, p. 30.
Publishers Weekly. CCXLIII, March 4, 1996, p. 44.
The Times Literary Supplement. October 4, 1996, p. 38.

ALIAS GRACE

Author: Margaret Atwood (1939-   )
Publisher: Doubleday (New York). 468 pp. $24.95
Type of work: Novel
Time: The 1830's to the 1870's
Locale: Canada

Atwood presents the story of Grace Marks, a young Irish immigrant who becomes involved in an infamous double murder in Toronto

Principal characters:
GRACE MARKS, an Irish-born young woman convicted of participation in a double murder in Toronto
MARY WHITNEY, her friend, a housemaid
THOMAS KINNEAR, a Canadian gentleman who employs Grace Marks
NANCY MONTGOMERY, Thomas Kinnear's housekeeper and lover
JAMES MCDERMOTT, a stablehand and servant employed by Kinnear who is convicted for the murders of Kinnear and Nancy Montgomery
JAMES WALSH, a farmhand employed by Kinnear
OLD JEREMIAH, a peddler, confidence man, and friend of Grace Marks
SIMON JORDAN, an American physician living in Toronto
RACHEL HUMPHREY, Jordan's landlady and erstwhile lover

Margaret Atwood is a novelist known for vividly imagining the present—and even the future—in her fiction. She is a writer who works primarily with the modern Canadian experience, who writes carefully crafted stories and novels describing the contemporary Canadian "wilderness" of social and sexual politics. In *Alias Grace*, however, Atwood shifts her perspective to the Canadian past and to the specific historical case of one woman in that past. Thus, the novel is a prime example of the historical novel, as Atwood makes of her novel (among other things) a study of history, of story, and of storytelling.

The "true story" of Grace Marks is the story of a young Irish immigrant (born in 1826) who comes to Canada with her family in the late 1830's, enters the world of domestic service, and becomes fatefully enmeshed in a scandalous double murder in 1843. Hired to join the household staff of Thomas Kinnear, and at first befriended by Kinnear's housekeeper, Nancy Montgomery, Grace gradually becomes aware of the true nature of the relationship between Kinnear and Montgomery. Grace also is drawn into the sociosexual tension that exists between Montgomery, Kinnear, and the servant James McDermott. It is McDermott who ostensibly involves Grace in his murderous revenge against both Kinnear and Montgomery, who flees with Grace into New York State, and who is arrested there with his "accomplice." At trial, both are found guilty of murder; McDermott is hanged, and Grace is sentenced to life imprisonment.

Atwood has worked with this story before, in her television play *The Servant Girl*, which was aired by the Canadian Broadcasting Corporation in 1974. The particular historical milieu is also familiar to Atwood; one of the extratextual, historical "voices" readers hear from in the novel is Susannah Moodie, who wrote two nonfiction accounts of nineteenth century Canadian life. In one of those accounts, *Life in the Clearings*, Moodie commented contemporaneously and at length on the case of Grace Marks. (Atwood has made previous use of Moodie's work and life in her own poetry.) Moodie's writing is just one of several historical "documents" Atwood uses to annotate her novel and to give it a certain historical texture and depth. Articles from the Toronto *Mirror*, excerpts from the *Punishment Book* of Kingston Penitentiary (where Grace Marks is imprisoned), passages from poems and songs about the murder, and other writings from the period all serve as voices participating in the telling of Grace's story.

One of the aims of *Alias Grace* is to study the very nature of story and of storytelling. The narrative center of Atwood's novel is Grace Marks herself. Much of the novel is told in Grace's first-person voice, as she tells her story both to the reader and to a young American doctor, Simon Jordan, who comes to study, to understand, and (he hopes) to explain her case. From the very beginning, Grace's experience—and her narrative of that experience—is fraught with ambiguity and contradiction. Her own court testimony runs counter to the accounts both of McDermott and of witnesses in the case. Most disturbing, however, is Grace's lapse of memory; significant gaps exist in her story where her memory of events simply (or not so simply) fails her. The cause of this failure becomes an important object of study and discussion within the novel, for it is necessarily linked to motive and to responsibility: Is Grace Marks's forgetfulness expedient and conscious, or is it spontaneous and induced by psychological trauma?

Responses to that question vary. The members of the jury hearing the case interpret the gaps in Grace's story as conveniently placed omissions designed by the storyteller to free herself of moral complicity; they judge Grace guilty of the act of murder. Members of the Canadian community react with varying degrees of acceptance or doubt of Grace's innocence, and many of these reactions are determined by individual perceptions of gender and class. Indeed, the whole matter of the female mind and of the female nature comes to occupy the fictional and critical discussions in this novel. The question of the "nature of a woman's heart and sensibility" is one to which many of her nineteenth century characters believe they possess the answer, and it is certainly a question Atwood has examined before in her fiction. In *Alias Grace*, however, that question is framed within the social, sexual, and intellectual dynamics of the Victorian Age.

Thus, Atwood is careful to delineate the world of Victoria Age-Canada, filling her novel with the details of that world. Grace Marks is quite clearly a person of her class and of her station. Born into a northern Irish family dominated by a brutish father, Grace suffers an Atlantic crossing during which her beloved mother dies and is buried at sea. Resettled in the urban wilderness of Toronto, Grace is forced to assume the maternal role—one of several roles she will adopt—with her younger siblings. Economic necessity eventually frees her from that role and launches her into the world of the Canadian working class.

Befriended by a young servant woman named Mary Whitney, Grace is brought into the "normalized" middle-class world of the Parkinsons, where she works with Mary on the household staff. This friendship with Mary becomes the most significant of Grace's life; the two women forge what is in some ways a shared existence and consciousness. When Mary is doubly victimized (a common plight of Atwood's women) by her employer's son—made both a physical and social victim—and impregnated, she seeks solution at the hands of a backstreet abortionist. When that abortion is botched and Mary dies, the experience comes to haunt Grace Marks in both her waking and her dreaming lives; when Grace later flees into the United States, she "becomes" Mary Whitney, using that name as an alias.

Grace, however, seems to adopt several aliases (thus, the title of the novel), so that the reader never does quite pin down the true Grace Marks. Nor does the visiting doctor from Massachusetts, Simon Jordan (Atwood's fictional creation), who comes to Toronto in 1859 to explicate the case of this "celebrated murderess" and perhaps to obtain for her a pardon. Despite his progressive, enlightened insights into the intricate world of the human psyche, Jordan never does satisfactorily penetrate the mystery of Grace's identity. As he listens to Grace's story—or to one version of that story, for Grace is a highly self-conscious and purposeful storyteller—Jordan struggles to remain detached and disinterested in that story and its storyteller. In one sense, the story becomes an act of seduction, as Grace draws Jordan into her narrated world and experience, into her version of the "true story." When that story complicates itself with gaps and contradictions, Jordan finds himself unable to resolve and to close that story; interestingly enough, closure is not a problem that seems to unsettle Grace Marks, the object of that story.

At the same time, Jordan involves himself in a sociosexual drama of his own, one which parallels the story related by Grace Marks. With a kind of inexorable fatality, Jordan becomes sexually indebted to his rather pathetic landlady, Rachel Humphrey. Class and socioeconomic differences highlight the impossibility of this relationship, particularly when Mrs. Humphrey begins imagining marriage—preceded by the premeditated murder of her long-absent husband—to the doctor. In her own way, Mrs. Humphrey becomes another of Atwood's victimized (and perhaps self-victimized) women, betrayed by sexual desire, economic want, and perceptual disparity. What Rachel Humphrey envisions as the truth differs greatly from what Simon Jordan envisions as the truth. Yet both characters play out this sad and tawdry drama to its end, seeking and finding separate resolutions.

The connections between Rachel Humphrey and Grace Marks are clear enough. In some ways, at least according to Grace's version of the story, Grace is drawn into a relationship with James McDermott against her will and made the resistant accomplice to his acts. There is even a sham marriage—Grace playing a double role, assuming the name of Mary Whitney and the part of McDermott's "wife"—when the couple attempt their escape from Canada. When their stories conflict as testimony, Grace gains some measure of satisfaction when her story seems to prevail in the legal (if not public and/or journalistic) consciousness. In the end, it is the story shaped by her lawyer that allows Grace Marks to elude the hangman's noose and to "win" imprisonment.

Grace spends twenty-eight years in prison and in lunatic asylums (she is first believed to be criminally insane), and Atwood does not let readers miss the point of Grace's incarceration in Kingston Penitentiary. Penitence becomes a major criterion for Grace's pardon, a visible sign of her rehabilitation, and Grace plays that role successfully. She even works her way back into the social world of the domestic servant and regains a certain degree of public trust. Yet she is always a sort of specimen and the object of study. She eventually comes under the sympathetic, though professional, scrutiny of Simon Jordan. Still later, she forms a "pact" with her old friend Jeremiah, who shows up in the disguise of a spiritualist doctor—Jeremiah as confidence man—who seeks to retrieve Grace's memory through hypnosis. While under Jeremiah's "spell," Grace speaks out in the voice of Mary Whitney, who seems to inhabit Grace's body and subconsciousness. Grace reveals a sort of multiple personality, what the Victorians called a "double consciousness," thus adding another layer (and another voice) to the stories being told. What is also added is another explanation for the nature and behavior of Grace Marks.

Eventually, Grace's story achieves a kind of resolution. She is abandoned by Simon Jordan who, doubly shaken by the turns of events in his relationships with Grace and with Mrs. Humphrey, returns to the United States; there, he suffers a severe head wound in the Civil War and, with proper irony, endures a loss of memory. Even without Jordan's help, Grace obtains a pardon in 1872, after twenty-eight years of imprisonment, of loss of privacy and freedom. Her immediately perceived need upon her release is the adoption of a new role, a new part to play in this drastically revised drama that is her life. She removes herself—or is removed by her friends—from Canada and is relocated in Ithaca, New York. In a prearranged construction of events, Grace is reunited with James Walsh, a former farmhand on the Kinnear estate and her longtime admirer; it was Walsh who provided Grace with her happiest memory of that time in her life. Grace and Walsh marry, designing a domestic existence from the odd parts of their emotional relationship. There is even the hint of a baby to come. These, too, are the details of Grace's story, as she relates them to Simon Jordan through her letters (the several epistolary narratives offer both a formal and a historical subtext to the novel), and they seem "true" elements of that story. In this way, Grace obtains temporary closure for her story up to that point.

Strikingly enough, however, Atwood refuses to allow Grace the final word in that story. Atwood's afterword provides a kind of metafictional commentary on the story that she and her character have just told. Because *Alias Grace* is a historical novel, Atwood somewhat carefully distinguishes between the historical and the fictional content of her story. Atwood turns from being the novelist to being the historian, adding a kind of footnote to this version of Grace Marks's story. As a result, readers are still left wondering about the problem of authenticity and reliability. Whose voice or voices have been heard in *Alias Grace*? What is the nature of that voice or of those voices? Ambiguity, complexity, contradiction: These, Atwood suggests, are the tools of the storyteller and even, perhaps, of the historian.

Gregory L. Morris

Sources for Further Study

Booklist. XCIII, September 15, 1996, p. 180.
Boston Globe. December 8, 1996, p. N16.
Library Journal. CXXI, November 1, 1996, p. 106.
Los Angeles Times Book Review. December 15, 1996, p. 2.
The Nation. CCLXIII, December 9, 1996, p. 25.
The New York Times. December 30, 1996, p. B1.
The New York Times Book Review. CI, December 29, 1996, p. 6.
Publishers Weekly. CCXLIII, October 7, 1996, p. 58.
Time. CXLIX, December 16, 1996, p. 75.
The Wall Street Journal. November 15, 1996, p. A12.
World Press Review. XLIII, December, 1996, p. 43.

THE AMERASIA SPY CASE
Prelude to McCarthyism

Authors: Harvey Klehr (1945-   ) and Ronald Radosh (1937-   )
Publisher: University of North Carolina Press (Chapel Hill). Illustrated. 266 pp. $29.95
Type of work: History
Time: The 1930's to the 1950's
Locale: Primarily the United States

A fascinating account of the first important American spy scandal of the postwar era

Principal personages:
PHILIP JAFFE, the editor of *Amerasia*
KATE MITCHELL, the assistant editor of *Amerasia*
ANDREW ROTH, a lieutenant in the Office of Naval Intelligence
EMMANUEL LARSON, an employee of the State Department
MARK GAYN, a journalist
JOHN SERVICE, a foreign service officer
LAUCHLIN CURRIE, a presidential adviser
BEN COHEN, legal counsel to the State Department
THOMAS CORCORAN, a Washington insider
J. EDGAR HOOVER, the director of the Federal Bureau of Investigation
    (FBI), 1924-1972
TOM CLARK, the attorney general of the United States, 1945-1949

As the Cold War recedes, distance is clarifying our understanding of many controversial episodes in that bitter conflict. The opening of archives, in Russia, the United
States, and elsewhere, has shed much light on these events, providing facts where
assertion and assumption once held sway. With the collapse of the Soviet Union, the
ebbing of Communism into irrelevancy, and the remorseless passing of generations,
the passions which once distorted any account of the struggle between East and West,
socialist and capitalist, are rapidly withering away. It is possible now to study those
days with the objectivity born of genuine detachment. Soon the story of the Cold War,
shorn of its ideological immediacy, will take its place in the larger stream of human
memory, becoming the stuff of tragedy and of comedy, providing provender for
philosophers and dramatists. Historians, whose concerns merge the philosophic and
dramatic, will also search the record of the Cold War for insights into the enduring
limits of the human condition.

Ronald Radosh and Harvey Klehr's *The Amerasia Spy Case: Prelude to McCarthyism* is a compelling product of this new era in Cold War historiography. Making
brilliant use of newly released Federal Bureau of Investigation (FBI) files, they vividly
re-create the first of the spy cases which rocked Soviet-American relations in the years
immediately following World War II. Yet the focus of their interest is less the fervent
political enthusiasms of the time, than the varied characters of the men and women
involved in the *Amerasia* case. In the hands of Radosh and Klehr, this tale of attempted
espionage becomes a meditation on pride, ambition, and greed. The story they tell is
not a pretty one, and neither old cold warriors nor their critics will be able to draw

much comfort from Radosh and Klehr's book. As the authors themselves point out, "it has few heroes, many villains, and more than a few knaves. None of the participants emerges with an unscathed reputation." What remains is a sobering study of corruption, both personal and political, a disheartening chronicle of idealism, and justice, gone awry.

Radosh and Klehr write with authority. Radosh is the coauthor of a ground-breaking study which argued that Julius and Ethel Rosenberg were indeed guilty of espionage. Although Radosh was vilified by partisans of the Rosenbergs when his book appeared, subsequent research has borne out his conclusions. Radosh's work was anything but a simple right-wing assault on two treasured icons of the left. At the same time that Radosh conceded the guilt of the Rosenbergs, he also criticized the unscrupulous tactics of the federal prosecutors in the case. Klehr is the author or coauthor of several books on the history of American Communism. He has been especially interested in showing the connections between the Communist Party of the United States (CPUSA) and the Soviet Union, with particular emphasis on the support officials of the CPUSA gave to Soviet intelligence agencies. Between them, Radosh and Klehr bring a wealth of knowledge to bear on their subject.

The *Amerasia* affair was set in motion in February, 1945, when the chief of the Southern Asia section of the Office of Strategic Services (OSS), the wartime precursor of the Central Intelligence Agency (CIA), picked up the January 26 issue of *Amerasia* and read an article on Thailand which had obviously been plagiarized from a highly classified report he himself had written. Alarmed at this breach in security, he notified the OSS's Domestic Intelligence Division. Agents were swiftly assigned to watch the offices of *Amerasia*. On the night of March 11, confident that nobody was working late, a team of operatives surreptitiously entered the offices. What they found astonished them. Scattered throughout the rooms were hundreds of government documents, many of them stamped "Top Secret." Among the documents were records of the locations of enemy warships and plans for bombing the Japanese mainland. The agents retrieved a few of the papers, believing that they would not be missed amid the clutter, and left as stealthily as they had entered. Their discoveries caused consternation in the upper reaches of the American government. The case was put into the hands of the FBI, which immediately began an elaborate investigation.

The prime suspect for the government was Philip Jaffe, the editor of *Amerasia*. Jaffe was a study in contradictions. Born in the Ukraine to a poor Jewish family, Jaffe came to the United States as a boy. He soon demonstrated remarkable energy and entrepreneurial skill. Forced to abandon youthful hopes of an academic career by financial pressures, Jaffe made himself a millionaire marketing greeting cards. Despite his capitalistic success, Jaffe early became an enthusiast for the Soviet experiment. Although he apparently did not join the Communist Party, he became a committed fellow traveler, actively laboring in a number of front organizations. Ironically, he was never much appreciated by the Party leadership.

Jaffe finally found his niche as editor of *China Today*, a small journal that parroted the Communist line on Chinese affairs. This began Philip Jaffe's transformation into an expert on the Far East. He was only able to visit China once, in 1937, during which he made a perilous journey to the Communist stronghold of Yenan. That same year, Jaffe founded *Amerasia*, a more scholarly, and slightly more independent, successor to *China Today*. *Amerasia*'s readership was small, but influential. For a time, Jaffe enjoyed the intellectual respect he craved. Yet a combination of the dislocations brought on by World War II, doubts about his pro-Communist editorial line, and Jaffe's own prickly personality dried up contributors to and contributions for *Amerasia*. By 1945, Jaffe and his assistant editor, Kate Mitchell, were writing virtually everything in the magazine. To generate material for his journal, Jaffe cultivated a small circle of contacts in Washington, D.C. Among them was Andrew Roth, a twenty-five-year-old lieutenant attached to the Office of Naval Intelligence (ONI). A Navy review board, after investigating Roth's background, had concluded that he was a Communist, and recommended that he not be assigned to the ONI. Despite this, he was posted to the ONI, and, by 1944, was the ONI liaison to the State Department. Roth introduced Jaffe to Emmanuel Sigurd Larson, a man who, while living a colorful life in China, had developed an encyclopedic knowledge of Chinese political figures. On the strength of this talent, he had been hired by the ONI. In late 1944, Larson transferred to a job in the State Department. Roth and Larson began passing documents to Jaffe, for use as background for his magazine. Jaffe was not the only person to benefit from this traffic in government documents. He gave some of them to a friend, Mark Gayn, a journalist who shared his political sympathies, and who published in such popular magazines as *Colliers* and *Time*.

While the activities of Jaffe, Roth, Larson, and Gayn were illegal, they did not initially constitute espionage. When the FBI first began tracking Jaffe and his associates, it appeared as if the case might merely concern an overzealous journalist and some profoundly indiscreet government employees. Yet late in April, events took a more ominous turn. On April 22, Jaffe held a meeting at his home, which was attended by a member of the Communist Chinese delegation to the United Nations conference in San Francisco. The FBI believed that this private gathering gave Jaffe a perfect opportunity to pass documents to the Chinese Communists. Even more disturbing, a former employee named Joseph Bernstein contacted Jaffe on April 30 and made a lunch date for two days later. According to the secretly recorded account that Jaffe gave to Andrew Roth, Bernstein identified himself as a Soviet agent and asked for Jaffe's help in acquiring information on the State Department's attitude toward China. After checking out Bernstein with some contacts in the CPUSA, Jaffe decided to cooperate with Bernstein. The FBI now had evidence that Jaffe was set on embarking on a career as a spy.

Complicating the case at this point was the entry of John Stewart Service. Service was the son of American missionaries in China. After spending most of his youth in China, he joined the State Department and quickly established himself as an able and promising foreign service officer. He became one of the "China Hands," a group of State Department experts on China who doubted the prospects of Chiang Kai-shek's Kuomintang government and advocated building better relations with Mao Tse-tung's

Communists. Service's anti-Chiang opinions finally brought him afoul of Patrick Hurley, a conservative Republican whom President Franklin Roosevelt had named ambassador to China. Hurley engineered Service's reassignment to Washington, D.C., in April, 1945. Almost immediately, Service was cultivated by Jaffe and his circle. Service responded warmly, so much so that Jaffe could not at first believe his success with this new contact. Service's generosity, however, was not a tribute to Jaffe's charm. After conferring with friends, including Lauchlin Currie, an adviser to the president, Service had decided to wage bureaucratic war against Hurley and his supporters in the State Department through a campaign of leaks. By passing on to Jaffe information embarrassing to Hurley and the Chiang Kai-shek regime in Peking, he hoped to help undermine their position and set the stage for a new direction in China policy. Service had no idea that he had decided to leak confidential information to a man who had decided to become a spy for the Soviet Union.

On June 6, the FBI arrested Philip Jaffe, Kate Mitchell, Mark Gayn, Emmanuel Larson, Andrew Roth, and John Service. The FBI's case was largely built on wiretap evidence, the legal validity of which was quite unclear in 1945. Nevertheless, FBI director J. Edgar Hoover and his subordinates believed that the bureau's extraordinary measures would be sustained in court for reasons of national security. Yet, almost immediately, the case began to unravel. One difficulty faced by the FBI and the Justice Department was the reluctance of other government agencies to allow confidential materials to be entered as evidence against the defendants. The government was caught in a dilemma; to protect its secrets, it would have to reveal them. Much of the most damning evidence against Jaffe and his associates was removed from consideration. Further, many members of the press perceived the *Amerasia* case, the full details of which could not be revealed, to be merely a rather heavy-handed attempt by the government to silence leakers. Maladroit public relations by government officials served to fuel this perception.

Philip Jaffe shrewdly retained as his legal counsel the law partner of Congressman Emmanuel Celler of Brooklyn, a Democrat well known for his weight with the Truman Administration. Kate Mitchell's doting uncle, a politically powerful attorney in Buffalo, New York, secured first-class legal representation for her as well. Most decisively, however, John Service's friend Lauchlin Currie intervened. He called Ben Cohen, a famous New Dealer who was legal counsel to the State Department. Anxious to avoid an embarrassing scandal, Cohen in turn enlisted his long-time associate Thomas Corcoran, a legendary political "fixer." Although out of government, Corcoran had lost none of his clout. He moved rapidly and effectively. Corcoran had reasons of his own for involving himself in the *Amerasia* case. He had business interests with the Kuomintang, and Chiang's men did not want a trial which might air criticisms of their regime.

Ironically, the FBI was listening in as Corcoran wrecked their case. Suspicious of the quintessential Washington insider, President Harry Truman had ordered an illegal wiretap of Corcoran's office phone. Corcoran cut a deal with attorney general designate Tom Clark. In return for assistance in guaranteeing Clark's confirmation, the Justice Department would back off charges against John Service and go easy with the other *Amerasia* defendants. A prosecutor was brought in from New York State who showed little enthusiasm for his job. Later, he would take a job as partner in Kate Mitchell's uncle's law firm. Espionage charges were dropped. In the end, Jaffe and Larson paid fines for a lesser charge. Service and the others walked away.

The *Amerasia* affair had a long afterlife. Conservatives smelled a rat, and, occasionally encouraged by an irate J. Edgar Hoover, made the case a symbol of "Red" influence in Washington, D.C. A series of congressional hearings followed, in which Democrats loyally covered up the true facts of the matter, and some Republicans concocted increasingly hysterical conspiracy theories. Ultimately, Senator Joseph McCarthy would make the case a centerpiece of his accusations of Communist infiltration of the State Department. Radosh and Klehr argue that the *Amerasia* case helped prepare the ideological ground for McCarthyism. One set of lies begat another. Lost in the machinations in Washington was the American people's right to the truth.

Daniel P. Murphy

Sources for Further Study

Chicago Tribune. June 9, 1996, XIV, p. 3.
Choice. XXXIII, July, 1996, p. 1859.
History: Reviews of New Books. XXV, Fall, 1996, p. 13.
Human Events. LII, July 12, 1996, p. 12.
Kirkus Reviews. LXIII, December 1, 1995, p. 1685.
The National Interest. Fall, 1996, p. 101.
The New York Times Book Review. CI, March 31, 1996, p. 24.
Publishers Weekly. CCXLII, December 11, 1995, p. 64.
The Times Literary Supplement. May 17, 1996, p. 8.

AMERICAN EXCEPTIONALISM
A Double-Edged Sword

Author: Seymour Martin Lipset (1922-   )
Publisher: W. W. Norton (New York). 352 pp. $27.50
Type of work: Essays; political science and cultural analysis

A collection of essays, reworked to shed light on the question of how American attitudes and institutions differ from those of Canada and Europe

Seymour Martin Lipset's long career as a sociologist and political scientist has focused on such institutions as trade unions, higher education, radicals and revolutions, American Jewry, Canadian politics, and problems of the welfare state. Born in 1922, Lipset has at last become something of an institution himself. Harvard University, Stanford University, George Mason University, the Progressive Policy Institute, and the Hoover Institution—these have been some of his academic way stations. One measure of his breadth of interest and achievement is the fact that he has served as the president of both the American Political Science Association and the American Sociological Association.

Lipset's interest in the problem of the uniqueness of the American national venture is of long duration. Indeed, as he states in the foreword of *American Exceptionalism: A Double-Edged Sword*, "My first book, *Agrarian Socialism* (1950), which was also my doctoral dissertation at Columbia University, took off from the issue 'Why no socialism in the United States?' " His major first statement on this topic was the important work, *The First New Nation: The United States in Historical and Comparative Perspective*, first published in 1963. The 1990 volume, *Continental Divide: The Values and Institutions of the United States and Canada*, sought to portray the cultural and institutional difference of "two countries which reflect the varying outcomes of the American Revolution in different sections of what had been British North America." Lipset's work on the history and cultural situation of American Jews has also placed exceptionalism in the foreground, as he tried to account for the relative absence of anti-Judaism in the nation's life.

What exactly is "American exceptionalism"? For such scholars as Louis Hartz, R. W. B. Lewis, George W. Pierson, Robert Bellah, and Lipset himself, the exceptionalism discussion springs from this question: "Is the United States an historically unique culture in ways that really matter?" Certainly America's national symbols and rhetorical heritage encourage such a view. The Puritan and biblical image of a "shining city upon a hill" was invoked in Ronald Reagan's presidential campaigns. The dollar bill contains the Latin phrase "Novus ordo seclorum"—a new order of the world. The Jeffersonian tradition pictures this country as a fresh start for humankind, one based on agriculture, scientific reason, educational opportunity, and the widespread ownership of productive property. "New Deal," "New Frontier," "New World Order"—such verbal formulas attest to the power of the idea of America's special destiny and historical novelty.

While such rhetoric can be both self-congratulatory and self-deceptive, the testimonies of foreign observers have often confirmed American exceptionalism. Over the years, Lipset has been particularly attentive to the nineteenth century writings of Alexis de Tocqueville and Harriet Martineau. The former's observations proved particularly astute, for with astonishing predictive power he linked the positive achievements of the new American democracy with certain quite unanticipated negative tendencies. Emancipated from the disciplining authoritative structures of social class, ecclesiastical power, and venerable tradition, the American was indeed the world's freest individual. Yet, observed Tocqueville, this very freedom makes the citizen subject to both the tyranny of majority opinion and the temptations of individualism.

"Individualism," in Tocqueville's account, is an exhilarating emancipation as well as an invitation to ignore the needs of the commonwealth. Americans are thus "naturally" inclined to lapse into subjectivism, solipsism, and the self-indulgent cultivation of private realms. What rescues them from a profoundly antisocial way of life is the countervailing tendency to form voluntary organizations for the solving of collective problems. The health of the "intermediate realm" of voluntary associations is therefore critical to the republic's survival, for these draw the individual into civic callings and require the tempering of egoistic, isolationist impulses. The most important free groups in America are religious ones, believed Tocqueville. For, in Lipset's gloss on the Frenchman's text, "voluntary religion fostered the myriad of voluntary associations. . . . These associations of what has come to be known as civil society create networks of communication among people with common positions and interests helping to sustain the moral order, political parties, and participation."

Tocqueville's brilliant insights about what made the United States a unique society sprang from research joined with preternatural philosophic genius. Lipset approaches Tocqueville's subject as a social scientist, one who must take account of a large critical literature as well as decades of empirical work. Hence, while he still finds Tocqueville generally accurate, Lipset ranges widely through a variety of evidence to build a richly documented and nuanced picture of the American difference. The reader is drawn into discussions of the difference between conservatism in Europe and America; the extraordinary weakness of the American state and the concomitant strength of Constitution-based individual rights; the feeble grip of political party discipline; the relation between the ethic of success in the United States and the country's exorbitant crime rate; the extreme inequality of wealth in the United States; its comparatively light tax burden; and the patriotism and optimism of its people.

One might have hoped for a magistrally systematic book from Lipset on this subject, but *American Exceptionalism* is actually a collection of previously published articles. While an attempt at editorial coherence is evident, overlaps, omissions, gaps, and odd transitions are plentiful. For example, early in the book Lipset excuses himself from discussing how the United States differs from other New World nations, saying, "I do not want to take on the issue of how exceptional the Americas are; dealing with the United States is more than enough." This is a costly refusal, however, for comparisons with other "settler nations" would certainly be revealing. American citizens have much to learn about their own "race problem" by considering its parallels in Brazil or Argentina. In his provocative work *The End of Racism: Principles for a Multiracial Society* (1995), Dinesh D'Souza does this very thing, with striking effect. Americans sense that learning about the Australian national experience can teach them much about themselves. Lipset, however, almost completely ignores this other English-speaking "New World."

Lipset devotes three chapters to "Exceptions on the Margin." In these he treats black-white relations, the history and present standing of Jews, and changing trends and fashions among American intellectuals. Much in these chapters is valuable and interesting, but one constantly senses that the discussion is veering too far from the topic of American cultural difference. Lipset clearly has other items on his agenda besides that of reaffirming exceptionalism. One of these is, simply put, a defense of historic American institutions and cultural practices. In his foreword, Lipset states that "there can be little question that the hand of providence has been on a nation which finds a Washington, a Lincoln, or a Roosevelt when it needs him." He further offers that "I write also as a proud American," one who, while not espousing national superiority, nevertheless "believes that the greatness of free politics lies in their institutionalization of conflict, of the continued struggles for freer and more humanely decent societies." Thus, *American Exceptionalism* actually shoulders two tasks: high-lighting essential national differences and celebrating key elements of that emergent portrait of difference. Put another way, Seymour Martin Lipset has apparently made the same journey to the right that has marked the careers of a number of important Jewish intellectuals.

This shift is nowhere clearer than in his treatment of the "cultural left." Chapter 6 is entitled "American Intellectuals—Mostly on the Left, Some Politically Incorrect." Only two paragraphs of this thirty-four-page excursion treat the interesting and challenging question of the cultural uniqueness of the American intelligentsia. Lipset is actually concerned to describe and evaluate key developments in the political left from the Depression to the present. In doing so, he is clearly defining his own evolution from a strong advocate of the New Deal (and European-style social democracy) to what has come to be known as "neo-conservatism."

As Lipset presents the matter, the starting point for critical later developments was the struggle in the 1930's and 1940's between leftists sympathetic to Stalin's brand of Communism and the more democratic and internationalist version offered by Leon Trotsky and his followers. Out of this split there developed an anticommunist, anti-Soviet tendency within the left, one that found clearest expression in the Demo-cratic Socialist movement, headed by the late Michael Harrington. With a clarity obviously born of much direct experience, Lipset details the misunderstanding that grew up between Harrington's sort of socialism and the student radicals of the 1960's and Marxist academics of the 1970's and 1980's—the architects of "political correct-ness." Lipset also shows how it happened that some of those who shared Harrington's enmity for Stalinism could have actually ended up as supporters of Ronald Reagan and the Republican Party.

For readers interested in the migration to the right of figures such as Norman Podhorez, Midge Decter, Gertrude Himmelfarb, Irving Kristol, and Jeane Kirkpatrick, the account supplied by Lipset is a lucid one. That he refrains completely from giving a straightforward indication of his own positioning, however, is a significant liability. For other vantage points on this history, readers should compare accounts by Irving Howe, Richard John Neuhaus, Paul Berman, and John Judis. While Lipset cites these writers, he does not make sufficient use of their insights. As new biographies of Michael Harrington begin to appear, new clarity on a signal development in American intellectual life will be possible.

For Seymour Martin Lipset, American exceptionalism is a "double-edged sword." What is meant by this? The extent to which the United States is still unique is, for Lipset, "astonishing." Its uniqueness centers in its ideology, "The American Creed," which is so fervently embraced by all parties that one can scarcely comprehend a nation which, like England, is held together more by traditional institutions than a consensus of values. This creed can be described in five terms, asserts Lipset: "liberty, egalitarianism, individualism, populism, and laissez-faire." In practice, the elements of this creed have been elaborated into a complex ethic of a liberal social order—one for which Lipset has the greatest admiration.

When pressed too far, however, the central passions arising from this creed can become dangerous. Populism and antielitism can engender lack of respect for authority, declining discipline in schools, and low electoral turnouts. Individualism can unleash an emphasis on achievement that makes crime a profound temptation for those shut out of accepted means of advancement. "In a country that stresses success above all, people are led to feel that the most important thing is to win the game, regardless of the methods employed in doing so," observes Lipset. By exaggerating the idea that the individual is self-made, the culture comes to look down on those who must rely on others—the weak and underprivileged. The creed is enshrined in Constitution-based individual rights, but such rights can become anticommunal, as the proliferation of deadly weapons shows. (No country in the world appears to face a gun problem so extreme as that seen in the United States.)

Thus, while American exceptionalism is generally seen in very positive ways by Lipset, he recognizes that in it also lies the source of most of the nation's problems. His writings on this subject are thus of immense value, for they help illuminate the special vulnerabilities that arise from the nation's strength. Readers interested in American exceptionalism should consider Lipset essential reading.

His works, however, ought not to be the only ones consulted. This is partly because Lipset relies heavily on terms dear to sociologists and political science—but not to general readers. One of these is "Protestant sectarianism." Lipset correctly sees that much in American life is conditioned by religious enthusiasms, but he seems quite deaf to the nuances and tones of real religious practices. His accounts of millenarianism, evangelicalism, revivalism, Baptist polity and Methodist discipline seem to come from someone who has scientifically studied these "phenomena," but does not really grasp them. He thus can contrast cultures dominated by a territorial church (Ireland,

Greece) with those offering a voluntaristic, congregational, pluralistic arrangement. Yet he rarely gets beyond this basic typology. He is content merely to invoke it as something that explains a great deal. One is left to supply the details and particularities oneself. The effect of this is to leave one uncertain about Lipset's adequacy as a guide in these important areas.

Leslie E. Gerber

Sources for Further Study

The Christian Science Monitor. April 29, 1996, p. 13.
Commonweal. CXXIII, September 13, 1996, p. 38.
Foreign Affairs. LXXV, March, 1996, p. 135.
Humanities. XVII, July, 1996, p. 4.
The Nation. CCLXII, May 6, 1996, p. 28.
New Statesman and Society. IX, March 29, 1996, p. 33.
The New York Times Book Review. CI, February 11, 1996, p. 7.
Publishers Weekly. CCXLIII, February 5, 1996, p. 75.
The Times Literary Supplement. March 29, 1996, p. 7.
The Washington Post Book World. XXVI, April 7, 1996, p. 4.

AN AMERICAN REQUIEM
God, My Father, and the War That Came Between Us

Author: James Carroll (1943-   )
Publisher: Houghton Mifflin (Boston). 279 pp. $23.95
Type of work: Memoir
Time: 1943 to the 1990's
Locale: Primarily the United States

Carroll describes his childhood relationship with his father, his adolescent and young adult struggle for personal identity, his decision to become a Catholic priest, his role as a dissident cleric during the Vietnam War, its effects on his relations with his father, his decision to leave the priesthood, and the final break between father and son that never healed

> *Principal personages:*
> JAMES CARROLL, an American novelist and former priest who was an
>   antiwar activist during the 1960's
> GENERAL JOSEPH CARROLL, his father, who began his career as an FBI
>   agent and went on to have a distinguished career in military
>   intelligence
> MARY CARROLL, his mother
> J. EDGAR HOOVER, director of the Federal Bureau of Investigation (FBI),
>   1924-1972
> CARDINAL FRANCIS SPELLMAN, a family friend who encouraged James
>   Carroll to enter the priesthood
> HANS KÜNG, a Swiss theologian who influenced James Carroll's
>   religious outlook
> GENERAL CURTIS D. LEMAY, a notable American military leader and
>   family friend of the Carrolls
> ALLEN TATE, a noted writer who tutored James Carroll when he attended
>   seminary school and encouraged his writing career

James Carroll is known as the author of nine well-received novels. *An American Requiem: God, My Father, and the War That Came Between Us*, however, is a work of nonfiction in which the author lays bare the tragic story of his relationship with his distinguished father, General Joseph Carroll. Joseph Carroll held important positions in U.S. Intelligence throughout the 1950's and 1960's and therefore during much of the Vietnam conflict that did much to create and deepen the estrangement between father and son.

The course of the relationship between father and son is in great measure the story of the younger Carroll's attempts to establish his own identity while simultaneously preserving the paternal bond. The problem confronting him, Carroll writes, was how to be "both a man and a son." In the end, perhaps inevitably, the task was beyond reach, leaving deep wounds that Carroll exposes in this poignant, often gripping, memoir.

Because of Joseph Carroll's high position in American government, *An American Requiem* takes the reader on a panoramic tour of American history in the first decades following World War II. Carroll's childhood encompassed his father's triumphs as an FBI agent and his personal elevation by Director J. Edgar Hoover himself, who brought Joseph Carroll to Washington, D.C., and made him the agency's chief troubleshooter.

The elder Carroll's accomplishments led to his appointment as director of the U.S. Air Force's Office of Special Investigations (OSI) followed by appointment to head the Defense Intelligence Agency (DIA), which under its new director became a powerful counterfoil to the Central Intelligence Agency. The first appointment resulted in Senator Stuart Symington, a key congressional backer who had been the first secretary of the Air Force, becoming General Carroll's mentor; the second brought him into close association with Secretary of Defense Robert McNamara. Joseph Carroll led the DIA until 1969, when his refusal to misinform Congress on the state of Soviet strategic doctrine led to his ouster and retirement. In 1991, suffering from Alzheimer's disease, he died at the age of eighty.

In the intervening years, Joseph Carroll's career in the FBI and the military took his family from Chicago to the nation's capital in 1947, at the outbreak of the Cold War. From there, in the 1950's, they traveled on temporary assignment to Germany; and, returning stateside before the end of the decade, arrived in Washington in time to live through the heady days of John F. Kennedy's presidency. They were therefore also in time for the emergence of the Civil Rights movement, and the tragic history of assassination followed by a war that divided America and eventually destroyed Lyndon Johnson's presidency.

During this period, James Carroll moved through childhood and adolescence to young adulthood. His career path had been laid out for him by his father's unspoken, but clearly understood, expectation that he would enter the priesthood, a vocation Joseph Carroll had rejected for himself on grounds of his unworthiness. Religion in the Carroll household—Joseph, his wife Mary, and their five sons—betokened a world of suffering and asceticism. Sex was unmentioned. This traditional Roman Catholic world jarred badly with James's early libidinal stirrings. Although James joined the Paulist Fathers and was ultimately ordained a priest, collision with a church he came to see as "rigid, morose, and moralistic" became unavoidable. More fundamentally, he came to feel that the choice of a clerical life was not his own. To become a man, he must defy his father's expectations and leave the priesthood.

From within the church, Carroll's sub rosa filial rebellion proceeded at one remove from its hidden paternal focus. Radicalized by new winds of liberation theology, the Civil Rights movement, and, especially, the Vietnam War, the dissident priest could not prevent tensions with General Carroll, followed by open breach and his father's declaration that he would not speak to his son again. The author's account of this history is, by turns, loving, agonizing, and heartbreaking, its final act of separation seemingly beyond hope from the outset. It is the stuff of Greek tragedy.

Along the way, readers meet some of the familiar names of the era's political and social history. Carroll begins his journey of self-discovery and separation from the expectations of an emotionally repressive family through popular music, especially that of Elvis Presley, whom Carroll once glimpsed at a club frequented by GIs in Germany. He meets J. Edgar Hoover, whom he later considers his personal enemy, and Cardinal Francis Spellman, a family friend who wished to ordain him. He dates Lynda Bird Johnson, daughter of Lyndon Johnson, cruising the Potomac on the vice presidential yacht with the girl's parents. His family has an audience with Pope John XXIII (a "counter-Elvis"); Joseph Carroll frequents the White House, dealing with President Kennedy, whom James Carroll meets and admires. General Curtis D. LeMay is a neighbor and family friend, an early idol of James, but despised by the rebel-priest of the mid-1960's as infamous warmonger.

After James's entrance into the Paulist Fathers' seminary, readers hear renowned Swiss theology professor Hans Küng's clarion call to church reform, with descriptions of church officials as fallible, sinful human beings, that thrilled young Turk seminarians but was ultimately suppressed. Readers even get to *The Dick Cavett Show*, if not to Cavett himself, where Carroll denounced the Vietnam War.

Carroll's narrative has occasional recourse to "psychologese," speaking of his "Oedipal" situation, a reference to Sigmund Freud's "Oedipus complex"—sons' predicament in wishing to overthrow (psychically "murder") their fathers as familial potentates, their unconscious guilt over the wish, and their consequent emotional conflict. Despite such references, the author omits psychological theorizing and simply recounts his story, exposing his feelings and motives. Carroll does, however, indulge in exhibiting his residual rebellion, refusing to conform to the prose of priests and purists by gratuitously interjecting the "f" word. He also leaves self-conscious markers of his continuing loyalty to antiwar radicalism, labeling the Paris peace accords America's "surrender document."

The tension and poignancy of Carroll's exploration of this story flow from his skill in arousing sympathy for father as well as son, re-creating in the reader the very conflict the author seeks to expiate in himself. How he loves his father and longs for a return to the sweet bond of masculine affection! He relates how as a priest he was taken with the claim that Jesus called God "Abba" ("father" or "daddy") and that He came to understand Himself by understanding this "father." The dissident priest missed his deep tie with earthly "daddy": "My nostalgia for a lost bond . . . was like everyone's nostalgia for a Garden of Eden." Yet James Carroll found the bond increasingly remote as the sense of a separate identity—especially moral identity—solidified.

The drama of Carroll's torment over his rebellion against paternal authority and his deep filial love and loyalty shifted from the family to the Roman Catholic church. As a priest, he was bound to hierarchical obedience in a structure of church government, essentially unchanged from its medieval origins, that enforced dogma laid down by the Council of Trent in the sixteenth century. Absolutist paternal authority sat no better with Carroll in a religious context than it did within the family.

In important ways this is a book about authority. It presents a somewhat one-sided view of the matter, however, for authority is an essential need of society. Every society, including liberal democracy, requires public authority. Yet democracy in particular requires acceptance by the individual of an inner authority, constructed from "authority figures" such as parents, clergy, or teachers. Woe betide democracy when the inner authority of self-discipline (most often learned and transmitted in the family) breaks down under the lash of primal urges. In the absence of internal self-control, some degree of social disorder is unavoidable. As political philosophers have known for millennia, the arrival of universal license is followed quickly by the heavy hand of authoritarianism.

As forces of change were unleashed during the turbulent years of the 1960's and into the 1970's, they were bound to collide with the Joseph Carrolls of the nation and were likewise destined to clash with the Cardinal Spellmans of the Roman Catholic hierarchy. In James Carroll's ecclesiastic world the old authority was being challenged by the likes of Professor Küng, a latter-day Martin Luther, who urged fundamental reform of church government that meant challenging its traditional authority structure.

The end of obedience is the beginning of politics—in the family, in societies that reject obedience to monarchs and choose democracy instead, or, as here, within a church in which democratic forces arose. Carroll's increasingly radical rebellion throughout the 1960's were mirrored in his theological politics. His image of the Catholic church expressed a growing rebellion over his status as his father's child who had chosen the priesthood for him and his search to define his manhood for himself; and it expressed his dissatisfaction with the hierarchical, authoritarian structure of the church, his support for the Civil Rights movement, and his moral revolt against the Vietnam War.

Readers learn that Carroll tried to restore his broken bond with his father, replacing it by a bond with his God, fulfilling the Latin etymology of "religion"—to "bind again that which is broken." The theology which supported the idea of obedience to God, however, also supported rigid adherence to a church conceived as a pyramid. At the commanding heights were cardinals headed by the Holy Father himself, while at the foot were the people themselves.

Carroll was led with his dissident allies to a radical confrontation with this concept of the church. Stern patriarchy should be replaced with unrepressive fraternity and sorority. Rather than a pyramid, the church should be conceived as "a people," its members as equals. Finally, Carroll rebelled theologically against "God" the Father in the name of the Son—"Jesus, the only God."

In the end, however, the strategy did not work. It did not change church government, and it did not release Carroll's sexuality, his need for women. Finally, his own well-being demanded he give up his father's choice for one that was authentically his own: Like many others, he left the priesthood and married. His father, hurt beyond words, refused to attend the wedding. The end between them, however, had already come following Father Carroll's arrest at an antiwar occupation of the U.S. Capitol. After a night in jail, he called home: "He doesn't want to talk to you *again*!" his mother told him.

Rebellion is often glorified in American culture. The American nation began its existence in rebellion. The bloody horror of the Civil War, however, should give pause to praise of unrestrained rebellion. There are, after all, degrees of rebellion, as Albert Camus, author of *L'Homme révolté* (1951; *The Rebel*, 1956), knew. In the context of rebellion, Camus called for "limits"—there shall, he argues, be limits under the sun.

An American Requiem shows, however, a certain surpassing of limits and its consequences.

As Carroll tells readers, those consequences can never be undone and were indeed tragic. They illustrate only too well the terrible aftermath for American society of the emotions that knew no boundaries unleashed by the Vietnam War—as illustrated by the self-immolations of war protesters recalled by the author. In the protest politics of one family, James Carroll and his father Joseph paid the price for the son's exceeding limits, for going "too far" in the father's eyes. That extreme of rebellion broke his father's heart. And, Carroll tells readers, it broke his own heart, too.

Charles F. Bahmueller

Sources for Further Study

America. CLXXIV, June 8, 1996, p. 24.
Boston Globe. May 19, 1996, p. B38.
Chicago Tribune. July 14, 1996, XIV, p. 3.
The Christian Science Monitor. May 23, 1996, p. B1.
Commonweal. CXXIII, July 12, 1996, p. 25.
Library Journal. CXXI, May 15, 1996, p. 67.
Los Angeles Times Book Review. May 19, 1996, p. 2.
The New York Times Book Review. CI, May 19, 1996, p. 36.
Publishers Weekly. CCXLIII, May 27, 1996, p. 52.
The Washington Post Book World. XXVI, June 16, 1996, p. 11.

ANGELA'S ASHES
A Memoir

Author: Frank McCourt (1930-   )
Publisher: Scribner (New York). 364 pp. $24.00
Type of work: Memoir
Time: 1930-1949
Locale: Mostly Limerick, Ireland

Brooklyn-born Frank McCourt recalls with a wry and sustaining innocence his poverty-scarred youth from age four to nineteen in depressed Limerick, Ireland, lowlighted by an improvident father, sickly mother, death of siblings, foul housing, and near-starvation

Principal personages:
FRANK MCCOURT, the harried youth through whose acute, physically impaired vision this memoir is conveyed
MALACHY MCCOURT, his father, a man addicted to drink and imagined tales of Ireland and Cuchulain, Eamon De Valera and Franklin D. Roosevelt
ANGELA SHEEHAN MCCOURT, his desperately put-upon mother
MALACHY GERARD MCCOURT, the second son, one year younger than Frank
OLIVER and EUGENE MCCOURT, twins who die in infancy
MARGARET MCCOURT, the fifth child and only daughter who dies in her pram at seven weeks in Brooklyn
MICHAEL "MIKE" and ALPHONSUS "ALPHIE" MCCOURT, Frank's youngest siblings
PADDY CLOHESSY, the biggest and toughest of Frank's schoolmates
FINTAN SLATTERY, a Bible-quoting dandy who curls his hair with hot iron tongs
MIKEY MOLLOY, a slightly older friend of Frank and an "expert in the lane on Girls' Bodies and Dirty Things in General"
MRS. LEIBOWITZ,
MINNIE MACADOREY, and
ANGELA DIMINO, Brooklyn neighbors who pen a letter to Angela's grandmother to bring McCourts back to Ireland
MR. O'NEILL, Frank's teacher at Leamy's School in Limerick
THERESA CARMODY, sharer of Frank's first "excitement"
MR. TIMONEY, Frank's first mentor, an admirer of Jonathan Swift
MR. HANNON, a hard-working Limerick coal and turf hauler who advises Frank to quit his job and go to school in the United States

Poverty, the mournful familiar of Frank McCourt's *Angela's Ashes: A Memoir*, has always occupied the thoughts of great writers. During the first century A.D., Juvenal wrote that "bitter poverty has no harder pang than that it makes men ridiculous." In his preface to *Major Barbara* (pr. 1905), George Bernard Shaw declared that "the greatest of our evils and the worst of our crimes is poverty." More recently, American poet William Carlos Williams, who was a practicing physician, expressed delight at the "anarchy" he found among his poor clients in Rutherford, New Jersey.

In *Angela's Ashes*, Frank McCourt dramatizes poverty's victims, destitute lives made ridiculous, criminal, and anarchic. Yet he also carries from the pitiable circumstances of his youth in Ireland a reconciliation that is never self-pitying, always able to allow the comic in, and, above all, can say, with fellow writer Harry Sylvester, that "the memory of the heart is the longest."

True, the book's anchoring sentiment is contained on its opening page: "When I look back on my childhood I wonder how I survived at all. It was, of course, a miserable childhood: the happy childhood is hardly worth your while. Worse than the ordinary miserable childhood is the miserable Irish childhood and worst yet is the miserable Irish Catholic childhood."

Yet, like his countryman James Joyce in *A Portrait of the Artist as a Young Man* (1916) eighty years before him, McCourt has chronicled a painful but ultimately rewarding growing up. *Angela's Ashes* pronounces, finally, a bittersweet "yes" to life. Frankie McCourt's story, the longest of shots, has a happy ending.

Nothing in the memoir's first two hundred pages gives promise of happiness. Rarely since *Les Miserables'* Jean Valjean was imprisoned for stealing a loaf of bread to feed his starving family has the want of some one thing so defined sadness: a piece of bread for one kind of sustenance, Frankie's; a pint of stout for another, his father's; a penny to refresh; a pair of shoes to replace his rubber-tire ones; a job for his father so his mother will not have to beg and the family go back on the dole.

The McCourts dub their flooded-out and foul-smelling downstairs "Ireland" and the upstairs "Italy" where "it's warm in the bed with the six of us and I love the glow of the fire the way it dances on the walls and ceiling and makes the room go red and black, red and black, till it dims to white and black and all you can hear is a little cry from [the baby] turning in my mother's arms."

Frank believes Angela when she tells him there is an angel on the seventh step. He finds solace in conversation with God's emissary: Will the angel bring a baby or is this just a visit? Three of his siblings die in the first eighty pages. At ten, Frank himself nearly succumbs to typhoid. His four-month hospital stay leads to his first significant conversation with a girl, Patricia Madigan, in the next room. The nuns rightly dictate that typhus and diphtheria shall not meet, but the slightly older Patricia, mortally ill, lives long enough to share her beloved book of poems and read him his first "bit of Shakespeare."

"Every day I can't wait for the doctors and nurses to leave me alone so I can learn a new verse from Patricia and find out what's happening to the highwayman and the landlord's red-lipped daughter." Thus was born Frank McCourt's love of language, so evident in this memoir.

Frank's father is the book's most memorable figure, although it is Malachy McCourt's recklessness that continually denies his family for his pint. Sent to Coventry during World War II to work in a munitions factory, he sends home only one paycheck in three years. Still, for all his profligacy, only his father, who cannot help Frank with his Irish because he is from the North, can transport his imaginative oldest son out of the lane to lands where everyone is a different color and everything is upside down and backward.

"I think my father is like the Holy Trinity with three people in him, the one in the morning with the paper, the one at night with the stories and the prayers, and then the one who does the bad thing and comes home with the smell of whiskey and wants us to die for Ireland."

Throughout his memoir, Frank McCourt attributes wry commentary on the events of his youth that must be credited to the adult looking down a fifty-year time corridor. Preparing for First Confession and First Communion, Frankie thinks of his sister and twin brothers who are dead: "The master says it's a glorious thing to die for the Faith and Dad says it's a glorious thing to die for Ireland and *I wonder if there's anyone in the world who would like us to live.*" [italics added]

Later, during Frank's slow recovery from typhoid, the nurses and nuns severely restrict his reading. At night, he escapes into happy thoughts about Tom Brown at Rugby and the comic creations of P. G. Wodehouse. "It's lovely to know the world can't interfere with the inside of your head."

Such interpolations are among the book's strongest passages. They provide the wisdom of hindsight as the memoirist allows them to overlay the remembered spirit of the youth's actual adventures. In semiautobiographical fiction, the first-person narrator dare not lose verisimilitude by giving an adolescent persona insights beyond his or her perceived capability. The memoir, if written with the skill of a Frank McCourt, permits a leavening palimpsest on remote memory.

The author devotes more than 300 of the memoir's 364 pages to Frankie's desperate years in Limerick, from age four to nineteen. The first thirty-five pages, however, reverse the conventional story of post-turn-of-century immigrants who made good. They describe the early years of the Great Depression in which, for the McCourts in their adopted Brooklyn, conditions were as bad as those they had left. Although McCourt never ties himself down to specific years—there are no dates—a good guess, reinforced by the chronology reckoned by Denis Donoghue in his review published in *The New York Times Book Review*, would be that Malachy McCourt immigrated to America from Ulster after the Irish civil war of 1922-1923. Donoghue doubts the story, so proudly and charmingly told by Frank, of his father's escape from Northern Ireland with a price on his head.

On March 28, 1930, Malachy and Angela Sheehan, a recent emigrant from the slums of Limerick, were married. On August 19 of the same year, the couple had their first child, Frank. The fact of bastardy is provided the reader early—on page 17—but Frank learns about it 250 pages later, in early teens, when he discovers his birth certificate while scouring his mother's trunk for her "red flapper dress" from America whose patterned hearts he will cut out for his football team's insignia.

Frank's awakening to his premature origin is, of course, innocent, but it provides clues to the boy's reliance on Roman Catholic reference: "[I am told] the father and mother have to be married nine months before there's a sign of a child. Here I am born into the world in half the time. That means I must be a miracle and I might grow up to be a saint with people celebrating the feast of St. Francis of Limerick." He goes to his pal Mikey Molloy, who is sixteen and knows all about "dirty things." Mikey tells him that "all bastards are doomed. . . . like babies that weren't baptized. . . . sent to Limbo for eternity."

McCourt's inventiveness in such scenes is extraordinary. It gives voice to a generosity of spirit that redeems the stench of toilets shared by an entire street, the insults of truant officers and barflies, the ubiquity of fleas in the mattress and rats on the floor.

In the spirit of the "life" novel—the story of passage, the experience of a spiritual education—*Angela's Ashes* arrives at a point when the hero's odyssey takes a turn for the better. With the entry of the United States on the side of hated Britain, many Irishmen, as Donoghue puts it, "decided that the war was not England's usual mischief but a worthy cause." Malachy, among many, went south to beef up the war industries whose work forces had been depleted. Although the father drank up his wages rather than send money home and the McCourts lived on charity, the oldest son takes a variety of jobs, from cleaning chamberpots to being an assistant to a coal hauler. For the first time, he can turn over three shillings to his mother. For the first time, Frank rises in his own estimation as "more than a scabby-eyed blubber gob dancing Jap."

In Mr. Hannon, Frank meets a Mr. Micawber figure who values him as an assistant hauler but also for his promise. "Mr. Hannon says, Up you get, and I climb up on the float like any workingman. . . . I'll take the reins and when he hands them over I'm sure I'll hear the boys gasping."

At fourteen, looking at himself in a mirror, Frank almost shuns his first "big" job, that of telegram boy at the post office. He is Pip without great expectations. He wishes he could be like the young Mickey Rooney as a happy delivery boy in *The Human Comedy* (1943), along with James Cagney and the Dead End Kids, his favorite from the Hollywood motion pictures he saw at The Lyric. When he finishes his calls, Frank visits the ancient monastery graveyard where his mother's relations are buried, sits on the highest wall of the ruins of Carrigogunnell Castle, watches the Shannon flowing on its way to America. Now he dreams of returning.

Frankie becomes the senior boy in the post office at about the same time he endures his ceremonial "first pint" at sixteen. He also enjoys his "first excitement" with a consumptive redhead named Theresa Carmody who, like Patricia Madigan six years earlier, seems to die on cue, providing his Catholic conscience still further guilt. Going on nineteen, he comes into a windfall with the death of an old woman, Mrs. Finucane, for whom he wrote letters for hire. Frank appropriates her informal "legacy" of fifty-seven pounds. For reasons not explained, he feels it is money due him. He can now book passage to New York.

McCourt compresses his late teens, climaxed by arrival by tugboat in the harbor of Poughkeepsie, into nine pages. The nineteen-year-old is ushered into a brothel by, of all people, a priest. He enjoys his second "excitement" before returning to the *Irish Oak* for the final leg of his journey.

"I stand on the deck with the Wireless Officer looking at the lights of America twinkling. He says, My God, that was a lovely night, Frank. Isn't this a great country altogether?" Frankie's answer, the single-word final chapter: "'Tis."

A book such as *Angela's Ashes* helps raise the currently expanding genre, the memoir, to new literary heights.

Richard Hauer Costa

Sources for Further Study

Boston Globe. August 25, 1996, p. N13.
Chicago Tribune. October 22, 1996, V, p. 1.
The Christian Science Monitor. December 4, 1996, p. 13.
Los Angeles Times Book Review. September 29, 1996, p. 6.
The New York Times Book Review. CI, September 15, 1996, p. 13.
Newsweek. CXXVIII, September 2, 1996, p. 68.
Publishers Weekly. CCXLIII, July 1, 1996, p. 49.
Time. CXLVIII, September 23, 1996, p. 76.
USA Today. September 10, 1996, p. D10.
The Washington Post Book World. XXVI, September 29, 1996, p. 1.

ANGUS WILSON
A Biography

Author: Margaret Drabble (1939-   )
First published: 1995, in Great Britain
Publisher: St. Martin's Press (New York). Illustrated. 716 pp. $35.00
Type of work: Literary biography
Time: 1913-1991
Locale: Primarily Great Britain and the United States

This first biography of Angus Wilson establishes his high place among postwar English novelists for maintaining the moral authority of fiction while challenging the sexual taboos of his native Britain

>   *Principal personages:*
>   ANGUS FRANK JOHNSTONE-WILSON, the British novelist
>   ANTHONY GARRETT, his companion of forty years
>   WILLIAM THOMAS FRANK JOHNSTONE-WILSON, his father
>   MAUDE ELLEN CANEY JOHNSTONE-WILSON, his mother
>   CLIVE JOHNSTONE-WILSON, one of five older brothers
>   COLIN JOHNSTONE-WILSON, second older brother
>   FREDERICK WILLIAM JOHNSTONE-WILSON, oldest brother, model for
>   characters in Angus' works

The product of five years of meticulous and exhaustive research, novelist Margaret Drabble's second literary biography—her first was of Arnold Bennett—may help restore the once-high reputation of Angus Wilson. The decline in his standing and popularity has been exaggerated, the biographer has written elsewhere, while having to admit that none of his eight novels was in print in America when her book appeared. Drabble, who came to know her subject as a friend from 1971 until his death twenty years later, acknowledges in her preface that "I came to this task as a committed admirer of Wilson's works. I have long considered him one of the major novelists of the post-war world, indeed of the century." She always refers to him, the literary hero of her student years at Cambridge University, as "Angus." Wilson made no secret of his homosexuality. This volume is in part a history of gay liberation and the decreasing need for discretion. Well into her lengthy biography, however, Drabble writes: "Coming out was not easy [for Angus]." By demonstrating the truth of this statement, Drabble, a noted novelist in her own right and editor of the fifth edition of the *Oxford Companion to English Literature* (1985), has conveyed the courage of one who dared to challenge the sexual taboos of his native England and, from the start, deal with them in his fiction.

That start was delayed until his middle thirties by circumstances that, in combination, made Angus Wilson a rare example of one who, in effect, turned to creative writing as therapy after mental breakdowns; he discovered as Somerset Maugham had before him that writing about disturbing matters enables the writer to deal with them.

Angus Frank Johnstone-Wilson was born in August, 1913, in the seaside resort of Bexhill, Sussex, between Hastings and Eastbourne. His parents were in early middle age when he was born, the youngest of six brothers, the nearest in age to him, Colin Frank, being thirteen years his senior. During the Great War, his mother communicated to her youngest her anxiety for three of his siblings who were involved in fighting on the other side of the Channel. Parental worry ran in tandem with patriotic bigotry. Once, when Angus was five, his mother ordered his twice-wounded brother out of the house because he expressed doubts about German barbarity.

Much later, Wilson would describe the many households of his parents and brothers as characterized by "genteel poverty" but also by shouts, screams, kicking—a lifestyle, in short, that contained memorable material for the unplanned stories he would write. Between the ages of seven and eleven, Angus Wilson also experienced the world of his mother's girlhood when the family immigrated to Durban, South Africa, in 1920. Although the country had changed much during her thirty-two-year absence, her people—the Caneys—had prospered. So, too, did the young Angus. As Drabble puts it, "Angus found himself greeted by a vast new array of cousins, much nearer in age than his own brothers, and by a country that struck him as thrilling and exotic."

By 1924, when he was eleven, Wilson and his parents were back in England, they to the careful middle-class world of small hotels in the Kensington area of London, he to a preparatory school at Seaford, Sussex, run by his second-eldest brother. After Angus left Seaford, where he distinguished himself less in academics than as an actor who persuaded the dancing mistress to teach the boys the Charleston, his mother died unexpectedly. The effects on him of the loss of this "sad-eyed, embittered, courageous but snobbish woman," who was typical of those displaced home colonials his fiction would bring to life, never really left him. She died during Angus' third year as a day boy at Westminster, one of England's oldest and most distinguished public schools. At Westminster, he discovered that his gift for "impressionistic mimicry," which he later called "my principal natural asset as a writer," and his shock of yellow hair topping a body that was always in motion conferred on him the affectionate tag of "mad boy."

Ironically, it was an inheritance from his mother that enabled Angus to be the first of his family to go to university. Having failed to obtain one of the closed scholarships available only to Westminster boys, he took up in 1932 a commoner's place at Merton College, Oxford, where most of the undergraduates were less rich, to read Medieval History. Drabble writes that Wilson's "long evident" homosexuality predated university. The early 1930's at Oxford were what Isaiah Berlin, contrasting it with the Golden Age of Harold Acton and Evelyn Waugh and his own slightly later Silver Age, calls the Leaden or Copper Age when apprehension over the rise of Adolf Hitler and Benito Mussolini led to moral earnestness. "Certainly Oxford was for me something quite apart from active sexual life," Wilson wrote later. Privileged self-indulgence often ruled. More important, however, Wilson came to know working-class students whose beliefs reinforced left-wing ideas he had drawn from some of the Westminster masters. Oxford widened his social framework and developed his sympathy for ordinary people which would surface thirty years later in *Late Call* (1964). In that novel, his fifth, he forged new novelistic territory and, in the flashbacks of his sixty-four-year-old female narrator, relived the traumas of his youth. Sylvia Calvert's early mental history can be said to reflect Wilson's crucial wartime crackups which led to his turning to fiction-writing. The notion of a creative breakdown is at the core of his writings. "Beneath the satire, the wit, the brilliant parodies and the acute social observation lies a sense of the self in search of the self," Drabble writes. "For a novelist the conviction that self-deception was no longer permissible . . . made for a brave agenda."

While acknowledging that her subject's crucial wartime service in Foreign Office Intelligence has never been satisfactorily reconstructed, even by Wilson himself, Margaret Drabble believes Wilson was a psychiatric casualty of the war even though he was nowhere near the fighting. Her chronicle reveals that he suffered a crippling identity crisis among his coworkers of both sexes at Bletchley Park, a government code and cipher school. The unkempt, irreverent young man became a "character" at Bletchley, but his ills, according to Drabble, had much in common with the wide range of psychiatric troubles and neuroses in British civilians and armed forces alike.

A year after the war ended, he was thirty-three years old and was working as a beginning cataloger at the British Museum when, on a Sunday morning in 1946, he sat down and wrote a short story about a little boy who is befriended by two eccentric ladies and becomes witness to their cruel killing of a bullfinch. The story took him eight hours, he titled it "Raspberry Jam," and the first important British novelist to make his debut after World War II was born.

From his first major review by Sean O'Faolain of the 1949 collection *The Wrens Set and Other Stories* ("a new writer of the first rank . . . a satirist with a lyrical touch; trenchant, ruthless, often very funny, sometimes very frightening; and he can write as a duck can swim"), Angus Wilson found himself a center of attention. It was the first time since his happy days at Westminster. He enjoyed his celebrity; he was seen everywhere. He was promoted to deputy superintendent of the British Museum Reading Room, the place, he told Maugham, where he learned all about the under-world.

Angus Wilson was in his fortieth year, having published a second story collection and a book on Émile Zola, when his controversial first novel, *Hemlock and After*, was published in 1952. The plot of this story of the narrowness of village life centers on the problems caused by the bisexuality of its married protagonist, the Grand Old Man of Letters, Bernard Sands, and on his conflicts at village level and finally beyond. The liaison between the middle-aged Sands and pretty young Eric Craddock, a would-be poet dominated by his attractive, intelligent mother, was partly autobiographical. Wilson appears to have modeled it on a developing relationship he was having with Anthony (Tony) Garrett, a probation officer sixteen years his junior. They moved in together the year *Hemlock and After* was published and were inseparable until Wilson's death forty years later at seventy-eight. He was not the first novelist to write about homosexuality, but he was one of the first to write candidly about matters such as "cruising" and "cottaging" some fifteen years before Britain's 1967 Sexual Of-fences Act made homosexuality between consenting adults legal.

"Angus [had] explored new territory," writes the biographer. "Here was freshness of insight and a questioning of sexual stereotypes: women as well as men welcomed this re-assessment of the normal. . . . It was as though we had known all along, but had not known we had known." Not everyone cared to be reminded. Wilson's American publisher declined *Hemlock and After*, but Viking snapped it up and reprinted it several times. Although, as Drabble demonstrates, Wilson was no liberator of sensuality on the D. H. Lawrence model, he was a mannerly man who disapproved of homosexuals such as André Gide or Norman Douglas, who married as a cover and then expected their wives to condone or even assist with their bizarre infidelities. He became the overage *infant terrible* to then long-known but un-self-acknowledged homosexual writers such as Somerset Maugham, E. M. Forster, W. H. Auden, and Stephen Spender, who regarded his candor with guarded interest.

Wilson retired in 1955 from his post at the British Museum. He was forty-two years old. For the next five years—or until he began accepting lucrative lectureships in his country and abroad, especially in the United States—he was able to devote himself wholly to writing fiction. *Anglo-Saxon Attitudes* (1956) and *The Middle Age of Mrs. Eliot* (1958), his best-known novels, accorded him a critical and popular stature that was comparable to those of the slightly older William Golding and slightly younger Anthony Burgess.

Anglo-Saxon Attitudes, twice the length of *Hemlock and After*, is the long novel of Victorian days Wilson had envisioned for a decade. Writing a continuing series for *The New York Times* just before her biography appeared, Drabble traces her discovery of *Anglo-Saxon Attitudes* to a Penguin reissue in 1958 while at Cambridge, when she found herself "in the company of a master." Five preliminary notebooks attest to the book's long gestation, about which Wilson told an interviewer, "An awful lot of . . . time was taken up just thinking." Elsewhere, interviewed by the American critic Michael Millgate for *The Paris Review*, Wilson disparaged his most famous book as "the most 'thought' of my novels and the least 'felt.'" Drabble shows throughout that evasiveness was not Wilson's grain. The poorest of self-promoters, he often aroused hostility in literary journalists.

Anglo-Saxon Attitudes and the slightly longer *The Middle Age of Mrs. Eliot* make their creator's value-distinction between thought and feeling ambiguous. Both present the individual facing up to midlife crises and doggedly meeting them. In the first, Oxford Don Gerald Middleton plunges introspectively into the past for a purging of self. In the second, Mrs. Eliot endures an exposed widowhood after having been in protective custody up to then. Averil Gardner, in the first book-length study of all eight of Wilson's novels, in 1985, anticipated Margaret Drabble's thesis (Chapter 13: "The Clearing in the Wild") that at the height of his powers in these novels Wilson was reflecting his personal situation in the mid-1950's since he had abandoned a "safe" job in exchange for the precarious life of the writer.

In the 1960's, however, he hedged his bets. He became a flourishing academic industry. Drabble charts with knowing compassion the decline of Wilson as novelist and rise as elder statesman of letters. By 1980, he had become Sir Angus Wilson. After prestigious lectureships at the University of California at Los Angeles and the

University of Chicago as well as the Northcliffe Lectures at the University of London, he accepted a part-time posting in English literature at East Anglia University. It lasted eight years. Constitutionally unable to say no, he became titular head of world societies under the names of the peers he worshiped and biographed, Charles Dickens and Rudyard Kipling, as well as the most powerful unread author of his day, John Cowper Powys. Of his visiting professorships at seventeen American universities, his favorites were the University of Iowa Writers' Workshop and the University of Delaware. Almost unique among transatlantic literati from the United Kingdom, Angus Wilson genuinely liked America and Americans. Los Angeles was his favorite American city and New York his least.

Writing of Wilson's last stand at Newark, Delaware, Drabble notes: "It was another term of interviews, honking geese, creative writing students, departmental picnics, faculty parties and visits to the pre-Raphaelites in Wilmington." The biographer allows the honkings and the rest to repeat and repeat. Tony Garrett recovered Wilson's voluminous notebooks, to which Drabble had exclusive access. Names of every person who had ever received an admiring glance, sponged on him, or cadged a favorable notice occur and recur. For one such as Angus Wilson, who had friendships everywhere, the only one that really counted, as Drabble makes clear, was the one of nearly fifty years with Tony Garrett, who made the living of his life possible.

Richard Hauer Costa

Sources for Further Study

Contemporary Review. CCLXVII, August, 1995, p. 108.
The Economist. CCCXXXV, June 17, 1995, p. 86.
London Review of Books. XVII, June 8, 1995, p. 3.
Los Angeles Times Book Review. June 9, 1996, p. 3.
New Statesman and Society. VIII, May 26, 1995, p. 24.
The New York Times Book Review. CI, August 11, 1996, p. 7.
Publishers Weekly. CCXLIII, March 4, 1996, p. 42.
The Spectator. CCLXXIV, May 27, 1995, p. 38.
The Times Literary Supplement. June 9, 1995, p. 24.
The Wall Street Journal. May 14, 1996, p. A18.

AN ANTHOLOGY OF CHINESE LITERATURE
Beginnings to 1911

Editor: Stephen Owen (1946-   )
Publisher: W. W. Norton (New York). 1212 pp. $39.95
Type of work: Literary anthology

An anthology of texts translated from the Chinese, with selections intended to give the general reader a sense of the tradition of Chinese literature

To the general reader, this mammoth undertaking may seem a bit daunting at first sight, but only until the first few pages introduce the voice of the editor and translator, Stephen Owen, a professor of Chinese and comparative literature at Harvard University. A gifted teacher, he makes it a positive pleasure to follow him through the hundreds of years of Chinese literature, over the seemingly unending succession of wars, changes of dynasties, and social turmoil from which the literature was born and against which it survived.

To cover so much in just one book inevitably entails simplification. On a topic for which, as the author points out, there may be some bad habits for a seasoned reader of Chinese literature to break, the outcome may be more instructive than not. Owens' point about translation, for example, only begins to suggest the choices to be made in such a project, and at the most basic level of words. The tradition of translation itself, as it were, includes the decision by some Western scholars to create a special dialect of English to meet the difficulties of translating from the Chinese, with the unfortunate result that the literary output of an entire culture may sound stilted and exotic in an excluding manner. To counteract this surface strangeness, Owen explains his choice to translate classical Chinese into English and the vernacular into American, thus allowing the more substantive rather than surface difference of Chinese literature to be accessible.

An even more difficult point to grapple with than translation difficulties is the concept of the "tradition" of Chinese literature. Owen gently deplores the conventional Western image of a changeless China, noting that the reader of a specific period would be aware of being historically situated as part of the reading process. At the same time, unlike the case of two poems written hundreds of years apart in English, two poems written in Chinese a thousand years apart might not, Owen explains, be essentially different. Elsewhere in the volume, he observes that cultural change in premodern China tended to be accretive, new styles getting added on to older ones in a manner quite different from the modern Western idea of change, in which the old is simply swept away by the new.

This collection, then, reflects the way in which the tradition of Chinese literature worked, and includes texts which have been considered to be part of the canon as well as those which were counter-canonical; the unifying concept for the editor and translator is that these are a selection of texts which respond to one another. Hence, though some pieces here may be familiar to the specialist, others will be fresh.

Literature lovers who are newcomers to Chinese literature will also be fascinated with tidbits of information about the production, transmission and preservation of words, as well as the occasional reference to a more familiar Western literary tradition for the comparative context, all helpful material to set off the treasury of poems, songs, stories, letters, excerpts from plays and novels, and literary theory. It is an additional marvel of this anthology that almost all of it was translated by Owens himself.

As with the literature of Greece and India, the earliest Chinese literature was produced and passed along orally. The physical medium for the written word evolved over time. From the second millennium B.C., writing carved into tortoise shells and bones survived, although the literature of this Shang or Yin dynasty, perhaps written on more perishable material, did not. Around the fourth and third century B.C., thin bamboo strips, bound with string into bundles, served as books, causing much difficulty if the string broke or rotted away and left piles of sentences incoherently separate on each strip of bamboo. During the Han dynasty, dating from approximately 206 B.C., silk was used and by the end of the second century A.D., the cumbersome bamboo strips were replaced with the more durable and usable scroll. Combined with the increasing standardization of the Chinese script, the scrolls helped to make literature more stable and accessible.

The functions of literature in China, as in other parts of the world, varied over time, too. Among the three hundred poems from *The Classic of Poetry* (*Shi-jing*), a collection from the Zhou dynasty (1020-249 B.C.) which constitutes the beginnings of the literature, are hymns which exhibit an important role of poetry: the naming of something so that it could play its role in rituals. The naming and describing served to guarantee that the rituals and social processes would continue. Another section of the collection consists of narrative poems which tell the stories of crucial periods in the formation of the dynasty. Interestingly, these stories avoid conclusion and point to continuation, an open-endedness that seems in the West to be such a late twentieth century postmodern characteristic. A distinctive feature appears in the poem "Spreading," which celebrates the group effort of building the walls of the Zhou capital; the closest Western equivalent would have been major public poems celebrating the building of the Egyptian pyramids or the European castles of the Middle Ages except, as Owen observes, that we know of no such poems in these other cultures.

A function of literature in China very familiar to the audiences of popular Chinese B-movies was as a means of social mobility. When the scroll gave way to a bound book of light paper in the Song dynasty, literature became even easier to store and use. Theoretically, any poor countryman who could manage to study and pass the national examinations could win a government post; so, very slowly, a meritocracy was introduced into the previously exclusive aristocratic circles.

Of particular comparative interest is a section on traditional literary theory, a subject area about which Owen has written before in *Readings in Chinese Literary Thought* (1992). It shows, for one thing, that certain literary concerns endure over time and distance. The early comments referred to the ethical power of literature, and the feeling that it could influence social and political behavior also led to some anxiety that there could be something dangerous in it. Also similar to Western concerns are the connections between the author's personality and style, the immortality granted by producing great works of art, and the impossibility of teaching literary talent.

Owen identifies the turn of the sixth century as at least one of the most glorious periods of Chinese literary theory and criticism. Lu Ji (261-303) wrote "The Poetic Exposition on Literature" (*Wen fu*), a poetic approach to writing that remains a distinctively original work of literary theory. Starting in prose and continuing in verse, Lu Ji pushes himself to express the process of writing, first steeping himself in the "classics of old," imagining and experiencing the sorrows and joys and beauty of the world, then knocking "upon silence, seeking its sound," as he attempts to put into words what goes "fleeting past."

The writings of a Buddhist scholar also provide a remarkable systematic account of the attitudes toward literature at the time. In the *Wen-xin Diao-long* ("The Literary Mind Carves Dragons"), Liu Xie (c.465-522) discusses the concept of *wen* (pattern). Starting with the observation that pattern began with the birth of Heaven and Earth, and that human beings are the mind reflecting their combination, he sees language becoming established when the human mind came into being and human language made the pattern manifest. It serves as an interesting insight into the difficult but important concept which can only be translated as "the Way," an attempt to describe the natural course of things.

Some literary situations may sound similar to late twentieth century audiences. For example, in the Qing dynasty, when the Manchus conquered China to become rulers of a multiethnic empire, they tried so hard to be good rulers that they became "more puritanically Confucian than the Chinese." In attempting to beep their ethnic identity, they vigorously censored anything that remotely cast aspersions on them, resulting in a cautious, anxious literature. Other conventions of the literary world appear less familiar: Owen notes that, until the twentieth century, it was the popular works that were printed with commentaries on literary techniques and structure, while the more scholarly forms were not.

The anthology ends at the beginning of the twentieth century, taking the May Fourth movement of 1919 as the start of modern Chinese literature. Although classical Chinese literature continued to be written, the protest of students on that day favored cultural reform, and the new literature was more influenced by Japanese and Western models. With this ambitious labor of selection and translations, Stephen Owen provides an ample and interesting introduction to the very long history of lively writing that preceded that change.

Shakuntala Jayaswal

Sources for Further Study

Choice. XXXIV, November, 1996, p. 451.

Library Journal. CXXI, May 1, 1996, p. 93.
The New Republic. CCXV, September 9, 1996, p. 38.
Publishers Weekly. CCXLIII, April 22, 1996, p. 64.
The Times Higher Education Supplement. December 6, 1996, p. SVIII.
The Washington Post Book World. XXVI, June 9, 1996, p. 13.

ANTS ON THE MELON
A Collection of Poems

Author: Virginia Hamilton Adair (1913-   )
Afterword by Robert Mezey
Publisher: Random House (New York). 162 pp. $21.00
Type of work: Poetry

A collection of poems, a distillation of life in six sections

Virginia Hamilton Adair's first published collection of poetry, has emerged when the author, at age eighty-three and blind, succumbed to the urgings of her longtime friend, poet, and neighbor in Claremont, California, Robert Mezey, and consented to participate in the winnowing of a lifetime of poetry writing. Mezey provides a graceful and illuminating afterword to this volume, outlining the principal biographical facts and locating the germ of his idea that she should "think about a book" in a reading she did at Pomona College in 1982. Adair, whose sight was failing at the time and who was still teaching at California State Polytechnic University, Pomona, a few miles to the west, was not to be hurried into such a project. After all, she had always read, written, and loved poetry; she had published poems in the 1930's and 1940's in such magazines as *The Saturday Review of Literature, The Atlantic Monthly,* and *The New Republic* and was always ready with a witty and clever poem on the occasion of a colleague's birthday or retirement from Cal Poly. Yet she was also quite busy raising a family of three children and running a household in Williamsburg, Virginia, and later, when her husband, distinguished historian Douglass Adair, accepted an appointment at the Claremont Graduate School, in Claremont, California. She taught at several local colleges, achieving the rank of full professor at Cal Poly, Pomona, where she enjoyed a solid reputation as an exciting, exacting, and charming teacher. She continued to write more poems and took care of her father, who lived to be ninety-four and who had been, Mezey points out, "both her chief audience and a continuous example of how poetry can sustain a life." After her husband's shocking and inexplicable suicide in 1968, such solace and sustaining as she could find was to be found in the lifelong and life-sustaining craft and practice of poetry. It is in the intensely personal nature of an acutely observed life rendered in technically masterful forms characterized by short lines, short stanzas, intricately rhymed, and carefully controlled meter that the grace she finds in poetry for her life is evident. Crowned with passion and garlanded with wit, these poems reward the reader with accessible experience and interpretation devoid of posturing and irritating mannerisms.

Arranged in six sections, the poems are linked thematically and somewhat chronologically. The first section, "Ants on the Melon," while in no way "sentimental" (Adair is far too strong a thinker to fall into that mode) is, as is the entire volume, full of sentiment (Adair has far too strong a heart to eschew feeling, passion, pain). This section plays in interesting ways with perception, the first perceptions of childhood, the perceptions bittersweet of adulthood. All is movement, all is change. The title poem, "Ants on the Melon," embodies these qualities, narrating a slight incident:

> Once when our blacktop city
> was still a topsoil town
> we carried to Formicopolis
> a cantaloupe rind to share
> and stooped to plop it down
> in their populous Times Square
> at the subway of the ants
>
> and saw that hemisphere
> blacken and rise and dance
> with antmen out of hand
> wild for their melon toddies
> just like our world next year
> no place to step or stand
> except on bodies.

What begins as a account of putting a delicacy on an ant den to watch the ants attack it, turns into a witty and finally sardonic observation on life, population growth, urban congestion, and an acute consciousness of mortality. Thus, it is a fitting end to the first section and a fitting title poem for the entire collection. Partly because of Adair's having lived a long and intense life, and partly because of her strong sense of craft and the requirements of form, individual poems and the volume as a whole always reveal the shadow as well as the sunlight, the frost as well as the warmth, usually in the last three or four lines of the poem. For instance, "The Shell" renders the poet's seeing in the border between sea and land a "wan shell. . . ./ Torn from the sea into the air./ Some other may lift it from the sand;/ I dare not. Never has my hot hand/ Held any substance so desolate and so rare." Or, in "Ashbury Park, 1915," a poem structured on memories of two experiences at age two and a half; one of seeing a cannon set amidst red cannas, an image preserved "on the picture-postcard of my mind,/ cannons and red flowers/ are forever one"; the other of her mother dragging the irrepressible Mary Virginia out of the Atlantic Ocean's surf, her father capturing the "rescue" on "sepia film./ For almost eighty years/ we have stood there on the sand,/ safe from the sea, in a black album." The second section, "By Old Maps," and the third, "Driving Westward," locate special and particular moments in her life as a woman busy with the details of travel, family, work, life.

The fourth section, "The Genesis Strain," provides a witty redaction of the Christian myth of Adam and Eve that begins "Not sure how I got there,/ But a perfect location: smogless,/ Free food & 4 unpolluted rivers." And moving to "That night I serve Adam Wisdom/ Thermidor made from the super-fruit,/ & we smoked the leaves, & WOW!" But, as we all know, that tree was forbidden. "What happened next is beyond me:/ Our landlord beating on the door,/ Asking these weird questions." And, sure enough,

We were evicted from Eden Gardens. . . .

How did I get here?—Via millennia,
Freezing my brains with our meatballs;
Vacuuming my soul with the wall-to-wall.

Tomorrow we run out of air and water.
Holy earth, you need the Maytag
More than our towels do. & A NEW MYTH.

This section celebrates a number of sacraments and their consequences, "Life in its awkward arc": marriage and its undoing, divorce; families and their tribulations; dying; love and lust; mysteries of gods and creation. "In Nomine" begins with a stunning stanza:

Ovarian vision, wisdom without words,
begins, pervades, maintains, links each with all,
ever-renewing as the oceans breathe
or fragments of lost planets reassemble
and round some central fire new orbits wreathe.

Moving from this complex image of the unity and connectedness of all creation (with that powerful second line of verbs that sums it all up), Adair visions in the next stanzas a "master choreographer" before whom "treetops and moons and holy dustmotes dance," "a vast cacophony of prayer" that summons "messenger molecules as angels" and "slits of matter and mind and sky/ where death is unceasing and irrelevant." Then she sweeps down to humankind ("higher than the Himalayas/ a little lower than the angleworm") and our modes of worshiping "the quintillion images of God." She ends this seven stanza, thirty-five line poem with a stirring acknowledgment that, in spite of the multiplicity of images, "God" is "the cyclone's eye, the seedling's heart;/ and yours the power and glory within us all," a powerful humanistic affirmation.

In the fifth section, "Exit Amor," Adair celebrates that affirmation further in the joyous sensuality of "Peeling an Orange" and tests it to the utmost in "One Ordinary Evening," the poem that most exquisitely and most painfully connects the "ordinary" joys of love and marriage shocked into stunned insensibility by the suicide of her husband. "I have never understood/ I will never understand." "One Ordinary Evening" is the first of ten poems that chronicle her attempts to understand, to explain, and to survive the misery of his inexplicable death. "Dark Lines" is a prayer cast as a villanelle that she may be able to draw "life from the cold sea" by writing poetry—"In this and many a poem I make/ to sound my dark identity,/ my line hold fast and do not break"—seeking solace in the last anguished stanza:

Forgive me, Life, the famished ache
to swing across eternity—
my line hold fast and do not break—
I do this for my hunger's sake.

In the poems of this section, one finds the incredible pain, passion, and bafflement that is our lot as human beings. There is always a powerful command of the technical aspects of form—rhyme, meter, stanza—of language, image, and metaphor. As one reads "The Ruin," "Exit Amor," "The Year After," and "Coronach" one comes to understand that, finally, loss is everything, a fact summed in "A Last Marriage." Here Adair catalogs her losses, the losses of anyone who, paradoxically perhaps, lives long enough: "The children gone, grown into other's arms,/ Man of her heart and bed gone underground/ . . . She came at last alone into her overgrown/ Shapeless and forlorn garden." Recalling the garden of "The Genesis Strain," perhaps, she "hacked and dragged away/ Horrors of deadwood, webbed and sagging foliage,/ Self-strangling roots, vines, suckers, arboreal/ Deformities in viperish coils." Yet in the agony of this despair, healing begins to emerge. This sequence of poems constitutes a powerful elegy for her husband, quoting some but not all of the norms of the traditional pastoral elegy. Nothing is simple about the "healing process," but it is a possible process. As Adair puts it in the second half, the turning half, of "A Last Marriage," "But day by day in the aftermath she recovered stillness," finding in the garden as reality and metaphor, as it renewed and took on new life, a "new marriage, reclusive, active, wordless/ . . . Now was a season to sit still with time to know,/ Drawing each breath like a fine crystal of snow."

The final section, "Make Light of Darkness," celebrates the gifts of memory, of poetry, of friends, and certainly of courage. Memory takes her back in "Return to Madison," when in 1936 she lived and studied at the University of Wisconsin, "the exaltation of learning, the sorrow and joy/ of that year of marvels pierce me:/ one all-night blizzard, and the dawn footprints/ leaving from my door, filling with fresh snow." "Red Camellias" begins with a memory of younger love and companionship, turned now into a dream, nine years after Douglass' death, segues into aphorism: "To survive we must unlearn much," and ends with a powerful image of transience: "The camellias are dropping,/ structures & colors come apart." She salutes poet-friends, Mezey and Borges; considers even here other lives that ended of their own volition such as the poet John Berryman's leap off that terrible bridge; and reflects on an unknown poet, Lorna Dee Cervantes, who drew her into her world where her "hand trembles, picking peaches/ in your poem where the two hummingbirds/ are stuck together." She celebrates—yes, "celebrates" is the right word after all—loss in the short, intense poem, "Slow Scythe."

> Slow scythe curving over the flowers
> In yesterday's field where you mow,
> My cool feet flicked
> The dew from the daisies, hours,
> Hours ago! Ages and ages ago
> They flicked the dew
> From the yellow and snow-colored flowers you leisurely mow.

The final poem in the book, "Take My Hand, Anna K.," acknowledges not only the physical limitations (imprisonment) of blindness but also that dependence on religion or even literature for comfort is a complex business. Her failing/failed sight is not only a physical fact but more fundamentally a psychological one: "My only home is in the poems I write/ Who now am exiled by my failing sight."

She continues a lifelong daily habit of writing poems on an old Olympic portable, of making sense out of all of life's character—passions, learning, friends, memories, losses—nothing denied except, remarkably, self-pity. In this exquisite volume, one finds then not only a superior craftsperson, keen in her sense of words and sounds and structures, powerful in her control of form, but also the wisdom of a brilliant mind and a passionate heart. Virginia Adair will be thanked by thousands of readers who will see in this distillation of her "lives" a whispering of the soul, as she puts it in the last two lines of "Strange Frequency":

> This is the sound that even we Gods find strange,
> Like a tear distilled from the deep eternal cold.

Theodore C. Humphrey

Sources for Further Study

Booklist. XCII, April 15, 1996, p. 1410.
Houston Chronicle. June 9, 1996, p. Z10.
The Kenyon Review. XVIII, Summer, 1996, p. 186.
Library Journal. CXXI, April 1, 1996, p. 83.
Los Angeles Times. March 29, 1996, p. E1.
The New York Review of Books. XLIII, May 23, 1996, p. 4.
The New York Times. August 7, 1996, p. C11.
The New York Times Book Review. CI, June 23, 1996, p. 9.
Publishers Weekly. CCXLIII, February 26, 1996, p. 103.
St. Louis Post-Dispatch. July 14, 1996, p. C5.
Time. CXLVII, May 27, 1996, p. 80.

ARK

Author: Ronald Johnson (1935-   )
Publisher: Living Batch Press (Albuquerque, New Mexico). 315 pp. Paperback $25.00
Type of work: Poetry

A long poem in three books, ninety-nine sections, that fuses epistemology, music, geography, art, and words to create an architecture

An "ark" is a boat that carries the survivors; the chest containing the Ten Commandments written on stone tablets, carried by the Hebrews during their desert wanderings, also called "ark of the covenant" and thus the Holy Ark; the boat built by Noah for survival during the Flood; or a place of shelter or refuge. Ronald Johnson's *Ark* calls to mind all of these definitions. Johnson tells readers in "A Note" at the end of *Ark* that the work is "Literally an architecture . . . fitted together with shards of language, in a kind of cement of music." A poetic edifice "based on trinities, its cornerstones the eye, the ear, the mind," it is "artifact rather than argument," Johnson's poetic Watts Towers, owing as much to Simon Rodia as to Louis Zukofsky and Charles Olson, "braving new schemes of language." Johnson reveals these elements to his readers in "A Note," but if one has worked his way through the "shards of language" that compose the three books of this intriguingly original and challenging poem, one sees again how "new" a vision a great poet weaves from the stuff he gathers from the physical, mythic, and psychological "places" of his being. While *Ark* is a "difficult" poem, it is also a rewarding one, a celebration of the extraordinarily complex composition of "America," the place, the idea, the dream. It is structured in three sections: "The Foundations 1-33 for Donald and Patricia Anderson"; "The Spires 34-66 for Jonathan Williams 'a solid, six-sided music'"; and "The Ramparts 67-99 for Guy Davenport Mover & Shaker." The structural components of the Foundations section comprise sections he names "Beams," usually verse arrayed in various patterns on the page suggesting a very free adaptation of what poets have traditionally called the ode, but sometimes the language is arrayed as sentences and paragraphs so that it looks like ordinary prose. Yet there is nothing "ordinary" in either the "prose" passages or the verse sections where the emphasis here is on "free" in that the tortured syntax and grammatical complexity of Johnson's use of the form often make Ezra Pound's verse seem accessible by comparison.

The "Foundations 1-33" section then is an examination of the various "beams" that support the structure of this Ark, this universe of meaning. These beams (which are also at least sometimes illuminations as in beams of light) are the phenomena of existence, the mind which knows (constructs) meaning and form out of these phenomena, and the constructions (physics, poetry, and so forth) of that mind that makes sense and shape of the (apparently) physical phenomena of existence. BEAM 15 for example, "Cornerstone," quotes Henry David Thoreau's *Walden* and alludes humans' need to know themselves, especially in their spiritual dimensions through the "living waters" of their own experience and thought, the serpent of error entering when they "drink" of the stagnant waters of others' experiences. In BEAM 17, Orpheus, Johnson asserts a number of propositions, the poem will illuminate, for example, "That one prism holds the spectrumed 'glory' as surely as whole populations of droplets strummed by sun./ That the action of the universe is metamorphosis—its articulation, metaphor. White crow, black swan, these are the hinges of Heaven." In a prose section of BEAM 17, he writes: "In the beginning there was the Word—for each man, magnetized by onrush, is Adam to his Tyger."

BEAM 18 is a palm print (one assumes of Johnson's right palm) the meaning of which seems related to the idea of man as maker—toolmaker, maker of music, maker of poetry, maker, indeed, of all meaning. Johnson says that it relates to one of the central myths of the poem, Orpheus and Euridice, and Jean Cocteau's handling of the "looking back" by visioning a mirror as a bath of mercury, Johnson's palm print being the "palm going into the mercury to get to the underworld." Even reading the poem then as an examination of man the maker, of the Ark as a vessel of meaning, one will inevitably ask why Johnson tortures grammar and syntax so? Perhaps he is arguing the inadequacy of "regular" linguistic and rhetorical rules to jar readers into meaning and understanding. Perhaps his "violations" of these rules comprise a meta-poem on the arbitrary (and insufficient) relationships among language, knowing, knower, and the known. Perhaps the most cogent view is to see the central myth of Orpheus creating and enacting the rhythmical, musical aspects of nature rather than the grammatical.

The structural components of the Spires section comprises sections Johnson calls "Spires," perhaps intending to suggest certain components of life and death. ARK 34, *Spire on the Death of L.Z.* argues that life, "as quick as a squirrel's tail" transforms into death "evenly distributed as nesting sights/ or silvery layers of film/ over rotifers." The closing images of ARK 34 move from the foundations on "this, red clay/ grassland" to "where the cloud steeds clatter out wide stars," asserting finally that "this is paradise . . . this is." ARK 37, *Spire called Prospero's Songs to Ariel (constructed in the form of a quilt from Roger Tory Peterson's A Field Guide to Western Birds)* is remarkable not only for its title but for the rendering in sound and visual imagery of bird life in the Kansas plains constructed, classified, described, rendered in all its aspects and stitched together by its music, a tour de force. The following poem, ARK 38, *Ariel's Songs to Prospero* is "the invisible Spire . . . a tape recording made with the assistance of sound technician Roger Gans. . . . [taking six months] with the end result being just over six minutes of 'musics' constructed out of recordings of songs of the birds of eastern United States." ARK 47, *Plow Spire*, figures the "dry red Kansas, country empty, even '*Great American* Desert'/ no mapped puddle skipped a pebble, but Flood" and the pioneers jostled in their covered wagons later.

The third and final section, "The Ramparts," comprises elements Johnson names "Arches," and these seem to refer pretty clearly to the architectural elements of structure, the social construction of realities by the conjoint efforts of poet and reader. Arches, one recalls, are among the oldest of engineering forms, strong, adaptable to and made from many materials, and often strikingly beautiful because of their lines and their strength. In ARK 69, Arches III, Johnson writes in three-line stanzas one of which reads: "wordsmith, way forth/ the old grammaire/ break dawn across foothills" suggesting that by breaking the conventional rules of syntax the poet "breaks" new light across the landscape(s) of creation, sings new music, calls forth new ways of reading, of constructing the world and, thus, of approaching the Ark itself.

ARK 71, Arches V, "Death of R.D." appears to be an elegy in function although unlike conventional pastoral elegy as it exists through the Romantic poets at least. Written again in three-line stanzas (the form suggests the Christian Trinity), the section alludes to Christian religion in a variety of ways—a section of hymns, citations of holy places, conjunctions of creation myths with "scientific" theories of origins, celebration of God's creations, allusions to Gerard Manley Hopkins and William Blake done in ways reminiscent of the ways musical composers will quote riffs or patterns from this or that predecessor. There is power in this section, one that speaks especially in the last twelve lines of the section

>light struck handsbreadth air—
>if life maintain not lift
>I wreath bequeath
>
>pressed into wall!
>trumpeter swan how signal dolphin
>abreast far outer spray
>
>wound into ball about us
>crow eclipse sky
>In the valley of the shadow of
>
>fair trial by fires, in vitro
>gathering life
>a breviary of universe

This section fairly illustrates some of Johnson's techniques: allusion, compaction, the metaphysical conjunctions of image sources with strong visuals and other sensory appeals create a form that does not invite the reader to participate in the construction of statement and meaning; rather they compel one to do so. One must read the spaces and the pauses and the breaks in syntax and metrical moves to make Johnson's daring and demanding moves accessible. A large number of his images strike with surprising force, as the last stanza quoted above: "fair trial by fires, in vitro/ gathering life/ a breviary of universe." Thus the poem becomes a "breviary of universe," a collection of hymns, offices, and prayers for the canonical hours, an ordered and regulated celebration of creation envisioned often in terms of the glorious great plains or at least its tattered remnants. "Intact as effigy,/ windmill stood face plain/ tablets applaud far climbs of man" compose a stanza compacting images that resonate with aspiration, law giving/discovering, mankind's strenuous efforts to achieve coherence even though alone and sturdy in the midst of history.

ARK 85, Arches XIX, moves readers closer to poet as maker, as architect, as carpenter and dancer (Johnson's father was, he says, a carpenter, his mother a dancer, his "main characters [of the poem] somehow" he calls them) as intercessor with whatever deities there might be as he begins with this triplet: "Craft, to seek renewal/ askew all question/ & exit in resonance genesis" and ends with "bluer as hillrise above hill/ apportioned lot, behave/ who Art in heaven." Throughout this final section, each Arch seems to rise higher and higher, the poetic intensity increasing, the claims for poetry and poet expanding. In ARK 97, Arches XXXI, for example, the last stanza reads: "quintessence in chorus/ sapphire Hemisphere/ deeps, crowned with stars," suggesting a convergence of music (of the spheres), of colors, of rule and government, of hierarchy, of connection, a kind of twenty-first century Great Chain of Being. In ARK 99, Arches XXXIII, readers find a closing exuberance: "Lo! *allegro non troppo*/ remake mankind/ a joyous noise into the void." *Ark* is that "joyous noise into the void" "all arrowed a rainbow midair,/ *ad astra per aspera*/ countdown for Lift Off," the movement of the entire poem from sunrise to sunrise captured here.

In "A Note" at the end of the volume, Johnson instructs readers on how to approach the poem, alluding to the sources of portions of technique and world view, arguing for his original take on the subject matter. Most interesting, however, is his assertion that "the idea of ARK came when I was able at last to conceive it as a structure rather than diatribe, artifact rather than argument, a veritable shell of the chambered nautilus, sliced and polished, bound for Ararat unknown." He sees himself as one who is constructing on the Kansas prairie an "Ozimandias of the spirit," an architecture "fitted together with shards of language, in a kind of cement of music." He asserts that the trinity of eye, ear, and mind are the constructing powers that erect the Ark, its foundations of thirty-three beams, the thirty-three spires on the top, and the arcades of the thirty-three arches encircling it about. It is instructive that a picture of Simon Rodia's Watts Towers graces the cover of the book, itself an architectural monument constructed from shards. One cannot help but think of the line from T. S. Eliot's *The Wasteland* (1922): "These fragments I have shored against my ruins," the salvation inherent in the creative act foremost in the figure.

Theodore C. Humphrey

Sources for Further Study

Chicago Review. XLII, Winter, 1996, p. 23.
Parnassus: Poetry in Review. XVII/XVIII, 1992-1993, p. 273.

ART AND AFFECTION
A Life of Virginia Woolf

Author: Panthea Reid (1940-   )
Publisher: Oxford University Press (New York). Illustrated. 570 pp. $35.00
Type of work: Literary biography
Time: 1882-1941
Locale: England

Drawing on the wealth of material available about Virginia Woolf and her circle, Reid reexamines the writer's personal relationships and literary theories

Principal personages:
VIRGINIA WOOLF, a British writer
LEONARD WOOLF, her husband
LESLIE STEPHEN, her eminent Victorian father
JULIA PRINCEPS DUCKWORTH STEPHEN, her mother
VANESSA BELL, Virginia's artist sister
CLIVE BELL, Vanessa's husband
VITA SACKVILLE-WEST, writer and Virginia's lover
ROGER FRY, artist, critic, Vanessa's lover and Virginia's friend

The lives of Virginia Woolf, her family, and her friends have been extensively documented. The letters and diaries of Leonard and Virginia Woolf have been published, Leonard's five-volume autobiography appeared in print in the 1960's, Regina Marler has edited a generous selection of Vanessa Bell's letters, Roger Fry's letters were published in 1972, the year Quentin Bell's definitive biography of his aunt Virginia appeared, Angelica Garnett and Clive Bell have written memoirs, and Woolf is one of the top ten subjects of literary investigation. Despite this vast amount of material, new interpretations and even new facts continue to emerge, and Reid has written an important addition to Virginia Woolf scholarship.

One of the themes that underlies this biography is Virginia's use of public writing to pursue private friendships. Other scholars such as Jane Dunn (*A Very Close Conspiracy: Vanessa Bell and Virginia Woolf*, 1990) and James King (*Virginia Woolf*, 1994) have noted, as Reid does, how Virginia as a child used writing to win parental approval. Her father, the eminent Victorian author Leslie Stephen, was more impressed with his daughter's literary talents than was her generally aloof mother, but Julia Stephen, too, at least once praised her daughter's efforts. Virginia reported that this recognition made her feel "like being a violin and being played upon." Reid observes that Woolf repeatedly used her talents to win attention and affection. In the early 1900's, Woolf's letters served to secure the fondness of Violet Dickinson, and Virginia wrote a biography of her friend in violet ink and bound it in violet leather.

After the birth of Julian Bell, Vanessa's first child, on February 4, 1908, Virginia began a biography of her sister, supposedly for Julian but actually as an attempt to recover Vanessa's attention. Virginia also wrote loving letters to her sister, letters more passionate, according to Vanessa, than any her own husband had ever addressed to her. Throughout her life Virginia used letters to keep her sister's (and other correspondents') love. In 1908, Virginia even contemplated a biography of Clive as a way of bringing her sister and brother-in-law closer to her. *Night and Day* (1919), Virginia's second novel, was dedicated to Vanessa, to whom Virginia wrote, "I think I'd rather please you than anyone, if only because I feel that its all your doing if I have any wits at all." Vanessa illustrated her sister's "Kew Gardens" (1919) and *Monday or Tuesday* (1921); Virginia's writing thus again brought the two women together. In response to Vanessa's praise of *The Waves* (1931), Virginia once more indicated how through her fiction she sought to keep Vanessa close: "Nobody except Leonard matters to me as you matter, and nothing would ever make up for it if you didn't like what I did. So its an amazing relief—I always feel I'm writing more for you than for anybody."

Roger Fry was another whom Woolf attempted to keep close through her pen. She had intended to dedicate *To the Lighthouse* (1927) to Fry, but he objected to the middle ("Time Passes") section. The work appeared without any dedication at all. Fry praised the novel once it was published, and Virginia wrote to thank him. She offered him an inscribed copy of the book and promised to compose a memoir of the artist. Woolf did not act on this promise until after Fry's death on September 9, 1934. The biography took six years, but its completion brought Fry back to her. As she recorded in her diary, "I feel very much in his presence at the moment: as if I were intimately connected with him; as if we together had given birth to this vision of him: a child born of us."

Orlando (1928), a fictionalized life of Vita Sackville-West, was a love letter of sorts undertaken to win back the affections of the book's subject. Virginia began the work as a response to suspicions—correct, as they proved to be—that Vita was having an affair with Mary Campbell. The book gave Virginia an excuse to probe Vita's life and to be with her. As Reid observes, "Virginia equated regaining Vita with writing *Orlando*."

Just as in *Roger Fry* Virginia used the written word to recover a dead friend, so she attempted to resurrect her nephew Julian Bell after he was killed in the Spanish Civil War in July, 1937. In 1936, the Woolfs had refused to publish Julian's memoir of Roger Fry, but in 1938 their Hogarth Press brought out *Julian Bell: Essays, Poems and Letters*, including the previously rejected biography. This volume was also another offering to Vanessa.

At the same time that Virginia was wooing her sister with letters and books, the two were rivals. Their contest began in childhood and persisted throughout Virginia's life. One way this conflict manifested itself was in an ongoing debate between the sisters over the relative merits of writing and painting. According to Reid, Virginia thought that if painting was important, then writing was not. Virginia and Vanessa followed their interests and talents in choosing their respective media, but Virginia may have in part been driven to literature because her older sister claimed art as her province. An early photograph (c.1892) shows the Stephen children grouped around Vanessa's easel; Virginia holds a book as an emblem of her separate identity. In the *Hyde Park Garden News*, a newspaper begun by the young Virginia and her brother Thoby (and thus an example of how Virginia used writing to draw herself close to someone she loved), Virginia declared, "Our correspondent [i.e., herself] is not an art connoisseur." When the "Manet and the Post-Impressionists" exhibition organized by Roger Fry prompted much conversation about paintings, Woolf remarked, "I don't think them so good as books," and she claimed to regard artists as "rather brutes." Jacob in *Jacob's Room* (1922) calls painting a "stupid art." Clive Bell reported that when someone observed in Virginia's hearing that standing at an easel for hours must be tiring for Vanessa, Virginia at once bought a tall desk so that she could stand and write.

In a letter to her sister, Virginia asked condescendingly, "Why are you artists so repetitious; does the eye for months together see nothing but roofs?" Similarly, she recorded in her diary, "If I were a painter I should only need a brush dipped in dun colour to give the tone of those eleven days [of sickness]. But painters lack sub[t]lety; there were points of light, shades beneath the surface, now, I suppose, undiscoverable." She urged her nephew Quentin Bell to give up a career in art and become a writer: "How in Gods name can you be content to remain a painter? Surely you must see the infinite superiority of the language to the paint?"

Vanessa, too, could be jealous, claiming, "You writers . . . do not know the joy of experimenting in a new medium," and writing that Virginia had not properly studied the pictures in the Accademia of Florence. Each sister occasionally threatened to invade the other's territory. "Shall I turn into a writer one of these days do you think?" Vanessa teased Virginia in 1910. Virginia earlier had declared that if she were badly reviewed she would turn from literature to art.

Despite this battle with artists, which Reid, following Leonardo da Vinci, calls *paragone*, Virginia was deeply influenced by the artistic theories of post-Impressionism. Her efforts at reforming the novel owe much to the ideas of Roger Fry and his circle. As she wrote to Fry after the publication of *To the Lighthouse*, "You have I think kept me on the right path, so far as writing goes, more than anyone—if the right path it is." The 1910 post-Impressionist exhibition prompted Virginia to revise "Melymbrosia" (which became *The Voyage Out*, 1915) to make the novel less conventional. In this and in subsequent works, she tried to achieve in language what the post-Impressionists were doing with paint: to offer the universal rather than the particular, to avoid photographic realism in favor of abstract representation. In her 1922 review of Percy Lubbock's *The Craft of Fiction*, she argued that books are not visible forms but emotions, a statement Reid links to Fry's defense of post-Impressionist artists who, he claimed, "do not seek to imitate forms, but to recreate form; not to imitate life, but to find an equivalent for life." Virginia and fry maintained that art is not about something but rather is something, creating its own reality.

In 1908, the rivalry between Vanessa and Virginia extended from *paragone* to Clive Bell. With Vanessa preoccupied with her first child, Bell sought to extend his friendship with Virginia to something more, and Virginia was willing to comply. Clive recommended the risqué eighteenth century novel *Les Liaisons dangereuses* to Virginia in an attempt to raise her sexual awareness. For Virginia's twenty-sixth birthday, he wrote her a poem speaking of her "emerald sleeping passions" that the poem hoped to awake. At St. Ives in April of 1908, the two took long walks together, and on

May 6, back in London, Virginia wrote to him, "I was certainly of opinion, though we did not kiss—(I was willing and offered once—but let that be)—I think we 'achieved the heights' as you put it." The affair, as Virginia called it, remained unconsummated and tapered off after 1912. Reid makes much of this relationship, finding in it a cause of Virginia's suicide in 1941 because after 1910 Virginia believed (with some justification, according to Reid) that her sister never trusted her again. Other students of Woolf's life place less emphasis on the affair. The sisters continued to exchange letters and visits, and after 1912 Vanessa turned her attention to other men, first Roger Fry and then Duncan Grant, father of her daughter, Angelica. Reid senses coldness in Vanessa's failure to include salutations in her letters to Virginia; Regina Marler sees in this mannerism the closeness of direct address.

In other matters, too, Reid seeks to revise earlier interpretations of Woolf's life. She plays down the early sexual abuse by Gerald and George Duckworth, Virginia's half-brothers, so much discussed by Roger Poole (*The Unknown Virginia Woolf*, 1978) and Louise A. DeSalvo (*Virginia Woolf: The Impact of Childhood Sexual Abuse on Her Life and Work*, 1989). Reid claims that Leonard Woolf chose to send Virginia's first novel to Gerald Duckworth for publication without Virginia's approval. James King disagrees, although it is clear that Virginia did not like to rely on Duckworth (or any other publisher). One reason for the Woolfs' establishment of the Hogarth Press was to free Virginia to publish what she liked. Reid's most persuasive argument concerns the conventional dating of Woolf's three suicide letters, two addressed to Leonard and one to Vanessa. Nigel Nicholson and Joanne Trautmann, who edited Woolf's letters, argue that the letter to Leonard dated "Tuesday" was written on March 18, 1941, and that the shorter, undated one to him was Virginia's last piece of writing. Reid claims that the short letter preceded the other two, and that the Tuesday of the dated letter is March 25, three days before Virginia drowned herself.

Reid tends to speculate beyond her data: the book contains many sentences qualified by "must have," "probably," "presumably," and "perhaps." Reid also can overwhelm with excessive detail, as when she discusses Virginia's mental collapse in 1915. "On 6 May, Virginia lay out in the garden and took no tranquilizers, and on 7 and 8 May, she was quiet but incoherent from time to time. Finally on 8 May [actually 9 May], her mind was clearer for a time, but then she became excited and angry." The sixty-six photographs enrich Reid's narrative, but the appendices dealing with the letters of Maria Jackson (Virginia's grandmother), with manic depression, and Leonardo da Vinci's attitude toward painting and writing seem gratuitous.

Reid's work will not replace Quentin Bell's as the biography of choice, and James King makes better use of Virginia's fiction as keys to her life. Indeed, Reid does little with Virginia's novels, although she examines Leonard's writings for clues about Virginia. Nevertheless, *Art and Affection: A Life of Virginia Woolf* makes a significant contribution to the ongoing study of Virginia Woolf and her circle.

Joseph Rosenblum

Sources for Further Study

Baltimore Morning Sun. November 3, 1996, p. F1.
Booklist. XCIII, November 15, 1996, p. 566.
Buffalo News. January 26, 1997, p. F8.
Library Journal. CXXI, September 15, 1996, p. 69.
Publishers Weekly. CCXLIII, October 14, 1996, p. 71.
Times Picayune. December 8, 1996, p. D6.

AT A CENTURY'S ENDING
Reflections 1982-1995

Author: George F. Kennan (1904-   )
Publisher: W. W. Norton (New York). 351 pp. $27.50
Type of work: Current history

Kennan offers his views on the twentieth century's East-West conflict

At a Century's Ending consists of a wide variety of papers, most previously published, written by George Kennan from the years 1982-1995. Although they concern a limited number of themes, the papers are diverse in form. They include addresses, articles, forewords to books by others, reviews, letters, and even one journal entry. Most selections concern East-West relations, though there are a few on other topics. The book's thirty-nine selections are arranged under five general headings: "Background," "The Cold War in Full Bloom," "Cold War, Its Decline and Fall," "Reviews and Introductions," and "Miscellaneous."

To Kennan, the century's most important history began in 1914 with the beginning of World War I and ended in 1989 with the fall of communism in Russia and the breakup of the Soviet empire. The great intervening events were the Russian Revolution in 1917; World War II, which he considers a continuation of World War I; and the Cold War, a result of the victors' failure to settle issues encountered in the conflict satisfactorily. The years before World War I and those after the fall of communism amount to prologue and epilogue to what Kennan perceives as a brutal, cruel century, yet one that permitted the continuance of a great western civilization.

George Kennan's career as diplomat and ambassador with the state department was not without its ironies. The best informed American statesman on Russian history and the Soviet Union, he knew personally many of the Soviet leaders from the 1930's through the early 1950's. During World War II, he served at the Moscow embassy as assistant to the American ambassador, W. Averell Harriman, and was ambassador himself during a brief period in 1952. Ironically, it was Soviet dictator Joseph Stalin who effectively ended his career by declaring Kennan *persona non grata*, primarily it seems because of his contacts with ordinary Russian citizens. When the administration of President Dwight Eisenhower found no place for him in government service, Kennan joined Princeton University's Institute for Advanced Study and put his expertise as a Russian historian to work. Except for a brief period as ambassador to Yugoslavia during the Kennedy administration, he has remained in that position, producing highly acclaimed volumes concerning the foreign relations of the United States, Russia, and Europe.

A further irony arises from his influence upon American policy toward the Soviet Union during the Cold War. In 1946, at the request of James Forrestal, secretary of defense, Kennan wrote a paper explaining what he expected Soviet behavior to be during the postwar period and how America might best meet the challenges it promised. In 1947, the paper, entitled "The Sources of Soviet Conduct" and written by "X," was published in the journal *Foreign Affairs*. The effort at anonymity failed, for shortly after publication its true authorship became widely known. In the article, Kennan depicted a Soviet Union ideologically driven, with leaders who were insecure, secretive, and highly suspicious. He pointed out that the Soviets would exploit any opportunity to advance communist ideology, particularly in Western Europe and Japan, and that it behooved the United States to remain involved in the foreign arena in order to counter those efforts. Kennan's paper became the most influential guide to the formation of America's policy of "containment," a word he first applied to the East-West rivalry. For his work, Kennan was appointed to the policy planning committee of the state department and was instrumental in formulating the Marshall Plan to provide aid to Europe following World War II.

Yet Kennan points out that his message concerning Russia became grossly distorted in the process of implementation. Never did he think that the Russians wished to become involved in a war against the West, or for that matter, even in minor wars on the fringes of their empire. Russia was too drained of manpower by the war and too depleted economically to risk another world war. The territories it had gained during the war were, for the most part, populated by citizens with no enthusiasm for communism, and all remaining world powers were allied with the United States. The Soviet threat was ideological, political, and perhaps economic, if the American-led West did nothing. Yet in the minds of Western political leaders, so little removed in time from the struggle against Nazi Germany, Russia appeared another dangerous aggressor led by a dictator who resembled Adolf Hitler. The perceived threat became a military one, and this view of the conflict triggered the dangerous and expensive arms race which Kennan deplores. Among its more costly and most dubious results was a massive build-up of military strength in Western Europe designed to counter a Russian threat that never materialized—the specter of Russian tanks sweeping into the West by the thousands.

Although he takes pains to distance his historical perspective from that of Arnold Toynbee, one cannot ignore how much Kennan's thinking bears the imprint of Toynbee's *A Study of History*, a work that depicted the course of history as shaped by an identifiable dominant civilization. In Toynbee's view, what matters most to the historian is not so much the efforts of individual leaders, but the rise and fall of civilization through intricate, complex influences over time. According to Toynbee, the modern era has been dominated by Western civilization, championed first by Greece and Rome, then by western Europe and most recently the United States. Kennan refers often to "Western civilization" in a similar way. He clearly sees the West as the dominant influence on the world, and largely ignores Africa, South America, Japan, China, and even the asiatic portion of Russia.

Collectively, the works reveal Kennan's views of international relations in general and especially those in the rapidly shifting East-West conflict. Like professional intelligence officers, professional diplomats acquire a somewhat different view of the world. They come to know their areas of specialization well and achieve a sympathy, even an affection, for the nations and peoples under their purview. They may feel more comfortable with colleagues in the foreign or opposing camp than with officials of their own government. Kennan reveals a profound knowledge and understanding of Russia and the Russian people and an appreciation of their culture.

Yet his is by no means an uncritical appreciation. Kennan views Russian history as a tragedy of diplomatic, social, and economic blunders at best, never achieving the means to marshall the country's vast resources to the benefit and prosperity of its citizens. In the twentieth century, past miseries were intensified through the cruelties of Joseph Stalin in his draconian measures before World War II and his squandering of lives during the war. Kennan holds out hope for improvement from leadership sufficiently enlightened, but does not underestimate the difficulties that lie ahead for the country.

Nor does he omit criticism of the West, for he believes that people learn more from their mistakes than from policies that proved successful. His criticisms of the United States are rather general but appear to be guided by the view that since the advantage in the Cold War belonged to the West, American leadership should have been able to shorten the conflict and thereby reduce its costs. He regards partizan politics, as practiced in the two-party system, as a necessary evil that either evades or distorts important issues and reduces public discourse to a "childish" level. In order to improve foreign policy, he reiterates his previous call for a bipartisan council of state consisting of experienced, balanced elders outside government who advise the national administration.

Like a modern-day prophet, he denounces the age for its transgressions. One can hardly quarrel with his identification of the major problems confronting civilization: the arms race, the threat of nuclear war, overpopulation, degradation of the environment in the northern hemisphere, the threat of nationalistic movements, and excessive public debt. The first four seem to him all the more alarming because no historical precedent exists for dealing with them. Never has the community of nations had to face such problems on such a scale. Kennan, too, seems to carry a legacy of the Cold War shared by many other statesmen. The problems it posed caused them to ponder not how a nation might accomplish great things, but rather how it might avoid disaster.

At his best, Kennan applies his profound knowledge of history in order to illuminate twentieth century conflicts. Through frequent analogies to Czarist Russia, he emphasizes the continuity of Russian attitudes and values under communist rule. In probing the recent crimes against humanity in the former Yugoslavia, he cites similar incivilities and atrocities during the Balkan Wars that preceded World War I. Anyone who doubts that his sense of the past enhances his powers as a prophet will find evidence to the contrary in his selection on Mikhail S. Gorbachev, which clearly shows that he understood the difficulty of the tasks Gorbachev had set himself and their probable results. His brief journal entry on American involvement in Somalia demonstrates both his grave misgivings and his prescience about the turn events in that country would take.

Prophets are not always correct, however, and Kennan's criticism of the course of history is sometimes errant. In an effort to derive sound generalities, which abound in his work, he ignores or overlooks important details and distinctions that might qualify his conclusions. In his criticism of Cold War rhetoric, especially American rhetoric, he appears to ignore evidence that while leaders were denouncing the Soviet Union most severely, they were giving private assurances to Russian leaders that campaign rhetoric should not be taken too seriously. This, to be sure, has serious negative implications for democracy, but it does blunt the edge of Kennan's criticisms. He also profoundly distrusts the military-industrial complex, with its overlapping interests that reach into all parts of society and its economic imperatives that drive a nation almost inexorably toward war. The drive is less inexorable, however, during an era of great productivity and economic prosperity. In all likelihood, he did not foresee the possibility either of widespread military base closings or relative reduction in the defense budget.

Further, some of his ideas appear quaint and outdated, as if the world had passed him by. At one point he expresses his sympathy for the baronial estates of East Prussia, with its agrarian lifestyle, paternalistic culture, and wealth, all utterly destroyed during World War II. This position, outlined in a foreword to a book written by a Prussian immigrant to the West, underscores his basically Eurocentric view of history. His perception that European civilization could not survive another major war, even a conventional one, lies behind much of his antiwar message. He laments the division of Europe into East and West, largely because it seems historically unnatural, yet he was apparently caught unawares by the rapid reunification of Germany and the sudden lifting of border restrictions that occurred after the collapse of the Soviet system.

The final essay, "The New Russia as a Neighbor," is perhaps the most timely and significant. Drawing upon Russian history, Kennan argues that there is no reason to assume that the new Russia will return to the aggressive expansionism of the Hitlerian-Stalinist period of history, a period he regards as an aberration. He believes it possible that Russia will successfully resolve the issues that threaten conflicts between it and the newly formed nations along its borders, and suggests, guardedly, that time now may be on the side of the peacemakers. He understandably leaves the impression that matters will likely turn out better if skilled and experienced diplomats are involved in the process.

In accordance with his diplomatic outlook, when he offers praise, Kennan names the individual, but he prefers anonymity when citing mistakes. The American ambassador who thought that Stalin's Moscow Trials were truly exposing guilty people remains anonymous, as does the secretary of state who dismissed Kennan. The book's style is marked by elegance and grace—a reflection of the man and a glimpse of the kind of world he would prefer.

Stanley Archer

Sources for Further Study

Booklist. XCII, February 1, 1996, p. 898.
Chicago Tribune. April 14, 1996, XIV, p. 6.
Commentary. CI, June, 1996, p. 59.
Foreign Affairs. LXXV, July, 1996, p. 145.
The New York Review of Books. XLIII, August 8, 1996, p. 4.
The New York Times Book Review. CI, April 7, 1996, p. 6.
Publishers Weekly. CCXLIII, January 29, 1996, p. 93.
The Times Literary Supplement. July 12, 1996, p. 27.
The Wall Street Journal. February 26, 1996, p. A10.
The Washington Post Book World. XXVI, February 25, 1996, p. 3.

THE ATLAS

Author: William T. Vollmann (1959-   )
Publisher: Viking (New York). 496 pp. $27.95
Type of work: Short stories

Short pieces set in a variety of countries with numerous characters

William T. Vollmann's newest collection of short pieces is a postmodern potpourri of legitimate short stories, vignettes, character sketches, prose poems, and stylistic exercises set internationally, from Cambodia to San Francisco, from Somalia to South Africa. With this international scope, readers should expect to encounter a variety of perspectives, approaches, and insights into a complex world. While approaches to the varied subject matter distinguish this volume, however, there is little by way of insight, variety of perspective, or even borrowing of cultural identities to distinguish the setting of one story from another. Instead, one voice is apparent throughout, and despite the conscious craftsmanship of the author, readers may enjoy what they read without knowing exactly what they were supposed to experience.

Throughout this collection, like his previous works, content is not Vollmann's strong suit. There are few memorable situations, although scenes such as the boy watching sex on a bus and the killer mosquitoes of America are engaging, surreal, and humorous. Yet such scenes are surrounded by thinly sketched characters undistinguishable in themselves or their surroundings, frequently drawn in seeming suspended animation with no action before or after a moment to give context to the portraits. What matters here is style, and Vollmann is an experienced craftsman and experimenter with an eye for the beauty, flow, rhythm, and interweaving of words, sentences, and paragraphs, particularly his musical metrical lines, a distinctive poetic voice in prose clothing. One example is the following set of images:

> So I let my shadow lead me down to the stain, even though you wouldn't hold my hand (I was only your symbiont). They say that the Cross with the anchor means salvation, that the olive branch is a symbol of hope. I found those symbols scraped into white shards of marble in the dark tufa walls of Saint Callisto's. I found them in the graves shelved with cool earth. Man-worms bored these caves into the world, some rounded, all so low that my head met the shadow of my head. Looking up into a skylight now very far above, I saw moss around that hole from which I'd been born from within my marble pillar of secretness.

Further, Vollmann is clever in his organization of material, claiming the pieces are juxtaposed thematically with early passages paralleling later refrains. This may be true—although pinning down just what Vollmann's themes are may take more effort than the individual stories warrant—but, again, such techniques only emphasize Vollmann's interest in method rather than what the stories are meant to convey.

This penchant of Vollmann's has been noted before, despite critics' praise for his first three books, comparing the author to such innovative American novelists as Thomas Pynchon. In his novels and previous short-story collections, Vollmann used complicated plots and numerous character types to critique human behavior, the nature of political power struggles, and the dynamics of history. In *The Atlas*, Vollmann can no longer be accused of complexity, and this is perhaps why his stories seem unrelated and not interwoven and integrated parts of a whole dependent on each brush stroke to make a volume fulfilling his clear intentions to link the disparate settings in *The Atlas*. Part of the problem, too, is that Vollmann is reworking subjects and themes from earlier, fresher volumes that were more important because of their then new innovations. Beginning with *You Bright and Risen Angels* (1987), reviewers observed Vollmann liked large, sprawling, disorderly canvases that operate on many levels suggesting many interpretations.

Touted as ingenious, bizarre, playful, ambitious, and crafted by a virtuoso, Vollmann's second book, *The Rainbow Stories* (1989) explored Vollmann's themes of death and alienation in more depth, a single-setting opus in which a frank and disturbing exploration of the lives of prostitutes, derelicts, and criminals which are determined, in Vollmann's perspective, by the spectrum of colors suggested in the book's title. Despite the descriptive detail, *The Rainbow Stories* also was criticized for its lack of character development and Vollmann's detached view of his subject, a detachment again evident in *The Atlas*. Similarly, his subsequent *Seven Dreams* volumes (including *Fathers and Crows* and *The Rifles*, reviewed in *Magill's Literary Annual*, 1993 and 1995, respectively) were credited for being adventurous, particularly for his symbolic interpretations of American history, but the book was widely viewed as being unmemorable, a flaw clearly recurring in *The Atlas*. So far in his career, beyond style, there is little for readers to sink their teeth into.

All this being said, Vollmann is an artist worthy of experiencing at least once, and *The Atlas* is as worthy an introduction into the author's quirky world as any of his earlier efforts. His ambition is greater than any contemporary that comes to mind, and his gift for sound and phrasing make his works perhaps better suited for reading aloud than for following along on the printed page. The pictures are beautifully drawn, expertly honed, and pleasing to the senses. Ultimately, Vollmann seems destined to find what it is he wants to say, will involve his heart as well as his mind, and will invest his talents into characters who are more than caricatures of each other. *The Atlas*, like his previous volumes, heralds a writer of immense potential and possibility worth watching.

Wesley Britton

Sources for Further Study

Booklist. XCII, February 1, 1996, p. 899.
Boston Globe. May 9, 1996, p. 94.
Chicago Tribune. August 11, 1996, XIV, p. 9.
Kirkus Reviews. LXIV, January 15, 1996, p. 97.

Library Journal. CXXI, March 1, 1996, p. 95.
The Nation. CCLXII, May 6, 1996, p. 72.
Publishers Weekly. CCXLIII, January 15, 1996, p. 441.
The Review of Contemporary Fiction. XVI, Summer, 1996, p. 154.
San Francisco Chronicle. May 5, 1996, p. REV9.
The Washington Post Book World. XXVI, May 26, 1996, p. 7.

AUDEN

Author: Richard Davenport-Hines (1953-   )
First published: 1995, in Great Britain
Publisher: Pantheon Books (New York). Illustrated. 406 pp. $30.00
Type of work: Literary biography
Time: 1907-1973
Locale: England; New York City; Berlin; Ischia, Italy; Kirchstetten, Austria

This biography of the greatest English poet of the twentieth century is also a history of some of the pressing and largely unresolved human and literary problems Auden faced in his lifetime

Principal personages:
   WYSTAN HUGH AUDEN, the British poet and critic who lived most of his
      career in New York City
   CONSTANCE ROSALIE AUDEN, his overbearing mother
   DR. GEORGE AUGUSTUS AUDEN, his father, a distinguished physician
      and professor who had a positive influence in his life
   CHESTER KALLMAN, a minor American poet, Auden's early lover and
      lifetime partner
   CHRISTOPHER ISHERWOOD, the British poet, a childhood friend who later
      collaborated with Auden on several early plays

There is little question of W. H. Auden's importance to Anglo-American literature. His poetry—in a career that ran from the late 1920's through the early 1970's—was not only a model of formal grace and flexibility, but illuminated several of the most important issues of the century: the role of ideology (especially in the Depression and World War II), the nature of love and sexual relationships, and the difficulties of the spiritual quest. This new biography by Richard Davenport-Hines presents Auden's life in some detail, but also manages to include long analyses of the poetry and descriptions of Auden wrestling with these crucial human issues.

Auden's early years were representative of a number of privileged British poets of his generation. His family provided motivation toward music and religion, but this biography is the first to stress not just Constance Auden's dominant and negative role in the poet's life, but his doctor-father's important influence in furthering Auden's intellectual and imaginative development (his lifelong interest in psychology, for example).

Education, first at St. Edmund's preparatory school, and then at Oxford (1925-1928), may have been less important for its academic legacy than for the friends Auden made there—Christopher Isherwood, Cecil Day Lewis, and Stephen Spender, most prominent among them—who would become "the Auden generation" of younger poets through the 1930's. After early influences on his verse from William Wordsworth, Thomas Hardy, and William Butler Yeats, Auden was most affected in the 1920's by T. S. Eliot, but, as Davenport-Hines shows, this influence was largely "contaminating" to Auden and other younger Anglo-American writers. Auden's first poetry was as difficult and inaccessible as his model's, and the most beneficial thing he inherited was Eliot's theory of the impersonality of poetry. Auden's best poetry would be formally complex and thematically symbolic, both clear inheritances from Eliot. Auden's life was a journey, Davenport-Hines shows, with few permanent stops, and no home until the end of his life. In the late 1920's he spent time abroad, not, as was typical, in Paris, but in Berlin. In the 1930's, he traveled to Iceland, to China, and to Spain. Recognized early for his poetic talents (he first published *Poems* in 1930), Auden's career had the standard interwar trajectory, and the twin flirtations with Freudianism, and then with Marxism.

In 1938, Auden made a crucial decision and emigrated to the United States and to a series of shabby apartments in New York City, where he would spend most of his creative life until his last few months, when he foolishly returned to Oxford. It is interesting that the two most influential poets of the twentieth century in effect exchanged places: Eliot, born in St. Louis, emigrated to England before World War I, to become a British subject, while Auden fled to New York before World War II to become an American citizen. As Eliot found comfort in conservative British institutions (such as royalty and the Church of England), Auden found something stimulating and supportive in the dynamic energy of New York, and his best work was produced there (he would win the Pulitzer Prize in 1948). As Davenport-Hines describes it, exile and isolation assumed important creative functions in Auden's career. His permanent sense of estrangement, and the suffering that feeling produced, fueled some of his best poetry.

Auden's career for the next thirty years would be full and productive, if not terribly happy. In addition to his poetry, he produced anthologies (of light verse, aphorisms), he worked in the theater, he and Chester Kallman wrote librettos for operas (as for Igor Stravinsky's *The Rake's Progress* in 1947)—he even helped to translate the journal of Dag Hammarskjöld, the secretary-general of the United Nations who was killed in 1961. Auden produced more than three dozen books of poetry and prose in an extraordinarily rich and fruitful career.

Apart from his poetry, his most influential work may have been his criticism, for Auden helped to define the role and significance of modern poetry in a changing world. "The primary function of poetry, as of all the arts," he wrote in 1938, "is to make us more aware of ourselves and the world around us." His first collection of critical essays, *The Dyer's Hand and Other Essays* (1962), is one of the most important volumes of twentieth century poetry theory, for it helps to anchor that theory at mid-century; "Poetry is reflective art," Auden wrote; "its existence is proof that man cannot be content with the outbursts of immediate sensation and that he wants to understand and organize what he feels." Auden taught briefly at a number of American universities (such as Bennington and Swarthmore)—"For an Englishman coming over here to teach, the rudeness of the students is quite shocking"—but managed to support himself and Kallman with his writing for most of his life. He also continued to travel, to search almost restlessly for a permanent home, as for spiritual meaning.

The most important element in Auden's search was his return to Christianity toward the end of the 1930's. He befriended Charles Williams, a poet and religious writer for Oxford University Press, and through discussions with him and with others, and through inordinately wide reading, Auden became—again as Eliot before him—one of the most important religious writers of the twentieth century. After that reconversion, he was often wrestling in his poetry with some essentially theological questions (for example, "Horae Canonicae," in 1954).

Related to his religious quest and perhaps the central issue of Auden's life was his search for love, and the agony of its failure. He met and fell in love with Chester Kallman early in his move to the United States; although they did not stay lovers for long, Kallman was the object of Auden's devotion for the rest of his life. Together, they shared vacation homes in Italy and Austria and traveled together extensively. This quest for love, which went finally unfulfilled with Kallman, sparked some of Auden's best poetry. "Auden was neither an equable companion nor a sympathetic, imaginative, soothing lover," Davenport-Hines reports, but it was not an easy time to be either. Certainly Auden's homosexuality was always a struggle: Homosexual acts were criminal in Britain until 1967, and persecuted by the police for years after that. Auden's peak productive years in New York in the 1940's and 1950's were also a period of the return of repressive, puritanical social attitudes. Davenport-Hines indicates that some of the negative reviews Auden received in his lifetime were probably for that lifestyle and not for the work.

Auden was at heart a poet of ideas, and Davenport-Hines is best at capturing the complexity of Auden's intellectual poetic struggles.

> This is another great feature of Auden's thought and work: he was always striving for integration, struggling to unify experience and objects, synthesizing the ideas of traditional religion and twentieth-century psychoanalysis. It was as if he hoped to heal the schisms of human knowledge and feeling. He wanted, in the end, an all-arching reconciliation.

Davenport-Hines goes to great lengths to prove how "Auden often wrote at his best when he was reacting against himself. His work was a public dialogue of private ideas; it was strongest when these ideas were not static."

Auden's final years were not happy ones. He returned to Oxford, but found himself now too American for the British academic scene. He had also become by now extremely self-centered, and his relationships were strained by what Davenport-Hines calls his "emotional pedagogy." Auden, who had been youthful looking for most of his life, suddenly developed a deeply wrinkled face; his emotional life had a similar collapse. His abuse of tobacco, alcohol, and amphetamines probably contributed to his early death.

> In the six years before 1963 Auden's poetry was the least exciting of any period of his life; but his dying fall proved glorious, with many rich, luxuriant poems brimming with courage, consolidation, gratitude and hope; steady, patient wisdom and sharp political comment interspersed with sparkles of campiness and rumbles of grumpiness. Gratitude provided the abiding note. He still rejoiced at his fortune in being alive and was startled at the ingratitude of others.

"The four necessary human relationships," Auden wrote in 1936, are "to love; to be loved; to be a teacher; to be a pupil." His poetry, while never confessional, could play all four roles easily. He had two compelling visions in his life, Davenport-Hines reports: a vision of human wholeness that came one evening in the English country-side, and a vision of violence and "of the ubiquity of human horror" which appeared before him during a visit to a Finnish whaling station. His poetry in a sense assumes both visions. Suffering was crucial to Auden, for it was almost always a part of his life, and it became an underpinning of his poetry and informed his best work ("Musée des Beaux Arts," "The Sea and the Mirror," "The Shield of Achilles"). Yet the horror did not stop Auden in his search for human and divine love. "Suffering (so he believed after his return to Christianity) was integral to God's love and the forgiveness of sins."

What is unique about this biography is the balance between the life and what it produced: the poetry and the ideas. Davenport-Hines is admirable in his analyses of the poetry (of the often misunderstood "September 1, 1939," for example), and he is clearly interested in Auden's ideas not only for their own sake, but for how they are expressed in the poetry. He has no ax to grind with Auden (although he tends to favor his own psychological approach—for example, Auden's "strong identification with his mother had created in him a narcissistic tendency which led him to choose men like himself as sexual objects"), and he certainly deals with Auden's sexual life in an open and objective way. The weakness in the biography is that Davenport-Hines is a little vague on the details of the life, how Auden supported himself, for example, and how his money was earned. Frank about the sexual life, he seems reticent about the financial. Yet it is a small enough criticism in an otherwise outstanding biography of an important English writer. In this sense, he is like Auden, who wrote, "To me the only good reason for writing is to try to organize my scattered thoughts of living into a whole, to relate everything to everything else."

While Davenport-Hines defines Auden's life as a journey, he also details the ways in which it was a journey for many people in the middle of this century as well: through the Depression, World War II, and into what Auden himself labeled "The Age of Anxiety," and through the struggles over war, sexual relationships, spiritual quests—issues with which the modern world is still wrestling. Auden's best poetry retraces those journeys, and this biography plays them back.

David Peck

Sources for Further Study

Commonweal. CXXIII, October 11, 1996, p. 23.
The Economist. CCCXXXVII, November 4, 1995, p. 91.
London Review of Books. XVII, November 16, 1995, p. 3.
Los Angeles Times Book Review. March 3, 1996, p. 3.
The New York Times Book Review. CI, March 31, 1996, p. 9.
The Observer. October 8, 1995, p. 16.
Publishers Weekly. CCXLII, December 4, 1995, p. 48.
The Spectator. CCLXXV, October 21, 1995, p. 43.
The Times Literary Supplement. October 27, 1995, p. 3.
The Wall Street Journal. February 13, 1996, p. A13.

THE AUTOBIOGRAPHY OF MY MOTHER

Author: Jamaica Kincaid (Elaine Potter Richardson; 1949-   )
Publisher: Farrar Straus Giroux (New York). 228 pp. $20.00
Type of work: Novel
Time: The 1920's to the 1990's
Locale: Dominica, a Caribbean island

A tough, lyric tale of a seventy-year-old woman recalling her often harsh and humorless life

> *Principal characters:*
> XUELA CLAUDETTE RICHARDSON, a Carib woman who is telling her
>   story
> HER FATHER, a half-Scottish, half-African man
> HER STEPMOTHER, Xuela's father's second wife, a woman who distrusts
>   Xuela and is jealous of her
> JACK LABATTE, a friend of Xuela's father with whom Xuela lives for a
>   while
> LISE LABATTE, Jack's wife
> PHILIP, a doctor Xuela marries
> ROLAND, a married man with whom Xuela has an affair

Jamaica Kincaid begins her tough, ironic, and lyrical novel by having her narrator, Xuela, a seventy-year-old resident of the Caribbean island of Dominica, announce that "My mother died at the moment I was born, and so for my whole life there was nothing standing between myself and eternity." Such a beginning promises the reader that an examination of big themes—life, identity, meaning—will surely follow, and in this respect, *The Autobiography of My Mother* does not disappoint.

Beginning with the subtitle, "a novel," appended to the title on the front cover of the book's dust jacket, the ironic self-contradiction is transformed by this work into a literary probe for exploring beneath the smooth surface of things. Besides juxtaposing the words "autobiography" and "novel," the title conceals a deeper irony: The main character is childless and aborting her pregnancy at the age of sixteen. Furthermore, these ironies of the novel's name are reflective of the ironies of Xuela's life. For instance, Xuela loves only one man in her life, Roland, who is already married; she marries a doctor named Philip who worships her, but she refuses to love him. If at times such irony can seem to be pretty thin gruel for nourishing a novel, the writing is richly evocative enough that the fruits of a life sustained by irony seem alternately refreshing and bleak.

The heavy layers of irony and the problematic title will not seem too surprising to longtime readers of Jamaica Kincaid. Since her debut collection of short stories, *At the Bottom of the River* that (1983), she has made a literary career out of mining the relationship between a mother and a daughter for every bit of irony and pathos it can offer. If her fiction has been narrow in its focus, it has also penetrated deeply.

Jamaica Kincaid—who was born Elaine Potter Richardson—created a lyrical beauty in *At the Bottom of the River* that she has never quite matched since. Not only the much reprinted "Girl," which seems to condense a young life's frustrations into a mouthful of overbearing, motherly instructions, but virtually every story in the collection has a compactness that seems to do more work than words normally can. The reader does not merely read the words of these stories; the images are also seen, felt, and experienced, but not always easily. The highly poetic prose of that work strips away the comfort of narrative, much as some of the best prose of Virginia Woolf and James Joyce does. Her follow-up novel, *Annie John*, was still highly lyrical in style, but was written in a much more conventional prose style. Because the two works cover much of the same ground—the development of a creative young girl as she matures, suffers a nervous breakdown, then recovers and leaves her native island (presumably Kincaid's native island, Antigua)—they are almost inseparable complements of one another. *Annie John* provides a key to some of the more obscure passages of *At the Bottom of the River* without reducing the rich complexity of that earlier work, or sacrificing its own beauty.

Though her follow-up works—the memoir of growing up in a colonized land, *A Small Place* (1988), and the novel which follows a character very similar to *Annie John* into adulthood, *Lucy* (1990)—both contain powerful writing, the pains of childhood which ignited the writing of her first two books are replaced by an anger of adulthood. Though Kincaid's writing was still well crafted, many readers found it less satisfying to follow where this new extension of her subject matter took her.

In contrast to her earlier fictions, which focused on a well defined portion of a life, in *The Autobiography of My Mother*, Kincaid for the first time takes it as her task to survey the entire shape of a character's life. The childhood sections of the novel convey the same type of wonderment, longing, and loneliness of Kincaid's first two books, and if she has ratcheted the emptiness and longing up a notch or two, one result is that the wonderment comes into greater relief. One incident which neatly captures the essence of this narrative contradance occurs early in the novel, as Xuela is describing her daily walk to school with a number of neighborhood companions whom she does not consider to be friends, but merely necessary companions. One morning when they come to a stream they have to cross, they see a naked woman bathing in the stream. One boy swims out to her until he exhausts himself and disappears without a trace; the woman disappears too. "That woman was not a woman," the narrator tells us; "she was a something that took the shape of a woman." For the other children who were there that day, this story entered into the realm of myth they did not really believe, "like the virgin birth or other such miracles"; a belief in this apparition "was the belief of the illegitimate, the poor, the low." Because she identifies herself as an outcast, though, a belief in this apparition is important to Xuela; "I believed in that apparition then and I believe in it now." Terror becomes an affirmation in outcast powers, which in turn becomes an affirmation of herself.

The pain of living as a colonized subject is an important theme in all of Kincaid's fiction, but in *The Autobiography of My Mother*, this theme gets its fullest artistic treatment in her work so far. School, as it was in portions of *Annie John*, is presented as a training ground in the subtleties of colonization. The first words Xuela learns to read are words she sees written across a map she sees on her first day of school: "THE BRITISH EMPIRE." Xuela's teacher is described as a woman "of the African people . . . and she found in this a source of humiliation and self-loathing." In her classroom, the students speak only English, although among themselves they speak a French patois. When her father remarries, Xuela's stepmother will speak to Xuela in patois, although English is the language of the house, and Xuela recognizes this not as friendliness, but as "an attempt on her part to make an illegitimate of me."

Once, her stepmother makes what seems to be a gesture of warmth when she gives Xuela a necklace to wear. Xuela is not fooled a moment; she puts the necklace around the neck of a dog and is unsurprised that he goes mad and dies. When the stepmother has her own children by Xuela's father, her murderous rage toward Xuela seems to halt, but she brings up her children to distrust Xuela. Xuela tells us she did not hate this sister, though; "her tragedy was greater than mine; her mother did not love her, but her mother was alive." This refusal to feel one negative emotion—hate—by replacing it with a distantly felt pity is typical of the refusal of strong emotions that characterize both Xuela's young life and her adult existence. While such reactions allow her to be emotionally self-possessed, this self-possession comes at the cost of emotional self-amputation.

This relationship between self-possession and self-amputation becomes clearest in Xuela's relationships with men. At the age of fifteen, she is sent by her father to live with a wealthy couple named Monsieur and Madame LaBatte, ostensibly to live there while she continues her schooling, but in fact to serve as his mistress—a scheme in which his wife fully cooperates. After their initial encounter, it begins to rain heavily, and Xuela goes into an apparent depression (somewhat reminiscent of a depression endured by the main character in *Annie John* at about the same age, though for different causes). It is only when she emerges from this depression (as his more or less full-time mistress) that she reveals to the reader her name, and she does so in a roundabout way, asking herself about the various sources of her full name, Xuela Claudette Richardson: "Who are these people?" "Your own name," she asserts, "eventually was not the gateway to who you really were." In part this is a comment on the confusing and contradictory threads that a colonial identity must coordinate: Each of her names represents a different cultural heritage. In part, though, it shows her backing into an almost God-like statement of existence as pure will: She is that she is.

Not coincidentally, this statement of the nature of her own existence leads to her most assertive statement of her own will—her decision to abort the pregnancy from this union. After some time, she comes to a disquieting acceptance of this action: "I would never become a mother, but that would not be the same as never bearing children. . . . I would bear them in abundance; they would emerge from my head, my armpits, from between my legs . . . but I would destroy them with the carelessness of a god." Self-will and self-negation are ultimate complements of each other.

As an adult, she has an affair with Roland, a married man, and when his wife confronts her and slaps her face, Xuela retreats into an ironic, distanced, musing: "Why is the state of marriage so desirable that all women are afraid to be caught outside it? And why does this woman, who has never seen me bore, to whom I have never made any promise, to whom I owe nothing, hate me so much?" Any answers to her questions—for instance, that marriage is closely tied to economic and personal sustenance, and that a person who threatens the marriage relationship is thus threatening the most personal realm of a married woman—are so obvious that the question cannot help but seem insincere. Yet from the above-it-all position that Xuela has constructed for herself, this refusal to understand cannot help but be sincere, even if it is intentional.

When Xuela herself marries, it is only after she is well past her childbearing years, and then to a doctor and friend of her father, "a man," she says, "I did not love," but who virtually worshipped her. Because she identifies him as "of the victors," that is, the British, she takes a cruel satisfaction in this unequal balance of affection: "He grew to live for the sound of my footsteps, so often I would walk without making a sound; he loved the sound of my voice, so for days I would not utter a word." Yet if her feelings toward him never coalesce into love, neither are they without tenderness. In the end, she says, "He became all the children I did not allow to be born, some of them fathered by him, some of them fathered by others"—surely a touching description for a seventy-year-old woman (Xuela's age at the end) to use of her late husband, but horribly complicated when one remembers her will to destroy her unborn children "with the carelessness of a god."

In "My Mother," a story in *At the Bottom of the River*, Kincaid ends by describing a college age girl's view of her now distant mother as almost godlike. In *The Autobiography of My Mother*, she allows this god to tell her own story, which turns out to be a story of lonely, loveless heights. Her will has shaped her own life so completely that the end finds her longing to meet death, "the thing"—perhaps the only thing she can conceive of—"greater than I am, the thing to which I can submit." In writing this story of a woman who never submits to things anything greater than herself—not to pain and certainly not to love—Jamaica Kincaid has written a bleak, powerful tale of survival, and the psychological costs paid.

Thomas Cassidy

Sources for Further Study

Essence. XXVI, March, 1996, p. 98.
Los Angeles Times Book Review. January 14, 1996, p. 3.
Maclean's. CIX, April 8, 1996, p. 72.
Ms. VI, January, 1996, p. 90.
The Nation. CCLXII, February 5, 1996, p. 23.
New Statesman and Society. CXXV, October 11, 1996, p. 45.
The New York Review of Books. XLIII, March 21, 1996, p. 28.
The New York Times Book Review. CI, February 4, 1996, p. 5.
The Times Literary Supplement. September 20, 1996, p. 22.
The Wall Street Journal. February 2, 1996, p. A8.

BABEL TOWER

Author: A. S. Byatt (1936-   )
Publisher: Random House (New York). 635 pp. $25.95
Type of work: Novel
Time: The mid-1960's
Locale: England

The third of a quartet of novels set in different mid-century time frames, each reflecting personal and historical crises peculiar to the time period

Principal characters:
FREDERICA POTTER REIVER, an educated woman caught in an abusive marriage; the novel's protagonist
NIGEL REIVER, her husband, a wealthy businessman
LEO ALEXANDER REIVER, their son
BILL POTTER, her father, a retired teacher
DANIEL ORTON, her brother-in-law, a clergyman
MARCUS ORTON, a professor and naturalist, Daniel's brother
JUDE MASON, the author of *Babeltower*, a controversial philosophical novel
AGATHA MOND, a civil servant, unmarried mother, landlady, and friend of Frederica
JOHN OTTOKAR, Frederica's student and lover
RUPERT PARROTT, the publisher of *Babeltower*

Babel Tower, like all of Antonia Susan Byatt's fiction, examines the lives of middle-class Britons, even as it focuses on a central female character. As in *Angels and Insects* (1992), Byatt develops a clever extended comparison between the societal life of lower animal forms and that of people, and she integrates this metaphor into her narrative. The moths and butterflies of *Angels and Insects* have their counterpart in the snails of *Babel Tower*. The changes which environment produces within their similarity becomes the key to understanding the evolutionary processes which take place in her characters' lives. *Babel Tower*, like Byatt's novel *Possession* (1991), also examines the nature of love. As in that earlier novel, Byatt finds that love is as often manipulative, exploitive, and abusive as it is necessary.

Byatt's *Babel Tower*, on one level, is an impressive intellectual exercise. One finds interesting facts about zoology, religion, the Marquis de Sade, mid-twentieth century British jurisprudence, censorship, spousal abuse, and a wealth of details on 1960's popular culture. More than this, however, it is an extraordinarily good novel with an artful, taut, and coherent narrative, which its author maintains for more than six hundred pages. It is, in fact, a prose epic, the third volume of an intended quartet, and following upon *The Virgin in the Garden* (1978) and *Still Life* (1985). Each of these attempts to re-create life as lived in Britain during a different mid-century time frame, focusing upon what Byatt considers essential to the given period. She leaves it for her readers to conclude that time creates difference that is merely accidental.

Amorality and idealism conflict repeatedly in Byatt's re-creation of the 1960's. The obscenity trial surrounding *Lady Chatterley's Lover*, the John Profumo-Christine Keeler sex scandal, the Moors Murders, and the beginnings of the Vietnam War protest movement make the comparable concerns of Byatt's characters logical and provide background against which to understand the three legal actions that provide the novel's climax. Nevertheless, the timelessness of human behavior supersedes all these elements. Humanity, like the hundreds of snail species, continues to blunder along making the adaptations necessary for survival, if not happiness.

The central plot of Byatt's novel is simple enough. Frederica Potter, a Cambridge University graduate with a background in English literature, has married Nigel Reiver, a wealthy businessman, and has retired to Reiver's country home. They have a son, an intelligent boy named Leo, but what might superficially appear a happy life soon emerges quite otherwise. Nigel is away from home on business for weeks at a time, and Frederica finds herself dominated by Nigel's unmarried sisters Olive and Rosalind as well as by their housekeeper Pippy Mammott. Intellectual life at Bran House, Nigel's country seat, is virtually nil. Nigel's sisters resent Frederica's education, and Nigel forbids visits from her Cambridge friends, mostly from jealousy since the educational demographics of the 1960's have provided her with an exclusively male circle of acquaintances. Desperate to maintain some form of intellectual life, Frederica retreats to a private world of serious reading. This withdrawal further estranges her from the inhabitants of Bran House, who criticize her for what they perceive as snobbishness and exclusivity.

Frederica's chance encounter with Hugh Pink, one of her Cambridge friends, brings the situation to a head. Nigel rudely dismisses a group of Frederica's friends who follow upon Pink's visit, refuses Frederica permission to begin doctoral studies, and forbids even excursions to London. Worse, he turns violent and seriously wounds her with an ax he throws during one of his possessive rages. Ultimately, Frederica escapes Bran House with the assistance of her friends. She takes her son Leo, but only reluctantly, when the boy intercepts her as she leaves and accuses her of attempting to abandon him. Frederica obtains two part-time positions in London, as a teacher and as a reader of manuscripts submitted for publication. What follows is Nigel's attempt at reconciliation, supported by expensive Christmas gifts and played out in the home of Frederica's parents. Nigel's charm almost convinces everybody, even Frederica. It is only subsequently that those close to Frederica see and even become victims of Nigel's violence.

Byatt cleverly interweaves a second narrative in the form of extended excerpts from a controversial book the reader subsequently discovers is entitled *Babeltower*, a massive utopian novel set at the time of the French Revolution. Its author, a disheveled misfit who has taken the name Jude Mason, describes the attempt of exiles fleeing from the Reign of Terror to establish an ideal society. What eventuates is individual cruelty, tribalism, and ultimately murder, all in the name of personal freedom.

Frederica meets Mason at the art school at which she teaches literature. It is here that Mason earns a meager income as an artist's model for an avant-garde project that echoes the themes of poet-artist William Blake. Frederica finds Mason repellent on every level, yet she thinks his book fascinating, considers it a literary breakthrough, and obtains its publication by the publisher for whom she works. Its publication leads to a public prosecution for obscenity.

Mason provides the link to another aspect of the plot. His unhappy personal life has caused him to become a regular and particularly exasperating caller of the counseling service run by St. Simeon's Church. Daniel Orton, a clergyman volunteer and Frederica's brother-in-law, receives most of these unsettling calls and has dubbed the anonymous Mason "Steelwire" because of the unsettling effect he has on the St. Simeon's staff. Orton engages in fruitless debates with Steelwire on the existence of God, and these particularly trouble the clergyman because he is experiencing his own crisis of faith. His wife Stephanie, Frederica's sister, died in a bizarre kitchen accident, and Orton's immediate reaction following her death was flight. In doing this, he effectively abandoned his children by Stephanie, Marcus and Mary, to the care of Frederica's agnostic parents.

On a fundamental level, Byatt's novel explores the imperfect nature of communication on personal and public levels, belief that is personal, institutional, and theological, and the larger question of whether life holds any genuine signification. None of the avenues the book explores (traditional religion, fundamentalism, mysticism, or secular humanism) appears to offer much to its adherents. The desire for freedom, common to all in every era, holds the promise of significance, yet this passion creates its own Tower of Babel when some speak in ways others cannot understand.

People do evil things in Byatt's novel, yet they are not villains. Essentially, the problem is that they cannot learn the language of those they harm. Nigel, for example, loves both Leo and Frederica and would be a good father to his son. His violent behavior stems from his frustration, his inability to see that Frederica cannot live her life exclusively on his materially pleasant terms. Spouses and lovers, children and parents, written works of literary genius and the general public, professional acquaintances and their associates—in Byatt's novel none breaks the barrier language imposes.

To underscore this thesis in mythic terms, Byatt provides extracts from Mason's *Babeltower* within her own *Babel Tower*. They are substantial and constitute a short novel within the larger work. Mason's protagonist, identified only as Culvert, has led a group of his followers away from the Terror, among them his beloved Roseace, to what will presumably be a better life in a sequestered retreat called La Tour Bruyarde, as its name implies, a towered building, complex in its construction and superficially impressive and impregnable. What begins as an experiment in total equality and absolute freedom, an existence comparable to the one Frederica had sought at Bran House, soon degenerates into an amoral and sadistic world in which even murder can be tolerated lest the experiment appear to fail. What happens at La Tour Bruyarde is similar to what often occurs in human relations. Having constructed an elaborate edifice—whether a government, a social code, literary standards, definitions of decency, or norms for married life—people often harm others to preserve the structure.

When Roseace can no longer endure the excesses of La Tour Bruyarde, she attempts to escape with her new and younger lover. Culvert brings her back forcibly. Rather than kill her immediately, he has a hideous needle-filled device inserted in her vagina, and engineers a slow, internal, painful death as both a lesson for her and as warning and entertainment for the community. Roseace's fate thus metaphorically parallels that of Frederica, at least what it would have been had she returned to Nigel.

Frederica does escape Bran House and finally wins her divorce from Nigel and primary custody of Leo, but not before two painful court actions. Her divorce does not, however, free her from life's Towers of Babel. Her affair with John Ottokar, a twin whose brother resents and perhaps envies Ottokar's relationship with Frederica, causes new problems of communication. Her support of the publication of *Babeltower* involves her in the obscenity suit, and this brings her, unwillingly though with compassion, to an understanding of its author's unhappy pact.

Any reader with an acquaintance of 1960's social history and popular culture will discover an uncanny number of resonances to this period in Byatt's *Babel Tower*. These are as different yet as characteristic of the time as the music of the Beatles, the poems and lifestyle of Alan Ginsberg, the protest movement against the Vietnam War, and the psychedelic gospel of Timothy Leary. Yet, there is more: details on the French Revolution, on utopian communes, cult, ritual, twentieth century British jurisprudence, phenomenology, the philosophy of Friedrich Nietzsche, approaches to teaching English and wasteful government committees that evaluate these approaches, a classic portrait of abusive marriage, and the pathetic situation of an educated woman caught in such a marriage at a time when many considered female independence extreme and eccentric. Hardly least, Byatt's masterful novel provides fascinating information on the social behavior of snails. With sardonic regret, a reader of *Babel Tower* will probably agree that crustaceans have more efficient and possibly more just social codes than the human race.

Robert J. Forman

Sources for Further Study

Los Angeles Times Book Review. June 16, 1996, p. 6.
New Scientist. CL, May 18, 1996, p. 50.
New Statesman and Society. IX, May 3, 1996, p. 40.
The New York Review of Books. XLIII, June 6, 1996, p. 17.
The New York Times Book Review. CI, June 9, 1996, p. 7.
Publishers Weekly. CCXLIII, March 25, 1996, p. 62.
Time. CXLVII, May 20, 1996, p. 76.
The Times Literary Supplement. May 10, 1996, p. 24.
The Wall Street Journal. May 6, 1996, p. A12.
The Washington Post Book World. XXVI, May 12, 1996, p. 3.

BAD LAND
An American Romance

Author: Jonathan Raban (1942-   )
Publisher: Pantheon Books (New York). 324 pp. $25.00
Type of work: Current history
Time: 1907-1995
Locale: Ismay, Mildred, and other small towns of eastern Montana

> *Raban reconstructs the settlement of the Montana plains, from the first immigrants struggling with weather conditions at the beginning of the twentieth century, to their few heirs holding on into the twenty-first*

Principal personages:
JONATHAN RABAN, the writer who puts together the histories of these
   original settlers in eastern Montana and visits those who live there in
   the 1990's
PERCY WOLLASTON, son of one of those original settlers and the author
   of a memoir of the region that Raban draws upon
EVELYN CAMERON, the famed photographer who settled in the region
   and captured its forbidding landscape

From the spring of 1907 through the fall of 1908, the Milwaukee Road railroad worked its way through the Dakotas into eastern Montana. As the line advanced across the land, it created cities with unlikely names such as Ismay and Mildred. No one lived in these towns until the railroad agents distributed pamphlets all over the United States and Europe describing the fertile terrain, and the government—with the railroad's help—passed the 1908 Homestead Act. Then the settlers came, by train, and settled on the land and filled up the towns. For the first years, the weather was good, the rainfall abundant, and the people prospered. After a few years, however, the land returned to its normal pattern of inadequate rainfall and sub-zero winters, and this area of the Great Northern Plains reverted to what it has also been called: the great American desert.

Jonathan Raban recaptures the unique ninety-year history of this piece of Western America in a book that is part memoir, part history, and always fascinating. Raban describes his own identity with this area in the opening chapter: how, as a British immigrant, recently resettled in Seattle, he finds a certain affinity with the refugees who migrated to this region. Driving through its inhospitable terrain, he finds the original ruined farmhouses, and in the parlor of one abandoned home picks up journals, letters, and schoolbooks that belonged to the first settlers. He returns to Seattle with these materials, and the research and writing begin—as well as the visits to the region where he can see what has happened to the survivors of this experiment in American homesteading.

The first settlers believed the railroad pamphlets and bought into the myth created in a book called *Campbell's Soil Culture Manual*, which told them that they could be successful in this semiarid landscape, and the related theory of Louis Agassiz that rain would follow the plough (settlement would bring its own good weather). For the first few years, the theories seemed adequate. Raban imaginatively re-creates the lives of the people on the trains moving west, people looking for a chance to make it in America, people who had read the propaganda and come to eastern Montana to live out their role in the dream.

> The extraordinary fertile benchlands around Ismay and Mildred promised adventure, space, nature, escape at the same time as they offered the comforts of village life with its intimate gossip and its twin guardians of church and school. To have a home with no landlord, no rent, no mortgage. . . . To be the lone ploughman of one's own acres.

Here was another example in the long American tradition of Emersonian self-reliance acted out again and again through the nineteenth century as migrants pushed back the frontier. "They had bought into the idea of the West as the last refuge of the pioneering individualist (as the government had encouraged them to do)." The homesteaders built schools and churches, farms sprang up on the landscape, and communities grew. Then the weather turned. The early settlers did not realize that their success had been built on unnaturally good rainfall and a half inch of soil they soon exhausted.

Their history is also a chronicle of what has gone wrong with farming in America. The banks, betting on the first good crops, encouraged these early Montana farmers to mortgage their land. Then the farmers got hooked—as many other consumers in the 1920's did through the new language of advertising—by the marvels of technology, and they began to invest in machinery such as tractors. The first years were good, but then the double attack of cold winters and lack of rain showed them what this land was really like. The normal cycle—including hail, cyclones, fires, and grasshoppers—returned. By 1919, the trains that had brought them in began to take them out. Not all at once, for some remained, in debt to the land and to their dreams of making it here. Those who stayed even survived the 1930's and the Dust Bowl conditions of the Depression that wiped out so many other farmers across the Great Plains.

Those that left headed west again, and Raban follows them and finds evidence of them, in Great Falls, Montana, and then in Lincoln, and then in Thompson Falls (where he locates the graves of the Wollastons, one of the original homesteading families). Finally, he makes it to Wenatchee, Washington, an abundant valley where some of the original settlers found success. Continuing west, Raban reaches Seattle, the original end of the Milwaukee Road line, and his own new home.

As the government agents and bankers had explained to these new homesteaders how to farm in the 1910's and 1920's, after the disasters of weather and failure, the evangelists started to explain to them another version of what had happened. Some of the most intriguing parts of *Bad Land: An American Romance* take place in the 1990's, as Raban traces the results of the failure of the American Dream, not only when it dried up in the scorching sun and freezing wind of eastern Montana in the early decades of this century, but later, in Ruby Ridge and Waco, when the last Emersonian ideal finally died out in the West in a hail of bullets and fire. Raban effectively links the first failure in Ismay with the anger and frustration of contemporary Middle America.

Lincoln is the home of Theodore Kaczynski, and when Raban passes through it, tracing the westward migration of these settlers, T-shirts proclaim it "home of the Unabomber." The Freeman militia live nearby.

In the early 1990's, new settlers to Ismay rename the town "Joe," in a futile effort to lure the quarterback of the 1993 Kansas City Chiefs (Joe Montana), and thus the accompanying media, for a celebration. It is a tragicomic story. "Not since around 1910 had Ismay been the focus of such publicity." The residents get the brief publicity, but when it dies they are left where they had started: with the farms which cannot be supported on this flat and vacant landscape.

Raban sees the beauty of this land and admires those early pioneers, as he admires many of the more recent immigrants. He also understands the anger at the failure of their American Dream. "In 1909, the government *did* drop people on to an expanse of land which looked suspiciously like the surface of the moon. The scheme *had* been pushed through Congress largely for the benefit of the powerful railroad companies." The story of eastern Montana is the story of the collusion between these forces, but it is also a story of courage and heroism, and Raban tells it in a series of poignant pictures: the scene of the early settlers tapping their fence wire to make crude telephones to talk to each other, for example, or the image of Percy Wollaston's mother "on her knees every day, crying and praying for rain."

Raban makes the story poetic in his own vivid and personal style and in the metaphors he uses to carry this history. In nearly every stage of the story, he finds an artist or writer who crossed these plains and left lasting images: the nineteenth century paintings of Frederic Remington and Albert Bierstadt, for example, that capture a landscape with bulk and flatness, but no vistas, or Claude A. Barr's *Jewels of the Plains*, a work of flower taxonomy "so engaging, so improbably well written, that I found myself staying up until 3 A.M. one morning for the pleasure of reading it cover to cover." Later, Raban re-creates the story of Evelyn Cameron, an early British settler who became a famed photographer. Her images of eastern Montana and its inhabitants are some of the best that remain, for, as Raban notes, she first caught "the treeless breadth and vacancy, more space than place, of the nearby plains." If Cameron's photographs drew more settlers, popular literature at the turn of the century was an even more powerful force in the settlement of the West. Raban shows how books such as *The Virginian* (1902), Jack London's *The Call of the Wild* (1903), and even *Rebecca of Sunnybrook Farm* (1903) created the romantic notion that one could make it in any landscape, no matter how barren.

At times, unfortunately, Raban's literary and artistic explorations take readers some distance from the history, and it appears that this arid land is not even able to sustain a full-length book, and Raban has padded his original *New Yorker* article to flesh out the story. Finally, however, the digressions weave together and deepen and embroider the book, for Raban proves that this story of historical failure is also a story of the continuing power of the American Dream.

It is an interesting fact of American literary history that some of the most accurate portraits of the United States have come from foreign visitors and refugees who have the fresher and clearer sight to see America for what it is. From Alexis de Tocqueville in the eighteenth century through Charles Dickens in the nineteenth to Evelyn Waugh and Aldous Huxley and dozens of other foreign visitors in the twentieth, Americans are often best able to see themselves through others' eyes. Raban continues this tradition. A recent immigrant himself, he is able to accurately depict what the United States has been in the past and what it has become today.

This in fact is not his first description of the United States. In *Old Glory: An American Voyage* (1981), Raban piloted a small outboard the length of the Mississippi River, in the wake of Huck Finn and in search of an America he found that still harbored anger and racial hatred in its heart. In the more recent *Hunting for Mister Heartbreak* (1991), Raban explored a more diverse America, from New York City through Guntersville, Alabama, and Key West, Florida, to Seattle.

Some of the best recent American nonfiction has come from writers examining the lives of Americans who people this country between the more populated coasts and whose stories have rarely been told. The model is probably James Agee and Walker Evans' *Let Us Now Praise Famous Men* (1941), a study of Alabama sharecroppers in the Depression. Recently, John McPhee, in *Rising from the Plains* (1986), and Ian Frazier, in *Great Plains* (1989), have described the hardy and heroic folk who settled the Great Plains. With *Bad Lands*, Raban joins this company in another study of the folly and courage, the dreams and disasters that are part of the history of this region. It is not always an inspiring story, but it is one that is worth telling, again and again, for its themes and images continue to reverberate.

David Peck

Sources for Further Study

Booklist. XCIII, November 15, 1996, p. 568.
Boston Globe. November 21, 1996, p. E2.
The Economist. CCCXLI, November 16, 1996, p. 6.
Library Journal. CXXI, October 1, 1996, p. 110.
Los Angeles Times Book Review. November 24, 1996, p. 4.
The New York Times Book Review. CI, November 10, 1996, p. 11.
Publishers Weekly. CCXLIII, September 30, 1996, p. 66.
The Spectator. CCLXXVII, October 19, 1996, p. 47.
Time. CXLVIII, November 25, 1996, p. 118.
The Washington Post Book World. XXVI, December 1, 1996, p. 1.

BALKAN ODYSSEY

Author: David Owen (1938-   )
First published: 1995, in Great Britain
Publisher: Harcourt Brace (New York). 389 pp. $25.00
Type of work: Current affairs
Time: 1991-1995
Locale: Former Yugoslavia

A detailed narrative and analysis of efforts to bring peace to the former Yugoslavia by the co-chairman of the International Conference on the Former Yugoslavia

Principal personages:
CYRUS VANCE, cochairman of the International Conference on the
    Former Yugoslavia
THORVALD STOLTENBERG, Vance's replacement in 1993
SLOBODAN MILOSEVIC, the president of Serbia
FRANJO TUDJMAN, the president of Croatia
ALIJA IZETBEGOVIC, the president of Bosnia-Herzegovina
RADOVAN KARADZIC, the leader of the Bosnian Serbs
RATKO MLADIC, commander of the Bosnian Serb army

David Owen, a member of the British Parliament from 1966 to 1992 and the holder of several cabinet positions (notably as minister of the navy and foreign secretary), joined in 1992 with former American secretary of state Cyrus Vance to create a plan for peace in the former Yugoslavia. The Yugoslav republic of Slovenia had declared its independence. Then Croatia also declared itself a sovereign nation, and a war with Serbia ensued. The Serb minority in Croatia feared for its life in an independent Croatia, remembering the Croatian Ustashas (Fascists) massacres of Serbs during World War II. Serbs also distrusted the plans of Croatian president Franjo Tudjman, who they suspected of attempting to create a "greater Croatia." Croatia was equally concerned about the fate of Croats in Serb-dominated parts of the former Yugoslavia and were fearful that Serbian president Slobodan Milosevic (in alliance with Croatian and Bosnian Serbs) was seeking to create a "greater Serbia." To complicate matters further, both Serbs and Croats fought over the disposition of land in the former Yugoslav republic of Bosnia-Herzegovina. Muslims formed the majority population in Bosnia but significant minorities of Serbs and Croats threatened the polyglot and multicultural existence of Bosnia and its central city, Sarajevo. If Bosnia were to become a separate country, whose country would it be? The Muslim majority was vulnerable and could not secure the whole of Bosnia-Herzegovina either by the people's consent or by military force. When war spread to Bosnia-Herzegovina, the complexity and contradictoriness of the civil war was increased enormously: Serbs attacked Croats and Muslims, Muslims attacked Serbs and Croats, and Croats attacked Serbs and Muslims. Cyrus Vance and David Owen were charged by the European Community to form a peace plan that (it was hoped) would also draw full support from the United States and the United Nations.

When Owen joined Vance, he took a position close to what the United States would maintain throughout his tenure as cochairman of the International Conference on the Former Yugoslavia. He believed that pressure (economic sanctions and air strikes) should be brought to bear on the main aggressor, Serbia. Of all the armies fighting in the former Yugoslavia, the Serbian was the best equipped and most destructive. It engaged in what came to be called "ethnic cleansing," the process of pushing out (and often killing) Croat and Muslim populations and replacing them with Serbs. It is generally acknowledged that Croats and Muslims also engaged in such atrocities, but their culpability has been deemed minimal compared to what many critics called the Serbian genocide of Croats and Muslims. The evil genius behind the Serbian depredations was thought to be Slobodan Milosevic, president of Serbia, who was brutally assisted by Bosnian Serb leader Radovan Karadzic and Serb general Ratko Mladic.

Owen soon saw his dilemma if he demonized the Serbs. The single most powerful figure in the former Yugoslavia was Milosevic. If Owen and Vance did not deal with him, the war would continue—with both the Croats and the Muslims fighting until they had regained the ground lost to the Serbs or exhausted themselves—in the process killing thousands and thousands of innocent people. It seemed unlikely that either the Muslims or the Croats could roll back the Serb advance very far, especially since attempts to unify Muslim and Croat forces kept breaking down and resulting in battles between themselves.

Owen discovered that compared to Karadzic and Mladic, Milosevic seemed reasonable and willing to strike a deal with Croatian president Franjo Tudjman. Owen's view is that Milosevic was never truly a Serbian nationalist, but only used nationalist feelings to secure his power base. In person, Milosevic (who had lived in the United States) seemed to Owen far more sophisticated and more responsible than Karadzic, who in Owen's book is represented as a craven war criminal capitulating to the worst instincts of his followers. Owen had no illusions about Milosevic as humanitarian; rather he suspected that the economic sanctions against Serbia and its isolation in the international community had persuaded Milosevic that the Serbs could gain nothing more from military activity.

With the support of presidents Tudjman and Milosevic, and the grudging cooperation of the Muslim side led by Alija Izetbegovic, Vance and Owen developed a map for a new Bosnia that gave approximately 51 percent to the Croats and Muslims and 49 percent to the Serbs. It would be one country based on a loose confederation of three separate entities for the Croats, Muslims, and Serbs. The plan would rectify the worst excesses of ethnic cleansing, although it could not reverse all the Serb gains. Yet then Vance and Owen were certain that no strategy could be devised that would return Bosnia to its former state. Besides, Vance and Owen recognized that however blameworthy the Serbs might be, their aggression had been prompted by legitimate concerns for their safety.

Owen is convinced that if President Bush, been reelected, something like the Vance-Owen Peace Plan (VOPP) would have been implemented in 1992-1993. Yet the change in American administrations doomed the VOPP. Clinton had campaigned on the premise that the Bush administration had not done enough to check Serb aggression. Milosevic and the Serbs had been portrayed in the U.S. media as the prime villains in genocide. Any plan that was perceived as rewarding the Serbs would be rejected by the new administration. Even worse, when Owen had the opportunity to meet with the new secretary of state, Warren Christopher, he was dismayed to learn that Christopher had not grasped the essential features of the VOPP. Owen attributed Christopher's ignorance to his intense participation in Clinton's transition to the White House. The new secretary of state had simply not had enough time to absorb the intricate VOPP or to think through its consequences. Soon it became clear that the United States would not support the VOPP. Indeed, it was advising the Muslims to hold out for more territory, and it resisted Owen's position that a peace plan had to be imposed on all parties. If a country as powerful as the United States favored one of the parties in the dispute, then no peace was possible, Owen concluded.

Owen's nuanced and complicated tactics were then criticized by the U.S. State Department and soon became distorted in the press. He was viewed as pro-Serb for his effort to put pressure on the Croats and Muslims to settle. Yet Owen was convinced that Milosevic was ready to strike a deal—a deal that the U.S. government and the American press simply could not accept. How could such a war criminal be believed? The fact that Milosevic, Karadzic, and Mladic continued the war seemed to contradict Owen's assertions.

Yet Owen saw a widening gap between Milosevic and his two putative henchmen. The interests in Serbia were not identical to the interests of Bosnian Serbs. Owen also saw Milosevic's own hold over the Bosnia Serbs continuing to slip as he put pressure on Karadzic to accept the Vance-Owen initiatives. Karadzic often seemed to yield under this pressure only to renege on agreements or to charge the other side with bad faith. The closer Owen studied the war, the more he saw that all sides had committed war crimes. Muslims had even shelled their own people to create more international outrage against the Serbs. The Muslims at one point paid off Croats to shell the Serbs. Moreover, the interfighting between Muslims and Croats was as fierce as anything the Serbs had perpetrated against Muslims and Croats.

This degraded situation did not make Owen a moral relativist. He still acknowledged that the Serbs had committed far more crimes than any other side, and he believed in the war crimes tribunal that would bring the criminals to justice, but the facts on the ground militated that a settlement, however dishonorable, was desirable rather than perpetuating war.

The irony for Owen is that when the United States finally began to engage directly in finding a peace settlement, it criticized Owen for not adequately acknowledging in realpolitik terms that the Serb advances could not be reversed. In other words, U.S. policy had turned 180 degrees. Only when the United States started to put pressure on the Muslims (exactly what Owen was criticized for) did a real movement for peace become feasible. Owen is quite resentful that it took the United States so long to come to a realistic sense of what peace would look like in the former Yugoslavia. Peace in reality meant virtually a partition of Bosnia-Herzegovina into separate ethnic enclaves—in effect, a ratification of ethnic cleansing that went way beyond what was contemplated in the VOPP.

Why did it take the United States so long to see things Owen's way? It was, of course, far easier to be moralistic about what was happening in the former Yugoslavia than to become intimately involved with enforcing the peace plan by committing U.S. troops to it. The U.S. had just suffered a devastating failure in Somalia and had pulled its troops out. The overwhelming sympathy for the Muslims would have made it difficult for any U.S. administration to strike a deal with Serbs. Owen would add that the Clinton administration had a particular penchant for scapegoating him and the United Nations as cover for a lack of a firm policy.

Owen's critics certainly view his book as hostile to the United States. He makes a powerful case, however, and realizes that the Europeans, including himself, made many mistakes. He speaks of President Clinton more in terms of regret than animosity. Clinton, he believes, was immersed in domestic policy and did not give foreign affairs the attention they deserved. When he did focus on the former Yugoslavia, Owen found that Clinton's judgment was quick and shrewder than his dilatory advisers.

Why did the Europeans fail to act on the VOPP themselves? Why did America, once again, have to come to the rescue of Europe? Owen has a very wise and balanced reply to these questions. Quite aside from the difficulty of getting Europeans to act as a single majority, there is the fact that the United States cannot be ignored any more than Russia can be in solving issues as significant as the civil war in the former Yugoslavia—a war that has threatened to spread to Greece and to Turkey and thus beyond the Balkans, involving both U.S. and European allies. Even if Europe tried to go it alone, in other words, the United States would have its say—as it did in advising the Muslims not to accept the VOPP. In effect, the United States has a virtual veto over European foreign policy, and Europeans must consult closely with the United States whether they wish to or not. It is almost beside the point to criticize Europeans for not solving their own problems when the Muslims and Croats, for example, looked to the United States to aid them.

Owen's book is extraordinarily detailed and may put off some readers because of its relentless accounts of meetings, timetables, redrawn maps, and passages studded with acronyms. A chronology of events, a list of acronyms and terms, and a dramatis personae tries to keep the narrative clear. Yet there is no denying that it is a hard task to assimilate all the details. On the other hand, Owen's careful and restrained account—truly remarkable considering the vicious attacks made on him—should give pause to those who take a purely moralistic view of foreign policy. As an insight into the workings of international diplomacy, and as an account of how personalities and policies clash and sometimes cohere, Owen's book is indispensable.

Carl Rollyson

Sources for Further Study

The Christian Science Monitor. March 28, 1996, p. B2.
The Economist. CCCXXXVII, December 16, 1995, p. 7.
Los Angeles Times Book Review. February 18, 1996, p. 10.
The New Republic. CCXIV, March 11, 1996, p. 34.
New Statesman and Society. VIII, December 8, 1995, p. 31.
The New York Review of Books. XLIII, February 29, 1996, p. 8.
The New York Times Book Review. CI, January 21, 1996, p. 12.
Publishers Weekly. CCXLII, December 11, 1995, p. 64.
San Francisco Chronicle. April 28, 1996, Section 10, p. 1.
The Times Literary Supplement. November 24, 1995, p. 10.
The Washington Post Book World. XXVI, March 10, 1996, p. 1.

THE BEAUTY OF MEN

Author: Andrew Holleran
Publisher: William Morrow (New York). 272 pp. $24.00
Type of work: Novel
Time: 1995
Locale: Northern Florida and Manhattan

A lonely middle-aged New Yorker keeps remembering dead homosexual friends and lovers while caring for his dying mother in dreary northern Florida

> *Principal characters:*
> LARK, a male homosexual in his late forties
> LARK'S MOTHER, an eighty-three-year-old woman who is completely paralyzed and bedridden
> BECKER, a handsome homosexual in his thirties with whom Lark is in love
> SUTCLIFFE, one of Lark's homosexual friends from his Manhattan past

Lark is a sophisticated New Yorker stuck in provincial northern Florida since his mother became completely paralyzed in a household accident twelve years before. He visits her at the nursing home, where he wheels her around the corridors or sits at her bedside watching television shows such as *Murder, She Wrote* and *Jeopardy.* On weekends, he brings his mother to their family home and takes care of her like an infant. During his free time, he tries to pursue what seems to be his only interest—"cruising" for sexual encounters with other homosexuals.

Lark does most of his cruising by automobile on the highways and back roads between Gainesville and Jacksonville. Much of this slow-paced, autobiographical novel consists of flashbacks to the gay life his hero led in Manhattan. Lark is haunted by memories of friends and lovers who died of what homosexuals generally refer to as "the plague" (AIDS—the acquired immune deficiency syndrome epidemic), a horrible aftermath to the gay liberation movement of the 1970's.

There is a sharp contrast between cosmopolitan New York of the past and still largely agrarian northern Florida of the present. Andrew Holleran (the pseudonym of an author who remains unidentified even after publishing three novels and a collection of essays) has a special talent for evoking a sense of place. His technical virtuosity is evident in his ability to interweave contrasting scenes, especially scenes of past and present.

In contrast to the permissive atmosphere of the Lower East Side Manhattan of Lark's spring of hope, he finds Florida homosexuals a furtive minority harassed by police and hated by the "straight" majority. "We're like roaches, he thinks; we're a problem in pest control. We find a place to gather, we gather, they notice us, they eradicate. Gather, eradicate; gather, eradicate."

In addition to scenes of gay Manhattan and scenes of the rudimentary gay life of northern Florida, Holleran paints many scenes of life in a nursing home. Lark's mother can do nothing but lie in bed in whatever position she has been placed. She has to beg to have an arm moved or a fly brushed away from her forehead. Her life seems hardly better than no life at all. She often wishes she were dead. The nursing home is not a house of horrors by any means, but the staff is overworked, underpaid, and inured to the suffering they see every day. They often handle patients roughly. Paralyzed elders sometimes sit staring at the wall because no one thought to turn their wheelchairs around. Intelligent men and women may be forced to watch idiotic animated cartoons on television because no one bothered to switch channels.

Lark's mother literally lives for her son's visits. He knows she wonders why he has never married. On one occasion she asks him directly if he is a homosexual, and he quickly replies, "Of course not." He realizes to his chagrin that if he was ever going to "come out" to his mother, he has waited far too long. In spite of his best intentions, he frequently becomes impatient and handles her with the same hostile efficiency she is accustomed to at the nursing home. He cannot bring himself to admit that he is waiting for her to die.

Being in enforced daily contact with the most decrepit segment of the population only adds to the depression Lark feels in his exile from Manhattan. At the same time, he realizes that the Manhattan he knew has become "a vast cemetery" because of the plague. He realizes he would probably be dead himself if his mother's condition had not forced him to move to Florida.

The only motivation that keeps this intensely subjective, almost claustrophobic narrative creeping forward is Lark's obsession with a suntanned young construction worker with whom he once shared a single night of ecstasy. Becker is living in a straitlaced little town with his junior-high-school-aged daughter and trying to blend into the community for her sake. Although it becomes obvious that the younger man was only interested in a one-night fling, Lark refuses to accept this unflattering truth. Like many homosexuals, he lives in a world of illusions, dreaming of the ideal lover that most gay men will never find.

One of the many cruel paradoxes of homosexuality is that gay men are not often attracted to men like themselves but are looking for that elusive, almost mythical individual—the really masculine man who happens to prefer men to women as lovers. Although Becker is definitely and promiscuously gay, he is a powerfully built outdoorsman who comes as close to the mythical ideal as Lark is ever likely to find. The fact that Becker actually fathered a child adds to his aura of normal masculinity.

On many a lonely night Lark will drive for miles out of his way to park across from Becker's house and stare at the lighted windows, trying to imagine the humdrum domestic life going on inside and wishing he were part of it. He knows Becker's telephone number but has been discouraged from calling by several chilly receptions. No doubt if Lark had been able to have a longer relationship he would have become disenchanted, as he has with so many other lovers in the past; it is the unattainability of this one man that makes him more desirable than any other he has ever met. Lark visits parks and bars where homosexuals congregate, hoping to encounter Becker but taking anyone else he can find. During his regular health checkup, he confesses to having twenty-four sexual encounters with ten different partners in the past year.

On one occasion, Lark sees Becker and his daughter swimming in a lake and watches from a concealed vantage point, adoring every muscle of the young proletarian's body and fantasizing about being part of his life. He is mortified when Becker unexpectedly confronts him and says, "You've been staring at me all afternoon. I've seen you drive by my house. I've about had it. You've got to leave me alone." Like so much gay fiction, *The Beauty of Men* shows the influence of Marcel Proust, and Lark's crushing disillusionment recalls the harrowing scene in which Monsieur de Charlus is publicly denounced and humiliated by his young protégé Morel in *La Prisonniere* (*The Captive*, 1923).

The increasing popularity of gay novels is hard to account for in view of the fact that they tend to be so much alike. "What is there to say about being gay?" Lark asks himself in one of his many interior monologues. "Coming out is the central story, told over and over again, like people describing how they found Christ." There is another story in addition to the one about coming out of the closet: It is the story about the "aging queen" who finds himself all alone with his memories of the fascinating promiscuous world he belonged to in his youth. The prototype is undoubtedly Christopher Isherwood's once shocking novel *A Single Man* (1964), which was avant garde in technique and subject matter when it appeared.

Lark questions himself as to whether there is divine retribution for the "sin" of homosexuality. Those who somehow manage to avoid contracting some fatal disease often end up, like himself, alienated from both the homosexual and heterosexual worlds. Surrounded by sophisticated, gregarious homosexuals in New York, it was easy enough for him to avoid such painful introspection; confined to northern Florida, however, where the norm is marriage and family, he feels conspicuously "queer"—an urbanite among rustics, a gay among straights, an aging queen haunting the gathering places of the young, a sensitive, intelligent man making a fool of himself like Proust's Monsieur de Charlus.

Lark sees himself and his own future in the old men who congregate at a certain bath house, where they are ignored by the clique of young homosexuals as if they were totally invisible. Some of the "manatees" in their seventies and eighties have not given up the impossible dream of finding the ideal lover—or at least someone to replace the companion who died. Lark himself is beginning to feel invisible. He knows that when his mother dies he will not find freedom but will only fade away.

Homosexuals characteristically experience a sense of liberation when they decide to come out of the closet. Holleran makes it clear, however, that there is no turning back. The aging homosexual who finds himself rejected by his chosen world has no one, nowhere, nothing to go back to. Lark's case calls to mind Proust's description of Charles Swann entering "a mysterious world to which one never may return again once its doors are closed."

Gay novels are written by homosexuals for homosexuals. The rare heterosexual reader may wonder about many peculiarities of the genre. For one thing, it is hard to understand why the characters are so obsessed with sex and with cruising. They seem to have little interest in anything else. Their many disappointing or even traumatic experiences with strangers only seem to whet their appetites for more. In fact, many seem to enjoy the degradation more than the questionable gratification. Most heterosexual men are happy to compartmentalize their sex drive through marriage so that they can devote their time to their careers. The AIDS epidemic has forced a certain amount of monogamy on gay men, but these monogamous relationships are often unsatisfactory and not even safe. Many gay men are so addicted to cruising that they bring home the dreaded disease which frightened them into monogamy in the first place.

Allied to the obsession with cruising for the dream lover who never appears, the characters in gay fiction rarely seem to have any work to do. In *The Beauty of Men*, the practical-minded reader will not find a single mention of how the protagonist pays his bills. All of Lark's witty, pleasure-loving friends in Manhattan seemed to exist as perpetual non-rent-paying roommates. They were "circuit queens" who subsisted on cocktails, hors d'oeuvres, and drugs in a dizzying round of nightlife. A moralist might argue that they would not be so obsessed with sex if they had jobs. Here again there is a strong resemblance to Proust, whose characters had nothing to do but search for love.

Judging from Holleran's novel, contracting AIDS does not stop most gay men from having sex. Many gay men who have contracted AIDS become even more promiscuous because they feel they have nothing to lose. It would not be unreasonable to assume that such men feel guilty and doomed, so that they not only expect to die of the dreaded disease but actually look forward to it.

Lark is haunted by guilt. Like James Joyce's Stephen Dedalus, Lark cannot lay down the cross of his early Catholic upbringing. He recalls conversations with Sutcliffe, one of his Manhattan friends, who vehemently denied what conservatives have been delighted to identify as divine retribution. "It's very hard to remember," said his friend and mentor, "its very hard not to get a little crazy over all of this, but try to repeat—it's just a germ. It's *not* God's judgment on us, it's *not* what we deserve, it's *not* what everyone thinks it is—divine justice—it's a germ that used to live in a green monkey in Africa, and decided to come to New York. Why not? New York is fun."

Holleran's highly acclaimed "post-Liberation" novel, *Dancer from the Dance* (1978), tells about the time when New York was truly fun for liberated homosexuals. Edmund White, the dean of gay fiction writers, said that the book "accomplished for the 1970's what *The Great Gatsby* achieved for the 1920's . . . the glamorization of a decade and a culture." To pursue the comparison with F. Scott Fitzgerald, *The Beauty of Men*, like Fitzgerald's best short story, "Babylon Revisited" (1931), is a haunting echo of a gaudy decade and an ill-fated subculture.

Bill Delaney

Sources for Further Study

Booklist. XCII, June 1, 1996, p. 1643.
Boston Globe. July 28, 1996, p. N15.
Library Journal. CXXI, June 15, 1996, p. 91.
Los Angeles Times Book Review. July 28, 1996, p. 2.
The New York Times Book Review. CI, June 30, 1996, p. 7.
Publishers Weekly. CCXLIII, June 17, 1996, p. 42.
USA Today. July 8, 1996, p. D4.
The Washington Post Book World. XXVI, June 9, 1996, p. 5.

BERTRAND RUSSELL
The Spirit of Solitude, 1872-1921

Author: Ray Monk
Publisher: Free Press (New York). Illustrated. 695 pp. $35.00
Type of work: Biography
Time: 1872-1921
Locale: Cambridge and other locations in England

This first volume of a projected two-volume biography covers the first half of Bertrand Russell's long life

Principal personages:
> BERTRAND RUSSELL, the most eminent of all twentieth century British philosophers
> ALYS RUSSELL (NÉE PEARSALL SMITH), his first wife
> DORA BLACK, his second wife
> LADY OTTOLINE MORRELL, his first long-time mistress and companion
> LUDWIG WITTGENSTEIN, the Austrian-born philosopher whose genius intimidated even Russell
> D. H. LAWRENCE, the British novelist whose frank appraisal of Russell's psychological motivation stunned Russell
> JOSEPH CONRAD, the Polish-born novelist with whom Russell formed a close friendship
> ALFRED NORTH WHITEHEAD, Russell's collaborator on *Principia Mathematica*
> VIVIEN ELIOT, T.S. Eliot's first wife, with whom Russell had a difficult relationship

Ray Monk is a philosophy professor whose first book was a biography of Ludwig Wittgenstein, the Austrian-born philosopher whose brilliance unsettled even the haughty Bertrand Russell. This first volume of a planned two-volume life of Russell covers the first forty-nine of his ninety-eight years, from 1872 through 1921. Writing Russell's life is a daunting task in that the *Bibliography of Bertrand Russell* contains more than three thousand entries, and the Russell Archives hold more than forty thousand letters as well as many journals, manuscripts, and other documents. In many of these materials, Russell is concerned mostly with himself, creating a record of "detailed self-absorption" that Monk judges matched only by that of Virginia Woolf.

In working with this rich trove, Monk, unlike previous biographers, provides a full account of Russell's philosophical work and social thought. Monk organizes his story around the three powerful forces he locates at the root of Russell's behavior: "his need for love, his yearning for certain knowledge, and his sometimes overpowering impulse to become involved in the great political issues of his day." These three passions were often in conflict with one another, and in Monk's analysis they issue from a terrible loneliness exacerbated by a haunting fear of madness. The events in Russell's life that shaped this difficult emotional history began very early in Russell's childhood.

Bertrand Arthur William Russell was born on May 18, 1872, in Monmouthshire,

England, in the most privileged circumstances. He was the third child and second son of Viscount Amberley and his wife, Kate. The Russells were an old family in a proud Whig tradition. Russell's grandfather, Lord John Russell, was a younger son of the sixth Duke of Bedford, and Lord John's highly principled political career included promotion of the Great Reform Act of 1832 and two terms as Queen Victoria's prime minister. Bertrand Russell was well aware all his life of the role expected of a Russell in public affairs.

Russell's family began to abandon him early in his childhood. When he was two years old, first his mother, and then a few days later his sister, died of diphtheria. Russell's heartbroken father died eighteen months later when Russell was three. He was taken in by his grandparents, only to have Lord Russell die when he was six and leave him to wonder when his grandmother would die too. Russell's extremely intelligent and rational mind set him off immediately from most people, and the combination of mental brilliance and his childhood losses burdened him with the "spirit of solitude" (the phrase is from Percy Bysshe Shelley's poem "Alastor") and the need for love that Monk captures so well.

Assuagement from his loneliness came in 1889 when he met Alys Pearsall Smith, staying with her well-to-do Philadelphia family near the farm of Russell's Uncle Rollo on the border between Surrey and Sussex. The following summer Russell entered Trinity College, Cambridge, and for the next few years he was preoccupied with mathematics and afflicted with sexual ache for Alys. He passed his Cambridge exams in 1893, and he married Alys in 1894 despite Lady Russell's opposition and her warning of hereditary insanity, a specter that haunted Russell's imagination all his life. After a flirtation with Baruch Spinoza's pantheism and a spell of allegiance to Friedrich Hegel's Absolute Idealism, by 1898 Russell had converted to the young analytical school of philosophy which he found compatible with an intense passion for Plato's world of shining abstract Forms.

By 1899, Russell was writing *The Principles of Mathematics*, but his discovery in 1900 of the mathematical logic of Giuseppe Peano convinced him that all mathematics is built on logic and he completely rewrote his manuscript. In 1901, he discovered "Russell's Paradox," the puzzling case of the class of all classes that are not members of themselves (if this class is a member of itself, then it is not, and if it is not, then it is), an insight that he feared might be fatal to the notion of a "class" that was vital to his construction of a logical base for mathematics. Russell's struggle with his paradox, not convincingly solved by his early "theory of types," pursued him into his "long night," Russell's own term for the period from 1904 to 1910 during which he was laboring intensively with Alfred North Whitehead on their *Principia Mathematica*. One product of this period was Russell's effort to resolve his paradox in his famous article "On Denoting" (1905), in which he argued that a concept is denoted by a description, not by a name. The paradox followed, he thought, from phrases that led to a contradiction and therefore could not refer to anything real. These phrases (synonymous in Russell's mind with classes) have meaning in his "Theory of Descriptions" only when they are embedded in a proposition, and if a whole proposition and its converse are both false without creating a paradox ("The present King of France is bald" and "The present King of France has hair on his head"), then it follows that there is no "class of classes which do not belong to themselves" and thus no paradox. Classes disappear; only individuals and universals remain: This was Russell's "substitution theory."

This solution soon collapsed under attack from Henri Poincaré, who demonstrated that the paradox was but a variant of the ancient Cretan liar paradox that has Epimenides the Cretan asserting "All Cretans are liars." Russell responded to this criticism by reviving his theory of types to describe "levels of truth" (first individuals, then classes, and so on), with accompanying levels of propositions. The resulting "ramified" theory of types was both intricate and ponderous (Monk speaks of "the utter unintelligibility of the theory of logic at the heart of *Principia*") but it was the best Russell could do. The crushing finale to the long effort put into *Principia* came in 1931, when the logician Kurt Gödel proved that Russell and Whitehead's project was doomed from the start since all formal theories of mathematics are demonstrably incomplete. Monk believes, however, that *Principia* advanced the study of mathematical logic significantly by preparing the way for the work of Alan Turing and John von Neumann that led to computer theory.

Russell's coldness and disingenuousness in treating women emerges not only in his brutal severance of affectionate ties with Alys, but also in his unforgivable exploitation of Helen Dudley and Vivien Eliot. Helen Dudley, daughter of a Northwestern University professor and surgeon, had met Russell briefly when she was at Oxford, and when he visited Chicago in 1914 they had a brief, passionate affair that led to Russell's suggestion that she come live with him in England. Yet when Ottoline Morrell learned of Helen, "she discovered a hitherto unknown sexual passion" for Russell, and he consequently refused even to see Helen when she arrived in England. In 1919, Helen returned to Chicago, where she came down with multiple sclerosis and went insane.

The precise details of Russell's difficult relationship with Vivien Eliot remain cloudy, in part because of a paucity of surviving letters from her in the Russell Archives that Monk regards as "rather suspicious" given Russell's habit of keeping everything. In a letter of October 30, 1917, to Constance Malleson, Russell says of Vivien: "at last I spent a night with her. *It was utter hell*. There was a quality of loathsomeness about it which I can't describe. . . . it has come out since in horrible nightmares which wake me in the middle of the night & leave me stripped bare of self-deception." The letter continues in this distraught vein. It is probably fair to conclude that, given Vivien's emotional problems, any relationship with a philanderer as ruthless as Russell could not have comforted her long. Unlike some women to whom Russell kept returning, particularly Ottoline Morrell and the actress Constance Malleson who were too cool and worldly to be hurt much by a man whose weaknesses they saw through immediately, more susceptible women could be broken by Russell's sexual exploitation and subsequent disdain.

Three talented men, creative and powerful in their own ways, swayed Russell's sensibility. Russell saw the brilliant Ludwig Wittgenstein as his natural successor in the study of mathematical logic, and their friendship persisted despite Wittgenstein's frank rejection of much of Russell's work. Wittgenstein dismissed Russell's Theory of Types, for example, arguing that only things exist and that philosophy's task is to learn how to talk about them. Their personal tie was close but their philosophical differences were profound.

Of the two novelists to whom Russell was drawn, D. H. Lawrence and Joseph Conrad, the intense Lawrence stirred Russell most devastatingly. Russell and Lawrence met at the Morrells' home in 1915, and Russell was immediately struck by Lawrence's uncanny insight into human motives. Their intense friendship soon faltered, however, and Lawrence wrote Russell a letter that stunned him. After sneering at Russell's essay "The Danger to Civilization," condemning its high-minded sentiment as "a plausible lie," Lawrence attacked: "The enemy of all mankind, you are, full of the lust of enmity. It is *not* the hatred of falsity which inspires you. It is the hatred of people, of flesh and blood. It is a perverted, mental blood-lust. Why don't you own it." Something of their relationship is re-created in Lawrence's short story "The Blind Man."

The outbreak of war in 1914 led Russell to participate in forming the Union of Democratic Control (UDC) even though he was not a pacifist. His position was that it was a terrible mistake for England, France, and Germany to be at war for they represented all that there was of civilization, and he was especially concerned to dampen anti-German sentiment. Lawrence's hope for a dictator to settle Europe's problems repelled Russell, who in 1916 spelled out his own ideas in eight lectures published as *Principles of Social Reconstruction*. Nevertheless, it was partly the influence of Lawrence that led Russell to reject the utilitarian arguments of Jeremy Bentham and John Stuart Mill as naïve about the unconscious motives that impel people. For Russell, the problem was to find a means of diverting these blind impulses away from destructive outlets and toward useful goals, toward something like William James's moral equivalent of war.

Russell's radical championing of the No-Conscription Fellowship led to a not particularly uncomfortable stay at Brixton prison in 1918. In 1919, he met Dora Black, a radical twenty-five-year-old student of French literature who in 1921 was to become his second wife shortly before bearing his first child, John Conrad. While he was sorting out his feelings for Dora, Russell made the customary liberal pilgrimage to Russia, where the new socialist heaven disappointed him. Russell's innate contempt for collectivist visions soured him on what he saw, and he was one of the few intellectuals of his day to foresee precisely what the outcome would be. In October of 1921, however, Russell and Dora arrived in China on a lecture tour that proved uncommonly gratifying for Russell until he came down in March with a serious illness that kept him near death for three months. Dora's devotion and a tough Whig constitution pulled him through, and in August, 1921, he rounded off roughly the first half of his life by docking in Liverpool.

Monk has produced a superb biography that is certain to pique the interest of scholars and general readers alike.

Frank Day

Sources for Further Study

The Economist. CCCXXXIX, April 20, 1996, p. 5.
London Review of Books. XVIII, April 4, 1996, p. 7.
Los Angeles Times Book Review. November 3, 1996, p. 4.
Nature. CCCLXXXI, June 20, 1996, p. 657.
The New Republic. CCXV, December 2, 1996, p. 46.
The New York Times. December 6, 1996, p. C15.
The New Yorker. LXXII, December 9, 1996, p. 104.
Publishers Weekly. CCXLIII, August 5, 1996, p. 419.
The Spectator. CCLXXVI, April 20, 1996, p. 39.
The Times Literary Supplement. June 21, 1996, p. 5.
The Wall Street Journal. September 27, 1996, p. A16.

BIRDSONG

Author: Sebastian Faulks (1953-   )
First published: 1993, in Great Britain
Publisher: Random House (New York). 402 pp. $25.00
Type of work: Novel
Time: 1910-1918, 1978-1979
Locale: Amiens, Beaumont-Hamel, Auchonvillers, Plombieres, St.-Remy-de-Provence, Bethune, Colincamps, Arras, Rouen, Thiepval, and Boulogne, France; London, Twickenham, Dover, Leamington Spa, Folkestone, Burnham Market, Buckinghamshire, and Southend, England; Brussels

A graphic depiction of the horrors of war, Birdsong *explores the effects of love and death on a handful of characters in France during World War I and their legacy in the 1970's*

Principal characters:
STEPHEN WRAYSFORD, the protagonist, a British army officer
ISABELLE AZAIRE, his lover, a manufacturer's wife
JEANNE FOURMENTIER, her sister, later Stephen's wife
ELIZABETH BENSON, his granddaughter, operator of a clothing firm
JACK FIREBRACE, an English soldier
MICHAEL WEIR, Stephen's best friend, an English officer
AZAIRE, Isabelle's husband
ROBERT, Elizabeth's lover
GRAY, an English officer
BRENNAN, an English soldier
LEVI, a German soldier
FRANÇOISE WRAYSFORD BENSON, the daughter of Stephen and Isabelle and the mother of Elizabeth

The horrors of World War I and the resulting disillusionment meant more to the British than to any other nationality, yet there are few major British novels dealing with the Great War. The most lasting fiction about this experience has been created by Americans—*Three Soldiers* (1921) by John Dos Passos, *The Enormous Room* (1922) by e. e. cummings, *Through the Wheat* (1923) by Thomas Boyd, *A Farewell to Arms* (1929) by Ernest Hemingway, *Paths of Glory* (1935) by Humphrey Cobb—and a German—*All Quiet on the Western Front* (1929) by Erich Maria Remarque—while the British are notable for the war poetry of Wilfred Owen, Siegfried Sassoon, Edmund Blunden, and Robert Graves and such memoirs as Graves's *Good-bye to All That* (1929). Sebastian Faulks remedies this gap with a graphic vision of World War I. *Birdsong*, however, is more than a war novel as Faulks blends such topics as sex, love, alienation, nature, and death into the fabric of his narrative.

Stephen Wraysford is just twenty when he visits Amiens in 1910 to study French textile manufacturing methods for his English employer. Staying with Azaire, owner of the local textile factory, Stephen is slowly drawn to Isabelle, his host's haunting young wife. Their attraction soon develops into an affair, and they run away after confronting Azaire, who has neglected and abused his wife. Isabelle is uncertain whether she loves Stephen or is just sexually attracted to him. When she becomes pregnant, she leaves him and returns first to her family in Rouen and later, uncomfortably, to a forgiving Azaire, who merely wants to reestablish the facade of a happy family for the sake of his place in the community. (Stephen does not discover his daughter's existence until after the war.)

Stephen continues his self-imposed exile in France, working at various jobs in several villages until the war begins. Quickly promoted to lieutenant, he develops a friendship with Michael Weir, an officer in charge of a group of "miners," men who burrow beneath the trenches to try to detect enemy mines. Stephen's experience of the war alternates with that of Jack Firebrace, one of Weir's miners. Stephen catches Jack asleep on duty but declines to take any measures against him. Later, when Stephen is badly wounded and assumed to be dead and his body is tossed amid a pile of corpses, Jack rescues him. Jack is well acquainted with death, having seen several friends killed and been informed of the death of his young son back in England. At the very end of the war, Stephen and the severely wounded Jack find themselves trapped underground for several days before being rescued by German soldiers, including Levi, whose beloved brother has died in combat. Between battles, Stephen meets Isabelle's older sister, Jeanne, and develops a friendship which intensifies after he finds Isabelle again and learns she is in love with Max, a German officer.

Another strand of *Birdsong* follows the more mundane travails in the 1970's of Elizabeth Benson, Stephen's granddaughter, who has been told little of her family's past by her mother, Françoise. Managing director of a clothing company and nearing forty, Elizabeth is dissatisfied with her life. In love with the married Robert, she realizes he will never divorce his wife. Elizabeth tries to make some sense of her ennui by investigating Stephen's life, including visiting the sites of battles in France and having a friend's husband decipher her grandfather's coded journal. Happy, regardless of Robert's plans, to find herself pregnant, she learns that Jeanne is not her grandmother.

Faulks, a former journalist who has written three previous novels, depicts war as the most harrowing of human experiences. Stephen, in his self-pity, is foolish to think that this chaos will help him forget his misery. The war only brings a sharper sense of pain. Faulks might be criticized for overdoing the scenes of blood and dismemberment, but his excess is intentional to make these horrors as vivid as possible. Helping a wounded soldier reach the stretcher bearers, Stephen becomes drenched in blood and almost chokes on the butcher's-shop smell. As the man is being carried away, the bearer is hit by shrapnel, and his blood splatters Stephen even more. A gruesomely burned soldier tries to scream at his pain but has lost his voice. Standing in a shell hole, Stephen feels something move beneath him: the face of a man whose brain is sliding out his eye socket. When he begs to die, Stephen shoots him.

Sixty years later, Elizabeth recognizes her responsibility not to forget the past and to honor those who have suffered. She forces herself to become friends with Brennan, one of the few remaining survivors among those who served with her grandfather. Brennan found his brother's headless body and has spent the years since the war in an institution.

The war teaches Stephen the grimmest of lessons: "It was not all the tens of thousands of deaths that mattered; it was the way they had proved that you could be human yet act in a way that was beyond nature." More than lives are being lost. A way of life is being destroyed. After a particularly brutal battle, Weir cries, "We've done something terrible, we'll never get back to how it was before." On leave in England, back where life is supposedly normal and ordered, the unusually sensitive Weir cannot abide the contrast with the battlefields he has left. Even more he cannot forgive the refusal of his parents and other civilians even to begin to contemplate the reality of the war. Weir wishes all such people dead.

On the sixtieth anniversary of the armistice, Elizabeth realizes her inability to grasp it all: "The topic seemed too large, too fraught, and too remote for her to take on at that moment." She is shocked at the number of British names on a French war memorial: "My God, nobody told me." Faulks uses her to emphasize the necessity of understanding the past.

Death permeates *Birdsong* even before the war as Faulks employs images of death to unify the novel. On a Sunday outing with the Azaires and friends, Stephen is "repelled by the water gardens: their hectic abundance seemed to him close to the vegetable fertility of death. . . . What was held to be a place of natural beauty was a stagnation of living tissue which could not be saved from decay." Stephen even feels similarly about sex: "The sensation of desire seemed indistinguishable from an impulse toward death."

Stephen, at this stage, is uneasy with nature and natural impulses because he is too innocent about the complexity of life—and death. The novel's title refers to the changing meaning, for Stephen, of birds and their sounds. He associates them with danger because of a lifelong nightmare of being trapped in a room full of frightened starlings. After a pigeon scares Isabelle, he confesses to hating birds since touching a dead crow and seeing maggots beneath its wings. Faulks ties birds to the war several times as when Stephen's men march by the graves being dug for the soon-to-be dead and the sudden quiet is filled by the songs of birds. Are the caged canaries taken into the tunnels singing from happiness or fear? When they stop singing, death is nearer. When Stephen and an injured Weir try to make their way out of a tunnel, they want to kill the canary so that it will not give them away to the enemy, but neither can do it. When Stephen emerges from underground to find the war ended, birds are heard. After the pain of the war, what he feared before has taken on a different meaning.

Faulks presents the war as a symptom of the general chaos and alienation of the twentieth century with Stephen and Elizabeth representative of the aimlessness of their times. Stephen's rootlessness stems in part from a Dickensian childhood. He never knew the man who impregnated his mother, and she later ran off to Scotland with another lover. Stephen lived with her parents until his grandfather was sent to prison. After time in an institution, he went to live with a stern social reformer. That he becomes the father of an illegitimate child without knowing it is typical of Faulks's ironies as is Elizabeth's continuing the family tradition though in a completely different social context.

In the war, the prematurely gray Stephen is considered strange by his men, distant, uncaring, a law unto himself and is reprimanded by Captain Gray, the company commander, for telling a soldier the war will become worse before it gets better. Stephen justifies his fatalistic attitude to Weir: "This is not a war, this is an exploration of how far men can be degraded. I am deeply curious to see how much further it can be taken. . . . If I didn't have that curiosity I would walk into enemy lines and let myself be killed." Faulks avoids such clichés of war literature as having his hero learn a hard moral lesson, experience some spiritual enlightenment, or undergo some other personality change. Faulks's war is more realistic, is much too complex to be reduced to platitudes. Stephen merely survives and, like his world which has permanently lost any pretension of innocence, will never be the same.

Birdsong was first published in England in 1993, and Faulks was named Author of the Year by the British Book Awards. The novel has some defects, such as indicating that Jack Firebrace will receive attention equal to Stephen during the war scenes only to disappear for long sections, such as sentimentalizing the effect of parenthood on Elizabeth—implying that her life is incomplete without a child. (The Elizabeth sections seem particularly trite next to the graphic depiction of war, and Faulks does little to counteract this imbalance of tone.) Faulks's tale is notable for avoiding sentimentality elsewhere, as with showing that the specter of Isabelle will forever tarnish the Stephen-Jeanne marriage. Stephen's self-pity over losing Isabelle is depicted as a character flaw eventually to be consumed by the fire of battle. Abandoned by Isabelle, he becomes wedded to the war. Faulks's deft handling of complicated emotional attachments and the awesome power of his evocation of war make *Birdsong* a triumph. Faulks acknowledges, however, the puniness of language in confronting war: Stephen's journal ends, "We will seal what we have seen in the silence of our hearts and no words will reach us."

Michael Adams

Sources for Further Study

Booklist. XCII, February 15, 1996, p. 990.
The Guardian. October 19, 1993, p. 13.
Kirkus Reviews. LXIII, December 1, 1995, p. 1652.
Los Angeles Times Book Review. April 7, 1996, p. 4.
New Statesman and Society. VI, September 17, 1993, p. 40.
The New York Times Book Review. CI, February 11, 1996, p. 11.
The New Yorker. LXXII, April 1, 1996, p. 97.
Publishers Weekly. CCXLII, December 11, 1996, p. 58.
The Spectator. CCLXXI, September 18, 1993, p. 39.
The Times Educational Supplement. November 5, 1993, p. 12.
The Times Literary Supplement. September 10, 1993, p. 21.
The Washington Post Book World. XXVI, February 18, 1996, p. 3.

BLACK ATHENA REVISITED

Editors: Mary R. Lefkowitz (1935-   ) and Guy MacLean Rogers (1954-   )
Publisher: University of North Carolina Press (Chapel Hill). Illustrated. 221 pp. $55.00; paperback $19.95
Type of work: Essays

A collection of twenty scholarly essays responding to issues of history and historiography raised by Martin Bernal in Black Athena

The publication of the first volume of Martin Bernal's *Black Athena* in 1987 shook the very foundations of the classical world to its historical and archaeological under-pinnings. In both this book and in a second volume, published in 1991, Bernal, a professor of political science and an expert on China, uses a wide range of arguments to call into question not only generally accepted views on the origins of Greek civilization but also the very methodological assumptions of the discipline.

Bernal's position, in brief, is that ancient Greece was colonized in the second millennium B.C.E. by Egyptians and Phoenicians and that ancient Greek culture was essentially Levantine, a mixture of Egyptian and Semitic influences. In support of this thesis, Bernal cites the witness of ancient Greeks themselves, especially the fifth century historian Herodotus, as well as Greek myths in which the Egyptian Danaus and the Phoenician Cadmus settle in Greece. Bernal ties these myths of colonization with hypothetical invasions of Greece, not only by the seventeenth century B.C.E. Hyksos rulers of Egypt, but also by the earlier, twelfth dynasty Egyptian pharaoh Senwosret I (1959-1914 B.C.E.), whom Bernal identifies with the Egyptian ruler Sesostris I reported by Herodotus to have led a major expedition as far north as the Black Sea. Bernal modifies this "Ancient Model" only to acknowledge an invasion of Greece by Indo-European speakers in the fourth or third millennium B.C.E.

In the "Revised Ancient Model" of *Black Athena*, Bernal emphasizes an Egyptian and Phoenician presence in Greece and argues that a significant portion of the ancient Greek language is Semitic or Egyptian in origin and that the sources for most of Greek culture can be traced to the Egyptians and Phoenicians. As suggested by both the title of *Black Athena*, as well as its subtitle *The Afroasiatic Roots of Greek Civilization*, Bernal's view of Greek culture is essentially an externalist one which weighs contri-butions from the Near East and Egypt more heavily than those of the Indo-Europeans. Much of the archaeological and documentary evidence for this "Revised Ancient Model" appears in the second volume of *Black Athena*, where Bernal cites irrigation works around Lake Kopais in Boeotia and a pyramid-like hill in Thebes as proof of an Egyptian presence in Greece in the third millennium B.C.E. A third volume on linguistic evidence and an unspecified fourth volume are promised by the author.

Bernal's quest for external sources for Greek civilization is not entirely new. Scholars have long acknowledged foreign, especially orientalizing, influences on Greek culture, and recent archaeological and historical work has provided increasing confirmation that Greek civilization developed in the midst of dynamic trade and cultural exchange in the eastern Mediterranean. Such widely accepted scholarly explanations often differ from Bernal's only in emphasis. Where Bernal tends to see invasions and colonizations, other scholars acknowledge no more than trading contacts, but the interaction of various Mediterranean cultures, including Greek, Mesopotamian, Phoenician, and Egyptian, has rarely been doubted. For scholars of the ancient world, the question has not been so much whether Greek civilization was influenced from the outside, but how these influences took place and from what part(s) of the Mediterranean. Were they based upon conquest, as Bernal suggests, or were they part of extended and broad cultural exchange? Did this influence go only in one direction or did the Greeks leave their marks on other early cultures?

If Bernal had only dealt with these historical questions, the reaction to his work would have been much more muted. However, in the first volume of *Black Athena*, aptly subtitled *The Fabrication of Ancient Greece*, Bernal broadens the debate to include historiography. He wounds the pride and questions the professionalism of scholars of the ancient Mediterranean by tying his "Revised Ancient Model" to suggestions that the historical methodology of modern European scholarship, especially its objective and scientific analysis of the ancient evidence, has been flawed for centuries by racial bigotry and anti-Semitic assumptions. Bernal argues that the original "Ancient Model," unchallenged by Europeans until the eighteenth century, was displaced in the nineteenth century by an "Aryan" one centered on the Indo-Europeans in order to avoid sharing any of the glory that was Greece and the splendor of Western civilization with a "black" Egypt or a Semitic Near East.

Scholarly and public reaction to *Black Athena* has been swift and loud. In 1989 Bernal defended his thesis at a colloquium sponsored by the American Philological Association. Some of the papers read at this colloquium were published in the same year as *The Challenge of "Black Athena,"* edited by M. M. Levine and J. Peradotto. Lefkowitz, the coeditor of *Black Athena Revisited*, has been especially prominent in this debate. She introduces this volume with "Ancient History, Modern Myths," an essay which originally appeared as "Not Out of Africa" in *The New Republic* in 1992. In 1996 she published *Not Out of Africa*, which grew out of the earlier article and which raises a number of objections to Bernal's diffusionist view of the ancient Mediterranean.

Black Athena Revisited, which Lefkowitz edits together with a colleague in the Department of Classics at Wellesley College, brings together responses to the *Black Athena* controversy by professors of Egyptology, archaeology, Classics, linguistics, German, Near Eastern Studies, the history of science, and history. All of the fields represented by these scholars have been affected in some way by Bernal's thesis. While some of the contributors are somewhat sympathetic toward Bernal's general premise and purpose, nearly all question the validity of his methodology and his interpretation of the literary, archaeological, and linguistic evidence. The twenty contributions are organized thematically under the headings Egypt, race, the Near East, linguistics, science, Greece, and historiography. Readers new to the *Black Athena* controversy will appreciate the presence in *Black Athena Revisited* of several chronological charts, maps, and site photographs.

The contributors to *Black Athena Revisited* challenge Bernal on a number of fronts. His disregard of the influence of Mesopotamia on the Mediterranean is especially highlighted. Mesopotamian science, mathematics, astronomy, and even governmental structures were so important in the ancient Mediterranean that Bernal's African or Levantine model could easily have been a Mesopotamian one instead. Such widespread cultural exchange actually argues for a Mediterranean model.

Bernal's Egyptian etymologies for Greek words are also questioned in *Black Athena Revisited*. Although Bernal can read hieroglyphics, his attempt to derive the name of the mythic Cretan king Minos from the Egyptian god Min or the goddess Athena from Egyptian Hwt-Nt (House of Neith) is doubted convincingly by Egyptologists.

Another criticism of Bernal which contributors raise in *Black Athena Revisited* is his acceptance of Greek myths at face value. Bernal uses the story of Danaus, who migrated from Egypt to Greece, as evidence of Egyptian colonization of Greece, yet, as a descendant of the Greek woman Io who goes to live in Egypt, Danaus can also been seen as the descendant of a Greek colonist to Egypt.

Contributors to *Black Athena Revisited* also draw attention to two recent archaeological discoveries which cast into doubt Bernal's model of Egyptian colonization of Greece and which, in fact, may suggest just the opposite. At an Austrian excavation of the ancient site of Avaris (Tell el-Dab'a), once the Hyksos capital of Egypt in the Nile Delta, a 1991 discovery of fragments of Minoan painted frescoes strongly suggests a Minoan presence in Egypt, and even some cultural influence, at the very period when Bernal hypothesizes an Egyptian colonization of Greece. This pattern is reenforced by the discovery, also in 1991, of a painted Minoan floor with flowers from the sixteenth century B.C.E. at Tell Kabri in Israel.

Even Bernal's impression that white racism and anti-Semitism were dominant among European historians from the eighteenth through the twentieth centuries is called into question in *Black Athena Revisited*. Several contributors prove Bernal to have quoted historians of the period out of context and to have overlooked other prominent scholars, such as Johann Gottfried von Herder (1744-1803), who had strongly antiracist views. The picture is thus much more complicated and ambiguous than Bernal suggests.

Such is the case, especially, in regard to the racial and ethnic questions implied by the title *Black Athena*. Bernal himself admitted at the American Philosophical Association colloquium in 1989 that his publisher changed the book's original title, *African Athena*, for marketing reasons. Bernal himself apparently accepts the equation of the terms "Egyptian," "African," and "Black" which this title suggests. Contributors to *Black Athena Revisited*, however, cite ample evidence that the population of ancient Egypt was stable from Neolithic times, with little evidence for significant ties with the peoples of sub-Saharan Africa. Furthermore, the racial and ethnic self-identity of the ancient Egyptians does not support a "black" Athena hypothesis. The people of ancient Egypt tended to distinguish themselves from the darker-skinned peoples to the south and the lighter-skinned peoples to the north and to consider themselves "Egyptian" rather than "African" or "Black."

Indeed, the very identification of "Africa" and "Black" in the context of ancient Egypt unfortunately ties Bernal's challenge with modern ideological issues of race which blur the historical reality and perspectives of anyone attempting to deal objectively with these issues. Bernal's condemnation of racism and anti-Semitism, especially among some nineteenth and twentieth century historians is certainly legitimate, but his revisionist history of the origin of Greek and Western culture has imposed a false sense of legitimacy upon a school of pseudohistorians, especially in the United States and Africa, who have blindly claimed that all cultural, technological, and scientific accomplishments of the West have been stolen from a black Egypt. The subtitle of G. G. M. James's *Stolen Legacy* (1954), *The Greeks Were Not the Authors of Greek Philosophy, but the People of North Africa, Commonly Called the Egyptians*, illustrates this claim, for which the essays in *Black Athena Revisited* offer no support.

Bernal's challenge is not directed to scholars alone. In volume 1 of *Black Athena*, he admits that he hopes his work will diminish the cultural arrogance of Europeans (and Americans). Yet, contributors to *Black Athena Revisited* argue that, in trying to identify an African (Egyptian and Phoenician) source for European civilization, Bernal has unwittingly reenforced the very Eurocentrism he has struggled to undermine. An unspoken premise of his book is that African civilization can only celebrate its greatness to the extent that it is the source of Western civilization. That is, only Europe matters in the end. Bernal's African model is, in itself, based on racist assumptions.

As a modified diffusionist, Bernal rejects the possibility of evolutionary autonomy in the Mediterranean. Like many nineteenth century comparative mythologists who searched for an Ur-myth, a single source myth for all later myths, Bernal assumes the existence an Ur-Kultur, an original culture which was a common parent of at least the Egyptians, the Phoenicians, and the Greeks. It is also possible that the cultures of the ancient Mediterranean worked out their accomplishments independently.

The contributors to *Black Athena Revisited* offer a balanced response to Bernal's work. While questioning some of his conclusions and his methodology, they welcome his fresh interpretations of the evidence as an opportunity to reconsider long-standing assumptions about the ancient world and the origins of Western civilization. Bernal's revisionist history offers an Afrocentric alternative to a traditional, Eurocentric view of history. The contributors to *Black Athena Revisited* take Bernal's work one step further. By emphasizing the multicultural nature of the ancient Mediterranean world they argue for a more wide-ranging view of human history. The roots of Western civilization are not merely Greco-Roman. They are also Egyptian, Phoenician, Hebrew, and Mesopotamian. *Black Athena Revisited* is not the end of this debate, only one of many noteworthy mileposts on a long, multicultural quest.

Thomas J. Sienkewicz

Sources for Further Study

American Journal of Archaeology. C, October, 1996, p. 781.
Library Journal. CXXI, May 1, 1996, p. 108.
The Nation. CCLXIII, October 28, 1996, p. 42.
New Scientist. CL, June 22, 1996, p. 45.
The New York Review of Books. XLIII, June 20, 1996, p. 67.
The New York Times Book Review. CI, February 25, 1996, p. 6.
The Wilson Quarterly. XX, Spring, 1996, p. 79.

BLACKWATER

Author: Kerstin Ekman
First published: Handelser vid vatten, 1993, in Sweden
Translated from the Swedish by Joan Tate
Publisher: Doubleday (New York). 434 pp. $23.95
Type of work: Novel
Time: 1974-1992
Locale: Far northern portion of Sweden, near the Norwegian border

An unsolved murder outside a small Swedish town near the Norwegian border turns the lives of several people upside down, first when it occurs, and then again eighteen years later when a second murder unexpectedly unravels the first

Principal characters:
    ANNIE RAFT, a schoolteacher who, on her way to join her boyfriend, Dan Ulander, living on a commune, stumbles across two dead bodies
    MIA RAFT, her daughter
    JOHAN BRANDBERG, a teenager who has been picked on by his older half brothers, he is widely believed to have committed the murder of the bodies Annie discovered, although he is never charged
    DAN ULANDER, a member of the Starhill commune and Annie's boyfriend
    BIRGER TORBJORNSSON, the district doctor, whose estranged wife has an affair with Dan Ulander
    GUDRUN BRANDBERG, Johan's overly protective mother
    YLJA, a woman who picks up Johan up as he is hitchhiking and hides him for several days
    PER-OLA,
    BJORNE,
    PEKKA, and
    VAINE BRANDBERG, Johann's older half brothers who torment him into running away

    In the second half of part 1 of Kerstin Ekman's *Blackwater*, it appears clear that the novel is going to be about how a murder that is never solved changes the lives of several people. The main characters of this first part, Annie Raft, Johan Brandberg, and Birger Torbjornsson all have their own secrets to protect, but in each case, their secrets are their hopes and fears which get bruised and abused by the investigation and apparent cover-up going on around them. Indeed, that is the nature of part 1 of the novel: It is less a murder mystery than a novel about the rippling waves that a murder causes. Part 2, however, becomes a bravura detective story when, eighteen years after the first murder, a second murder occurs. Facts that were obvious but insignificant eighteen years ago suddenly seem to be significant, and people who refused to talk after the first murder easily open up their secrets.
    This novel, translated so seamlessly into English that it is hard to believe it is a translation, begins when Annie Raft recognizes that the man who drives her twenty-three-year-old daughter Mia home one night is the same man she and Mia glimpsed

in a forest one night eighteen years ago, a night they stumbled upon a murder scene. Annie has always believed that this man, Johan Brandberg, who was a teenager at the time, was responsible for the murders, although she has never known his name until Mia tells it to her. This triggers the narrative flashback which constitutes the core of part 1 of the novel.

As a flashback, the material in part 1 is unconventional in that it does not stick to a single point of view. Ekman's narrator roams freely, touching on the lives of Annie and Mia arriving in Blackwater, a small town in the far northern region of Sweden, Johan Brandberg, trying to escape his bullying brothers, and a variety of other characters, most notably Birger Torbjornsson, the district doctor, whose narrative role in the plot takes a while to become clear.

It takes sixty-three pages before the discovery of the central murder of an unknown man and woman who were camping in a tent. Even before that, however, the writer does a good job of creating an air of mystery and menace. Annie Raft has arrived in Blackwater to join her boyfriend, Dan Ulander in living at the Starhill commune, a back-to-earth group (this portion of the book is set in 1974), but Dan never appears. Following a map, she drags her daughter through the thick forest, trying to make her way up to the commune she has never been to; it is in the woods that she encounters the mysterious (to her) young man, Johan Brandberg, who seems to be fleeing.

The reader, meanwhile, has also been following Johan's story, as he was roughed up by his older half brothers, who believe that he ratted on his father for hitting an obnoxious neighbor. His brothers lower Johan into an empty well with a rope and leave him there. In one of the more interesting symbolic moves in the novel, the author describes an eel who has also been living in the little bit of water in this well, probably having been placed there when the well was active to keep it clear of insects. Johan wraps the thick, old eel in his shirt and takes it with him as he determinedly climbs up out of the well. Figuratively, the eel seems to represent Johan's own manhood, which he now believes he is taking control of, having determined to leave his overprotective mother and his bullying brothers behind. It is this bloodied, determined, and near desperate young man that Mia later believes to have committed a murder. Part of the success of the narrative is that, although readers of the novel know Johan well and cannot understand how he could have committed these murders, Ekman creates a confused character pushed to a far enough extreme that readers cannot completely discount the possibility.

As the investigation into the murder turns up nothing—no identity for the male victim, no suspects, no solid clues—Johan's and Mia's fates seem to distantly echo each other, in that both fall in with people who are not quite what they seem. Yet it is also unclear if the true nature of their secrets is in any way connected to the unsolved murder. Johan gets picked up by a mysterious woman who calls herself Ylja, though she also hints that that is not her real name. She offers to give him shelter for a few days in a shed, where she brings him food and meets him for sex. When he demands an explanation of what she wants from him, she claims that she is a part of a secret cabal of women; he is to be their new "traveller," the designated man in this group of women. Half believing this (as perhaps only a teenager discovering sex would), half convinced she is manipulating him, he searches her room when she is gone and has to jump from a window to avoid detection when she comes back in. Afterward, she barely notices his broken foot, but when she sees a newspaper story about the unsolved murder in Blackwater, she hastily tells him it is time for him to leave. She also shakes free the eel he has been keeping in a cage into the lake; so much for his illusion of manhood.

Meanwhile, Annie Raft finds that everyone in the Starhill commune, especially her boyfriend Dan, seems to be keeping secrets—and every time she thinks she has discovered the truth, she stumbles into more secrets. It may or may not have been an accident that no one came to meet her at the bus when she arrived in town; the members of the commune may or may not have discovered the dead bodies before she stumbled across them; they may or may not know some secrets about who the dead people were and how they died. Finally, Annie, who is pregnant again, gets sick of the deceit and sets out on skis to escape from this commune. For Annie as for Johan, the attempt to escape into another world, an alternate reality, fails miserably; both characters have to go back home.

If the first part of the novel is the story of how an unexpected shock of a seemingly senseless accident tears apart the lives of many different people, the second part is the story of the shocks of revelation when the seemingly senseless and disparate acts of years ago begin to make sense and show connections. The biggest shock of the novel is when the reader discovers in part 2 of the novel, eighteen years later, that the second murder of the novel is the murder of Annie Raft herself. Again, this murder seems to be completely senseless; but its occurrence so soon after she had seen Johan again argues for a connection between the two murders. Johan and the doctor Birger Torbjornsson (who it turns out has been a romantic partner of Annie for some time) slowly begin to investigate. Birger discovers that Mia has known for many years the name of the male murder victim; she learned it from the other children of the Starhill commune. Meanwhile, Johan, who has discovered from a library book that the myth of the "traveller" is a real myth determines to track Ylja down to learn her part in this affair. Together, the two of them set about piecing together the secrets of eighteen years before.

That the narrative succeeds in pulling together seemingly unrelated elements, and linking them all to the murdered man, if not to the actual murder, is a stunning narrative achievement in itself. Along the way, however, readers also get to know enough about the life that Annie Raft has been living for the last eighteen years to want to know her better. This is certainly intended by the author as a strategy to make us feel the loss of life that her death represents; Ekman is so effective in this that one might almost wish she had dispensed with the murder mystery plot completely and instead written a novel about Annie Raft, single mother and creative teacher.

The mature professional that Annie becomes after her experiences with Dan Ulander and the Starhill commune is such a compelling figure that it seems a shame to let the reader barely glimpse her life before killing her off to satisfy the demands of the genre; yet making the reader feel her loss in that way is precisely the success of this artistically rendered novel.

Kerstin Ekman knows her region and her people well. She knows the subtle tensions between Swedes and Norwegians and Finns, and the psychological cost of the ethnic tensions in border regions, such as in the town of Blackwater. Despite the clarity of her main characters, however, the sheer size of her cast and her untethered narrative perspective, which unexpectedly plunks readers down into the life and the mind of a character they did not expect to be asked to follow so closely, makes this a book that can be confusing to read, especially during the first half of part 1. Nevertheless, a guide to the principal characters included after the title page goes a long way toward dispelling this confusion.

Ekman is not the pompous kind of writer who will demand that her characters engage in sophomoric conversations about the essential goodness of humankind or the nature of evil. She does, however, have an understanding of the causes of what we call evil, and those looking for ideas in her writing will find them. Her ideas, however, are to be found in the way her characters live more than in what they say: in the secrets they hide that they should not, in the secrets they try to keep hidden but cannot, and in the sometimes tragic and sometimes merely frustrating confusion that results when too many people are trying too hard to protect these secrets.

Although *Blackwater* is Ekman's first novel to appear in English, it is her seventeenth novel overall, and the dust jacket lists a number of prestigious awards she has won for writing them. Judging her work on the basis of this engaging sample, it is easy to see why she has been so successful. She is a careful, artistic novelist in full command of her craft who has taken the outrage of murder as her subject matter, but who gives away almost nothing to the expectations of the murder mystery genre.

Thomas Cassidy

Sources for Further Study

Booklist. XCII, December 15, 1995, p. 667.
Bookwatch. XVII, March, 1996, p. 5.
New Statesman and Society. VIII, April 21, 1995, p. 37.
The New York Times Book Review. CI, March 17, 1996, p. 24.
The New Yorker. LXXII, June 17, 1996, p. 100.
The Observer. April 23, 1995, p. 20.
Publishers Weekly. CCXLII, December 4, 1995, p. 51.
Twin Cities Reader. XXII, January 31, 1996, p. 20.
The Washington Post Book World. XXVI, March 3, 1996, p. 9.
The Women's Review of Books. XIII, July, 1996, p. 38.

BLAKE

Author: Peter Ackroyd (1949-   )
First published: 1995, in Great Britain
Publisher: Alfred A. Knopf (New York). Illustrated. 399 pp. $35.00
Type of work: Literary biography
Time: 1757-1827
Locale: London

A penetrating biography of the Romantic poet and artist William Blake that shows the depth of Blake's frustration at the neglect he suffered during his lifetime, as well as the powerful nature of his visionary genius, which triumphed only posthumously

> *Principal personages:*
> WILLIAM BLAKE, the British poet, artist, and engraver
> CATHERINE BLAKE, his wife
> ROBERT BLAKE, his younger brother
> THOMAS BUTTS, Blake's patron
> GEORGE CUMBERLAND, Blake's friend
> JOHN FLAXMAN, a sculptor and friend of Blake
> HENRY FUSELI, an artist and friend of Blake
> WILLIAM HAYLEY, Blake's patron
> JOHN LINNELL, an artist and friend of Blake in his old age
> SAMUEL PALMER, an artist and friend of Blake in his old age
> THOMAS STOLHARD, an artist and friend of Blake

Dismissed in his own day as nothing more than a journeyman engraver with eccentric ideas and wild visions, and as the writer of some unintelligible poetry, William Blake is a titanic figure in modern times, hailed by many as the greatest of the Romantic poets and with a popular appeal that stretches far beyond the confines of art history or literary criticism. Yet he has had to wait until the 1990's for a biographer who can truly do him justice. Until well into the twentieth century, the general view of Blake's life was based on Alexander Gilchrist's *Life of William Blake*, which was published in 1863. Gilchrist had the advantage of talking directly to people who had known Blake, but his picture of the otherworldly artist pursuing his prophetic visions in lonely splendor was a gross distortion of the truth. It was not until David Erdman's *Prophet Against Empire* was published in 1954 that the full extent of Blake's engagement with the political and social issues of his time was realized. Erdman's book was a critical rather than biographical work, and a major biography that presents the many-sidedness of William Blake, taking into account all his complexity and contradictions, has been long overdue.

What Peter Ackroyd conveys most memorably is not only the gigantic nature of Blake's artistic and poetic achievement but also the pathos of the man: his insecurity, his neurotic fears, his troubles with authority figures, his mild-mannered passivity, which was counterbalanced by explosions of anger whenever he thought he had been slighted (which was often); his tendency to feel victimized, his resentment at being accused of being mad; and his continually thwarted hopes for worldly success. His friends and acquaintances referred to him as "poor Blake," so ill-suited did he seem for success in his worldly enterprises. Yet through it all he kept up his heroic, lifelong effort to maintain his belief in his own genius and his destiny, even when the world stubbornly refused to confirm them. Sometimes this led him into grandiloquent claims for his own work; at other times, the only way he could think of to preserve his sense of his own worth was to bluntly demand more money for some piece of hack work. Sometimes, in spite of all his efforts, he sank into despair. It is impossible not to be moved by Peter Ackroyd's compelling narration of Blake's story.

William Blake was born, the son of a hosier, in London in 1757. He remained a Londoner all his life, leaving the city only once, for a three-year stay at a cottage on the South Coast. Ackroyd, who is the biographer of another famous Londoner, Charles Dickens, brilliantly re-creates the sounds and sights and smells of England's capital city and the changes it underwent during Blake's lifetime. According to Ackroyd, Blake's art springs from the variety and energy of the city; Blake once referred to himself as "English Blake" but he might equally well be known as "London Blake." It was a London not seen by his contemporaries, in the sense that Blake, a natural visionary, always saw through the surface realities, the teeming, everyday world of a great city, to the spiritual dimension, what he called "the spiritual fourfold London," which was its true, essential reality.

Blake always had his eye on eternity, even as a young boy—at the age of four he had a vision of God and not many years later he saw a tree full of angels in the fields at Peckham Rye. He began writing poetry when he was twelve, and his drawing ability was so early manifest that his father decided to apprentice him for seven years to a well-known engraver. Engraving was how he made his living for the remainder of his life, although for the most part Blake viewed this kind of work as daily drudgery; his real interests lay elsewhere, in art and poetry.

One of the few blessings Blake had in life was his marriage, to Catherine Boucher. Catherine was the illiterate daughter of a market gardener, but she proved a loyal and devoted wife to Blake, helping him color his designs and imbibing from him his gift for seeing visions. It is refreshing to find that Ackroyd takes the contemporary evidence of the harmony of the Blakes' marriage at face value. Unlike some literary critics, he does not try to read tensions into it based on the fact that Blake's mythology expresses considerable conflict between male and female principles, and a particular horror of what Blake calls the "female will," which should be understood in a metaphysical rather than literal sense.

Ackroyd is most illuminating when he discusses Blake's work as an artist rather than as a poet. One salient point he emphasizes several times is how Blake's art so often seems to radiate a kind of spiritual light. This is first discernible in two pen sketches, "The Complaint of Job" and "The Death of Ezekiel's Wife," which were completed in the mid-1780's. Ackroyd notes their "extraordinary luminescence" and comments that "The light within Blake's paintings and watercolors is often the most immediately noticeable characteristic; it represents the light of understanding, the light of eternity suffused through material reality." This recalls the comment of another

Blake scholar, Kathleen Raine, that the subtle yellows that make up many of the backgrounds in the designs to Blake's *Songs of Innocence and of Experience* (1794) seem almost to reflect the light of heaven itself. These effects cannot usually be seen in reproductions.

This sense of light as a kind of spiritual revelation was something Blake discovered as an artist before he incorporated it into his poetic myth. Ackroyd notes its occurrence once more in the engravings Blake made to illustrate "The Grave," by Robert Blair. These relief etchings were executed entirely in white line (that is, white against a black background), which tends to create the effect that "there is a light to be found in all things," an effect that was not understood or appreciated by Robert Cromek, who had commissioned the etchings, but who removed Blake from the project when he saw the results. It was not the first time that Blake's work was not in keeping with contemporary tastes.

According to Ackroyd, a similar impression of light is made by two series of Blake's later works: the woodcuts illustrating Virgil, and the engravings Blake made in illustration of the Book of Job. In the former, Ackroyd notes that fields and streams seem to be illuminated by the sun, and yet the scene depicted is lit by moonlight only. As a result, "there must be some other source of brightness here, since Blake well understood the spiritual dimension of light." In the latter, one of Blake's last works, there is a "radiant brightness . . . an extraordinary silver light that comes from a very fine distribution of highlights and burnishing as well as the delicacy of the engraved lines."

This information is enlightening (if that word may be used in this context), but Ackroyd does not always give the same detailed attention to Blake's poetry that he does to Blake's art. When he does so his comments are rewarding, in spite of the fact that he offers mostly conventional interpretations. Yet those readers who admire Blake's epic poetry, or prophecies, may find Ackroyd's discussions of them lacking in completeness. This applies in particular to the masterwork *Milton: A Poem* (1804-1808), in which Blake seeks to correct what he sees as the mistakes made by John Milton, the great epic poet in whose footsteps Blake sought to follow. It contains some of Blake's finest poetry, and Ackroyd might profitably have devoted more space to elucidating it. The poem also has biographical interest: The long episode known as the Bard's Song, for example, might have been used to throw light on the troubled relationship between Blake and his patron, William Hayley.

Ackroyd gives a slightly more detailed account of Blake's last major epic poem, *Jerusalem: The Emancipation of the Great Albion* (1804-1820), although his comment that it is the most accessible of Blake's prophecies may surprise the reader who has attempted to read that tough book. (Milton is usually thought to be easily the more accessible of the two.)

In the context of the whole biography, however, these are small criticisms indeed. As are the errors that have crept in, of which there seem to be three. First, regarding the Gordon Riots of 1780, in which mobs rampaged through London for several days protesting the easing of restrictions on Catholics, Ackroyd states that the rioters passed within a few yards of Blake's own home on Broad Street. This is not so. There were two Broad Streets in London, one in the city, leading to Holborn and St. Paul's Cathedral, the other a good half mile away in Westminster. The rioters surged down the former; Blake lived in the latter.

Second, Ackroyd states that one of Blake's engravings was included in *The Conjurer's Magazine* in 1792. Yet G. R. Bentley, Jr., Blake's bibliographer, has pointed out that there is no plate signed by Blake in any issues of this magazine, or its successor, *The Astrologer's Magazine*. The error weakens only very slightly the case Ackroyd makes for Blake being aware of contemporary ideas about the efficacy of magic. The real question is what credence Blake gave to a magical view of the universe. The majority of Blake scholars, at least in the United States, usually argue that Blake's worldview does not make room for magic. Ackroyd begs to differ, and the examples he produces offer a challenge to the conventional view.

Third, in Ackroyd's discussion of the influence of the German seer Jacob Boehme on Blake—which is important and accurately described—he states that Boehme was an influential figure during all the religious disputes among the radical sects in England in the mid-sixteenth century, but these disputes date from the mid-seventeenth century.

Blake: A Biography may well become the standard biography of Blake for many years to come. Nevertheless, there is another work on the way. Aileen Ward, the biographer of John Keats, has been working on a biography of Blake for more than ten years, and the results of her research are eagerly awaited. She has already published an article in which she makes a persuasive case for the date of birth of Blake's favorite brother Robert to have been 1761, not 1767. The latter date has been accepted by scholars for nearly thirty years, and Ackroyd follows this convention. Ward's findings may have been published too late for Ackroyd to make use of, but it is intriguing to think that there may still be more "Minute Particulars" about the life of that self-described "Mental Prince," William Blake, for the future biographer to tease out.

Bryan Aubrey

Sources for Further Study

The Economist. CCCXXXVII, November 11, 1995, p. 4.
London Review of Books. XVIII, February 22, 1996, p. 16.
Los Angeles Times Book Review. May 19, 1996, p. 4.
New Statesman and Society. VIII, September 8, 1995, p. 36.
The New York Times Book Review. CI, April 14, 1996, p. 5.
The Observer. September 3, 1995, p. 14.
Publishers Weekly. CCXLIII, February 26, 1996, p. 90.
The Times Literary Supplement. October 20, 1995, p. 3.
The Wall Street Journal. April 9, 1996, p. A16.
The Washington Post Book World. XXVI, May 12, 1996, p. 1.

THE BLUE DEVILS OF NADA
A Contemporary American Approach to Aesthetic Statement

Author: Albert Murray (1916-   )
Publisher: Pantheon Books (New York). 238 pp. $23.00
Type of work: Essays

Observations on the nature of the creative process, especially in music, art, and literature, define and develop the blues aesthetic as the possible basis for an affirmative, even heroic, response to the harsh actualities of experience

For someone who has established himself as one of the most formidable presences in contemporary African American letters, Albert Murray came late to a literary career. His first book, *The Omni-Americans*, an eloquent affirmation of African American culture in itself and in its importance for American culture at large, was published in 1970, when Murray, who had retired from the Air Force as a major in 1962, was fifty-four years old. This was followed in 1971 by *South to a Very Old Place*, a book that grew out of a series of articles commissioned for the "Going Home" series inaugurated by Willie Morris, then editor of *Harper's*. This probably remains the work for which Murray is best known, but he has done impressive work as a literary critic in *The Hero and the Blues* (1972), and as a music critic in *Stomping the Blues* (1976), for which he received the 1977 ASCAP-Deems Taylor Award for music commentary from the American Society of Composers, Authors, and Publishers (ASCAP). In 1985, *Good Morning Blues: The Autobiography of Count Basie as Told to Albert Murray* was published to widespread acclaim. Murray's first novel, *Train Whistle Guitar* appeared in 1974. It was the first of a series of novels focusing on the experiences of Scooter, Murray's intermittently autobiographical protagonist. The second novel of the series, *The Spyglass Tree*, was published in 1991. A third novel, *The Seven League Boots*, was published simultaneously in 1996 with *The Blue Devils of Nada*. Although at least one reviewer has referred to *The Seven League Boots* as the last novel of a trilogy, published comments by the eighty-year-old author give readers reason to hope that they have not heard the last of Scooter.

All this constitutes an impressive body of work, notable not only for its quantity and consistently high level of merit, but also for the wide range of interests and competence it reflects. Murray is certainly no one-note writer. Yet his work, both fiction and nonfiction, is informed by certain recurrent themes which are present as well in *The Blue Devils of Nada*.

There is, first of all, the blues. Murray uses this term rather more broadly than is customary. The blues idiom, for Murray, is incarnated in all forms of jazz that remain linked to dance and good times. The function of this music is not, as a common misunderstanding would have it, lamentation; a blues composition is not a torch song. The function of the music called the blues, or of the blues idiom, is to keep the emotional state called the blues at bay, while honestly accepting the inevitability of its return. Even as the lyrics may wail a tale of woe, the music remains at some level life-affirming, heroic. Borrowing a term from the American literary and cultural critic Kenneth Burke, a major influence on his thought, Murray finds that the blues idiom provides humans repeatedly with equipment for living.

The blues idiom is in origin black, and Murray is an African American. In praising the music, he is then affirming his own cultural heritage. He is also clearing up a few things about that heritage. From *The Omni-Americans* on, Murray has made it part of his mission to challenge the view that the history of the African American may be adequately viewed as a history of victimization. As a man of letters, he has scornfully dismissed most protest fiction or, to use one of his preferred terms, social science fiction. While acknowledging that African Americans have sufficient and legitimate historical grounds for anger, he will not be moved by writers who are merely angry, without being innovative or insightful. By Murray's standards, even such respected African American writers as James Baldwin and Richard Wright are ultimately unsatisfactory. What he calls for, and what he tries to practice in his own work, is not a denial of the harsh realities of experience, but an affirmative disposition toward those realities. In the obstacles individuals must overcome, both those that belong to the universal human condition and those that belong to the black experience in particular, Murray perceives what he calls a cooperative antagonism: We are forced to extend and to realize ourselves in the very struggles we cannot escape. "[An] affirmative disposition toward the harsh actualities of human existence . . . is characteristic of the fully orchestrated blues statement."

A further point Murray wants to clear up is suggested by his willingness to discuss a black musical tradition in terms borrowed from a white critic such as Kenneth Burke. Murray insists that African American culture simply cannot be understood or appreciated or affirmed in isolation from American culture at large. There is, Murray observes, no "White" American culture. As he pointed out initially in *The Omni-Americans*, mainstream American culture is mulatto, the product at all points of racial interaction. (Multiculturalists of America, take note.) Hence Murray's rejection of all forms of separatism; black people who separate themselves from mainstream American culture are, in Murray's view, separating themselves from what is rightfully their own. There is, furthermore, no "Black" culture, if by that is meant a culture of African Americans that does not reflect their interaction with Americans of all ethnic heritages. The blues idiom is itself not "African," but arises out of the confrontation of African and European musical elements in the transforming context of America.

These, then, are the major organizing themes of Murray's work, and all of them find expression in *The Blue Devils of Nada*. Of the eight essays (plus "Prologue" and "Epilogue,") that make up the book, five focus on three masters of the blues idiom, Louis Armstrong, Count Basie, and Duke Ellington. Although all these essays are informed by Murray's knowledgeability about the music, none are especially analytical in their approach; there is not a single musical quotation in the book. There are, to be sure, some eloquent impressions of what it is to experience this music, but music criticism of the technical sort is not what Murray is up to here. It is rather the significance of the music, the meaning of the blues idiom in American, including

African American, culture that he is trying to articulate. This in turn establishes the context for his celebration of the three artists who concern him.

Each of these artists clearly has his own statement to make, but each becomes as well an instance of Murray's interests. Ellington, for example, grew up in Washington, D.C., during the administration of Woodrow Wilson, a bleak time for black people. In his autobiography, *Music Is My Mistress*, however, Ellington does not define himself as a victim or his art as a form of protest. Rather, he treats whatever obstacles he had to overcome as challenges to creativity. The music itself exemplifies that affirmative disposition toward harsh realities that Murray has identified as characteristic of the blues idiom. Ellington makes the whole orchestra a personal instrument without thereby frustrating the expressiveness of the individual musicians in the group. Along with that of Armstrong, his work in the blues idiom amounts to a musical equivalent of what Murray calls the representative anecdote (another term derived from Kenneth Burke), which reflects, suggests, embodies, or summarizes a basic attitude toward experience or outlook on life. Ultimately, according to Murray, Ellington must be acknowledged as the quintessential American composer, and it is not an accident that Murray says "American," rather than "African American."

Among bandleaders only Count Basie has charisma comparable to that of Duke Ellington, and one of Murray's major projects was his collaboration with Basie as the "as told to" partner of *Good Morning, Blues*, Basie's autobiography. The essay "Comping for Basie" is illuminating on just what is involved in such a collaboration, at least in this very successful instance, and provocative on the notion of autobiography as fiction. It also offers an engaging informal portrait of Basie himself. Again, Murray stresses the importance (on his account, to Basie as well as to himself) of not reducing the autobiography of a complex and creative individual to a polemic about racism. His comparison of the art of Basie to the fiction of Ernest Hemingway and to the late cutout compositions of the French modernist painter Henri Matisse reasserts Murray's refusal to ghettoize the accomplishments of African American artists.

In exploring the manifestations of the blues aesthetic in the music of these three giants, Murray is dealing, however insightfully, with a fairly obvious subject. In the last two essays of the book he moves into less clearly charted territory.

The first of these essays examines the art of Romare Bearden, perhaps the finest African American painter of the century. While Murray reveals a sophisticated familiarity with some of the more influential art historical concepts associated with modernism, emphasizing, for example, the importance of flat surface painting in Bearden's work, it is the embodiment in that work of the blues aesthetic that is Murray's true subject. He persuasively traces the African American roots of Bearden's art and underlines Bearden's conscious awareness of the relationships between his creative process and jazz musicianship. It is the sort of irony that Murray is especially ready to appreciate that it was a white painter, the American abstractionist Stuart Davis, who first pointed out to Bearden the possibilities for visual statement implicit in the jazz aesthetic. Murray also traces the many lines of influence and of mutual illumination between Bearden's art and that of many European masters. He even suggests that some of the specifically African elements in Bearden's work may be derived from sources such as Picasso's *Demoiselles d'Avignon*, rather than directly from African art. This crossing of cultural lines, Murray has suggested, is entirely typical of the blues idiom. For all the interweaving of influence, however, Murray concludes that Bearden could only be idiomatically American, by which (again) Murray does not mean merely African American.

Murray's examination of the blues idiom in music and as extended into the paintings of Romare Bearden suggests both the complexity of the idiom and its pervasiveness in the art of African Americans, at least, Murray might add, in the best art of African Americans. The longest and most ambitious essay in the book, however, is devoted to the fiction of Ernest Hemingway in the light of the blues aesthetic. Murray argues that the fundamental sense of life consistently expressed in the fiction of Hemingway is identical with that which underlies the spirit of the blues. It is not Murray's claim that Hemingway wrote in terms of the blues, but that what he wrote can be regarded as the literary equivalent of blues music. Facing the harsh actuality that all stories, if carried far enough, end in death, Hemingway affirms in the light of that hard knowledge the value of each moment and experience. He celebrates the joys of the sensual without making the mistake of thinking that the sensual is all there is to reality. Murray's close friend Ralph Ellison (who also admired Hemingway) once said that the blues "express both the agony of life and the possibility of conquering it through sheer toughness of spirit." This is very like the vision that, in Murray's reading, informs the work of Hemingway. Yet the blues can be felt in Hemingway's style as well, for example, in his rhythmic repetitions and riffing on words. Murray notes that Hemingway worked as a journalist in Kansas City; thus his prose style and the musical style of Count Basie were formed in the same city. It may be suggestive that both styles, as Murray sees it, are characterized by comparable qualities of brevity, vigor, and positive accentuation. Murray also compares these artists, it will be remembered, in his essay on Basie.

What Murray helps readers to recognize, finally, is that the blues aesthetic, derived from the art of African Americans, can help to illuminate much that is most vital in that American culture he has described, has praised, as mulatto. It can therefore provide interpreters of that culture with a valuable instrument. Perhaps more important, it can shape the work of young artists, black, white, or other, as they strive to realize what is for Albert Murray one of the most important functions of art: keeping the blues at bay.

W. P. Kenney

Sources for Further Study

American Heritage. XLVII, September, 1996, p. 68.
Booklist. XCII, February 15, 1996, p. 980.
Boston Globe. February 18, 1996, p. B36.

Chicago Tribune. March 17, 1996, XIV, p. 5.
Library Journal. CXX, December, 1995, p. 111.
The Nation. CCLXII, March 25, 1996, p. 25.
The New York Times Book Review. CI, March 10, 1996, p. 4.
The New Yorker. LXXII, April 8, 1996, p. 70.
Newsweek. CXXVII, February 5, 1996, p. 60.
Publishers Weekly. CCXLII, December 18, 1995, p. 35.
The Village Voice Literary Supplement. February, 1996, p. 17.
The Washington Post Book World. XXVI, February 4, 1996, p. 7.

BREAKING THE NEWS
How the Media Undermine American Democracy

Author: James Fallows (1949-   )
Publisher: Pantheon Books (New York). 296 pp. $23.00
Type of work: Current affairs

A respected journalist takes his mass media colleagues to task for "undermining" American democracy and offers proposals for improving performance in the future

In *Breaking the News: How the Media Undermine American Democracy,* James Fallows accuses most of his colleagues in the mass media of failing to hold up their end in the quest to fulfill the dream of American democracy. As Washington editor for *The Atlantic Monthly,* a regular commentator on National Public Radio's *Morning Edition,* and author of an award-winning book on national defense, Fallows is in a position to criticize the media as a respected insider. As a result, this book has drawn considerable media attention. Whether it will make a lasting impression remains to be seen.

Although a particularly shortsighted commercialism appears to be the main fountainhead of the media's failure to perform, Fallows' critique is multifaceted. For an opener, Fallows condemns the media's pervasive emphasis on the "horse race" aspects of politics at the expense of serious analysis of public policy issues. As examples, Fallows cites not only election coverage, which focuses on who is leading by how much and the strategies employed to capture public support, but also on policy debates such as that over President Clinton's health care reform bill in 1993-1994. According to Fallows, media coverage of this debate never really came to terms with the technical merit of Clinton's proposal or any of the numerous counterproposals which were offered in Congress. Instead, the media focused on tactics employed to promote and defeat various health care proposals, while the American public remained largely ignorant as to the potential consequences both of health care reform and the failure to enact reform.

Connected to this is the media's unrelenting cynicism toward public figures and even government institutions as a whole. Since the focus is on tactical wheeling and dealing rather than on the substantive differences between candidates and bills, politics is seen primarily as an enterprise in public relations, with manipulation and subterfuge being the name of the game. Members of the media compound this serious distortion of what politics is really about by exhibiting deep—indeed, one might even say, dogmatic—skepticism. Conveying belief in a program, party, or individual is considered far too risky or subjective. Instead, reporters and commentators take on what they see as a more sophisticated attitude—one of wary suspicion. While Fallows does not urge media operatives to become true believers or political cheerleaders, he does argue that a more balanced view of political motives and performance would be far better for public morale and also more accurate.

Corollary to the fashionable skepticism of media coverage is the inability or unwillingness of contemporary reporters to get beyond the surface of stories in order to understand their true meaning. Reporters not only lack the depth of knowledge to carefully gauge the sincerity of politicians and government officials, they also lack apparent incentives—commercial or otherwise—to acquire such knowledge. As a result, an air of cynicism becomes a handy and economical substitute for the difficult work of boning up on the fine points of public policy.

This convenient superficiality leads in turn to news coverage which emphasizes novelty, entertainment, and controversy for its own sake. On the other hand, in-depth analysis is in severely short supply. The public instead gets a confusing abundance of images and facts, along with incessant scandal and squawking. News coverage is bereft of much needed historical context or other forms of explanation. Also lacking is any substantial follow-up to current headlines. Stories come and go, remaining in the public eye only until the novelty has worn off. Although Fallows credits the media for making some progress in the quest for meaningful background, he believes that the political world conveyed by the media still usually lacks coherence and perspective.

Personal greed and ambition are also factors in the failure of mass media, according to Fallows. More specifically, Fallows faults selected media "stars" for putting monetary gain and fame ahead of professional ethics and personal integrity. He has in mind particularly those celebrities who do the Sunday morning scene on shows such as *Firing Line* and *The McLaughlin Group*. These journalists maintain their popularity (and disparately high incomes) on the tube by emphasizing controversy for its own sake and preparing quick quips on every issue that is likely to come up, whether they are knowledgeable on the topic or not. Fallows also doubts the objectivity of journalists who take large speaking fees from corporations and interest groups upon whom they might someday have to report.

The result of all this collective and individual dereliction of duty is to seriously undermine the foundation of American democratic institutions. Nor do the mass media themselves prosper. For the irony is that, while news coverage erodes public faith in government, public opinion polls show increasing dissatisfaction with news sources themselves; dissatisfaction with all the negativity, sensationalism, and exploitiveness alluded to above. Thus, mass media are also undermining their own long term credibility in the quest for short term commercial success.

There is hope, according to Fallows, in an emerging commitment to what he calls "public journalism." By public journalism, Fallows means news coverage and analysis which gauges and addresses the deeper concerns of communities and citizens rather than pandering to the public's all too apparent appetite for scandal and controversy for their own sake. As in many books such as this one, however, the section on solutions is highly speculative and fragmentary.

The book has other weaknesses as well. While most readers will readily recognize the sorts of media behavior singled out for criticism by Fallows, there is a lack of systematic evidence needed to support the broad conclusions he draws about the overall image of American politics cast by the media. True, one can find plenty of horse race type coverage, news stories lacking sufficient background, and television commentators who cast more heat than light. Yet one also can find wonderfully informative articles in the better newspapers and magazines. In-depth coverage of politics on C-Span I and II is also available to members of the public who are interested enough to commit themselves to the search for thorough information.

The fact that not that many citizens are so committed brings up the most fundamental oversight of Fallows' book, which is his failure to deal thoroughly with the complex triangular relationship between the media, political institutions, and the American people. For, even if the media fall short on a daily basis in all the ways noted by Fallows, it is also true that, on an equally daily basis, politicians provide an abundance of "probable cause" for skepticism regarding their words, deeds, and motives; and also that the American public, as a whole, exhibits little interest in taking the time necessary to make themselves well informed about politics and public affairs.

Likewise, Fallows fails to seriously examine the irony that current media practices simultaneously increase circulation while reducing public approval of the media. Here, the effect is much like that of negative advertising in political campaigns. The public proclaims disgust at negative advertisements, yet candidates and consultants continue to use them because they appear to be effective; that is, the public responds to them. In the case of media sensationalism, negativity, and superficiality, the public expresses disdain, but they stay away in droves from serious programming and, as consumers, vote for the very sort of unsatisfactory news coverage they claim to dislike.

Coming at it from another angle, Fallows blames the media for the public's disaffection from and disinterest in American politics. Yet one might consider whether the relationship is not actually reversed. Perhaps it is the lack of an aggressive, committed citizenry which has produced the media the United States has today, and which threatens American democracy. This question is skirted by Fallows, perhaps because it provides a far more troubling scenario for those, like himself, who believe, or at least wish to believe, that democratic institutions can not only survive but also proceed toward ever greater perfection.

Connected to this is Fallows' failure to look systematically at the relation between inadequate journalism and the profit motive, this despite the fact that he links much of his critique to the media's self-defeating commercialism. If mass media officials are in a position where they must choose between thorough, penetrating journalism or satisfying a mass audience demanding crass entertainment, then "public journalism" of the sort advocated by Fallows probably will not become the norm. The truth is that much of Fallows discussion appears to assume just such a situation. In short, with regard to the political and economic context within which the mass media must perform, Fallows' own analysis suffers from a lack of depth.

Despite these criticisms, Fallows' book makes a substantial contribution to public debate about the condition and contributions of mass media in the United States. If nothing else, it offers a compelling alternative to the images of the media which dominate public discourse: that is, on the one hand, the media's smug self-image as the nation's conscience, and, on the other, the common right-wing image of the media (or national media, anyway) as an insidious liberal, or left-wing, conspiracy. To those who hold the first view, Fallows offers a chilling wake-up call. You are not doing the job, Fallows tells them, and, as a result, you are hurting American democracy, perhaps irreparably. To those who hold the second view (and who are probably far less likely to read this book), Fallows offers a similarly pungent reality check. Painting the media as essentially "liberal," he suggests, is misleading and, in some ways, even too kind, since media performance currently makes the job of all politicians—no matter what their ideology—tougher than it should be.

Finally, Fallows' book is valuable because it raises important questions about the real performance of American democracy, helping citizens to get beyond the uncritical self-praise that has marked their post-Cold War euphoria. True, Americans have outlasted the Soviet Union and won the Cold War. In that sense, the American way of life has triumphed. What Americans have not done so far, however, is to deal with the remaining distance between their democratic ideals and the reality of their far from flawless democratic institutions, including the mass media. Doing so will require much serious introspection of the sort contained in *Breaking the News*.

Ira Smolensky

Sources for Further Study

AJR: American Journalism Review. XVIII, March, 1996, p. 46.
The American Scholar. LXV, Summer, 1996, p. 472.
Booklist. XCII, January 1, 1996, p. 748.
Business Week. February 19, 1996, p. 14.
Columbia Journalism Review. XXXIV, March, 1996, p. 49.
Esquire. CXXV, January, 1996, p. 28.
Folio. XXV, May 15, 1996, p. 18.
Los Angeles Times Book Review. February 4, 1996, p. 3.
The Nation. CCLXII, February 5, 1996, p. 25.
The New York Times Book Review. CI, January 28, 1996, p. 8.
Publishers Weekly. CCXLIII, January 1, 1996, p. 67.
Time. CXLVII, January 22, 1996, p. 68.
Washington Monthly. XXVIII, January, 1996, p. 43.
The Washington Post Book World. XXVI, February 4, 1996, p. 4.

THE CASE AGAINST IMMIGRATION

Author: Roy Beck (1948-   )
Publisher: W. W. Norton (New York). 287 pp. $24.00
Type of work: Current affairs

A journalist attempts to argue the case for immigration restriction from a liberal, rather than a racist, position

Many Americans had, by the 1990's, come to look back nostalgically on the American economy of the period from 1945 to 1965, comparing it favorably with the economically stressful era that began in the early and middle 1970's. In the golden era of the two post-World War II decades, it was asserted, one breadwinner had been able to support a wife and children on a single income; in the last decade of the twentieth century, by contrast, the average American family needed at least two, and sometimes three or more, earners to make ends meet, as average real wages remained practically stagnant. By the 1990's, it was asserted, unemployment was more common than in the 1950's, and the condition of black urban ghettos was far worse than in the 1950's.

Journalist Roy Beck points out what he sees as one major cause of the harsher economic climate of the 1990's, compared with that of the 1950's: the renewal of mass immigration to the United States as a result of the enactment of a more liberal immigration law in October, 1965. The constant supply of fresh immigrant labor, he argues, allowed American employers to break the power of labor unions, depress wages, cut benefits, and deny workers decent working conditions. The high levels of immigration during the 1980's and 1990's, Beck concludes, benefited an affluent minority of Americans at the expense of both the poor and the broad middle class. The emphasis on immigration as a cause of the declining economic fortunes of middle-class Americans distinguishes Beck from another leading advocate of immigration restriction, Peter Brimelow, the author of *Alien Nation: Common Sense About America's Immigration Disaster* (1995; covered in *Magill's Literary Annual, 1996*); it also distinguishes Beck from most of those who have studied the malaise of the post-1973 American economy.

To make his case, Beck is not content to rest on generalities; he offers the reader the results not merely of library research, but also of his own journalistic legwork. Instead of confining his attention to the large cities that are often cited for evidence on the effects of post-1965 immigration, the author has taken the trouble of visiting small towns and rural areas in the Midwest and the South: Storm Lake and Hawarden, Iowa; Worthington, Minnesota; Garden City, Kansas; Cordova, Maryland; and Wausau, Wisconsin. The author interviewed scholarly experts and consulted scholarly books, articles, and newspaper reprints. It is his interviews with ordinary people in the areas affected by the new immigration, however, that provide especially valuable insights into the issue.

To counter the argument that it was foreign competition rather than immigration that undermined American workers' standard of living from the early 1970's onward,

Beck looks at industries that are relatively well-insulated from such foreign competition: The meat-packing industry is his favorite example. In the late 1980's, he tells readers, the meat-packing companies that had already relocated from big cities to small towns in an effort to cut costs and increase profits, began to make heavy use of immigrant labor (largely Southeast Asians and Mexicans, with some immigrants from eastern Africa). Such immigrant laborers, the author argues, made it possible for employers to destroy the once-powerful meatpackers' union, bringing an end to the middle-class prosperity that the union had provided for native-born American meatpackers and their families in such towns as Storm Lake, Iowa, and bringing back to the industry the substandard working conditions once exposed in Upton Sinclair's muckraking novel *The Jungle* (1906). In Cordova, Maryland, Beck alleges, the growing use of Mexican immigrant labor in poultry processing plants in the late 1980's and early 1990's robbed local African Americans of job opportunities that they had once had. In California, Beck argues, some of those most severely hurt by competition with recent Mexican immigrants were native-born Asian Americans and Mexican Americans as well as those Asian and Mexican immigrants who had arrived in the United States earlier.

Beck sees mass immigration as a threat, not only to the unskilled and the blue-collar workers but also to highly educated professionals. Against the notion, propounded by opponents of immigration restriction, that immigration is necessary to fill America's need for scientific and technological talent, Beck offers evidence that the United States had, in the 1990's, a surplus of trained scientists and a considerable unemployment problem among native-born scientists. He argues that American computer industry entrepreneurs, in their greed, have hired foreign technical and scientific talent because foreign professionals, like foreign unskilled laborers, are willing to work for less money. Although Beck does, all too briefly, take note of other factors (such as the end of the Cold War) that have reduced the demand for scientists in the United States, the casual reader may mistakenly infer that immigration is responsible for all the employment problems of native-born scientists in the United States, and that a halt in immigration would end those problems without producing any negative side effects. Yet foreign-born professionals do, after all, sometimes create new jobs (by founding new businesses) for the native-born as well as take existing jobs away from the native-born.

In the early 1990's, opponents of immigration in Canada, France, Great Britain, and Germany were openly racist; in the United States in the same decade, such advocates of immigration as Peter Brimelow were often accused of being racist. Partly in order to ward off such an accusation, Beck argues at length that post-1965 mass immigration has been particularly harmful to African Americans. Vehemently denying the contention of some conservatives that African Americans displaced by post-1965 immigrant competition were simply unwilling to work, Beck contends that native-born blacks, like native-born whites, can and will fill any job, however menial, if they are paid reasonable wages.

Immigrant competition for jobs with African Americans, Beck suggests, is not a completely fair contest. The post-1965 inflow of foreign labor, Beck contends, has given prejudiced employers a way to avoid hiring African Americans for jobs that they would otherwise have access to; the virtual disappearance of African Americans from the ranks of hotel janitors in the Los Angeles area is given as an example. Immigrant-founded businesses, Beck suggests, usually try to hire only fellow immigrants; such businesses are, in practice, unlikely to be affected by government-enforced affirmative action. Finally, the very affirmative action programs that were intended to help African American descendants of slavery have, the author points out, been used by immigrants, such as Cubans and Asian Indians, who never suffered discrimination as intense as that suffered by African Americans and who do not really deserve the special help that African Americans ought to receive. Unfortunately, Beck's distinction between legiti-mate native-born black beneficiaries of affirmative action and illegitimate immigrant beneficiaries of the program makes more sense for Southern California (where native-born blacks face immigrants from Mexico and Central and South America) than for the New York City area (where a good proportion of the immigrant population consists of blacks from the West Indies and Africa).

Beck is concerned with other negative effects of immigration besides the alleged harm done to the average American worker's pay and working conditions. He considers the population increase brought about by post-1965 immigration to be a serious threat to the quality of America's environment. Like other advocates of restriction, he sees mass post-1965 immigration as producing higher crime rates (especially from youth gangs) and greater welfare dependency, even though he sees such pathologies as a result of the process of unchecked immigration itself rather than as evidence of the inherent inferiority of any particular immigrant group. Not content to propound empty generalizations, Beck uses anecdotes from his journalistic travels to bolster such arguments. Thus, he shows readers how Southeast Asian immigration to Wausau, Wisconsin, led to higher taxes to pay for sharply higher welfare costs and the increased cost of public education, greater youth delinquency, and a general loss of community harmony as white Wausau's resentment of the newcomers grew. Beck also tells how Storm Lake, Iowa, found itself faced with an increase in crime as a result of the new immigration fostered by the meat-packing companies, even though the Southeast Asian and Mexican immigrants did have jobs.

To clarify the problems posed by the influx of foreigners into the United States in the 1990's, Beck goes beyond mere reportage, offering readers a sweeping interpre-tation of the history of American immigration from the late nineteenth century to the late twentieth century. Americans, he explains, have never given an unreserved welcome to immigrants. At the height of mass immigration from Europe during the period from 1880 to 1924, many Americans, appalled at the dire poverty of so many of the newcomers, demanded that immigration either be curtailed drastically or stopped completely. Unlike such opponents of immigration restriction as University of Maryland economics professor Julian L. Simon, Beck does not see unrestricted immigration as the key to American prosperity at all times. Instead, Beck views Americans' willingness to curtail immigration in 1924 as the answer to the riddle of why the years from 1945 to 1965 were characterized by such widespread good times for the broad middle class, and by such a strong sense of national unity and purpose.

In 1924, the U.S. Congress passed a law sharply reducing immigration levels; these remained relatively low until the passage of the Immigration Act of 1965. With less immigration from abroad, the American labor force grew more slowly. By the 1950's, Beck argues, the booming demand for workers, combined with the slow pace of labor force growth, made it possible for labor unions to win higher wages and better working conditions even for unskilled workers. Since all employers faced the same labor market conditions, being a benevolent employer was the profitable thing to do as well as the right thing to do. Higher wages gave employers an incentive to innovate technologically, making each worker more productive. The brisk demand for unskilled labor and the low levels of immigration enabled large numbers of unskilled African Americans from the rural South to secure relatively well-paying jobs in the mass-production industries of the North. Before the 1920's, competition from European immigrants had kept African Americans from getting a secure foothold in such industries. Partly because of the spread of middle-class prosperity and partly the result of the paucity of newcomers, the culture of the United States in the 1950's became more homogeneous than ever before or since. Paradoxically, Beck argues, individual immigrants were greeted more warmly by native-born Americans in the 1950's than was the case either before 1924 or after 1965. To prove his point, he cites the example of a Chinese refugee restaurateur, a resident of the United States since the early 1950's, whom Beck interviewed in Wausau, Wisconsin.

Readers could easily conclude that all that stands between the average American and the return of the boom times of the 1950's is the passage of a restrictive immigration law. Unfortunately, the author fails to give sufficient emphasis to other factors besides low immigration levels that made the prosperous America of the 1950's possible: the savings Americans had stored away during World War II; the heavy military spending, fueled by the Soviet-American Cold War that followed so rapidly on the heels of the end of World War II; the temporary absence of competition from the war-devastated industries of Japan and Western Europe; the improvements in productivity in agriculture as well as industry; and the introduction of jet travel and television.

The relative scarcity of labor in the 1950's owed something to the low birthrates of the Depression years (1929-1941) and to the high military casualties of World War II (1941-1945), as well as to the reduced influx of foreigners; likewise, the post-World War II baby boom swelled the supply of labor in the post-1973 economy as much as did post-1965 immigration. To be able to judge critically Beck's argument, readers must consult other books that explore the failure of the post-1973 American economy to deliver the broad-based prosperity of the 1950's and 1960's: Michael Elliott's *The Day Before Yesterday: Reconsidering America's Past, Rediscovering the Present* (1996), Jeffrey Madrick's *The End of Affluence: The Causes and Consequences of America's Economic Dilemma* (1995), Michael J. Mandel's *The High-Risk Society: Peril and Promise in the New Economy* (1996), and Robert J. Samuelson's *The Good*

Life and Its Discontents: The American Dream in the Age of Entitlement, 1945-1995 (1996; see essay in this volume).

The call for a general reduction in immigration levels, besides being of dubious value as an economic panacea, may also be politically impractical. Beck differs from fellow author Peter Brimelow in being more worried about the increase in the total volume of immigration since 1965, rather than in the shift in the ethnic or racial composition of the immigrant flow. Many Americans can be found who agree that immigration levels should be reduced, just as many can be found who agree that the federal deficit should be reduced; disagreement erupts when the question arises of which potential immigrants from which countries should be excluded. Two leading advocates of immigration restriction, journalist Peter Brimelow and economist George Borjas, were actually born abroad (Brimelow in England, Borjas in Cuba). Then, too, it is probable that many white New Yorkers and Bostonians do not view increased immigration from Ireland as a threat to their well-being. The Immigration Act of 1924, which Beck so praises, was the result at least as much of fear of particular immigrant groups (East Asians and southern and eastern Europeans) as of a general desire for lower population growth. As of election year 1996, it was still questionable whether a successful coalition for immigration restriction could be created by appealing solely to a desire to check the increase in the numbers of people living in the United States.

In stressing some aspects of the immigration issue, Beck slights others. Little is included on illegal immigration. In the text, Beck mentions briefly, and tantalizingly, that immigrants from Somalia, Ethiopia, and the Sudan have settled in the meat-packing towns of the rural Midwest. Readers gain no hint, however, of the special problems that immigrants from East Africa must face in adjusting to their new environment, or of how the meat-packing experience may have modified their traditional culture (the names of their countries are not even mentioned in the index). Readers who are less interested in the question of whether post-1965 immigration is good or bad for the United States, and more interested in learning something about the experiences of the post-1965 immigrants themselves, in their own voices, should consult Sanford J. Ungar's *Fresh Blood: The New American Immigrants* (1995) and Sarah J. Mahler's *American Dreaming: Immigrant Life on the Margins* (1995). Those interested in the impact of post-1965 immigration on American politics should read Georgie Ann Geyer's *Americans No More: The Death of Citizenship* (1996) and Dale Maharidge's *The Coming White Minority: California's Eruptions and the Nation's Future* (1996).

Beck's work contains relatively few aids to readers. Between pages 19 and 20, thereare three charts showing the effect of post-1965 immigration on American population growth. The index is only moderately useful. The endnotes do provide a mine of sources for further reading and research; the names of most of Beck's interview subjects, however, are cited only in the text itself and in the index. Unfortunately, Beck has failed to include any time line or red-letter dates in American legislation and executive action concerning immigration and the admission of refugees. There are neither photographic illustrations nor maps; the latter would have been helpful to readers who are unfamiliar with the American Midwest. These criticisms aside, Beck has provided an important contribution to the debate concerning American immigration.

Paul D. Mageli

Sources for Further Study

Business Week. XXII, April 22, 1996, p. 15.
Choice. XXXIV, September, 1996, p. 167.
Foreign Affairs. LXXV, July, 1996, p. 146.
National Review. XLVIII, November 25, 1996, p. 65.
The New York Times Book Review. CI, September 1, 1996, p. 18.
Publishers Weekly. CCXLIII, March 11, 1996, p. 52.
Times-Picayune. May 5, 1996, p. E7.
The Washington Post Book World. XXVI, July 21, 1996, p. 4.

THE CATTLE KILLING

Author: John Edgar Wideman (1941-   )
Publisher: Houghton Mifflin (New York). 212 pp. $22.95
Type of work: Novel
Time: The late eighteenth century and the 1990's
Locale: Philadelphia, Pennsylvania, and its environs

Wideman creates a self-reflexive fiction in which a contemporary African American writer shares with family members a newly finished manuscript about an eighteenth century former slave and itinerant preacher caught up in the racist repercussions of a 1793 outbreak of yellow fever in Philadelphia

Principal characters:
> ISAIAH, the contemporary writer who opens the novel
> THE PREACHER, an African American who has bought himself out of slavery, has converted to Methodism, and pursues an itinerant ministry until racist violence dissolves his faith
> LIAM, an African uprooted in boyhood by English slavers who secures his freedom and heads for the New World
> MRS. STUBBS, a white English servant girl who falls in love with Liam and accompanies him to America
> BISHOP RICHARD ALLEN, the historical founder of the African Methodist Episcopal (A.M.E.) Church, the first independent black Christian denomination
> DR. THRUSH, a fictional rendering of Dr. Benjamin Rush, the signer of the Declaration of Independence and a noted Philadelphia surgeon
> MRS. THRUSH, the doctor's blind wife
> KATHRYN, the African American woman who attends Mrs. Thrush and serves as her scribe
> J., the son of the contemporary novelist to whom the finished manuscript is shown and whose response helps complete the text

In this complex, layered fiction, John Wideman revisits favorite themes which here assume heightened clarity and resonance. Long a practitioner of modernist textual acrobatics—polyphonic narratives, unmediated disjunctions of time and place, elusive and elliptical voicings often cited by critics as prose variations on jazz improvisations—Wideman also acknowledges postmodernist doubts about the potential of any creative enterprise to relieve the artist's egotism or conjure up and communicate with its audience. Yet he escapes the postmodern temptation to repudiate claims of artistic "meaning" through the countervailing influence upon him of African American culture, with its insistence upon the life-affirming power of stories and the revitalizing grace accompanying their telling. Wideman regularly incorporates African myth into his narratives as a means of affirming continuity and connection across the ruptures of history, doing so, as he explains in his 1994 memoir *Fatheralong*, because the "truly dead" are "those who do not speak and are not spoken of, those not connected by vital words, those whom the stories have forgotten, who have forgotten the stories."

Accordingly, the title of Wideman's 1996 novel derives from a legend describing how the Xhosa people of South Africa were tragically duped by a prophetic vision instructing them to kill the cattle herds on which their whole civilization rested. They did so, they believed, as a necessary step toward ending their suffering under white European imperialism, but the act proved catastrophic, for the Xhosa unwittingly destroy their community from the inside as an adjunct to the assaults plaguing it from without.

Relating this lesson of the mythic past is no empty exercise in esoterica; it reveals a pattern within lived experience evident anew in the devastated inner cities of the America of the 1990's, where African American youths shoot each other down day after day like "panicked cattle funneled down the killing chute," only coming to recognize "too late" that "The cattle are the people. The people are the cattle." The contemporary writer whose imagination gives birth to all that follows "wanted every word of his new book to be a warning, to be saturated with the image of a devastated landscape. . . . Wasn't the stench of that ravaged countryside burning his eyes, his nostrils as he turned up Wylie Hill. His book beginning and ending here," on the brutal streets of Philadelphia where only the night before his arrival for an academic conference two black teenagers lay murdered.

This narrator, named Isaiah, quickly establishes his own anxieties as to the prophetic potential of art and his own credentials for the task. His nickname "Eye" puns not only on the assumed "vision" of the prophet but also on the inescapable danger that such visions may erupt more from the "I" of Ego than from the eye of unfettered sight. By alluding to the Old Testament prophet who kept alive in the Israelites of the Babylonian Captivity a belief that they would one day recover the Promised Land, Wideman blends Judeo-Christian and African frames of reference and recalls the generations of slaves who subversively aligned themselves with God's chosen people.

The narrative Isaiah has completed reflects his anguished desire to fashion a redemptive art for an era whose relentless brutalities mock the comforts and certainties of faith. He constructs his text achronologically, since "Sometimes . . . going backward in the story is more important than proceeding forward." These interlocking pieces are offered nightly by a male speaker who hopes to use them, in an intriguing variation upon the task of Scheherezade, to keep a bedridden female listener alive. The tale-teller reveals himself to be an unnamed former slave and former itinerant minister of the late eighteenth century who had been won over by Methodism's celebration "of the holy spirit dwelling in all God's creatures." A religion resting upon love and "cultivating the spark of divinity within any man, high or low" proved especially attractive to one who had been reared a slave and who had found in other churches only an indictment of humanity's irrevocable depravity.

Choosing to remain outside the reach of official religious institutions, he undertakes that prototypical American act, a purposeful wandering through the sparsely inhabited regions beyond the metropolis, and establishes a worship community of African Americans who seek spiritual renewal. Wideman's Preacher invites his flock to commune in nature and to recover both their human dignity and their joy in the love of God. The Preacher is set apart among these folks by his own attunement to a wide spectrum of insight into the nature of things, for he is subject to seizures that initially prompt him to deliver a torrent of abusive commentary on the absurdity of the world around him but then give way to an exhilarating moment of insight into the wholeness of creation, "sweet as it must have been, and still is, if we had but eyes to see it, before the Fall." His utterances following such epiphanies win for him awed respect as God's chosen messenger—the prophet as visionary poet.

During this time, he also encounters a biracial couple living an industrious life parallel to, but aloof from, the white world of rural colonial Pennsylvania. Immigrants from England seeking freedom from Europe's constrictive social forms, they quickly discover New World variants on Old World racism and choose to disguise their relationship behind that of mistress and servant. By doing so, they collude with the demeaning system of human valuation they had originally fled and find that as a result they are inexorably yet subtly divided from each other. Liam retreats behind a wall of silence, and his beloved becomes known to the reader only by her duplicitous pseudonym "Mrs. Stubbs." Liam's alienation, for years relieved only by the punishing labor of frontier life, begins to give way when the Preacher's arrival unlocks his tongue and prompts him to share stories he has long withheld. In the presence of another African, Liam's spirit revives, and he explains that he had come to America dreaming not only of an opportunity for unfettered love but also to unleash the artistic voice he felt nascent within him—an avenue by which, perhaps, to recoup the aborted promise of his early days as the son of an African "wizard" and one destined himself to become a "holy man" in his own right; here as elsewhere in the novel, Wideman explores and distinguishes between the soul-nourishing functions of art and religion.

Later as a slave in service to the painter and medical illustrator George Stubbs, Liam discovers equally compelling parallels between that artist's vivisectionist obsessions and those of his father, a butcher and tanner, and notes the commonalities linking both to the legitimized aggression of modern business, politics, and science. Ultimately, Liam proves unequal to the detached "ruthlessness" required to subdue life's messy energies to a static orderliness revealing "the truth . . . people ordinarily couldn't see." He comes to see the terrible incongruity artistic aspiration posed for a black man at this historical moment and in the context of an America deepening rather than repudiating its dependence upon slavery. For if the artist is one who, like the Preacher, responds to the "inner light" of truth and struggles to speak honestly of what he sees, how does he depict a culture that traffics in human beings?

Liam calls the racism that was both cause and effect of American slavery "the madness," and he cannot imagine finding his own voice in such a world, its very "air thick with blood and wailing." While the paintings he once longed to make have failed to materialize, another kind of artistic respite suddenly becomes accessible to him through the Preacher's two-year tenure in his home: Telling his tale to a seemingly ideal listener counteracts the fear that there is no way out of self and into meaningful engagement with the life of another. That the stunted Liam achieves such communion with the Preacher is inspiring; that it cannot save him, finally, from the eruption of racist panic that causes his death inside his burning home offers a somber reflection on the limits of art to effect anything grander than individual epiphany.

The apocalyptic fires that consume Liam and his mate also bear witness to the impossibility, even in a land still teeming with wilderness, of sequestering oneself beyond the polluting reach of society's pressure points. Philadelphia's yellow fever epidemic and its rumored association with African Americans unhinges neighbors who for years have left the couple to themselves. Liam had once described his existence apart from the white community as "quarantine," and with his death the equation of racial difference with contagion and eradication is completed.

The Preacher's own faith is rocked, though not altogether unmoored, by this early American lynching. He decides instead to take his anger to Philadelphia itself, where he will minister to the despised black poor deprived of medical assistance both by the lie that, as supposed carriers of the disease, they are immune to its ravages, and by white indifference to their suffering when they do succumb. On his journey, he encounters a black woman speaking a Caribbean dialect and toting a dead white child on her hip. He accompanies the seemingly deranged woman to the lake she has been determined to find, traversing a landscape even the wilderness-loving Preacher does not recognize. When she comes to it at last, she walks into its depths with the child, a seeming suicide but said by the Preacher to have merely "disappeared." In the course of the novel and in the progression of stories the Preacher shares with his still unnamed interlocutor, the Preacher theorizes that he had met her years before upon emerging from one of his seizures. A figure in blue, she had given him cool water and captured his attention, only to disappear yet again, this time into a swelling crowd of "more African people than I'd ever seen in one place at one time."

Ultimately the Preacher links these two apparitions of feminine devotion to the woman listening to his stories. Although she is never explicitly identified, textual clues indicate that she is Kathryn, a black servant and ladies' maid working in the home of Dr. Benjamin Thrush of Philadelphia. Having reached the city, the Preacher has quickly joined the service of Bishop Richard Allen, a man of God daring enough to challenge publicly the establishment church's practice of segregating its congregations. In delivering Allen's request that Dr. Thrush intercede to stop the broadsides claiming that blacks harbored and disseminated the deadly fever, the Preacher meets Kathryn, and a friendship blossoming into passion is born. Yet it unfolds amid a drama whereby the Thrush household continues to educate the Preacher in the folly of his idealism. Dr. Thrush eschews the potential damage to his newly recuperated reputation that might accompany his taking an unpopular stand against racist scapegoating. This, added to his culpability in disseminating the argument early in the days of plague that inherent racial differences gave Africans immunities to the disease, causes men such as Allen and the Preacher to despair of the supposed good will of liberal whites. Moreover, Thrush proves no more disciplined in his exercise of white male droit du seigneur than the smuggest Southern plantation owner. He regularly coerces Kathryn's acquiescence to his sexual demands, eventually fathering the child she is carrying even as her relationship with the Preacher ignites.

Wideman's handling of Kathryn's character goes beyond the familiar trope of victimized slave woman at the mercy of white male moral turpitude, however. He makes her not only the attendant to Thrush's blind gentlewoman wife but hands her a pen by which she serves as recording secretary for her mistress, transposing her unbearably sweet-tempered and uninformed nostrums about her world into a journal Mrs. Thrush will only be able to "read" when Kathryn "voices" it for her—a ventriloquism with provocative implications. Interpolated into the text its putative author will never see are the scribe's caustic remarks which not only announce her presence in the master narrative of white female privilege but permit her to expose its essential falsity.

Nor is Kathryn's testimony the only source of condemnation directed against the well-meaning but hapless Mrs. Thrush whose blindness, in a novel so laden with images of light and seeing, evinces a spiritual as well as physical handicap. In one of Wideman's many allusions to classic African American literary texts, she recalls the equally obtuse Mrs. Dalton in Richard Wright's *Native Son*. Needing to find an acceptable activity for her empty days, Mrs. Thrush takes up the cause of black children orphaned by the epidemic who now live in a home where they are virtual prisoners. Failing to recognize the abject realities of their lives, she goes among them (always accompanied by Kathryn, her "hands" as well as her eyes), and merges Christianity with the young republic's new secular "religion" of education by insisting on the Bible as their primer. She voices her disappointment with her charges' lack of enthusiasm for their lessons but does not perceive the rage she is engendering in one of her pupils, who pathetically focuses his energies on an act of arson that kills his fellow orphans but leaves the white woman who symbolizes his oppression untouched. For her, this act of self-destructive protest remains opaque; her punishment comes elsewhere, in the revelation of Kathryn's pregnancy and her husband's infidelity. Yet for the Preacher, who stands at the orphans' gravesite as Bishop Allen eulogizes them, the potential of religion to mediate such tragedies finally collapses.

He withdraws from Allen and from his former missionary quest and instead gives himself over to the task of devising life-saving stories from the marrow of his experience to heal Kathryn, abed with an ailment never disclosed but suggestive of the ubiquitous fever. If it is, the outcome of her pregnancy remains undisclosed, leaving the exact configuration of this potential new family mysterious. All that can be said for certain is that the Preacher's faith now resides in stories—stories by which strangers are illuminated to one another through brief but redemptive glimpses into the human heart.

Finally, *The Cattle Killing* offers an intricately woven meditation on the relationship of past to present and places at the center of each of its time frames an African American devoted to language as a counterforce to historical and cultural rupture: language, for all its limitations, as the raw material for the stories that just may weaken despair as they defeat death. The contemporary frame of the novel begins with the Wideman-like novelist on a quest to find his father and share with him his newest work; whether he accomplishes that mission is left unclear. Yet in the book's epilogue, a letter written by the writer's son reveals that he has read the manuscript and wants to contribute to it in the form of a document he has found from a black man who might have been the Preacher's long-lost brother. What follows that letter is a short "improvisation" on that theme—and thus *The Cattle Killing* becomes a collaborative tale spinning off new possibilities and directions even at the point where conventional narrative would be moving toward closure. For as Wideman repeats here and elsewhere in his work, "All stories are true."

Barbara Kitt Seidman

Sources for Further Study

Atlanta Constitution. October 24, 1996, p. D1.
Booklist. XCII, August, 1996, p. 1857.
Boston Globe. October 13, 1996, p. N16.
Chicago Tribune. December 8, 1996, XIV, p. 6.
Library Journal. CXXI, July, 1996, p. 164.
The Nation. CCLXIII, December 28, 1996, p. 58.
The New York Times Book Review. CI, November 3, 1996, p. 20.
Publishers Weekly. CCXLIII, August 12, 1996, p. 63.
San Francisco Chronicle. October 13, 1996, p. REV5.

CHARLES DARWIN'S LETTERS
A Selection 1825-1859

Author: Charles Robert Darwin (1809-1882)
Edited by Frederick Burkhardt
Foreword by Stephen Jay Gould
Publisher: Cambridge University Press (New York). 249 pp. $21.95
Type of work: Letters
Time: 1825-1859

Frederick Burkhardt presents a sample of Darwin's letters during his formative years as a person and as a scientist

Principal personages:
> CHARLES ROBERT DARWIN, a British naturalist, famous for his theory of natural selection
> JOHN STEVENS HENSLOW, a professor of botany at Cambridge University and Darwin's teacher and friend
> JOHN DALTON HOOKER, a director of the Royal Botanic Gardens, Kew, and confidant of Darwin
> THOMAS HENRY HUXLEY, a British naturalist
> CHARLES LYELL, a British geologist and one of Darwin's mentors

Charles Darwin is one of the half dozen or so scientists whose name is known to anyone who claims to be an educated person in the Western tradition. His theory of evolution through natural selection is one of the landmarks of Western thought. Like many modern scientists, Darwin left behind an abundant paper legacy. In addition to his many publications, he filled pages of notebooks and wrote thousands of letters to family, friends, and fellow scientists. He also received thousands of letters. *A Calendar of Correspondence of Charles Darwin, 1821-1882* (1985) lists nearly fourteen thousand items, some of which were published in his son Francis' *Life and Letters of Charles Darwin* (1887) and *More Letters of Charles Darwin* (1903). Much of his correspondence remained unpublished, however, for a century after his death.

The second half of the twentieth century witnessed the establishment of a large number of documentary editing projects, each dedicated to the collection and publication of the correspondence of either an individual, a group of individuals, or a social movement. In some cases, these editions were designed to replace nineteenth century life and letters volumes—which were often filled with silently corrected, silently edited, or even bowdlerized letters—with collections of correspondence which reproduced as closely as possible in printed form the manuscript document.

The correspondence of Darwin has been caught up in this documentary editing revolution. His most important correspondence began being published in 1985 in a multivolume edition, *The Correspondence of Charles Darwin*, edited by Frederick Burkhardt, who has been assisted by a staff in England and the United States. This edition targets a select scholarly audience of historians, philosophers, and sociologists of science, as well as biologists. In addition to providing contextual annotations drawing upon the most recent historical scholarship, *The Correspondence of Charles Darwin* has an elaborate editorial apparatus which furnishes a clear, easily readable version of the letter, while enabling readers, if they so desire, to reconstruct the manuscript version of the letter down to every cross-out, alteration, false start, and interlineation; hopefully, the reader can see the letter as the original recipient saw it. This edition has been highly praised for both its editorial policy and annotations.

Most nonspecialists do not need either the quantity of letters nor the elaborate editorial apparatus that appear in the volumes of *The Correspondence of Charles Darwin* to understand and appreciate Darwin through his correspondence. Fewer letters and a simpler apparatus would suffice. To serve an audience of casual readers of Darwin's correspondence, Burkhardt has selected a tiny fraction of Darwin's outgoing letters (no incoming correspondence is included in *Charles Darwin's Letters*) from the first seven volumes of *The Correspondence of Charles Darwin* (1985-1991). The sampling represents approximately 10 percent of Darwin's outgoing letters that appear in *The Correspondence of Charles Darwin*. Burkhardt presents this sample without most of the editorial apparatus of *The Correspondence of Charles Darwin*. The texts retain the original spelling and punctuation, but no effort is made to signal deletions or interlineations. The number of notes has also been reduced to a bare minimum. Editorial commentary between documents supplies missing facts, chronology, and context which would have been provided by annotation or documents in *The Correspondence of Charles Darwin*.

To assist the nonspecialist further, *Charles Darwin's Letters* includes a biographical register with succinct identifications, a bibliography of Darwin's publications, and some further readings—some historical, some scientific, and some biographical. The biographical register successfully captures the essence of an individual, at least in the context of Darwin's life, in a sentence or two. The list of readings—limited to books—is adequate for the general reader.

The index includes both names and subjects and is fairly detailed and analytical. It is also inconvenient, because it fails to highlight individuals as recipients of letters. For example, it is impossible from the index to distinguish between a letter to Asa Gray in which Darwin provides an outline of his theory, and a letter to a third party in which Darwin tells that third party that he had written Gray about the theory. Even worse is the situation when the contents of the letter have nothing directly to do with the recipient. When Darwin's eldest daughter Anne Elizabeth was terminally ill, Darwin wrote a series of letters from his daughter's bedside to his wife, who was pregnant and unable to travel. These letters provide a detailed record of his daughter's decline and a sense of the relationship between Darwin and his wife. The letters are not indexed under his wife's name except for two passing references to her pregnancy. Including an index subentry called something like "recipient of letter" would have been most useful, especially in relocating a specific letter.

The editorial commentary is rather thin, but it is supplemented by Burkhardt's introduction, which briefly sketches Darwin's life for those readers not already familiar with the basic structure of Darwin's life and work. Supplementing Burkhardt's editorial contributions is the foreword by Stephen Jay Gould. Gould's foreword, entitled "A Life's Epistolary Drama," is a delightful essay, typical of Gould, which not only extols the delights of epistolary books, but also highlights the major themes in the first five decades of Darwin's life, whether personal or scientific. It is an essay which ranks with Gould's best on the history of science.

Burkhardt arranges his selection of letters chronologically, starting with Darwin a student attending Edinburgh University, and ending shortly after the publication of the *Origin of Species* in November, 1859. The chronological arrangement results in the mixture of personal letters with professional ones; letters which show Darwin as a concerned father are printed next to those which show Darwin seeking technical information from colleagues in the scientific community in Great Britain or overseas. Thus the letters reflect the real world situation where there is no clear boundary between private and professional life.

The letters of the younger Darwin are the choicest. The opening letters from Scotland are family letters and give a wonderful picture of a young man at the university. Readers learn about his studies and his need for money (some aspects of college life never change).

There is also a wonderful collection of letters written while Darwin was on the voyage of the HMS *Beagle*. Darwin grows as a scientist before the eye of the reader. In letters to his sisters and to his professor at Cambridge, John Stevens Henslow, Darwin describes life at sea and his scientific discoveries. Enthusiasm and excitement are evident. So is pride in the discoveries he has made, mixed occasionally with some humility. In a letter to his elder sister Susan, Darwin writes that "I do not suppose any of you can be much interested in Geological details," then proceeds to provide her with the equivalent of a full printed page of geological descriptions and theories. He just cannot stop himself.

Readers also see Darwin the lover in letters to his cousin, Emma Wedgewood, whom he married in January, 1839. Three days after their engagement, he wrote her a delightful letter, full of love, plans for the future, and joy, which he himself describes at the end as "a very silly one," but sends it anyway because "I cant write a better one."

As a father, Darwin was, by the standards of his age, attentive, concerned, relatively sensitive, and sympathetic. He even told his son William, then a student at Cambridge University, "to let me know in good time before you run short of money." He signed his letters to William with some variation of "yours affectionately," and called him "my dear old man."

Yet Darwin is of interest to most readers because of his science, not because he was a Victorian father or a successful wooer of his cousin. By the time of his engagement, Darwin has conceived of his theory of natural selection, although he was to spend the next two decades developing it. His letters, however, throw no light on that original conception. That documentation can be found in private notebooks, not correspondence. Darwin was not yet ready to expose his idea to external criticism.

What these letters do elucidate is Darwin's development as a scientist. By the late 1830's, he had been accepted as a peer by the scientific community of London. Some of the greatest names in Victorian science appear among his correspondents: John Dalton Hooker, Charles Lyell, and Thomas Henry Huxley, later to gain fame as the fierce public defender of Darwin's theory of evolution.

Darwin appears in these letters as a synthesizer. He is picking the brains of experts, whether in zoology, geology, or botany. Or else he is using friends and relatives to aid in his search for information or specimens. Hooker is asked for information about the ability of seeds to survive exposure to salt water. Darwin would then turn to Asa Gray at Harvard for his knowledge of the geographical distribution of plants. He asks William Darwin Fox, a cousin, to organize a hunt for lizard eggs. John E. Gray, a zoologist at the British museum is requested to be a go-between in Darwin's efforts to learn more about Chinese agriculture. Darwin demonstrates a genius for the management of information and informants almost on a par with that of his drawing diverse threads of science together into a coherent theory.

This is not a volume to be studied or used for reference. It is a book to be read and enjoyed. The reader desiring detail, fuller context, and fuller knowledge of what Darwin's correspondents were writing to him must go to the volumes of *The Correspondence of Charles Darwin*. Those looking to gain a flavor of Darwin's own style of letter writing and of the man himself will find *Charles Darwin's Letters* sufficient.

Letters written by an interesting and lively individual writing about interesting things, and who is writing only for his correspondent and not with an eye on history, are a pleasure to read. Darwin, especially the younger Darwin, was such a letter writer: animated and unself-conscious. Gould's description of the letters dealing with the decision to publish *Origin of Species* would serve as an evaluation of many of the letters published in this volume: "the drama, the complexity, the moral struggles, are so much better told in Darwin's own words than through his biographers."

Marc Rothenberg

Sources for Further Study

Booklist. XCII, April 15, 1996, p. 1402.
Library Journal. CXXI, February 15, 1996, p. 172.
Natural History. CV, May, 1996, p. 6.
Nature. CCCLXXX, March 28, 1996, p. 300.
New Scientist. CXLIX, March 30, 1996, p. 46.
Scientific American. CCLXXV, October, 1996, p. 123.

CITIES OF MEMORY

Author: Ellen Hinsey (1960-   )
Foreword by James Dickey
Publisher: Yale University Press (New Haven, Connecticut). 69 pp. $17.00; paperback $10.00
Type of work: Poetry

A collection of poems that juxtaposes observation and vision, memory and reality, and history and society while it celebrates a connectedness which is fundamental to all those who believe in the commonality in human experience

Ellen Hinsey is a Massachusetts native who lives in Paris, France. She received a bachelor of fine arts degree from Tufts University in conjunction with the School of the Museum of Fine Arts, Boston. Her poems have appeared in various prestigious newspapers and magazines such as *The New York Times*, *The Paris Review*, *The New England Review*, and *The Missouri Review*. In 1995, *Cities of Memory* won the Yale Series of Younger Poets, an annual contest open to any American writer under forty years of age who has not previously published a volume of poetry. James Dickey was the judge of the competition. In the foreword to the book, Dickey writes:

> The need for roots, as Simone Weil reminds us, is fundamental to human kind; there is no one wearing our shape who has not felt it. But along with this condition, there are those who can take root in places where they do not expect to live out the rest of their lives and die.

Hinsey has traveled extensively in Europe. Her works are informed by her sensitivity to and interest in the cultural, political, historical, and geographical landscapes of Europe and by her eagerness to celebrate a connectedness which is fundamental to all those who believe in the commonality in human experience.

The poems collected in *Cities of Memory* can be divided into four groups: poems about events, poems about people, poems about places, and poems about objects and what Dickey calls "artifacts." The poem "March 26, 1827" is an elegy. It registers a historical moment. On March 26, 1827, the singer Lablanche, seeking news of Ludwig van Beethoven, arrived to find the latter in a coma and could make out but few words: "do you hear the tolling? Change the scene." According to Jean and Brigitte Massin, co-authors of *Ludwig van Beethoven* (1967), Beethoven's remark was a reference to the bells in the theaters of Vienna that, during this period, announced the changing of the acts. "March 26, 1827" opens with the description of people's fear that with Beethoven's death, "the last of sound would be carted off—/ the price exacted in recompense." It continues with the investigation of the dialectical relationship between sound and silence, between the past and the present, and between time and immortality. With the realization that "music is not the note/ but the interval—/ that it is not the note but/ the possibility that lies between," the poem ends with the description of Beethoven's funeral. Following the elegiac tradition in poetry, "March 26, 1827" praises the musician's achievement and laments the loss of someone who cannot be replaced. In "Lebensraum," the narrator compares the Romans' war against the Veii

and World War II. Veii was an ancient Etruscan city in central Italy. It was destroyed
by the Romans in 396 B.C. According to historian Michael Grant in *History of Rome*
(1978), the Romans' invasion of the Veii was instigated by their need of new land.
"Lebensraum" is a German term which literally means "living space." The term was
used by Hitler to describe his policy of acquiring enough land to create a nation of two
hundred million German people. The poem, by contrasting the tranquillity of nature
and the peacefulness of life and the cruelty and destructiveness of wars, calls readers'
attention to the natural and the unnatural, the part of the world which makes human
existence a beautiful experience and the decisions arbitrarily made to satisfy people's
twisted ego. In Part I of the poem, Hinsey describes how the Roman soldiers, on their
way to war, passed the "Temple of Janus." Janus was one of the principal Roman gods.
His shrine in the Forum in Rome had two doors. The doors were closed in times of
peace and open in times of war. Janus is represented as having two faces. They look
in opposite directions, symbolizing his ability to see both the future and the past. The
reference to Janus paradigmatically demonstrates the pernicious effect when people
fail to learn from their ancestors' mistakes.

    "Diptych," "Fantasie on the Church at Auvers," "Night in Clamart," "Paula Moder-
sohn-Becker at Worpswede," and "Canticle in Grey" trace European artists and
writers' footsteps in history to portray their struggles and celebrate their lives. Several
poems in the group extol female artists' indefatigable spirit and their eagerness to blaze
new trails in arts and poetry. "Night in Clamart" describes the Russian poet Marina
Tsvetayeva's brief exile in the Parisian suburb of Petit Clamart. The predominant color
in the poem is gray and dark and the tone somber. The dirty rains threaten to dissolve
the roads which are written like afterthoughts; the empty roads look for the poet's
shadow but to no avail. The poem describes Tsvetayeva's struggle with both her poems
and her loneliness, foreshadowing a life that would end tragically (Tsvetayeva returned
to the Soviet Union in 1939; in 1941, under harsh government reprisals, she committed
suicide). Paula Modersohn-Becker began her career as a painter in the small German
art colony of Worpswede. Her attempt to break with the prevailing visual idiom
took her to Paris four times during her lifetime. Worpswede is described in "Paula
Modersohn-Becker at Worpswede" as a place where "Each morning, from the same
palette/ the landlocked hamlet came to light./ Night had sketched the shadowy forms,/
and from its traces, birched, brace white,/ issued forth their line, laced the canal's
sinuous path." The natural beauty of Worpswede is contrasted, however, with the
"idiom of the place" which over time grows cold and depletes Modersohn-Becker's
creative energy. The artist eventually decides to give up "twilight, the pastoral figure/
in half-light, to pass into knowing." "Canticle in Gray" describes another Russian poet
Anna Akhmatova's struggle in life. Though persecuted by the Soviet government after
the Bolshevik Revolution in 1917, Akhmatova remained in the Soviet Union as a
witness to the atrocities of the Stalinist period. Her loneliness is accentuated in the
poem by the portrayal of both the political and the physical environment: "Winter
again: beneath frost's hand a spiraling trail/ of bodies held to relentless queues." Yet
Akhmatova is undaunted. She stays "as the prison wall like a sightless shore/ cast up

its victims in the snow. And through the dark" she remains "a bronze figure softened by rain/ who above a broken jug could praise the water's touch." Akhmatova's determination and tenacity are also strengthened by her awareness of her connection with a civilization which has lasted more than two thousand years.

Hinsey's poems about places represent some of her best. "On a Visit to Budapest" is a moving poem describing the narrator's love affair in Budapest. The narrator is a forty-year-old woman who falls in love in Budapest. The relationship has changed her perspective on life and human relationship. The experience is like seeing life from "the wrong end of a telescope." It turns her world upside down. What appears to be a triangle relationship involving the narrator, her lover, and her family, though, turns out to be the narrator's love affair with the city. She is glad to "walk the streets/ at night and listen to how dawn would light/ on her sill." "The Stairwell, Berggasse 19, Vienna" is another poem which was inspired by Hinsey's visit of a place of historic significance. From 1891 to 1938, Austrian neurologist and founder of psychoanalysis Sigmund Freud lived at Berggasse 19. It was the location of his consulting rooms and, one flight above, his private quarters. On March 15, 1938, the household was invaded by Brownshirts. According to the recollection of Freud's son, Martin Freud (*The Diary of Sigmund Freud 1929-1939*, 1992), Martha Freud, Freud's wife, treated the Brown-shirts "as ordinary visitors, inviting them to put their rifles down in the sections of the hall-stand reserved for umbrellas, and even to sit down." Freud, too, "had retained his invincible poise, leaving his sofa where he had been resting to join" Martha "in the living room where he sat calmly in his armchair throughout the raid." The poem portrays Freud as a calm and rational person. In contrast, the Brownshirts are those in whom: "Faustian elements gathered force,/ masses like dark water under bridges;/ thirsty as the primal horde, they bent/ together and lit their torches." The poem is interspersed with passages from Freud's representative works such as *The Interpretation of Dreams* (1965) and *Civilization, Society, and Religion* (1985). The device demonstrates the reciprocal relationship between history and theory: the former informs the latter whereas the latter helps explain the former.

The last group of Hinsey's poems deals with objects and artifacts. The poet's curiosity of the power of light, her attraction to the body in youth, and her strong feelings about the Berlin Wall provide her with opportunities to study the dialectical relationship between the predictable and the unpredictable patterns of life. "The Art of Measuring Light" uses impressionistic approach in its portrayal of the Pont-Neuf, Paris. "The light here has begun to pass and as it passes/ it will bend down to the Seine in the last of its/ winter gymnastics: unwrapping its hands from/ the white crevices of Saint-Germain-des-Près,/ giving a last honor to Sacré-Coeur." The poem then turns into a study of distance, physical and psychological, in relevance to space and time. Light is what connects the past and the present. Light is what enables the poet to live at Paris, France, and New Hampshire, the United States, simultaneously, for "that light/ that has passed here is light that will contrive/ to touch the white of wood on maple-lined streets,/ deep in New Hampshire, where snow is piling/ high, in the unbroken shadow of a new day." "The Body in Youth" connects the study of human physiology with that of metaphysical contemplation. The poem explores the relationship between the form of the body and the formless world, between body parts which provide the frame for the definition of human existence and the metaphysical contemplation which provides substance for that definition. The body in youth exudes energy and enthusiasm. It is powerful, muscular, and mysterious. Its imperfection is justified by its entitlement to dreams and desires which also help inform and define its very existence. The poem ends as mysteriously as it starts with lines which highlight the mischievous and willfulness of "the body in youth": "like a ship tide-persuaded," "the body drifted, abandoning what it sought/ to become, the body in youth lingering/ only a moment in its own folds." In the group, "From: The Seven Wonders of the Modern World" registers Hinsey's antagonistic feelings about oppression and separation. Using the Berlin Wall as a symbol, she criticizes a decision made in defiance of common sense and human beings' aspiration for communication and understanding.

Poetry uses metaphorical language to portray human experience that cannot be portrayed any other way. The juxtaposition of the exploration of abstract ideas and the portrayal of concrete images works in two ways. On one hand, concrete images are employed to reveal and reinforce poets' thematic concerns. In Hinsey's "The Art of Measuring Light," for example, light is used as an image to suggest the conquerability of distance created by space and time. Images are also used to concretize an experience which otherwise would remain largely metaphysical. In "Trains at Night," the train's shadowy corridor is compared to "an apology:/ a winding argument of thrusts and retreats,/ whose odd logic keeps the night/ navigator pinned by turns to the window's/ reflection, or cast up against compartments/ where the tremulous sleep, under a blanket/ of half-closed eyes." *Cities of Memory* is informed by the cultural, political, historical, and geographical landscapes of Europe. Hinsey's sensitivity, her longing for connectedness, and the musical quality of her poems help create a symphony whose notes will surely strike a common chord among those who share her feelings about place, about culture, and about history.

Qun Wang

Sources for Further Study

Booklist. XCII, June 1, 1996, p. 1667.
Library Journal. CXXI, June 15, 1996, p. 68.
Philadelphia Inquirer. May 28, 1996, p. C1.
Publishers Weekly. CCXLIII, June 3, 1996, p. 74.

CLEANTH BROOKS AND THE RISE OF MODERN CRITICISM

Author: Mark Royden Winchell (1948-   )
Publisher: University Press of Virginia (Charlottesville). 510 pp. $34.95
Type of work: Literary biography
Time: 1906-1992
Locale: The United States and Great Britain

A biography and study of the influence of Cleanth Brooks on the formation of modern literary criticism

Principal personages:
CLEANTH BROOKS, JR., the American critic who popularized the tenets
    of New Criticism
TINKUM BROOKS, his beloved wife
ROBERT PENN WARREN, an American poet and New Critic
JOHN CROWE RANSOM, the poet and critic who taught Brooks at
    Vanderbilt University

Mark Royden Winchell's *Cleanth Brooks and the Rise of Modern Criticism* is both a biography and a work of intellectual history dealing with Cleanth Brooks's central role in the rise—and fall—of the New Criticism. There are few biographies about literary critics or teachers, so this book, along with its mixture of literary history, is unusual. The life of Cleanth Brooks, Jr., however, was not marked by very much drama or even crisis; it was a serene and largely untroubled life. Biographers seldom choose such a subject.

The book begins with biography as it traces the background and parentage of Brooks. Cleanth Brooks, Sr., was a Methodist minister based in Memphis around the late nineteenth century and early twentieth century, and, although he worked hard, he was made redundant by a somewhat heartless church. Both Christian ideas and the South figure prominently in the thought of his son, Cleanth Brooks, Jr.

Cleanth Brooks, Jr., was born on October 16, 1906, in the town of Murray, Kentucky. Because his father often changed his residence as he moved from one Methodist church to another, young Cleanth lived in various towns in Kentucky and Tennessee in his early years. He attended the McTyerie school in Henry County, Tennessee, and he later became a student at the most prestigious college in the South, Vanderbilt University, in 1924. At Vanderbilt, Brooks received a traditional education in English and American literature; the emphasis was on philology and history. There was little discussion of a literary criticism or any analysis of poems in detail. Brooks's later career was, of course, based on such an analysis. Brooks took a class from John Crowe Ransom, the poet and critic then teaching at Vanderbilt, although he was not influenced by Ransom's critical views until later. Another critic and poet at Vanderbilt during these years was Brooks's fellow student, Robert Penn Warren. The careers and critical views of the two were to be linked in future years. Warren's life and career, however, was very different from Brooks. He was primarily a poet and only incidentally a critic, and there was enough drama and trouble in his life to fill a few biographies.

While Brooks's critical view were still unshaped, he did imbibe some of the Agrarian and Fugitive ideas that were prominent during his time at Vanderbilt. The Agrarian movement began in reaction to the urban and Northern dominance of American culture. In *I'll Take My Stand* (1924), a number of Southern intellectuals, including Warren, Ransom, Stark Young, and Allen Tate, declared their allegiance to the traditional and rural South against the urban and industrialized North. The "Fugitives" also dissented from the Northern and Eastern establishment. Their journal, *The Fugitive: A Journal of Poetry*, was the organ of traditional Southern and rural views. Winchell places a great deal of emphasis upon this movement and the influence of the South upon Brooks. At times, this seems to be excessive since Brooks spent at least half of his life out of the South and he never took part in any specifically Southern movement. He did edit the *Southern Review* at Louisiana State University, but the emphasis of that journal is more New Criticism than Agrarian. So Winchell seems to overrate the influence of the South on Brooks's criticism. One reason is that the book is part of the New Minds of the South series.

Brooks then went to Tulane University, where he was a graduate student in English and received a master of arts degree; the move was also intended to put him in a better position for a Rhodes scholarship. He did receive a Rhodes award in 1929. When he was at Oxford, Brooks attended lectures by one of the earliest New Critics, I. A. Richards. Brooks was not very interested in Richards' seminal book *Principles of Literary Criticism* since it stressed the psychological effects of literature upon a read, and it was theoretical. Yet the more pedagogical text of Richards, *Practical Criticism*, which taught readers to avoid stock responses, was to become a key text for him. It stressed the close reading of literary works, especially poetry.

After completing his studies at Oxford, Brooks took a teaching position at Louisiana State University in 1934 and was then able to marry his lifetime love, Tinkum. During their marriage, Brooks's parents continued to live with them, and the older man was very dependent on his more successful son. Brooks was joined at Louisiana State by his fellow student, Robert Penn Warren, a few years later. Louisiana State University was a backwater school at the time, although Huey Long, the notorious governor of Louisiana, did put a considerable amount of funding into the school. Also attending the university as a graduate student in English was the important American poet, Robert Lowell, and his wife, the fiction writer Jean Stafford. Winchell recounts some amusing anecdotes about Lowell and Stafford and even gives them brief biographies; their lives were, of course, lurid next to the staid Brooks.

In 1938, Brooks and Warren published *Understanding Poetry*. This text was to take the basic principles of the New Criticism and place them in a very teachable form. Its influence can be seen in the many colleges and universities throughout the country that adopted it; in fact, it is still in print after nearly sixty years. *Understanding Poetry*, and the later *Understanding Fiction* and *Understanding Drama*, were the authoritative introduction to literature texts. In 1939, Brooks wrote a more traditional scholarly work, *Modern Poetry and the Tradition*. This book clearly shows that Brooks inherited the critical views of T. S. Eliot and used them to reformulate the then accepted canon.

The dominant figure for Eliot and Brooks were the metaphysical poets, especially John Donne. Modern poetry was to be measured by the model of the metaphysicals, and Eliot's *The Waste Land* was the prime example of that poetry in practice. Brooks may have followed Eliot a little too closely in erecting what is, after all, a very selective tradition.

After his success with *Understanding Poetry* and other works, Brooks was invited to join the faculty of English at Yale University. Yale was and is a very prestigious institution, especially for the study of English. The dominant critical mode of the school when Brooks first became a faculty member there was historical. The specialty of the English department was editing the Boswell papers under the formidable Chauncey Brewster Tinker. Brooks did do some editing of the Boswell papers, but his major work was to teach and write about literature by using the principles of the New Criticism. He helped turn Yale's English department away from historical scholarship to literary criticism.

Winchell not only presents Brooks's contribution to the New Criticism, but he also brings out the challenges to it. The first challenge was that of a historical critic, Douglas Bush. Bush claims that the New Critics, and especially Brook, ignored the historical context of the poem. Winchell defends Brooks by claiming that his analysis of poetry, especially that of Andrew Marvell, does contain a recognition of the historical background. The primary thrust of the essay and of the New Criticism, however, is the autonomous text and not its background.

In 1944, Brooks found another subject for his critical analysis, the works of the Southern novelist, William Faulkner. His treatment of Faulkner emphasizes the Southern world that he constructed in his work. It is decidedly not a New Critical analysis. Brooks proceeded to map the novels and to see the world of Yoknapatawpha County as a whole, which was an important addition to the criticism on the novelist. Brooks wrote two books on Faulkner that helped provide readers with critical tools with which to read this complex novelist.

In 1947, Brooks published *The Well Wrought Urn*. It was both his fullest defense of the New Criticism and the best demonstration of its ability to analyze poetry. Brooks selected poems from various periods in order to show that it could read all types of poetry, not just the seventeenth century metaphysicals. The analysis of poems by Alexander Pope and William Wordsworth, however, is an attempt to demonstrate the "metaphysical" elements within them. These poems were then used to illustrate the favored devices of the New Criticism: paradox, irony, and ambiguity. The analyses are ingenious, but treating all poems as if they were metaphysical poems does lead to some distortion of literary history. It is Brooks's most important book and his most successful attempt to apply the principles of the New Criticism. The very success of the book, however, may have led other critics to react against and challenge that criticism.

In 1957, Brooks expanded his critical range by publishing, with W. K. Wimsatt, *A Short History of Literary Criticism*. It is a book that was meant to be used by students as it included examples from the earliest criticism of Plato and Aristotle up to the New Critic, I. A. Richards. The discussion of that criticism by Wimsatt and Brooks is cogent and represents informed critical opinion of the time. It is, like so many of Brooks's books, a useful text.

The sharpest challenges to the New Criticism came from Stanley Fish and E. D. Hirsch, Jr. Fish was a reader critic and claimed that New Critics were asking the wrong questions about the text. The meaning of a poem, according to Fish, was a process that takes place within the reader. The poem does not exist, he claimed, in the marks on a piece of paper. Hirsch located the authority for the validity of an interpretation on the author's intention. The "intention fallacy" had long been a staple of New Criticism. Hirsch says that the intention of the author can be seen in the genre he writes in not in his stated intention. Winchell does present the challenges to the New Criticism, but he believes that these critics do not destroy the theoretical principles of New Criticism.

In 1965, Brooks was invited to serve in England as a cultural attaché. He welcomed this return to the country where he had been a Rhodes scholar. It was a signal honor for a college professor, and Brooks enjoyed being in London and taking part in the intellectual debates of the period. He did give a lecture on the poetry of T. S. Eliot in which he described Eliot as an urban poet. Eliot was a very important poet for Brooks's critical views, but this poetry as Brooks acknowledged was far removed from the ideals of the Agrarians.

In 1975, Brooks retired from Yale after forty-three years of teaching. He was, by all accounts, an excellent teacher in the classroom. His manner was gentle but persistent as he pushed his students to question assumptions and to probe further in the poem. At the time of his retirement, however, very different types of criticism—deconstruction and feminist—were becoming dominant.

In 1986, Brooks's beloved wife Tinkum died. They had no children, and Tinkum had been a close part of everything Brooks had done through the years. Without her, his life was notably diminished, although he tried to maintain a vigorous intellectual life. Brooks died in 1992.

Cleanth Brooks lived a full and exceptionally successful life. He was a brilliant teacher and had an ideal marriage. His critical views are no longer in fashion, but his influence on the dissemination of the New Criticism was immense. His textbooks and articles taught a generation of teachers and students to read poetry more closely and more fully. He was not a literary theorist but a practical critic who was able to put theories into a usable form. His influence can still be seen in any introductory texts on poetry and literature. The literary criticism of the twentieth century would be quite different without his influence.

James Sullivan

Sources for Further Study

Library Journal. CXXI, March 15, 1996, p. 72.
The New Leader. LXXIX, August 12, 1996, p. 24.
Publishers Weekly. CCXLIII, April 29, 1996, p. 58.
The Washington Post Book World. XXVI, August 11, 1996, p. 3.

THE CLOISTER WALK

Author: Kathleen Norris (1947-   )
Publisher: Riverhead Books (New York). 384 pp. $23.95
Type of work: Memoir

A wise and informative account, this spiritual autobiography traces the liturgical year when the author was in residence at a Benedictine monastery

In her preface, Kathleen Norris writes that *"The Cloister Walk* is a result of . . . [her] immersion into a liturgical world," of various intervals of study that were to comprise one year but which, for her, took nearly three. This period corresponded to her preparation to become a Benedictine oblate, a lay member of the fifteen-hundred-year-old order of monks founded by St. Benedict, and the time of her residence at Saint John's Abbey and University in Collegeville, Minnesota. The author structures her book as if this period of time covered one liturgical year, beginning with September 3, the feast day of Saint Gregory the Great, and concluding near the end of August with "Night," a short meditation on Compline, the official night prayer of the Church. Although a practicing Presbyterian, Norris explores through seventy-five short chapters her affinity as a poet to the Catholic monastic tradition, the mystery of her spiritual journey, as well as her reflections on the relevance of Scripture and the lives of various saints to contemporary society. Interlacing chapters on monastic practice and tradition, autobiographical detail, and commentary on Scripture and the saints allows Norris to capture the rhythm of church seasons, thus creating a sense of time counter to the hurried pace of American life. The only flaw in *The Cloister Walk* is the occasional repetition of information, a result of the individual essays having been written at different times and published separately before compilation in one collection.

One of the central themes in *The Cloister Walk* is the relevance of Norris' experiences at St. John's Abbey to contemporary life, primarily her own but also the reader's. The people Norris met in the monastery were not escapists, but those who had deliberately chosen a simple life incurring confrontation with spiritual issues many seek to avoid. Practices such as the chanting of the Psalms from Scripture, even when these strongly reflect the militaristic and patriarchal culture of ancient Israel, become a means of transcendence for Norris, as she is able to find parallels between the subjects of the psalmist and her own moods as well as the conditions of life for the poor and disenfranchised in contemporary America. Norris writes of finding herself "immersed in poetry" during the chanting, an experience that fed her writing, as the book attests. The images of the Psalms, as she notes, are sensuous and earthy, not theological, thus close to contemporary poetry. Using extensive examples from the lives of the Benedictine sisters and monks she has known, Norris also demonstrates the healing function of the chanting.

Other chapters in *The Cloister Walk* offer commentary on readings from the prophet Jeremiah and the Book of Revelation. The former discussion leads Norris from an analysis of the communal method of *lectio divina*, a type of meditation based on close reading of Scripture—achieved in the monastery through oral reading of religious texts at meals—to the prophetic role of the contemporary poet. Norris' chapter on the Apocalypse becomes not so much a reading of Revelations as an insightful commentary on language and the use of metaphor. Finding hope in the reading of visionary literature, Norris points out that the word apocalypse, often misunderstood as meaning destruction, suggests, in fact, enlightenment and, thereby, hope. Just as listening to the Psalms immersed the writer in poetry, listening to the Book of Revelation immersed her in metaphor. Here Norris contends that those who misunderstand the Book of Revelation err by reading too literally. Fundamentalists try to control metaphor "with literal interpretations of prophetic and apocalyptic texts that deny the import of its metaphorical language," Norris maintains, while liberals try "to eliminate metaphoric images of plagues, punishment, the heavenly courts, martyrdom, and even the cross—that might be deemed offensive, depressing, or judgmental."

Applying her poet's awareness of language and rhythm to the reading of the Bible is one of the strong features of *The Cloister Walk*. Norris' comments also contain both blunt humor and subtle beauty. "Listening to Jeremiah," she writes, "is one hell of a way to get the blood going in the morning; it puts caffeine to shame." While Saint Jerome, whose feast day is September 30, "may have been one of the most irascible people who ever lived," the poets Louise Bogan, Anne Sexton, and John Berryman, all of whom longed for faith, are remembered tenderly on November 1 and 2, the feasts of all saints and all souls. Norris writes poetically after recounting their painful spiritual journeys: "They told it well, but darkly. Now the feasts wheel round, in the dark of the year. All Saints, All Souls, all song and story." In one chapter entitled "Trees," the author meditates on the scarcity of trees in the remote western area of South Dakota where she lives. Those trees that are present create a painted beauty:

> Here in the fall, the groves of ash and poplars planted as windbreaks glow in a golden, Italianate light, and I feel as if I am in a painting by Giotto, or Fra Angelico. A dusty, spare, but lovely place in Tuscany, or western Dakota.

Irony, too, becomes a recurrent feature in Norris' work. The clever title of one chapter, "Saved by a Rockette: Easters I Have Known," recounts stories both joyful and anguished, tracing the author's earliest memories of Easter as an occasion for fancy dress and singing in her church choir through a time in young adulthood when Easter weekend was marked by a bad drug experience and she was treated to a healthful breakfast by a friend, who happened also to be a Rockette. The joyful and solemn celebration of the faith-filled monks of Saint John's, where Norris once again is a member of the choir, the Women's Schola, culminates the spiritual transformation the author has undergone.

Norris is adept at conveying these personal transformations, and the role the monastic way of life has in her journey, as well as explaining monastic traditions and customs. For lay readers unfamiliar with monasticism, *The Cloister Walk* is a compendium of information ranging from the most widely known—the practice of chanting the Liturgy of the Hours, the official prayer of the Catholic church—to the unfamiliar—the robing of novices and the significance of the religious habit. Even the unexpected—the absence of strict rules to govern life in the monastery—can be found. Chapters on the Easter celebration, the Triduum, or three days of Maundy Thursday, Good Friday, and Holy Saturday, clarify the significance of this sacred time for the Christian. Moreover, Norris does not avoid complex, difficult issues. Writing with full awareness that some see celibacy, a requirement for priesthood and religious profession, as a repressive obstacle, Norris discusses the subject with wisdom and insight. Finding celibacy relevant to contemporary life, she points out that the practice is a conscious sublimation, not, as some may believe, a hatred of the flesh or a rejection of sexuality. Examples of both monks and nuns illustrate that celibates do fall in love, even while they struggle to remain faithful to their vows. Like their non-celibate counterparts, they experience infatuation and struggle with the total focus on another, instead of their vowed commitment to Christ. Indeed, as Norris notes, many of these celibates become excellent advisers to married persons precisely because they have worked through these struggles. Also, since all marriages have "times of separation, ill-health, or just plain crankiness, in which sexual intercourse is ill-advised," the skills of the celibate can be pertinent.

The benefits of the monastic way of life fill the pages of *The Cloister Walk*: the embracing of all visitors in response to the rule of hospitality, the recognition of Christ in every stranger; the monks' acceptance of themselves without the delusion that their way of life precludes a struggle with evil; the psychological boon of meditating on Scripture; the emotionally rich experience of chanting the liturgy, not as theology but as poetry. Norris writes:

> to sing, to read poetry aloud, and to have the poetry and the wild stories of scripture read to me. To respond with others, in blessed silence. That is a far more accurate description of morning and evening prayer in a monastery than what most people conjure up when they hear the word "church."

Norris returns repeatedly to this theme of the goodness of the monastic life, particularly to its simplicity and its healing properties, not only for the writer herself but also for American culture.

One of Norris' central purposes is to clarify the misconceptions that readers may have about the experience of church and, particularly, the monastic way of life and those who embrace it. However, Norris also writes as an astute commentator on American cultural assumptions. Her own journey took her from a notion of religion as comfort to one that recognizes agony and the joy of triumph over suffering, a transformation illustrated by the crucifixion and resurrection of Christ. Although nominally Christian, most Americans, Norris maintains, are not comfortable with anything but optimistic religion, nor with a way of life which seemingly denies competition and freedom. Monastics, as Norris points out, have chosen "to live . . . deprived of the autonomy and abundance . . . that middle-class Americans take for granted." Writing poignantly of this choice and its ramifications for the average

American, Norris raises essential questions for those seeking spiritual awareness in their own lives:

> What would I find in my own heart if the noise of the world were silenced? Who would I be? Who will I be when loss or crisis or the depredations of time take away the trappings of success, of self-importance, even personality itself?

As spiritual autobiography, *The Cloister Walk* offers many important insights. The meaning of hospitality is vividly defined when an aged priest who has suffered a fall is able to greet his hospital visitors graciously with a comment about the sweetness of life. The meaning of community, both in the monastery and in the small South Dakota town of Lemmon, where Norris and her husband make their home, is illustrated through descriptions of the Presbyterian church services that Norris participates in, often as a lay preacher, and by the tragedies that strike the community of sixteen hundred: the inexplicable murder of a young father, the death of an irascible town drunk. The early virgin martyrs as well as the twentieth-century saint Maria Goretti, the twelve-year-old who died resisting her rapist, serve as subjects for meditation on American views of women and girls and the obsession with their bodies as always "available" for sexual intercourse. Little escapes Norris' meditations: women's indi-vidualistic methods of doing laundry, the scarcity of trees in the Dakotas, the baking of cinnamon rolls for a convent of over two hundred, as well as Benedictine humor, storytelling, and satire. All serve to illustrate the beauty and interconnectedness of life. Indeed, one of the recurrent themes in *The Cloister Walk* is the unexpected similarities between the monastic life and the artistic, between life in a Benedictine abbey and life in a small town.

Because of the availability and popularity of recordings of liturgical chant by Benedictine monks in the 1990's, monasticism has experienced a revival of interest among the American public. It is difficult to say whether Norris' meditations on her monastic experiences will foster a renaissance of *lectio divina*, the method of scriptural meditation encountered in both monasteries and many religious retreat houses. Nevertheless, *The Cloister Walk* is a wise and informative book, offering moments of courageous insight and lyrical beauty.

Stella Nesanovich

Sources for Further Study

America. CLXXV, August 31, 1996, p. 29.
The Christian Century. CXIII, October 9, 1996, p. 940.
The Christian Science Monitor. May 30, 1996, p. 14.
Commonweal. CXXIII, May 17, 1996, p. 26.
Cross Currents. XLVI, Fall, 1996, p. 403.

First Things. December, 1996, p. 30.
Library Journal. CXXI, March 15, 1996, p. 76.
Los Angeles Times. May 21, 1996, p. E1.
The New York Times Book Review. CI, May 5, 1996, p. 12.
The New Yorker. LXXII, June 17, 1996, p. 100.
Publishers Weekly. CCXLIII, February 26, 1996, p. 95.
Sojourners. XXV, November, 1996, p. 56.
The Women's Review of Books. XIV, November, 1996, p. 26.

COLLECTED POEMS, 1956-1994

Author: Thomas Kinsella (1928-   )
Publisher: Oxford University Press (New York). 339 pp. Paperback $19.95
Type of work: Poetry

One of the best-known poets of the twentieth century, Irish-born Thomas Kinsella composes distinctive lyrical verse that dramatizes love, death, and the inexorable march of time

Wedged between the two other giants of twentieth century Irish poetry, William Butler Yeats and Seamus Heaney, Thomas Kinsella has always assumed a kind of modest stance as an artist. He does not champion specifically Irish causes in the manner of Yeats, nor does he attempt to speak for the common laborers and tillers of the sod in the fashion of Seamus Heaney. Indeed, much of Kinsella's career has a distinctly non-Irish profile—and even a nonliterary slant. Oddly enough, Kinsella devoted himself to the study of science when he began his university studies, and ultimately he graduated from Dublin College with a degree in public administration, becoming a member of the Irish Civil Service, employed first by the Land Commission and then by the Department of Finance.

Like T. S. Eliot, who worked in a London bank, and Wallace Stevens, who served as a vice president for an insurance company, Thomas Kinsella managed to write his poetry while fully employed in the workaday world. No stranger to the world of business and ordinary work, Kinsella chose to celebrate the professions of urban workers and to describe the streets, parks, and neighborhoods of his beloved Dublin. His sonorous lyrics somehow sprang from the hard cobblestones of this old Irish city.

When not employed by the Irish government, Kinsella also put a great deal of time into translating traditional Gaelic poems (even though his own work is never chauvinistic or mawkishly patriotic). Notable titles in this area include his translation of the bloody Irish epic *The Tain* (1969) and *An Duanaire—An Irish Anthology: Poems of the Dispossessed, 1600-1900* (1980). As if bureaucratic work and translating were not sufficient distractions from his primary vocation of poetry, Kinsella also edited the work of other poets, such as Austin Clarke, whose *Selected Poems* (1980) is perhaps Kinsella's most successful editorial enterprise.

So Kinsella's own poetic output is quite extraordinary, given these severe demands on his time. Between 1956 and 1991, for example, he brought out more than twenty volumes of his own poetry. And, as if to underscore the central place of poetry in Kinsella's life, many of those poems are concerned with the act of writing itself or with the transcendent quality of metaphors and other figurative language. This preoccupation with the artistic process is evident even in the opening poem of *Collected Poems, 1956-1994*, which bears the telling title of "Echoes":

> An echo deepens as the past recedes;
> Words like swans are swallowed into the reeds
> With lapping airs and graces.
> Speechless white necks dip in the fugal pause
> When streaming images transfigure the dove that was.

Many of these early poems employ a somewhat strange and contorted syntax, one more sign that the poet was experimenting with and testing the limits of language:

> Turns again in my room,
> The crippled leopard.
> Paw-pad, configured
> Yellow light of his eyes,
> Pass, repass, repass.

Somewhat less obliquely—and with a wry sense of humor—Kinsella examines the writer-figure behind the writing process, especially the obligatory roles and poses that the writer must assume:

> *I wonder whether one expects*
> *Flowing tie or expert sex*
> *Or even absent-mindedness*
> *Of poets any longer. Less*
> *Candour than the average,*
> *Less confidence, a ready rage*
> *Alertness when it comes to beer,*
> *An affectation that their ear,*
> *For music is a little weak*
> *These are the attributes we seek.*

Later, in *New Poems* (1973), Kinsella offers a confessional report of his own writing process, and the reader beholds the poet/editor/translator trying to compose at his kitchen table. "Many a time," he explains,

> I have risen from my gnawed books
> and prowled about, wrapped in a long grey robe,
> and rubbed my forehead; reached for my instruments
> .   .   .   .
> my book propped before me, eaten forkfuls
> of scrambled egg and buttered fresh bread
> and taken hot tea until the sweat stood out
> at the roots of my hair!

In a similar vein, Kinsella writes passionately and melodiously about the traditional theme of love, addressing many love poems to his wife, like the short but effective lyric entitled "*Je t'adore*":

> The other props are gone.
> Sighing in one another's
> Iron arms, propped above nothing,
> We praise Love the limiter.

Another love poem takes the form of a letter-prose poem that is addressed to his "Beloved" and concludes thus:

Love also, it seems, will continue until we fail: in the sensing of the wider scope, in the growth toward it, in the swallowing and absorption of bitterness, in the resumed innocence.

In *Song of the Night and Other Poems* (1978), Kinsella includes a poem entitled "Artists' Letters," in which the poet pokes around in a cardboard box, discovering an apparently lost packet of love letters secured with a rubber band. The letters are full of foolishness, but they resonate with a poignant full-heartedness that elicits this response from the now mature poet:

> There is one throw, no more, One
> offering: make it. With no style
> —these are desperate times. There is
> a poverty of spirit in the wind;
> a shabby richness in braving it.
> My apologies, but you are my beloved
> and I will not be put off.

If poems about artistic creation and the persistence of love are staples in the canon of Thomas Kinsella, it is not surprising to discover a parallel track of poems about death, the subject that ennobles and complements the theme of love. Death necessitates love and art, the most positive antidotes to the great negation of death. Most of Kinsella's poems on the subject of death are elegies, even if they eulogize in a somewhat informal or candid way. Chief among such poems is "Tear," a kind of pre-elegy that describes Kinsella's horrifying visit to his grandmother's deathbed. The room reeks of "disused/ organs and sour kidney," and the poet is trapped in a wave of nausea: "Was I to kiss her? As soon/ kiss the damp that crept/ in the flowered walls/ of this pit." Steeling himself for the experience, he is utterly surprised at the appearance of a single tear, which arrives like an unbidden guest: "a single drop// splashed. And I found/ what I was looking for."

The most famous poem on the theme of death is *Butcher's Dozen* (1972), a book-length poem inspired by the shooting of thirteen civil rights demonstrators by the occupying British soldiers in Derry on January 30, 1972—a well-documented event. Kinsella's poem is a radical departure for him, since the work takes the form of thirteen ghostly voices discoursing on their deaths and the general chaos in Northern Ireland. *Butcher's Dozen* is easily the most political poem in *Collected Poems*, but Kinsella handles his potentially inflammatory material with a certain philosophical detachment. It is plain that his sympathies lie with the slain demonstrators, but the poem becomes a universal statement against war and suffering rather than a topical indictment of British policy or Protestant intolerance. The tragedy will certainly continue unless radical change occurs, as one of the ghosts eloquently explains:

> 'My curse on the cunning and the bland
> On gentlemen who loot a land
> They do not care to understand;
> Who keep the natives on their paws

> With ready lash and rotten laws;
> Then if the beasts erupt in rage
> Give them a slightly larger cage
> And, in scorn and fear combined,
> Turn them against their own kind.'

Kinsella also penned three famous elegies, each one addressed to a personal hero or role model: *Vertical Man* (1973) for the Irish musician and composer Sean O'Riada; *The Good Fight* (1973) for President John F. Kennedy; and "Memory of W. H. Auden" in homage to the English poet whose elegance and formal phrasing played a formative role in Kinsella's artistic development. For Sean O'Riada, Kinsella has these words:

> I thought we had laid you to rest
> —that you had been directed toward
> crumbling silence, and the like.
> It seems it is hard to keep
> a vertical man down.

Of John Kennedy, scion of an Irish emigrant family that did well in the new country of America, Kinsella notes that, after his assassination, "great numbers of people":

> couldn't sleep, and lost appetite. Children experienced
> alarm at the sight of their parents crying.
> There were many who admitted
> they expected the President's ghost to appear.

Kinsella also experiences a kind of vision of the craggy-faced, chain-smoking poet W. H. Auden, who dominated the literary landscape in the 1930's, still exerting considerable influence at the time of his death in 1973. For Kinsella, Auden becomes a true mentor, a sort of artistic father-figure, all the more painful to lose:

> staring down out of the Thirties
> —rapt, radiant with vision and opinion,
> flawed with the final furrows.
> Secondary father, with cigarette.

Even though these poems about art, life, and death tend to provide a thematic framework for the collection as a whole, careful readers will notice that, subject matter notwithstanding, the poems tend to become progressively looser, less formal, and more conversational. At the same time, Kinsella seems to penetrate deeper and deeper into the texture of his life, trying to replicate the innerness of his dream-life and psychic states. Much of this shift in attention can be attributed to his study of the Swiss psychologist Carl Gustav Jung. In the poem entitled "C. G. Jung's 'First Years,' " Kinsella speaks of the "disappearing particulars" of dreams and tries his best to recover them in later poems, especially *Songs of the Psyche* (1985), the title poem of which contains these haunting images of the ephemeral nature of dreams:

> Night foxes
> body masks
>
> tilted up, eyes
> a city of lights
>
> a cistern hiss
> in their erect ears
>
> they are dreaming
> one another.

"Dream," from *Open Court* (1991), contains this eerie transcription of a dream. The reader is asked to imagine a "stony desert, baked and still," where

> A creature scuffles among the rocks
> and stops, harrying its own vitals.
> Another figure stands still on one foot,
> pulling its head down between its shoulders,
> torn by a great extinct beak. Other shapes
> are lying here and there in the dust.

There are probably many influences in this poem besides that of Jung; one suspects at least some—possibly unconscious—encouragement from the neo-primitivism of British Poet Laureate Ted Hughes and his monumental book of archetypal poems, *Crow* (1971). These dream-poems may seem to exist at a far remove from Kinsella's earliest work, but the sensitive readers will observe that the early lyrics and nature poems are themselves conceived in dream-language, or at least in dream states. They are, in short, visionary poems. The title poem of *Another September* (1958) offers a graphic example of sensory perception, rich assonance, and an aura that is not quite of this world:

> Dreams fled away, this country bedroom, raw
> With the touch of the dawn, wrapped in a minor peace,
> Hears through an open window the garden draw
> Long pitch black breaths, lay bare its apple trees
> Ripe pear trees, brambles, windfall-sweetened soil,
> Exhale rough sweetness against the starry slates.

Kinsella envisions the city of Dublin in much the same way in "Baggot Street Deserta," his most frequently anthologized poem. A "shy"

> Gasp of waters in the gorse
> Is sonneting origins. Dreamers' heads
> Lie mesmerised in Dublin's beds
> Flashing with images, Adam's morse.

Poetry, that special morse code "flashing with images," is Thomas Kinsella's privileged speech. What makes the appearance of this American edition of *Collected Poems, 1956-1994* especially welcome is that fact that many new readers can now discover the pleasures of a mature and fascinating poet.

Daniel L. Guillory

Source for Further Study

South Atlantic Quarterly. XCV, Winter, 1996, p. 145.

THE COLLECTED STORIES OF MAVIS GALLANT

Author: Mavis Gallant (1922–   )
Publisher: Random House (New York). 887 pp. $45.00
Type of work: Short stories

Fifty-two stories, all but one first published in The New Yorker, *by an acclaimed modern master of the short-story form*

Mavis Gallant is one of those troublesome authors often referred to as "a writer's writer." The designation is double–edged, for on the one hand it suggests someone whose writing is so professional and polished that it is best appreciated by those who are themselves capable of writing highly crafted prose; on the other hand, it often suggests someone who is seldom read by anyone else but other writers. Gallant's case is further complicated by the fact that of the fifty–two stories in this collection (out of the more than one hundred stories she has written since 1950) all but one of them originally appeared in *The New Yorker* magazine. Furthermore, until his retirement in the mid-1970's, all were personally accepted by the editor and author William Maxwell, a short–story writer himself, whose themes, characters, and styles are quite similar to those of Mavis Gallant. Although *The New Yorker* is notorious for capturing authors and holding on to them—John Updike and John Cheever are two of the most famous examples—Gallant's literary situation presents a strange, but not unheard of, case of the total output of one author being sustained in print almost solely by the taste of another author.

This may account for the fact that all of Gallant's stories, at least the fifty percent of them she has chosen to include in this hefty collection, sound very much alike. It is as though she found her literary milieu very early (Maxwell published her first story in 1950 when she was in her late twenties) and has stuck to it untiringly ever since. In her preface to *The Collected Stories,* Gallant insists, quite rightly, that short stories are not chapters of novels and should not be read one after another as if they were meant to follow along. Although a number of her stories focus on the same characters as they develop over time and therefore could be read together as if they were chapters in a novel, it would indeed be exhausting to read a great many of Gallant's stories one after another; although the plots and characters change, they change only slightly, and the rhythm of the prose is fairly consistent throughout this volume.

An example can be seen in two stories that focus on the same characters, "Speck's Idea" and "Overhead in a Balloon." The first focuses on Sandor Speck, who runs an art gallery in Paris. As are most art fanciers in Gallant's stories, Speck is more interested in artistic reputations than in artistic merit. The plot concerns his ineffectual efforts to revive interest in a forgotten artist so that he can profit by a renewed interest in his gallery. Yet in this comic satiric story that reads much like minor Henry James, Speck, after much wrangling with the artist's widow for a number of his canvases, fails to bring off his artistic/commercial coup. "Overhead in a Balloon," the title story of one of Gallant's collections, centers on Speck's assistant Walter. Speck never appears in the story but is unflatteringly referred to throughout by Walter as "trout face"; the character Walter is so similar to Speck that with a name change they would be relatively indistinguishable. Like his boss, Walter is also made the ineffectual victim of an artist who, like Walter and Speck, is more concerned with the practical matters of establishing reputation than he is interested in the integrity of art.

Four interrelated stories focus on Henri Grippes, a Parisian novelist, diarist, and critic, who, like Speck and Walter, lives on the fringes of the artistic life, and who focuses his attention on making a name for himself by capitalizing on the rising and falling stock of various literary and artistic fashions. In "A Painful Affair," Grippes is passed over to speak at the commemoration ceremony for a wealthy patron of the arts by a man that Grippes feels is only a minor critic and thinker. "A Flying Start" moves back in time to the story of how the lesser critic courted the favor of the benefactress and thus edged Grippes out of his moment of fame. The theme of changing fashions of what constitutes art and therefore what establishes fame is emphasized throughout the story by a sort of running gag about a planned dictionary of literary biography that over the years is constantly altered because of changes in literary taste and thus is never produced. In "Grippes and Poche," Grippes fights a continual battle with a tax auditor who, because he is an admirer, saves Grippes from financial harm; finally in "In Plain Sight," Grippes, grown old and crotchety, ironically complains about the increasing commercialization of the arty area of Paris where he has lived for so many years. These stories reflect a representative side of Gallant's work—her skill at creating comic satire about the artistic life—which partially explains why she is often referred to as a writer's writer.

Another series of four interrelated stories follows the life of a man, Edouard B., who, having married an older Jewish–born actress during World War II so she would not be captured by the Nazis, finds that, although he has never lived with her, he remains somehow responsible for her. Like many other male characters in the Gallant gallery, Edouard finds himself trapped by past romantic ideals. "A Recollection" recounts the story of the marriage and the couple's journey to safety in the south of France where they part company. The second story, "The Colonel's Child," deals with Edouard's meeting his second wife, Juliette; the third one, "Rue de Lillie," focuses on Juliette, who sees through to Edouard's first marriage with the actress Magdalena, as if they were characters in a fiction, albeit a fiction in which she too is entangled. The final story, "Lena," centers on a meeting between Magdalena and Edouard when they are eighty and sixty–five respectively, both still bound together by an idealistic gesture many years in the past.

Another significant series of four interrelated stories focus on the Carette family. The first, "1933," introduces Mme Carette and her two daughters, Berthe and Marie, shortly after the death of her husband has plunged them into genteel poverty. The strict social conventions of the Montreal middle–class Carette family is most clearly reflected by the mother's insistence that the children never refer to her as a seamstress, but must say instead, "My mother was clever with her hands." "The Chosen Husband" focuses on the family in 1949 after Mme Carette's receipt of a legacy of eighteen thousand dollars from a brother–in–law makes it possible for the daughters, now in their early twenties to marry. The plot of the story centers on Marie's courtship with Louis Driscoll, which provides an occasion for social satire in the fashion of Henry James or Jane Austen. For example, when Driscoll makes his first call and gets choked on one of his own chocolates, Gallant describes it delicately as, "He was in trouble with a caramel," and the Carettes look away so that the young man can "strangle unobserved." The last two stories of the Carette family, "From Cloud to Cloud" and "Florida," jump many years ahead to focus on Marie's son Raymond when he enlists in the American army during the Vietnam War and then later when he settles in Florida and marries a rather common (by old Montreal social standards) young divorcée. The story ends with Raymond storming out after a minor quarrel, leaving his mother and his pregnant wife once again without a man in the house, thus bringing the saga full circle.

Although Gallant is not a popular writer widely enough read to make any one of her stories well known (she is seldom anthologized in the ubiquitous literature anthologies that keep short stories alive for undergraduate and graduate students, nor are her stories chosen for the highly visible *Best American Short Stories* or *O. Henry Award Stories* collections), some of the strongest and most memorable works in this collection are the title stories of some of her earlier anthologies, such as "The Pegnitz Junction" and "Across the Bridge." The first, the longest story in *The Collected Stories* focuses on a young woman who becomes involved with an older man (not an unusual situation in a Gallant story) who is divorced and has custody of his young son. The story follows the threesome on a holiday trip that becomes a minor nightmare when, because of an airline shutdown, they must return home on a train that winds its way slowly and tortuously through the European landscape as the young woman tries to cope with a spoiled child and a man who cannot evenly divide his time and attention between his son and his lover. The title of the story, of course, refers to an important junction in the relationship of the three people.

"Across the Bridge" also has a metaphoric title. The bridge is at first merely a physical presence, for the story begins with the narrator Sylvie walking across a bridge in Paris with her mother who has the invitations to her wedding in a leather shopping bag. When Sylvie tells her mother she has her heart set on another young man, saying she has thoughts of throwing herself off the bridge if she is forced to marry the family choice instead of the man she loves, her mother dumps the invitations off the bridge into the water. The story develops in typical drawing–room comedy fashion with Sylvie falling in love with her family's original choice after all. It ends in romantic poignancy as Sylvie takes the long way home after seeing her fiancé board his train, for she thinks it unfair to arrive home before he does. She says she will never tell anyone about this, that it will remain a small and insignificant secret that belongs to the "true life" she is almost ready to enter. This is the bridge crossing reflected by the title of the story; it is a significant metaphor for many of Gallant's stories, for often small and seemingly insignificant secrets are what give her fiction its life.

Gallant's stories are often irresolute and seemingly unpatterned. When she was writing a weekly column about radio for the *Montreal Standard* newspaper in the late 1940's, she once described one writer's plays as being unlike the usual radio play because they did not come to a traditional fictional climax, defending this practice by arguing that real problems do not always resolve themselves in tidy ways and that if stories seem incomplete, that is because they are true. In spite of this seeming allegiance to the relatively ragged nature of reality rather than to the neat patterns of art, however, Gallant claims in one of her essays that style is intentional and inseparable from structure. Indeed, all of Gallant's stories reflect this apparent paradox. Whereas they seem relatively artless, simple sketches of minor characters caught in impasses of their own making, they are carefully crafted and highly stylized structures of rigid social patterns. Gallant has described her method of getting something on paper as a painfully precise play with the language: "I could not move on to the second sentence until the first sounded true. True to what? Some arrangement in my head, I suppose." In describing her "outrageous slowness," Gallant says that she sometimes puts aside parts of a story for months, even years. The story is finished when it seems to "tally with a plan I surely must have had in mind but cannot describe, or when I come to the conclusion that it cannot be written satisfactorily any other way, at least not by me." It is precisely this kind of care for the individual word and sentence that has lead to Mavis Gallant often being referred to as "a writer's writer."

Charles E. May

Sources for Further Study

Chicago Tribune. October 27, 1996, XIV, p. 7.
Houston Chronicle. October 27, 1996, p. Z23.
Library Journal. CXXI, August, 1996, p. 116.
Los Angeles Times Book Review. October 6, 1996, p. 1.
The New Republic. CCXV, November 25, 1996, p. 42.
The New York Times Book Review. CI, October 13, 1996, p. 11.
Publishers Weekly. CCXLIII, August 5, 1996, p. 431.
Saturday Night. CXI, October, 1996, p. 109.
Times-Picayune. November 24, 1996, p. D7.
The Wall Street Journal. September 16, 1996, p. A16.

COLLECTED WORKS
Volume I: 1956-1976

Author: Paul Metcalf (1917-   )
Publisher: Coffee House Press (Minneapolis, Minnesota). 591 pp. $35.00
Type of work: Fiction; history; collage

The work of a great American original is retrieved and made available to a wider readership

Paul Metcalf is one of the undiscovered treasures of American literature in the second half of the twentieth century, and the publication of his *Collected Works* by Coffee House Press is an occasion for rejoicing. This first volume, issued in the fall of 1996, will be followed by two more, the final volume planned for the fall of 1997 to coincide with Metcalf's eightieth birthday.

Metcalf's obscurity is not what is interesting about him—he should not be read *because* he is relatively unknown—but it is the necessary starting point. That which cannot be readily categorized is likely to be ignored, and it has been Metcalf's fate to write in a form that eludes familiar labels. He is not a poet, although his literary "fathers" are Ezra Pound, William Carlos Williams, and Charles Olson. He is not a novelist, though he began his career by writing fiction. He is not a historian, though many of his books are largely assemblages of historical source-material. He is an artist of collage—but he notes that "collage" suggests a static image, whereas his texts unfold in time, with a narrative drive. He proposes the unhelpful term "narrative hieroglyph," and compares his books to totem poles (see the essay "Totem Paul: A Self-Review," in *Where Do You Put the Horse?*, reviewed in *Magill's Literary Annual, 1987*).

One of the virtues of this first volume is that it allows the reader to observe the development of Metcalf's distinctive style. There's an excitement, apart from the pleasures of the individual works gathered here, in seeing how a powerfully original artist discovered his medium. Few readers could have predicted from Metcalf's first book, the novella *Will West* (1956), the riches that lay ahead. *Will West* is Metcalf's closest published approach to conventional fiction. (An earlier work, a conventional novel, "failed to move the hearts of New York editors," Metcalf recalls.) The protagonist, Will West, is a young Cherokee Indian pitching in the minor leagues. He meets a white woman on a sunny, deserted beach, where they make love and frolic in the waves—and where, suddenly, Will chokes her to death. After the murder, he returns home briefly to his mother's cabin in the Smokey Mountains, then—wounded by police—flees west. Intercut with this narrative are passages set in italics. At first these are stream-of-consciousness passages that open a window to Will's thoughts, but as the novella proceeds these counterpoint sections are unidentified excerpts from historical texts, ranging from early Spanish encounters with Indians in America to scenes from the Civil War.

As a novella, *Will West* does not succeed. The interplay between the fictional narrative and the historical extracts seems contrived, and the fictional scenes, despite some local intensity, lack verisimilitude. There is a curious affinity between this book and the French *nouveau roman*, not a matter of influence but of imaginative convergence: like Alain Robbe-Grillet and Claude Simon, Metcalf displaces the attention of the reader accustomed to plot and character (there is a lot of attention to geography in *Will West*).

From *Will West* to Metcalf's second book, *Genoa: A Telling of Wonders*, written in the 1950's but not published until 1965, is an enormous jump. Metcalf's most complex book and his best known (though still it has never had anything approaching a large readership), *Genoa* resembles *Will West* to the extent that it combines a fictional narrative with extracts from other texts. Yet it is a far more audacious, more assured assemblage.

Three facts about Metcalf are essential background to *Genoa*. First, he is a great-grandson of Herman Melville, and he was reared in a home that became a shrine to the Melville revival, presided over by his mother, Eleanor Melville Metcalf. Growing up, Metcalf rebelled against all this, but ultimately (in part following the lead of Charles Olson) he reencountered Melville on his own terms. Second, Metcalf is an autodidact. He left Harvard in his first year there, and that—as he has proudly proclaimed—was the extent of his formal higher education. He is a prodigious reader who has acquired his knowledge independently, with the peculiar strengths and weaknesses of the self-taught (the latter outweighed by the former, but still to be noted). Third, he was an adept of Dianetics, the movement founded by L. Ron Hubbard and later transformed into Scientology. By that time, Metcalf has said, he had concluded that Hubbard was a con man, but he adds, "It is a truism that some of the most brilliant minds may be found in the heads of confidence men." So while rejecting Hubbard's promotion of Scientology as a quasi-religion, Metcalf retained from Dianetics "the notion that all memory is *theoretically* recoverable, from conception to the present," and extended this from the case of the individual to all of human history.

And so *Genoa* is both an extraordinary meditation on the life and work of Herman Melville (especially on Christopher Columbus' influence on Melville) and an interlacing of all manner of strange lore, framed by the story of the fictional brothers Michael and Carl Mills: Michael, the Melvillean narrator, and Carl, his monstrous *Doppelgänger*. A typical page of *Genoa* resembles a page of Pound's *Cantos*, Williams' *Paterson*, and Olson's *Maximus Poems*, juxtaposing texts from heterogeneous sources with different typefaces, playing against each other. (*Genoa* was published by Jonathan Williams's Jargon Press, the publisher of *Maximus*; its publication was subsidized by Metcalf's mother, even though she hated the book's dark view of Melville.) The sumptuous look of the first edition of *Genoa*—the poetry of the page layout—is lost to some extent in the smaller format of the Coffee House Press edition, as is true of *Patagoni* and other Metcalf texts, but that is a price well worth paying to have these works in accessible form.

If there is a single lesson to this wild tapestry of a book, it is that history matters. Not, Metcalf is quick to add, history as it is practiced by many academic historians, "who retreated thirty years ago into, let's say, the eighteenth century and [haven't] been heard from since" (see his essay "The Poet and History," in *Where Do You Put the Horse?*). Indeed, Metcalf writes, "History is important only insofar as it impinges on the present." This passionate engagement with history is Metcalf's antidote for the

vast world . . . inhabited by scientologists and science fictioneers, UFO seekers and Brooklyn Buddhists, evangelical Christians and home-study astrologers— . . . all of them, in this uncertain and corrupt world, escaping into constructs that avoid the hard and/or glorious realities of their own genetic and cultural heritage. History and evolution may appear to disappear—and it may be comforting to believe in the imminent end of the world. But the world, manifestly, does not end. And all that you are, past and present, once more comes into focus, every morning, when you awaken.

In *Genoa*, for the first time, Metcalf appended a bibliography at the end of the book to acknowledge the sources he had used. In subsequent works the bibliographies would become more extensive, though he continued to leave it up to the curious reader to track down, among the many titles listed, the source of any given quotation, believing that notes or similar citations "would have broken the flow, the rhythms." If *Genoa* was the book in which Metcalf found himself as a writer, establishing the form he would employ with variations through the rest of his career, it also marked a terminus. After this book, he dropped the scaffolding of fiction entirely. Never again did he plunge into psychological depths as he did here. And finally, while he continued to specialize in provocative juxtapositions, he simplified and clarified his designs. *Genoa* was one of a kind, a book into which he poured everything.

The remaining three works in this first volume, *Patagoni* (1971), *The Middle Passage* (1976), and *Apalache* (1976), show Metcalf writing the kind of books he had taught himself to write. (One cannot imagine anyone else writing them.) *Patagoni*, as Guy Davenport suggests in his introduction to this volume, "may be Metcalf's most congenial book." Here Metcalf explores contrasts and affinities between North America and South America, between twentieth century American culture and the culture of the Incas. In part this is playfulness; the dust jacket of the original Jargon Society edition of *Patagoni* features a photo of Henry Ford next to a photo of an Andean Indian, a la "Separated at Birth?" (The resemblance is striking, and in the text there are references to Ford's belief in reincarnation.) Yet Metcalf has a point to make as well.

In an essay titled "The Scene," Metcalf quotes from an interview with Robert Creeley, in which Creeley describes an encounter with an Indian in southern Mexico. For Creeley—and for Metcalf—this Indian embodies "the centering of physical being, the sensory system absolutely alert . . . vis à vis the awful success of the process of objectivity, the mind with almost no consciousness of the body it lives in" (ellipses Metcalf's). That comment might serve as a gloss for *Patagoni*, and for Metcalf's work as a whole. In *Patagoni*, Ford's intelligence is splendidly physical, suspicious of abstraction, working by touch. And in Metcalf's scheme this rhymes with the genius of Andean culture. (We also see this culture in its debased modern form, in letters and diary entries from a trip Metcalf took to South America in 1959. As with *Genoa*, there was a long hiatus between the writing of *Patagoni* and its publication.)

Metcalf's insistence on the physical as against the disembodied mind seems unbalanced in its own way, a corrective carried too far. (And the spiritual? It is not even on his radar, except as an object of scorn.) Yet it does energize his language. *Patagoni*— the same is true of *The Middle Passage* and *Apalache* and any other Metcalf text—is a feast for the tongue. Whether he is quoting from a geologist on the South American land or savoring Inca words, Metcalf is a connoisseur of language. Like Ezra Pound, he has an eye for the luminous detail and an unfailing ear for the rhythmic phrase.

That sense of language, in which the craftsman and the musician share equally, gives Metcalf's collages a classical gravity and beauty—a quality that sharply distinguishes his work from the typical productions of the contemporary avant-garde. *The Middle Passage* is a very short, intense book that, in its conception, sounds like a self-indulgence funded by an arts grant. Subtitled "A Triptych of Commodities," it considers in turn the futile Luddite rebellion against mechanized knitting ("Ludd"), the slave trade, and particularly conditions on the slave ships ("Efik"), and finally whales and whaling ("Orca"). Yet there is nothing self-indulgent about this work, nor is there any of the obscurantism that passes for art in many circles. *The Middle Passage* communicates with great clarity an overwhelming sense of tragedy, a deep awareness of the perennial human temptation to commodify everything.

Apalache is tragic too in its evocation of native peoples wiped out as European settlers crowded the eastern coast of North America, and its tracing of the legacy of slavery. In counterpoint, there are passages full of wonder at the bounty and the beauty of the American land, and stretches of geology turned into poetry, and strange Indian words, and a seasoning of Yankee humor. None of this is news, exactly; we may think we know it all. Yet the language of the texts Metcalf weaves together is fresh and pungent and gritty, and the juxtapositions are striking, as when in parallel columns we follow contemporary accounts of the abortive slave uprising planned by Denmark Vesey, a former slave who had purchased his freedom, in Charleston, South Carolina, in 1821-1822, and newspaper reports from 1961 concerning Robert Williams, a "militant Negro leader" in Monroe, North Carolina, who is charged with kidnapping a white couple during an outbreak of racial violence and who eventually flees to Cuba.

None of this is presented with a strident air. There is plenty to argue with in the implicit history of America that *Apalache* puts forward, but Metcalf does not cajole or wheedle or scold; he does not lecture or pontificate. He invites the reader to join him. Thanks to Coffee House Press, many more readers will have a chance to accept the invitation.

John Wilson

Sources for Further Study

Booklist. XCIII, November 15, 1996, p. 566.
Columbus Dispatch. November 10, 1996, p. G7.
Library Journal. CXXI, November 15, 1996, p. 65.
Publishers Weekly. CCXLIII, September 9, 1996, p. 29.
St. Paul Pioneer Press. November 12, 1996, p. C8.

THE CONSCIOUS MIND
In Search of a Fundamental Theory

Author: David J. Chalmers (1966-   )
Publisher: Oxford University Press (New York). 414 pp. $29.95
Type of work: Philosophy

Chalmers examines a variety of contemporary theories about human consciousness and provides his own fundamental theory, which rejects a reductionist approach and yet remains compatible with a modern scientific worldview

Can a relationship between consciousness and science be taken seriously? While such an esoteric topic may be off-putting to the reader untrained in philosophical navigation, David Chalmers has tried to make the waters floating his theory of human consciousness smooth. The book's crossover question represents an intriguing and ambitious project for a philosopher, whose kind do not often understand or concern themselves with the scientific world. For the nonprofessional reader, asterisks next to the titles of certain sections are included to alert him or her that the starred sections are written especially for those trained in philosophy and dedicated to the pursuit of some of its deeper questions. Reading the designated sections does not yield evidence that they were appreciably more difficult than the rest of the text, however.

In the first section of the book (chapters 1 and 2), the problems of trying to account for consciousness and the framework in which they can be studied are addressed. Although human beings experience consciousness in an intimately familiar way, its nature poses a difficult philosophical question: How can a system of functioning physical realities produce what we know as the experience of experiencing? The author is interested here in exploring the phenomenological dimension of the question rather than consciousness' psychological aspect. He examines the connections or dependency (supervenience) of consciousness on the natural order of things. He endeavors to go beyond a merely nominal, factual, or even a functional explanation of consciousness. In the early chapters Chalmers sets out to eliminate solutions which he judges inadequate. He notes, "Mere natural supervenience is ontologically expensive." Therefore he concludes that "it is fortunate that logical supervenience is the rule and natural supervenience the exception."

The second section of the book (chapters 3-5) asserts that an explanation for consciousness cannot be reduced to a mere scientific or materialistic calculus. Consequently the author selects a dualistic model to explain the phenomenon, tentatively claiming for his model some element of truth. His central insight, explored in chapter 4, designates "property dualism" as the only reasonable option to explain consciousness. He sets up four premises:

1. Conscious experience exists.
2. Conscious experience is not logically supervenient on the physical.
3. If there are phenomena that are not logically supervenient on the physical facts, then materialism is false.
4. The physical domain is causally closed.

Having set up his premises, he proceeds to dissect them cleanly, disposing of arguments that may be raised against each of them. At the end he has exposed the bones of his own option.

Yet it is clear that his "property dualism" solution to the problem of consciousness is not a totally satisfactory answer for many thinkers, especially for those who favor a reductively materialistic explanation. Yet Chalmers undercuts partisans for materialism with the quip, "You can't have your materialistic cake and eat your consciousness too." He dismisses holding a purely scientific worldview by arguing that his position "requires us to give up little that is *important* [emphasis his]. . . . It merely requires us to give up a dogma." He replaces such "dogma" with his own "credo": "If this is dualism, then we should learn to love dualism." Even in the labored exposition of very difficult material, the author does not forsake a sense of humor.

His thesis that consciousness is not a totally material phenomenon will likely be particularly intriguing to theologians. It appears to take natural law theory seriously. Generally, modern philosophers have dismissed natural law as a rather quaint and archaic relic of philosophical history, kept on life support by a few religious thinkers. Yet it is not altogether persuasive that, in the end, his theory really does go beyond the materialism he eschews.

Chapter 5 takes up the distinction between cognition and consciousness. Cognition is simply sensation, a basic awareness of encountered objects (this is a red book); consciousness is perception about things at a deeper level. In the act of perception the subject is engaged not only in a phenomenological task, but in an activity that stems from his or her psychology. The first order experience of the red book proceeds to a second order judgment about that experience ("I am having an experience or sensation of something red"). Finally, human consciousness has the capacity to reflect on the meaning of experiences for the subject ("Sensations are mysterious.") in a third order judgment. Not everyone who sees a red book will likely attribute the same meaning to that experience at this more personal reflective level. Sam's conclusion, "Red is marvelous—my favorite color," will not be congruent with Shana's "My favorite childhood book was red." Consciousness appears to function uniquely to determine for the particular individual what the ultimate content of experience will be for him or for her.

The concepts addressed here are by no means simple; they require the reader's careful attention, and often some rereading, to avoid losing the thread of the argument. Yet the author's dedication to thoroughness demands a rigorous pursuit of the arguments that support his thesis, as well as the disposal of counterarguments. It is not surprising, then, that the brunt of the latter portion of this chapter and others is given over to answering the arguments that could be mounted against his conclusions. Asterisks abound.

The coherence between cognition and consciousness, grounded in a set of psychological laws governing the relationship between consciousness and physically demonstrable systems, is the basis for the author's theory. The exposition of this connection considers the strong link between consciousness and cognition: persons' judgments that experience occurs appear to be connected to real experiences. If persons are asked what they perceive, their answers will provide reliable crumbs pointing the trail toward the nature of consciousness.

The direct correlation between coherence and cognition does not deny that it is possible to ignore what is perceived and thereby to be unaware of what is available in the nexus of an experience. This objection, however, does not negate Chalmers' hypothesis. Experience that persons can access data but in fact do not does not mean that a particular experience is not available to them. Further, it is also possible to be conscious of something that is not immediately present to observation. I am aware of my coat lying on the seat of my car, even though I am currently standing in the kitchen; I know who is currently president of the United States, although neither he nor accessible proof of that statement are available to me at the precise moment I make that statement.

The author finds parallels between what he proposes and contemporary scientific theories, particularly in the field of physics. He suggests that his theory, like some in physics, should be simple enough to be printed out on the front of a T-shirt—an interesting idea! His humorous asides consistently lighten the task for the persistent reader. As in earlier chapters, he sets forth his position and its alternatives and carefully eliminates the alternatives.

Where does the evidence to support his proposed "laws" originate? The author suggests the use of empirical data, gathered through the rather ordinary means of simply asking people about their own experiences. He understands that this methodology does not fully conform to the pure and rigorous model that characterizes scientific inquiry, but he believes it is sufficient for his purposes. His hypothesis, then, is: Where there is consciousness, there is awareness.

Even given its limits as a scientific process, Chalmers considers his theory useful as a pre-experimental basis for scientific inquiry into facts about experience. Every scientific investigation begins with some axiom. Used as such, Chalmers' theory bridges the gap to the physical components of knowledge about experience, even when they are not made explicit. Essentially this chapter details more fully what he has presented earlier in the book.

In the third major division of the book (chapters 6, 7, and 8) the reader finds the meat of the author's "positive theory of consciousness," in its coherence to cognition. Besides using empirical evidence, the author explores principles of plausibility, simplicity, and aesthetics. He advances what he calls "the principle of organizational invariance." Identical systems will process data in identical ways with predictably similar results. Within an entity, one can theoretically substitute one medium of information transfer for another (computer chips for neurons, for example) and expect the same results. The key is to replace the medium but to preserve the systematic interconnection of the elements.

With the groundwork laid, the author can move to the conclusion that, in theory at least, beings other than human persons have the potential for consciousness. If there is a cognitive and cohesive system present, it is logical to infer that such a system would be conscious. He believes, for example, that a computer could be constructed that would be aware of its own activity. This extension of the author's thesis may ultimately call into question his dualistic notion of consciousness and reduce it to materialism after all. The author does not seem to think so, however. In essence, the imaginary HAL lives, a logical extension of Chalmers' conclusion. The instances of such entities, those who could function as true agents or persons, is expected to be small, however. The exposition of the theory ends with a list of open questions.

The final chapters (9 and 10) are what the author calls his "dessert." In them he offers applications of his theory to central questions in the foundations of artificial intelligence and quantum mechanics. He argues the case for the aggressive computer technology that might give rise to the conscious mind, which he had mentioned earlier. He makes some connections to the field of quantum mechanics.

Chalmers has written a dense and lengthy work to thoroughly cover the subject in a systematic manner. He has rendered a difficult and obtuse body of material almost accessible. Footnotes enhance the text with rich auxiliary information and cogent alternative arguments. The reading is made easier by the author's sense of whimsy and his good use of examples. Cartoon characters (such as Calvin and Hobbes), zombies, and robots march across the pages to exemplify the author's ideas. Following his use of black-eyed pea salad as an illustration to make a point, for example, the author offers a footnote with the recipe for the dish, a tasty reward for the persistent reader who has the courage to investigate the scholarly apparatus at the end of the text.

The book claims to target a popular audience, even identifying the "harder," more technical portions to accommodate them, as noted above. The unsophisticated reader, however, will have to struggle mightily; the book is not at all the pulp equivalent of easy-listening music heard in the dentist's office. While it can be conquered, success will come only at the price of some patience and effort. The question for one who does not share Chalmers' burning desire to solve the nature of consciousness is whether the battle is worth the effort. Readers who resonate with his passion, "in their bones," will no doubt devour it greedily.

Dolores L. Christie

Sources for Further Study

Choice. XXXIV, December, 1996, p. 625.
Library Journal. CXXI, July, 1996, p. 119.
Nature. CCCLXXXI, May 9, 1996, p. 123.
New Scientist. CLI, August 31, 1996, p. 40.
The New York Times Book Review. CI, December 29, 1996, p. 22.
Science News. CXLIX, June 15, 1996, p. 370.
Time. CXLVII, March 25, 1996, p. 50.
The Times Literary Supplement. June 21, 1996, p. 3.

CROSS CHANNEL

Author: Julian Barnes (1946-   )
Publisher: Alfred A. Knopf (New York). 211 pp. $21.00
Type of work: Short stories

Ten short stories exploring more than four centuries of cross-cultural exchange between Britain and France

The ten works constituting Julian Barnes's first collection of variously touching, provocative, and lighthearted short stories will inevitably reinforce in the reader a truth all but self-evident: that despite their relative geographical proximity and nearly a millennium of continual contact (not always under ideal circumstances), the French and English of the late twentieth century are only nominally closer to understanding one another and to sympathizing with each other's foibles than they were in the days of William the Conqueror. While Barnes's engaging volume directly traces this rivalrous relationship only as far back as Henri IV's Edict of Nantes, a 1598 decree granting religious tolerance for the Protestant Huguenots (and the backdrop for "Dragons"), a sense of the ongoing historical friction as well as the interdependence between these two fiercely chauvinistic nations conspicuously permeates every aspect of his book.

Pierre Chaigne, the main character in "Dragons," cannot refrain from generalizing the French position—be it the murderous icy wind, the livestock-devouring Beast of Gruissan, the commissioners from the Paris court who first explain Henri IV's proclamation, or the three Irish dragons who overrun his house and pressure the population to convert to Catholicism: "Everything bad came from the north." In "Junctions," the only other piece in *Cross Channel* presented from a decidedly French perspective, Dr. Achille, his wife Mme Julie, and the medical student Charles-André gawk at the beef-eating, hard-swearing British navvies imported to construct the Rouen-Le Havre railway while the narration coolly notes the familiar mundanity of the arrangement—after all, British captives under the Roman emperor Claudius had built the first road linking Lyon and Clermont-Ferrand way back in A.D. 45-46. The surprise these three worldly characters experience at not being set upon by gypsies, bandits, or locusts during their Sunday strolls through British work sites in the early 1840's provides the reader with a glimpse of the more relaxed cultural rapprochement between the two countries already looming on the horizon. This narrowing of distance is made especially manifest at the story's close, where Napoleon III awards the British engineer Brassey the Cross of the Légion d'honneur for his invaluable service to France.

In spite of its early twentieth century time frame, though, the collection's opening piece strikes the emblematic chord of sustained cultural estrangement for the nine stories to come. In "Interference," the dying English composer Leonard Verity hopes to hear his final work and putative masterpiece played on British Broadcasting Corporation (BBC) radio in the remote French village of Saint-Maure-de-Vercelles, where he has lived with his common-law wife for many years in self-imposed exile. The "interference" of the title, the reader learns, has at least three distinct meanings, only two of which are explained directly in the story: first, there is the static caused by the modern electrical apparatuses in the vicinity, which threatens to impair the quality of the broadcast; then there is the arrogant Verity's belief that the artist as creator is above the niceties (that is, interference) of societal responsibility and intercourse. Unspoken, though, is the third and most blatant example of interference, that of Verity's own implacable and uncompromising presence in a village where he has made little effort to act in a neighborly fashion toward the French inhabitants. For all Verity's pretensions to be a citizen of the world, the story's close confirms his standing as an unassimilated man without a country, alienated as much from the bourgeois, God-fearing England he despises as from the France he never considered home.

"Melon," in contrast, treats predictable Anglo-Gallic culture shock with greater irony and poignancy. Divided into three sections, the story opens with a letter home from Hamilton Lindsay, an English student traveling through France, to his beloved Evelina, the cousin and sweetheart he later marries. In this bright-eyed correspondence, the young Hamilton recounts the strangeness of the titular fruit there; his difficulty in growing accustomed to Catholic fast days; the impossibility of coming across hot water with which to prepare tea, and the unappetizing quality to the small bloody birds one is served for supper. Still, Lindsay, who is referred to as "Sir" in the second section of "Melon" and as "General" by the third (in which he awaits a prisoner exchange while interned in France during the Napoleonic Wars), blithely enjoys his reputation for being a "Galloman," due to his lifelong cultivated fondness for things French. This in spite of his extreme Britishness and the impoverished relationship to his second country he must endure in the diminished capacity of his declining years.

Another story highlighting the inevitability of cultural division brought to bear by history and custom is "Hermitage." In this work, Florence and Emily, a lesbian couple eager to leave behind the stuffy provinciality of their native Essex, and wholeheartedly open to the charms of France's wine country, wonder whether their revitalizing presence at the château and vineyard they have purchased will really produce any lasting or palpable change. While these two independent-minded British ladies are quickly accepted as somewhat eccentric fixtures by the local population, they nevertheless come to realize that all their attempts to improve the cultivation and processing of the estate's wine have, in fact, had little impact on its quality. Age-old traditions, as well as the inscrutable methods of the French natives who work the vineyard, it seems, ultimately undermine any chance of permanent English influence taking root there.

The exploration of national characteristics and the inevitable clash of cultures these produce hardly constitute new terrain for Julian Barnes. His novel *Flaubert's Parrot* (1984) wryly recounts the efforts of an English doctor, a Gustave Flaubert aficionado, to determine which of two stuffed parrots residing in separate French museums is actually the one the French realist author kept on his desk while writing. Similarly, Barnes's *The Porcupine* (1992) follows the trial of a deposed Communist leader after the collapse of the Berlin Wall who cunningly challenges the capitalist ideology and hidden motivation of his ambitious young prosecutor, exposing in the process the same hypocrisy and self-interest in the new regime as existed in the old. Barnes's entertaining collection of essays, *Letters from London 1990-1995* (1995) also provides piquant insights into the collective sensibilities of his own compatriots.

Yet, at no point are Barnes's unique takes on a nation's peculiar disposition more perceptive than when they target the insurmountable barriers of language and their effect on both individual and collective alienation. If the British navvies and their fellow French workers in "Junction" somehow manage to make themselves understood (when necessary) through an indecipherable *lingua franca* of their own invention, Dr. Achille nevertheless finds himself unwilling to romanticize this glimpse into a possibly harmonious future world order. Their patois will neither doom poetry nor put an end to war, as his strolling companions remark, but simply lead to new versions of both. In "Evermore," the lexicographer Miss Moss fears that the world's fading memory of the Great War will doom her brother's ultimate sacrifice to meaninglessness and oblivion. Recalling the inscription on a monument erected to honor the World War I fallen in France, which she has visited annually for fifty years, Miss Moss, in her meticulous work on an English-language dictionary, fights against designating her cherished definition of the story's title word ("for all future times") as "obsolete."

In a lighter vein, the narrator's garrulous, though predictable Uncle Freddy in "Experiment" appears incapable of fixing his explanation of how he managed to be invited to participate in a Surrealist conference on sexuality attended by some of France's most infamous artists of the 1920's. Is it because this wax polish salesman tells them his product is *cire réaliste*, or that as a racing enthusiast he declares, "Je suis, sire, rallyiste?" Similar linguistic intricacies provide a subtle shading to the sexual dimensions of the middle-aged Englishwomen of "Hermitage," as well. After Emily, with her annoying attention to detail, catalogs various types of viticultural malady, Florence asks her what *cryptogamia* might be. The daunting word of Greek origin turns out to mean literally "concealed wedlock," and is a fungus, Emily explains, included in Linnaeus' taxonomy among the last (that is, lowest) class of plants. In a wink to the reader, Florence expresses her sincere hopes that this classification does not entail any moral judgment.

While most of the stories in *Cross Channel* are rooted in historical realism, at least two are of a more whimsical nature. "Gnossienne," in particular, tends toward fantasy with its account of the English writer Clements, whose claim never to have attended a single literary conference is belied by a seemingly intimate knowledge of their proceedings. Usually averse to requests to participate, Clements becomes intrigued by an unexpected invitation he receives which requires no response, but suggests cryptically that "attendance is performance." After some difficulty in arriving at the town where the mysterious conference is to be held, Clements is met, curiously, by its mayor and a marching band, led to his hotel, and instructed to appear at seven-thirty that evening for a dinner and discussion. The session is moderated by one Jean-Luc Cazes, whom Clements later learns is a writer invented by the OULIPO group of artists and intellectuals who espouse "pataphysics," that is, the "science of imagining solutions!" Recalling an earlier interview for French television in which he was asked to comment on myth versus reality, Clements' final utterance in "Gnossienne" is the reiterated claim never to have been present at a literary conference in his life.

Cross Channel ends on a ludic note with "Tunnel," the only story set in the future (2015), which serves as a summational coda to the nine earlier pieces in the volume. At first glance, the work appears simply to recount the observations of an elderly British writer traveling on business to Paris aboard the efficient Eurostar. As "Tunnel" progresses, however, familiar echoes from the preceding stories begin to be heard in oblique references now recombined coherently into an entirely new narrative. By the time the collection closes with the sentence: "And the elderly Englishman, when he returned home, began to write the stories you have just read," the reader should hardly be surprised as to the tenth story's function. Dispersed elements here—an adolescent outing to France, a concern about senility and the presence of an alembic—had all already appeared in "Melon." Speculation that another traveler, a sportswriter, may be covering the Tour de France, and that an older woman may once have been a cabaret performer at the famed Crazy Horse dance hall in Paris, leads the reader back to the British cyclist Andy and his stripper girlfriend in "Brambilla." The view of a World War I cemetery on the French side of the titular tunnel brings to mind "Evermore"; the imagined presence of an engineer recalls "Junction"; the Meursault wine the English writer takes along with him, "Hermitage." If mention of the hooligan fans of a British football club called the "Dragons" seems to turn the final integrating impulse of "Tunnel" into a forced conceit, the elderly author is there to sound this concluding justificatory note—the writer, he explains, "was meant to thrive on knowing and not knowing, on the fruitful misprision, the partial discovery and the resonant fragment." The sentiment might have served *Cross Channel* as its epigraph.

Gregary J. Racz

Sources for Further Study

Booklist. XCII, February 15, 1996, p. 988.
Chicago Tribune. April 21, 1996, XIV, p. 3.
Kirkus Review. LXIV, February 1, 1996, p. 151.
London Review of Books. XVIII, January 4, 1996, p. 22.
Los Angeles Times Book Review. March 17, 1996, p. 2.
The New Republic. CCXIV, June 24, 1996, p. 40.
New Statesman and Society. IX, January 19, 1996, p. 39.
The New York Times Book Review. CI, April 21, 1996, p. 12.
Publishers Weekly. CCXLIII, February 19, 1996, p. 204.
The Spectator. CCLXXVI, January 6, 1996, p. 28.
The Times Literary Supplement. January 19, 1996, p. 24.
The Virginia Quarterly Review. LXXII, Autumn, 1996, p. 132.

CULTURAL SELECTION
Why Some Achievements Survive the Test of Time—and Others Don't

Author: Gary Taylor
Publisher: BasicBooks (New York). 325 pp. $26.00
Type of work: Cultural and literary criticism

An exploration of cultural memory explaining why certain innovations are valued by societies, while others are forgotten

Cultural Selection: Why Some Achievements Survive the Test of Time—and Others Don't incorporates recent research into the nature of human memory, arguing that the "editorial function" of society is more often an accident of context than a recognition of genuine superiority. According to Taylor, the plays of Shakespeare are read and performed, not because they are inherently better than other plays, but because they both suited a particular niche at the time of their composition and have been presented to succeeding generations as something "important" and worthy of respect. Likewise, other works of art, music, and literature became classics when they were viewed by dominant social classes as embodying the values that justified their own hold on power.

Taylor's perspective is shaped in large part by the discipline known as "cultural studies." (Cultural studies analyze and interpret cultural artifacts in the light of the social ideology they contain.) The limits of Taylor's own objectivity may be seen in his dismissal of traditionalists as acting "like a herd of incompetent automatons programmed by one mad white pig" and his statement that he seeks "to offer an interpretation of culture compatible with a more progressive social agenda." It is never clear in *Cultural Selection* why an interpretation of culture need be compatible with *any* political agenda, rather than with the facts, sound reasoning, or the best evidence available. Taylor's answer is that an apolitical interpretation of culture is simply not possible. Any explanation of society or its achievements must, he believes, be colored by an author's worldview, historical background, social class, and cultural assumptions. To Taylor, academic objectivity is an illusion, a mere pretense of impartiality that masks an inevitable desire to advance some particular political, social, or economic agenda.

At times, Taylor seems uncomfortable with the *reductio ad absurdum* that this implies. He notes, for instance, that even students who adamantly refuse to label one theory right and another one wrong "realize that this logic will not convince the police, and few of them try to apply it in their math classes." In a well-chosen phrase, Taylor notes that "relativists are absolutists about relativism." Nevertheless, *Cultural Selection* does not clearly distinguish the author's own "moderate" relativism from the views of these extremists. Unwilling, for example, to draw a line between literature and popular culture, Taylor sees no contradiction in discussing *Hamlet* alongside *Casablanca*, the *Odyssey* alongside *The Terminator*, and Ludwig van Beethoven alongside Marvin Gaye. Since any idea or work of art may come to be regarded as great by future generations, he treats all products of a culture as equally important and as worthy of serious intellectual consideration.

In support of this view, Taylor concludes, "Look at how most of us respond to our children's taste in music." His reasoning appears to be that, while artistic or ideological innovations may be rejected at the time of their introduction, later generations sometimes find great value in them. Thus certain tunes from the 1960's that were dismissed as "noise" by the World War II generation came to be accepted as "standards" within a very short time. In much the same way, Taylor would have us believe, any idea or work of art may gain respect someday, if it fits the needs of a future generation. Scholars thus should not exclude any work or theory from their consideration since no one can know what our descendants will regard as great.

Unfortunately, Taylor's own evidence undermines this premise. By calling the reader's attention to shifting tastes in music, Taylor underscores the very distinction between high art and popular culture that *Cultural Selection* seeks to minimize. If, for instance, popular tunes and other transitory songs are capable of becoming classics worthy of serious academic study, then which popular tunes of the 1650's, 1750's, or even 1850's are widely remembered today? An academic specialist in popular song may be able to name a dozen or two such pieces, but the vast majority of people will not be able to recall any at all. What people *will* have heard of are the works of Joseph Haydn, Felix Mendelssohn, Giuseppe Verdi, and so on, even if they recall no more than the composer's names. No one doubts that there have been popular songs throughout history and that many of these were widely known in their own day. Nevertheless, what remains influential beyond a brief period is rarely if ever popular culture. What society ends up remembering are works sufficiently complex that they repay multiple performances, viewings, or study. The more levels of meaning in a work, the more likely it is that it will survive not for just a few decades (the span from the 1960's until the publication of *Cultural Selection*, for instance), but for many lifetimes.

Taylor also fails to realize that music is poor evidence that "memory is a function of social power." Johann Sebastian Bach's *Organ Fugue in G minor*, Johannes Brahms's *Fourth Symphony*, or Béla Bartók's *Concerto for Orchestra* were not remembered because they contained ideologies that endeared them to the ruling classes. Nor is it true that these works were preferred to popular music only because Bach, Brahms, and Bartók all happened to be white males (repeatedly treated as villains in *Cultural Selection*). It must be remembered that the vast majority of the popular song composers living side by side with Bach, Brahms, and Bartók would have been white males as well.

Although Taylor does not admit it, most music has no ideology whatsoever. This is why it has proved more resistant to deconstruction and cultural studies than have literature and art. *Cultural Selection* may dismiss the traditional view that achievements become timeless when successive generations find that they elevate and enrich the human spirit, provide sufficient technical challenge to warrant interpretation by highly skilled performers, and recombine familiar components in innovative and complex ways. Nevertheless, Taylor has no real alternative to offer.

Even if it were true, as the author suggests, that the popular culture despised today may become the celebrated art of tomorrow, this would hardly prove that dominant social forces have dictated cultural tastes. There are numerous examples of new theories, doctrines, or styles—such as heliocentrism, Christianity, and Impressionism, to name only three—that were quickly accepted despite vigorous repression from those in authority. In each case, the innovation triumphed, not because it was imposed upon society from above, but because it helped explain known phenomena, offered a greater message of hope and human dignity to those who needed it, or transformed the way in which people viewed their world. Even Taylor's earlier example of popular tunes that were condemned by one generation only to become the cherished songs of the next disproves his thesis that standards are often set by "dominant social groups."

Although Taylor is uncomfortable with Michel Foucault's political interpretation of culture or Jacques Derrida's deconstruction, he never really offers an alternative approach in *Cultural Selection*. At one point, for example, Taylor states that "if you have heard of Shakespeare's play *Othello*, it is because many mediums [*sic*] between the early seventeenth century and the late twentieth century chose to reproduce and circulate that representation of a seemingly civilized, Christian black man who collapses in the end back into his natural state of barbarism." For an author who has already published a major work on William Shakespeare (*Reinventing Shakespeare: A Cultural History from the Restoration to the Present*, 1989), this appears to be a strange and narrow misreading of *Othello*. How, after all, does Taylor account for Iago or for readers who may "have heard" of *Macbeth*, *Hamlet*, and *Romeo and Juliet*? Does Taylor believe that the forces of social dominance found it in their own self-interest to reproduce and circulate these depictions of corrupt or violent Caucasians? Once again, the author is highly selective of the evidence he is willing to consider.

Early in the book, Taylor suggests that he views culture as operating in a Darwinian fashion. Particular ideas and works of art survive, not because they are better than others, but because they are "fittest." As Taylor himself points out, fitness is only a relative term. Something may be fit for a single purpose or social niche and not for another, and the needs of society change throughout history. As a result, Taylor repeatedly reverts to the very same relativism that he had rejected in others. He seems not to understand the difference between an evolution in social values and the complete abandonment of all earlier values. After all, continuity in human culture is precisely what makes *The Epic of Gilgamesh*, *Oedipus the King*, and *Macbeth* meaningful to each generation in turn. Content, rather than mere accident, has made these works worth remembering. On the other hand, it is unlikely that films such as *Carrington* (1995) and Oliver Stone's *Nixon* (1995) or popular songs such as "I Heard It Through the Grapevine" or Melissa Etheridge's "Ruins"—all of which Taylor cites with great earnestness—will be remembered for more than a brief period.

Taylor's reluctance to grant superior status to any idea or work of art means that *Cultural Selection* shifts continually from topic to topic. Television shows are analyzed with the same intensity as tragedies, editorial cartoons are mentioned in the same breath as Renaissance paintings, and major historical figures are treated no more respectfully (and often a good deal less respectfully) than modern-day celebrities. Taylor's unwillingness to impose values may conceal nothing more than an inability to edit. No insight is too trivial to mention. He includes endless details about himself and his family, what he happened to read in the newspaper that morning, and a host of his most fleeting impressions. At one point, he states, "These are my personal memories; they probably mean nothing to you." Then why, a reader is forced to wonder, does Taylor bother recording them? His answer appears to be that, if anything has even a remote chance of being important, then it is worth preserving for posterity. *Cultural Selection* ends up being crammed with insignificant detail. The irony is that, for a book that purports to deal with memory, so little of the work ends up being memorable.

The impact of *Cultural Selection* is further diminished by a number of factual and typographical errors. Reference to Kenneth Clark's *Civilisation* as Kenneth Clarke's *Civilization* compresses two spelling errors into only three words. (It may also be that Taylor has confused Lord Kenneth Clark, the late art historian, with Kenneth Harry Clarke, the more recent chancellor of the Exchequer.) The composer of the *Ring* cycle is misidentified as Richard *von* Wagner. Horace's famous line *dulce et decorum est pro patria mori* (literally, "it is sweet and proper to die for one's country") is garbled by Taylor as "precious and proper it is, for the fatherland dying." Jargon (including "hierarchize," "exaptation," and "chunking"), substandard forms (such as "arsoned" and "legitimated"), and the excessive use of parenthetical phrases give *Cultural Selection* a stylistic weakness that will distract readers from its argument.

More important, however, are the questionable observations that Taylor makes throughout the book. He regards the author of the *Iliad* and the *Odyssey* as the blind bard of legend, apparently unaware that this view is treated skeptically by academics. He regards Minoan civilization as having been "devastated by a massive volcanic eruption on the island of Thera," although this theory has now been soundly rejected. He calls the journal *Representations* "the most influential journal in the humanities," a conclusion that should be regarded as debatable at best. As a result, neither Taylor's facts nor his interpretation of them should be approached without extreme skepticism.

Jeffrey L. Buller

Sources for Further Study

Booklist. XCII, March 15, 1996, p. 1225.
Kirkus Reviews. LXIV, February 1, 1996, p. 214.
The New York Times. April 5, 1996, p. C27.
The New York Times Book Review. CI, May 26, 1996, p. 17.
Publishers Weekly. CCXLIII, February 5, 1996, p. 71.
Times-Picayune. June 30, 1996, p. E7.
The Washington Post Book World. XXVI, April 7, 1996, p. 7.

DAMNED TO FAME
The Life of Samuel Beckett

Author: James Knowlson
Publisher: Simon & Schuster (New York). Illustrated. 800 pp. $35.00
Type of work: Literary biography
Time: 1906-1989
Locale: Ireland, France, Germany, and England

Knowlson retraces the personal development and literary evolution of the unique playwright and novelist, known to many as an innovative practitioner of the Theater of the Absurd and creator of unique worlds inhabited by solitary individuals imprisoned in a world devoid of coherent communication

Principal personages:
SAMUEL BECKETT, recipient of the Nobel Prize in Literature in 1969
SUZANNE DESCHEVAUX-DUMESNIL, his wife, whom he married in 1961
PEGGY SINCLAIR, his first cousin, with whom he had a romantic liaison
JAMES JOYCE, Irish poet and novelist with whom Beckett developed a
    long-lasting friendship
THOMAS RUDMOSE-BROWN, a professor of Romance languages at Trinity
    College, Dublin, who played an important role in Beckett's academic
    formation and future career

James Knowlson, chair of French at the University of Reading, England, and the official biographer and long-time friend of Beckett, retraces in great detail and with an evident understanding of Beckett's foibles and strengths, idiosyncrasies and philosophy, the path that led him to be celebrated as one of this century's greatest writers.

Samuel Beckett was the second of two sons born to May Roe and Bill Beckett in Foxrock, County Dublin, on April 13, 1906. The Becketts were descended from Huguenots who emigrated to Ireland from France in the eighteenth century. Samuel's mother, a strict and demanding figure, possessed a rather rebellious nature and stubborn streak which Samuel was to inherit. His father, a member of a successful quantity surveying firm, was a lover of the outdoors and instilled this joy in his son, who had inherited the athletic prowess of his father's family.

At the age of thirteen, Beckett was enrolled in Portora Royal School, where, withdrawn, moody, and introspective, at first, he did not fit easily into the schoolboy community. His violent temper and skills in self-defense, as well as his qualities as a witty companion, characterized his adolescent social demeanor. Beckett was an excellent pupil in Latin and French, and was an avid reader of Arthur Conan Doyle's stories and those of the humorist Stephen Leacock. The latter's wit, parodies, wordplay, and interest in unusual words appealed to Beckett's intelligence. Generally, Beckett ended up adapting well to school life. This was greatly facilitated by his abilities as an all-around athlete. Rugby, rowing, swimming, cricket, and boxing were Beckett's preferred sports, activities in which he excelled. The formative years spent at Portora Royal School encouraged Beckett to become aware of his strengths and limitations. During this time, Beckett came to form a set of demanding standards to which his somewhat puritanical nature aspired.

When, at the age of seventeen, Beckett entered Dublin's Trinity College in 1923, he was a shy, retiring undergraduate intending to study for an arts degree. Still involved in sports, it was his passion for words, literature, and art that was to develop most dramatically at Trinity College. Thomas Rudmose-Brown, professor of Romance languages, exerted significant influence over Beckett, both in the context of his academic formation—reading and discussing literature—and in reinforcing the ideal of individual freedom. Rudmose-Brown, keenly interested in modern French literature, and in poetry in particular, was admired by Beckett because of his knowledge of the Paris literary scene of the time. It was he who introduced Beckett to the work of the poet Jean-Pierre Jouve, as well as to the works of Surrealists such as Paul Éluard, André Breton, and René Crevel. Later, Beckett would translate some of the works of these poets. During this period, Beckett developed a deep love for French and Italian, which were his honors subjects, and for theater, cinema, and art.

In the summer of 1928, on his return to Dublin from a year teaching French and English at Campbell College in Belfast, Beckett met his young first cousin, Peggy Sinclair, with whom he developed a romance. Beckett's parents were violently opposed to such a relationship, and when Peggy enrolled in a program of study at a school of music, dance, and movement in Austria, Beckett visited her, contrary to the wishes of his parents. The affair eventually ended because of Beckett's unwillingness to have a physical relationship with Sinclair.

Following his stay in Vienna, Beckett took up a position as lecteur d'anglais at the prestigious École Normale Supérieure in Paris. Here Beckett made the acquaintance of James Joyce whose works—*Dubliners*, *Portrait of the Artist as a Young Man*, *Ulysses*, and various poems—he greatly admired. Both men had degrees in French and Italian. Both shared a fervent anticlericalism, a passionate love of Dante and of words—sounds, rhythms, etymologies. They also shared a keen interest in the work of Franz Schubert, Paul Cézanne, and the films of Charlie Chaplin. Beckett became a part of the Joyce circle, celebrating family birthdays, attending receptions at the Joyce apartment, and developing a friendship with Joyce's daughter, Lucia. When Lucia Joyce realized that Beckett did not have any romantic interest in her, partially because of her wild and disturbing mood fluctuations that would later become more acute, Beckett became *persona non grata* at the Joyce apartment. Joyce's wife blamed Beckett for leading Lucia on; Joyce played the role of outraged father and banished Beckett from the household. Beckett was devastated by his rift with Joyce, which was eventually repaired when Joyce came to recognize how ill his daughter was.

Paris was a revelation to Beckett. Far from the academic stuffiness of Trinity College, he felt a strong sense of release, not entirely disassociated with guilt. He became enthralled with the atmosphere of innovation and experimentation that surrounded Surrealism whose manifesto had been published in 1924. Beckett was very interested in innovative German painters belonging to the "Die Brücke" group and members of the Bauhaus who exhibited in smaller Paris galleries. He also adored contemplating works by Rembrandt and Poussin in the Louvre.

Upon returning to Trinity College in 1930 to take up a lectureship in French, Beckett, for whom speaking in public was excruciatingly painful, lacked the confidence to overcome such a difficulty, and, consequently, chose to resign his post in 1932. Once again living in Paris, Beckett began what would become *Dream of Fair to Middling Women*, eventually to be published in 1992. The work deals with the experiences, ideas, and inner life of a young man named Belacqua. The structure of the novel, complex and fragmented, lacks linear form and unity. Such an aesthetic is a characteristic of Beckett who condemned the "chloroformed world" of Honoré de Balzac's novels, in which he believed characters are turned into "clockwork cabbages." Since life is complex and mysterious, Beckett chose to reflect such an image by actively dismantling the underpinning of the conventional novel.

Devastated by the death of his father in 1933, and guilt-ridden for having failed to live up to his father's expectations, Beckett began intensive psychotherapy at the Tavistock Clinic in London. His symptoms included severe anxiety, arrhythmic heart, night sweats, shudders, breathlessness, and at times total paralysis. Beckett became clearly convinced that his physical problems were caused in part by his own attitude of superiority and an isolation from others that resulted from a morbid, obsessive immersion in self. Painting helped Beckett to contemplate the relationship between the artist, his work, and the outside world. What Beckett saw in twentieth century art reinforced his own view of the world. Cézanne's landscapes, which he saw at the Tate Gallery, served to bring to the fore visually concepts he had formulated in relation to his view that landscape had nothing to do with man, that man was alien to landscape and in fact was severed from the outside world.

In 1937, Beckett left both his home and the country of his birth for Paris, his permanent home for the next fifty-two years. In Paris, Beckett began writing poetry in French. He viewed this time as a period of "lostness, drifting around, seeing a few friends—a period of apathy and lethargy." Nevertheless, it was a time when he was in contact with painters and writers at the cutting edge of the avant-garde. It was in Paris that his future wife, Suzanne Deschevaux-Dumesnil captured his heart. Six years older than he, she was an accomplished pianist who had studied at the École Normale de Musique in the 1920's, had an interest in literature and theater, and a voracious appetite for music and concertgoing. She had great respect for Beckett's talents and total belief in his genius.

The German Occupation of Paris saw Beckett and Deschevaux-Dumesnil seek refuge in a small village in the Vaucluse, an isolated and relatively safe haven during the war. War-ravaged France and a very grim looking Paris to which they returned in 1945 became indelible images in Beckett's psyche. Henceforth, he would draw on his own inner world for the subjects of his writing. He would allow his imagination to create alternative worlds to those of conventional reality. Beckett was becoming more sure of his vision, technique, and voice.

The remarkable success of *En attendant Godot* (1952; *Waiting for Godot*, 1954) confirmed Beckett's originality and his expertise in theatrical productions. Throughout his life, he was actively involved in the production of his plays, for which the requests for permission to translate or to adapt them into other languages were constant and extremely lucrative for Beckett. His material future as well his place, not only in modern French literature, but also in world literature, were, therefore, assured. When in 1954 his brother, Frank, died of lung cancer, Beckett, despite the renewal of certain physical symptoms of profound anxiety that had earlier caused him to seek psychotherapy, felt paradoxically a huge surge of creative energy that resulted in the writing of *Fin de partie* (1957; *Endgame*, 1958), which, although not autobiographical, does evoke the experience of the sickroom and of waiting for someone to die. The anticlerical nature of this play, as well as certain words deemed not suitable for public consumption, caused great consternation for the British Lord Chamberlain, who threatened to refuse to license the play for public performance although the play had already been performed without censorship in France, Germany, and the United States. Eventually, an agreement was reached to replace the word "bastard" with "swine," thereby assuaging the sole objection by the Lord Chamberlain that Beckett was willing to address.

Increasingly, as Beckett's work became more and more in demand, Deschevaux-Dumesnil saw her role as unofficial literary agent assigned to others. She played a less vital role in Beckett's literary life, but never wavered in the respect and admiration with which she viewed him. Eventually, in 1961 the two married, and they would remain constant companions in a relationship, unconventional perhaps in its attendant freedoms.

The awarding to Beckett of the Nobel Prize in Literature in 1969 was strangely seen by the recipient as a catastrophe for, in his eyes, this award meant inevitably that his long-term future would be permanently disrupted by the celebrity. Not wanting to be publicly discourteous, and displaying a mixture of humility and pride, he accepted the award. Beckett's extraordinarily rapid rise to such a pinnacle of world recognition bespeaks the profound lucidity and uniquely captivating nature of his voice.

During the last years of his life, Beckett contemplated compelling questions such as mortality, time, political brutality, and the impossibility of understanding human existence. Frail at the end of his life, he died in Paris at the end of 1989, several months after the death of his wife, beside whose body he was interred in the Cimitière Montparnasse.

Knowlson's biography is written in a direct, sometimes expressive style, communicating a vast amount of information, from the mundane to the aesthetic and the philosophical. James Knowlson has succeeded in painting a portrait of Beckett from the inside, sharing insights and anecdotes that reveal a shy, proud individual, driven by his vision, and compelled to be true to his inspiration. A strong supporter of human rights, often erroneously perceived as melancholic, persnickety, and self-absorbed, Beckett is eloquently portrayed as a self-aware, resilient, and compassionate soul, whose unique inspiration created postmodern images and extraordinary uses of language, complex in its simplicity, that capture the essence of humankind's struggle to understand the gift of life.

Kenneth W. Meadwell

Sources for Further Study

Boston Globe. December 8, 1996, p. N17.
The Guardian. September 12, 1996, II, p. 18.
Houston Chronicle. October 27, 1996, p. Z22.
Kirkus Reviews. LXIV, August 1, 1996, p. 1123.
Library Journal. CXXI, September 15, 1996, p. 69.
The New Republic. CCXV, December 30, 1996, p. 29.
The New York Times Book Review. CI, November 24, 1996, p. 14.
Publishers Weekly. CCXLIII, September 30, 1996, p. 72.
The Times Literary Supplement. September 27, 1996, p. 3.
The Washington Post Book World. XXVI, October 13, 1996, p. 1.

DANCING AFTER HOURS

Author: Andre Dubus (1936-   )
Publisher: Alfred A. Knopf (New York). 234 pp. $23.00
Type of work: Short stories

Fourteen tales by one of the masters of the modern realistic and moralistic short story

Of the nine books of fiction Andre Dubus has published in the last twenty years, seven of them are collections of short fiction; thus he is usually included as part of the so-called renaissance of the short story that has taken place since the 1970's. However, Dubus' fiction is neither like the self-reflexive experiments of Donald Barthelme, nor the minimalist realism of Raymond Carver. Rather, Dubus' short fictions are more like the kind of stories that Bernard Malamud would have written had he not been Jewish, Flannery O'Connor would have written had she not been southern, or Raymond Carver would have written had he been Catholic. In short, Dubus' stories have always manifested a hopeful spirituality and an optimistic humanism that has marked him as thematically old-fashioned and technically conservative among younger short-story writers.

As it has been for Dubus' fiction in the past, most of the short stories in *Dancing After Hours* are based on the conviction, belief, or hope that most human beings are seeking love rather than sex, relationships rather than one-night stands, and the security of family rather than the adventure of the temporary thrill. Perhaps because Dubus himself is nearing sixty, most of the men and women in these stories are middle-aged or older. Perhaps because an accident caused him to lose a leg and be confined to a wheelchair in 1986, several of these stories focus on men who have been physically disabled and are trying to find a way to cope with their inability to walk. Perhaps because Dubus' third wife left him a few months after his accident, most of these stories focus on men and women nostalgically looking backward to a time when they loved and were loved or hopefully looking forward to a time when they will love and be loved again.

As in his earlier Paul Clement series of stories, which focused on the coming-of-age of a young man, Dubus here features the same character in more than one story. In "Falling in Love," readers meet the young Ted Briggs, who has come back from the Vietnam War with a wounded leg that forces him to use a cane. After impregnating a liberated and independent young woman, he is filled with rage when she refuses either to marry him or to have the baby. He bitterly complains to a friend, who, like him, is also alone and getting older, that he will never have sex with another woman who insists on killing his baby. As if this statement has left a gap that needs closing, in a later story in the collection, "All the Time in the World," readers learn of LuAnn Arceneaux, a woman who has had many lovers but no real love and who also fears growing old alone, who meets the now-mature Ted Briggs. In what seems a match made in heaven, LuAnn, like Ted, does not want a relationship that begins with sex, nor does she want to conceive a child that she does not want. When Ted makes a token sexual overture she puts him off, and he is glad. She is filled with joy at the possibility of loving and being loved by Ted, and the story ends with her eagerness and anxiety about the future, knowing that love will bring her both joy and pain.

Ted and LuAnn appear again in "The Timing of Sin," the central theme of which is announced in the opening sentence: "On a Thursday night in early autumn she nearly committed adultery." LuAnn is forty-three in this story and works part-time at a home for teenage girls. Surrounded by young women who have been neglected or abused and now are troubled and alone, she becomes attracted to the soft-spoken director of the girls' home. Most of the story is a conversation between LuAnn and a friend who tells her about her previous adultery and the breakup of an earlier marriage, a breakup that she still regrets. LuAnn describes her own almost-adultery that took place in a car. In the process of the encounter, as LuAnn and the director try to get her jeans off, she sees herself walking into her house and not finding her husband Ted or her children there, and she knows she cannot be unfaithful. As she tells her friend, it is not that she was being good, it was the jeans that saved her. Had she been wearing a skirt, there would not have been those few seconds of thoughtful hesitation. Knowing now how easy adultery is and hard relationships are to maintain, she dismisses the triviality of being saved by jeans and asserts that it must have been God or grace that saved her.

The last story about LuAnn and Ted, "Out of the Snow," is the most powerful one. It is the year following the almost-adultery, and the relationship between husband and wife is intimate and loving. Little happens in the story until LuAnn comes home from the grocery store and is shocked to discover that she has been followed into her house by two men. Seeing herself stripped naked, struck, choked, and raped, with every bit of herself taken away from her, she is filled with rage and fiercely strikes back. In three tense and highly detailed paragraphs, Dubus describes a woman defending her whole self with such ferocity and yet cold-blooded control that the reader cannot help but be completely caught up in it. Making use of a teakettle and a skillet on the stove, LuAnn smashes the men, breaking bones and bringing blood until they crawl pitifully away. In some ways, the scene is a cheap revenge convention, typical of a Charles Bronson film in which one gets back at the scum who terrorize innocent people; it is at the same time, however, the stimulus to a catharsis that makes the reader want to cheer. LuAnn is intelligent and honest enough to know that when she struck out it was not for Ted or for her children, but for herself, to continue living. "And if it is that easy," she says elliptically, leaving the implied question unanswered, "if evil can walk through the door and there's a place deep in our hearts that knows how to look at its face, and beat it till it's broken and bleeding, till it crawls away. And we do this with rapture." The story ends with Ted and LuAnn sitting side by side, their bodies touching, in front of the fire. As in many of Dubus' stories, the final epiphany, although it suggests ambiguous complexity of both fears and hopes, ferocity and gentleness, is almost too easy, dependent as it is on the simple goodness of the characters and the moral simplicity of the conflict.

Many of these stories have the sympathetic tone of the humanistic storyteller and thus the simple structure of a domestic parable. For example, the very brief piece, "A

Love Song" introduces us to the central female character whose husband has left her for another woman with the line, "When her heart truly broke, she was thirty-seven years old." Dubus does not underestimate the significance of the mid-life loss of love; the woman feels the experience has undercut the significance of her life. However, she begins to go out with female friends and find happiness in being a mother to her daughters. She also discovers a relationship with a lover. The story ends with the narrator describing her attending her two daughters' weddings, three years apart, and feeling the old hope in her breast that so fills her body that she can hardly contain it. The story is thus about the loss of the old hope that marriage brings as well as the realization that it is only hope.

Another brief piece, "Sunday Morning," builds on the prototypical and parabolic scene of two lovers in bed together on Sunday morning. As usual in these stories, neither are young; he is thirty-seven and she is thirty-six. She has begun to fear that she will never have children and that she will grow old and die alone. He tells her a story about a couple he knew in which the husband killed his wife when she was three months pregnant because he wanted the insurance money. The two lovers, frightened by this cautionary tale, want some assurance that they are loved and will not be deceived. They want to feel that comfortable security and intimacy of a marriage that is absolutely sound. But once again, they know that the best that it can be is a hope and a dream. The story ends with the woman looking at the man's face on the pillow beside her in a moment filled with both longing and fear.

The male character in "The Lover," aged fifty-five, has three former wives and five children. He has given up on love and now wants women who will take him into their hearts but not keep him. When he asks a younger woman, a waitress at the restaurant where he eats, to go home with him, the sexual encounter is described as if it were his rediscovery of some old magic that he thought he had lost forever. At the end he cries in her arms, saying he feels he has missed something somewhere, but that he knows he cannot start over again. She holds him, and he knows that is all one can do, ultimately, "hold and touch and speak, watch and listen, and wish the pain would end."

In one story in which the comfortable intimacy of married life is ultimately affirmed, "The Colonel's Wife," that desired interdependency seems partially possible because the Colonel has two broken legs from having a horse fall on him. He knows his knees will never fully recover and he will always have difficulty walking. An older man having served in two wars without injury, he is now humiliated by his helplessness. His wife must wipe him after he has used a bedpan, and he feels dirty and embarrassed, even though his wife performs this task with good humor. The story concludes when he finds out that she has been having an affair, which has just ended. She says it is not her first affair, and he says he has also had affairs. Again, as is typical in a Dubus story, the reader must fully accept the basic goodness of the characters and the premise that love heals all wounds to believe the Colonel when he says that he is glad the horse fell on him, for it made him sit still long enough to look at his wife.

The two most communal stories in the collection are "Blessings" and the title story. In the former, a family goes on a fishing trip and the boat capsizes because of the captain's neglect. The story is told from the perspective of the mother one year after the family survived the accident. The means by which the family survive are described in precise detail, much as LuAnn's defense of herself in "Out of the Snow," as if there were some sort of incantatory magic about those events. The story is about what gives people character and what holds them together. It ends with the husband and wife, in one of those intimate moments of togetherness that no one can break through, agreeing that it was the worst day of their lives and yet the best day also. In the title story "Dancing After Hours," a forty-year-old female bartender who, because she is not pretty, still lives alone, finds renewed hope when she shares a communal party with a small group that includes a man in a wheelchair who continues to live life with gusto in spite of his disability.

These stories show readers nothing new in the world of Andre Dubus (one of the stories, "The Intruder," is his first published story), except that his world is past middle age and his characters are often alone. As usual, Dubus' stories are about hope and faith and union; they are romantic and religious, and some may even call them corny. It seems appropriate that in the title story, the characters listen to old Frank Sinatra songs on the jukebox, for Dubus' stories affirm that love and marriage do go together like a horse and carriage. The problem is, Dubus' world often seems too simply a long-lost horse-and-carriage world.

Charles E. May

Sources for Further Study

America. CLXXIV, June 8, 1996, p. 25.
The Antioch Review. LIV, Summer, 1996, p. 380.
Booklist. XCII, January 1, 1996, p. 786.
Boston Magazine. LXXXVIII, April, 1996, p. 140.
Chicago Tribune. March 10, 1996, XIV, p. 3.
The Christian Century. CXIII, May 22, 1996, p. 591.
Commonweal. CXXIII, May 17, 1996, p. 24.
Library Journal. CXXI, February 15, 1996, p. 177.
Los Angeles Times Book Review. February 18, 1996, p. 2.
National Catholic Reporter. XXXII, May 24, 1996, p. 26.
The New York Times Book Review. CI, February 25, 1996, p. 13.
Publishers Weekly. CCXLIII, January 1, 1996, p. 58.
Time. CXLVII, March 4, 1996, p. 66.
The Washington Post Book World. March 3, 1996, p. 8.

DEATH IN THE ANDES

Author: Mario Vargas Llosa (1936-   )
First published: Lituma en los Andes, 1993
Translated from the Spanish by Edith Grossman
Publisher: Farrar Straus Giroux (New York). 276 pp. $24.00
Type of work: Novel
Time: The 1990's
Locale: The Andean highlands of Peru

Two members of the Peruvian Civil Guard sent to investigate mysterious disappearances and deaths in an Andean village discover many layers of horror and complicity with Shining Path terrorism

> Principal characters:
> LITUMA, a corporal in the Civil Guard
> TOMÁS "TOMASITO" CARREÑO, Lituma's adjutant in the Civil Guard
> DIONISIO, barkeeper in the Andean town of Naccos
> ADRIANA, Dionisio's wife
> MERCEDES "MECHE" TRELLES, Tomás Carreño's girlfriend

Like Mario Vargas Llosa's earlier novels, *La casa verde* (1966; *The Green House,* 1968) and *Conversación en la Catedral,* (1969; *Conversation in the Cathedral,* 1975), *Death in the Andes* is an ambitious novel about Peru in the last part of the twentieth century. The central question in *Death in the Andes,* to which there are no simple answers, is the following: What is it about Peru and about Peruvian culture and beliefs that has allowed the phenomenon of Shining Path guerrillas to represent part of its national identity? The basic structure of the novel is that of a conversation between two men—Lituma and his young aide, Tomás Carreño—who have been posted to the remote Andean town of Naccos to investigate three disappearances thought to be evidence of Shining Path action in the area. The two Civil Guardsmen hate being in this baffling, dangerous place but do their job conscientiously. To stay sane, they talk to each other. These two primary voices are dramatically different from each other: Lituma's serious pursuit of the horrifying truths about violence and death in the Andes is contrasted throughout the novel with young Tomasito Carreño's romantic love story. In the end, Lituma deciphers the truth and Carreño gets his girl. Yet Lituma's detective work uncovers the ever shadier and murkier underside of human nature, whereas Carreño manages to ignore or brush aside any complexities that might mar his sunny world of idealized romance. Carreño totally refuses to consider that his beloved Mercedes might be less than perfect: He is a committed knight errant who dedicates himself fully to the adoration of his love object. Everyone around him thinks he is crazy, but in the end, his love prevails. Carreño's tenacity, refusal to entertain doubt, and total obsession pay off: His beloved seeks him out even in remote Naccos. He has insisted upon believing in a fiction, and the fiction becomes reality (within the fiction of the novel).

Lituma, who has appeared in many of Vargas Llosa's earlier novels, is a listener, an observer, a good-hearted but not a clever man. He is accustomed to obeying rather than formulating orders. Yet in this novel, stranded in a mountain village in a declared emergency zone, with a love-struck boy as his only fellow Guardsman, Lituma is forced into an unaccustomed and unwelcome leadership role, and he spends his time looking for someone who can tell him what to do or at least explain the situation to him.

As in Vargas Llosa's *¿Quién mató a Palomino Molero?* (1986; *Who Killed Palomino Molero?*, 1987) which also pairs a police inquiry into a mysterious death with a soap-opera-like love interest, one effect of the dual story line is to emphasize the enigmatic and perhaps ambiguous nature of issues of truth and justice, and the obsessional, single-mindedness of sexual passion: Truth is complex and love is simplistic. As in *Palomino Molero*, the detective story is an inquiry into the state of the Peruvian nation while the romance focuses upon individual fantasy and obsession. Those who seek justice must try to understand its complex national scenario, whereas love is blind and self-absorbed. Lituma struggles with the effort to understand ideas which are alien to him and to adjust his definitions of reality if need be, but Carreño's love is fueled by his desire to make reality conform to his idealistic (however silly and romantic) vision.

While Lituma's and Carreño's stories provide comprehensible, familiar continuity, four other narratives compete vigorously for the reader's attention from the outset. These are related to the Shining Path guerrilla movement, pre-Greek Dionysiac beliefs, pre-Columbian Andean rituals, and Catholic convictions.

Like all of Vargas Llosa's novels, *Death in the Andes* is carefully crafted. Part 1 is composed of five chapters which recount five instances of Shining Path incidents, sandwiched between segments of the ongoing Lituma/Carreño plot. Thus the five shocking Shining Path accounts are cushioned between chapter beginnings and endings in which a stable, reassuring, chronological continuity engages our interest. The five Shining Path incidents embedded among segments of Tomás and Lituma's ongoing conversation are: the deaths by stoning of two French travelers and others traveling on a bus near Andahuaylas; the slaughter of a herd of vicuñas tended by Pedro Tinoco in Pampa Galeras, near Auquipata; killings and beatings in the town of Andamarca, from which the town lieutenant-governor, Medardo Llantac, escapes by chance; the deaths of idealistic reformers, Hortensia d'Harcourt and others, organizing a reforestation project near Huayllarajcra; and the apparent execution of Casimiro Huarcaya by a Shining Path leader in Accra, south of Ayacucho. The protagonists of three of these incidents (the second, third, and fifth) survive to become the three missing people whose disappearance the two Guardsmen have come to Naccos to investigate, although this information is withheld until the end of the book.

All five of these are stories of Shining Path "justice," and in each case, the Shining Path rationale is presented clearly and explicitly, although unsympathetically. Each incident portrays the victimization of the innocent by the brutal—and often barely comprehensible—force unleashed, provoked, or inflicted by Shining Path groups which manipulate the fear, poverty, ignorance, and superstition of Andean villagers.

The distinction between victims and victimizers seems reasonably straightforward in part 1, but Lituma makes no progress in his investigation of the missing-person cases in the area under his jurisdiction.

The four chapters of part 2 feature accounts of supernatural and superstitious beliefs. Lituma's pursuit of truth leads him in each chapter to a new episode in which rational explanation is insufficient. Dionysiac excess, beliefs in Andean spirits (*nacaqs, apus, mukis, pishtacos*), and superstitions about outsiders complicate Lituma's desire for a simple solution. The chapters of part 2, like those of part 1, also sandwich accounts of unfolding horrors between two Lituma segments. The continuing saga of Tomás' love story is spaced at wider intervals, at the end of each chapter. This contrast with part 1 increases the tension and anxiety level of Lituma's search; he is getting closer to the truths he seeks, and the love story, like a continuing soap opera, is displaced from prime time, as it were. In the lengthy epilogue, where the various strands of the story all come together, it is the love story that is resolved first, with Mercedes' arrival and reunion with Tomás. The two Guardsmen receive their new posting orders, and only then does Lituma learn the truth about what has happened in Naccos.

References to Greek myth and to Andean spiritism are interwoven prominently— even flamboyantly—throughout *Death in the Andes,* although they are not emphasized as deliberate parallels until part 2. Right from the beginning, the supernatural is a presence in this fragile Andean outpost buffeted by storms, earthquakes, and terror of guerrilla assaults. Lituma and his adjutant, depressed and baffled by the three missing-person cases reported to them, feel like outsiders. From the beginning of the novel, major sites and preoccupations are fused: Andean superstitions; the idea of expiation, placation, and sacrifice associated in the book with Greek, Andean, and Christian beliefs; the storytelling in Dionisio's cantina, where the barkeeper and his fortune-telling wife, Adriana, hold forth; and Lituma's difficulty in relating to all this. Even the name Dionisio tips readers off, or should tip them off, to the Greek reference. Dionysus, the youngest of the Greek gods, the son of Zeus and the mortal Semele, who died when Zeus revealed himself to her in a blaze of lightning, was a nature god of fruitfulness, vegetation, and wine, the god of the erect phallus, and of orgiastic and barbarian rituals. The myth recounts his wide travels as he taught the mysteries of his worship in song and dance, and how to cultivate grapevines. He was followed about by a group of maenads who danced by torchlight and indulged in ritual feasts in which living victims were torn apart and eaten. Eventually Dionysus (here Dionisio) married Ariadne (here Adriana), who had come to Naxos (Naccos) with Theseus (Timoteo), whom she helped to escape from the labyrinth after killing the minotaur (*pishtaco*) in Crete (Quenka). Dionysus is associated with thunder, earthquakes, and phallic healing ceremonies, all prominent in *Death in the Andes*. This Greek myth is a central narrative force in Vargas Llosa's novel; reconsidered within the context of the Dionysiac, Shining Path atrocities become somewhat comprehensible in a new way.

Offerings, sacrifices, and beliefs in the immediacy of the supernatural are mentioned frequently in *Death in the Andes*. The epitaph from William Blake's "The Ghost of Abel" ("Cain's City built with Human Blood,/ not Blood of Bulls and Goats") forewarns the alert reader. There is repeated mention of ancient pre-Incan beliefs in earth gods and spirits which roar in thunder and can cause earthquakes and rock slides (precisely the powers ascribed to Dionysus by the Greeks) unless placated. Woven into this narrative line about offerings and sacrifices is a related and often indistinguishable narrative which shares the mythological rhetoric but refers to Shining Path killings. Sent to the state-declared emergency zone, Lituma and Carreño feel that they are being offered up as living sacrifices. The series of Shining Path incidents in which victims are stoned to death are clearly rituals. The orgiastic rites of the Greek Dionysus are also associated with deaths by stoning. Dionisio in *Death in the Andes* speaks both of mountain spirits and of the guerrillas, saying: "They'll stone us to death, too."

While part 1 of *Death in the Andes* is densely interlaced with references to beliefs in mountain spirits and to "sacrifice," part 2 begins with Lituma's rapt attention to the Danish anthropologist Stirmsson's revelation about pre-Incan Andean human sacrifices. Lituma is theoretically willing to accept that the three missing men have been sacrificed to the *apus,* and he pursues this line of investigation, but he is resistant: This explanation is repugnant to him. He longs for the simpler life of Piura, for the comfort and reassurance of the Lituma-Carreño plotline of ignorance and romance found in part 1.

Only when Lituma is nearly killed in a huge rockslide is he sufficiently shaken out of rational composure to get drunk at Dionisio's. In the brilliantly assembled chapter 8, forward narrative and flashbacks alternate and overlap, and what Lituma hears fuses with his retrospective imaginary projection of what he thinks must have happened to Casimiro Huarcaya. The past and the present fuse; what Lituma knows and what he imagines are synthesized into one nearly seamless revelation. Lituma lives (in his imagination) what he has been trying and failing to make into rational, ordered sequence. Like participants in Dionysiac orgies, he experiences apocalyptic, intuitive truth. Pedro Tinoco, marked as sacrificial lamb (here, a vicuña) by Dionisio's "kiss of Judas," is carried off like a "patron saint of the fiesta." Lituma imagines this as a religious procession complete with priest and incense. This is followed by Adriana's account of the apogee of Dionysiac celebration when the joyous fervor of dance and drink possessed everyone "until all Naccos was a whirlwind of drunk, happy people. Nobody knew who was who anymore, where one person began and the other ended, who was man, who was animal, who was human, who was woman." Catholic rite fuses with pagan healing ceremony when Demetrio cures the men of Muquiyauyo: "instead of a saint on a platform, they carried a clay prick made by the best potter in Muquiyauyo. The band played a military march for it, and the girls decorated it with wreaths of flowers" and the miracle of healing occurs.

At the novel's conclusion, Lituma, again very drunk, seeks and chooses to know the heart of darkness. He has gradually accustomed himself to accepting that the three missing men were sacrificed to the *apus* by being hurled live down a mine shaft. Yet the final man he interviews has something worse on his conscience. Not only were the three individuals sacrificed but their genitals were eaten by the assembled communicants, who are later unable to forget their participation in such a horror. Graphic description of the bloody ceremony nauseates Lituma, who regrets he ever began the inquiry but cannot now regain his innocence.

Christian communion in which flesh and blood are consumed, Shining Path rituals of execution by stoning, Andean belief in cannibalistic *pishtacos* and expiatory rites involving human sacrifice, Greek accounts of human beings sacrificed to minotaurs or torn apart and eaten in orgiastic rituals by maenads: all of these are fused by Vargas Llosa into one powerful meditation on the irrational in human civilization and specifically on the force of the irrational in the Andean areas of Peru.

Mary G. Berg

Sources for Further Study

The Atlantic. CCLXXVII, March, 1996, p. 122.
Chicago Tribune. March 3, 1996, XIV, p. 6.
Library Journal. CXXI, January, 1996, p. 146.
Los Angeles Times Book Review. February 11, 1996, p. 3.
The Nation. CCLXII, February 12, 1996, p. 28.
The New York Review of Books. XLIII, May 9, 1996, p. 16.
The New York Times Book Review. CI, February 18, 1996, p. 7.
The New Yorker. LXXII, April 15, 1996, p. 84.
Time. CXLVII, February 12, 1996, p. 75.
The Times Literary Supplement. June 21, 1996, p. 22.
The Wall Street Journal. February 16, 1996, p. A8.
The Washington Post Book World. XXVI, February 25, 1996, p. 1.

DEMOCRACY'S DISCONTENTS
America in Search of a Public Philosophy

Author: Michael J. Sandel (1953-   )
Publisher: The Belknap Press of Harvard University Press (Cambridge, Massachusetts). 417 pp.
$24.95
Type of work: Philosophy; current affairs

The author surveys the history of the interplay of classical liberal and classical republican strands of America's public philosophy and finds the predominant classical liberal interpretation insufficient for current needs and suggests it be supplemented by classical republicanism emphasizing civic obligation and revitalization of decentralized arrangements for self-government

When the United States of America emerged from its eighteenth century crucible to become the world's first modern constitutional republic, its public philosophy was composed of two competing strands. One was classical liberalism, the doctrine which emphasized the rights of the individual and the dependence of legitimate government on the consent of the governed—consent that the governed were free to withdraw at their pleasure. Political obligations, that is to say, are by nature "voluntarist." They are *chosen* by the free will of those who submit to this or that government to protect their interests—their "rights"—and not because government necessarily merits obedience. This is the substance of what, famously, Thomas Jefferson, writing as representative of an entire revolutionary generation, set down in the Declaration of Independence: "all Men are . . . endowed by their Creator with certain unalienable Rights, . . . That to secure these Rights, Governments are instituted among Men, deriving their just Powers from the Consent of the Governed."

This liberal strand, whose foundation rested on the idea of the uncoerced consent of the free individual, was, however, not the only element of the new American republic's philosophical self-conception. A second strand was classical republicanism, inherited from ancient Greece and Rome. This republican philosophy entered the American world both directly, through such authors as Aristotle and the Roman statesmen Cato the Elder and Cicero, and, indirectly, through modern apostles of republicanism such as the Florentine diplomat Niccolò Machiavelli, Swiss-born philosopher Jean-Jacques Rousseau, and French aristocrat Baron de Montesquieu, among others.

Republicanism differed markedly from its fraternal twin liberalism in its fundamental assumptions and consequently in its moral emphasis. Rather than rights, it emphasized the obligations of republican citizens, for republicanism is concerned, above all, with the well-being of the common political enterprise that the republic represents. Rather than the pursuit of individual private happiness, republicanism places its greatest regard upon the common good and the public happiness of those who live among their fellows and see themselves primarily as members.

Republicanism looks to a political enterprise that is not so much chosen as born into, part of what one ineluctably is. It looks to communal solidarity, springing naturally from common experience and common identity, as a moral guidepost, teaching men and women that their fate and happiness depend primarily on the common good. Above all, if the grand shared civic enterprise is to flourish, the common good must take precedence in citizens' lives.

Indeed, the republican tradition, looking back to the revered figure of the Roman republican citizen-soldier Cincinnatus, who left the safety of family and farm to defend his country, teaches citizens that sacrifice of the private to the public good is sometimes required. Such devoted sacrifice is the highest ideal of republican citizenship. It is civic virtue epitomized, a natural and inescapable part of self-government.

The story of the American nation from its eighteenth century roots to the twenty-first century can be interpreted as the history of the tension between and fate of these two orientations—private or public; rights or obligations; individual separateness or the solidarity of membership; individually chosen ends or the purposes set forth by a public philosophy which sets limits to individual liberty and marks out the space within which choices may be made.

Michael J. Sandel, professor of government at Harvard University, has undertaken just such an interpretation of American public life, the explicit public philosophy of its most prominent leaders and jurists, and the ideas implicit in the principal features of its political and constitutional history. In doing so he has written a compelling, sensitive, and learned, if sometimes troubling book that is at once provocative and profoundly engaging for those concerned with the difficult present and future well-being of American democracy. His work has implications, too, beyond American shores, for democracy as practiced in the West, which is to say liberal democracy.

Sandel's argument is that while the tension between the two strands of American public philosophy was maintained in the nineteenth century, in the century that followed, it was broken decisively, and unwisely, in favor of the notion of sovereign individual "selves" exercising their wills to pursue private happiness. This occurred with the triumph of what the author terms the liberal "procedural republic" over civic republicanism. The orientations of these two strands of American political ideas are very different. The liberalism of the procedural republic safeguards the liberties of each individual through the rule of law, backed by the courts' power of judicial review, declaring null and void laws they find contrary to the U.S. Constitution. American liberalism, like liberalism elsewhere, declared that the state should be neutral with regard to the ends that people pursue.

This liberalism can trace its pedigree to Thomas Hobbes, who declared in *Leviathan* (1651) that there is no "utmost aim, nor *summum bonum*, greatest good, as is spoken of in the books of the old moral philosophers." Since there is no "good life," there are only the differing goods that individuals choose for their personal ends. The state is to be neutral with respect to these ends, so long as they allow others their ends. Instead, government "should provide a framework of rights that respects persons as free and independent selves, capable of choosing their own values and ends." Sandel calls these arrangements the "procedural republic." What is right according to the procedural justice ensured by a neutral liberal state takes precedence over a shared concept of the

Good Life; or, as Sandel puts it, today the state "asserts the priority of the right over the good."

By contrast, civic republicanism lives by a shared public philosophy about the nature of the good life. Its political discourse includes moral-religious language and ideas. Policies that conflict with the public philosophy's notion of the Good Life are to be discarded. Republicanism asserts the good over the (procedural) "right."

Sandel discusses at length the debates of American political history in terms of the clash between liberal proceduralism and civic republicanism—from the early republic to the Jacksonian era and the Civil War period and after, when civic republicanism had a considerable following and was expressed in public discourse, as Sandel shows in examining nineteenth century debates which he terms "free labor versus wage labor." The twentieth century saw the eclipse of republicanism in favor of the procedural republic, in which nearly all of the Bill of Rights has been extended by the courts to cover state law, not federal law alone, as originally intended.

In the process, the idea of civic obligations not chosen by the individual has been progressively excluded. In place of republican citizens, in Sandel's interpretation, are "sovereign selves" without ties or obligations, save those freely chosen. Gone, too, is the republican notion that liberty is impossible for those who fail to participate in self-government—in making public policy. But in a thesis central to this book, however, Sandel argues that the procedural republic, lacking a public philosophy of the Good Life, "cannot secure the part of liberty bound up with self-government."

There are consequences to Sandel's position that some may find disturbing, however. In the case of controversial issues, the recognition in law and political discourse of a civic republican public philosophy would be attractive to majorities. But in a pluralist society such as the United States, where deep divides bifurcate or fragment society, minorities may find Sandel's vision of a civic republic oppressive.

The philosophy and practice of classical republicanism was, after all, developed by and suited to small, preindustrialized states with homogeneous populations. Those living close together in similar conditions can be expected to have a common outlook translatable to a shared notion of the Good Life. Law and policy adhering to this public philosophy would enjoy public support. Yet the complex postindustrial economies of modern republics create citizens with far less in common. James Madison, "father of the Constitution," explicitly contrasted small ancient republics with modern, extended, commercial versions, such as the one envisioned by the Constitution. Might Sandel be misappropriating the philosophy of ancient republics, applying it to circumstances where its place must be modest?

Sandel is aware of this criticism but offers no solution, because there is none. The enactment of a philosophy of a "good life" would be widely viewed among those in the minority on key questions as a "tyranny of the majority," which the liberal thrust of the Constitution and the addition of the Bill of Rights was designed to thwart. A majority which replaced contemporary liberal freedoms with a public philosophy derived from religion-based traditional morality would, among other measures, eliminate access to nearly all abortions, suppress much erotica, and ban the practice of various consensual sexual eccentricities. Forms of expression banned by college "speech codes" before they were overturned as unconstitutional by the "procedural republic" also might be banned when the political pendulum swung to the left. Nor would a republican political philosophy hesitate to interfere more extensively in modern market outcomes.

Be this as it may, Sandel argues that if people participated in large numbers in the reestablishment of a legally enforced public morality, they would secure their liberty. Does he, then, embrace Rousseau's "paradox of freedom"? Are the losing minority "forced to be free"?

Sandel has been criticized for expecting too much from modern men and women, who are harassed by economic insecurity, pressed from all sides for their time and attention, anxious to escape the pressures and dangers of a society that seems unable to control its destiny. The new global environment may be helping to foster public passivity among a citizenry that cannot grasp the social and economic forces that form the context of their lives. It is just such passivity that Sandel wishes to diagnose and counter. In doing so he does not hanker after a lost American past or, worse, the reconstruction of the long-dead classical republic.

Sandel is no polemicist; he levies criticism when he believes it warranted, but his tone is muted and his prose is marked by civility, candor, and an evident effort to think arguments through and abandon directions which appear inviting but on closer scrutiny are found wanting. Thus, Sandel ponders the views of "globalists" who, in so many words, call for the dismantling of the American republic in the name of a new, inchoate world government. In the end, he declines to follow a course that would amount to turning back from the experiment in self-government Lincoln described as "the last, best hope of mankind."

After considering this and other road maps to the future, adapting his vision from the rich tapestry of American constitutionalism, Sandel fastens his gaze on the possibilities for an enriched and publicly engaged republican citizenship found in the architecture of American federalism. He looks to new forms of community and communal self-direction and, like others, sees self-government not just in formal politics but also in civil society, the autonomous, self-organizing part of society that is separate from public institutions and the state. This prescription, which has the distinct advantage of nonpartisanship, surely points in the right direction.

Whether the jeremiads of a Harvard philosopher will be heard by the American public is another matter. Social forces tend to be impervious to academic messengers, however thoughtful and timely. Americans in great numbers participate actively in civil society, but it is doubtful that many will give up more time to public activity. Modern life is too frenetic to expect that weary commuters use more precious leisure for citizenship. As political philosopher Duane Smith of the University of California at Los Angeles has stressed, people believe they have better things to do than to spend more time at civic chores.

Whether the quality of democracy's conversation in the nation's public life will decline further in the face of the uncertainties and complexities of modern society is the subject of debate. Michael Sandel, however, has made a notable contribution to its elevation.

Charles F. Bahmueller

Sources for Further Study

Commentary. CII, August, 1996, p. 97.
Commonweal. CXXIII, November 22, 1996, p. 26.
Foreign Affairs. LXXV, March, 1996, p. 135.
The Nation. CCLXII, May 6, 1996, p. 34.
The New Republic. CCXIV, April 1, 1996, p. 39.
The New York Times Book Review. CI, May 19, 1996, p. 6.
Newsweek. CXXVII, May 13, 1996, p. 82.
The Times Literary Supplement. October 18, 1996, p. 14.
U.S. News and World Report. CXX, April 15, 1996, p. 65.
The Washington Post Book World. XXVI, May 5, 1996, p. 6.

THE DEVIL PROBLEM
And Other True Stories

Author: David Remnick
Publisher: Random House (New York). 404 pp. $25.95
Type of work: Current affairs; essays

Remnick writes perceptively, and at times hauntingly, about the lives of famous and powerful people, who become, in his stories, extraordinarily ordinary, or perhaps more accurately, just as complicated as most ordinary folks, only more interesting for their fame, talent, or power

David Remnick has compiled a series of essays he wrote earlier, mostly for *The New Yorker*, into a book that is easy to read and hard to put down, especially for those of us (and alas, there are far too many) who are morbidly curious about the lives and foibles of the powerful and famous. This is like a "best-of" *People* magazine, but in the style of *The New Yorker*. Remnick has a gritty, honest style which at first is refreshing, but at length has a tired Old World, we-aren't-afraid-to-use-bad-language aspect which is slightly depressing. Perhaps the articles were not meant to be read all at once. Something about them is too rich, too much.

An example of this heaviness is Remnick's use in two adjacent articles of the description of certain things as having "the color of dried blood" (referring to the border of a tie on page 338, and referring to a carpet on page 356). This is what happens when you bring together articles from different times or places. The first article was originally written in 1987, while the second was originally written in 1994. An author's inventory of words and phrases is not infinite, and what were striking images used once now look tired or even strange when they appear repeated within the space of twenty pages.

Yet perhaps this criticism is missing the forest for the trees. Remnick is counting on his readers' fundamental interest in the people he writes about and their stories, and here he has an unerring eye for the story line which will draw the reader into the narrative life of the each of his protagonists. There is a bit of the ancient theater in what Remnick is doing, and he is aware of this also. His first section is called "Forms of Exile," and is about politicians (and one athlete), marginalized in one way or another, mainly by their own actions (Gary Hart, Marion Barry), but also with a sense of fate about their lives. Whether it is watching Reggie Jackson age or Mario Cuomo apparently miss political opportunities, regret is mingled with resignation over what must be, given the character of the hero. Perhaps this is why Americans are not shocked at the lack of repentance from Gary Hart and Marion Barry, or the lifelong insistence of innocence on the part of Alger Hiss. Even Gerry Adams (of the Irish Republican Army's political wing Sinn Féin) does not seem anymore the anarchist, the ultimate individual, when Remnick is through with him, but rather a sad and inevitable product of ages of hatred and violence.

Remnick here strikes just the right balance between the twin metaphors of individual responsibility (sin) and social determination (sickness). His characters never lose their responsibility for their actions, but readers become more sympathetic with them (even the ones Remnick obviously dislikes, interestingly) as their stories are told. They are not excused, but they are understood, even pitied (in the best sense of the word). To read Remnick aright is to see oneself reflected, even if dimly, in the lives of those he writes about. Their passions are real, their mistakes are stupid, their ambitions are strong, their minds are clear (if at times one-tracked). They are like us, only larger.

In part 2 of his book, titled "Artists and Scholars," Remnick deals with various writers and academics, as well as with two basketball players (Michael Jordan and Dennis Rodman). It is here that one wonders whether there is some deeper principle of organization that is not so obvious, or whether (as seems to be the case) Remnick simply did not pay much attention to how his book was put together. Not only are several of the characters in this second section candidates for the first section (particularly writer Ralph Ellison and sociologist William Julius Wilson), but he could have had another section entitled "Athletes," and put Jackson, Jordan, and Rodman together. Perhaps what Remnick is trying to show is more of a Greek mythic sense of things, tragedy in the first act, comedy (in the theatrical sense of a cathartic or happy ending, not in the sense of being funny) in the second. Drama comes last, as can be seen below. Certainly the second section stories are generally more upbeat, and usually end on a more positive note, at least with regard to their main characters.

Elaine Pagels comes the closest to gaining sainthood in the book. (Her article is titled "The Devil Problem," from which comes the title of the book itself.) Hers, along with several others in this section, is a story of overcoming great hardship (the death of both son and husband in a short span of time), of affirming Life and the True and the Beautiful in the midst of the death and lies and ugliness of ordinary human experience. Nobel Prize-winning author Kenzaburo Oe and his son Hikari come in a close second to Pagels for canonization. A thoroughly modern Japanese man highly critical of his own countrymen's traditions, Oe nevertheless comes across as a deeply spiritual man, and spiritual in a deeply Eastern way. His connection to his severely mentally handicapped son is profoundly mystical and inexplicable by any Western standards, yet fits perfectly in the world of Eastern tradition he inhabits and under which he chafes.

Joseph Brodsky also gets into the Pantheon, but mostly by his work, not his life. He stood for the best in internal intellectual anti-Soviet critique, it is true, but Remnick cannot resist constantly quoting his poetry over giving details of his life, as if to say, "For a writer, his words are his life." If this is so, it makes Remnick's treatment of Steve Sohmer and Mary Ann McGrail all the more pointedly pathetic (here again Remnick seems to have misplaced his article, but perhaps his readers may be looking for too much organization, or the wrong kind). This is the story of a minor Shakespeare scholar and a screenwriter-turned-amateur Shakespeare scholar fighting over what may turn out to be a rather meager bone—the idea that the Bard was using *Hamlet* as a sort of undercover apologetic for Luther and the Protestant Reformation (each claims the idea as his or her own, and therein is the story). As is often the case with biblical scholarship as well, it looks to the casual observer that this is indeed much ado about nothing, or at least, about very little. With so much time being spent by so many people on so little literary real estate (comparatively speaking), it is inevitable that the exegetical canons expand to include the ingenious, even fantastic theorizing of the interpreters themselves. It is the old nemesis of a certain kind of rabbinical exegesis. Midrash (the allusive, metaphorical interpretations of biblical texts engaged in by Jewish scholars—mostly ancient) can be found in any text, but is it the midrash of the text or of the interpreter? If it is clever enough, it is difficult to prove—or disprove, for that matter (and many flee into the arms of science).

To return to the basketball players. Remnick presents them in a manner consistent with the section in which he puts them—as comic heroes, life-affirming in spite of character flaws (especially in the case of Rodman). Yet these athletes seem prisoners of their own ambition even more than do the petty scholars and the politicians. Their addiction to competition may entertain audiences, but Remnick does not question (at least for these two) where it leads for the addicts themselves. Perhaps he will return to that theme in a later series.

In his last section ("The News Business"), Remnick deals with reporters, publishers, and columnists. Some he admires (Ben Bradlee of *The Washington Post*, Murray Kempton of the *New York Post*), some he does not, or at least seems ambivalent about (Al Neuharth of *USA Today*). Yet here Remnick is most at home. These are his people, this is the writing he understands, the genre, the values, the excitement of "being there." It is clear this is where he is comfortable, where he lets his own feelings out. Whatever traces of admiration for Neuharth's business acumen he might have, Remnick tells readers how he really feels in the endnote (on page 355) to "Good News Is No News," the article on *USA Today*: "There are precious few cities now where *USA Today* is not the best paper in town. God help us."

Remnick portrays clearly throughout this section the impression that he thinks that literate culture at some level is dying in the United States, or maybe even in the West or in the world. He does this by mourning the passing of his heroes (Bradlee and Kempton) as well as sadly chronicling the rise of the new media-conscious, icon-and-entertainment-driven publishers such as Rupert Murdoch or editors such as Al Neuharth. There is nobility and baseness, a war between high and low culture (if not good and evil). Here, then, is the section on drama to go with the first two on tragedy and comedy, giving Remnick his full range of human experience to explore and of which to tell the tale.

Remnick loves good writing and strives for a straightforward, almost in-your-face style which does not always feel congruent with the depth of his analysis or the profundity of his exploration of human character. It is an aggressive mix which probably goes down better in New York City than many other places. Still in all, he writes interesting stories about interesting people, and that will get him read. He quotes Pete Hamill (on page 356) of the *New York Post* as saying "You wanna know what I think would be God's paper?" "It would be a tabloid that's smart and hip, knowing."

Remnick tries, and mostly succeeds, in writing in a way that is smart and hip, knowing. Whether or not that makes him God's writer is for his readers to decide.

Robert A. Bascom

Sources for Further Study

Atlanta Journal Constitution. October 6, 1996, p. L10.
Booklist. XCII, August, 1996, p. 1875.
Denver Post. August 25, 1996, p. I6.
Kirkus Reviews. LXIV, June 15, 1996, p. 884.
Library Journal. CXXI, August, 1996, p. 85.
Los Angeles Times Book Review. November 17, 1996, p. 14.
The New York Times Book Review. CI, September 8, 1996, p. 22.
Publishers Weekly. CCXLIII, June 24, 1996, p. 39.

D. H. LAWRENCE
Triumph to Exile, 1912-1922

Author: Mark Kinkead-Weekes
Publisher: Cambridge University Press (New York). Illustrated. 943 pp. $39.95
Type of work: Literary biography
Time: 1912-1921
Locale: Germany, Italy, and England

The second volume of the Cambridge Biography of the British novelist, tracing in exhaustive detail his experiences from his elopement with Frieda von Richthofen and the publication of his first major novel, Sons and Lovers, *through his severe disillusionment and alienation during World War I and his renunciation of his native land*

Principal personages:
> D. H. LAWRENCE, an English novelist, poet, and polemicist
> FRIEDA VON RICHTHOFEN WEEKLEY LAWRENCE, his German-born wife
> ERNEST WEEKLEY, Frieda's first husband, a professor of philology
> LADY OTTOLINE MORRELL, a prominent society hostess to artists and
>   intellectuals
> LADY CYNTHIA ASQUITH, a friend of Lawrence, the daughter-in-law of
>   Prime Minister H. H. Asquith
> S. S. KOTELIANSKY, a Russian émigré, literary translator, and close
>   friend of Lawrence
> JOHN MIDDLETON MURRY, a literary journalist and editor, friend and
>   betrayer of Lawrence
> KATHERINE MANSFIELD, a short-story writer and friend of Lawrence and
>   Murry
> BERTRAND RUSSELL, a philosopher and antiwar collaborator with
>   Lawrence
> HILDA DOOLITTLE (H.D.), an American-born imagist poet and friend of
>   Lawrence
> RICHARD ALDINGTON, Hilda's husband, a man of letters, friend, and
>   early biographer of Lawrence
> WILLIAM HENRY HOCKING, a Cornish farmer and friend of Lawrence
> ROBERT MOUNTSIER, Lawrence's American agent

D. H. Lawrence: Triumph to Exile, 1912-1922 is the central panel in what will eventually be an enormous biographical triptych. The first volume, *D. H. Lawrence: The Early Years, 1885-1912*, by John Worthen, was favorably received upon its publication in 1991. The third volume, written by David Ellis, will concentrate on the last eight years of Lawrence's relatively brief but productive life. In volume 2, spanning ten pivotal years in the middle of the novelist's career, Mark Kinkead-Weekes mines the wealth of information recently made available by the publication of new and authoritative editions of Lawrence's complete letters and works by Cambridge University Press. (Indeed, Kinkead-Weekes is the editor of the Cambridge edition of one of Lawrence's major novels, *The Rainbow*.) The result is an exhaustively detailed account that, in its methodical recording of virtually all Lawrence's known actions—almost a week-by-week log of his whereabouts, the company he kept, the words he uttered, the debts he owed and paid—aims to convey "some sense at least of what it may have been like to live as Lawrence did."

This immersion in detail is not the only way in which the Cambridge Biography differs from previous lives of Lawrence written by Richard Aldington, Harry T. Moore, and Jeffrey Meyers. In a jointly penned authors' preface, Worthen, Kinkead-Weekes, and Ellis lay claim to attempting not just a new biography of Lawrence but "a new kind of biography" altogether. The division of the project into three parts each produced by a different author is only the first departure from custom. Although the three biographers have shared materials and "collaborated very closely" on their work, each has his own interpretation of the subject, his own style and emphasis. That three somewhat different Lawrences may emerge from these volumes is not a cause for apology. Rather, the cobiographers see their approach as well suited to an age that remains skeptical about "the idea of a personal core or centre, an 'essential self.'" Avoiding "the genetic fallacy" by which one explains a complex phenomenon—in this case, a remarkable character—after the fact, as a direct result of its origins, the biographers disavow any attempt to impose a single "definitive" pattern onto their subject. They further justify this poststructuralist approach, as it may be called, by invoking Lawrence's own vitalist aesthetic, which preferred open-ended, improvisational narratives, tales responding readily to fluctuating currents of feeling and impulse rather than to a preconceived formal design.

An immediate consequence of this particular biographical experiment is the deliberate sacrifice of narrative speed and economy. If it is the biographical analogue to a relay race, the course followed here is like that of a marathon or a steeple chase. Kinkead-Weekes, for his part, asserts that biographical "summary and generalisation should go to the . . . devil; since the life of things tends to be found in detail, variation and change through time; though that story takes longer to tell." As if to demonstrate his premise, Kinkead-Weekes devotes his first hundred pages to a complete reprise of events already fully presented in the preceding volume. At first glance, there does not seem to be a compelling reason to go over this ground again, except that doing so enables the biographer to include one of the most dramatic events in all of Lawrence's life: his "elopement" in the spring of 1912 with Frieda Weekley, a married woman and mother of three, and their flight from home in Nottinghamshire to the Continent. Beginning with the image of Lawrence and Frieda on the ferry from Dover to Ostend, Kinkead-Weekes sets the stage for his concluding set piece which finds the Lawrences again setting forth, a decade later, for foreign parts, this time en route to Ceylon (modern Sri Lanka) and Australia. The dual images of Lawrence in transit effectively frame the period in which most of Kinkead-Weekes' volume takes place, the years when Lawrence's movements were most often confined to his native land.

The primary focus of this volume is the transformation brought about in Lawrence by a disastrous series of events that he endured during World War I. (A more streamlined account of this experience appeared in Paul Delaney's 1978 biography, *D. H. Lawrence's Nightmare*.) One of the most memorable junctures in the biography occurs when Kinkead-Weekes "freezes" his narrative after describing a well-known photograph of Lawrence, Frieda, and their friends Katherine Mansfield and John Middleton Murry on the day of the Lawrences' wedding, July 14, 1914, and speculates about "how *different* the lives and characters of Lawrence and Frieda might have become if their world had allowed them to live as they planned." After the modest critical success of *Sons and Lovers* (1913), Lawrence had matured as both a man and an artist and developed a new approach to the novel. Henceforth, he would eschew "the old stable *ego*" of character and vividly created "scenes" in favor of a deeper and less predictable method of composition—one that he first attempted in his "Brang-wensaga" that would eventually become *The Rainbow* (1915) and *Women in Love* (1920). The growth of his imaginative powers paralleled—and no doubt was closely related to—the strengthening of his bond with Frieda. After weathering the hurt and anger of her jilted husband, Ernest Weekley (who had been one of Lawrence's professors at the University of Nottingham), the pain of separation from her children, and the resistance of both their families to their living together, the high-born Frieda finally committed herself to this miner's son. Although the relationship was notoriously volatile, Lawrence drew strength from it, as though he thrived on her opposition to his will. Moreover, after returning to London from the Continent, Lawrence found increasing acceptance among the most "advanced" artists and intellectuals of the day. He soon formed ties to such luminaries as Lady Ottoline Morrell, Lady Cynthia Asquith (the prime minister's daughter-in-law), Edward Marsh, E. M. Forster, Bertrand Russell, Aldous Huxley, and "H.D.," as well as the aforementioned Mansfield and Murry. Lawrence's future seemed promising, his prospects bright both professionally and personally, and he was essentially secure in his connection with his homeland.

All this would change utterly after the hostilities of August, 1914, commenced. First, the Lawrences found they could not return to Italy as planned because "war conditions" complicated any movement across national frontiers. Frieda's German origins and sympathies were bound to arouse suspicion, and Lawrence's early vocal opposition to the war further drew fire from the "patriotic" establishment. In the fall of 1915, the popular press virulently attacked *The Rainbow* as "immoral" on both sexual and political grounds. Lawrence's publisher, Methuen, made no attempt to defend the novel or its author, and only a few of his friends and fellow writers were willing to offer public support. In time, important friendships and collaborations such as those with Murry and Russell foundered. Lawrence began to find himself increasingly isolated from the social and intellectual circles to which he had been admitted only a short time before. After the official suppression of *The Rainbow* (the novel could not be legally purchased in England for another fifteen years), Lawrence had difficulty marketing his other work. Although that novel's sequel, *Women in Love*, was essentially finished by 1917, it would not be published until well after the war and then only in the United States. Lawrence's chief source of income thus dried up, and he was forced to borrow from friends and family merely to subsist. As the war dragged on and became ever more bloody, Lawrence's depression—exacerbated by poverty and illness—grew apace. When his wish to emigrate to America fell through, the Lawrences moved to the remote westernmost coast of Cornwall. Eventually even that retreat failed them. His notoriety as the perpetrator of "dirty" books, his antiwar activities, and Frieda's familial ties to Manfred von Richthofen, the famous "Red Baron"—all these factors conspired to arouse official suspicion that the Lawrences were, at best, German sympathizers and, at worst, enemy spies. Thereafter, they were hounded relentlessly by the authorities. Although obviously unfit for military service (he had already been diagnosed as consumptive), Lawrence was three times subjected to humiliating medical examinations under threat of conscription. Their house was searched, the mail opened, his manuscripts tampered with. Finally, in October, 1917, they were officially evicted from Cornwall as suspected spies. Yet still they were not permitted to leave England and had to wait out the rest of the war, dependent upon his family back in the Midlands.

Subjected to this unremitting barrage of blows, Lawrence bitterly turned against his homeland. Finally in November, 1919, after the armistice, he and Frieda departed for Italy and, sixteen months later, for Ceylon, Australia, and America in search of a new beginning. Never again would they live in England, nor would Lawrence write again for the English public. Although he sporadically worked on novels begun before or during the war—*The Lost Girl* (1920), *Aaron's Rod* (1922), and *Mr. Noon* (published in 1984 but written in 1920-1921 and never finished)—Lawrence was casting about for fresh inspiration and a different audience. These he would find eventually in America, but even then he was essentially recasting the experience of being spiritually uprooted and starting over in a new world.

In addition to tracking Lawrence's inexorable progress from "triumph to exile," Kinkead-Weekes provides very ample discussions of all of his writings during the period. "We should remember," he tells readers, "that Lawrence's was . . . a writing life, lived perhaps as vividly on paper as with people." This means not only that the biographer patiently paraphrases and comments on even the most obscure essay or poem but also that he recounts the sometimes mundane dealings with literary agents, editors, and publishers. More interesting are Kinkead-Weekes' observations about Lawrence's often difficult relations with fellow writers, especially with modernists such as Ezra Pound, Ford Madox Ford, Wyndham Lewis, and T. S. Eliot. Despite several similarities, Lawrence's art parted company with that of the modernists in that he did not deliberately strive, as they did, for formal perfection but instead sought "life surging itself into utterance at its very well-head," knowing "no finality, no finished crystallisation." Even more telling, as Kinkead-Weekes points out, "where Modernist emphasis fell on the artist-self as creator, Lawrence emphasised the *transformation* of the self at the hands of the Other." It was an experience he had come to know all too well.

Readers of modern literature will doubtless welcome this carefully executed "middle" relay in the ongoing Cambridge biographical marathon that has already added much to our knowledge of one of the century's indispensable voices.

Ronald G. Walker

Sources for Further Study

Choice. XXXIV, December, 1996, p. 614.
The New York Times Book Review. CI, December 15, 1996, p. 30.
The Spectator. CCLXXVII, August 31, 1996, p. 27.
The Times Literary Supplement. August 23, 1996, p. 3.

DINOSAUR IN A HAYSTACK
Reflections in Natural History

Author: Stephen Jay Gould (1941-   )
Publisher: Harmony Books (New York). Illustrated. 496 pp. $25.00
Type of work: Science

In a series of essays in natural history, Gould uses evolutionary theory to discover surprising interconnections among such widely diverse physical, biological, and human phenomena as solar eclipses, mass extinctions, and the eugenic ideas of Luther Burbank and the Nazis

Stephen Jay Gould thinks that evolution is the most exciting truth that any scientist has ever discovered. Since 1974, he has written numerous essays, most of them for his monthly column in *Natural History* magazine, in which he has explored the power of Darwinian theory to shed light on a variety of biological, environmental, and historical topics. He has collected these essays into six previous books, and in *Dinosaur in a Haystack: Reflections in Natural History*, his seventh, he has cast his net of evolution over an even broader range of subjects than before, with a new emphasis on social, political, literary, religious, and ethical subjects. Gould appears well on his way to becoming, with Isaac Asimov and Carl Sagan, one of America's great popularizers of science in the twentieth century.

While Gould's essays are not personal in the conventional sense, he makes such extensive use of his own experiences that readers learn much about his character and life, in addition to his work. The heroes of his youth were his father and Charles Darwin, and his favorite author was D'Arcy Wentworth Thompson, whose *Growth and Form* has been called the finest work of literature in all of science. Gould, who teaches biology, geology, and the history of science at Harvard University, is a creature of intense enthusiasms and antipathies. He likes dinosaurs, Bach's B-minor Mass, the Yankee baseball team, old books, and the bus driver who, thirty-eight years ago, wrote in his autograph book: "A man of words and not of deeds/ Is like a garden full of weeds."

He dislikes the ladder image for evolution, those who make science too orderly, and publishers who neglect papers claiming negative results. He depicts himself as a reasonable and tolerant humanist, but in some of his essays he seems a bit like Henry Higgins in George Bernard Shaw's *Pygmalion*—a scientist blissfully unaware of his pride and arrogance. Indeed, he has much to be proud of, for an essay in this collection marks the completion of twenty years of writing his magazine column, having never missed a month, even through his battles with cancer. Critics have noticed a considerable variety in the tone of his essays: whimsical, melancholic, meditative, self-congratulatory, preachy, pedantic, and professorial, but this is to be expected for essays written at different times and for various purposes. Furthermore, he does not want his critics to consider him "just a science writer"; he sees himself as an "essay machine" in the tradition of Michel Eyquem de Montaigne.

Gould attributes the success of his books of essays to his ability to discover insightful connections that harmonize the apparently inharmonious. The thirty-four chapters of *Dinosaur in a Haystack* provide ample evidence of such interconnections. For example, Gould's joy is almost palpable as he uses the plot of Giuseppe Verdi's *Un Ballo in Maschera* and the appearance of the botanist Carl Linnaeus and the Swedish King Gustav III on opposite sides of the fifty-kronor note to help readers understand how Linnaeus developed his system for classifying plants by their sex organs. In a chapter entitled "Cordelia's Dilemma," Gould moves from Cordelia's silence before King Lear to the evolutionary theory of punctuated equilibrium that he and Niles Eldredge developed in 1972. This theory argued that, contrary to popular conception, evolution is not gradual change but long periods of nonchange punctuated by bursts of rapid change. Similarly, in the chapter that supplies the book's title, he moves from a favorite statement of Darwin ("the best one-liner ever penned") to an investigation of mass extinctions in the late Cretaceous period. This statement—"How odd it is that anyone should not see that all observation must be for or against some view if it is to be of any service!"—leads to a discussion of the two-way street that must exist between scientific ideas and observations if human understanding of nature is to deepen. The theoretical must be saturated with the actual, but fascinating oddities, which pique the reader's curiosity, can also be used to elucidate such grand ideas of evolutionary biology as change and stasis.

Some of the essays are mystery stories. Was Edgar Allan Poe guilty of plagiarism when he wrote a textbook on conchology (the study of mollusks and shells)? Why are students wrongly taught that medieval people believed the earth was flat? As in any good mystery, Gould subjects his readers to a series of digressions and surprises, and the mystery is sometimes made more mysterious before all is explained. Like the hero in classic detective stories, Gould, the intellectually confident scientist, is often the puzzle solver, although his confidence weakens when ethically complex human problems are involved.

Dinosaur in a Haystack has eight parts, with three to six chapters per part. Although it is difficult to see any narrative momentum from part to part, there is a vague trend from the physical through the biological to the human as the reader proceeds in order through the essays. For example, in part 1, Gould depicts the impact that the solar eclipse on May 10, 1994, had on him and many other people in New York City. For a short time highly disparate people, through their shared curiosity, brought their common nature to light. Another essay in this first part introduces the theme of science and religion, which plays an increasingly important role in later essays. This chapter, alliteratively titled "Dousing Diminutive Dennis's Debate (or DDDD = 2000)," is concerned with the question of when humanity should celebrate the twenty-first century's birth. Because the monk Dionysius Exiguus ("Dennis the Short") decided, in the sixth century, to start the Christian era in A.D. 1 (and not the year zero), scholars have insisted that centuries must end in a double zero, and, indeed, Americans celebrated the start of the twentieth century on January 1, 1901. Yet Gould believes that because of popular culture's present power, Americans will bring in the new century when 1999 turns into 2000.

Dionysius Exiguus believed that biblical stories explained both the universe and human history. By the nineteenth century, another narrative—the scientific—was ascendant. During the seventeenth and eighteenth centuries, the founders of this scientific vision—Nicolaus Copernicus, Johannes Kepler, Galileo Galilei, and Sir Isaac Newton—did not think of their story as a replacement for the great Judeo-Christian narrative but as an extension of it. Newton, whose discoveries were made in the service of God, conceived of God as a great mathematician. By the time Pierre-Simon Laplace wrote the five volumes of his *Méchanique céleste* (1700-1825; *Celestial Mechanics*), God was on the way to becoming a dead metaphor. When Napoleon asked Laplace how he could write about the operation of the heavens without once mentioning God, he is supposed to have replied that he had no need of that hypothesis. Gould points out that the story is most likely apocryphal, but it has become a staple in many histories of science and textbooks because it symbolizes the role that determinism played in classical science. Many scientists continued to believe in God, but it was a God who made the clockwork universe, wound it up, and then let it run without interruption. Dionysius Exiguus would certainly have been displeased, because it was the supremely important intervention of Jesus Christ that was responsible for his new system of naming years.

Gould is aware that religion and science have been at odds over the meaning of the universe, but in his quest to reconcile these traditional antagonists, by limiting each to a specific domain (science to the empirical world, religion to ethics and values), he misses both substantial differences between them and some areas of profound agreement. In "The Late Birth of a Flat Earth" Gould analyzes the writings of John W. Draper, who saw the relationship between religion and science as conflict, and Andrew Dickson White, who saw the relationship between theology and science as warfare. Both Draper and White believed that medieval thinkers espoused the idea of a flat earth, but Gould shows that most medieval thinkers, including the Venerable Bede, Thomas Aquinas, Roger Bacon, Jean Buridan, and Nicholas Oresme, among others, affirmed the earth's sphericity. In telling their tale of how rational science was victorious over superstitious religion, Draper and White ignored the aforementioned scholars and relied on insignificant writers such as Cosmas Indicopleustes, who believed in a flat earth. For his part, Gould wonders how there can be conflict between two subjects with such different areas of authority.

In his struggle to get his theory of evolution as punctuated equilibrium accepted by the scientific community, Gould has had direct experience of the power of these social forces. When Gould and Eldredge proposed their theory, many scientists resisted it, though they should have known, from the fossil record, that nonchange of species was the rule rather than the exception. Punctuated equilibrium, on the other hand, does not mean that Gould rejects all gradual change of species. For example, he accepts that, in the evolution of horses, their toes did get fewer and their bodies bigger. Paleontologists certainly had evidence of dramatic changes in the geological record. The Cambrian explosion of multicellular life that took place from 535 to 530 million years ago introduced the basic structures and functions of many species that have dominated life ever since.

Ironically, Gould was initially skeptical about a new discovery that supported punctuated equilibrium. When, in 1979, physicist Luis Alvarez and his collaborators first published their idea that a large extraterrestrial object, an asteroid or comet, had collided with the earth at the end of the Cretaceous period and caused massive extinctions of life, most paleontologists were inclined to reject it. Gould's skepticism was the result of his ignorance about the tremendous explosive energies involved in such a collision. Despite these doubts, Alvarez had proposed a testable theory, and scientists began work to uncover evidence that either verified or falsified his idea. For example, iridium, an element scarce on earth but abundant in asteroids, was found in high concentrations in rock layers associated with the extinctions. Before Alvarez's theory, many paleontologists believed that the dinosaurs had become extinct long before the time that the boundary layers of rock between the Cretaceous and Tertiary periods were deposited. Evidence of rare species becoming extinct at this K/T boundary was difficult to find. It was like looking for a single small needle in a very large haystack (the title of Gould's book comes from this search for rare dinosaur bones in large amounts of rock). By systematically searching strata near the K/T boundary, scientists were able to discover, in the late Cretaceous rocks of Montana and North Dakota, evidence of dinosaur bones up to the K/T boundary.

Alvarez's theory ultimately provided answers to a series of paleontological questions about the extinction of dinosaurs and other ancient species of life that occurred sixty-five million years ago, but it was unable to shed much light on interactions between science and human values, issues of particular concern to Gould in the final chapters of his book. For example, Gould was surprised by the eugenic views of Luther Burbank, the plant breeder famous for creating the stoneless plum, the white blackberry, the Shasta daisy, and the Burbank rose. Most people have categorized eugenics as an ideology of political conservatives who wanted to reform society by improving hereditary traits through controls on breeding and restrictions on immigration, but Burbank was a eugenicist of the political left who encouraged immigration because he believed that mingling races would bring about "the finest race the world has ever known." Basing his arguments on Jean Lamarck's evolutionary views, Burbank believed that characteristics acquired by plants and animals through good breeding could be transferred to offspring. Just as he had succeeded, by careful rearing and selection, in making better plants, so, too, he wanted to improve the human stock. He was wrong, however, since a good environment does not strengthen genes any more than a bad environment dilutes them.

Despite Gould's sympathy with Burbank's civil libertarian views, he sees this great horticulturalist making the same error that most eugenicists did. As Gould puts it, three-and-a-half billion years of evolution provide no basis for what constitutes morally good human behavior. These false eugenic ideas even influenced a good man, Burbank, to advocate bad laws on the prohibition of marriage for the "unfit." The natural world is amoral, and its processes, authoritarian and cruel, cannot serve as moral models for human beings.

These considerations serve to introduce readers to Gould's reflections on the nature of *Homo sapiens*. He believes that human beings, using their intelligence, can transcend nature through morality. Yet the same capacity that grounds human choices for good may also allow humans to choose evil, and Gould is deeply troubled by the destructive role that false biological ideas can have on human behavior when they become associated with political power. He deals with these issues in his chapter on the Wannsee Conference of January 20, 1942, whose purpose was to develop solutions to what the Nazis called "the Jewish Question." In reading about this infamous conference, Gould was horrified by Adolf Eichmann's use of Darwinian arguments of natural selection in explaining why the Nazis would have to be particularly vigilant about the Jews who survived the rigors of the forced-labor camps, since they would be the products of natural selection and especially tough and dangerous. They would, if freed, act as founts of a Jewish revivification. Gould denounces Eichmann's misuse of Darwin's ideas, while conceding that this misuse was not restricted to Germany. In the 1930's, Hitler's laws of enforced sterilization for the unfit were actually based on American laws (which had been upheld by the Supreme Court in 1927).

What happened in interwar America and in wartime Nazi Germany forces Gould to confront that most impenetrable of all mysteries—human evil. Here the power of evolutionary theory, which has formed the basis or the background for many of Gould's essays, falls flat, as does his evolutionary view of the human being as a fortuitous cosmic afterthought. For him, the human animal is but a tiny twig on the richly branching bush of life. To the question of how human life began, Gould answers, by accident; to the question of how the human species will end, Gould answers, by accident. On the other hand, to many people the accidental life is not worth living; they are searching for life's meaning.

Gould promises to keep telling his scientific tales until the new millennium, which begins in 2001. Since he writes a volume every two or three years, this means he hopes to give his readers two more books of essays. These readers have grown comfortable with this author who symbolizes much of the modern scientific mind—intelligent, self-sufficient, skeptical, ironical, and splendidly trained for the great game of solving the puzzles of nature. Since consciousness began, humans have been weaving their experiences of themselves and of their physical and biological worlds into stories that have provided a basis for systems of values, and every generation has passed on its ways of valuing human life. As new generations have encountered more of the world and its complexities, they have had to reinterpret the stories of the past. All accounts of the universe and human struggles within it—scientific, religious, mythical, evolutionary—tell of human error and frailty. The best of these stories, however, are told in ways that inspire a deep sense of moral responsibility and of stewardship for the earth. In the future books that Gould has promised to write, readers must hope that his tales will encourage his fellow human beings to grow in understanding of their wonderful universe and in the wisdom needed to make life-enhancing choices.

Robert J. Paradowski

Sources for Further Study

Booklist. XCII, December 1, 1995, p. 595.
Canadian Geographic. CXVI, March, 1996, p. 81.
Chicago Tribune. March 3, 1996, XIV, p. 9.
Library Journal. CXX, December, 1995, p. 151.
Los Angeles Times. October 8, 1996, p. E1.
The Nation. CCLXII, May 20, 1996, p. 25.
Nature. CCCLXXX, March 28, 1996, p. 300.
New Scientist. CXLIX, March 30, 1996, p. 46.
The New York Review of Books. XLIII, October 17, 1996, p. 33.
The New York Times Book Review. CI, January 21, 1996, p. 9.
Publishers Weekly. CCXLII, December 4, 1995, p. 48.
Sci Tech Book News. XX, March, 1996, p. 19.

THE DISCOVERY OF HEAVEN

Author: Harry Mulisch (1927-   )
First published: De ontdekking van de hemel, 1992, in The Netherlands
Translated from the Dutch by Paul Vincent
Publisher: Viking (New York). 730 pp. $34.95
Type of work: Novel
Time: 1967-1985
Locale: Holland, Cuba, Rome, and Jerusalem

In a densely plotted tale in which supernatural beings manipulate the lives of individuals in order to bring about the destruction of God's Mosaic covenant with humankind, novelist Harry Mulisch develops a metaphysical treatise on the impact of materialism and technology on the modern world

Principal characters:
ONNO QUIST, an iconoclastic philologist and son of a prominent Dutch politician
MAX DELIUS, astronomer and womanizer
ADA BRONS QUIST, cellist who falls in love first with Max, then with Onno
SOPHIA BRONS, Ada's mother and Max's lover
QUINTIN QUIST, natural son of Max and Ada who is claimed by Onno as his son

It is unfortunate that English-speaking readers know Dutch writer Harry Mulisch from translations of his popular novels *The Assault* (1985) and *Last Call* (1989). These represent only a fragment of his prodigious output, which includes nearly four dozen books of fiction and philosophy. Nevertheless, the few works available in English suggest that Mulisch is concerned with more than mere entertainment in his novels. For example, in *The Assault*, he uses his own experience as a survivor of World War II and the Holocaust as a backdrop for exploring the presence and consequences of evil in the modern world. In *Last Call*, a novel ostensibly about the theater, he turns his attention to the nature of reality and the power of art to preserve and transform the world. The subjects of *The Discovery of Heaven* are even more complex and controversial: the nature of human existence, the possibility of the existence of God, and the relationship between humankind and its Creator. Tackling such subjects would be sufficiently challenging for most novelists, but Mulisch goes even further in his exploration of the human condition, exploring the nature of politics, the implications of scientific discovery, and the impact of technology on humankind in the twentieth century.

Mulisch's philosophical musings are ensconced in a densely plotted novel reminiscent in some ways of *Don Quixote* and *Tom Jones*. His story opens in 1967, when philologist Onno Quist meets astronomer Max Delius on what they perceive as a chance encounter outside Amsterdam. The two are unlikely soulmates. Although Onno leads a bohemian existence, he is descended from a prominent family active in Dutch politics for generations, while Max is the son of a Jewish woman killed in the

Holocaust after being betrayed by her husband, a Nazi war criminal. Their unusual friendship is strengthened, however, by conversations on matters of politics and philosophy. A chance encounter in a bookstore begins Max's relationship with Ada, a young cellist. When their affair comes to an end, Ada eventually takes up with Onno. When Ada gets a chance to travel to Havana to perform a concert as a guest of the Communist government, Max and Onno decide to accompany her. In Cuba they are mistaken for revolutionaries and made to participate in a worldwide political conference sponsored by Fidel Castro. On the last day of their visit, while Onno is secretly visiting a prostitute, Max takes Ada swimming; at sea, overwhelmed by an unexplainable passion, they make love; the result of their lovemaking is Quintin, a child Onno believes is his, since he too makes love to Ada later the same day. When the trio returns to Holland and Onno learns Ada is pregnant, he agrees to marry her.

A reformed Onno decides to enter politics, and Max continues his career as an astronomer bent on discovering the mysteries of the deepest parts of the universe. All of their lives are altered tragically when, upon learning that Ada's father is dying, they dash off to Amsterdam from the country so she can be with him. On the way, a freak auto accident sends Ada into a coma; Onno rushes her to the hospital and sends Max to tell Ada's mother Sophia, who is now a widow, of Ada's condition. In a scene of macabre irony, Sophia ends up seducing Max in her own home. Weeks later, doctors are able to deliver the comatose Ada's baby when it is close to term. Overcome by the tragedy, however, Onno is unable to see himself in the role of father. Max agrees to raise the child and convinces Sophia to live with him—ostensibly as housekeeper, but really as his lover. The young Quintin, deprived of a mother who remains in a coma for the next two decades, grows up thinking Onno is his biological father. Although not a good student in school, he learns much about the world from Max and from tenants in the castle-turned-apartment house in which he lives with his foster father and grandmother.

Mulisch continues to complicate the plot by having Onno disgraced by a political rival who exposes his participation in the Cuban convention at a most inopportune time. Crushed, Onno leaves Holland just at a time when Quintin, an unusual child grown to an unusual teenager, most needs his fatherly consultation. For years, Quintin is obsessed by a recurrent dream in which he sees a building which he believes is the center of the universe; convinced the dream has some significance, he looks to various adults for assistance in interpreting it. Unfortunately, few can help him, not even Max, whose work in astronomy has begun to lead him to some unusual speculations of his own about the nature of the universe. Ironically, just as he is about to assimilate his disparate ideas into a coherent theory about the possibility of a divine presence behind the physical world, Max is killed by a falling meteor. Bereft, Quintin feels he has no choice but to leave his grandmother to search for his absent father.

Quintin's search takes him to Rome, where by chance he discovers Onno. Sightseeing in the city, they stumble upon St. John Lateran Church, which is the embodiment of the building from Quintin's dream; inside, they find a small sanctuary zealously guarded by the clergy, and Quintin becomes convinced that the secret to his dream lies buried there. A series of conversations with his father and others, and several discoveries in old histories and documents, convinces Quintin that hidden in St. John Lateran are the original tablets Moses brought down from Sinai. Father and son engage in a bizarre plot to rob the church. Successful in gaining entry, they find there two dusty tablets; almost caught in their crime, they escape across the continent to Jerusalem. There, Quintin manages to "return" the tablets to their original hiding place in the desert, and for his troubles he is rewarded with immediate apotheosis.

All this sounds much more strange in summary than in the pages of Mulisch's novel. The novelist makes the absurd coincidences acceptable in a variety of ways. First, the bohemian lifestyles of Max and Onno lend credence to the episodic nature of the plot. Second, and more important, Mulisch includes two characters outside—actually above—the story of Max, Onno, and Quintin, who control the action of these earthlings. Called Sparks, these angel-like creatures, whose conversations form brief interludes between major segments of the principal story, are seen manipulating events to bring about the climax of the tale in which Quintin discovers and eventually destroys the Mosaic tablets. The Sparks take credit for bringing together first Quintin's grandparents, then his father and mother. They arrange for Ada's accident, and for Max's death. They act, in their opinion, from the highest of motives: to create on earth a messenger from the divine world who can sever the relationship between God and the creatures who are no longer worthy of God's attention.

Through the Sparks Mulisch introduces one of the major themes of the novel: the movement of the human race toward the discovery of the divine. As readers learn from the Sparks, and from conversations between Onno and Max and later between Quintin and his two fathers, the human race has been moving inexorably to replace belief in the divine with reliance on technology. Through both his heavenly and earthly characters, Mulisch cleverly assigns the start of this process to the actions of sixteenth century scientist and philosopher Francis Bacon, who is supposed to have entered into a Faustian pact with Satan, exchanging knowledge for salvation. Bacon's pact is not merely personal, however; his actions condemn all humankind to a path where technological progress will lead to a severing of the original compact God made with his people more than two thousand years earlier.

The story of Max, Onno, and Quintin's metaphysical journey is told against a backdrop of modern European and global history that gives *The Discovery of Heaven* a realistic dimension which grounds Mulisch's metaphysical premise. From the characters one gains a sense of the impact on Europe (and on the world at large) of World War II, the Communist revolution, the Vietnam War, and the advances in technology which have brought humankind closer to understanding the physical universe. Mulisch is able to introduce these topics unobtrusively in conversations among his principal characters. He is also quite adept at creating what might be appropriately called situational irony, as evidenced, for example, by his placing Holland's new astronomical observatory on the site of the abandoned World War II holding camp where Jews were assembled for shipment to concentration camps in Germany and Poland.

Mulisch is also a master at characterization, and the cast he assembles in *The Discovery of Heaven* rivals those in the novels of Henry Fielding, Charles Dickens, Stendhal, Balzac, Thomas Mann, or William Faulkner. Onno Quist may remind one of Miguel de Cervantes' Knight of the Mournful Countenance. Max Delius, a character with autobiographical overtones, shares affinities with great Romantic searchers such as Julien Sorel. Sophia Brons is a quintessential Earth Mother, combining the qualities of lover and protector. The supporting cast is equally memorable, a collection as differentiated and interesting as Chaucer's pilgrims. Mulisch is also exceptionally adept at combining the excitement of the detective and adventure genres with the qualities of the philosophical tale, making comparisons to his Italian contemporary Umberto Eco both apparent and appropriate. Like Eco, Mulisch handles the more technical aspects of novel writing with subtlety and skill; for example, the recurrent references to music and harmony provide a symbolic substructure to the novel without being so obtrusive as to detract from the story.

If there is a weakness in the novel, it lies in Mulisch's handling of his supernatural characters. The interludes in which the Sparks appear seem contrived and are largely expository conversations in which philosophical and religious background seems ladled in. Their presence is slight, however, by comparison to the principal story; and when one considers the amazing array of topics covered in a novel which holds readers' interest for more than seven hundred pages, this is but a small fault. Mulisch's analysis of the cultural, political, scientific, and political dimensions of the twentieth century make *The Discovery of Heaven* a novel worthy of multiple readings and significant study.

Laurence W. Mazzeno

Sources for Further Study

Library Journal. CXXI, October 15, 1996, p. 91.
Los Angeles Times Book Review. November 10, 1996, p. 2.
The New Yorker. LXXII, November 25, 1996, p. 115.
Publishers Weekly. CCXLIII, September 23, 1996, p. 55.
The Wall Street Journal. October 30, 1996, p. A20.
The Washington Post Book World. XXVI, October 27, 1996, p. 5.

DRAWN WITH THE SWORD
Reflections on the American Civil War

Author: James M. McPherson (1936-   )
Publisher: Oxford University Press (New York). 258 pp. $25.00
Type of work: History
Time: 1860-1865
Locale: The United States

An insightful series of connections on the American Civil War, focusing on its origins, reason for its outcome, and its enduring impact on American life

Principal personages:
ABRAHAM LINCOLN (1809-1865), sixteenth president of the United States
ROBERT E. LEE (1807-1870), Confederate general
ULYSSES S. GRANT (1822-1885), Union general
FREDERICK DOUGLASS (1817-1895), African American author and leader

The American Civil War remains a source of enduring fascination and endless debates, and not merely for those in the academic discipline of history. Hundreds of thousands of Americans continue to read and argue about the war, its causes, conduct, and outcome, while thousands of others annually reenact its bloody course in carefully rehearsed battles fought in uniforms meticulously correct down to the last divisional patch, the precise brigade button. Clearly, as James McPherson notes in his splendid collection of essays, *Drawn with the Sword: Reflections on the American Civil War*, the American Civil War is truly "the war that never goes away."

Why this fascination? What caused it? Why has it endured? How did the war change both its own scope during its career and the nature of America? And ultimately, why is there the inability of Americans to come to final closure with this war and agree upon its causes and meanings? Those are the fundamental questions McPherson turns to in his selection of essays, and his answers move beyond the practice of history to a broad and sometimes moving reflection not merely on the Civil War itself, but of ourselves as Americans.

Few authors could be more fitted to that task. Long a distinguished professor of history, with his specialty in the era of the Civil War and Reconstruction, McPherson won the Pulitzer Prize in 1989 for his one-volume narrative of the conflict, *Battle Cry of Freedom: The Civil War Era*. In that volume, he accomplished what for modern historians had seemed an all but lost cause itself: the restoration of narrative history to an honored place where the sweep of events did not displace a thoughtful discussion of causes, and where the military account reinforced, and did not overwhelm, the social, economic, and even personal stories of the men and women involved.

Still, a narrative history to be manageable must be selective, and *Battle Cry of Freedom* could only touch upon some matters of essential importance. With *Drawn with the Sword*, McPherson turns to the essay form to give these points the more leisurely review they deserve. The reader is richly rewarded as a result.

Of the first question, why the fascination with the Civil War? McPherson suggests that the answer is an innate, almost instinctive realization that the American Civil War was somehow fundamentally different from all other conflicts. This realization came to Americans as a people early, if hazily: "More than 50,000 books and pamphlets have been published about the Civil War since the guns ceased firing," McPherson informs readers, and indicates that the stream gives no indication of slowing, let alone drying up.

There are several obvious reasons for the fascination, McPherson notes. There were dramatic changes wrought by the Civil War, most notably the end of slavery, and McPherson has thought-provoking insights into a relatively new question here, the intriguing one of exactly who was responsible for the freeing of the slaves—Lincoln, the Union army, or the slaves themselves? His provisional answer: It took all three to effect such a monumental change, but slavery was ended.

Americans also remain fascinated by the Civil War because of the immense toll it exacted, a toll which continues to be felt, especially in the South. McPherson notes that, "Two percent of the American population of 1860 were killed in the Civil War; the same proportion in the 1990's would exceed 5 million." The effects of such massive human misery remain potent, despite the waves of immigration during the latter part of the nineteenth century and the greater mobility of modern Americans. Much of American soil remains uniquely hallowed ground.

Finally, Americans are drawn to the Civil War for the simple reason that human beings have always been attracted to such tales: From the siege and fall of Troy to the stubborn, unyielding defense of Stalingrad, people have ever responded to stories of courage and endurance under combat. The Civil War is the American epic, the great national parable which is central to Americans' sense of self and identity, but about which they can never fully agree.

Their disagreements begin with its cause. In 1861, Abraham Lincoln in his first inaugural address as president stated the conflict as one to restore the Union; by 1862, he had expanded it to become, at least in a strictly limited sense, a crusade against slavery, something many others in the North had wanted all along. Such a crusade was precisely what the South had feared, and terming a potential assault on "states' rights" used it as justification for seceding from the Union. The circular arguments reveal not a confusion of logic or terms but a conflict between systems and cultures.

"The War of Southern Aggression," one of McPherson's finest essays in the volume, picks through this particularly volatile minefield with precision and skill. By the 1850's, he notes, the language spoken by North and South was, in many ways, not a common language at all. It had become "an instrument of division, not unity." The epithets which the two societies hurled at each other can be, to some extent, disregarded. More serious, however, were the differing meanings which indicate a serious, perhaps unbridgeable division between what the two sides thought about serious political issues.

States' rights, for example, was the ultimate argument of the South in its long quarrel with the rest of the nation. From John C. Calhoun to Robert E. Lee to modern apologists for the Confederacy, the strictly limited relationship between the states and the federal government has been cited as justification of the South and its actions. Yet, McPherson notes, "When Yankee citizens harbored fugitive slaves, Southerners in Congress passed a Fugitive Slave Law that gave the national government greater powers than it had ever before possessed to reach into Northern states and capture the fugitives (so much for Southern commitment to states' rights)." When political language becomes so arbitrary, the response to arms grows increasingly likely.

Nowhere was this linguistic division more evident than when Northerner and Southerner used the term "freedom." For the North, by the 1850's that word had come increasingly to mean its literal definition, a state where no human being was subject to ownership by another. The South had a different, and more abstract reasoning. "Freedom," men such as South Carolina's Senator James H. Hammond explained, meant that there had to be a class of people (the "mud-sill of society" was Hammond's metaphor) condemned "to do the menial duties, to perform the drudgery of life," so others could be truly free. The North hired its "mud-sill," Hammond sneered; the South had adopted the more natural and sensible use of black slavery, thus lifting the entire white race to freedom.

"If slaves are freed, whites will become menials," another South Carolina politician warned. "We will lose every right and every liberty which belongs to the name of freemen." In other words, as McPherson accurately notes, the South went to war, at least in part, because it believed that "Freedom is not possible without slavery." That this proposition could be seriously adopted then—and now—as justified under the doctrine of states' rights is yet another—and sobering—source of fascination for the American Civil War.

As the war wore on, it changed its character and, eventually and inevitably, it changed the United States and American society. Part of McPherson's purpose in *Drawn with the Sword*, and one which he accomplishes with brief, suggestive remarks in several essays, is to link the military, the racial, the economic, and the social aspects of the war, to show how interconnected and intertwined they are—and how they all changed as a result of the conflict.

In his second inaugural address, Lincoln noted the efforts of many men, North and South, to avoid the conflict, all to no avail: "And the war came." Lincoln's hammer-stroke words give an air of inevitability to the Civil War, and Americans are inclined to accept the inevitability of its outcome as well. Yet, as McPherson clearly demonstrates in several of his more impressive essays, the South nearly won and the North came close to losing the struggle.

The outcome was as it was because the nature of the war and the nature of American society changed. From a war limited in purpose and scope, it transformed itself into a total war, and while Northern armies were more extensive and successful in bringing the war and its devastating effects to the civilian population, the South lacked mainly the opportunity, rather than the inclination, to do so. Robert E. Lee, as much as Ulysses S. Grant or William T. Sherman, understood that civilian morale was key to the war effort; thus the Confederate army's desperate attempts in 1864 in defensive battle after defensive battle whose purposes were fundamentally not military but political: to inflict enough Union casualties to defeat Lincoln at the polls.

The greatest shift from limited to total war was in respect to the slaves. Frederick Douglass, among other black leaders, had long urged that the Union army make use of the manpower of freed slaves. When the war was not resolved quickly, slavery was doomed, for Lincoln was determined to use any weapon to restore and maintain the Union. By issuing the Emancipation Proclamation and authorizing the recruiting, training, and eventual use of black troops, Lincoln (admittedly, in large part, forced by events) transformed the conflict.

The destruction of chattel slavery, however it came about, was an obvious result of the war, but there were others, so various and pervasive that, in a sense, the true national "reconstruction" came during the war, not after it. The old Union, a compact between individual states, was dissolved in a way the South never anticipated. In its place was a new nation, consisting of a compact between individual human beings. Even more than the revolution, McPherson maintains, the Civil War remade America. Those who lived during the time agreed. One of them was George Ticknor, a Harvard professor, who said the Civil War represented "a great gulf between what happened before in our century and what has happened since. . . . It does not seem to me as if I were living in the country in which I was born." Ticknor was right.

Ultimately, McPherson touches on the question of why Americans seem unable to come to final closure with this war and agree upon its causes and meanings. He posits first that great issues were at stake, issues which fundamentally reworked the American Republic through an ordeal by fire into its modern form; second, these issues, while resolved on one level (no, secession is not an acceptable answer to internal political disputes) remain unresolved on others (slavery being ended and overt discrimination outlawed, yet how do Americans resolve the racial differences in their society?). In short, the Civil War reformed Americans from the early American Republic to the modern United States. What, exactly, does that mean? Americans still are not certain and that is why that question remains the most fought-over battlefield of the Civil War.

McPherson's central thesis, woven throughout the book like a scarlet thread that binds all the essays together, is an essentially simple one: Although the end of the Civil War is never in doubt, its meaning is constantly debated and discussed. For that reason, if nothing else, this is indeed "the war that never goes away." It remains, and it remains to be discussed, studied, and examined. *Drawn with the Sword* sets a high standard for any further discussion, study, or examination.

Michael Witkoski

Sources for Further Study

America's Civil War. IX, January, 1997, p. 87.
American Heritage. XLVII, May, 1996, p. 113.

Booklist. XCII, March 1, 1996, p. 1119.
Forbes. CLVII, May 6, 1996, p. 24.
History: Reviews of New Books. XXV, Fall, 1996, p. 7.
Library Journal. CXXI, March 15, 1996, p. 82.
The New York Times Book Review. CI, April 21, 1996, p. 27.
Publishers Weekly. CXLIII, February 26, 1996, p. 92.
The Virginia Quarterly Review. Autumn, 1996, p. 116.
The Washington Post. April 17, 1996, p. C2.

EDGE EFFECT
Trails and Portrayals

Author: Sandra McPherson (1943-   )
Publisher: Wesleyan University Press/University Press of New England (Hanover, New Hampshire). 84 pp. $22.50; paperback $11.95
Type of work: Poetry

Sandra McPherson's poetry combines science and passion in poems which explore the relationship between natural history and folk art

Edge Effect: Trails and Portrayals is Sandra McPherson's twelfth book of poetry. McPherson's personal and yet intellectual style has become widely known since she was featured on the PBS television series hosted by Bill Moyers, *The Language of Life*, which introduced a variety of contemporary poets and types of poetry to the American public. *Edge Effect* was published in the same year as another, *The Spaces Between Birds*, and the two together represent the two sides of McPherson's art. The direct intensely personal side dominates in *Spaces*, poems about her experiences raising an autistic daughter; her meditations are interspersed with the daughter's own poems. The more indirect but nonetheless felt poetry of *Edge Effect* uses precise description of natural history and folk art to comment on the essential force of spontaneous creativity she finds in both.

The double vision that is McPherson's most definitive characteristic surfaces in *Edge Effect*. McPherson's gift from her first work has been an ability to superimpose factual accounts of natural processes on some element of human experience so that the one mirrors the other and the two become one image. In her earlier collections such as *Radiation*, natural processes not very familiar to nonscientists are described in such a way as to make them apt metaphors for human concerns. In her later book *The God of Indeterminacy*, it is two forms of art—blues and the quilt—which comment on each other and on the general question of what creativity really is. Her poems in the later books circle around the mysterious center all generative power seems to have, and to ask if this power is a god or a blind force, and how it manifests itself.

Edge Effect parallels two distinct realms: the natural world and the art of folk or "outsider" artists. Their areas overlap—natural art reflects the artistry of nature. The book demonstrates the scientific and emotional truth Allan A. Schoenherr, in *A Natural History of California,* refers to as the "edge effect": "The zone where two communities overlap, called an ecotone, shares characteristics of both communities and therefore is diverse. That is, the edge of a community is more diversified than its center, a phenomenon also known as 'edge effect.'"

To reflect the two realms, the collection is divided into two sets of poems. Those included as "Portrayals," examine the art and celebrate the artistry of self-taught folk artists, while "Trails" are mysteriously linked journeys through and into nature. This collection needs to be read as a whole, complete with epigraphs and concluding notes, rather than browsed. It is more centered than most poetry collections, and McPherson's capsule sketches of the folk artists and brief quotations from nature studies enhance the reading of the poetry. The two sections are preceded by a poem of invocation, "Choosing an Author for Assurance in the Night," which recalls McPherson's early poem "Wanting a Mummy." In "Choosing an Author," a dead woman speaks to and through the living poet in a mystical communication that assures the message will be received and heard. In the first of the many reversals or inversions or turnings upside-down that constitute this book, the "lean idol of this Day of the Dead" types:

> Death makes me direct,
> with a little ornamental nonsense
> of elbows and knees,
> if you call this death:
> my twaddle still counsels
> though I have no ears to hook a mask on.

This is the muse McPherson calls forth to lead into the collection, and her serious yet playful irony surfaces throughout the book. "Portrayals" introduce and examine art that is not studied, but is a direct result of emotion expressed through some medium without regard to the rules or conventions of a craft. These artists' idiosyncratic visions are "read" as having their own integrity outside the system, and, in fact, as being in themselves arguments against accepted definitions and standards of art. For the "outsider" artists, passion and vision are not diluted by a need to meet expectations. "Justin McCarthy, Naive" describes a Pennsylvania artist who lived from 1892-1977 and, according to McPherson's note, "received no recognition for his work until quite late in his life, when folk art supporters began to take him seriously." Such work as McCarthy's comes close to being unmediated:

> Tormented
> by grace,
> he had to
> scratch at it,
> leave
> the marks
> of his enthusiasm,
> his best
> imperfect
> penstroke.

McPherson's minimalist style in this poem suggests the stripped-down directness of McCarthy's art. The brief, simple description of his startling, unschooled, but evocative work is followed by the comment that "Facility/defaces longing." Too much study proves an obstacle between the dream and the representation:

> Longing is
> the one expression
> skill masks,
> polish ravages.

Although one might want to dismiss or at least to qualify this premise, it is convincingly argued in the poem. Many of the other "portrayals" support the position that what art needs is singlemindedness and commitment, effort and honesty. What it does not need is adherence to artistic principles or "workshopping." Except in "Justin McCarthy" these notions are understated; what the "portrayals" present is for the most part the art itself, empathetically observed and responded to by another artist. The speaker learns to unlearn, to re-envision, from this nonstandard art. "Outsider: Minnie Evans" begins with a statement of lessons learned: "Now, because of you, symmetry and asymmetry interest me equally." McPherson describes Evans' art and dips into the source of her art, a kind of effusion from the unconscious world. The art of the woman who, according to McPherson's note, "painted her dreams and waking visions while working as a gatekeeper at a public garden" enriches the poet's own work, as the poet taps into the same source and recognizes a commonality.

The "Trails" are journeys into nature, focused on specific locations. These poems manifest two kinds of nature knowledge, the exact observation that constitutes direct experience and also the nature lore of the botanist. Thus they recall the work of McPherson's teacher Elizabeth Bishop and also of Marianne Moore, who also created moving poems which incorporated intricate scientific detail. More involved with botany than zoology, the poems in "Trails" abound with words unfamiliar to the nonspecialist, but rich with sound and suggestion: xeric, filaree, minisci, penstemon. McPherson's early experience as a technical writer serves her well; her poetic goals seem to include the precise description of intangibles, through exactness of natural detail and hidden, hinted-at correspondences between surfaces and depths.

"Trails" leads through various landscapes where the plants and animals of the locations as well as the natural laws that make the place a system combine to reveal something about the relationship between self and world. The titles are suggestive of revelations: "Ocean Water Absorbs Red, Orange, and Yellow Light"; "Path Through a Few Things That Must Be Said for Putah Creek, at the Foot of Monticello Dam," "Genius of Fog at Ecola Creek Mouth." The places that the speaker of these poems travels to or through seem alive as individual sentient beings with their own identities. And the speaker slips in and out of each place, melding its identity with her own and then separating to become the observer again.

In general, then, the "Trails" provide a gentle dissolving of the boundary between self and other, so that nature's surfaces and the boundaries of the body are almost indistinguishable. "Paths Rounding Timberline, Mt. Hood, Last Week of Summer" begins with such a blurring of the edges:

> All-mantling, the grit—
> scoured and beaten
> and rinsed
> by glacier sap,
> . . . clean rock
> to eat—
> not like dust,

> not like zest
> shaved and bowled on a table
> to taste,
> but an ascendant
> snack
> of rock essence,
> its core of dryness
> crisp-cased,
> a spark on the teeth.

The hiker is literally invaded by the grit, but what would be expected to be a negative experience comes across instead as an epiphany. Thus it tends to be as well in the rest of these poems: Nature's laws, which would seem to many inevitable proof of the blank materiality of the universe, become instead suggestions of a natural metaphysics that is glimpsed now and then through the surface of the world. The world strikes sparks in its contact with the self, and these sparks are a kind of mutual recognition.

In "Ocean Water Absorbs Red, Orange, and Yellow Light" the scientific explanation of how colors appear in water opens out into a commentary on desire and human loves in general. Ocean water "allows only the green and blue/ to penetrate the depths./ As we love deeply those we love/ they are our blue and green." The emotional, the physical, and indeed the spiritual swirl together in this poem in a variegated maelstrom. The poem asks and answers the question, in the face of death, why love? Of what good is physical beauty of any kind, since it must die? The answer is that in this world everything belongs to beauty, even death. After richly image-filled explorations of this felt truth, the poem concludes by imagining the skeletons of lovers as appropriate to the natural scene. She describes the "red and yellow femurs" as perhaps "tossed at last on shore/ among carnelians and agates drying."

> arousing
> color when wet, even the inexpressive
> skull seen to be homely
> as an ecstasy of gaping mouth
> returned to the wild
> as the outermost open mind.

The playfully ironic conclusion nevertheless gives the poem positive implications. If the physical world adds up to beauty, skull and all, then it must have meaning. In fact, beauty is meaning—with a metaphysical slant in a somewhat different direction from John Keats's "Ode on a Grecian Urn": "Beauty is truth, truth, beauty—that is all/ Ye know on earth, and all ye need to know."

McPherson's speculation about a natural, unpredictable metaphysic—an undefinable deity—was present in her previous collection, *The God of Indeterminacy*. In the "Trails" section of this collection, she focuses more on nature and on natural history as areas in which the force of creativity, the "god of indeterminacy," manifests itself.

In "Portrayals," the same force works through human artists, but especially through those who are naïve or unschooled enough to allow it to work.

McPherson's combinations of natural and personal, outer and inner, continue to challenge the reader and open areas of speculation. Moreover, her recent works redefine a poetry collection as something other than merely a group of poems put between covers. *Edge Effect* in particular is an organic whole that has qualities of the long poem or even the personal essay as well as consisting of a series of separate meditations.

Janet McCann

Sources for Further Study

Booklist. XCII, March 15, 1996, p. 1236.
Library Journal. CXXI, March 1, 1996, p. 81.
Publishers Weekly. CCXLIII, February 26, 1996, p. 102.
San Francisco Chronicle. June 22, 1995, p. E1.

EMERSON AMONG THE ECCENTRICS
A Group Portrait

Author: Carlos Baker (1909-1987)
Introduction and epilogue by James R. Mellow
Publisher: Viking (New York). 608 pp. $34.95
Type of work: Literary biography
Time: 1832-1882
Locale: Boston and Concord, Massachusetts

This biography of the most prominent American man of letters of the nineteenth century is also a portrait of the writers who were drawn to his genius and made up the influential Transcendentalist circle

Principal personages:
RALPH WALDO EMERSON, who left his Unitarian ministry to become the leading Transcendentalist essayist and poet
LIDIAN EMERSON, his second wife, who, despite poor health, was married to the writer for forty-five years and finally outlived him
HENRY DAVID THOREAU, Emerson's friend and student, who built his Walden cabin on Emerson property
MARGARET FULLER, the fiery writer and activist, who tested Emerson's emotional limits
NATHANIEL HAWTHORNE, the novelist and short-story writer and Emerson's sometime neighbor in Concord
AMOS BRONSON ALCOTT, teacher and friend of Emerson and father of Louisa May Alcott
WILLIAM ELLERY CHANNING, another Concord writer and friend

When Carlos Baker died in 1987, he left the manuscript of this work virtually completed; James R. Mellow has provided introduction and epilogue as a frame for Baker's book, to tie the unfinished manuscript together. The work is organized into five sections of some fifty chapters, one section for each of the decades of Emerson's life Baker focuses on, from the 1830's through the 1870's (Emerson died in 1882). Each chapter averages about ten pages in length, and each centers on an episode in the life of one or another of the figures in the Transcendentalist movement of the middle of the nineteenth century. Yet each chapter functions almost as an independent piece, with little or no overlap with other chapters. Rather than a continuous biography, then, *Emerson Among the Eccentrics* reads like a collection of short stories. Had Baker lived, one suspects he might have found a stronger framework than the one Mellow has provided readers here, and linked the different stories together more effectively.

Certainly Baker had fascinating material with which to work. The period from 1840 to 1860, which has come to be known as the American Renaissance, produced America's first important writers—Edgar Allan Poe, Emily Dickinson, and Walt Whitman among them—and several at one time or another lived and worked in and around the small town of Concord, where Ralph Waldo Emerson did his most important writing. Henry David Thoreau, Margaret Fuller, and Nathaniel Hawthorne were just a few of the writers who were drawn to the flame of genius and friendship which Emerson burned throughout his life. Baker's "group portrait" not only sketches in the details of the life of the leader of this philosophical and literary movement, but gives full-length portraits of its other major figures, and describes their complex (usually supportive but occasionally acrimonious) interrelationships.

Baker begins with the turning point of Emerson's life when, at age twenty-seven, and after the death of his first wife, Ellen, Emerson left for Europe. When he set sail for Malta aboard the brig *Jasper* on Christmas Day, 1832, Emerson could look back upon two years in which, however he tried, he had found much to be endured and little to be enjoyed: the death of his spirited young wife, his voluntary resignation as pastor of the Second Church of Boston, the nagging illnesses of three of his four brothers, and a debilitating sickness of his own that had finally persuaded him to see what an ocean voyage and a prolonged change of scene might do for his enfeebled constitution.

The change, as Baker knows, would make all the difference. Emerson met Thomas Carlyle, Samuel Taylor Coleridge, William Wordsworth, and other English Romantic writers on his tour, and he began formulating the Transcendental philosophy which would permeate his life and writings. Emerson's first book, *Nature*, and the first and best exposition of this philosophy, was published in 1836, but his career would continue for almost another half-century. Settled in Concord, with his second wife Lidian and an expanding household, Emerson became the center of a growing number of writers who were developing their romantic, Transcendental ideas, often through the *Dial* journal (1840-1844). Thoreau grew up and died in Concord, and lived at the Emerson house at different times in his adulthood; Margaret Fuller, author of *Women in the Nineteenth Century* (1845), among other works, often stayed there; Nathaniel Hawthorne lived in Concord for several periods; Ellery Channing and Bronson Alcott were other neighbors. The list of the people who came through Emerson's Concord—from Theodore Parker through Henry Wadsworth Longfellow to Walt Whitman—is a catalog of the leading thinkers and writers of the mid-nineteenth century.

Unlike later literary periods, there were no elaborate dinner parties or witty salons in Concord; rather, these Renaissance writers walked and talked, and often through the woods by Walden Pond where Thoreau would soon build his cabin and live out his unique experiment (1845-1847). Throughout these early years, Emerson was writing his best essays and poems, and giving his most influential lectures: "The Divinity School Address" (1838), "The American Scholar" and "Concord Hymn" (both 1837, the latter poem the source of Emerson's most famous line, "And fired the shot heard round the world").

Baker shows what a good friend and mentor Emerson was, in letter as in person. He supported many of the younger writers around him, not only intellectually and morally but also financially. There would always be something of the preacher about him: While he championed Walt Whitman, he also urged Whitman to tone down the racier passages of *Leaves of Grass* (1855). Emerson's mark can be found on so many of the major works of the American Renaissance—even by its absence. Several of his friends shared the Brook Farm communal experiment (and Hawthorne wrote *The*

Blithedale Romance about it). Hawthorne and Melville met in Lenox (and *Moby Dick* was significantly altered as a result), but much of their fiction can be seen as an attempted antidote to the optimistic tenor of Emerson's Transcendentalism. Thoreau lived in Emerson's house (and played with the Emerson children as if he were one himself), and then went off to build his cabin on property Emerson owned on Walden Pond.

These were truly "eccentrics," as Baker demonstrates, less for their behavior, perhaps, than because they were part of the first generation of writers and intellectuals to break the Puritan stranglehold on American thought (reinforced in a series of religious revivals in the late eighteenth and early nineteenth centuries), and develop an American philosophy which reflected the energy and expansiveness of the continent. Emerson first saw the limitations of Protestant Christianity, or of the church which bore its name: The excellence in Jesus, Emerson wrote in the essay "Character," was that "he affirms the Divinity in him and in us." In all of his lectures, Emerson taught one doctrine, he claimed: "the infinitude of the private man." In poems such as "Brahma" (which so influenced Whitman), and in essays such as "Self-Reliance" (1841), Emerson translated Eastern mysticism and British Romanticism into a uniquely American philosophy which stressed human goodness and potential, and the immanent spirituality of all life. The "world is emblematic," Emerson wrote in *Nature*, and

> behind nature, throughout nature, spirit is present. . . . It does not act upon us from without, that is, in space and time, but spiritually, or through ourselves. Therefore that spirit . . . the Supreme Being, does not build up nature around us, but puts it forth through us, as the life of the tree puts forth new branches and leaves through the pores of the old. . . . Who can set bounds to the possibilities of man? Once inhale the upper air, being admitted to behold the absolute natures of justice and truth, and we learn that man has access to the entire mind of the Creator, is himself the creator of the infinite.

Such a philosophy—which eliminates priests and churches and elevates human understanding at the same time—would be an underpinning for much of the best writing produced in the next half century, from Thoreau's natural history to the abolitionist tracts of Alcott, Parker, and others. Yet Emerson's influence would continue to be felt through the twentieth century, in writers as different as John Steinbeck, Ralph Ellison, and the Beats.

Baker is less interested in ideas for their own sake, however, than in a description of what life was like for their inventors. One picture that emerges freshly here is the fragility of their lives. Emerson's first wife dies early; his second wife, Lidian, is sick for much of their marriage, and their daughter Ellen becomes their housekeeper-nursemaid for most of her adult years; their first son Waldo dies at an early age; Emerson's brother is confined to a mental hospital for most of his life; friends and neighbors, and their children, get sick and die regularly. Proof of the strength of Emerson's Transcendental philosophy is that he could hold it in the midst of such a precarious existence. Increasingly in the later chapters of Baker's book, the stars are falling: Margaret Fuller drowned in a shipwreck off Long Island in 1850, Thoreau dying of tuberculosis in 1862, Hawthorne in 1864. Emerson outlived all of his disciples by decades, and his last years showed a sharp decline. Baker's portrait is the darker or reverse side of *Little Women* (1868-1869): On the surface, large families gambol on the sunny lawns, but, just below, funerals and memorial services are held for young and old alike.

Baker does a fine job of giving a sense of the social and historical conditions in the middle of the nineteenth century: about slavery, for example, and particularly the Abolitionist movement (John Brown was one of the Transcendental heroes, and he spoke in Concord); about the Civil War, and what it felt like for a small town to see its young men go off to be wounded and to die. Baker also is not afraid to describe the limitations of the personalities here: Hawthorne's shyness, for example, or Thoreau's prickliness, and even the emotional limits of Emerson's own life, which did not allow people entrance very often or very far. Emerson wrote that Thoreau "wants a little ambition in his mixture. Fault of this, instead of being the head of American Engineers, he is captain of a huckleberry party." Thoreau, for his part, responded in his journal,

> I had two friends. The one offered me friendship on such terms that I could not accept it, without a sense of degradation. He would not meet me on equal terms, but only be to some extent my patron. He would not come to see me, but was hurt if I did not visit him. He would not readily accept a favor, but would gladly confer one.

Emerson's "long dream of a cooperative assemblage of gifted individualists" was lost—as it nearly always is—"by their inability to get along with one another."

Carlos Baker started this biography in the 1970's, and its more traditional form shows through. It is a work virtually untouched by recent developments in historical writing, and, while a penetrating portrait of the Transcendentalists emerges, much else is missing: significant analysis of their ideas, and of the interconnections of those ideas with the social and ideological struggles of their era. What is best about this work is that readers get to see these figures as men and women, in the fullness of their families and their friendships. *Emerson Among the Eccentrics* fills out the picture of this unique period in American literary history.

David Peck

Sources for Further Study

America. CLXXV, October 19, 1996, p. 26.
Chicago Tribune. April 7, 1996, XIV, p. 3.
The Christian Century. CXIII, October 9, 1996, p. 943.
The Economist. CCCXXXIX, June 15, 1996, p. 4.
The New York Times Book Review. CI, May 19, 1996, p. 9.
The Virginia Quarterly Review. LXXII, Autumn, 1996, p. 125.
The Wall Street Journal. April 4, 1996, p. A10.
The Washington Post Book World. XXVI, March 31, 1996, p. 4.
The Wilson Quarterly. XX, Spring, 1996, p. 85.

THE END OF SCIENCE
Facing the Limits of Knowledge in the Twilight of the Scientific Age

Author: John Horgan (1955-   )
Publisher: Addison-Wesley (Reading, Massachusetts). 308 pp. $24.00
Type of work: Science

A science writer questions prominent scientists on the issue of whether there are any more major scientific discoveries to be made

Is there anything significant left for scientists to discover? Will there be any more Albert Einsteins, Charles Darwins, or James Clerk Maxwells changing our understanding of the natural world in fundamental ways? Will there be any more scientific revolutions, or will future scientists be reduced to solving trivial puzzles? John Horgan, a staff writer for *Scientific American,* asks some three dozen scientists and philosophers whether we have reached the limits of empirical scientific research, and if so, what does that ultimately mean for the future of the human race. The scientists he interviews are drawn from a variety of scientific disciplines, including physics, cosmology, evolutionary biology, and the social sciences. Among them are some of the best-known names in science, mostly individuals who have made serious efforts to communicate with the general public, including the cosmologist Stephen Hawking; the particle physicist Steven Weinberg; the biologists Stephen Jay Gould, Lynn Margulis, and Francis Crick; and the sociobiologist E. O. Wilson. Included among the philosophers are Karl Popper and Thomas Kuhn. With few exceptions, his interviewees are the men and women who symbolize science to nonscientific audiences in the English-speaking world.

Not surprisingly, the answers given by these men and women vary. Some are afraid humans may have reached the limits of scientific knowledge; others are confident that those limits have not yet been reached. Some are very optimistic about the future; others are pessimistic. Above all, Horgan detects ambivalence as the dominant emotion.

What the scientists believe, however, is only part of the story of this book. Unlike most books by science journalists based on interviews with scientists, Horgan neither attempts to fade into the background, allowing the scientists to tell readers about their work, nor strives to serve as the spokesperson for the general public, asking the interesting questions that readers would ask these leading researchers if given the chance. He explicitly rejects the strategy of leaving it to readers to discern which scientist made the best argument and the most sense. He also makes no pretension that nonscientists are able to fully comprehend what some of these scientists are really saying in their equations. Instead, the interviews serve as opportunities for Horgan either to expand upon the opinions or conclusions of the interviewees with whom he agrees, whether scientists or philosophers, or to rebut those with whom he disagrees. The interviews are vehicles for the articulation of Horgan's own beliefs. The words of the scientists are text which Horgan annotates. As the author admits in his introduction, this book is "overtly judgmental, argumentative, and personal." The interviews are debates, but debates in which the outcome is controlled by one of the debaters, who takes every opportunity to comment on the answers of his opponent.

Horgan is more of a columnist than a reporter, and this book should be viewed more as an opinion piece than a factual report. Horgan claims that he likes scientists, but that is sometimes difficult to believe on the basis of this book. Coloring our perspective are Horgan's commentaries on the appearance, voice, and gestures of these men and women. Even when Horgan agrees with their views, his word pictures of the scientists are not particularly sympathetic or pleasant.

Horgan is convinced that science, by which he means the ability to create and prove grand theories that explain significant questions—how was the universe created; how did life begin; what is the nature of consciousness—has reached the limit of its power to explain. Either humans already know the answer, or the answer is unknowable using the methods of scientific inquiry. Science is to him not a body of knowledge but the process of discovering knowledge. If we can discover no new knowledge, then we no longer have science.

To provide an organizing principle for his criticism of individual scientists, Horgan identifies a mode of scientific activity he calls "ironic science." He defines it as a "speculative, postempirical mode" of scientific activity. (Science enters the postmodern age.) To clarify what he means by ironic science, Horgan draws on literary criticism. He uses the word "ironic" in the sense that literary critics speak of texts as ironic: "they have multiple meanings, none of them definitive." He then draws two different analogies between science and literature. First, he asks what can a modern poet do when faced with the "perfection" of the work of William Shakespeare or Dante. One solution for modern poets has been to accept that their predecessors have mastered language and emotion, but "strive to transcend [that mastery] through various subterfuges, including a subtle misreading of the predecessors' work." Likewise, there are scientists who misread the theories which are considered fundamental for their respective disciplines in order to transcend them. (It is not entirely clear what he means by "misread.") In his second analogy, ironic science is to scientific discovery what literary criticism is to literature. It offers opinions and points of view which lead to discussion and debate, but no real knowledge. It is the generation of heat without light. The ironic scientist will often point to what we do not yet know to show how much further science has to go. Horgan, however, sees this as a deceptive strategy, because he believes that much of what humans do not yet know will never be known.

Horgan identifies two forms of ironic scientist. The worse form is the "naïve" ironic scientist. These individuals produce scientific speculations which cannot be empirically validated, but despite their inability to prove their speculations, the naïve scientists strongly believe in the truth of their theories. Horgan uses the word "faith" in describing the relationship between these scientists and their theories, and the word fits. Their belief is an act of faith. These scientists do not even acknowledge that underlying their speculations is a philosophical position or belief system. His example is the particle physicist Edward Witten, one of the leaders in the development of superstring theory, a man not widely known to the general public but held in high esteem by his fellow physicists.

In contrast, Horgan labels as "sophisticated" ironic scientists those who are cognizant that their speculations are based upon a philosophical system. An example is Stephen Weinberg, who has written extensively for general audiences.

Horgan is not happy about these ironic scientists. An English major who came to dislike the uncertainty of the knowledge offered in the humanities, Horgan embraced science because "Science . . . yields durable insights into the nature of things. It gets us somewhere. . . . Science addresses questions that can be answered." In science, there are right and wrong answers. Some of his ire is evident in his commentary on individual scientists. For example, he draws an implicit analogy between "James Joyce's gobbledygookian tome *Finnegans Wake*" and Witten's superstring theory. In Horgan's worldview, the multiple interpretations possible of Joyce's book is one of its worse sins. To compare a theory to that book is to condemn it.

Horgan is not sympathetic to the cultural constructionist view of science, which asserts that all knowledge systems, including science, are culturally determined or constructed. In his words, scientific theories "are true, empirically true, in a way that no work of art can be." Science is a superior knowledge system. Yet he realizes science is not a superior knowledge system when practiced by ironic scientists. Their form of science may be intellectually stimulating and amusing, but it does not provide truth. It is not different from other forms of knowledge systems. Although Horgan does not discuss this, the scientists themselves, especially sophisticated ironic scientists, have given comfort to the cultural constructionist argument.

After interviewing philosophers and scientists, Horgan ends the book with an interview of a theologian in a chapter entitled "The Terror of God." Here he makes a grand leap into what readers, according to their truth-systems, might call the mystical, the metaphysical, or the theological, providing a brief discussion of the nature of God. He also probes the question of whether humans are more comfortable knowing or not knowing.

The chapter should have been left out or greatly expanded. As it now stands, it is superficial. In a book that is on occasion self-indulgent and manipulative, this chapter is the worst. Rather than provide a description of his psychotic experience, Horgan should have explored the issues he raises with more theologians. For example, it might have been quite informative to have interviewed Roman Catholic priests/scientists to see how they handle some of the issues.

Two questions may arise in readers' minds as they read *The End of Science*. The first is relatively minor: How representative is Horgan's group of interviewees? Science is an international activity, but Horgan's sources are primarily Americans with a sprinkling of English scientists. All sorts of comparisons are possible. Do the Continental scientists share the feelings of their counterparts in Great Britain or the United States? Is ironic science also practiced on the Continent? What about the views of scientists from behind the former Iron Curtain? Would lesser-known figures in the scientific community provide a different perspective? Horgan himself suggests that the answers to such questions might prove interesting by acknowledging that his British scientists are more "immune to metaphysical anxiety" than their American counterparts. He asks whether this is the result of some characteristic of British culture, but does not explore the issue any further. Perhaps he should have.

The second question was whether the significance of science is in the great fundamental theories or in the details. Horgan is convinced that humans already know the truth about most of the big questions in science and that the little ones are not very important. Yet the concept of science involves understanding the world in all its detail—both great and small. Perhaps scientists do not really know as much about the universe as Horgan contends. In some fields, fields he seems uninterested in, facts and theories are in great flux. For example, because of developments in instrumentation and other breakthroughs, much of what was "known" about the solar system thirty years ago has proven to be wrong, from the number of satellites of the planets, the number of planets with rings, to the nature of atmospheres and surfaces. Water at the bottom of a lunar crater and life on Mars are two issues that arose after the publication of this book. There is always the possibility that a new "fact" may be discovered which challenges our comfortable assurance that science has already learned all the answers.

Marc Rothenberg

Sources for Further Study

Bulletin of the Atomic Scientists. LII, November, 1996, p. 60.
Business Week. July 29, 1996, p. 12.
The Economist. CCCXL, July 20, 1996, p. 11.
Nature. CCCLXXXII, August 29, 1996, p. 769.
New Scientist. CL, June 22, 1996, p. 45.
The New York Times Book Review. CI, June 30, 1996, p. 11.
Publishers Weekly. CCXLIII, April 22, 1996, p. 55.
Science. CCLXXII, June 14, 1996, p. 1594.
Time. CXLVIII, September 9, 1996, p. 56.
The Wall Street Journal. June 19, 1996, p. A18.

ENDANGERED DREAMS
The Great Depression in California

Author: Kevin Starr (1940-   )
Publisher: Oxford University Press (New York). 402 pp. $35.00
Type of work: History
Time: 1930-1940
Locale: California

In this fourth installment in his series of books about California history, Starr describes the bitter conflicts between haves and have-nots during the 1930's, culminating in a temporary truce with the completion of a spectacular array of public works on the eve of World War II

To many Americans, the Great Depression in California is almost synonymous with John Steinbeck's novel *The Grapes of Wrath* (1939). Steinbeck had the genius to see the epic qualities in the great migration of dispossessed farmers across the plains and deserts in their overladen jalopies. He also had a passion for social justice that gave his book a strong thesis. The novel was doubly effective because it was made into a beautifully photographed, highly successful film by famous director John Ford. In *Endangered Dreams: The Great Depression in California*, Kevin Starr discusses Steinbeck's novel from the perspective of the 1990's and makes it clear that *The Grapes of Wrath*, though an inspired work of fiction, told only a tiny portion of the story of California's Depression years and a distorted one at that.

For example, Steinbeck charged that California fruit and vegetable growers were papering the Dust Bowl with handbills in order to attract more pickers than they needed, thereby forcing down wages to the near-starvation level. According to Starr, no one has ever been able to produce a single handbill of the kind Steinbeck described, although they might be valuable collectors' items by now. Starr is persuasive when he argues that it would have been foolhardy for the big agricultural interests to attract such a potentially revolutionary army of indigents to California for a short-term windfall profit. He claims that the influx of "Okies" from Oklahoma, Missouri, Texas, and Arkansas in some cases caused taxes to double in order to pay for such services as public health, policing, welfare, and education.

Starr's story of the Great Depression in California is far more complicated than Steinbeck's. Starr also tries harder to remain impartial, although his sympathies are more with the forces of free enterprise than with those of organized labor and paternalistic government. He is a member of the elitist Bohemian Club of San Francisco and has been active in the business world as both a consultant and an entrepreneur. Steinbeck's novel had a large cast of characters and the action covered much of the state; but Starr's history has a much larger cast of characters (the index itself runs to eighteen pages), a longer time span, and a setting that includes California's two great metropolitan centers as well as the Central Valley.

The first two chapters of *Endangered Dreams* serve as a prelude to the Crash of 1929 and the pivotal decade that followed. The Communist Party USA, under the direction of the Soviet Union, was heavily involved in the radicalism of the period.

This involvement had good and bad features for both labor and the monied interests Starr persistently refers to as "the oligarchy." Communist agitators gave the labor movement direction and rhetoric but also offered the oligarchy plenty of opportunities to frighten small farmers, lower-middle class business and professional people, and California's many conservative retirees with the specter of revolution and dictatorship.

Chapter 3 deals with strikes in rural California involving Mexican, Filipino, and Dust Bowl migrants and organized by young Communists. In 1935, however, the Communist Party USA dissolved its unions under orders from Moscow.

Chapter 4 covers the famous San Francisco Waterfront and General Strike of 1934 in which the ascetic, resourceful Australian immigrant Harry Bridges emerged as a powerful spokesman for organized labor.

Chapter 5 describes the 1934 gubernatorial campaign of eccentric, idealistic, brilliant Upton Sinclair, who might easily have become governor of California and initiated his program to End Poverty in California (EPIC) if he had not been sabotaged by the unscrupulous tactics of the oligarchy.

In chapter 6, Starr tells how the oligarchy, frightened by Sinclair's near victory and the growing strength of organized labor, counterattacked with legal, paralegal, and strictly illegal violence in what Starr calls "the fascist alternative."

Chapters 7 and 8 describe California's efforts at recovery under the New Deal. Of particular interest are the Townsendites and Ham and Eggers, both of whom promised pensions for any Californian over the age of fifty. Chapter 8 discusses conditions in migrant camps. Between 1930 and 1934 some 683,000 migrants flooded California in jalopies, creating problems for federal, state, county, city, and private agencies.

In chapter 9, "Documenting the Crisis," Starr discusses *The Grapes of Wrath* as one of the important works to come out of California during the Great Depression. He also recommends many other important works which are not so well known, including *Factories in the Field* (1939) by Carey McWilliams and *An American Exodus* (1939) by Paul Taylor and Dorothea Lange. Starr devotes many pages to praising the artistry and dedication of photographer Dorothea Lange, whose *Migrant Mother* is "one of the best known photographs in history." Several of Lange's photographs are included in the section of illustrations.

Chapter 10 narrates the history of the Hetch Hetchy Project which brought a bountiful supply of Sierra Nevada water to San Francisco and made it possible for the Bay Area to grow into one of the major metropolitan areas of the world.

Chapter 11 discusses the water problems of Southern California and describes the construction of Hoover Dam and the Colorado River Project which made Los Angeles the premier city of the entire American Southwest.

In chapter 12, titled "Completing California: The Therapy of Public Works," Starr describes California's other major public works, crediting them for alleviating the unemployment problem.

Chapter 13 tells how the Great Depression ended with the billions of dollars being pumped into national defense by the Roosevelt Administration and then became a subject of history when the Japanese bombed Pearl Harbor on December 7, 1941. The conscription of millions of men into the military and the enormous demand for labor in the shipyards, aircraft factories, and other California war industries quickly solved the unemployment problem and squelched labor unrest.

Endangered Dreams contains twenty-eight pages of endnotes and annotated bibliography, making it a rich reference source. Starr seems to have read virtually everything available on his subject, including such characteristically weighty and detailed government reports as the six-volume *Hearings Before the Select Committee to Investigate the Interstate Migration of Destitute Citizens, House of Representatives, Seventy-Sixth Congress* (1941), known as the Tolan Report.

Starr quotes Congressman John Tolan as asking the committee members: "Well, it all comes down to the question again as to whether the Federal Government owes a duty to people who are hungry or naked or on account of circumstances over which they have no control, are in need. Do we owe that duty or do we not?" The Great Depression in California brought that controversial question into the forefront of American politics. It still remains unanswered. Does any government have the right to take property from the haves and give it to the have-nots? If so, what is the philosophical basis of that right? Does such government intervention discourage enterprise? Does it encourage a welfare mentality? Essentially the same question had brought Adolf Hitler, Benito Mussolini, and Joseph Stalin into power in their respective countries and had led to World War II.

Starr presents his story of California in the 1930's as a struggle between the haves and the have-nots, the left and the right. Although this is an effective way of marshaling facts and making a nonfiction work dramatic, it has been criticized as an oversimplification. William H. Chafe, a professor of history and dean of the faculty at Duke University, charges in a review published in *The New York Times Book Review*, that "the contending forces are written too large. It is as if every significant figure carried the burden of representing Good versus Evil."

Starr does indeed have a tendency to color and dramatize his history. This touch of the New Journalism may annoy specialists but has made him popular with the general public. He often uses striking and surprising figures of speech, as in the following examples: "That such a Darth Vader figure [as Philip Bancroft] could win the senatorial nomination in the Republican primary only testified to the strength of the Right by 1938." He borrows audaciously from the fantastical science-fiction *Star Wars* film trilogy to title one of his chapters "The Empire Strikes Back." He calls the 1916 conviction and death sentence of Tom Mooney and Warren Knox Billings for the bombing of a Preparedness Day parade "the Dreyfus case of mid-twentieth-century California." He refers to a consortium of California business organizations and financial interests as "the usual suspects."

It would seem that Starr's newspaper experience has taught him the value of featuring personalities and anecdotes in his histories. The reader may occasionally feel overwhelmed by the relentless stream of factual detail but will be entertained and amused by the thumbnail profiles of such characters as the irrepressible Utopian

Socialist Upton Sinclair and the intrepid union leader Harry Bridges in this cavalcade of individualists. The diligent reader of *Endangered Dreams* will definitely come away with a good grasp of the dynamics of California history during this troubled decade.

In all of his books on California history, Starr has depicted the state as a land of dreamers. Hollywood was built on celluloid dreams. The television industry, centered in Southern California, broadcasts prefabricated dreams to the rest of the United States and other parts of the world. More than a billion viewers watch the Academy Award presentations each year, a motion picture/television spectacular event about the fulfillment of the dreams of some of Hollywood's most successful dreamers.

There were many different kinds of dreams in Depression-era California, and they often brought the dreamers into conflict. The 1930's California microcosm mirrored the troubled globe on the brink of war. Socialists dreamed of creating a cooperative society. The state's many retirees dreamed of finding peace and security in an idyllic climate. California's writers and artists had their dreams of fame and fortune or of a Thoreauvian life of independence and creative freedom. The "Okies"—those pathetic dispossessed subsistence farmers immortalized by John Steinbeck—dreamed of owning a piece of rich farmland and putting down new roots. Factory workers, merchant seamen, stevedores, and teamsters dreamed of dignity, decent wages, and humane working conditions. The lower-middle class dreamed of enrichment and upward social mobility in a land of opportunities. Politicians of leftist and rightist sympathies dreamed of becoming mayors, senators, governors, and presidents.

The oligarchy had grandiose dreams and the power to get them fulfilled in such modern wonders as Hoover Dam, the Golden Gate and Oakland Bay bridges, the All-American Canal, the Hetch Hetchy Aqueduct, Shasta Dam, Rainbow Bridge, and the network of freeways that eventually transformed California into a unique civilization dependent upon cars and trucks.

Starr concludes his book with a description of the Golden Gate International Exposition of 1939, for which an entire four-hundred-acre island was created in the middle of San Francisco Bay. Treasure Island was intended to become an international airport after the fair ended, but the eruption of World War II changed the strategically situated island into the most important naval base on the West Coast. San Francisco's World's Fair was officially held to commemorate the completion of the Bay Area's great bridges; according to Starr, however, it symbolized the end of the Great Depression, the beginning of California's emergence from an agricultural province into international prominence, and the assertion of its leadership role among the newly developing markets of the Pacific Rim.

Endangered Dreams is the fourth in a series of scholarly books on California history with the omnibus title of *Americans and the California Dream*. The previous volumes were *Americans and the California Dream, 1850-1915* (1973); *Inventing the Dream: California Through the Progressive Era* (1985); and *Material Dreams: Southern California Through the 1920's* (1990). The author is state librarian of California, a contributing editor of the *Los Angeles Times*, and a member of the faculty at the University of Southern California.

The book is illustrated with many black-and-white photographs, including a shot of Pan America Airways' luxurious state-of-the-art four-engine *China Clipper*, which began regular service in 1935 and was expected to facilitate business relations between the United States and the Far East.

Bill Delaney

Sources for Further Study

Bookwatch. XVII, February, 1996, p. 6.
Choice. XXXIII, May, 1996, p. 1546.
Civilization. III, January, 1996, p. 76.
Kirkus Reviews. LXIII, October 1, 1995, p. 1413.
Library Journal. CXX, October 15, 1995, p. 74.
Los Angeles Times Book Review. January 21, 1996, p. 1.
The New York Times Book Review. CI, February 18, 1996, p. 19.
Publishers Weekly. CCXLII, November 20, 1995, p. 63.
The Washington Post Book World. XXVI, February 11, 1996, p. 6.

THE ENDS OF THE EARTH
A Journey at the Dawn of the Twenty-first Century

Author: Robert D. Kaplan (1952-   )
Publisher: Random House (New York). 476 pp. $27.50
Type of work: Current affairs; travel
Time: The mid-1990's
Locale: West Africa; Egypt; Turkey; Central Asia; the subcontinent; Southeast Asia

An account of a global journey by an experienced journalist and provocative thinker who articulates many of the most urgent and telling questions facing the human race at the end of the twentieth century

Robert D. Kaplan's cover article in the February, 1994, issue of *The Atlantic Monthly* "The Coming Anarchy"—claiming as it did that large areas of the world were fast going from bad to worse and that West Africa was succumbing to neotribalism and war for its own sake—sparked a storm of controversy, bringing down on its author ire from across the political spectrum. Writing in the establishment Canadian newspaper *The Globe and Mail*, Marcus Gee (in an essay reprinted in *World Press Review*, July, 1994) took care to speak respectfully of Kaplan and his work before massaging an assortment of dubious official statistics to support his comforting counterargument. "Africa is an exception to the rule, a dark chapter in a much larger story," claimed Gee. "Despite all the looming troubles, so eloquently recounted by Kaplan, life for the majority of the world's citizens is getting steadily better in almost every category."

Alexander Cockburn on the other hand, writing in the leftist weekly *The Nation* (March 28, 1994), wasted no time with courtesies, launching directly and unabashedly into an anti-Kaplan diatribe. Citing Kaplan's "lurid predictions" and "catastrophist impressionism," accusing him of "data-free" analysis and, tacitly but unmistakably, of racism, describing him as a "rabid Malthusian" and calling his analysis "vacuous to the point of imbecility," Cockburn wrote: "Above all, Kaplan has no faith in people or politics." At a time when the rebellion in the southern Mexican state of Chiapas against Mexico's central government had been under way less than three months, Cockburn concluded: "Scenarists of horror like Kaplan cannot imagine that political will might challenge and repel the evils they discern or predict. Most recently the Maya of Chiapas put the lie to all that."

The responses of Gee and Cockburn, mutual anathema though they certainly be, share several telling traits. Both reflect a belief that the world should be and can become a better place than it is. Both prescribe instrumental solutions to human ills—"progress" in a bland, liberal sense in Gee's case; social revolution in Cockburn's—and purport to demonstrate that such solutions are possible and desirable. And, in marked contrast to Kaplan's article, both are based more on wishful speculation than on experience.

The shrillness of Cockburn's attack—and "attack" is the only appropriate word—prompts a suspicion directly contrary to what he would like us to believe: that Kaplan may well have articulated disturbing, genuinely prophetic insights that fundamentally challenge notions and categories that prevailed during the half-century following

World War II. Evidently, writers of Cockburn's persuasion would rather defend a long-cherished ideology than debate Kaplan's case respectfully and on its merits.

The Ends of the Earth: A Journey at the Dawn of the Twenty-first Century is Kaplan's fleshing-out of "The Coming Anarchy," but it is more than that; he goes several steps further, discussing and depicting his visits to parts of the world not treated in the article. Kaplan's only mention in the book of "The Coming Anarchy" is admirably diffident, expressing at once both called-for humility and well-earned pride, and nicely highlighting the contrast between his approach to understanding the world and those of many of his detractors:

> In 1994, immediately after this article was published, I began a journey by land—roughly speaking—from Egypt to Cambodia: through the Near East, Central Asia, the Indian subcontinent, and Southeast Asia. While "The Coming Anarchy" was being debated at home, I was already engaged in the mop-up operation. This mop-up operation did not so much disprove "The Coming Anarchy" as it showed me how culture, politics, geography, history and economics were inextricable. Rather than a grand theory, the best I could now hope for was a better appreciation of these interrelationships.

The Ends of the Earth is the account of a particular journey of global scope by an experienced, thoughtful, and impressively well-informed journalist, at a particular historical moment. It is important to make this observation, because the book's true subject is a cluster of big, complex patterns and truths. Kaplan himself emphasizes the particularity of what he has done. "This is a travel book," he writes in a preface. "It is concrete to the extent that my ideas arise from personal experience. It is subjective. . . . It is idiosyncratic. . . . Think of it as a brief romp through a swath of the globe, in which I try to give personal meaning to the kinds of issues raised in Paul Kennedy's *Preparing for the Twenty-first Century*."

Tactically, and rightly, Kaplan thus scales down the rhetorical scope of his claim to authority. His authority nonetheless remains substantial, because of both the very particularity of the journey he narrates and the extent of knowledge and previous experience he brings to it. Thus, when he arrives in Pakistan, he is able to note almost in passing that "This was not my first but my tenth trip to Pakistan." Most travel writing depends on a tone, often either forced or cloying, of naïve discovery. Kaplan has done far too much homework to pull off this tone, and to his credit he scarcely tries. *The Ends of the Earth* is less a "travel book" than a guided tour, an eyewitness depiction of our world at the moment just before the time of huge upheavals that already was beginning in the 1990's. The brilliance of its conception and execution is its author's success at depicting and explaining large geopolitical and demographic truths by way of concrete, particular events and experiences.

Kaplan's refusal to accept the claimed validity of received categories allows him to articulate questions that are important precisely to the extent that they undermine cherished notions. Thus, in a fascinating chapter on Iran, he writes:

> While U.S. policymakers were still obsessed with Iranian-sponsored terrorism, I sensed that the outlaw behavior of Iran's current regime was one of those problems that would soon be submerged—under the pressure of greater, tectonic forces gathering at the turn of the twenty-first century, forces driven by the ability, and inability, of various cultures to manage dwindling resources.

A running theme is Kaplan's insistent refusal to read maps as if they portrayed objective reality. The book's endpapers, which feature a metaphorically borderless world map, elegantly summarize the author's project quite nearly in its entirety. At the end of his first chapter he reproduces a map of Africa that hangs in the entrance hall at Thomas Jefferson's home and asks: "Would that 1802 map at Monticello someday turn out to be more useful than the present ones?" Similarly, he asserts that "To imagine the map of the emerging world you should travel backward from the latest CD-ROM version of the Encyclopaedia Britannica to the eleventh edition, published in 1910. The subject headings in these brittle, yellowing pages still correspond to the world of the late 1990's: 'Russia in Asia,' 'Turkey in Asia,' 'India (with lesser Frontier States.' . . . Pakistan, of course, is absent. Its components fall under the rubric 'lesser Frontier States.'" Kaplan knows that every map is a metaphor, and he is determined to replace inadequate existing metaphors with ones he can accept as more nearly true.

The chapter on Thailand is the least strong; in it, Kaplan fails in ways that highlight his notable successes elsewhere in the book. Evidently physically tired near the end of what plainly was a long and arduous journey, on arrival in Bangkok Kaplan lets down his critical guard. This is unfortunate but understandable: any traveler who has arrived in Bangkok from both clean, orderly Hong Kong and frustrating, exhausting India knows that whether or not Thailand ranks as a "success story" is very much in the eye of the beholder. The trouble with Kaplan's chapter on Bangkok is that although he subtitles it, appropriately, "Environmental and Sexual Limits," he bases it far too much on secondhand sources, including a local newspaper not known for being unfailingly authoritative.

This is especially jarring because so much of the rest of the book is based so directly on the writer's own experience. "In Bangkok," he writes, "I experienced travel more through the reading of monographs than through conversations in the street or in buses—because here was one of the few places where accurate figures existed *on location* [Kaplan's emphasis]." The observation reads like a cop-out and is puzzling: Is Kaplan saying he would prefer to read monographs than to do his own work as a journalist? Surely not. Another unhappy lapse is his use of the book *Behind the Smile: Voices of Thailand* by Thai writer Sanitsuda Ekachai. Following a common practice, he refers to the author as "Ekachai." Ekachai is indeed the writer's surname, but can Kaplan not have known that the Thai custom is always to refer to people, even in formal contexts, by their given names? If he did not know, he should have, if he was going to write about Thailand and borrow a Thai writer's authority. He also is inconsistent in this matter, since he refers to think-tank thinker Twatchai Yongkittikul rightly as "Dr. Twatchai" and to Singaporean dictator Lee Kuan Yew as "Mr. Lee."

Much ink has been spilled detailing similar minor complaints about the journalism of V. S. Naipaul, a writer Kaplan admires and seems to emulate. To point out errors of fact or interpretation is one of the valid purposes of criticism. Even so, it is difficult to avoid the conclusion that many of Naipaul's critics envy his stature and privilege theory or ideology over experience. To dwell overmuch on those few places where Kaplan stumbles would be to distort his larger purpose and achievement. To point out, then, that his chapter on Thailand is relatively thin and weak is only to say that other writers have as much experience of Thailand as he does of Pakistan and the eastern Mediterranean. In Thailand Kaplan slips, but from a very high standard. The book's last chapter, on Cambodia, is much better and nicely completes the circle of his experience and musings that had begun months earlier in West Africa.

Perhaps the greatest of Kaplan's many accomplishments is that he has realigned the intellectual and geographical landscape in such a way as to compel other journalists henceforward to refer to his work, whether they want to or not. "The Coming Anarchy" first, then *The Ends of the Earth*, made the name "Kaplan" a kind of byword: In informed circles in the mid-1990's, simply saying the name aloud sufficed to spark an animated discussion. On particular matters as well Kaplan points the way for other writers. His chapter on China, approaching that huge and complex country as it does through the geographical back door (from Central Asia), should prompt serious rethinking. In a very amusing chapter titled "Strategic Hippie Routes," he wonders if the large numbers of budget tourists in Central Asia might be an indicator of coming strife in that region. (Backpackers, he writes, "went to medieval locations that had been suddenly exposed to outside influences. . . . And places like this, moving from the fifteenth century to the twenty-first, were likely candidates for upheaval.")

It is unfortunate that Kaplan did not visit Burma; his thoughts on that blighted land surely would have been most interesting. On the other hand, it is precisely the applicability of his thoughts on Uzbekistan to the plight of Burma that best illustrates the scope of what he has done, as well as the troubling nature of the big questions that faced the human race as it limped into the twenty-first century. Citing Uzbek president Islam Karimov's ugly human rights record, Kaplan writes: "Karimov, the Nigerian generals, and others like them are betting that democracy is not the final word in political evolution. The West believes they are wrong. But what if they are right, or even partly right—in their cases? For us it's a matter of principle; for tens of millions threatened by the spectre of civil conflict, it is a matter of life and death."

The tone is characteristic. As in all of his work, rather than flinching when faced with difficult questions, Kaplan articulates them. It is the mark of an important writer.

Ethan Casey

Sources for Further Study

Los Angeles Times Book Review. March 17, 1996, p. 1.
The New Republic. CCXIV, April 15, 1996, p. 32.
The New York Times Book Review. CI, March 31, 1996, p. 7.
The New Yorker. LXXII, April 8, 1996, p. 96.
Technology Review. XCIX, November, 1996, p. 70.
The Wall Street Journal. March 27, 1996, p. A20.
The Washington Post Book World. XXVI, March 3, 1996, p. 1.
World Policy Journal. VIII, Spring, 1996, p. 83.

ESSAYS IN APPRECIATION

Author: Christopher Ricks (1933-   )
Publisher: Oxford University Press (New York). 363 pp. $24.95
Type of work: Literary criticism

With emphasis on style, Ricks analyzes specific literary works and explores larger critical issues

Although Christopher Ricks furnishes no subtitle to his book, an appropriate one might be "Beyond the New Criticism," for he writes primarily in the new critical tradition. This school of critics became popular during the 1940's through the writings of Cleanth Brooks, Robert Penn Warren, Alan Tate, and numerous others. More a methodology than a critical theory, the movement stressed the integrity of the individual text over biographical, historical, or generic influences. It suggested that through explication—a systematic analysis of plot, characterization, style, tone, and themes of a poem or work of fiction—one might gain a more reliable understanding of the text. While the new critics did on occasion use their analytical approach to call attention to defects of a literary work, their chief aim was to uphold the organic unity and artistic integrity of a poem or short story. Their system of criticism, though it did not supplant other critical and scholarly approaches, became the primary pedagogical approach in English departments for more than two decades.

While it largely achieved its original purposes, the New Criticism revealed certain weaknesses. By ignoring biographical analysis, rejecting consideration of outside evidence of authorial intention, and downplaying conventions of literary genre, it sometimes appeared too narrow in its approaches. Further, its emphasis upon subtlety and irony in individual texts worked to the detriment of specific groups of authors, most notably those of the Neoclassic and Romantic periods. More important, meticulous analysis of all parts of a work meant that dramas, novels, and long narrative poems presented tasks too formidable for thorough explication. One came to expect that the New Criticism would explicate poems and short stories and little else. Later critics in the tradition met this objection by limiting their analyses to one or two approaches. Ricks belongs to the generation of new critics who attempt close but limited analysis of texts. One could, for example, analyze an epic poem such as *Paradise Lost* through a close reading of style, as Ricks did in *Milton's Grand Style* (1963).

The word "Appreciation" in the title is also important, for Ricks at his best enhances the reader's appreciation of literature by exploring meanings and stylistic subtleties that might otherwise be overlooked. Among his predecessors in twentieth century criticism, he has consistently admired William Empson, Donald Davie, F. R. Leavis, T. S. Eliot—indicating his allegiance to Great Britain—but his effort to enhance appreciation reveals an allegiance to a legacy that extends to Matthew Arnold, Samuel Taylor Coleridge, and Samuel Johnson.

Essays in Appreciation is a collection of essays, most previously published, beginning with literature of the Renaissance and ending with twentieth century works and critical controversy. The book analyzes a diversity of poems, prose works, and dramas by major authors such as Christopher Marlowe, John Donne, George Eliot, and Jane Austen, as well as by lesser-known writers such as George Crabbe, the Earl of Clarendon, and E. C. Gaskell. In his writings on lesser-known works in particular, Ricks seems intent on pointing out merits that have been overlooked.

Only one selection, "A Note on Hardy's 'A Spellbound Palace,'" offers a fully realized explication of a poem in the manner of New Criticism, and even in that selection Ricks moves on from explication to compare Hardy's poem with T. S. Eliot's "Sweeney Erect." Citing similarities in the diction and imagery of the two poems, he amasses a number of close analogies, suggesting that the aging Thomas Hardy borrowed from Eliot. More typical of Ricks's critical analysis is the book's opening essay, "*Doctor Faustus* and Hell on Earth," an analysis of Christopher Marlowe's best-known tragedy. What one expects in Ricks is identification of recurrent words or phrases that somehow reveal important points of emphasis or meanings that have been previously obscured. By doing so he presents a sharply focussed critical discussion and often makes sometimes exciting discoveries about the meaning of a work. In his discussion of Marlowe's drama, he centers upon references to the plague, the "hell on earth" of the title. Historical analysis of the plague during Elizabethan times and references in other fiction and drama suggest that the disease was deeply feared, with good reason. Thus, Ricks suggests, when Mephistopheles assures Faustus twenty-four more years of life in exchange for his soul, the bargain would not have seemed as trivial to Faustus and Marlowe's audience as it does to modern readers. Given the grim realities of the time, Marlowe's hero could not have expected to live twenty-four additional years, and thus his fatal bargain becomes more plausible.

When Ricks turns to longer works, his criticism is necessarily even more tightly focused. Three essays concern lengthy Victorian biographies: E. C. Gaskell's *Life of Charlotte Brontë*, James Anthony Froude's eleven volumes on the lives of Thomas and Jane Carlyle, and Hallam Tennyson's *Alfred Lord Tennyson: A Memoir*. Since all three were written by persons closely associated with the principals, Ricks explores the challenges they faced in being artistic and truthful at the same time. Gaskell and Froude were close friends of their subjects; Hallam Tennyson was an only surviving son. Ricks cites numerous quotations from Gaskell's work to demonstrate that her style admirably fits the subject and is sufficiently supple to deal appropriately with the varied experiences, especially the numerous misfortunes, of the Brontës. Froude, however, faced a more difficult task, for he confronted the choice of dealing with only the pleasant aspects of the Carlyles' lives, as the standards of his time encouraged him to do, or, by presenting a truthful narration, doing what he thought Carlyle would have wished. He braved censure for not acceding to the Victorian preference for hagiography and revealed the truth about the Carlyles' marriage. By contrast, Hallam Tennyson, writing the biography of his father, performed an act of piety, yet one truthful to the subject. From Ricks's analysis, the reader acquires an appreciation for the difficulties that the biographers overcame and for their artful narration—largely evidenced in admirable adaptation of style to content. By paying homage to the achievements of biographers whose works, if not forgotten, are at least seldom read, Ricks carries out the function of the critic in making meritorious but obscure literary works more familiar.

Toward the work's close, Ricks includes a series of four essays more generally concerned with literary study and criticism. The first, "Literature and the Matter of Fact," is a sensitive, thoughtful exploration of problems that arise from authors' misuse of facts in fiction. The essay represents a kind of touchstone for Ricks's adherence to the great critical tradition that harks back to Dr. Johnson. Some critics believe that mistakes of fact are of no consequence to imaginative writing. Why should anyone care that Chaucer, anachronistically, puts dukes in ancient Athens or that Shakespeare has a clock strike in imperial Rome? Ricks makes the point that when anachronisms and other factual errors are distracting to readers, as they sometimes are, for example, in realistic novels, then they do create problems. After George Eliot described a character as wearing an item of clothing that was not available at the time of the novel's setting, a reader called the mistake to her attention. In response, Eliot simply altered the text in a subsequent edition to correct the blunder. Yet for a contrasting example, Ricks cites William Golding, in *Lord of the Flies* (1954), who had the boys use Piggy's glasses to magnify sunlight and start a fire. A reader pointed out to him that Piggy was myopic and that lenses for myopia could not focus light to create heat. Because the glasses contributed to important symbolism associated with the characters, however, Golding was convinced that he could not make a change without doing aesthetic damage to the text. He left the factual error in the hope that most readers would not notice it or, if they did, would not find it distracting. Ricks reaches a commonsense conclusion: Factual accuracy is significant but not of overriding importance.

In the final three selections, two of them very brief, Ricks assails postmodernism in literary criticism, particularly as it has developed in the United States since the late 1960's. The movement, which might be traced in American academic writing to Stanley Fish's *Surprised by Sin: The Reader and "Paradise Lost"* (1967), began with reader-response criticism that placed the reader at the center of critical concern. Often drawing upon avant-garde thinking from France, it has continued through major movements such as structuralism, deconstructionism, and New Historicism and minor ones such as semiotics and Marxian analysis. Highly theoretical, these movements derive their intellectual substance from philosophy and social sciences—linguistics, anthropology, psychology, and sociology. With the possible exception of Marxism, these critical trends have made little headway in England, where Ricks spent most of his academic life. He makes no effort to discredit the individual theoretical schools of postmodernism; instead he centers upon fundamental principles and, as one might expect, matters of style.

In assessing the major concerns of theoretical criticism, he advocates principle over theory. In accord with the long critical tradition in England that extends back to Johnson, principles that can be expressed in the manner of proverbs or maxims seem more fitting for art than theory. Ricks reasonably inquires what the role of theory is in criticism of painting or music and suggests that the teachable portion of literature concerns rhetoric, a term that embraces his own area of strength, stylistics. Yet beyond style, Ricks believes that grasping literature's emotional content is only hindered by theoretical approaches. As for the theorists' often proclaimed assertion that all thinking is theoretical, Ricks points out some of the differences between speculating and theorizing. Theory has one meaning in science, another in the social sciences, still another in the humanities. Yet theory may be distinguished from speculation by its intellectual rigor, complexity, and consistency. Ricks clearly believes that theory borrowed from social science is incapable of accounting for what really matters in a literary work.

His attack on critical style demonstrates that what theoretical critics would describe as a new openness and inclusiveness is really another form of dogmatism and that the rhetoric they employ gives this away. He assails the jargon so frequent in writings of literary theorists: "canon," "marginalize," "mystification," and "empowerment." He cites enough "jokey" titles and exaggerated claims to present a caveat, but for the most part his examples do derive from the best writing by theorists.

In exploring concepts of the canon, he suggests that the issue is not so much what is meritorious but rather what can be taught in the time allotted for literature in the system of education. Some texts, he urges, are marginal, not marginalized, and the reasons are not those of race, gender, or class. In English classes, where most literature is taught in English-speaking countries, one can do little more than teach selected texts from the national literatures of Great Britain and the United States, in reality many fewer titles than most teachers would prefer. The list of frequently taught texts has changed over time, not because of the efforts of professional critics, but because neglected works have often been rediscovered by creative writers. Although he does not quite do so, Ricks seems to dismiss literary theory on the grounds that it is irrelevant to pedagogy and to creative writers.

Ricks evinces scintillating style enriched with literary allusions, especially to Shakespeare and Milton, and repetitive wordplay. Despite occasional preciosity and excessive repetition, the book makes for rewarding reading. Although it includes too many citations and quotations to fit the category of *belles lettres*, the insightful, sensitive interpretations Ricks provides place the book in the limited category of critical writings with appeal beyond a narrow academic circle. In large measure he achieves the critic's function—enhancing the reader's appreciation for well-known works and making manifest the merits of lesser-known titles.

Stanley Archer

Sources for Further Study

Boston Globe. March 31, 1996, p. B42.
The Guardian. July 19, 1996, p. 16.
London Review of Books. XVIII, August 1, 1996, p. 15.
Publishers Weekly. CCXLIII, March 4, 1996, p. 48.
The Spectator. CCLXXVII, August 24, 1996, p. 27.
The Times Literary Supplement. November 29, 1996, p. 6.

EUROPE
A History

Author: Norman Davies (1939-   )
Publisher: Oxford University Press (New York). Illustrated. 1365 pp. $39.95
Type of work: History
Time: From antiquity to the 1990's
Locale: Europe

Norman Davies discusses the changing concepts of Europe and explores its long history

Europe: A History is an ambitious, contentious, and massive history of the continent which appropriately begins with the myth of Europa, who was seduced by Zeus in the guise of a white bull and carried on his back from Phoenicia in the Middle East to the Aegean islands where she became the mother of Minos of Crete, the founder of European civilization. Norman Davies is a professor of history at the University of London and is the author of a highly acclaimed two-volume history of Poland, *God's Playground* (1981). The history of eastern Europe plays a prominent part in this work as well, and its often superficial treatment in many other studies of Europe is one of the criticisms Davies directs at his fellow historians, past and present.

In an almost fifty-page introduction to this extremely long history, Davies discusses his aims in writing *Europe*. He points out that only in the eighteenth century, the era of the Enlightenment, did the term "Europe" begin to replace "Christendom" as the general designation of the continent, this at a time when religion was becoming the bane of such writers as Voltaire. The problems with using the term "Europe" are numerous. Does it include Great Britain? The British have often been reluctant to identify themselves with the Continent and its tribulations. Does it include Russia, or is Russia largely part of Asia? The Russians have often been divided on the wisdom of being part of European civilization. The sea borders of Europe are readily apparent, but where should the line be drawn in the east—is there geographically something called Europe rather than Eurasia?

Davies attacks the general use of the term "Western civilization," claiming, with considerable validity, that too often "Western civilization" is merely a cover for discussing the history and culture of western Europe, especially France, Britain, Italy through the Renaissance, and certain periods of German history. Eastern Europe is largely ignored except to contrast its economic paucity and tyrannical rapacity with the supposedly more civilized west. This, he argues, has been prevalent even through-out the twentieth century, and especially during the Cold War. Much of *Europe* is thus devoted to reasserting the balance between western and eastern Europe, and in choosing to do so Davies has inevitably opened up new areas, persons, and events for many readers of his work. It might even be claimed that Davies' *Europe* is symbolically a reflection of the demise of the post-World War II conflict and the beginning of the reunification and reintegration of the continent.

He is also critical of many of the claims of cultural pluralism. Although he agrees that traditional Eurocentrism—the belief that Europe and its accomplishments are the focus of civilized progress—can be fallacious, Davies argues that European history, culture, and civilization form the significant roots of the United States in its commitment to individual rights, freedom of thought, and toleration. He scorns the supposed bias against dead white European males. Davies admits that the so-called great books lists have always included mostly Europeans—too often limited to western Europeans in Davies' opinion—but to replace those figures merely because they are politically incorrect to a later generation because of ethnicity and gender is unconscionable, as Davies notes that there is no African Aquinas, Mexican Mill, or Vietnamese Virgil.

Following his argumentative introduction, Davies divides his work into twelve chronological chapters, divisions which generally correspond to those of most histories of Europe. A chapter on environment and prehistory is followed by chapters on the Greeks, the Romans, the birth of Europe during the era of the barbarian invasions, the Middle Ages, and its decline at the time of the Black Death, the renaissances and religious reformations, absolutism and the enlightenment, the eighteenth century revolutions, the nineteenth century when Europe reached its pinnacle of power, and two chapters covering the twentieth century, divided at 1945 with the end of World War II.

Europe as a shared culture came into existence toward the end of antiquity with the mingling of Roman civilization, the barbarian invasions, and the emergence of Christian civilization. Yet, Davies states, there is no single Europe either. There is, he claims, a European culture and shared historical experiences, but there also have been historic divisions across the continent such as the division between Roman and non-Roman Europe, the later split in Christendom between Roman Catholicism and Eastern Orthodoxy, and most recently Winston Churchill's Iron Curtain of the Cold War. In the author's opinion, commonality but pluralism, unity but divergence have been the history of Europe. If Davies' chronological approach and chapter divisions are traditional, what is more unusual is that at the end of each chapter is a specific historical event which suggests a possible summary or interpretation of that chapter in just a few pages. These choices are obviously subjective, as Davies admits, but it can assist the reader in bringing together some of what has been previously read. For example, at the end of the chapter titled "Environment and Prehistory," Davies focuses upon Knossos, in Crete, in 1628 B.C., and the fall of Minoan civilization possibly as a result of the volcanic eruption of the Aegean island of Thera. In line with Davies' concern to restore the balance between the east and west in Europe, the chapter on Rome is concluded by several pages on the dedication of Constantinople, the new Rome in the east, in A.D. 326. The era of the enlightenment and absolutism are encapsulated by the premiere of Mozart's "Don Giovanni," in Prague, on October 29, 1787. Europe's most influential century, the nineteenth, is brought to an end on Monday, August 3, 1914, at the British foreign office in London, as Europe begins its fall into the quagmire of the Great War. These set pieces are useful codas and something of a respite from the hectic pace and factually full pages of the rest of the narrative.

One of the highlights of *Europe* is what Davies designates as "Capsules." There are about three hundred distributed throughout the work. They, too, are subjective choices by the author, but are frequently fascinating in their information. Rarely concerned with high politics or international war and diplomacy, these capsules are a recognition of the impact of social history, such as by the French *Annales* School of historical writing, which stresses an interdisciplinary approach and explores topics often ignored by past historians. Davies' capsules reflect such interests. They include a discussion of "Brie," traceable back to Charlemagne in 774 when he was presented with a local cheese by the monks at the Abbey of Meaux on the Plateau de Brie. "Jeans" comes from the French name for Genoa and the style of pants worn by Genoese sailors. Serge de Nimes was the traditional name for a blue sailcloth manufactured in the French town of that name. Levi Strauss, a Bavarian immigrant to the United States, in meeting the needs of the prospectors during the California gold rush of 1849, used the French cloth with the Genoese style, reinforcing the pockets and seams with brass rivets. The result was a garment which in time became one of the most popular throughout the entire world. In "Genug" ("enough") are quoted the last words of a number of prominent Europeans from Agrippina (mother of the Roman emperor Nero), to H. G. Wells. Others include such varied topics as "Anno Domini" and "Apocalypse," "Condom" and "Chastity," "Sarajevo" and "Syphilus," to "Vendemaire" and the origins of the French Revolutionary calendar and "Vlad," the story of Vlad the Impaler, also known as Dracula. Any reader of *Europe* could find entertainment and enlightenment in merely perusing the many capsules.

In the introduction, Davies notes that one of the significant elements of the European tradition is its musical heritage. A number of the capsules include music topics, such as "Musike," "Nibelung," "Cantus," "Missa," "Angelus," "Baletto," "Opera," "Flamenco," "Sonata," "Strad," "Cantata," "Freude" (Beethoven's Ninth Symphony), "Strassburg" ("La Marseillaise"), among many others. The premier of Mozart's *Don Giovanni* in Prague in 1787 is referred to above, and at the end of his chapter on the French Revolution, Davies begins his set piece of Napoleon's first abdication at Fountainbleu on April 20, 1814, by noting the trumpeters played the "Fanfare de l'Empereur" when Napoleon appeared, and as in his earlier discussion of Mozart, Davies includes musical notations from the piece. Unfortunately, the reader is not so well rewarded when it comes to the visual arts. There are more than seventy illustrations included in *Europe*, but most are not easily identified without searching through the index, and some, such as Adolf Hitler portrayed as a medieval knight in armor, seem inappropriate and irrelevant considering Europe's rich heritage in art and architecture.

The volume contains numerous maps. Many of them have been turned, however, so that north, instead of appearing at the top of the page, is frequently on the right. After a time the reader gets used to this eccentricity, but there seems no particular reason for such an arrangement other than possibly shaking the reader's prior perceptions and thus seeing Europe with a new awareness. It hardly seems necessary. In addition to chapter notes, capsule notes, and notes on the illustrations, there is a large appendix, or "Historical Compendium," of subtantially more than one hundred pages and which includes more than one hundred items, graphs, maps, charts, and lists covering such topics as "Minoan Scripts," "Pythagorean Food Classification," "The Chicago 'Great Books Scheme,'" "European University Foundations," "Paris *Rentes*, 1420-1787," "Grand Opera, 1607-1969," "The Papal Index, 1559-1952," "Queen Victoria's Relatives," and "The Gulag Archipelago." Much is fascinating although at times overwhelming, and some not as clear and understandable as it might be.

For the general reader who has some previous knowledge of Europe or, dare it be said, "Western civilization," *Europe* contains many rewards, especially on topics and in areas—particularly the east—that are often not covered by many histories which, as Davies compellingly argues, often concentrate primarily on western Europe. Because the entire history of Europe is confined to a single and extremely long volume, the vast number of names, dates, and events can become confusing. Many of the events could easily be expanded but then the history of the Continent could not be contained between just two covers. Unfortunately there is another criticism which can be made of Davies' *Europe*. In such a monumental work, some errors of fact are possibly to be expected. Nevertheless, here there seem to be too many. For example, the Donation of Constantine was discovered to be a forgery in the fifteenth century and not in the sixteenth; the first manned flight by the Wright brothers took place in Kitty Hawk, North Carolina, not in Dayton, Ohio, where they were born; the United States Congress did not choose the English language over German by one vote during the Civil War; and the British House of Lords did not block three Irish Home Rule Bills in the nineteenth century, but only one—the first was defeated in the House of Commons, and the Home Rule Bill introduced into Parliament in 1912 was the third and not the fourth. Other inaccuracies could be listed. This suggests a certain carelessness on the part of the author and the editor. Additional fact checkers should have been included in the project.

Still, *Europe* is well worth reading and much of it is notably impressive. Davies has strong opinions, and his writing generally reflects great style and wit. The last set piece at the end of the final chapter is "14 February 1992, Summertown" (near Oxford, England), the date and place where Davies completed his history. He writes that the Soviet Union has only recently collapsed and that all of Europe must be profoundly affected. His final comments are cautiously optimistic: "Europe is not going to be fully united in the near future. But it has a chance to be less divided than for generations past. . . . Europa rides on."

Eugene Larson

Sources for Further Study

The Economist. CCCXLI, November 16, 1996, p. 3.
The Guardian. October 17, 1996, II, p. 9.
Los Angeles Times. January 17, 1997, p. E2.

The New York Times Book Review. CI, December 1, 1996, p. 15.
Publishers Weekly. CCXLIII, August 26, 1996, p. 83.
The Times Literary Supplement. December 20, 1996, p. 3.
The Wall Street Journal. November 18, 1996, p. A10.

THE FACE OF THE NATION
Immigration, the State, and the National Identity

Author: Keith Fitzgerald (1956-   )
Publisher: Stanford University Press (Stanford, California). 285 pp. $39.50
Type of work: Political science; history; current affairs
Time: 1879 to the 1990's
Locale: The United States

A study of the intricate decision making, often carried out at cross-purposes, that accounts for the otherwise baffling inconsistencies of U.S. immigration policy

In the preface to the second edition of their excellent book *Immigrant America: A Portrait* (1996), Alejandro Portes and Rubén G. Rumbaut speak of "the sharply politicized and increasingly acrimonious public debate on immigration in the 1990s." Noting that "the twenty million foreign-born persons counted by the 1990 U.S. Census formed the largest immigrant population in the world, and admissions during the 1990s appear certain to eclipse the record set in the first decade of this century," they register at the same time higher levels of "public alarm and nativist resistance" to immigration.

Readers who have followed immigration issues for a decade or more will recognize a familiar paradox here. It was in the 1980's that attention began to be focused on the enormous surge of immigration following the landmark Immigration Act of 1965, including as well more than one million refugees from Southeast Asia. Critics of U.S. policy warned of dire consequences if immigration continued at such high levels; in response, immigrant advocates denounced the critics for nativism and xenophobia and often added the charge of racism as well, since the "new immigration" was substantially non-European. When Congress finally got around to updating and revising immigration policy at the end of the 1980's, the result (the Immigration Act of 1990) was actually a higher ceiling for legal immigration.

So it has gone in the 1990's as well. In 1995, the U.S. Commission on Immigration Reform, chaired by Barbara Jordan, recommended that legal immigration be cut by roughly a third. President Bill Clinton initially endorsed the commission's recommendation, but as immigration reform bills wound their way through Congress, with the final compromise signed into law on September 30, 1996, the Clinton Administration backtracked, shifting the focus to illegal immigration. With regard to *legal* immigration, far from following the Jordan Commission's call for a substantial reduction, the 1996 law deals with procedural issues such as sponsorship, seeking to ensure that sponsors of new immigrants would indeed have the means to support them if necessary rather than adding to the burden of public assistance. Even these measures were denounced by immigrant advocates as "harsh."

Here then is a puzzle. Americans hear of a "backlash" against immigrants—and in the next decade immigration increases to record levels. Public opinion polls repeatedly report that a majority of Americans would like to see immigration reduced—and the much ballyhooed reform bill does nothing to bring that about. Americans are told that immigration will be a major issue in the 1996 presidential campaign; as it plays out, however, there is virtually no mention of reducing legal immigration, let alone sustained debate on the subject.

Why is there this seeming disparity between rhetoric and reality, between public opinion and policy? Is the direction of U.S. immigration policy from 1965 to the present the result of choice or inadvertence? Or, as Keith Fitzgerald puts it, "Can a polity effectively choose its identity?" Immigration policy, Fitzgerald adds, "is about the face of the nation, or providing character to the national community." How and why are the decisions that determine "the face of the nation" being made?

A good place to begin wrestling with those questions is Fitzgerald's *The Face of the Nation: Immigration, the State, and the National Identity*. On the big shelf of books on immigration published in 1996, Fitzgerald's is one of the most valuable. Nevertheless, let the reader be warned: This book does not yield its riches easily. Its pages of tiny type are filled with jargon-infested sentences. Moreover, Fitzgerald is a maddeningly repetitive writer. He tells readers what he is going to say three or four times before he says it, and then when he is done he repeats what he just said.

Fitzgerald's point of departure is the observation by various critics—among them the Cornell University economist Vernon M. Briggs, Jr.—that U.S immigration policy is "meandering" and "aimless," indeed irrational. Briggs wrote in 1986 that "The absence of any serious effort to forge an immigration policy based upon labor market considerations means that immigration policy today functions as a 'wild card' among the nation's array of key labor market policies. . . . This is a situation that no sensible nation can allow to continue." Yet in the decade since, nothing has changed. "Why," Fitzgerald asks, "did immigration increase during the recession of the early 1990s?"

The absence of any clear labor market rationale is only one of many anomalies. Having established that on the surface U.S. immigration policy is incoherent, Fitzgerald seeks to uncover the logic of the decisions that cumulatively constitute this policy. To do so, he makes two analytic moves. The first is to differentiate among three kinds of immigration: admission of refugees, admission of nonrefugee immigrants through official channels ("front-gate" immigration, in Fitzgerald's usage), and unsanctioned immigration ("back-door" or illegal immigration). Each of these types of immigration raises a different set of issues, so that to speak of "immigration policy" as a unitary subject is often misleading.

Fitzgerald's second analytic move is to consider three theoretical approaches that attempt to account for the baffling inconsistencies in immigration policy. The first, the "pluralist" model, focuses on individuals acting in concert through organized interest groups. From this perspective, inconsistencies in immigration policy reflect the differing and often contradictory agendas of competing interest groups. So, for example, "one might expect to see employers pushing for labor migration, especially during wage spikes and boom times. Labor unions might try to reduce labor migration, especially during times of wage contraction or recessions."

The second approach Fitzgerald considers, the "class conflict" model, is neo-Marxist. A good example of this approach (not specifically cited by Fitzgerald) is *The New Asian Immigration in Los Angeles and Global Restructuring* (1994), a collection of essays edited by Paul Ong, Edna Bonacich, and Lucie Cheng. These essays consider post-1965 Asian immigration in the context of the global restructuring of capitalism. Asian immigration has been "bipolar," with many unskilled, poorly paid workers on the one hand and, on the other, many highly trained managers and professionals. Why has U.S. immigration policy encouraged the admission of both? Paul Ong finds the answer in the "two prongs" of capitalist global restructuring: "cheapening labor and pursuing innovation."

Both of these approaches treat politics as a neutral medium in which the real forces that drive social change are expressed, or as a mask for what is "really" going on. In short, while pluralist and class conflict analyses offer useful insights, both treat politics reductively. Fitzgerald prefers the third model, "state-centered" or "realist" (the latter term used here in a special sense). This approach is representative of the "new institutionalism," a school of thought which, in Fitzgerald's words, "puts politics back at the center of policy explanation." It emphasizes the way in which contingent historical circumstances—in particular, the structure, logic, and self-interest of bureaucratic institutions—shape the formation of policy. Fitzgerald's own approach, which he calls "improvisational institutionalism," is a variant of this third model.

Now to anyone who has seen the film *Advise and Consent* (1962), or has merely served on a church committee, this theoretical debate may seem like much ado about nothing, a squabble among academics and of academic interest only. Obviously at every level, from the local school board to the U.S. Congress, policy is shaped in part by institutions. And yes, politics matters; that give-and-take is not just an elaborate show. Yet Fitzgerald's book is not simply a theoretical treatise, for after laying this foundation he applies his approach by tracing the evolution of U.S. immigration policy. This "thick description" superbly conveys the byzantine twists and turns of lawmaking and administration related to all three varieties of immigration (front-gate, back-door, and refugee).

One example out of many will have to suffice here. Following the Hungarian uprising of 1956, about 200,000 Hungarians fled their native land. They dispersed all around the world, with the largest number (38,000) settling in the United States. The manner in which they were admitted perfectly illustrates Fitzgerald's emphasis on the role of bureaucratic institutions, improvising policy in response to contingent circumstances.

Most of these Hungarian refugees were not, strictly speaking, "political" refugees (that is, most had not actively participated in the revolt), but they were fleeing communist tyranny, and the State Department favored refugees from the communist bloc. About 5,000 of the Hungarian refugees were admitted under the provisions of the Refugee Relief Act of 1953. That act, however, required a security check (to avoid admitting subversives who came in the guise of refugees), which most of the post-uprising refugees did not have the documentation to pass.

These remaining refugees could not be admitted through the front gate. The national-origins quota system codified by the Immigration Act of 1924 was still in place, and by 1956 front-gate Hungarian immigration had already "borrowed" from the annual quota of future years to such an extent that several decades of quotas were "mortgaged." Faced with this dilemma, the Justice Department responded by making use of an obscure parole provision of immigration law, originally "intended to meet such situations as the provision of emergency medical care or allowing in a witness to aid prosecution." It was never intended to accommodate large-scale admissions. "Nevertheless," Fitzgerald writes, "the attorney general used the parole provision to allow 15,000 Hungarians in before Congress could even convene to consider the question." Given the outpouring of public sympathy for the refugees, Congress was not inclined to dissent, and ultimately almost 30,000 of the Hungarian refugees were admitted under the parole provision.

This action, which developed not from any central planning but rather was an improvised institutional response to a particular event, had far-reaching consequences. As Fitzgerald observes, "an astonishing precedent was set enabling the executive branch to admit large numbers of aliens outside the ordinary legal framework of immigration policy." Moreover, with the Hungarian refugees, "For the first time, the United States government actually helped immigrants assimilate by coordinating resettlement programs." And so the Hungarian case established precedents that influenced refugee policy for decades.

Fitzgerald's account should arm the reader against sweeping, simplistic generalizations about U.S immigration policy. Yet there is one respect in which his own study is strangely reductive. Like many of the scholars with whom he is debating on theoretical grounds, Fitzgerald debunks what might be called the founding story of American immigration, imaged by the Statue of Liberty. "The evidence . . . provides persuasive documentation that immigration policy in the United States contrasts with the values crystallized by the immigration mythology," Fitzgerald writes in his concluding chapter; indeed, "the evidence shows that the public authority that regulates immigration defies the liberal and democratic beliefs that the immigrant myth celebrates." And so on. What makes this reductive judgment strange is that it is so thoroughly contradicted by the nuanced story Fitzgerald himself has told, in which discrimination, exploitation, and the interests of the state are interwoven with a genuine commitment to freedom and equality. If the admission of the Hungarian refugees reflected in part the state's interest in the Cold War (as it surely did), it also reflected precisely those cherished "liberal and democratic beliefs" about America as a haven for the oppressed.

Thus we return to the paradox with which we began. Amid all the talk—the jeremiads of the immigration-control faction, and the victim-talk of the immigrant advocates—people keep coming to America, in greater numbers than ever before. The face of the nation is changing; that much is certain. Yet exactly what that will mean in the America of the twenty-first century, no one knows.

John Wilson

Source for Further Study

Choice. XXXIV, December, 1996, p. 688.

FAME AND FOLLY
Essays

Author: Cynthia Ozick (1928-   )
Publisher: Alfred A. Knopf (New York). 289 pp. $26.00
Type of work: Essays

A collection of seventeen essays by the author of Art and Ardor, The Messiah of Stockholm,
and The Shawl

Like runners, most writers have preferred distances. Cynthia Ozick is most at home in mid-length forms. Her most memorable fiction has been in *Bloodshed and Three Novellas* (1976) and *The Shawl* (1989) and the short novels *The Cannibal Galaxy* (1983) and *The Messiah of Stockholm* (1987). With few exceptions, the most impressive essays in her two previous collections have been the ten- to twenty-page ones: extended examinations of Edith Wharton, Virginia and Leonard Woolf, Bernard Malamud, Harold Bloom and "a new Yiddish" in *Art and Ardor* (1983), and of Cyril Connolly, Primo Levi, Theodore Dreiser, Sholem Aleichem, S. Y. Agnon, and the Book of Ruth in *Metaphor and Memory* (1989).

In her foreword to *Art and Ardor,* Ozick acknowledged that most of the reviews, essays, articles, talks, and journalism collected in that book were "instigated or invited," the products of stimuli that were "inevitably external." In most cases, in other words, she chose neither their subjects nor their length. The work in *Metaphor and Memory* was similar: mainly short pieces, written at the request of others. Since Ozick is a thoughtful, often surprising writer and a sensitive, book-obsessed reader, she is almost totally incapable of being uninteresting, regardless of length. Yet beginning with its first essay—a forty-seven-page meditation on "T. S. Eliot at 101" which deservedly attracted a good deal of attention when it first appeared in *The New Yorker*—it is obvious that *Fame and Folly* contains essays that are fundamentally different from those in her earlier collections. These essays grow out of her own interests rather than assignments, and their lengths have been determined by her rather than by editorial constraints. The effect has been liberating, so that in *Fame and Folly* her particular passions and persistent concerns are placed in bold relief.

Cynthia Ozick is a self-consciously Jewish American writer. She is also a connoisseur of failure and disappointment, whose every essay is an exercise in disguised or undisguised autobiography. The ones that stand out in *Fame and Folly* all seem inspired by a peculiar, occasionally discomfiting, combination of envy and sympathy. The careers of other writers—their ascents and declines, fame and infamy, wisdom and folly, success and neglect—obviously fascinate her. In part, it seems, because she cannot help but comparing them to her own.

Her memoir "Alfred Chester's Wig" and her essay on Eliot are the most obvious examples of this autobiographical slant. In the memoir, she spends nearly as many pages as she devotes to her essay on the most influential poet of the first half of the twentieth century dissecting her rivalry with a minor American writer who is now almost totally forgotten. She and Chester started out together at New York University in 1946 as precocious and ambitious readers and writers. In the 1950's and 1960's— while Ozick was struggling with a three-hundred-thousand-word first novel that she ultimately abandoned—Chester quickly gained publication, reputation, literary friendships, and a small portion of cultural power. His work appeared in *Commentary*, *Partisan Review*, and *Paris Review*; he was an editor of the avant-garde little magazine *Botteghe Oscure*; he was included in one of *Esquire* magazine's annual reports on the "Red Hot Center" of American writing; he traveled abroad, living for several years first in Paris and then in Morocco. By the early 1970's—as Ozick was just beginning to gain recognition—he self-destructed, dying at forty-two of drink, drugs, and dissipation.

Why, she asks, did he fall apart? She does not seem to ask because she is searching for an answer but because she is already sure she knows it. Based on the several years that they spent together in their youths, Ozick is convinced that it was because of the insecurities and crises of identity created by the childhood illness that left him bald and led him to wear terribly obvious, sadly comic, wigs as a young man; because he was rejected by women he loved and turned to homosexuality in response; because he turned from the friends (like her) who might have supported and sustained him to friends who helped him to destroy himself. Her confidence that she understands Chester's psychology and sexuality better than he did is startling and more than a little presumptuous—especially since she demonstrates so little knowledge of or empathy for homosexuality.

Finally, this memoir is as much about Ozick as Chester, an effort to disentangle and differentiate her fate and career from his. In her mind, they were rivals. "He was better than I was!" she thinks at one point, but "I was stronger." She portrays herself as the tortoise to his hare. He speeds ahead into bohemia, only to lose control of his literary style and his life; she plods along among the middle class, quietly laboring to perfect her craft at the little Sears Roebuck desk that she has used since high school, eventually establishing her reputation and surviving into her sixties.

Yet she also sees that they shared a common fate. In literary history, Ozick observes early in her memoir, there is no middle class. "The heights belong, at most, to four or five writers, a princely crew; the remainder are invisible, or else have the partial, now-and-then visibility that attaches to minor status. Every young writer imagines only the heights; no one aspires to be minor or invisible, and when, finally, the recognition of where one stands arrives, as it must, in maturity, one either accepts the limitations of fate or talent, or surrenders to sour cynicism." Like Chester, most of the writers "who on occasion reminisce about Chester have by now lived long enough to confirm their own minor status," she writes at the end. Clearly, she includes herself among their number.

For most of this century, T. S. Eliot has been at the head of the "princely crew." Perhaps the most fascinating aspect of Ozick's treatment of Eliot, however, is that she reads him in much the same way she reads Chester, linking his writing and his biography in an essay which focuses on his meteoric rise to prominence and the decline of his literary and personal fortunes. Like her essays on Henry James, her examination of Eliot is most appealing in its ability to make us see the young man just starting out: Henry James before he became "Henry James," the Master; Tom Eliot before he became "T. S. Eliot," poetry incarnate.

She again begins with the decline, again goes back to recall and try to understand his rise, and again connects his fall, like Chester's, to flaws in his character. Along the way, she draws on and brilliantly synthesizes the findings of the several volumes that have helped readers to penetrate the facade of impersonality that Eliot so assiduously cultivated in his prime—Lyndall Gordon's *Eliot's Early Years* (1977) and *Eliot's New Life* (1988), Peter Ackroyd's *T. S. Eliot: A Life* (1984), and Valerie Eliot's edition of *The Letters of T. S. Eliot, Vol. I: 1898-1922* (1988).

Exaggerating more than a little, Ozick claims that Eliot's fall is evident in the fact that only "The Love Song of J. Alfred Prufrock" continues to be taught in the college and university English departments he and the New Criticism once dominated. In part, she suggests, this is because of anti-Semitic passages in his poetry and prose that readers are no longer willing to ignore or excuse; in part, it is because the poetic principles that he espoused so vehemently—"the objective correlative," "the impersonality of poetry"—have been rejected by his poetic successors and exposed as absurdly irrelevant to his own work by the recent biographies.

"The prodigy of Eliot's rocketlike climb from termite to superman" by the age of thirty intrigues her even more than Chester's smaller success did. "What was it," she asks, "that singled Eliot out to put him in the lead so astoundingly early? That he ferociously willed it means nothing. Nearly all beginning writers have a will for extreme fame; will, no matter how resilient, is usually no more efficacious in the marketplace than daydream." To Ozick, the size of his oeuvre—fifty-four poems— would seem to doom him to minor status. Yet he became "a god"—creator not only of poetic works but of a method for reading them. What singled him out, she proposes, was what singled out the young James: early "sovereignty," a voice that conveyed an erudition that awed and cowed.

In *Art and Ardor*, Ozick wrote of how Leonard Woolf's long-suffering and selfless nursing made Virginia Woolf's art possible. In *Fame and Folly*, Eliot becomes Leonard's mirror image: his first wife Vivien's mental illness was the "seizure that animated the poetry," his failure to save or stand by her was the moral nightmare that both prompted and haunted his greatest work and led to the weaknesses she finds in his later poems and plays.

The same focus on the rise and fall of literary reputations is evident in the other major essays in the collection. Trollope captures her attention and earns her sympathy and defense because he, too, is an underrated minor writer whose works have fallen out of fashion. The "nervous breakdown" that Henry James suffered following the public humiliation accompanying the performance of his play *Guy Domville* captures her, becoming an explanation for the mystery at the center of his later, "modern" style. Isaac Babel's personal and literary impersonations capture her, because they challenge her to understand how continuing to write in the language he loved could lead a Jewish writer to complicity in pogroms conducted by the same anti-Semitic state that would eventually execute him. Mark Twain, in the *fin de siècle* Europe of Karl Lueger's Vienna and France's Dreyfus Affair, intrigues her because of the way that his "The Man Who Corrupted Hadleyburg" could offer a clear-eyed commentary on that anti-Semitic culture while his essay "Concerning the Jews"—written at the same time—could demonstrate how he himself was blinded by stereotypes about the Jews. Salman Rushdie gains her sympathy because the *fatwa* transforms him from a fashionable, highly successful, rigidly Third World figure who refused to sign a protest against Middle Eastern terrorism at a PEN conference in New York in 1986 into "a little Israel"—a writer hunted, isolated, yet unbowed, who deserves her support and that of anyone who cares about freedom of expression.

Two other pieces in this collection deserve special mention. "The Break" is a moving fictionalized confession in which Ozick's obsession with literary reputations and with the status of her own achievement in relation to that of other writers is painfully raw and undisguised. In it, a "terrifying operation" divides the "I" into two imaginary alter egos: a still ambitious younger self who imagines that her career lies ahead, full of possibility, and a depressed and defeated older self who acknowledges that "She is little known or known not at all, relegated to marginality, absent from the authoritative anthologies. . . . She knows that she does not matter. . . . she has been in rooms with the famous, and felt the humiliation of her lessness, her invisibility, her lack of writerly weight or topical cachet. . . . she has not written enough. She is certainly not read."

"Saul Bellow's Broadway" is a reading of *Seize the Day* which makes the extraordinarily wrongheaded assertion that "*The Adventures of Augie March* struck out on a course so independent from the tide of American fiction that no literary lessons could flow from it: it left no wake, and cut a channel so entirely idiosyncratic as to be uncopyable." An entire generation of Jewish American novelists who began writing in the 1950's and early 1960's, inspired by Bellow's yoking of the street and the library, attest to the absurdity of this claim. (For a more accurate assessment of the influence of Bellow's style, see Philip Roth's essay "Imagining Jews.")

"What we think we are surely going to do, we don't do," Ozick wrote in her foreword to *Art and Ardor*; "and what we never intended to do, we may one day notice that we have done, and done, and done." To readers, what truly matters is that what Cynthia Ozick has done—both in fiction and in the essay—bears the unmistakable stamp of her particular and provocative intelligence. Like her earlier collections of essays, *Fame and Folly* is an important part of her continuing claim to our attention.

Bernard F. Rodgers, Jr.

Sources for Further Study

Boston Globe. May 8, 1996, p. 50.
Chicago Tribune. September 1, 1996, XIV, p. 3.

Kirkus Reviews. LXIV, March 1, 1996, p. 357.
Library Journal. CXXI, June 15, 1996, p. 66.
Los Angeles Times. May 3, 1996, p. E10.
The Nation. CCLXII, February 26, 1996, p. 34.
The New York Times. May 7, 1996, p. 17.
The New York Times Book Review. CI, June 9, 1996, p. 32.
The New Yorker. LXXII, May 13, 1996, p. 88.
Publishers Weekly. CCXLIII, April 1, 1996, p. 65.
San Francisco Chronicle. April 28, 1996, p. REV3.
The Wall Street Journal. May 22, 1996, p. A20.

FATHER AND SON

Author: Larry Brown (1951-   )
Publisher: Algonquin Books of Chapel Hill (Chapel Hill, North Carolina). 347 pp. $23.00
Type of work: Novel
Time: 1968
Locale: Rural Mississippi

A Mississippi man returns to his rural hometown after serving a prison sentence for killing a child in a drunk driving accident, and methodically takes revenge on people of the town he believes have wronged him

> *Principal characters:*
> GLEN DAVIS, a convict just released from the state penitentiary
> RANDOLPH "PUPPY" DAVIS, his younger brother
> VIRGIL DAVIS, their father
> MARY BLANCHARD, Virgil's lover
> BOBBY BLANCHARD, the sheriff, Mary's son
> JEWEL, the mother of Glen's young son

Larry Brown's stark and vivid rendering of the inner lives of poor, hard-living white Southerners has commanded the attention of serious readers since his first disturbing stories came onto the literary scene in small magazines and in the story collections *Facing the Music* and *Big Bad Love*. He has followed it with the novels *Dirty Work* and *Joe*, and the short haunting memoir *On Fire*, about the seventeen years he spent as a fireman and emergency rescue technician in the hometown he shares with William Faulkner: Oxford, Mississippi, which is sometimes called, only partly in jest, "the Vatican of Southern writing."

Though Brown's work follows the basic settings, speech, and themes of traditional Southern fiction—the tangled loyalties of family and community, the pressures of history, soul-grinding poverty and economic struggle, and Southerners' visceral bond with the land—his work is remarkable for what it does not contain. Both stereotype and sentimentality are virtually absent from Brown's writing, as is, strangely, the kind of lyrical exalted language that has become synonymous with Southern authors from Faulkner on down.

Larry Brown achieves his sometimes stunning dramatic effects not by soaring turns of phrase but by the gradual accretion of an undeniable reality, a vision that is severe and tender in equal measure, as in this description of a sheriff going to a remote place where a child's body has been found:

> They got into the cruiser and drove out into the country to meet the coroner and his helpers at a lonely and rain-swept crossroads where the hawks had folded their wings to sit in the fence posts and regard the sky with their cold bright eyes. Shoals of water were riffling off the fields and the day was gray and dark, the creeks rising, foaming, the beavers swimming strongly with sticks in their mouths as the men crossed the little bridges in their cars and cast a glance down into the muddy currents. In a small procession they drove to that place where he had already been and unloaded their shovels, and they went down through the woods.

Father and Son, set in 1968, takes Brown's familiar fictional territory to a new level of scope and complexity, with the slow-motion crime spree of a "bad seed" named Glen Davis bringing into focus the interconnected loves, hates, and betrayals of three generations of families in a small Mississippi town whose name is never given.

"Puppy" Davis, ever-hopeful peacemaker between the estranged Glen and their father Virgil, picks up Glen at the local bus station after his release from prison and gives him the requisite pep talk about making a fresh start and putting his life back together.

By nightfall on the first of the five days the novel covers, Glen has already openly taunted the sheriff who arrested him, vandalized and stolen from a bar owner he feels has mistreated him, and purchased a case of beer with the intent to drink it while considering his next move.

The stark final sentence of that chapter sets the stage for what is about to happen: "While he was sitting there thinking everything over, he figured he might as well finish it, now that it was started."

"It" is the tragedy that Glen seems to have been advancing toward from an early age. As the narrative unfolds, readers learn that his father—likewise a heavy drinker who had violent brawls with the young Glen—was a prisoner of war in Bataan during World War II and still suffers physically and mentally from that long-ago torture, as well as from more recent wounds. Glen, while not yet a teenager, accidentally killed a third brother while playing with a shotgun he thought was unloaded. Virgil's wife Emma has died while Glen was in prison.

Before Glen reluctantly pays his father a visit, at Puppy's urging, he stops by the town diner to see Jewel, who works there. He and Jewel had a son before he left, and she promised to wait for him. Even though Glen spends his first night home with her, he brushes off her attempt to make him acquainted with David and lets her know he is after sex, not marriage. "No talk of marriage again," Glen muses. "He'd explain to her that it wasn't good, that it promised things it couldn't deliver, that it led to people hating each other and doing bad things to each other and then there were children and things could happen to them so that what you wound up having was not what you'd hoped for to start, a long life, happiness, good times, no. You could rock along for a while and think everything was just fine and then turn around and you were in the g———n penitentiary."

Glen moves in temporarily with his father, and shortly begins the crime spree that everyone who knows him is already half expecting. From his actions, and his gritty and convincing inner dialogue, readers learn that Glen is violent, calculating, and cosmically angry: a "natural born killer." Yet one of the triumphs of Brown's writing is that Glen's bizarre and paranoid reasoning, and his grudges both real and imagined, make sense to readers on their own terms; they follow him with a mixture of revulsion and hope, that somehow he will be able to break the chain of tragedy that seems to be in his very genes:

He lay there alone in the black bed in the blackness of the house with the dark walls around him. . . .
He'd stripped the bloody sheets off and they lay piled in a pale white bundle in one corner. There
was just the rough ticking of the mattress against his skin, a loose button that dug into his ribs if he
turned the wrong way. He'd had neither drink nor the comfort of another's hand. Just the endless
roaming over the roads and the ceaseless cigarettes and the music that he was already tired of hearing.
And how many nights had he lay like this already? In the saw and whine of a thousand sleeping
throats he'd imagined a world different, a better place than the one that had been his for so long, as
if stepping out of those iron gates would free more than his physical body and allow him to regain
some sort of balance, quell his anger, drive away the bad memories, make possible all the things he
wished could be. But he saw now that it wasn't going to be like that.

Although similar characters and situations have long been the potter's clay of
Brown's fictional world, *Father and Son* is a breakthrough for him, almost Shake-
spearean in its dramatic scope and the larger questions it raises. Like Pete Dexter's
Pulitzer Prize-winning novel *Paris Trout* (1988), it moves readers to look past the
conventional concept of law and order and consider the role of each individual in a
community that is openly threatened by such a criminal: Where does personal
responsibility end and collective responsibility begin? The answers are endlessly
refracted through the prism of the narrative's changing viewpoints.

Glen's chief nemesis is Sheriff Bobby Blanchard, a kind and patient man who in
many ways represents the community's conscience. Yet even that relationship, like so
many in *Father and Son*, has dark roots in the past. Readers learn that Bobby is Glen's
illegitimate half brother, a child Virgil had with Mary, a town schoolteacher, while
married to Glen's mother. Moreover, Bobby has long been in love with Jewel, so Glen's
hatred of both mother and son runs especially deep.

Glen's violence moves inexorably forward—some of it methodical, such as the
shotgun killing of a bar owner who once offered to buy Jewel a drink, and some on
impulse, as in the rape of a teenage girl who flirts with him at a lunch counter. The
alternating paths of Glen and Bobby, as the sheriff suspects Glen's handiwork and
slowly realizes what he feared is coming to pass among the patchwork of other crimes
in the county, form the backbone of the narrative. When Glen finally fixes on an act
of revenge that will wound both mother and son, readers see the foreshadowing and
recognize its inevitability from the beginning.

Although *Father and Son* is filled with violence, the descriptions of it are never
gratuitous or melodramatic. Even the threat of violence is a constant harrowing
presence in Glen's story, as when he passes his sleeping father's bed with a shotgun:

He cocked the hammer now and swung the barrel up to his father's head and held the black and
yawning muzzle of it an inch away. He tightened his fingers on the checkered pistol grip. The old
man slept on, father and son. Some sense of foreboding told him to pull back and undo all of this
before it was done. Yet he put his finger on the trigger, just touched it. He already knew what it
would look like.
Virgil moved in his sleep, made a small sound almost like a cough. The puppy whined outside. The
house was quiet but for that.
He raised the barrel and caught the hammer with his thumb and eased back on the trigger, letting it
down. He went out the door, lighting a cigarette, hurrying.

Part of *Father and Son*'s richness lies in the subtle parallels and connections woven almost invisibly through the story. Virgil's time in the POW camp on Bataan was three years, the same as Glen's in the state penitentiary. Just at the periphery of many conversations is what one father calls "that mess over there," referring to the escalating war in Vietnam.

Glen's warm memories of fishing trips when he was younger are echoed by the eagerness of Jewel and Glen's son to go fishing with his grandfather. During a brief respite from his trail of violence, Glen goes fishing with an old friend who is taken aback when Glen decides to release a prize fish he has caught because he cannot stand to see something so beautiful die: "You're a good man, Glen," Roy said to him. "No I ain't," he said to the water. Shortly afterward, Glen confronts Jewel at the diner about the amount of time Bobby has been spending at her house. "He'll be sorry," Glen tells her. "And you will, too." Jewel threatens to call the police and Glen leaves, setting the final showdown in action.

By the time the novel is resolved, it is clear that the outcome is less the result of chance than of the legacy of all that has gone before—in the phrase of reviewer Bernadine Connelly, writing in *Newsday*, "Despite miles of thick, uncharted forests, and crystal-blue lakes, neither anonymity nor starting fresh is an option."

Brown's harsh, clear-eyed, and ultimately loving account of the intersection of these lives in a Southern town is a memorable achievement, one that promises much and sets an impressive standard for his books that are yet to come.

Carroll Dale Short

Sources for Further Study

Atlanta Journal Constitution. September 29, 1996, p. M3.
Booklist. XCII, July, 1996, p. 1779.
Boston Globe. October 20, 1996, p. M16.
Chicago Tribune. October 9, 1996, V, p. 3.
Library Journal. CXXI, August, 1996, p. 110.
New York. XXIX, October 21, 1996, p. 54.
The New York Times Book Review. CI, September 22, 1996, p. 11.
Publishers Weekly. CCXLIII, June 24, 1996, p. 44.
USA Today. November 21, 1996, p. D7.
The Washington Post. September 26, 1996, p. C2.

THE FIGURED WHEEL
New and Collected Poems, 1966-1996

Author: Robert Pinsky (1940-   )
Publisher: Farrar Straus Giroux (New York). 300 pp. $30.00
Type of work: Poetry

A collection of lyrics and long argumentative poems that use memory to explore the urban and everyday world

Robert Pinsky's *The Figured Wheel* is an impressive collection of poems which includes a number of new poems, three of his earlier volumes, and a few translations. The organization of the book is curious; it begins with a group of Pinsky's recent poems and moves from there to his recent books of poems and ends with his earliest poems. So it is, perhaps, best to read the book backward and start with Pinsky's earliest book and trace his development from there to his latest poems. Pinsky is an unusual contemporary poet in his use of discursive and narrative elements in his poems. There are a number of long poems in the collection that, in some ways, do not differ significantly from an argumentative essay. He uses imagery extensively—and strikingly—but does not make the image the poem but subordinates it to the narrative or argument. In addition, he uses rhyme and a loose iambic meter in some of the poems, especially in the earlier ones. What is, perhaps, more important is his use of the poetic line, especially in the way he uses run-on lines, even run-on stanzas and run-on sections of poems.

Sadness and Happiness (1975) is Pinsky's first book of poems; it is divided into five distinct sections. The first section is called "The Time of Year, The Time of Day," and the poems in it are various, although there is an emphasis on the people and places of Pinsky's early life in Long Branch, New Jersey. The first poem, for example, is "Poem About People." The speaker first describes types of people: "Women in grocery stores . . . " and "Balding young men in work shoes." He feels for these types a "diffuse tenderness"; however, that vague feeling is contrasted to the demands made by a unique "Soul." He then uses popular art—music and film—to affirm the theme. What is being asserted is the self against the type, the individual against the group. "*Hate my whole kind*, but me/ Love me for myself." The poem ends with an image to define the permanent "wide spaces between us." The movement of the poem from a sentimental "tenderness" to the fact of separation is a strategic opening for the book and the collection as a whole. It also touches on the theme of "desire" that is at the core of Pinsky's poetry.

The title poem of the section, "The Time of Year, the Time of Day," continues the problem of our connections to others. In this poem, the bond between man and woman is to "alleviate,/ The weather. the time of year, the time of day." That need is defined by an incident in adolescence when the boy returning home, "cold" even in July, is overwhelmed by the burden of using the time. This desire is, for Pinsky, what sends humans to "bodies," to "kitchens," or in a very different reference that sends the settlers of the plains to "couple in a fury/ To fill the width of their tillable fields." Desire is disturbing and, at times, destructive, but it is the source of all created things.

The next section, "Sadness and Happiness," is made up of one long poem with linking parts. Pinsky has each part run on into the next since the last lines have no end punctuation. The effect is of a meditation as the poet-speaker sorts out the place of sadness and happiness in human lives. First of all, sadness and happiness are only found in memory and in that mode they cannot be distinguished. They do, however, "organize" people's lives into the patterns they create. The speaker of the poem varies his tone; at times he is serious while at other times he mocks himself and his false idealism. For example, in part 6, he comments on the expectations others had for him to become a "Jewish-American Shakespeare." He also mocks his chivalric and idealistic attitudes in love. At the end of the poem, he sees that sadness and happiness are only an attempt to escape from the finality of art or nature; these emotional states that seem to be so real are a process or illusory "games." The poem as a whole is interesting in its taking on different points of view as it wends its way through the argument. In Pinsky's critical book on poetry, *The Situation of Poetry*, he spoke of the need for poetry to "help us." Placing sadness and happiness in a proper context is an example of how poetry can accomplish that.

The next two sections are devoted to memories of people and of "The Street of Furthest Memory." Pinsky is a poet of memory, and his evocation of his father in his shop and the world of childhood in suburban New Jersey is very powerful. The most interesting section, however, is the last one called "Essay on Psychiatrists." It is a long poem with linked parts and is very discursive. Indeed, it is saved from prose only by a sharp use of imagery and the tone of the poet. It is also a poem that attempts to sort out the role and place of the psychiatrist in modern life and times. One way to place the psychiatrist in a context and so understand his role better is Pinsky's use of Euripides' *Bacchae*. He compares a psychiatrist to both Pentheus and Dionysius, although the cunning and withholding God may be a more appropriate model for the psychiatrist. Pinsky also compares the psychiatrist to a figure in the comics—Rex Morgan. Rex is like Pentheus, completely unflappable and untouched by what goes on around him. Pinsky often uses images and allusions to popular arts such as jazz, popular songs, and the comics. He has a wide range of reference and a humor that makes the poems interesting and amusing. In the last part of the poem, he speaks of having failed to distinguish psychiatrists from "the rest of us." That failure becomes the final assertion of the poem: "Grace evoke the way we are all psychiatrists,/ All fumbling at so many millions of miles." The conclusion of the "essay"—"we are all psychiatrists"—is not interesting in itself; it is the journey and the various ways in which the topic is dealt with that is the point of the poem. This is one of the ways in which it is a poem rather than merely being a prose essay.

The next book of poems is *An Explanation of America* (1980). The title poem has long discursive sections, and its method is to sort out the essential nature of the country. The first part is addressed to Pinsky's daughter and is the weakest and least compelling part of the poem. The poem defines America by its inclusiveness. In "IV Contraries and Explanations," for example, he compares America to the three parts of the Russian troika speeding on its way. More significantly, he sees the nation in terms of its historical changes: "Boston before it was Irish or Italian." One of the most interesting sections is Pinsky's use of a poem by Horace and a discussion of Horace's life; Horace's father was a slave but became a freedman and sacrificed everything for his son's education. This desire for the child's success is connected to Pinsky's wishes for his daughter. He also alludes to the amusing definitions of a nation offered by Leopold Bloom in James Joyce's *Ulysses*: "The same people living/ In the same place" "Or different people living in different places." This use of Joyce points out one of the strengths of the poem, the light and humorous approach to a serious subject.

One of the most interesting sections is in part 2, where Pinsky sees America in terms of the emptiness of the prairie. This leads to an assertion that what he wants for his daughter is a "mystic home," one that is imagined rather than merely bounded by reality. This is continued in part 3, where he uses a memory of his daughter performing in William Shakespeare's *The Winter's Tale*. At the end of the play, that imagined world is seen as a "dream," an "elsewhere" that like America is "So large and strangely broken and unforeseen." The poem as a whole is flawed, and some of the sections are less moving, but Pinsky's final vision of an America that is imperfect but contains imaginative possibilities is very effective.

Pinsky's next book of poems is *A History of My Heart* (1984); it includes two long poems and a number of fine lyrics. The long title poem, "History of My Heart," also relies on memory as it shows the emotional development of the speaker. The central incident is the appearance of Fats Waller at a downtown department store witnessed by his mother before he was born. He compares that joyful moment to an adolescent one when dancing with a girl and suddenly feeling that "she likes me." The poem does have an interesting movement from childhood to adolescence to adulthood. There is another fine scene of the speaker of the poem roasting meat in the woods with his friends and escaping the control of the parents. The ending of the poem is an evocation of "desire" in a very general manner that comes from "The pure source" but is "poured out and away." There is, however, the "giving of desire" which is sufficient, "nothing more wanted." In the book, desire is often frustrated or is selfish; here, however, it is the "giving" that marks the emotional development in the poem.

The title poem of the collection, "The Figured Wheel," shows another dimension of Pinsky's poetics, his use of myth. The Figured Wheel rolls over all stories and tales through time. It is universal but also personal as it rolls "over the haunts of Robert Pinsky's mother and father/ And his wife and children and his own sweet self." It includes all myths, all gods, and all religions as it rolls through time. Pinsky is a poet of inclusion and transcendence, and this poem brings out those aspects of his poetry most fully.

The Want Bone (1990) does not have any long discursive poems but it does continue the theme of "desire" and has some of his most powerful lyrics. "The Shirt" is a social poem that traces the origins and history of a shirt he is wearing. The lines of the poem are short and nouns dominate the even shorter sentences: "The back, the yoke, the yardage. Lapped seams,/ The nearly invisible stitches along the collar." After defining the elements and terms of the shirt, Pinsky connects it to the historical fire at the Triangle Shirtwaist Factory early in this century. Moreover, he connects the shirt to its "cost" to those who made it in sweat shop conditions and finally brings together the inspector and himself both seeing the same object. "The shape/ The labor, the color, the shade. The shirt." Pinsky's poems do take place in a social world, and "The Shirt" is one of his most effective and powerful poems.

"The Want Bone," the title poem of the book, is another poem on "desire." It begins with images of the sea which are very common in Pinsky's poems and then shifts to the bleached out jaws of a shark. They form the "shape of birth and craving." This O shape sings a song that begins in love but then defines itself more clearly: "But O I love you it sings, my little my country/ My food my parent my child I want you my own/ My flower my fin my life my lightness my O." Love is superseded by the demand for possession as it asserts only its own self; it is the dark side of desire.

New Poems has a number of important poems about the city, and Pinsky is a very effective urban poet. For example, "The City Dark" portrays the "broken city dark," but that darkness is alleviated by images of "glimmering" light and the process of "generation." The light alleviates and clarifies that darkness in the "glittering slabs" under the dark pavement of the city. There is a similar if less powerful use of "illumination" in "Avenues" where Pinsky celebrates the overlooked mass of people: "These theys I write."

The Figured Wheel along with his recent translation of Dante's *Inferno* clearly demonstrates the importance of Robert Pinsky as a contemporary poet. The poems in this collection are complex and challenging but never lose their moorings in the lives and places of ordinary people. In *The Situation of Poetry*, Pinsky made a compelling case against the "nominalism," or surrealism, of many contemporary poems. In this collection, he shows that statement, the discursive and evocations of feeling still have an important place in contemporary poetry.

James Sullivan

Sources for Further Study

Booklist. XCII, April 1, 1996, p. 1339.
Chicago Review. XLII, Spring, 1996, p. p. 122.
Library Journal. CXXI, April 1, 1996, p. 88.
The Nation. CCLXII, April 29, 1996, p. 25.
The New York Times Book Review. CI, August 18, 1996, p. 9.
Publishers Weekly. CCXLIII, March 18, 1996, p. 65.
The Yale Review. LXXXIV, July, 1996, p. 173.

THE FLAMING CORSAGE

Author: William Kennedy (1928-   )
Publisher: Viking (New York). 209 pp. $23.95
Type of work: Novel
Time: 1884-1912
Locale: Albany, New York

The sixth novel in William Kennedy's "Albany Cycle" probes a tortured marriage and explores tensions arising from class and ethnicity in the city Kennedy has made his literary property

Principal characters:
> EDWARD DAUGHERTY, playwright
> KATRINA TAYLOR DAUGHERTY, his wife
> EMMETT DAUGHERTY, his father
> JACOB TAYLOR, Katrina's father
> GERALDINE TAYLOR, Katrina's mother
> THOMAS MAGINN, journalist
> MELISSA SPENCER, actress and Edward's mistress
> GILES FITZROY, physician
> FELICITY, Giles's wife
> CULLY WATSON, a tough

With the publication of *The Flaming Corsage*, William Kennedy extends one of the important American literary projects of the later twentieth century. *The Albany Cycle*, a collective title dreamed up as a marketing device by an editor at Viking, Kennedy's publisher, originally applied to three novels: *Legs* (1975), *Billy Phelan's Greatest Game* (1978), and *Ironweed* (1983). Following the success of *Ironweed*, Viking hoped to awaken interest in the two neglected earlier novels by suggesting their function as parts of a larger design; the three novels were issued in a single binding in the later 1980's, and the *Cycle* thus became a reality.

It is now clear that the three novels were in turn part of a still larger whole. Three further novels have appeared since *Ironweed*: *Quinn's Book* (1988), *Very Old Bones* (1992), and *The Flaming Corsage*. *The Albany Cycle* has been accepted as the collective title of all six, and the end is not in sight. There is no reason to suppose that Kennedy as a literary artist will ever leave Albany. He has said in the past that he realizes he is the sort of writer for whom the sense of place is crucial and that there is no place he will ever know any better than he knows his native Albany. Staying thus at home permits him to explore how the inner lives of human beings are shaped by the experience of living in a particular time and a particular place. Since this kind of experience shapes everyone, Kennedy's examination of particulars manifesting themselves through highly individual, often idiosyncratic, characters, can, when successfully carried through, point toward what is most universal in us.

The Flaming Corsage begins with a melodramatic episode: a shooting in a Manhattan hotel suite. On a night in 1908, a man identified as "the husband" kills his wife and wounds a second man in the room; a second woman manages to escape unharmed.

The husband then turns the gun on himself. Who these people are and what has brought them to this fatal confrontation is a mystery that the narrative will gradually resolve.

While the scene, if a touch overblown, is undeniably an attention getter, and while the mystery it generates promotes a curiosity that will help to focus the reader's response for much of the novel, the episode itself proves to be something like what the film director Alfred Hitchcock called a "maguffin": a device for focusing the audience's (in this case, the reader's) attention while the story's real center of interest lies elsewhere.

"Elsewhere," on this occasion, means the relationship of Edward Daugherty and Katrina Taylor, the woman Edward marries in 1886. The marriage is an unlikely one in the Albany of the period, since Edward is an Irish Catholic, of working-class origins, while Katrina is of English ancestry, a member in good standing of Albany's Episcopalian ruling class. Both families are predictably aghast at the thought of marriage between these two, Katrina's parents because they consider the Irish infinitely beneath them (Edward's mother had worked as a servant at the home of friends of the Taylors), and Edward's father because he knows how the Taylors feel and because of the role Jacob Taylor played in labor struggles in the past.

It seems, though, that neither Edward nor Katrina can be defined by such affiliations. Edward is an artist, a writer, and artists, according to one view at least, transcend the ordinary categories of class and ethnicity. As for Katrina, her very involvement with Edward testifies to her liberation from the narrow attitudes of her parents' generation. Her actions can seem so spontaneous that it is hard to conceive of them as links in any kind of sociocultural causal chain, as when she astonishes Edward by giving herself to him sexually one Sunday afternoon in the Angel of the Holy Sepulchre cemetery. Her response to a comment by Edward's father seems to define a spiritual independence that approaches the sublime: "I do what I think I should do, so I can become what I think I must be."

Yet it is not so easy to deny the power of the past and the attachments, personal, cultural, ideological, that it entails. By the night of October 16, 1908, the marriage of Edward and Katrina is in trouble. The Taylors' acceptance of their son-in-law has never been more than formal and superficial, and Katrina for her part has surprised in herself a need to reembrace her father and the comforts among which she was raised in the Taylor family home on Elk Street. Still, Edward, now enjoying success as a writer, continues his campaign to overcome these obstacles to a happy union. On this night Katrina's parents, her sister Adelaide, and Adelaide's husband Archie Van Slyke are the dinner guests of Edward and Katrina at the Delavan House, Albany's most elegant hotel. Moreover, Edward bears gifts: for Katrina's mother, a stunning sealskin coat; for her father, ownership of a horse he has coveted.

The promise of the evening comes to nothing as a disastrous fire breaks out. The hotel is destroyed. Fourteen people are killed. The Daughertys and their party manage to make their way out of the hotel, but not unscathed. Katrina's corsage has been set aflame by a flaming stick flying through the air, leaving her breast scarred. On the seventh day after the fire, Adelaide dies of internal injuries sustained in a desperate jump from one of the hotel's upper floors. Katrina's father suffers a fatal heart attack soon after.

The marriage of Edward and Katrina has also sustained fatal injuries. Accepting her mother's evaluation, Katrina blames Edward for the death of her father and sister; it was Edward, after all, who brought them all to the hotel that night. Yet Katrina will also blame herself, both for marrying Edward in the first place and for the need for reconciliation with her family that had motivated Edward's peacemaking gesture. This complex of blame makes authentic reconciliation with her husband impossible.

Much of this material is covered in approximately one-third of the novel's length. The rest of the novel traces the gradual and irreversible disintegration of the relationship of Edward and Katrina, while leading readers by indirection to a resolution of the mystery established by the opening episode of the novel. Consistently rejected by his wife, Edward takes as his mistress the beautiful young actress Melissa Spencer. (Readers of *Very Old Bones* will remember her sexual encounter with Edward's son Martin in that novel.) A complicated set of interrelationships develops, involving Edward and Katrina, Melissa, and the Fitzroys, Giles, a former suitor of Katrina, and his wife Felicity. Always somewhere in the picture is Thomas Maginn, a cynical journalist and Edward's friend since they were both newspapermen together. Readers first meet Maginn when he is leading Edward on a search for whores in the tent city on the outskirts of the state fair of 1885.

The shooting with which the novel began arises out of these relationships. While there remain some ambiguities regarding exactly who was doing what and to whom, the broad outline of a solution to the mystery gradually emerges. It involves adulteries, including Edward's, as well as other forms of sexual experimentation. Yet it involves as well the humiliation of Maginn as the result of a practical joke played on him by Giles Fitzroy with the reluctant participation of Edward. Maginn's revenge is a still more brutal practical joke which in fact leads directly to the death of Fitzroy and his wife and the wounding of Edward. As Edward comes to understand it, he was Maginn's real target. Before the novel ends, there will be some kind of settling of accounts between these two. The story of Edward and Katrina will also reach its resolution in her death by fire, "her element," as Edward says.

Like all Kennedy's Albany novels, *The Flaming Corsage* offers a generous share of brilliantly realized episodes. The first sexual union of Edward and Katrina is one; the fire at the Delavan is another. A barroom brawl in which an ear is partly ingested and a darker outburst of violence on board an excursion boat are at the very least impressive set pieces. The scene in which Edward, presenting himself to the Taylors as a suitor for their daughter, generously forgives his social superiors for being English is a comic gem. The deathbed scene of Edward's father fuses humor and sentiment with a uniquely Irish Catholic blend of piety and irreverence.

As always with Kennedy, too, Albany itself is a felt presence in this novel. The complex crossing and recrossing of social and ethnic lines sharply defines the character of the place. The crossings, inevitably entailing blurrings, suggest a city very much in process, and the development of Albany's political culture is one of the novel's subjects. The beginnings of the McCall family's dominance of local politics, treated elsewhere in *The Albany Cycle*, are located here in the election of Grover Cleveland in 1884.

There are, then, many rewards here, both for those who know the other novels in *The Albany Cycle* and for those who will be entering the city of Kennedy's imagination for the first time. Yet both groups, and especially the latter will encounter problems as well. Three key developments in the novel depend on qualities in the characters that are never fully realized in the text. First, much flows from the practical joke Giles Fitzroy plays on Maginn, but there is little to establish that the impulse to play such a joke arises from Giles's character, rather than from the novelist's need to get his story moving. Maginn will finally reveal himself as a monster, yet the Maginn readers know from most of the novel seems less monstrous than unfocused, disorganized. The author's attempt to suggest that Maginn is to be understood as a creative cripple, driven by resentment at his own failure to equal Edward as an artist, seems a desperate attempt by the author to impose coherence on an underrealized character.

The greatest failure is Katrina. While she is often a vivid presence, she remains less a character than an idea for a character. Her change of heart after her marriage to Edward is announced, rather than dramatically rendered. It is possible to argue that she represents the power of class differences even over those who seem to have risen above them. Yet this remains an abstraction; there may be a general truth to it, but the unique truth of Katrina eludes the author and the reader. Since her reaction to the fire is at the heart of the narrative, Kennedy's failure to give her full imaginative life constitutes a major flaw in the novel.

It may be argued that Kennedy's intention is to let the reader know these characters as Edward does, neither more nor less. The technical objection to this possible defense is that Edward is not consistently a viewpoint character; readers are not necessarily limited to his perceptions. The deeper objection is that, whatever the author's technical choices, the reader simply must know these characters if the novel is to work. Still, any reader who has come this far with *The Albany Cycle* will certainly want to read this latest installment. Readers who have not yet discovered *The Albany Cycle* are advised to do so, but with this warning: William Kennedy can be habit forming.

W. P. Kenney

Sources for Further Study

America. CLXXV, September 14, 1996, p. 28.
Boston Globe. May 12, 1996, p. B38.
Chicago Tribune. June 16, 1996, XIV, p. 3.
Commonweal. CXXIII, September 13, 1996, p. 36.
Library Journal. CXXI, April 15, 1996, p. 52.
Los Angeles Times Book Review. July 14, 1996, p. 6.

The New York Times. May 2, 1996, p. C19.
The New York Times Book Review. CI, May 19, 1996, p. 7.
Publishers Weekly. CCXLIII, March 4, 1996, p. 52.
San Francisco Chronicle. May 5, 1996, p. REV1.
Time. CXLVII, May 13, 1996, p. 92.
The Washington Post. April 26, 1996, p. B2.

FLYING HOME AND OTHER STORIES

Author: Ralph Ellison (1914-1994)
Edited, with an introduction, by John F. Callahan
Publisher: Random House (New York). 173 pp. $23.00
Type of work: Short stories

A collection of thirteen short stories, six of them previously unpublished, by the author of Invisible Man

Shortly before he died in 1994, Ralph Ellison told his literary executor John F. Callahan that he wanted to publish a collection of his short stories and hinted that he had some unpublished stories that no one had ever seen. After Ellison's death, as Callahan began to review the thousands of pages of manuscript of Ellison's long-awaited unpublished second novel to see if they could be brought together into a final text, he discovered a box that was full of old magazines, clippings, and duplicate printouts from the novel. At the bottom of the box he found a brown imitation-leather portfolio with RALPH W. ELLISON embossed in gold letters on the front; inside, there was a manila folder labeled "Early Stories" bulging with manuscripts typed on crumbling paper, brown with age. While some of these manuscripts were fragments or unfinished stories, Callahan determined that six of them were worthy of publication.

The discovery of these six stories made publishing a book of Ellison's stories possible: Without them, there would not have been enough short fiction for a collection. In the fifty-seven years between his first story and his death, Ellison published a total of only twenty-two pieces of short fiction: eight pieces between 1937 and 1944, two of which were excerpts from an abandoned novel called *Slick*; and just fourteen stories in the fifty years after 1944, all but one of them excerpts from *Invisible Man* (1952) or his novel-in-progress.

In the four hundred pages of *Conversations with Ralph Ellison* (1995) and the eight hundred fifty pages of his *Collected Essays* (1996), Ellison's references to his short stories add up to less than a few pages. In describing his relationship with Richard Wright in several interviews he mentions "Hymie's Bull" as his first story, written at Wright's invitation to appear in a magazine he edited called *New Challenge* (the magazine folded while the story was in galleys and the story was not published until 1996); there is a sentence or two about "Flying Home" in a 1971 interview with David L. Carson, noting that its publication in the 1944 *Cross Section* anthology was his first appearance between hard covers and confirming that its title came from a jazz piece of the same name; and he refers briefly in his thirtieth anniversary introduction to *Invisible Man* to "In a Strange Country" (without naming it) as an outgrowth of the unfinished novel he abandoned to write his masterpiece.

In other words, Ralph Ellison decided early that the short story was not the form that interested him and abandoned it when he began writing *Invisible Man* in 1945. ("A Coupla Scalped Indians" was published in 1956, but it is not clear when he actually wrote it or whether he originally conceived of it as an excerpt from his novel-in-progress rather than a free-standing story.) Since he was an inveterate collector and reviser who appears to have kept copies of every draft of decades of effort on his second novel, it is hardly surprising that Ellison kept copies of his early unpublished stories at the bottom of an old box. In spite of his comment to Callahan, however, it is still hard to believe that Ellison would have really wanted these unpublished stories to be presented to his public. He chose not to publish them during the forty-two years separating *Invisible Man* and his death, although he had ample opportunity to do so. His self-critical attitude toward his own work was legendary: Long after it had become a contemporary classic, he wondered aloud whether *Invisible Man* would continue to be read; and in spite of the encouragement of many writers and critics he respected, he was never satisfied enough with his novel-in-progress to allow it to be published.

Yet readers owe John F. Callahan a debt of gratitude for preparing this volume, and for all the painstaking work he has undertaken as Ellison's literary executor. Like *The Collected Essays of Ralph Ellison*, *Flying Home and Other Stories* is part of Callahan's effort to make long unavailable Ellison materials easily accessible to all those who care about one of the most important figures in modern American literature. Just as readers may look forward with anticipation to publication of the version of Ellison's second novel that Callahan is preparing—knowing that the best it can be is a sensitive editor's approximation of what Ellison intended rather than the final text of the author himself, and that Ellison did not consider the book ready for publication—they may read *Flying Home* with interest and pleasure for what it is.

It is a collection of apprentice work which reveals the development of Ellison's talent, technique, and vision. In a 1974 interview with John Hersey that suggests how these early stories should be read, Ellison said that when he began writing his first stories he approached writing as he approached music: "I knew you didn't reach a capable performance in whatever craft without work. . . . I wrote a hell of a lot of stuff that I didn't submit to anybody." He went on to say that one of the particular problems that he was working on in these stories was "how to render AfroAmerican speech without resorting to misspellings—to give a *suggestion* of the idiom." "Some of the first things were embarrassing," he confessed. "You go from something that you've read, until you find out how *you* really feel about it."

The six previously unpublished stories in *Flying Home*—"A Party down at the Square," "Boy on a Train," "Hymie's Bull," "I Did Not Learn Their Names," "A Hard Time Keeping Up," and "The Black Ball"—show what he meant by these statements. So do the four published stories about two young Oklahoma boys, Buster and Riley—"Mister Toussan" (1941), "Afternoon" (1940), "That I Had Wings" (1943), and "A Coupla Scalped Indians." From the beginning, the territory seems Ellison's own. In all these stories, however, he is still trying to find his own voice. Their voice is obviously imitative, shaped by his reading of Mark Twain, William Faulkner, and especially Ernest Hemingway—three of the writers he frequently cited in his essays and interviews as early influences on his own fiction.

"A Party down at the Square," for example, is an exercise in the kind of innocent, child's eye, first-person point of view that is so effective in stories such as Hemingway's "My Old Man" or Sherwood Anderson's "I Want to Know Why." Told by a white boy, it vividly describes a lynching and conveys a sense of the moral and social chaos surrounding it. In his introduction to *Flying Home*, Callahan quotes an undated meditation by Ellison in which he writes of the importance of Hemingway's prose style to his own early work: "when I started trying to write fiction, I selected Hemingway for a model." The model is apparent in the simple words, sequence of "ands," and multiple meanings of the word "party" in the story's opening paragraph:

> "I don't know what started it. A bunch of men came by my Uncle Ed's place and said there was going to be a party down at the Square, and my uncle hollered for me to come on and I ran with them through the dark and rain and there we were at the Square.

It also appears in the plainspoken, deadpan reaction of the boy as he becomes morally complicit when he watches the "Bacote nigger" burn: "I had enough. I didn't want to see anymore. I wanted to run somewhere and puke, but I stayed. I stayed right there in front of the crowd and looked."

Hemingway's voice echoes throughout these early stories: in "Boy on a Train" ("The train gave a long, shrill, lonely whistle, and seemed to gain speed as it rushed downgrade between two hills covered with trees. The trees were covered with deep-red, brown, and yellow leaves"); in "I Did Not Learn Their Names" ("It was chilly up on top. We were riding to St. Louis on a manifest, clinging to the top of the boxcar. It was dark, and sparks from the engine flew back to where we were riding"); and in "A Hard Time Keeping Up" ("The streetlights and the neon signs made you think of Christmas as they sparkled on the whiteness. It was pleasant to think about the snow."

In the Buster and Riley stories—the stories in which Ellison is attempting to find a way to render African American speech—the Mark Twain of *Adventures of Huckleberry Finn* (1884) is just as clearly a model. "I hope they all gits rotten and the worms git in lem," the first story begins. Yet Ellison goes beyond Twain as "Mister Toussan" progresses, using the vernacular to introduce the boys' love of language and riffing into his narrative: "Ole Toussan was too hard on them white folks, thass why/ oh, he was a hard man!/ He was mean . . . / But a good mean. . . . / Toussan was clean . . . / . . . He was a good, clean mean. . . . / Aw, man, he was sooo-preme."

These early stories do not compare with the mature Ellison in complexity, originality, or style, but they certainly show that Ellison's powers of characterization and description developed quickly. In *Shadow and Act* (1964), Ellison observed that when he began to write he was forced "to stare down the deadly and hypnotic temptation to interpret the world and all its devices in terms of race." His overcoming this temptation seems to have come quickly, too. With the glaring exception of "Black Ball" (the only truly embarrassing piece in *Flying Home*), while all of these stories engage questions of race in one way or another, none of them reads like propaganda rather than literature.

The best stories in *Flying Home*, by far, are the final three—all published in 1944 as Ellison was about to begin *Invisible Man*, and all expressing his unique voice and vision. There is a value in gathering the apprentice work of a great writer, but the value is as much historical and biographical as literary. Restoring "King of the Bingo Game," "In a Strange Country," and "Flying Home" to print, however, makes this collection an important literary event. Unlike the earlier work, each stands on its own as a masterful short story that would deserve to be published even if Ralph Ellison were not its author. At the same time, reading them together is particularly fascinating because they reveal Ellison beginning to work out the style, themes, and images that would emerge fully formed in his novel.

In "King of the Bingo Game," which describes a desperate man trying to hit the jackpot at a motion picture theater's bingo game, Ellison has already gained control of the blend of realism and surrealism that characterizes the Battle Royal, Golden Day, and Liberty Paint factory episodes of *Invisible Man*. Both "In a Strange Country" and "Flying Home" are stories set during World War II about the conflicts felt by black servicemen fighting for a country that spurns them. In "In a Strange Country," Parker leaves his ship for shore leave in a small Welsh town feeling "the excited expectancy of entering a strange land . . . in the morning he would see the country with fresh eyes, like those with which the Pilgrims had seen the New World." As he walks into the town, he is glad to hear the other American voices of a group of soldiers bunched at a curb—until they spring out of the darkness and attack him, yelling, "It's a goddam nigger." A Welshman and his friends rescue him, take him to a pub, treat him with respect and kindness, and invite him along to a concert at a private club where the beauty of their folksongs touches him deeply. "*I believe in music!*" he thinks, "*in what's happening here tonight.*" When the Welshmen try to honor him by singing "The Star-Spangled Banner," Parker suddenly hears his own voice singing along: "it was like the voice of another, over whom he had no control," and, "for the first time in your whole life," he thinks, "the words are not ironic." In just nine pages, Ellison captures the complexities of Parker's emotional vulnerability, his defensiveness, his hope, his love of music, and his unrequited sense of his own Americanness.

In "Flying Home," a black aviator from a nearby base crashes his plane in a Macon County field. "Now the humiliation would come," he thinks. "When you must have them judge you, knowing that they never accept your mistakes as your own but hold it against your whole race." Ashamed to be associated with the old black fieldhand Jefferson who tries to help him, abused by the local white landowner Mister Graves who has him placed in a straightjacket, the aviator Todd also finds himself "in a strange country"—the South, America, a land where he can never feel at home. In its frank treatment of an educated black man's ambivalence toward the pull of racial solidarity, its symbolic use of Jefferson's folktale of flying in heaven, its allusions to the spirituals, its combination of realism and surreality, its control of its central imagery, and its use of several narrative voices, "Flying Home" is Ellison's most impressive story. A prelude to *Invisible Man* and culmination of all the experiments with the short story that preceded it.

Bernard F. Rodgers, Jr.

Sources for Further Study

Booklist. XCIII, October 15, 1996, p. 379.
The Chronicle of Higher Education. September 20, 1996, p. B3.
Library Journal. CXXI, December, 1996, p. 149.
The New York Times. April 18, 1996, p. C13.
The New York Times. December 10, 1996, p. C19.
The New York Times Book Review. CII, January 19, 1997, p. 13.
Publishers Weekly. CCXLIII, October 28, 1996, p. 57.
Time. CXLIX, January 13, 1997, p. 76.
USA Today. January 3, 1997, p. D4.

FOOTPRINTS

Author: Shelby Hearon (1931-   )
Publisher: Alfred A. Knopf (New York). 191 pp. $21.00
Type of work: Novel
Locale: Mead's Mill in upstate New York; Texas; Florida
Time: The mid-1990's

The death of their daughter in a car accident and their decision to donate her heart to save another life lead Nan and Douglas Mayhall to reevaluate their marriage and their own attitudes toward life

Principal characters:
> DOUGLAS MAYHALL, a science professor who specializes in the study of
> consciousness and the brain
> NAN MAYHALL, his wife of twenty-five years who gave up her science
> career plans to support his
> BETHANY MAYHALL, their daughter who was accidentally killed at age
> twenty-two
> BERT MAYHALL, their younger son, a deep-sea diver
> ALISON, Bert's girlfriend
> JESSE, Douglas' widowed stepmother who lives on the ranch in Texas
> where Douglas and his brother grew up
> CAROLE, Bethany's former English professor and Douglas' friend
> DORIS, a faculty wife and Nan's friend

Footprints is Shelby Hearon's fifteenth novel, following the highly acclaimed *Life Estates* (1994) and *Owning Jolene* (1990), which won an American Academy of Arts and Letters Literature Award. In *Footprints* Hearon continues her careful attention to detail, her rich command of language, and her clear insights into the human condition, especially the condition of women who struggle in their personal relationships. Nan Mayhall, the first-person narrator and protagonist of *Footprints*, is a forty-nine-year-old woman who apparently has a stable and contented life with her husband of twenty-five years. Yet the accidental death of their daughter, Bethany, plunges both parents into separate griefs, and Nan finds herself reevaluating her life, particularly her connection with her husband Douglas.

Bethany Mayhall, age twenty-two, had been killed on Thanksgiving Day in Texas, struck down by a drunken driver as she was driving to see Jesse, her grandfather's widow, at the Mayhall ranch. Her parents agreed to allow Bethany's organs to be donated to help save other lives. As the novel begins, Nan and Douglas Mayhall are attending a barbecue in Houston which has been arranged to honor donor and recipient families. Nan is uncomfortable, upset by the sentimentality of the occasion, but Douglas is anxious to see who has his daughter's heart and is delighted when he meets the recipient, the Reverend Calvin C. Clayton, and finds that he and Clayton are the same age, born the same week fifty years ago. Despite his career as a biology professor and researcher of the brain, he is emotionally caught up in the idea that somehow

Bethany lives through Clayton, and that by befriending the preacher he can still have his daughter. This notion seems foreign and unfathomable to Nan, and she resents her husband's enthusiasm, just as he cannot understand her ways of dealing with Bethany's death. As Nan muses, "Grief cut a canyon there was no crossing."

Nan and Douglas visit Jesse, "Daddy Mayhall's widow," on the ranch near Houston, and she repeats a favorite story about the first time she met Douglas, age seven, and his brother Walter, a year older, who later became a bomber pilot and was killed in action. Jesse thought they were exceptionally serious and intellectual children. Although she did not take the Mayhall name, she married and helped raise the boys and was always supportive of Nan and the grandchildren. Recognizing that Nan and Douglas may need a change after the loss of Bethany, Jesse gives them the property on Florida's Sanibel Island where the family had spent several vacations. Before they leave the ranch, Nan and Douglas make love as they had done on previous visits, and Nan notes that Douglas strokes her stomach and calls out "baby, baby, baby," the way he used to do when he was hoping she would become pregnant.

When they return to the cold winter of upstate New York, Nan has a moment of panic when she gets out of the car, wishing she could hail a taxi and leave for anywhere. It reminds her of the first time she came to Mead's Mill, where Douglas had a job at the university; Douglas had finished his Ph.D. at Northwestern University in Chicago where they met, but Nan, a year younger, had agreed not to complete her dissertation and instead to move with him to his new position. She had experienced a similar panic then, wanting to go on with her own studies of fossils and her own life rather than be merely Douglas' wife.

The Mayhalls host a dinner party in an attempt to act as they have in the past, and among the guests are Carole, Bethany's favorite professor, and Jay, from another university, who is working with Douglas on a research project. Nan finds herself attracted to Jay, particularly since as a new acquaintance she will not have to discuss the loss of her daughter with him. The next morning, she decides to leave for the vacation house on Sanibel Island off the west coast of Florida. Before she leaves, Douglas brings Carole to the house to tell Nan their plans to establish a memorial at the university in memory of Bethany. Nan sees that Carole and Douglas are becoming close.

On Sanibel, Nan observes the varied wildlife and swims in the ocean. She is especially pleased when her son Bert, a diver who is studying the physiology of breathing, comes from the east coast of Florida for a visit, bringing his girlfriend Alison. Nan has asked Douglas to telephone while Bert is there, but he does not do so; clearly he and Bert are estranged even more than he and his wife.

Nan's friend Doris phones to say she is having surgery, and Nan decides to go back to Mead's Mill for a visit. She has talked with Jesse, who had predicted Douglas would probably be wanting to father another child, and Douglas admits that he had tried with Carole. Nan is furious that he would use another baby as a replacement for Bethany. She sees Doris, and they discuss the affairs their husbands had had years ago and how they had each dealt with it, Nan by having a brief affair herself and Doris, at Nan's suggestion, feeding her husband rich and spicy foods that put on the pounds and gave him heartburn, discouraging his philandering.

Nan accompanies her husband to a conference where Jay has asked him to speak. She and Jay continue their brief flirtation, but Nan realizes that it would only complicate her life to have an affair with him. Instead, she uses her time to go back to a quarry where she had long ago found some trilobite fossils. She feels that if she can find even one it will be a sign that she can start over, that all is not lost. She does find a specimen, and she acknowledges to herself that she wants to go back to school and resume her paleontology studies. She also has a sudden remembrance of the trip the family had taken the previous summer, their last vacation together. When she had asked Douglas about it he had simply listed the highways they drove and the cities they visited. She did not seem to be able to recall anything. Yet now she remembers that Douglas had controlled everything, telling her she should not take up their time with her little hobby of fossil hunting, that Bethany should not do her running, and definitely Bert should not risk his neck with his dangerous diving.

Nan returns alone to Sanibel. Douglas flies down to see her, and just before he arrives Nan gets a call from Alison saying that Bert has had an accident while diving. As Nan and Douglas anxiously wait, Alison and Bert arrive—Bert is not injured. Nan is relieved, but Douglas shouts at Bert furiously. As he continues his emotional outburst, it becomes clear that he worried so much about his children because of his own experience as a surviving son. Daddy Mayhall destroyed every trace of Walter, except for one picture of him in his uniform, and refused ever to talk about him. Douglas had never been able to work through his feelings of grief for his brother or the burden his father put on him to live and make up for the loss. After Bethany died, his impulse to father another child was because he knew first hand the pressures felt by the surviving sibling. It is a moment of insight and understanding for all of them, Douglas included, and they are all able to embrace.

Nan had asked the surgeon if she could sometime watch a heart transplant, and she does so, in the Houston hospital where Bethany had died. The instant the heart starts beating in the recipient's body, she feels comforted at the thought of new life. As she leaves the operating area, she finds Douglas with Mrs. Clayton; the Reverend Clayton has just died. Douglas at first takes it personally, as though Bethany's heart should have done better, but everyone reassures him that organ rejection is common, and that at least Clayton had four extra months of life to appreciate. Nan reminds him that it is not Bethany who has just died; Bethany died in November. As the novel ends, Nan and Douglas are driving out to the ranch to see Jesse.

The novel addresses serious topics yet also includes humor and a close observation of human character. What emerges is not only the difficulty of human relationships but strategies for dealing with problems. Jesse, for example, listens to others and thinks of ways to help them even before they realize how much they need it. Her repeated story about Douglas and Walter as little boys is a way of giving Douglas back his brother, of recognizing his loss. She deeds the house in Sanibel to Douglas and Nan because they need a change, and she does it with kindness and generosity, as though they are doing her a favor by taking care of it. Nan's friend Doris, whom she had met when she first arrived at Mead's Mill, is a member of a covert group called Lemonade Stand organized specifically to provide support for faculty wives. The message is clear that love and loyalty and kindness are important, and not only within the family unit.

Another major theme is the need for individuals to pursue their own dreams. Bert does this deep sea diving, despite—and in some ways precisely because of—its dangers. Nan realizes that she supported her husband and identified with her children at the cost of abandoning her own interests and her sense of herself. Douglas, although successful in his academic career, carries the image of himself as second best to his missing brother and feels he had to do what his father wanted him to do rather than to satisfy himself.

Shelby Hearon does not specify the meaning of the title, but "footprints" appears twice. Once is in the context of the need for selfhood and independence, when Nan is wondering why Bethany was not as eager as Nan had been to "set her footprints on a broader trail" and leave home as soon as she could. The second time is at the end of the novel, when Nan is watching the heart transplant surgery. She muses that in her particular area of science, the study of the long extinct trilobites, she could observe only their "footprints," not the creatures themselves, quite unlike the beating heart and the living body in the operating room. The surgical team must literally dare and risk to involve themselves with the living, and they must also demonstrate caring and cooperation. Nan understands more fully than ever the truth that these same qualities are necessary for her and for all living beings.

Lois Marchino

Sources for Further Study

Boston Globe. March 24, 1996, p. B36.
Chicago Tribune. March 31, 1996, XIV, p. 3.
Kirkus Reviews. LXIV, February 1, 1996, p. 159.
Library Journal. CXXI, March 15, 1996, p. 95.
Los Angeles Times Book Review. May 5, 1996, p. 14.
National Catholic Reporter. May 31, 1996, p. 14.
The New York Times Book Review. CI, March 31, 1996, p. 30.
Publishers Weekly. CCXLIII, January 22, 1996, p. 58.
San Francisco Chronicle. April 7, 1996, p. REV8.
Writer. CIX, July, 1996, p. 3.

FORBIDDEN KNOWLEDGE
From Prometheus to Pornography

Author: Roger Shattuck (1923-   )
Publisher: St. Martin's Press (New York). 370 pp. $26.95
Type of work: Literary criticism; literary history

In defiance of what he regards as the bias of modern culture, a respected literary scholar dares to explore the possibility that there are things humans should not know

One could hardly accuse Roger Shattuck, University Professor and Professor of Modern Languages and Literature at Boston University, of courting fashion. As president of the Association of Literary Scholars and Critics, Shattuck leads a countermovement of academic traditionalists against perceived excesses and irresponsibility in the current academic study of literature. In his article "Nineteen Theses on Literature," published in *Essays in Criticism* in July of 1995, Shattuck has declared without any trace of doubt or ambiguity his allegiance to such old-fashioned notions as the belief that literature may serve as a mirror of human expression and feelings, providing authentic insights into the human condition. It is doubtful, however, whether Shattuck has ever more directly challenged cultural fashions than in *Forbidden Knowledge: From Prometheus to Pornography*. The first sentence of the book is a question: "Are there things that we should *not* know?" Moreover, this is for Shattuck a real question. Against what he would regard as the overwhelming tendency of advanced thinkers in modern and postmodern culture to answer his question in the negative, Shattuck urges readers to reexamine the issue. His strategy in the first part of his book is to trace the theme of forbidden knowledge in myth and literature into the present century; in the second part, he offers "case studies" meant to illuminate the status of the concept, and the implications of that status, in contemporary culture.

In spite of its superficially neat two-part division, the book is by no means rigidly systematic. Although Shattuck offers an enumeration of six categories of forbidden knowledge, he does so only in an appendix; the categories therefore scarcely organize the argument in the mind of the reader. On several occasions, in fact, Shattuck offers what amounts to an apology for his book's structural looseness. Even a sympathetic reader may find at times that it is only on a second reading that the relevance of a particular passage to the overall design of the book becomes clear. Still, a patient and attentive reading will discern that there is a design after all.

Shattuck first undertakes to establish the antiquity of the concept of forbidden knowledge. He reminds readers of the foregrounding of the theme in some of the founding myths of Western culture. The story of Prometheus, for example, is the story of the theft of fire from the gods; Prometheus takes on a knowledge and power meant for gods alone. In spite of the grim penalty he suffers, Prometheus is usually ranked among our mythic heroes, representing in the customary interpretation a justified rebellion against limits arbitrarily imposed by an unjust authority. Shattuck does not quarrel with this interpretation, but he reminds readers that there is more to the myth.

Zeus sends Pandora, the first woman, in retaliation for the insubordination of Prometheus. When Pandora's unchecked curiosity leads her to open the lid of the fateful box, she unlooses grief, cares, and all evil. As a consequence of Pandora's failure to accept limits on what she is allowed to know, the benefits bestowed by Prometheus' defiance are effectively canceled out.

In the Judeo-Christian tradition, the story of Adam and Eve stands as the archetypal account of the consequences, in this case expulsion from the Garden and the entry of Sin and Death into the world, of the refusal to accept limits to knowledge. Shattuck affirms the cultural importance of the biblical account, but he devotes more sustained attention to the elaboration of that account in Milton's *Paradise Lost*. He articulates the full implications of Raphael's urging Adam to be "lowly wise," locating in that advice evidence of the continuing vitality of the concept of limits to human knowledge. Shattuck also defines the four stages of the "downward path of wisdom" as delineated by Milton: innocence, fancy, experience, wisdom. As he makes clear in a later chapter, however, Shattuck acknowledges the possibility that wisdom may in certain circumstances be attainable without the necessity of the perilous passage through experience.

Before reaching that stage of his argument, however, Shattuck turns his attention to literary incarnations of the Faust myth, for many the central myth of secular Western culture. He traces the myth from its earliest appearances at the threshold of the Renaissance to its culminating expression in Goethe's nineteenth century masterpiece. In the course of this development, Shattuck observes, a most revealing change occurs. The Faust whose damnation provides the denouement of the story as dramatized, for example, by Christopher Marlowe in the sixteenth century, has become in the later era the Faust who earns salvation because of his "striving." The rejection of limits, the refusal to acknowledge that any knowledge is legitimately forbidden, becomes a defining feature of the myth as humans enter the Romantic era, from which, many would argue, they have yet to emerge.

Forbidden Knowledge would have been a more clearly organized book if Shattuck had made certain choices at this point. He has traced the evolution of the Faust myth, relating it provocatively to the figures of Don Quixote, Don Juan, and Frankenstein. He has also demonstrated in that evolution the marks of the revolutionary shift in cultural values, which culminates in the modern rejection of the idea that there may be such a thing as forbidden knowledge. Shattuck might have moved directly to the issue of the bearing of this evolution on his concerns regarding contemporary culture, the primary topic of the second part of the book. Instead, having used myth and literature to establish that the idea of forbidden knowledge, although it may have lost its hold over humans in the course of the last two centuries, has been from antiquity an important part of human self-definition, Shattuck takes two more steps before jumping to the present.

Shattuck offers one of his apologies for the structure of his book as he turns to his discussion of the seventeenth century French novel *La Princesse de Cleves*, by Madame de La Fayette and of the poems of the nineteenth century American poet Emily Dickinson. Yet the function of the discussion is finally clear. If the issue has been whether it is necessary that some knowledge be regarded as forbidden, the topic now becomes the positive benefits that can arise from abstinence and asceticism. Each in her own way, these authors (that both are women may or may not be incidental) affirm the emotional and spiritual intensity that can achieved through the rejection of direct experience. They represent, then, forbidden knowledge as a positive value, rather than as simply a limit that must be accepted. They also suggest that the path to wisdom need not lead through experience. To fancy, or imagine, an action is not necessarily to do it and may at times be more profoundly satisfying than the action itself could possibly be.

Shattuck's discussion of Albert Camus' *The Stranger*, which he compares to Herman Melville's *Billy Budd*, may seem at first merely a case of a professor's getting a few things off his chest about a novel his students seem unable to understand. Yet even here Shattuck is advancing his argument. The misunderstanding with which he does battle arises from the attitude most familiarly expressed as, "To understand is to forgive." He finds his students, and perhaps Camus himself, too willing to forgive the murderous protagonist of *The Stranger*. The moral error arises from a failure to understand understanding. Readers find it possible to forgive the murderer because they think they can arrive at an unlimited understanding of another human being, an understanding that explains, indeed explains away, whatever might be reprehensible in human behavior. What Shattuck wants to suggest is that this kind of knowledge is forbidden, not in the sense that some authority figure announces a taboo, but in the sense that it is simply not attainable. The belief that humans have attained such complete knowledge can therefore only be a sentimental fiction, and judgments based on that belief will inevitably manifest the moral confusion Shattuck finds in his students and in some of their mentors.

In the second part of the book, Shattuck turns to contemporary issues in science and literature. He identifies the Manhattan Project, which led to the atomic bomb, and the Human Genome Project, which opens up far-ranging possibilities of genetic engineering, as two instances of scientific inquiry that raise troubling questions about where scientific knowledge may take humanity if pursued with no sense of limits—that is, with no acknowledgement of the possibility of forbidden knowledge. His reflections on these matters lead Shattuck to the proposal that scientists devise an equivalent of medicine's Hippocratic Oath. Scientists, he suggests, must acknowledge as a guiding principle, "Above all, do no harm." Shattuck is not himself a scientist, but his observations on these matters may acquire additional moral weight from his identification of himself as one of those veterans of the war in the Pacific whose life may have been saved by the dropping of the atomic bomb.

The longest chapter in the book focuses on the Marquis de Sade and, more centrally, on the vicissitudes of his literary reputation. Simone de Beauvoir wrote in 1952 an essay entitled "Must We Burn Sade?" Her negative answer to the question and her generally laudatory account of Sade's work are in Shattuck's view only too typical of what has happened to Sade's reputation and, by extension, to the values embodied in much of contemporary literature and, perhaps to an even greater degree, in the contemporary critical study of literature. For Shattuck, the question has been improperly framed. The issue is not, "Must we burn Sade?" but, "Should we rehabilitate Sade?" To the first of these questions, Shattuck is sufficiently a man of the modern age to answer, "No." Yet he answers "No" to the second question as well. Sade "represents forbidden knowledge that we may not forbid." If we are in our time powerless to forbid, we are all the more responsible for our critical judgments, in themselves and in their consequences. This includes our judgment of the possible consequences of the texts we criticize. Shattuck's complaint is that critical fashion, permeated with relativism, renders us only too ready to abdicate that responsibility.

Shattuck's book can be criticized for its organizational weaknesses. It is also possible to argue with it on more substantive points. Most of the early reviews of the book have come from literary scholars. While most of these have found the chapter on issues in science highly persuasive, one awaits the response of the scientific community. Moreover, Shattuck may overrate the importance of Sade, and the issues surrounding his work, to contemporary thought. On the basis of figures he himself provides, sales of Sade's works have fallen off dramatically in recent years, and he never makes clear just how widely Sade is studied in American universities and in what ways.

Even if one finds *Forbidden Knowledge* entirely persuasive, one may ask what follows from its argument. If we are not to burn Sade, if we can no longer forbid the forbidden, what has Shattuck given us beyond an exercise in moral and intellectual nostalgia? While scientists may be open to the idea of a version of the Hippocratic Oath, Shattuck seems under no illusion that literary scholars would tolerate similar restraints.

Shattuck's accomplishment, though apparently modest, is by no means insignificant. If there is one defining feature of modern secular thought, at least in its academic incarnations, it may be the shared and unquestioned conviction that the pursuit of knowledge must be unfettered. In that context, what Shattuck has done is to renew readers' consciousness of ways of thinking that have for several generations been virtually unavailable to the intellectual community. A responsive reader of this book is forced at least to entertain thoughts that had become virtually unthinkable. What the reader now does with the thoughts Shattuck has provoked remains precisely the reader's responsibility. It seems that awakening readers to their responsibility has been Shattuck's project all along.

W. P. Kenney

Sources for Further Study

Booklist. XCIII, September 15, 1996, p. 204.
Boston Globe. September 19, 1996, p. N15.
The Christian Science Monitor. October 23, 1996, p. 15.

Commentary. CII, December, 1996, p. 68.
Library Journal. CXXI, October 1, 1996, p. 77.
The New Republic. CCXV, November 4, 1996, p. 34.
The New York Times Book Review. CI, October 27, 1996, p. 17.
Publishers Weekly. CCXLIII, August 5, 1996, p. 424.
The Wall Street Journal. September 23, 1996, p. A18.
The Wilson Quarterly. XX, Autumn, 1996, p. 86.

THE FORTUNES OF THE COURTIER
The European Recognition of Castiglione's *Cortegiano*

Author: Peter Burke (1937-   )
First published: 1995, in Great Britain
Publisher: Pennsylvania State University Press (University Park, Pennsylvania). Illustrated.
   210 pp. $40.00; paperback $16.95
Type of work: Literary history
Time: 1528-c.1900
Locale: Europe

Burke uses the European reception of Castiglione's The Courtier *to illustrate historical and cultural shifts, particularly in the century following its first publication*

Principal personages:
BALDASAR CASTIGLIONE, courtier and author
ROGER ASCHAM, English humanist
PIETRO BEMBO, Venetian patrician and Platonist
COUNT LODOVICO DA CANOSSA, Veronese nobleman
ELISABETTA GONZAGA, duchess of Urbino
LUKASZ GÓRNICKI, sixteenth century Polish courtier and author
THOMAS HOBY, translator of *The Courtier* into English

The son of a courtier, Baldasar Castiglione was born in 1487 at Casatico, Italy. On his mother's side he was related to the Gonzagas who ruled Mantua. Following his father's profession, Castiglione served his kinsman Francesco Gonzaga (1499-1503); then, from 1504 to 1513 he was at the court of Urbino, the setting for his treatise on the ideal courtier. In 1524, he became papal nuncio to Emperor Charles V of Spain, who sacked Rome in 1527. Although Castiglione claimed that *The Courtier* was the product of a few days' effort, he may have begun writing it as early as 1508, fully two decades before its publication. By 1518, he had completed a first draft, which he revised in the early 1520's. *The Courtier* appeared in Venice in 1528, shortly before its author's death in Toledo on February 8, 1529.

Burke's study is a response to Sir Ernest Baker's 1948 comment that "it would be a fascinating study to examine comparatively the different national tinctures" given to Castiglione's book, particularly during the century following its initial printing. This exploration of reception illuminates three other issues: the response to the Renaissance outside Italy, the history of the book, and changes in cultural attitudes.

Burke notes that Castiglione's work belongs to a long tradition of conduct books that dates from the beginnings of Western literature. Homer's *Iliad* and *Odyssey* (c. 776 B.C.), though presenting different versions of the hero, illustrate the eighth century B.C. ideal of excellence. Aristotle's *Ethics* and Xenophon's *Cyropedia* in the fourth century B.C., Cicero's *Des officiis* (of duties), even Ovid's *Art of Love* provide other classical examples that sought to teach a code of behavior. In the early Middle Ages, such manuals concentrated on the clergy; the title of St. Ambrose's *Des officiis clericorum* (of the duties of the clergy) reveals the refocusing of Cicero's concern from the secular to the religious world. By the High Middle Ages the emphasis had changed again, as *chansons de geste* and romances taught chivalry and courtesy to new lay elites. Courtesy books also reappeared. Castiglione drew on all of these predecessors, quoting from or alluding to many of these in his text.

Yet as Burke observes, *The Courtier* was not originally an instruction manual. Castiglione's book is a dialogue, in which diverse individuals offer conflicting views. This form is as old as Plato and was adopted by Cicero and Lucian; it was revived by such fifteenth century humanists as Leonardo Bruni, Poggio Bracciolini, and Lorenzo Valla. Dialogues are not necessarily open: some of Plato's, for example, are little more than showcases for Socrates to expound his (or Plato's) views. Others, however, allow for alternative positions, and Castiglione's belongs to this category. In the third book, Giuliano de' Medici argues that women can understand as much as men, but Gasparo Pallavicino claims that women are "a mistake of nature," and Cesare Gonzaga asserts that a woman's role is to inspire male achievement. *The Courtier*'s very structure reveals its open quality. At the end of the fourth evening, which comprises the fourth and final book, the speakers disperse, promising to resume their conversation; but they do not. Yet Castiglione does stress certain qualities that the courtier and court lady should exhibit: honor, *gentilezza*, *modestia*, liberality, elegance, affability, discretion, grace. The most famous characteristic that Castiglione discusses is *sprezzatura* or spontaneity—hence the author's claim to have dashed off his book in a few days.

The popularity of *The Courtier* peaked in Italy in the 1530's and 1540's; Burke counts thirteen editions in each decade. Ten more editions appeared in the 1550's, nine in the 1560's, four each in the 1570's and 1580's, two in the 1590's, three more between 1600 and 1606, and then none again for more than a century. Judging from the list of owners Burke includes in appendix 2, purchasers of these editions ranged across the social and geographical world of Italy. Aristocrats from Ferrara and Siena, Florentine critics, Venetian authors, a lawyer from Sicily, the Benedictine monk Vincenzio Borghini and the humanist bishop Paolo Giovio all owned copies. Nor was the book's appeal limited to men; Castiglione presented copies to nine women, and Irene di Spilimbergo, a noblewoman from Friuli, ranked her copy with Petrarch.

As *The Courtier* was reprinted in the course of the sixteenth century, it acquired additional materials intended to help the reader. The 1547 Aldine edition (Venice) added an index as well as a summary of the qualities a courtier should possess. The 1560 Giolito edition (Venice) provided a different index and a summary of each book. Other editions added marginal notations. The unintentional consequence of these accretions was to turn Castiglione's open text into a closed, monologic instruction manual. In Book Two of *The Courtier*, Federico Fregoso asks for rules, but another speaker argues that circumstances alter cases. Castiglione's sixteenth century editors nevertheless provided what Fregoso had wanted. Thus, Vittoria Colonna praised Castiglione's maxims, and the lawyer Argisto Giuffredi urged his son to follow the precepts of *The Courtier*. Burke illustrates how the medium affects the message.

Castiglione was writing in an Italian context. In choosing Italian (rather than Latin), he was participating in the debate about literary language. Castiglione may also have been defending principalities in general and Urbino in particular from ambitious neighbors. Castiglione's life was framed by the French invasion of Italy in 1494 and the Spanish sack of Rome in 1527. In *The Courtier*, Lodovico da Canossa laments the ruin of Italy, and the Fregoso brothers bemoan Italy's becoming a prey to foreigners. Yet the book also has a larger context. It appeared at a critical time in the development of European courts. Charles V, Francois I, and Henry VIII all came to the throne early in the century. Erasmus' *Education of a Christian Prince* appeared in 1519. Pope Pius II's *On the Miseries of Courtiers*, written in 1444, was published at this time, as was Ulrich von Hutten's *The Court*.

Interest in *The Courtier* thus extended beyond Italy. Between 1528 and 1619, about sixty translations appeared, and many people across Europe would have read the work in the original. Burke found ninety non-Italian owners of the Italian text, even after translations were available. Another measure of the work's popularity is the praise it elicited. Roger Ascham commented that carefully reading and following the advice of *The Courtier* for one year at home would benefit a young man more than three years of travel abroad. In 1608, an English traveller made a pilgrimage to Castiglione' tomb. Montaigne's friend Jacques-Auguste de Thou likened *The Courtier* to Cicero's *Orator*, an equation that also struck Henry Howard. Howard's marginalia cite parallels between Castiglione's text and four by Cicero. The Spanish humanist Cristóbal de Villalón wrote a treatise on education, *El scholástico*, a dialogue in four books covering four days and set in 1528, an obvious tribute to Castiglione. Recognizing the similarities between his book and *The Courtier*, Villalón felt compelled to deny the charge of plagiarism, but he concluded that if anyone still thought that he had drawn too heavily from his Italian precursor he had no objection, since Castiglione "is one of the wisest men of whom learned Italy may worthily be proud."

Castiglione's courtier came to be seen as an ideal. In 1548 William Patten praised Sir John Luttrell of Dunster as a man "such . . . as Count Balthazar the Italian in his book of Courtier doth frame." Pietro Bizzarri called John Astley "the only courtier on Castiglione's model," and Gabriel Harvey concurred. Sir Philip Sidney was another regarded as the embodiment of Castiglione's vision.

Translations not only illustrate the popularity of *The Courtier* but also show how ideas can be modified as they cross borders. The Spanish version of Castiglione omitted the terms *cittadino* and *civile* because, as Burke observes, Spain lacked the kind of civic culture that characterized Renaissance Italy. Burke examines in particular the way translators dealt with the key terms of *cortegiania*, *grazia*, and *sprezzatura*. Thomas Hoby's choice of "disgracing" for this last term raises the question of his response to the text, since the English word was pejorative even in the 1500's.

Equally revealing of cultural differences are imitations of *The Courtier*. Lukasz Górnicki's *Dworzanin polski* (Polish courtier), published in 1566, shifts Castiglione's dialogue from Urbino to Pradnik (near Cracow), the court of Samuel Maciejowski, bishop of Cracow and chancellor of Poland. The speakers are nine Polish noblemen. The omission of women is significant. Górnicki justified this change by claiming that Poland, unlike Italy, lacked learned women. Also, the presence of women may have seemed inappropriate for the court of a bishop. Reflecting the ecclesiastical milieu is the removal of some of Castiglione's jokes about the clergy. Górnicki did not discuss painting and sculpture because, he noted, those arts were not well known in Poland, and he eliminated the treatment of music because the Polish nobility did not play instruments.

Nicolas Farget's *Honnête homme* (1630) also eliminates the discussion of music and painting as inappropriate for the gentleman. Farget expands the treatment of religion, demonstrating the influence of the Counter-Reformation. Francisco Rodriguez Lôbo's *Côrte na aldeia e noites de inverno* (court in the village and winter nights) of 1619 emphasizes the etiquette of letter-writing and visiting, suggesting that these matters were important in seventeenth century Portugal.

Despite the popularity of *The Courtier*, its European appeal was not universal. Burke finds no owners among the Norwegians, Finns, Russians, Bulgarians, Serbians, Moldavians, Wallachians, or Irish. The absence of readers in eastern Europe is especially revealing, coinciding with other observations that this region did not experience the Renaissance but remained in the Middle Ages until the Enlightenment. Burke also found critics of the work. In the late sixteenth century the Catholic church objected to aspects of Castiglione's book and ordered the preparation of an expurgated version, first published in 1584. The reviser, Antonio Ciccarelli, deleted references to fortune, secular uses of theological terms, and jokes about the clergy. Some Protestants also felt uncomfortable about Castiglione because they thought he advocated hypocrisy. Attacking *The Courtier* also became a metonymy for attacking any court and Italy.

Burke focuses on the fortunes of *The Courtier* in its first century, but he briefly examines the book's subsequent reception. By the middle of the seventeenth century interest in Castiglione's book had declined, in part because of religious objections, in part because the kind of court that Castiglione described had ceased to exist. In the absolutist courts of Europe's nation-states success required not grace but conformity. Castiglione continued to be read, but now as a guide to private rather than public life. The 1685 Dresden edition called the work *Gallant Night Conversations*, implying that the book could teach the art of conversation. *De volmaeckte hovelinck* (1662), the first Dutch translation, appeared at a time when the rich merchants of the Netherlands were trying to learn to act like aristocrats.

The early eighteenth century witnessed what Burke calls the "renaissance of the Renaissance," with the reprinting of many important Italian authors of the 1400's and 1500's, including Castiglione. This renewed interest persisted. For Jacob Burckhardt in *The Civilization of the Renaissance in Italy* (1860) Castiglione represented the *Zeitgeist*. Sir Walter Raleigh in his 1900 edition of *The Courtier* called the book "an abstract or epitome of the chief moral ideas of the age," and William Butler Yeats referred to Urbino as "That grammar school of courtesies/ Where wit and wisdom learned their trade."

The Fortunes of the Courtier is an important contribution to intellectual history and to the history of the book. It demonstrates how bibliography, textual criticism, and library history can illuminate the mentality of an age. Burke's methodology is as significant as his findings, confirming the observation of Terentianus Maurus, "Pro captu lectoris habent sua fata libelli" (through the reader's fancy books have their fates). By studying the fate of books one can learn much about the past.

Joseph Rosenblum

Sources for Further Study

AB Bookman's Weekly. XCVII, January 8, 1996, p. 96.
History Today. XLV, April, 1995, p. 52.
Publishers Weekly. CCXLIII, January 15, 1996, p. 458.
The Times Literary Supplement. May 10, 1996, p. 30.

FOUNDING FATHER
Rediscovering George Washington

Author: Richard Brookhiser (1955-   )
Publisher: Free Press (New York). 230 pp. $25.00
Type of work: History
Time: 1776-1799
Locale: The United States

A search for the real Washington behind the myth, one of the truly great men of history, the man who personified America's finest hopes and aspirations and continues to challenge Americans to live up to his example

> *Principal personages:*
> GEORGE WASHINGTON, an American general, farmer, and first president of the United States, 1789-1797
> JOHN ADAMS, an American diplomat, first vice president, and second president of the United States, 1797-1801
> ALEXANDER HAMILTON, a prominent Federalist leader and first secretary of the Treasury under Washington
> THOMAS JEFFERSON, an American diplomat, secretary of state under Washington, and third president of the United States, 1801-1809
> JAMES MADISON, father of the Constitution, secretary of state under Jefferson, and fourth president of the United States, 1809-1817

Modern intellectuals, with their ignorance and contempt of the past, have condemned Washington to the realm of children's stories. They have destroyed his reputation with simple statements: he was a rich man, he was a slave holder, he was a womanizer, he was cold and unfeeling, he was nothing more than a figurehead. It was as if the pendulum had swung from nineteenth century adulation to twentieth century skepticism, cynicism, and smugness. This is the attitude that Brookhiser takes head-on. Noting that great statesmen are rare enough, he comments that modern individuals have gone even further, to "believe that they are mythical, like unicorns."

Brookhiser's biography is not a "life" of George Washington. That life has been recorded by fine scholars whose books are opened most often only by other scholars. Brookhiser, instead, writes what he calls a "moral biography" in the tradition of Plutarch; and like Plutarch, he organizes his study into discrete sections: Washington's public actions, his private life, and an assessment of the man and his achievements. Brookhiser intends his book to have an impact on the public appreciation of the man who seems to have been first placed upon a pedestal, then neglected, and finally despised. There is nothing the modern age needs as much as an authentic hero, and few men and women in all of history, if any, fulfill the role better than George Washington.

Nothing came easily to Washington. When he was named commander in chief of the Continental Army, his officers were inexperienced, his men undisciplined. Time after time the troops were outmaneuvered and outfought—when Washington could get them to stand and fight long enough to be beaten. When he presided over the

Constitutional Convention, the delegates were badly divided. When he became president, there was less administrative tradition and experience than there were theories about the nature of government and of men, and he faced an immediate crisis in the wars of the French Revolution. Had America been a nation of saints, anybody could have been the Founding Father. Among the three million Americans then living, however, there was but one Washington. He was the indispensable man.

Yet what made him indispensable? Brookhiser posits three characteristics. First, there was his physical appearance. In an era of short men and poor medical knowledge, Washington was tall, healthy, and vigorous. To his natural strength he added perfect posture, self-control, and studied dignity. When he walked among his officers, nobody had to ask who was in command; when he rode a horse, he was the model of control and grace; when he danced, everyone marveled at the balance of talent and training. Strong? The width of the Rappahannock may vary, but the height of the Natural Bridge in the Shenandoah Valley remains at 215 feet. One cannot encourage anyone to attempt to duplicate Washington's having thrown a rock up to it, but experienced baseball players might look up at it and wonder if he would not have made a marvelous center fielder.

Second and third were his ideas on morality and government—ideas which were not as far apart as his contemporaries (and ours) wished us to believe, and, therefore, have to be discussed together. Underneath everything lay Washington's desire for a good reputation. Some acts were simply dishonorable, some bad manners, and others merely stupid. A gentleman who wanted respect avoided all three as best he could. The preventives were called honesty and courage, courtesy and civility, and the combination of reading, intelligent observation, and forethought. One avoided thoughtless words and promises by saying little, drinking less, and by an unwavering politeness to friends and enemies alike. Such behavior was not easy for Washington, for he was a sensitive man who possessed a fiery temper, and he had an exquisite vocabulary of unprintable words which could be effectively employed on the proper occasions—all the more reason for him to exercise his famous self-control.

Washington had the big man's self-confidence, the easy laugh, the consciousness of always being on display, but he was not disturbed by the public intrusions into his everyday life. He enjoyed company, was an active sportsman, and a conscientious manager. It helped that he was reared an aristocrat, with an awareness of the importance of social life, a thorough knowledge of proper manners, and an appropriate stock of small talk. These virtues too often mislead modern readers to conclude that he was shallow. An athlete's grace, a monarch's charm, a politician's readiness for any situation make the difficult seem simple, the deepest fords easy to cross—Washington possessed all these traits.

Washington's political ideas have become platitudes, so commonplace that most Americans do not recognize them as his. Well-read rather than widely read, conversant in the original sense of the word with the great constitutional thinkers of America, Washington's deep belief in the need for self-government led him to risk his life and fortune in his country's service—without ambition for enrichment, offices, or titles.

(Fame is another matter.) At the Constitutional Convention, he guided the oft-meandering discussions back to the main stream, and as president he was aware that every day he set precedents. His precepts live on despite our best efforts to subvert them. It was not reporters from *The Washington Post* who brought down Richard Nixon. It was the memory of George Washington and his confession about the cherry tree: "Father, I cannot tell a lie."

Washington was a universalist in political theory. If nature's law applied in England, it applied in America; if it applied here, it applied elsewhere. The main issue was education of the public. Hence, his support of a national university, best founded right in the nation's capitol, where students could observe the statesmen of a free republic gravely debating the nation's business. Even though he was disappointed in Congress' behavior, he remained a realist, who understood that these particular laws of nature were executed by men; moreover, by men unaccustomed to the tasks and temptations facing them. He understood that men, like a fine horse, needed guidance—and not the spur, but a firm and gentle hand. In his Farewell Address (a document that the author recommends for wider and closer study) Washington's long third paragraph praises the generosity of Providence, the richness of the land, the opportunities that await, and the knowledge available (thanks to what is now called the Age of the Enlightenment), but he concludes with the terse and gloomy warning that if the citizens of United States are not completely free and happy, it will be their own fault.

It was in this very mood that he contemplated the central paradox of American history, that men who had just made themselves free continued to hold slaves. Others had slaves—several European states which did not have domestic slavery permitted it on their sugar islands, Africans sold slaves, Turks bought them, and Chinese felt free to castrate theirs. Yet these others had no political philosophy based on the principle of liberty. Washington could only divide his actions into public and private spheres—while remaining acutely aware that these spheres overlapped. As commanding general of the Continental Army, he would do nothing unless sanctioned by Congress (his was not the way of Cromwell). As president, he would do nothing that would split the new nation. Slavery was simply too heated an issue to attempt to resolve at this moment. As a private person, he had to be concerned with his livelihood. His various attempts to find ways of managing Mount Vernon without slaves all failed. The best he could do was to avoid buying slaves as best he could and never to sell a slave. The slaves who had served him as president were freed so quietly that the fact was not discovered until a recent biographer went through his private papers. His treatment of the slaves at Mount Vernon was exemplary—there is no credible evidence of his ever having slept with slaves or mistreated them; moreover, they were freed upon Martha's death and the older slaves were given pensions. This was not a heroic solution, but it was more than reconciling oneself to live forever with an existing evil. He had done what he could and, as suggested by the third paragraph of his Farewell Address, the rest was up to the nation.

Although his resolution of the slavery issue was unsatisfactory, it provides deep insights into Washington's innermost thoughts. Had he been a political radical determined to end every oppression on the face of the earth or die in the process, he would have been a failure. Had he been unconcerned with the problem of liberty, he would have stayed home when called to serve. Instead, Washington was a man who believed in process and progress. Unless his generation grounded the principles of liberty solidly in political life and on a foundation of moral principles, nothing could be achieved; once such a government was in existence, however, and the moral principles universally accepted, nothing could prevent their being logically extended to include others outside the original compact. First principles demanded that the country be firmly established; afterward, steps could be taken to rectify failings in the human institutions of society. Washington's task was to found the nation. Brookhiser demonstrates that the title Founding Father was apt then and apt now.

One could not anticipate a future filled with tall men or even the assistance of divine providence. What can compensate for all shortcomings is character. Character is developed by training—based on moral concepts of what constitutes good and evil, and hard discipline along proven lines to prepare oneself to deal with the temptations that both will bring—and models of behavior, good and bad, with appropriate lessons from each drawn from history. Washington left the example of a good man's complete life. Unlike some other great figures, he did not die prematurely. His was a full career—varied, challenging, frustrating, rewarding. Yet nothing distinguished his various careers and triumphs as his leaving them behind. From command of the Continental Army, he went home; from the Constitutional Convention, back to private life; and once again after two terms as president he retired to Mount Vernon. So rare was this characteristic among public figures that for a comparison contemporaries had to scour history to find the semihistorical Cincinnatus in ancient Rome.

What he left Americans, his true posterity (he had no children of his own), includes an awareness of a parent's true role: one cannot be a father (to remain within the metaphor) without governing one's children; one cannot govern others unless one can govern oneself; one can govern oneself only by adhering to unchanging principles of right and wrong. Modern Americans seem to be floundering in a moral morass, unsure of principle, resentful of restraints, scorning all types of patriarchy. Washington lives to remind Americans that liberty does not involve being freed from duty, good manners, or laws.

Even his death was appropriate to a man steeped in good manners and civility: in contrast to Joseph Stalin and Adolf Hitler, Washington died with dignity. No contemporary disagreed with Henry Lee's summary of Washington's significance: "first in war, first in peace, and first in the hearts of his countrymen."

William Urban

Sources for Further Study

American Heritage. XLVII, May, 1996, p. 110.
Commentary. CI, May, 1996, p. 69.

Forbes. CLVIII, December 2, 1996, p. 26.
Kirkus Reviews. LXIII, December 1, 1995, p. 1678.
Los Angeles Times Book Review. March 24, 1996, p. 10.
National Review. XLVIII, March 11, 1996, p. 61.
The New York Review of Books. XLIII, February 29, 1996, p. 11.
The New York Times Book Review. CI, February 18, 1996, p. 8.
The New Yorker. LXXI, February 5, 1996, p. 68.
Publishers Weekly. CCXLIII, January 8, 1996, p. 55.
The Wall Street Journal. February 8, 1996, p. A12.

FRAME STRUCTURES
Early Poems, 1974-1979

Author: Susan Howe (1937-   )
Publisher: New Directions (New York). 122 pp. Paperback $12.95
Type of work: Poetry

A collection of poems revealing the author's emotional and ontological attachment to history

Since the release of Susan Howe's *The Nonconformist's Memorial* in 1993, many readers have eagerly been waiting for her next book. *Frame Structures* turns out to be a collection of Howe's early poems written and published between 1974 and 1979. It is only appropriate that a person whose inspiration derives as much from her interaction with the present as from her attachment to history decides to republish some of her earliest poems in the forms which she cares to have them last. It is a revisionist approach firmly grounded in what Howe believes should be permanent, a leitmotif which melodiously and rhythmically threads some of the poet's best poems together. Howe is a professor of English at the State University of New York at Buffalo. She started writing poetry in earnest in 1972, after she moved to Connecticut with her husband. Her training in the visual arts had laid a solid foundation for her development as a poet. In quite a few of her poems, not only does she use words to create mental images for the reader, she also uses them to draw pictures literally. Fascinated with history and the landscape of the Long Island Sound area and the Atlantic Ocean around Massachusetts, Howe deals with both themes in poems which are collected in *The Europe of Trusts: Selected Poems* (1990), *Singularities* (1990), and *The Nonconformist's Memorial*. Besides poetry, she is also interested in postmodernist criticism. She is a two-time winner of the Before Columbus Foundation Book Award for *Secret History of the Dividing Line* (1978), a collection of poems, and *My Emily Dickinson* (1985), a postmodern critical study.

Frame Structures includes poems from Howe's four early chapbooks: *Hinge Picture* (1974), *Chanting at the Crystal Sea* (1975), *Cabbage Gardens* (1979), and *Secret History of the Dividing Line* (1978). In the "Preface" written specifically for the collection, Howe discusses Paul Demund Evans's book, *The Holland Land and Company* (1924), describes her relationship with her father, recalls her family's tie to the New England area, and ponders the intricate connection between history and literature. The juxtaposition of history, literature, and personal memoir suggests a cohesiveness between history and the present, between primitivity and modernity, and between family and country. For "in the cold drama of moral lucidity there is primitive reason just as in the calm dicta of moral lucidity there is personal reason." Everything, indeed, starts in primitive forms; everything starts with the individual; everything starts with the family.

It is quite apparent that Howe's painstaking study of her family pedigree in the "Preface" represents an effort to reclaim her sense of identity by (re)connecting with history. The title of the book, however, suggests that she is interested in both history per se as well as the way it is "framed." In the context of poetry, the only way a person can "frame" history is with the help of words. Howe has expressed doubts about the reliability of words. According to Geoffrey O'Brien, she once questioned: "Words are the only clues we have. What if they fail us?" Her affection for words, nevertheless, is revealed by her belief that the past can only live through the way we read it. In *Frame Structures*, Howe's interest in words moves beyond their conventional use. In one of the examples she presents in the "Preface," what looks very much like a working manuscript with deleted, overtyped, congested, and incomplete lines, in effect, represents a "trajectory in imagination where logic and mathematics meet the materials of art." The congested lines present a visual display of history's potential, whose reconstruction can be just as confusing as human hermeneutic interpretation. It is an expressionistic approach placed in a new historical form. By combining words and imagery, the poet has turned form into message.

Frame Structures is divided into four parts. In "Hinge Picture," the author uses the Bible as a bedrock for her study of history. If Howe's previous book, *The Nonconformist's Memorial*, takes a deconstructionist approach to the study of religion, *Frame Structures* uses religion as a means to facilitate its poetic representation of history. It provides the author with one of several lenses through which history is viewed, reviewed, reiterated, and reconstructed. In the very core of its highly subjective perception lies the very foundation Howe wants to build her edifice. The central image in "Hinge Picture" is the sea. If the sea emblematizes time and history, the voyage is what connects both. In between the past and the present, between distance and connectedness, and between the visual and the literal, the voyage is what weaves a picture with which the author attempts to make an emotional connection with the reader. Words are also used in this section to represent movement in history, not in a linear line but in the form of exchange back and forth between historical facts and human interpretation. In some parts, the author uses words to create what looks very much like the picture of a ship whose movement coincides with that of the narrative.

In "Chanting at the Crystal Sea," Howe shifts her topic from that of the storm at the sea to that of the storm of human relationship. Throughout the section, a person can feel the presence of danger and the narrator's high level of anxiety. It starts with the description of the besiegement of Captain Stork and ends with a governor's proclamation: "I will not yield my ground until annihilation." In contrast to the previous section which is narrated from a third person's detached, omniscient point of view, the voice in this section belongs to a female who takes the center stage. She plays in turn the role of a child, an innocent observer, and that of a participant in the creation of history. Unlike the male figures in the poem who are very much involved in the fight for control and superiority the narrator, chanting the line: "I told them to lie down and put their mouths in the dust," is more concerned about her family's safety as well as the loss of innocent lives. The narrator's description of her family life reveals Howe's close tie to the Confessional School in contemporary American poetry.

"Cabbage Gardens" portrays the conflict between war's cruelty and those who are innocently involved. In the epigraph, Howe quotes Samuel Johnson: "You know there is already *The Hop-garden, a Poem*: and, I think, one could say a great deal about cabbage. The poem might begin with the advantages of civilized society over a rude state, exemplified by the Scotch, who had no cabbages till Oliver Cromwell's soldiers introduced them; and one might thus show how arts are propagated by conquest, as they were by the Roman arms." The paradoxicality implied in Johnson's statement constitutes the center of conflict in "Cabbage Gardens." Ostensibly, the poem is narrated from a cabbage's point of view. The narrator's innocent view and the cruelty of war it witnesses: fire, blood, and homeless people, creates the very foundation of the tragic conflict. "Cabbage Gardens" also exemplifies Howe's experiment with words to create visual images. Sometimes, the stanzas form a picture resembling that of a stem on a cabbage leave cut in half; other times, they look like sad human faces. It is in the correspondence of the natural world and the human world, people see a similarity eradicable only by human ignorance, deliberate or otherwise. Hence the paradoxical nature of the cabbage's experience and the human sufferings it witnesses. Typical of her practice in the other sections, Howe does not hesitate to split words into separate lines. In the following stanza, for example, she sacrifices several words apparently for the perfection of a picture:

> Life la
> nd friend
> no lighthous
> marin
> ere
> people of the
> Land
> Darkened
> Perilous
> mana
> cled with ice
> to a torn floor
> Let my lea
> ves
> press ankl deep
> into full fur
> rows
> howls a wind
> ow stil
> lness in rooms
> sombre and slo

The separation of the words is partially necessitated by the perfection of form and partially required by content. In both cases, the stem of the leaf, if the picture indeed represents that of a cabbage leaf, is what connects the form and the content, enabling a person to see panorama through singularities. The forced separation, besides vividly representing the cruelty of war, also reminds readers of, among other things, the arbitrariness of the arrangement of words themselves.

In "Secret History of the Dividing Line," Howe consummates her poetic rendition of history by venturing into the study of what is divisible and what is indivisible. The section examines the division as well as the indivision of the past and the present, distance and connectedness, and displacement and reconnection. The horizon, for example, represents the ultimate freedom. Yet the horizon is also what condemns humans into an existence which belies their true selves. "Secret History of the Dividing Line" is about restriction and freedom. It is about spiritual exile from a person's true self into territories which are marked by property lines and cage like family life. It is about the "quintessential clarity of inarticulation." For the "dividing lines" threaten to eradicate "numerous singularities." Just like a "CLOSED FIST" can withhold "AN OPEN PALM," however, the narrator starts to see the positive side of the horizon at the end of the poem. She wakes up one "sunny morning" watching "a new line of earthworks/ in the rear of the old ones" and decides to take refuge in the "Ancient of Days," "hint of what light/ the open sky."

As one of the country's leading experimental poets, Susan Howe has consistently shown her interest in finding a medium to make emotional engagement with the reader. *Frame Structures* marks the beginning of a journey in search of such a medium. As has been demonstrated in many of her poems, Howe's affection for words underlines a tie closer to the School of New Criticism and Deconstructionism than to those who believe in the omnipotent power of content. Poet and critic T. S. Eliot once posited that the "only way of expressing emotion in the form of art is by finding an 'objective correlative,'" "a set of objects, a situation, a chain of events which shall be the formula of that *particular* emotion; such that when the external facts, which must terminate in sensory experience, are given, the emotion is immediately evoked" ("Hamlet and His Problems," *An Introduction to Poetry*, 1986). Scholars who belong to the so-called School of New Criticism concur. The group, once headed by literary critic and scholar John Crowe Ransom, has vehemently been arguing that it is the nonlogical texture, but not the logical core, which distinguishes poetry as a literary genre. Howe knows that there is a "war-whoop in each dusty narrative" and words have the power to emancipate a person from the manacles of one's false self; they have the power to connect the present with the past and form with content. Besides providing the author with a vehicle to con- nect with readers at the visual, emotional, and rational level, words in Howe's poems also play a role similar to that of a hinge. They provide history with a frame, rendering "a pure past that returns to itself unattackable," which enables individuals to relive the past, makes it possible for them to record and interpret historical facts, and underlines the connectedness of human existence. For the whole history is like a "Beast found/ descended from harmony/ enduring in unity/ far back in some story/ heard long ago."

Qun Wang

Sources for Further Study

Chicago Review. XLII, Spring, 1996, p. 103.
Publishers Weekly. CCXLIII, March 18, 1996, p. 65.

THE FREQUENCY OF SOULS

Author: Mary Kay Zuravleff (1960-   )
Publisher: Farrar Straus Giroux (New York). 244 pp. $23.00
Type of work: Novel
Time: 1992
Locale: Rockville, Maryland

George Mahoney's attraction toward his new coworker, Niagara Spense, leads to an exploration and renewal of his life

> *Principal characters:*
> GEORGE MAHONEY, a thirty-nine-year-old refrigerator designer
> JUDY MAHONEY, his wife
> THE VETERAN, his recently retired office mate
> NIAGARA SPENSE, a newly hired refrigerator designer working with
>   George
> SHACKELFORD, George and Niagara's boss at Coldpoint

Mary Kay Zuravleff's first novel, *The Frequency of Souls*, exhibits her command of language and talent for characterization. The plot is linear, uncomplicated, and leavened with humor. Her work was supported by the D.C. Commission on the Arts, the National Endowment for the Arts, the James Jones Society, and the Ragdale Foundation.

The novel's protagonist is George Mahoney, through whose mind and vision a third-person narrator relates the story. A refrigerator engineer at Coldpoint for fourteen years, George claims his career matches his total faith in the material world and logic. He is the American suburban male prototype: handsome, tall, happily married and still sexually attracted to Judy, his wife of sixteen years. He has a twelve-year-old son, Harris, and a six-year-old daughter, Sheridan, and with this family he lives in an upper-class neighborhood on the outskirts of Washington, D.C. That his life is a good one goes unquestioned until his office mate of fourteen years, the Veteran, retires and is replaced by Niagara Spense. Soon it becomes clear first to the reader and eventually to George that he is stalled in neutral, in a passive, unquestioning mindset and situation. Symbolically, his only refrigerator redesign has been the automatic ice-maker invention.

George and his wife Judy believe they know each other well. Judy, a successful Washington, D.C., real estate agent, has become the planner of their lives—somewhat obsessively, so George thinks. Nevertheless, he enjoys his freedom from this responsibility, which he perceives as a healthy contentment. The only friction in their family comes from George and Judy's differing opinions about their son Harris' need to lose weight and how to plot the life of this apparent genius.

The novel covers seven days in which George, willy-nilly, awakens from his passive stupor. The story begins when he does the unthinkable: invites his new and much younger office mate, Niagara Spense, for lunch, not in the Coldpoint cafeteria but in a nearby restaurant.

Newly out of Caltech graduate school, Niagara is as bizarre as George Mahoney is typical. She is six feet, two inches tall, has an extra large frame, and wears garish homemade dresses, thick glasses and thicker makeup, and a hearing aid. Although George's fellow employees make jokes about Niagara, her individuality attracts rather than repels George. Later in the novel, she also attracts a younger man, a musicology professor who is a son of the Veteran.

Niagara's characterization defies or deconstructs the woman type so prevalent in American literature and popular culture. She is not a shrew; she is not a seductress. Large, homely, and gentle, she is not a reincarnated Dame Van Winkle or Hemingway bitch-goddess. She bites her nails and she is very intelligent, but she is not in any way self-conscious or affected. She is direct, polite in responses when she can hear questions, that is, when her hearing aid is working. She is honest and humorous. She is quite human. When George at the novel's end, himself realigned with his wife, family, and past, asks Niagara how she can reconcile her attempts to communicate with a mistreated dead scientist and her plans to marry a young, hippylike musicologist, she says, "Well, I can't kiss a dead man, can I?"

There is a magic in the way Zuravleff creates and develops these two unlikely friends, just as there is magic in the way she finds all her thematic and symbolic material in the world of refrigerator engineering and electricity.

Niagara's role as a catalyst in George's life begins when she asks why he has chosen engineering as a life's vocation. Anchored as he is in the physical, George resists answering even such a slightly probing question, even as he follows his attraction to Niagara. A few passionate kisses and George decides he will leave his wife and family for Niagara, forever. Yet this sudden fall from almost twenty years of fidelity to his loved and loving wife will not happen, because the physical is not the real substance of Niagara's force. The real electricity of Niagara is metaphysical. Powered by this force, George reshapes the principles of his life.

This level of connection is moved forward when, having given some superficial responses to Niagara's questions about his refrigeration vocation, George demands that she explain her decision to work on refrigeration. Niagara immediately answers: She needs the job to pay for her real life goal, an experiment in electricity. As a graduate at Caltech and now late at night in her rickety, hidden trailer-lab, she listens in on the frequencies of old cabinet radios, believing that she will some night connect with the wavelength on which the dead speak, that is, the frequency of souls. George finds this project incomprehensible.

At the same time, Niagara's questions start George dreaming of his early years, and speaking to Niagara about them. Thus Niagara brings forth from George not just sexual fantasies but new images and expressions of himself. That is, because of these dreams George relates to Niagara his psychological scars and his soul's guilt: the cruel putdowns he suffered from his mother; his father's passivity; the sudden disappearance of his pregnant teenage lover; his achievement of what he calls his life's only goal, the death of his mother, when he and his father unplug his brain-dead mother from life-sustaining machines. George also dreams and speaks of an important early positive experience. A nurturing couple, the Harrisons, hire him during his high school days to assist them in running Dino Park, a low-budget operation in which he displays his knowledge of dinosaurs and expands his mechanical and electrical talents. Through them, it seems, George finds enough self-esteem to succeed as an adult: finish college, pursue a career, marry, raise children.

During his conversations and other escapades with Niagara, George sharpens both his speaking skills and his listening powers, previously weakened by the familiarity and routine of his life at work with the Veteran and at home with his family. At first George does this so that he will not make a fool of himself with Niagara, but soon because he wants her to understand him and he wants to listen to what she says. In responding to Niagara's own direct and playful speech, George's more logical and reticent speech becomes direct and playful. Ironically, although she is hearing disabled, Niagara is a good listener, via her battery-powered hearing aid. That both George and Niagara connect with the metaphysical frequency—the frequency of souls—before the book's end, is made plausible from the ongoing interaction of these characters.

Their soul listening comes about first because George's former office mate, the retired Veteran, has a stroke. Niagara and George visit him in the hospital, where he is wired to life-support systems. That night, Niagara hears the Veteran's voice on one of her radio frequencies. He tells her is that he is dead, he wants the plugs still connected to his body to be pulled, and he wants to be cremated. The next morning, Niagara learns that when she heard the Veteran's voice, he was already dead. George scoffs at Niagara's story when he hears it; he is still not totally adept at listening.

Then comes George's own contact with the souls of the dead. On the day of the Veteran's funeral, attended by George's fellow employees and their spouses, including Judy, George's boss gives his workers the afternoon off. George and Judy change the day's plan: She goes off to work; he stays home to welcome Sheridan after school. Then George changes the planned dinner menu, and all are surprised but pleased. In this peaceful family setting, George resolves to give up Niagara and to stay with his family.

Late that night, dreams of Niagara and his mother waken George. In the early morning hours, he drives to Niagara's trailer to declare his love. Through the window he watches Niagara with his younger rival, the musicology professor who is the Veteran's son. When they leave, George starts vandalizing Niagara's treasured ancient wooden radios in a fit of jealousy. Always the engineer, however, he stops and plays with her radio frequencies. He hears two women in dialogue and realizes they are his dead aunt and dead mother. George's mother's confessions via the radio frequency heal George's inner trauma, but his listening poses a dilemma: How can he both disbelieve that there is a frequency of souls, or any metaphysical reality, and have such an experience? Whatever the outcome, George knows he no longer desires Niagara's physical gifts, for unexpectedly she has given him a spiritual one that reshapes his life even as he stays connected to his refrigeration job, his conventionally beautiful wife and matched-set offspring, and his suburban lifestyle.

In the novel's final scene, the major characters gather to watch George and Judy's son, Harris, present his science fair project, a machine through which sound waves generate cold temperatures. It is both a brilliant project and an expression of Harris' love for his father. Harris asks George to select the musical tape to start the machine, and though George chooses an unfamiliar one, the words that activate Harris' machine also express what George has experienced with Niagara. Meanwhile, Niagara leaves Coldpoint to take a research job in the religious studies department at the university where her musicologist boyfriend teaches.

Music, as in this last scene, is an important element throughout the novel. George loves gospel music, not, he says, for its religious meanings but because it connects him to his Kentucky roots. Yet during his period of metamorphosis from dullness to liveliness, from false contentment to new enthusiasm, he remembers or hears gospel music words that match his awakening experience. These words come to him on electrical frequencies.

Finally, the novel contains several allusions to Ralph Ellison's *Invisible Man* (1947), a novel overflowing with black spirituals, blues, and jazz. In *The Frequency of Souls*, there is only one black character, Shackelford, and his name perhaps refers to the shackles of slavery. As George's boss, Shackelford has resisted any real change in refrigeration design, thus contributing to George's passivity. Also George's middle name, Bledsoe, mentioned just once, recalls the school leader by that name in Ellison's novel. In *Invisible Man*, Bledsoe is a figure of the assimilationist and humble Booker T. Washington style black leader, who asks for no real change in the status of blacks in racist America. Most significant, Ellison's protagonist ends his journey underground and stealing his electricity from the power and light company that services New York City. He listens to black music, he is at rest, but he threatens to explode into the racially violent world above, some day. The last line spoken by Ellison's narrator is: "Who knows but that, on the lower frequencies, I speak for you?"

The Frequency of Souls succeeds in linking to refrigeration design and old radios its theme of listening to metaphysical frequencies for voices from within, for as Niagara tells George, perhaps in hearing his mother's voice he was really listening to his own buried truth. One can anticipate further literary fiction from Mary Kay Zuravleff, an unexpected descendant, perhaps, of Ralph Ellison.

Francine Dempsey

Sources for Further Study

Chicago Tribune. July 28, 1996, XIV, p. 5.
Los Angeles Times. June 12, 1996, p. E4.
New Scientist. CLI, July 6, 1996, p. 43.
The New York Times Book Review. CI, July 28, 1996, p. 19.
The Times Literary Supplement. May 17, 1996, p. 23.
The Washington Post Book World. XXVI, August 25, 1996, p. 11.

FROM BONDAGE
Volume III of *Mercy of a Rude Stream*

Author: Henry Roth (1906-1995)
Publisher: St. Martin's Press (New York). 397 pp. $25.95
Type of work: Novel
Time: The 1920's and 1990's
Locale: New York City, the Catskills, and Albuquerque

In the third of six projected novels, the first one to be published posthumously, Henry Roth continues to trace the sentimental education of alter ego Ira Stigman through his college years

Principal characters:
IRA STIGMAN, an eighty-nine-year-old author reflecting on his youth
M, his dead wife, a composer
MINNIE STIGMAN, his sister
STELLA, his cousin
MAMIE, his aunt and Stella's mother
ZAIDA (BEN ZION FARB), his pious maternal grandfather
LARRY GORDON, his best friend during college years
EDITH WELLES, a professor at New York University who befriends Larry and Ira
MARCIA MEEDE, a pioneering anthropologist
LEWLYN CRADDOCK, a sociologist, Marcia's husband and Edith's lover
ECCLESIAS, Ira's word processor

Some write for love, some for lucre, some for fame, others as a stay against oblivion. But shame is the engine that drives *From Bondage*, whose aging, arthritic narrator—like his author?—has been suffering from a "moral canker" for seven decades. Alone at the word processor he personifies as "Ecclesias," eighty-nine-year-old Ira Stigman exorcises the sordid secrets of a legendary, decades-long writer's block that he comes to attribute to incest and alienation.

If he had not been born, in Austro-Hungarian Galicia in 1906, Henry Roth might have been invented as a gloss on Moss Hart's remark that American lives lack second acts. When *Call It Sleep*—the classic American novel of the immigration experience, presented through the eyes of David Schearl, a sensitive, traumatized little boy— became a surprise best-seller in 1964, exactly thirty years after its debut, Roth had long since abandoned literary ambitions. It was not until 1990 that he published a second novel, *A Star Shines Over Mt. Morris Park*, the first installment of a cycle called *Mercy of a Rude Stream*. A sequel, *A Diving Rock on the Hudson*, followed in 1995, when Roth was eighty-nine. *From Bondage* is the third of the novels to trace the sentimental education of Ira Stigman, though the book can be read independently, and compulsively. Three additional volumes, completing the series, await publication. Set in the 1920's, volume 3 of *Mercy of a Rude Stream* is a Jewish-American *Künstlerroman*, a portrait of the thwarted artist as an anxious young man. Cross-cut with Ira's experiences during the mid-1920's, in his late teens and early twenties, and set in a different typescript are his current reflections as octogenarian author, alone with Ecclesias.

"This is a work of fiction," announces the copyright page, disingenuously. "This novel is certainly *not* an autobiography, nor should it be taken as such." Like *The First Man*, a book by Albert Camus not published until 1995 though he died in 1960, this first posthumous work by Roth, who died October 13, 1995, is a transparent nonfiction. Like the actual author, who was married to a musician named Muriel for more than fifty years, Ira Stigman has been widowed for five years from the woman he calls M. Their two sons, Herschel and Jess, sound much like Roth's own offspring Hugh and Jeremy. Like Roth himself, Stigman raised waterfowl in Maine after his early first novel enjoyed only modest success in New York.

Stigman and Roth both resumed writing in New Mexico, but *From Bondage* is a memoir of the period when each lived with mismatched parents on East 119th Street in East Harlem while attending the City College of New York (CCNY). That college's magazine *The Lavender* published "Impressions of a Plumber," a promising story that nevertheless earned Roth and his fictional alter ego a "D." Ira's best friend Larry Gordon, like Roth's buddy Lester Winter, is a dilettante who flits from poetry to sculpture to acting and becomes the lover of an English professor at New York University. Like her real-life prototype Edna Lou Walton, Edith Welles introduces the callow youths to intellectual celebrities such as Marcia Meede (Margaret Mead) and Louise Bogan (Louise Bogan). Not all names are changed to protect the innocent; though naïveté abounds, innocence vanished when the twenty-one-year-old Ira began vile, incestuous relations with his sister Minnie and his cousin Stella, ages eighteen and seventeen, respectively.

Ira, who shares a cottage with Edith and Larry during an exhilarating summer in Woodstock, New York, covets his buddy's lover, though he fears that domestic lechery has rendered him unworthy of the older, more sophisticated Gentile. Although he expects Edith to tire of the shallow Larry, who suffers from premature ejaculation, he does not count on her involvement with other men, including Lewlyn Craddock, a sociology instructor and Anglican priest. Ira is both exhilarated and dismayed to find himself treated as a neutral confidant, a mere and mediocre undergraduate made privy to remarkable romantic triangulations: Edith, Larry, and Lewlyn; Lewlyn, Marcia, and Cecilia; Marcia, Lewlyn, and Robert.

Before Edith and Ira become lovers, Edith serves as the uncouth young Jew's mentor, initiating him into the mysteries of James Joyce and T. S. Eliot, whose arcane texts he admires and then despises, for emotional sterility. Despite their dazzling stylistic virtuosity, the modernist masters abandoned, Ira comes to realize, the common people from whom art derives its power. His initial rapture over *Ulysses*, an outlawed work that he reads in a copy that Edith smuggles back from Europe, is undercut by his recognition that the novel was "an evasion of history; its author *resolved* to perceive nothing of the continuing evolution of Ireland, refusing to discover anything latent within the seeming inane of a day in 1904. History may have been a nightmare, but the ones who could have awakened him were the very ones he eschewed: his folk." Ira resents his feckless father Herman, a failed milkman turned waiter, for having forced the family to move away from the Lower East Side, a neighborhood in which it was much easier to feel part of the Jewish community. Although he flirts with Marxist abstractions, Ira comes to understand that he can overcome his creative aridity only by returning to the kindred ordinary Jews whom he sought to transcend and sexually abused. Late in life, he realizes that incest is a symptom of the arrested development that enabled him to devise a child's-eye masterpiece but obstructed other writing. Ira attributes his inability to achieve a sexual relationship with a mature woman outside his family to the same cause that prevented him from following up on his youthful novel of prepubescence: "his continued, his prolonged *infantilism.*" *From Bondage* diagnoses the emotional captivity from which Ira learned to liberate himself only much later and through his writing.

For Ira Stigman, as probably for Henry Roth behind him, the writing of a book that integrates the perspectives of an older author with his younger self is an attempt to overcome the "grave and disabling discontinuity" following the publication of his ambitious first novel. Roth, neglected for thirty years but revered now as a master of American Jewish literature, had spent much of the past three decades trying to explain why he had never published a book after *Call It Sleep*; yet his fictional Stigman spends much of *From Bondage* trying to justify writing *this* shocking, shameful book. He asks himself: "why was he doing this, demeaning himself—and perhaps Jews, the multitude of Jews who had transformed one previous novel into a shrine, a child's shrine at that—to the extent he was?" Is writing this lacerating good for the Jews? From an initial ambition to transcend the limitations of his origins in a poor family of immigrant Jews, Stigman eventually learns that the only way to attain the universal for which he yearns is through embrace of the parochial. He credits the renewal of literary creativity in his eighties to his belated identification with the Jewish people, particularly with the revived Jewish state, what he calls "the midwife of his rebirth: *Israel.*" He explains that: "It was Israel that had rescued him from Joyce, had rescued him from alienation, modified him even to tolerating the Diaspora. It was late in happening, true, but it *had* happened, and it succeeded in altering the orientation of the once withdrawn individual." From an individualist aesthete, Stigman sees himself transformed into a voice for his people, and it is by discovering and cultivating that voice that he is able to overcome his artistic and human obstructions, to write a novel very like the one that Roth constructs about him.

From Bondage, however, is not nearly as schematic or tendentious as this outline might suggest. It immerses its reader in the felt life of an earnest bounder, bound to move beyond the meager cold-water tenement of his uneducated parents into the enchanted intellectual bohemia that he imagines Edith inhabiting. A glossary at the back assists the Anglophonic reader in negotiating the Yiddish-speaking world that Ira Stigman meticulously, affectionately evokes decades after rejecting. Ira's menial jobs as a clerk in a fancy candy shop and as a grease monkey on a repair crew of the New York subway system are vividly rendered. So is the old man's frank desire for death; the Cumaean Sibyl's announcement *Apothanein thelo*, "I wish to die," is what the aging author asks to be inscribed and hung in his study in New Mexico. Yet suffusing and exalting all is Stigman's literary mission and his love for M, the musician he met at the Yaddo artists' colony so long ago and who is the object of the passionate homage expressed in the novel's final sentence.

When both are in their twenties, Ira envies the facile fertility of Larry, as well as his assimilation into middle-class America. "Larry could relate his adventures; they slipped easily through regular channels. His didn't, his were deformed, fitted no channel, could never be told." They are told, many years later, in *From Bondage*, a novel very much like the one that Ira Stigman, dying, struggles over in his agonizing, solitary sessions with Ecclesias. It is a book that overpowers with the force of delayed revelation and the hope of ultimate but earthly redemption. Whether or not the fictional author's mortifying disclosures are autobiographically accurate, Roth's book is a more enduring achievement than Larry's kind of conventional writing, which slips easily through regular channels, and into literary oblivion.

Roth begins and concludes this valedictory volume with allusions to Samuel Taylor Coleridge, under the sign of the Ancient Mariner—with an initial epigraph from the famous poem about an aging, obsessive storyteller and a concluding discussion of the line "He prayeth best, who loveth best." Like Coleridge's Wedding Guest, readers will be spellbound by vivid evocations of assignations, conversations, and job assignments seventy years ago. A tense nocturnal scene in Aunt Mamie's apartment, in which Ira slinks past "Zaida," his pious grandfather, and Mamie after an illicit tryst with his Cousin Stella is consummately constructed. Also memorable is a sequence in which Ira accompanies Edith to the pier in Hoboken, New Jersey—to see her lover Lewlyn off to England, where he intends to join another woman—and returns to sleep chastely beside Edith in her Greenwich Village bed. Puns and rhymes in Roth's trademark stream-of-consciousness are sometimes self-indulgent, and, in some extended dialogue, the aged author nods. Yet no non-nonagenarian has a right to patronize this man. Who touches this book touches a man in touch with the mysteries of creation and redemption. Roth once announced his ambition "to die with one's books on." Mixing memory and desire with revulsion and purgation, *From Bondage* is worthy raiment for final thoughts.

Steven G. Kellman

Sources for Further Study

Booklist. XCII, May 1, 1996, p. 1489.
Boston Globe. July 14, 1996, p. B33.
Kirkus Reviews. LXIV, April 15, 1996, p. 557.
Library Journal. CXXI, June 15, 1996, p. 94.
Los Angeles Times. September 18, 1996, p. E2.
The Nation. CCLXIII, September 23, 1996, p. 25.
The New York Times Book Review. CI, July 14, 1996, p. 6.
Publishers Weekly. CCXLIII, April 22, 1996, p. 59.
The Wall Street Journal. July 11, 1996, p. A12.

FULL HOUSE
The Spread of Excellence from Plato to Darwin

Author: Stephen Jay Gould (1941-   )
Publisher: Harmony Books (New York). 244 pp. $25.00
Type of work: Science

A persuasive case for rethinking evolution in terms of variety, not progress

Since he began writing a column for *Natural History*, Stephen Jay Gould has distinguished himself as one of America's foremost interpreters of Darwinian evolution for both the scientist and the general reader. He has a knack for making recent scientific findings accessible and interesting without condescending to the reader, often by fixating on one component of nature such as the panda's thumb or the taxonomy of wasps and using it to illustrate some principle of evolution. *Full House: The Spread of Excellence from Plato to Darwin* was written in conjunction with *Wonderful Life* (1989) to persuade his readership to reconsider their conception of humanity as the crowning achievement of evolution. Gould posits a complete reversal of this anthropocentric view in which animals adapt over time into more complex, superior forms. Instead, he claims evolution is fundamentally passive and does not progress at all.

To help readers understand the basis of his theories, Gould returns again and again to Charles Darwin's *Origin of Species*, much of which sets out to prove three basic principles, which Gould lists as follows:

1. All organisms tend to produce more offspring than can possibly survive.
2. Offspring vary among themselves, and are not carbon copies of an immutable type.
3. At least some of this variation is passed down by inheritance to future generations.

From these inferences, Darwin can conclude that "survivors will tend to be those individuals with variations that are fortuitously best suited to changing local environments." Thus woolly mammoths are hairy because hair best suits the cold Siberian climate. Interestingly, Gould points out how Darwin disliked the word "evolution," since it emphasized progress. The word "adaptation" better captures the passive nature of species changeover.

To modify the contemporary perception of evolution, Gould focusses on variations within entire systems which can be graphed out statistically. Gould's graphs show that any consideration of an average life form ignores the wide assortment of variations surrounding it. After giving his lay readers a crash course in statistics, Gould then provides multiple examples of wrong-headed "ladders" needing to be replaced with the broader picture of a full house of variation, a methodology which applies equally well to help analyze changes in baseball, cancer prognoses, and trapeze artistry, as well as to the evolution of different species. His examples of complex organisms that inhabit the earth in the late twentieth century—humans, horses—are only incidental offshoots of a gigantic "bush" that could just as easily have not produced humans.

Gould painstakingly teaches the reader his conceptual apparatus. For example, a bell curve suggests an even distribution of something, like a selection of graded assignments that can be "curved" to cover all grades equally. In nature, however, distributions are more often skewed in one direction with a "wall" forming one limit of possibility and a "tale" stretching beyond the frame of the graph. Given the assumption that life began in primordial soup billions of years ago as single-celled organisms, life had no way to evolve but toward multicellular creatures. The fact that life was just beginning formed one "wall" of variation while more complex multicellular organisms evolved along the opposite side of the graph. Any time some activity produces a variety of results, be it biological or cultural, a graph depicting the contraction and expansion of that variation provides a better picture of reality than a study of some average arbitrarily chosen within it. Thus Gould debunks the idea of a Platonic ideal man since it leads people to ignore all the variant humans that nature randomly produces.

To a large extent, Gould reports his findings in opposition to any essentialist view of the world. In keeping with the search for some ideal form, scientists in the past have looked for average samples which make all variations mere aberrations of nature. Thus, classical thinkers thought that there was just one sex, male, and the female sex was a degraded variation of the ideal male. More recently, people still tend to think that homosexuality is an aberration on the "ideal" heterosexual impulse, whereas nature produces multiple forms of sexuality. This search for the fallacious average or ideal takes the statistical form of tracing means, modes, and medians plotted along the rates of distribution. Gould uses his personal experience of learning that he was likely to die of cancer in eight months to show that all such averages can easily mislead scientists or doctors when they fail to take in account the entire system of variation. Upon learning that he had only eight months to live after a diagnosis of abdominal mesothelioma, Gould figured out that his proposed life expectancy was skewed, and that in his particular case he had a far better chance of survival, which proved correct. All he had to know was where he stood on the graph. Little wonder that political spin doctors use exactly the same statistical methods to prove contradictory claims about the economy or a president's polls. The average can easily falsify the true variety of any kind of data.

Once he sets up his methodology, Gould uses it to prove the fallacy of earlier interpretations of Darwin's theories. He critiques the "scientific" representations of prehistoric times chronicling evolution that jumps from invertebrates to reptiles in a dramatic display of progress. In their desire to create a ladder of increasingly complex animals, the artists neglect to show that invertebrates thrive to this day and in some cases have proven more adaptable to their environment than vertebrates have. Next, he takes apart the famous charts prepared by Othniel C. Marsh and William D. Matthew showing the horse's evolution from small three-toed animals to the "superior" animals of today. Looking at the evolution of horse species as a whole, one finds a complex "bush" of different species growing larger and smaller, while the contemporary horse just happened to survive as a small twig on a much larger but now extinct bush of related species.

Possibly worried that all these graphs might alienate his general readership, Gould spends one quarter of his study showing how baseball statistics indicate contemporary baseball's general superiority to the era between 1900 and 1930 when players such as Ty Cobb and "Shoeless" Joe Jackson sometimes exceeded a .400 batting average. While sports commentators have decried the disappearance of the .400 batting average since the 1930's with elaborate theories and presuppositions of the decline of the modern athlete, Gould simply graphs out the narrowing of variation along a skewed distribution. Batters fail to bat above .400 because the rest of the game—pitching and outfielding—has markedly improved and, therefore, reduced variation in batting averages. Professional baseball batters are thus not worse but better in a more fine-tuned game, and anyone who eventually does beat the .400 level will have accomplished far more than his peers sixty years ago. Just as he triumphantly figures out that he can survive cancer, so Gould also shows how baseball has actually improved even though players no longer maintain a .400 batting average.

Given Gould's criteria, rats, bats, and antelopes share a successful evolutionary growth amongst the mammals, but he ultimately finds bacteria the most fundamental and adaptable creatures of all. Not only is bacteria the most dominant, the most varied, the longest lasting species on earth, they even digest the food consumed by humans. Gould claims that since the beginning of life on the planet, there has been just one "Age of Bacteria." Bacteria can survive deep within the earth's crust and may even inhabit other supposedly barren planets. At the same time, bacteria lack the charismatic appeal of dinosaurs, pandas, and jellyfish. If they provide the new model for Darwinian excellence, they also pose a problem for the direction of Gould's theories. One might find it difficult to get excited about the evolutionary superiority of bacteria, even if the graphs prove it to be so.

Gould makes a persuasive case for rethinking how evolution works, but he may at times leave his popular readership behind. In places, this book would better suit as a monograph for scientists, such as E. O. Wilson, who disagree with Gould on this issue. Gould seems to know this, hence his modest proposal for readers to bear with him and they will benefit by the end of the book. The technical nature of statistics, even when applied to baseball records, confronts readers with mathematics and skewed distributions when they might have been expecting charming examples of animals illustrating Darwinian principles. Gould does bend over backward to help readers by supplying multiple examples proving his thesis, by reiterating and summarizing major aspects of his methodology, and by drawing on popular culture, sports, and even his personal crisis for illustrations. Since his principle method relies heavily on mathematics and graphs, however, such sophisticated use of figures may frustrate and confuse some readers.

Furthermore, Gould fails to work out the many possible implications of his findings for us. His brief epilogue only marginally considers the implications of his study for human culture. Having pointed out that technology definitely progresses, Gould admits that humans still share much the same physical makeup as their earliest ancestors. Physically, biological limitations bind humans as technology grows with a distinctively unnatural virulence. Thus, circus trapeze artists have already reached a wall or statistical limit with four somersaults in the air. Writers may reach a given limit in exploring a style of speech. Yet the key question of how this new interpretation will affect the way humans see themselves remains unanswered.

Gould hints at the difficulty of working out these implications when he discusses Darwin's ambivalence on this issue in *Origin of Species*. Living in a period when Victorians viewed progress as key to their understanding of the world, Darwin waffled. He seemed to know the radical implications of his study, but still bowed to societal pressure when he wrote "all corporeal and mental endowments will tend to progress towards perfection." Darwin tries to unite science with a prevailing ideology, but Gould does not attempt this for his view of a passive nature. Gould wants to temper the arrogance of humans with respect to their position in the world, but what alternative can he offer to replace it? A resigned acceptance of humans' evolutionary inconsequentiality? A grudging admission of the evolutionary superiority of bacteria?

Readers can sense some of Gould's ambivalence over the implications of his study in his subtitle to his book *The Spread of Excellence from Plato to Darwin*. The word "spread" refers to the spread of variation within the full house of statistical analysis, but where does "excellence" fit into this schema and why is Plato included at all? Platonic theories of the ideal are summarily discarded by Gould's new paradigm; they are now seen as delusions wiped away by science. Finally, "excellence" seems a strangely hierarchical term to apply to a vision of nature that prioritizes variation over the ideal. If the entire spread of variation is excellent, what is left to be inferior? The full house of skewed distribution implies a new democratization of all species. Only survival and the amount of variation determine excellence, a principle that can apply as easily to parasites as humans. In the end, Gould just touches on some of the implications of the paradigm-shift he proposes. Perhaps he intends for readers to decide what to do with his findings.

Roy C. Flannagan

Sources for Further Study

Audubon. XCVIII, September, 1996, p. 112.
The Chronicle of Higher Education. XLIII, September 6, 1996, p. A23.
Library Journal. CXXI, July, 1996, p. 149.
Los Angeles Times Book Review. October 20, 1996, p. 10.
Nature. CCCLXXXIII, October 31, 1996, p. 771.
New Scientist. CLII, October 5, 1996, p. 46.
The New York Review of Books. XLIII, October 17, 1996, p. 33.
The New York Times Book Review. CI, September 22, 1996, p. 9.
Publishers Weekly. CCXLIII, June 24, 1996, p. 36.
The Wall Street Journal. September 5, 1996, p. A14.

GENESIS
Translation and Commentary

Author: Robert Alter (1935-   )
Publisher: W. W. Norton (New York). 324 pp. $25.00
Type of work: Literary criticism

A new version of the Book of Genesis underscores its lexical and narrative subtlety

Robert Alter's translation of Genesis is one of several to appear recently—along with versions by Everett Fox (1995) and Stephen Mitchell (1996)—that has attempted to restore accuracy and power to modern versions of the text, qualities that have been lost in theologically tendentious or verbally stilted renderings. The inaccuracies of the immensely powerful and influential King James Version have to be confronted, as well as the problem of matching or overcoming its high tones that have been indelibly etched in the English imagination. Alter's work addresses these problems and raises new ones.

Scholars and general students of the Bible, even those with little knowledge of ancient Hebrew, have benefited from Alter's powerful studies *The Art of Biblical Narrative* (1981) and *The Art of Biblical Poetry* (1985), in which he has pointed to the immense subtlety and skill of the writing of the Hebrew Bible, qualities of verbal resonance and structure that cannot be separated from its message. His account, for example, of the story of Judah and Tamar of Genesis 38 reveals how a seemingly spurious story in the midst of the Joseph narrative actually complements the main story in both its underlying structure and in very definite verbal leitmotifs. Alter provides a very important antidote to the assumptions made by Stephen Mitchell in his recent version of Genesis that the additions of a redactor interested in making a coherent narrative mar the essential power of the "original" stories. It is certainly not easy to determine what is and what is not original in Genesis, who are the various authors, and where an editor or editors may or may not have added something. As a book, Genesis occupies an extremely powerful place in human culture, and Alter's assumption of narrative complexity and coherence is far more compelling than Mitchell's tempting metaphor of an original canvas that has been painted over and needs to be restored. The fact is that Mitchell's own vision finds much in Genesis that is disturbing or contradictory and would better be left aside.

Much in Genesis is disturbing, contradictory, and obscure, and much of its power derives from holding unresolved contradictions in tension, from allowing readers to sense—as the great critic Eric Auerbach has pointed out—the shadows and silences looming in the background of everything in it. It invites, if not demands, commentary and speculation. Alter has tended to make his insights literary as opposed to theological. He wants readers to see the thematic and verbal warp and woof of the tapestry as a way into its meaning, leaving theology and theodicy to those so inclined. Alter's approach also makes translation a particularly fruitful vehicle for interpretation. Yet there is a problem with his approach that can also be found in the other recent translations of Everett Fox and Stephen Mitchell: What does it mean to talk about Genesis or the Bible as literary work or as stories? In his very clear and forceful introduction, Alter writes:

> Our own cultural preconceptions of writers scrupulously devoted to finding exactly the right word are associated with figures like Flaubert and Joyce, who meticulously chose terms of their narratives from a large repertory of finely discriminated lexical items. Biblical prose often exhibits an analogous precision within the severe limits of its primary vocabulary.

Alter makes the case for the precision of biblical writers quite convincingly. Nevertheless, the language and style of the Bible has to be considered in relation to a vision of the subject matter and cultural place of the book: Genesis is a book about the origin of the world, God and man's relation to God, and has been and for many still is a sacred text. These facts should come into play in any translation if it is to be meaningful and powerful. The sense of the terror and mystery of its primary character—God—and the moral power and depravity of some of its most important characters—Adam, Eve, the serpent, Abraham, Jacob, and Joseph—need to be conveyed in a way that recognizes its difference, intrinsically and extrinsically, from almost all other books. At the very least, the translator needs to convey the book's central force—immense power and mystery seen through haunting simplicity. If the elevation and highness of the King James Version is not true to the text, it still lends the book some measure of power. On the lexical level, Alter gives readers much that is fresh, clear, and important. Ultimately, however, it is not as compelling as one would expect, and some of the problems seem to be a result of some of Alter's literary concerns and a diffidence or lack of inspiration that comes through at the aural level.

There are a couple of important places in the translation when things seen to be inexplicably flat or suffering from copyediting problems. One passage occurs in the very beginning. What the King James Version—not to mention the New Jerusalem Bible, Fox, and Mitchell—gives as "In the beginning God created the heavens and the earth," Alter renders as "When God began to create the heaven and earth. . . . " His version places emphasis on the state of things at that time rather than on the mystery conveyed by the phrase, which suggests both a definite and indefinite origin as well as announcing the supreme, encompassing power of the creator. Both translations are permitted by the grammar of the Hebrew, although the verb *bara* expresses an act of creativity distinct from that of man. Alter rarely fails to footnote his important decisions, and one is surprised to find there is no accounting of this one.

The rendering of Eve's encounter with the serpent (Genesis 3:1-5) reveals ways in which Alter's concern with accuracy seem to interfere with drama. The serpent's first words to Eve are translated "Though God said, you shall not eat from any tree of the garden. . . . " Alter justifies this reading as the beginning of a false statement ("though" being more accurate than the traditional "truly") interrupted and corrected by Eve. Yet the punctuation and wooden tone of Alter's version tend to force readers to the footnote for clarification. They need to hear the serpent's cunning, which may indeed include false premises or a clever way of directing Eve's attention to the taboo. Although

Mitchell's translation has other problems, his rendering of the serpent's pick-up line contains a world of convincing drama: "Did God really say that you're not allowed to eat from any tree in the garden?" This is colloquial and more sinister because of it. The passage also suggests the intriguing possibility that a conversation might have been in progress before the narrative begins. The rest of Alter's version has powerful and provocative parallel diction, that the forbidden tree was "lust to the eyes . . . and lovely to look at." The passage is marred, however, by what can only be taken as an error in punctuation: "And the serpent said to the woman, 'You shall be doomed to die.' For God knows that on the day you eat . . . " By ending the serpent's dialogue after the word "die," Alter's translation appears to be inserting a third voice into the narrative. Surely there are enough voices in Genesis that there is no need for another. This error underscores what is obvious to many who have dealt with trade and university presses alike—the lack of care and responsibility in the copyediting stage of production.

One place where Alter paradoxically succeeds and fails at the same time is in what is both literally and metaphorically the central story of the book, Abraham and Isaac. Alter recognizes and underscores the important motif of vision and sight in this story that begins when Abraham goes to the mountain as God commanded him: "On the third day Abraham raised his eyes and saw the place from afar." In the haunting moment when Isaac wonders where the sheep is for an offering, Abraham responds with a line of infinite tension, "God will see to the sheep for the offering, my son." "See to" is usually translated "provide," and Alter sacrifices the idiomatic force of that word for an underscoring of its fossil poetry—the notion of flight which is then echoed in the naming of the mountain, "on the mount of the Lord there is sight." One gets the lexical thread and other ambiguities but in a way that hardly seems idiomatic. In another moment in the same story, Abraham is seen directing his servant (or slaves) about his sons: "And Abraham said to his lads, 'Sit you here with the donkey and let me and the lad walk ahead and let us worship and return to you.'" All the "lads" makes this sound like an anecdote about the Beatles. Certainly, the King James Version uses "lad" but allows for a distinction in this passage between "lad" and "boy" in reference to Isaac. Alter points out in his commentary that the repetition points to an irony about the relation of Isaac to the slaves and to his father, but this subtlety should be left to the commentary and find less clumsy language in the text. Alter might better have gone for readability and force in the text and left the unpacking to the commentary, which in his case is almost always clear and thoughtful (and, happily, available at the bottom of the page rather than at the back of the book).

Alter has given readers a Genesis that will be very useful to students who want to approach the book with a minimum of theological cant and who want to appreciate the subtlety and complexity of its composition. He avoids the problems of Everett Fox's emphasis on recovering all of the sonorities of the Hebrew, thereby creating a version which can be described as the scaffolding or notes toward a supreme translation but, as it is, remains between two languages. Although Stephen Mitchell has an excellent ear and a vision of the stories of Genesis, his inability to accept the book as whole mars his translation. If Mitchell's ear could combine with Alter's sense of lexical precision and narrative, we would be on the way to a truly great translation. Yet the ideal translator of Genesis is also going to have to risk a vision of what this book means, of what God means, in the life of our culture.

Robert Faggen

Sources for Further Study

Booklist. XCIII, September 1, 1996, p. 38.
Boston Globe. October 13, 1996, p. N16.
Library Journal. CXXI, August, 1996, p. 77.
The National Review. XLVIII, December 9, 1996, p. 61.
The New York Times Book Review. CI, December 15, 1996, p. 7.
Publishers Weekly. CCXLIII, November 4, 1996, p. 46.
San Francisco Chronicle. October 6, 1996, p. REV1.
The Washington Post Book World. XXVI, December 8, 1996, p. 5.

THE GIANT'S HOUSE
A Romance

Author: Elizabeth McCracken
Publisher: Dial Press (New York). 259 pp. $19.95
Type of work: Novel
Time: The 1950's to the 1990's
Locale: Brewsterville, Cape Cod, Massachusetts

A small-town librarian falls in love with a young boy afflicted with gigantism, although she knows he will live an unnatural life and die at an early age

Principal characters:
PEGGY CORT, a young, unmarried librarian
JAMES CARLSON SWEATT, the "giant" of the novel
MRS. SWEATT, his mother, an alcoholic
CALVIN SWEATT, his father
CAROLINE STRICKLAND, Calvin's effervescent sister
OSCAR STRICKLAND, her husband, a would-be artist

As both a former professional librarian and a writer trained in her craft, Elizabeth McCracken is doubly aware of the need for order. Having spent several years dealing with overdue books and irrational patrons, McCracken is well aware that even with the best of systems, one is frequently faced with irregularities. In her fiction, McCracken emphasizes the fact that in this respect, the larger world is no different from any library. She likes to create characters who defy norms, such as the tattoo artist, the casual levitator, the armless mother, and the various sideshow performers in her short-story collection *Here's Your Hat, What's Your Hurry* (1993), and the boy who cannot stop growing in *The Giant's House*. McCracken's focus, however, is less on such characters than on how their presence affects those around them. The more human beings depend on predictable patterns, McCracken suggests, the more they are threatened by the inevitable confrontations with people who do not fit the norms. Often they respond with unfeeling curiosity, even with unconcealed antipathy. Sometimes, however, through these encounters people catch a glimpse of a divine order that is not bound by human limitations. Sometimes, like the librarian in *The Giant's House*, they may even be transformed by the experience, forever changed through the redemptive power of love.

Peggy Cort, the narrator and the real protagonist of *The Giant's House*, is a small-town librarian who presents herself in somewhat stereotypical terms. At twenty-five, fresh from library school, she has found her identity in her library, much in the same way, she muses, that some women are possessed by their marriages. While she remembers often being overcome by hatred for the library building, which is as inadequate and as undependable as the worst of husbands, she has a peculiar fondness for it, as well as a deep love for the books it contains and the information that can be found in them. Indeed, the happiest moments in her rather prosaic life come when she is asked to find a reference for one of her patrons. For a librarian, Peggy explains, knowledge is the bond between people, and the gift of knowledge is an expression of love.

Unlike everyone else in Brewsterville, who seem aware only of James Carlson Sweatt's amazing stature, Peggy sees him as exceptional for very different reasons. While other eleven-year-old boys rarely come to the library, he is an avid reader. Moreover, he almost invariably returns his books on time and in good condition, and, best of all, he is one of the few patrons who makes use of Peggy's skills as a reference librarian. As soon as she recognizes these virtues in James, Peggy is already half in love with him.

Yet when she comes to know him better, Peggy sees that although James may be unique as far as his appearance is concerned, the two of them have even more in common than intellectual curiosity and a passion for books—they are isolated in a small town that only pretends to accept anyone who is different. In Brewsterville, James is viewed not as a human being, but as a freak, while Peggy is seen not as a living, breathing woman, but as a functionary, a useful piece of furniture, as she comments with some bitterness.

James and Peggy are alike in another way, too. Both of them have the capacity for love. By nature, James is kindly and unassuming; Peggy, on the other hand, is initially a bit waspish, but eventually her passion for James leaves no room for any unworthy feelings. In the second part of the novel, although Peggy still has her position at the library, she is devoting most of her energy to James's welfare. By the time he is seventeen, James is too large to fit into the furniture used by ordinary people, and it is obvious that he can no longer stay inside the house of his aunt, Caroline Strickland, and her kind-hearted husband Oscar, with whom Mrs. Sweatt and James have made their home ever since they were abandoned. It is Peggy who spearheads a drive for money to build a cottage for James behind the Stricklands' house, and, once he is installed in it, Peggy spends all of her spare time there. Although by now she knows that she is helplessly in love with him, she is not possessive. She encourages high school friends to stop by, and she even tries to supply him with a girlfriend of his own age. She also modifies her car so that she can take him on trips, including one to the wedding of the girl with whom she had tried to involve him and another to New York. Once in New York City, James stays at the Astor, appears in Madison Square Garden, and hurts Peggy's feelings by flirting with another exception to the human rule, a woman billed as the smallest in the world.

If McCracken had not chosen to use first-person narration, she would undoubtedly have remarked on how much her protagonist has changed. Since Peggy is telling the story, however, one has to look in her account itself to see the difference in her outlook on life. No longer is Peggy concerned with the failings of her patrons or her fellow workers, nor does she feel impelled to describe herself as a lonely and isolated person. She is too busy to think about herself. If she did have the inclination to reflect on her own life, Peggy might notice that she is no longer lonely. She not only has James but also has a family. From her first visit to their home, the Stricklands have accepted her without question, and now they involve her as fully in their dreams, their plans, their problems, and even their differences of opinion as if she were a blood relation. In the high-spirited but highly practical Caroline, Peggy has truly found not only a loyal friend but a sister.

Nevertheless, Peggy's happiness cannot last. Although she and James become engaged, his failing health makes it impossible for them ever to marry. In time, Peggy shares his bed, but James cannot consummate their relationship. There is one fall too many, and he dies, leaving Peggy to wonder whether love is worth such grief and pain.

At this point, it appears that Peggy's later life may follow the same pattern as that of James's mother, who never recovered from losing the man she loved. Having given herself wholly to him, somehow she lost track of herself. Her loss of identity is symbolized by the fact that no one seems to remember her given name; throughout the novel, even her sister-in-law always refers to her merely as "Mrs. Sweatt." Even though she loves her son, Mrs. Sweatt cannot find his existence or even his need for her sufficient reason for continuing with her life. While she occasionally functions as a mother, at least to the extent of going to the library to pick up books for James, Mrs. Sweatt leaves most of her maternal duties to Caroline Strickland. Her goal is to drink herself to death, and eventually she succeeds in doing so.

In the third and final section of the novel, however, Peggy evades the fate of James's miserable mother. Ironically, the agent of her liberation is the man who broke Mrs. Sweatt's heart. There is no hint of this happy outcome at Peggy's first encounter with Calvin Sweatt, for immediately after introducing him to Peggy, Caroline announces that his primary interest is the possibility of his having inherited some money from his son. Peggy soon finds that, although Calvin never provided any financial support for his son, he did at least keep in touch with him. The signatory initials in some of the correspondence she found among James's effects, she suddenly realizes, were those of his father. Calvin also tells her that he saw James and spoke with him by telephone during the trip to New York, a fact that James never mentioned to Peggy. Calvin also has a different explanation as to why he abandoned his family from that which Mrs. Sweatt had always given. It was not so much James's illness that drove him away, he says, as his wife's annoying habit of asking unanswerable questions and then hounding him for the answers.

As she processes this new information, Peggy is taking another significant step in her development. Already she has learned the importance of love; now she is coming to understand that no human being can ever learn everything about another. As much as she loved James, and as much they both loved facts, there were always things about him and his life which he would not, or could not, reveal to her. Her conversations with Calvin also make her aware of the limitations of all human knowledge, whether it is found within books or relayed in conversation. Although she will never be certain how much of what Calvin says about his motives is actually true, this new and wiser Peggy comes to like him on his own terms.

It is Peggy's encounter with Calvin which turns *The Giant's House* from a tragic story of the loss of love into a "romance," to quote the subtitle, in which unlikely events conspire to produce a story with a happy ending. In addition to forcing her to understand the limits of knowledge, Calvin fulfills two of Peggy's most pressing needs. As she comments, he is a very good listener, and since Calvin is just as interested in hearing about James as Peggy is in talking about him, Calvin provides her with an opportunity to vent her grief.

Moreover, by a strange twist of fate, Calvin also gives Peggy a reason to proceed with her life. At the end of his visit, he and Peggy find themselves in bed together. She later castigates herself for having become involved with any man other than James, and certainly with a man she still does not fully trust, and Calvin leaves with a puzzled, apologetic note to her, shortly thereafter to disappear as he had done so many years before. Some time later, Peggy discovers that she is pregnant. Being left with a baby and no husband could have made Peggy as disconsolate as the late Mrs. Sweatt. Nevertheless, the child proves to be her salvation. No longer encumbered by her old passion for accuracy, Peggy chooses to believe that James is the real father of the child she is carrying. Admittedly, even without Calvin in the picture, there is ample gossip, and eventually Peggy is dismissed from the library. In McCracken's romance, however, there is the expected happy ending. Thanks to Caroline's initiative, a private museum has been set up in the cottage, and Peggy is the obvious person to serve as curator. After the birth of her child, Peggy is blissfully happy, and even much later, when her daughter is grown and gone, Peggy can devote the rest of her life to telling the curious world about her beloved giant.

Rosemary M. Canfield Reisman

Sources for Further Study

American Libraries. XXVII, August, 1996, p. 15.
Booklist. XCII, May 15, 1996, p. 1569.
Boston Globe. July 14, 1996, p. B33.
Library Journal. CXXI, July, 1996, p. 165.
Los Angeles Times Book Review. September 15, 1996, p. 6.
The New York Times Book Review. CI, July 7, 1996, p. 8.
The New Yorker. LXXII, July 29, 1996, p. 74.
Publishers Weekly. CCXLIII, May 6, 1996, p. 66.
San Francisco Chronicle. July 14, 1996, p. REV 5.
The Washington Post Book World. XXVI, November 10, 1996, p. 6.

GIVING OFFENSE
Essays on Censorship

Author: J. M. Coetzee (1940-   )
Publisher: University of Chicago Press (Chicago). 289 pp. $24.95
Type of work: Essays

Coetzee provides a philosophical and political review of the concept and implementation of censorship in various Western and Communist regimes during the twentieth century

Giving Offense: Essays on Censorship is not a systematic analysis of the modern phenomenon of censorship. Rather, it is a collection of a dozen essays which appeared in a number of periodicals such as *Salmagundi, Mosaic, Neophilologus, Social Dynamics,* and *Raritan* during the period 1988-1993. As a consequence, the volume lacks a consistency of argumentation; however, this minor flaw (if it can even be called that) is more than compensated for by a clarity of vision and a deep understanding on the part of an author who has some firsthand experience with the subject: J. M. Coetzee is a distinguished novelist and respected academician who has lived in a country which, until 1993, officially sanctioned censorship. Coetzee is passionately opposed to any form of official censorship, and the essays in this collection detail the dangers of this practice to the creative process. This is not a "history of censorship," Coetzee insists; it is instead "an attempt to understand a passion with which" he has "no intuitive sympathy." The book is also a tribute to the men and women who have withstood the censor's gaze and defied official prohibitions to produce works of art which reveal aspects of the human spirit that some would rather see kept hidden from view.

Throughout his study, Coetzee deals with the philosophical and sociological implications of censorship. Relying primarily on the work of twentieth century politicians, philosophers, and literary theorists, he mines his considerable store of academic learning, bringing to bear as well the thoughts of classical, medieval, Renaissance, and Enlightenment figures who have confronted the phenomenon of censorship in their own times. Throughout, Coetzee is eloquent in his analysis of the mind of the censor and the reaction of the writer who knows he or she is being watched.

The initial chapters provide an overview of censorship in the modern world and expose Coetzee's personal biases. A liberal in the mold of English philosopher John Stuart Mill, Coetzee argues for a free-market approach to art and literature, convinced that works with no redeeming artistic value will have little impact on the public. In these introductory chapters the author is careful to lay the groundwork for exploring the two forms of censorship with which he will deal: the suppression of so-called pornographic materials, banned as a means of preserving the moral character of a society; and the squelching of political opposition through prohibitions on publication of literature that exposes weakness or corruption in the ruling government.

Coetzee follows this overview with a sensitive and balanced analysis of one of the most celebrated cases of censorship in the twentieth century: the suppression of

D. H. Lawrence's novel *Lady Chatterly's Lover*. Relying on both the public record of the outcry against the work and the novelist's own critique of the tale, Coetzee shows how the act of censorship is based on the naïve belief that such actions can have lasting effect. The censors are always wrong, Coetzee argues, because by their actions they assure the work a welcome among a reading public whose curiosity is heightened by the attention it has received. The endurance of Lawrence's work is testimony to the failure of official censorship, because it illustrates a principle Coetzee sees at the heart of such actions: "The more draconically the state comes down on writing, the more seriously it is seen to be taking writing; the more seriously it is seen to be taking writing, the more attention is paid to writing; the more attention is paid to writing, the more the disseminative potential to writing grows."

The same argument can be extended to other art forms, Coetzee argues, and in his fourth essay, "The Harms of Pornography," he takes on a group who have been decidedly liberal in most of their political activities, but who have recently come out in favor of censorship: the feminists. Like so many others on the political Left, feminists have vehemently criticized political censorship. Beginning in the 1960's, however, a number of feminist writers have been in the forefront of a movement to restrict production and dissemination of art, literature, and film which depicts women in demeaning ways. Coetzee deals with the issue head-on, choosing as his target the works of critic Catharine MacKinnon. Judging her argument to be simplistic, he shows how the strident rhetoric condemning the results of sexual exploitation is really overkill; in his opinion, she and her feminist colleagues overestimate the significance of pornography in shaping attitudes toward women (although he admits it is a pervasive influence in the United States).

Having rebuffed the feminists' arguments for censorship, Coetzee abruptly shifts gears and includes a lengthy commentary on the career and writings of the Renaissance writer Desiderius Erasmus. Using the writings of French philosophers Michel Foucault and Jacques Lacan as his guides, Coetzee explains how Erasmus' *The Praise of Folly* (1509) can be viewed as a way for the writer to enter into political debate while still shielding himself from the censor's grasp. There emerges from the essay a sense that Erasmus is Coetzee's Writer/Critic-as-Hero, a man who speaks the truth under the guise of folly and brings to light the foibles of both sides of a debate raging in the Renaissance humanist's lifetime. By far the most complex and dense argument in the book, "Erasmus: Madness and Rivalry" is a review of the nature of power and powerlessness, demonstrating ways a writer can turn the tables on powerful political figures through his manipulation of language. Coetzee's essay on Erasmus requires careful analysis to understand how the writer's understanding of madness, or folly, shapes his argument and allows him to rise above the political fray about which he writes.

The next two chapters focus on writers from the Soviet Union: the poet Osip Mandelstam and the novelist Aleksandr Solzhenitsyn. Like the previous essay on Erasmus, the one on Mandelstam offers a detailed examination of a single literary work. In his analysis of Mandelstam's "Ode to Stalin," Coetzee takes the controversial position that the work is actually first-rate art, even though it was written as a forced apology to Stalin by a poet threatened with exile and even death for works written earlier in his career which ridicule the Soviet dictator. The critique of the "Ode to Stalin" shows how writing in a climate of censorship affects the writer's psyche.

Coetzee's essay on Solzhenitsyn begins with an excellent summary of the history of Soviet censorship, tracing its roots to the eighteenth century. He also explains how *Novy Mir*, the curious publication sponsored by the government which claimed to promote avant garde writing did in fact serve as a form of "dissidence," even when its editor was forced to reject some of the more radical work submitted to him. Coetzee's portrait of Solzhenitsyn is not particularly flattering, however; the writer is presented as egotistical, self-centered, and convinced of the rightness of his political position. Defiant in his attitude toward the political bureaucracy, he seems to take pleasure in using others to assure that his works reach both the Russian reading public who had access to *samizdat* (writing circulated in manuscript) and to a larger audience in the West.

Coetzee rounds out his discussion of censorship behind the Iron Curtain with a brief analysis of the career of Polish poet Zbigniew Herbert. The trials Herbert faced in getting his work past the censor are another good example of what is required of an artist forced to work in a regime where censorship is the norm. The sensitive reading of Herbert's work and the equally sympathetic description of the poet's difficulties with the government serve as prelude to the final four chapters in the book, in which Coetzee turns his attention to his homeland.

Unquestionably, some of the greatest restrictions on writers have been imposed on those living in South Africa during the twentieth century. Motivated by a belief that only through strict control of art in all its forms could apartheid be preserved, the censors of South Africa have been stern in reviewing the works of novelists and poets who, predictably, have attempted to dramatize the evils of racial segregation. Perhaps the most intriguing essay in the entire collection is Coetzee's analysis of the works of Geoffrey Cronjé, a leading South African intellectual whose treatises on apartheid provide justification for the government's century-long effort to control the black and colored segments of the population and keep them separate from white South Africans. In the following chapter, Coetzee tries to get into the mind of the South African censor by examining the writings of J. C. W. Van Rooyen, a member of the Publications Appeal Board, which until the 1990's had final authority for judging the acceptability of literary works.

Having laid out the position of the censor, Coetzee turns his attention to the writers who have had to work under conditions imposed by a repressive government. He begins by reviewing the career of novelist Andre Brink, who, like Coetzee, took time away from writing fiction to explain the plight of the writer in South Africa in a penetrating examination of the phenomenon of censorship, *Writing in a State of Siege* (1982). The final chapter is an extended analysis of the poetry of Coetzee's countryman Breyten Breytenbach. Coetzee discusses several works by a poet whose writing was banned frequently by South African politicians who knew that beneath the metaphors and brilliant imagery there resides a strong strain of protest against the apartheid regime.

Most who write on censorship view censors as authority figures imposing their wills on writers, artists, and filmmakers. The censor is frequently described as a kind of father figure, a model popularized by Sigmund Freud. While not denying the appropriateness of that role, Coetzee, following the brilliant analysis of censorship by French philosopher René Girard, concentrates on the censor-as-rival. Both the writer and the censor see themselves in competition for the attention of the reader. Coetzee believes that, at the heart of censorship lies paranoia, an instinctual fear in the minds and hearts of the censors of the chaos and disorder which would inevitably follow if there were no censorship. The censors see themselves standing in the shoes of others, recognizing how a work of art might lead to moral corruption or political unrest; possessing (in their own minds, at least) a superior quality of judgment and superior strength of character to withstand the temptation of the works they are asked to judge. Coetzee finds the whole process logically inconsistent at best, devastating to the creative process when carried to extremes. Capable of self-reflection, the novelist-turned-essayist remarks on more than one occasion that his own prejudices against censorship may be leading him to be more critical and less balanced in his dismissal of the censors than he should be.

Anyone who remembers the intellectual challenge of reading Ludwig Wittgenstein's slim volume on the power of language in *Tractatus Logico-philosophicus* (1921), or moving slowly through Jean-Paul Sartre's highly technical, densely written analysis of the creative process in *What Is Literature?* (1949), will recognize that a book's modest size may belie its complexity. Such is the case with *Giving Offense*. This is a book for scholars or highly literate readers. The diction is formal, the vocabulary sophisticated and technical, laced with references to contemporary critical theory and peppered with allusions to writers from two millennia of Western thought. It is, in the best sense, thought-provoking, and worth the time and effort required to ponder the ideas Coetzee espouses with understanding and skill.

Laurence W. Mazzeno

Sources for Further Study

Booklist. XCII, April 1, 1996, p. 1328.
Hungry Mind Review. XI, Summer, 1996, p. 47.
Kirkus Reviews. LXIV, February 1, 1996, p. 188.
Los Angeles Times Book Review. April 21, 1996, p. 2.
The New Republic. CCXV, November 18, 1996, p. 30.
The New York Times Book Review. CI, September 22, 1996, p. 32.
The Washington Post Book World. XXVI, May 5, 1996, p. 5.
World Literature Today. LXX, Winter, 1996, p. 107.

GOD'S CHINESE SON
The Taiping Heavenly Kingdom of Hong Xiuquan

Author: Jonathan D. Spence (1936-   )
Publisher: W. W. Norton (New York). Illustrated. 400 pp. $27.50
Type of work: History
Time: The middle third of the nineteenth century
Locale: South China

Drawing on many previously untapped primary sources, Spence traces the humble provincial origins and awesome rise to power of the rebel Taiping theocracy that ruled many of China's wealthiest regions for more than a decade in the mid-nineteenth century

Principal personages:
> HONG XIUQUAN (originally named HONG HUOXIU; 1814-1864), the Taiping rebels' charismatic supreme leader who believed himself to be Jesus Christ's younger brother
> YANG XIUQING, the Taiping "East King" who coordinated most day-to-day military and civil affairs before his murder
> XIAO CHAOGUI, the Taiping "West King" who similarly combined shrewd military leadership with claims of divine inspiration
> SHI DAKAI, the Taiping "Wing King" who, unlike the East and West kings, remained alive to keep fighting the Manchus until well into the 1860's
> HONG RENGAN, the most Westernized Taiping leader who attempted in vain to win foreign support for the Taipings
> ISSACHAR ROBERTS, the temperamental Baptist missionary from Tennessee whose preaching and translations from the Bible influenced Hong Xiuquan in unanticipated ways

Lasting a decade and a half and costing in excess of twenty million Chinese lives, the mid-nineteenth century Taiping Rebellion stands as one of the most devastating civil wars the world has ever seen. Its desolation of entire counties in China's rich Yangzi valley provinces stunted that country's economic and societal development and weakened the central government to the advantage of provincial military leaders. More than any other conflict, the Taiping Rebellion signaled that the peaceful and prosperous era of eighteenth century China was but a distant memory. It also foreshadowed the bitter internecine clashes and struggles that would beleaguer China throughout much of the twentieth century.

God's Chinese Son: The Taiping Heavenly Kingdom of Hong Xiuquan builds upon a considerable body of existing research on the Taiping "Heavenly Kingdom," yet caters to the general reader by relegating the scholarly apparatus to the endnotes and bibliography. Acclaimed historian Jonathan Spence uses the present tense and an engaging prose style to make the book read more like a vivid assemblage of eyewitness accounts than a dry chronology of facts and events. Spence's balanced portrayals of Hong Xiuquan and other key historical figures on both sides of the struggle evince both sympathy for their strivings and criticism of their excesses.

Hong Xiuquan was a provincial Cantonese from a village about thirty miles north of Guangzhou (Canton), Guangdong Province's largest city and, until 1842, China's only trading port legally open to Western merchants. This crossroads of Chinese and Western culture proved to be a catalyst for a hybrid millenarian ideology that would foster a doggedly entrenched mass rebellion against the Manchu Qing court and its local officials and soldiers.

As Hong repeatedly failed the Confucianist civil service exams, his resentment took the form of a strong interest in the rival religious system of Christianity brought to Guangdong and other predominantly southeastern regions by Western missionaries. Hong was drawn to Protestantism's emphasis on personal religious experience mediated by one's own language or dialect and not dependent upon priestly intervention; no organized priesthood subservient to Rome or elsewhere could effectively deny any religious vision he might have. Nor would Hong defer readily to Protestants; the Baptist missionary Issachar Roberts delayed his planned baptism of Hong, expressing doubts about the Chinese convert's religious sincerity, but Hong never doubted himself, abruptly walking away from Roberts to preach in his own way and on his own terms. Hong Xiuquan even convinced many highly educated Chinese like his cousin Hong Rengan of the authenticity and significance of the former's hallucinatory vision of 1837 in which God recognized Xiuquan as Jesus Christ's younger brother and exhorted him to extirpate China's unbelieving "demon devils" (not explicitly identified as the Manchus and their followers until a dozen years later in 1849).

Like many Hakkas, or "guest people," whose ancestors had migrated south to China's southernmost provinces considerably later than the original Han Chinese inhabitants of Guangdong and Guangxi Provinces, Hong Xiuquan resented what bordered on second-class status for the Hakkas and became interested in nonmainstream religious movements such as Christianity and moralistic folk Buddhism. Spence convincingly shows how the millenarian and moralistic beliefs in these two religions strongly resonated with one another, making Hong's doctrinal claims much less exotic to his provincial revival-goers than they would have sounded to Confucian literati who tended to dismiss folk Buddhism as mere superstition.

Anti-Manchu secret societies, such as the Heaven-and-Earth Society and the Triads, also formed an organizational base for many Hakkas, who along with the Hong's "God-worshipers" formed the major nucleus of his increasingly militant millenarian movement. The movement's ranks swelled even further with the addition of erstwhile bandits and pirates yearning for a more secure existence in the wake of Manchu bandit suppression campaigns and the British navy's destruction of key coastal pirate lairs. Other new Taiping converts included destitute and desperate provincials who were fleeing famine and social unrest for the subsistence and relative safety they could find among the God-worshipers' camps.

The turning point of the God-worshipers' transformation from unruly but basically harmless bands of religious zealots into a self-proclaimed army fighting against the Manchus to establish a Heavenly Kingdom occurred in the winter of 1849-1850. Two prominent adherents were arrested by the local authorities in 1849 on trumped-up charges, and the tactics of appeals for clemency, arguments for the imprisoned men's innocence of any substantial wrongdoing, and generous bribes to magistrates and jailers no longer proved as efficacious as they had in the past. Both of the imprisoned God-worshipers soon died from mistreatment in jail; Hong Xiuquan and his followers vowed that the time for "patience and humility" in responding to government suppression was over. By the early months of 1850, the four Hakka-dominated bases for the God-worshipers in Guangxi were being described as "army" encampments that needed to be stockpiling guns and gunpowder with as much urgency as they had been storing up grain against threats of government siege for some time. Now styling himself the Taiping Heavenly King, Hong wrote a poem likening himself to the founders of the Han and Ming dynasties, and began to wear the yellow robes traditionally reserved for emperors alone. It was at the end of this fateful year that the first Manchu government officer died in combat with the Taipings, resulting in a tough policy of suppression.

The year 1851 witnessed the Manchu government's first concerted military campaigns to search out and destroy the Taipings, whose Heavenly Kingdom was officially founded in March. A few years passed before the Taiping armies and their generals were able to conquer a major walled city and defend it from Manchu sieges for years on end. The Taipings quickly learned the techniques of one type of warfare after another, however, showing themselves equally adept at besieging the enemy's cities, staving off the enemy's sieges, and breaking out of enemy encirclement. Whenever the Manchu forces appeared to be getting the upper hand in their struggle with the Taipings, the latter would elude catastrophic defeat via an end run or a strategic pullback, and manage to regroup somewhere less perilous. The Taipings also became proficient at transporting their army and its attached civilian population by land and by river, simply requisitioning the boats and carts they needed while moving from city to city. They conquered and occupied their first sizable walled city in September that year (Yong'an in Guangxi), although they were shortly forced to abandon it because of Manchu encirclement tactics. Unable to conquer either the major walled cities of Guilin in Guangxi or Changsha in Hunan, the Taipings simply cut their losses and broke out of Manchu lines to the north. Hubei Province's great river ports of Hankou, Hanyang, and Wuchang fell to the Taipings' quick and relentless assaults early in 1853, and later that year they conquered their biggest prize of all, the downstream port of Nanjing, which they made the capital of the Taiping Heavenly Country (literally, "Great Peace Heavenly Country").

At the fullest extent of their power, Taiping armies controlled most of the crucial Yangzi River valley, fought to within a hundred miles of the Manchu capital at Beijing, and were poised to conquer or at least lay waste to China's major commercial hub of Shanghai. By 1864, however, the remaining Taiping generals were either busy foraging for desperately needed grain supplies or else trying in vain to break the tightening Manchu blockade around Nanjing, which finally fell to the Qing siege in mid-July.

Spence's study highlights a number of factors which contributed to the Taiping debacle. Instead of setting up a viable and regularized system of justice and law, the

Taiping leaders preferred to handle such matters along the arbitrary lines of frontier or rebel justice, in which summary execution was typically meted out to the accused before evidence could be weighed and sifted in any systematic manner. Many of the European mercenaries who fought for the Taipings in the early 1850's departed in disgust over the plethora of indiscriminate beheadings during the middle of that decade, and the various provincial armies allied with the Qing against the Taiping included huge numbers of Taiping deserters and peasants who resented the Taipings for their harshness in conscripting coolie labor and confiscating village grain supplies. The Taipings' edicts that forbade private trade in Nanjing and elsewhere helped prevent the economic recovery of war-ravaged areas and encouraged the widespread military confiscation of foodstuffs and other essential products, which was certainly a heavy blow to the region's agricultural economy.

Hong Xiuquan and his right-hand king Yang Xiuqing seemed to ignore the egalitarian ideals they once preached when later cloistering themselves in luxurious palaces thronged with concubines, where the trappings of power and abstruse squabbles over theology distracted them from the more practical matter of improving long-term security and prosperity for their kingdom's subjects. For example, the Taiping rulers isolated their kingdom when rebuffing various European offers to regularize trade and diplomacy; the Taipings insisted on impossible preconditions that foreigners first break off relations with the Qing dynasty "demon devils" and follow the archaic tributary model of coming forward as a vassal nation of the overlord Taiping Kingdom. Not surprisingly, British, American, and other Western troops primarily fought against the Taipings when not maintaining a wary neutrality. However difficult Westerners may have found Qing officials to deal with at times, at least the latter did not claim to be infallible mouthpieces of God who enjoyed a monopoly on the truth. Even Western missionaries who initially were favorably disposed toward the Taipings generally came away disappointed, if not disgusted, at the Taiping kings' dogged adherence to what seemed heretical religious dogma, not to mention the draconian manner in which the kings' commandments were often enforced.

Foreign disapproval of the Taipings, however, was a very small factor in their demise compared to the internecine struggle that swept through the Taiping capital in the mid-1850's. As Hong Xiuquan's absorption with theology and the pleasures of his palace caused him to cede more and more control over military planning and day-to-day administration to his chief lieutenant, East King Yang Xiuqing, Yang came to have the ambition that his position as de facto chief of the realm be recognized with a title that put him on par with Hong. The fact that Yang was behaving more and more like an emperor and had sent all three of the Taiping generals most loyal to Hong on suspiciously distant military campaigns strongly implies that he was planning a coup to oust Hong. Ever since the death of West King Xiao Chaogui during a battle in 1852, Yang was the only other surviving Taiping king aside from Hong who regularly claimed to be serving as a direct mouthpiece of part of the Holy Trinity; Yang was thus uniquely qualified to serve as both the spiritual and temporal leader of the Taipings.

Hong astutely preempted Yang's coup plot by secretly ordering his three most loyal generals to return with stealth and set a trap for seizing Yang. Two of Hong's most zealous generals returned earlier than expected and managed to trap and kill Yang before he could flee or stage a counterattack. Yet the generals went on to conduct a bloody rampage, indiscriminately killing all of Yang's family members, concubines, servants, and clerks in his palace. Moreover, with Hong's blessing, the two generals used a ruse to trap the several thousand retainers still loyal to Yang who had managed to avoid the first bout of killings and massacred them all in turn, striking terror into much of Nanjing's population during the process.

When the third general, Shi Dakai, finally returned to Nanjing, he was so shocked at these brutal excesses that he criticized the two generals for unnecessarily creating divisions among the Taipings and thereby indirectly aiding the Qing enemy. The two generals furiously countercharged that Shi Dakai must have been a Qing spy himself to say such things, and proceeded to massacre Shi's wives and children and hunt down Shi himself. More fortunate than his murdered family members, Shi managed to escape from Nanjing, outside of which he assembled a huge Taiping army a hundred thousand strong; he threatened to attack Nanjing unless the two severed heads of the murderous generals were brought to him. Hong Xiuquan managed to arrange just that, thereby averting what might have been a suicidal, full-blown conflagration in Nanjing. The bloody coup shocked and demoralized the Taiping faithful, however, and the loss of literally dozens of capable military leaders and thousands of elite troops and loyal followers was a heavy blow from which the Heavenly Kingdom never fully recovered.

Spence insightfully notes that as the Taipings' military and economic prospects became more and more bleak in the early 1860's, the leaders' claims of bringing messages from divine sources dwindled to nothing. As famine conditions worsened in 1862, Hong Xiuquan's noble gesture of joining his subjects in supplementing their meager grain rations by gathering purportedly edible weeds led to the pathetic aftermath of a serious illness that finally killed the Heavenly King on June 1, 1864. His fourteen-year-old son, the Young Monarch Tiangui, ruled for only six weeks until having to escape from rampaging Manchu troops that had finally broken through Nanjing's formidable wall defenses. In spite of fleeing afar, shaving off his hair, and disguising himself as a farm laborer, Tiangui was captured by Qing troops in October. He begged to be released, arguing that he never shared his father's ambition to become an emperor and had no greater ambition than "to study quietly at the Confucian classics and try to gain the lowest degree, that of licentiate." Tiangui was probably oblivious of the irony of requesting to follow the very path his father had once taken for many years until resentfully rejecting it for more exalted callings. The young man's execution in November, 1864, marked the pathetic end of Hong Xiuquan's short-lived imperial line, but the Taipings' eagerness to countenance the destruction of millions of lives as a small price to pay for building a brave new political order would reappear in a twentieth century Chinese regime that has proudly apotheosized the Heavenly Kingdom as its revolutionary precursor.

Philip F. Williams

Sources for Further Study

America. CLXXV, August 17, 1996, p. 62.
American Spectator. XXIX, April, 1996, p. 69.
Asiaweek. XXII, April 5, 1996, p. 15.
Commonweal. CXXIII, August 16, 1996, p. 24.
First Things. LIV, June-July, 1996, p. 46.
Los Angeles Times. February 23, 1996, p. E4.
New Statesman and Society. IX, May 24, 1996, p. 38.
The New York Review of Books. XLIII, February 29, 1996, p. 39.
The New York Times. January 24, 1996, p. B5.
The New York Times Book Review. CI, February 4, 1996, p. 6.
Publishers Weekly. CCXLII, November 27, 1995, p. 62.
The Times Literary Supplement. October 25, 1996, p. 4.
The Virginia Quarterly Review. LXXII, Summer, 1996, p. 80.
The Wall Street Journal. January 5, 1996, p. A7.
The Washington Post Book World. XCII, January 21, 1996, p. 1.
The Wilson Quarterly. XX, Winter, 1996, p. 85.

THE GOOD LIFE AND ITS DISCONTENTS
The American Dream in the Age of Entitlement, 1945-1995

Author: Robert J. Samuelson
Publisher: Times Books (New York). 293 pp. $25.00
Type of work: History; current affairs
Time: 1945-1995
Locale: The United States

Assessing why so many Americans feel discontented, Samuelson argues that an overly optimistic American Dream led to pessimism that can be relieved only if expectations become more realistic and responsible

American public opinion polling in the 1990's consistently reveals a society anxious about the future and apprehensive about priorities that seem out of whack. The polls also show that Americans are alarmed by the society's moral decline. At the same time, ambivalence abounds about how to cope in these circumstances. Americans want freedom for the individual, but they are unhappy about how people use freedom. They want a high standard of living and financial security. Americans also claim that family life and friendship are most important to them, and then they feel conflicted when the race for prosperity robs them of time for care and love. Americans are skeptical about government programs but not likely to stand by calmly—especially if *their* perks are up for grabs—when talk about budget deficit reduction gets serious. Consuming desires for more and more collide with recognition, however faintly felt, that unending attempts to fulfill unsatisfied desire are unsustainable. Even when individuals think that their personal lives are going well—a feeling shared by 80 percent in some polls—Americans often say that the state of the union is headed in the opposite direction. Ironically, the happiness that Americans pursue, the good life that many of them enjoy, strangely leads to discontent in spite of all that they possess and accomplish.

How did Americans become so discontented? What can be done about this melancholy? Robert J. Samuelson, an astute columnist for *Newsweek* and *The Washington Post*, seeks answers to those questions. *The Good Life and Its Discontents* grew out of his journalistic studies about the economic, political, and social development of the United States in the fifty years after World War II. Identifying a peculiarly American "dis-ease," Samuelson's book has three major parts plus an epilogue. The three parts diagnose the malady; the epilogue makes a modest attempt to prescribe steps toward health. According to Samuelson, American discontent results from an inflated sense of entitlement, a naïve optimism about capitalism, and a glut of "overpromise." Straightforward and sober, the remedy—greater realism and responsibility—will be difficult for American dreamers to achieve, but failure to use the prescription, Samuelson judges correctly, is not a chance that the United States should take.

Samuelson's governing question—How did Americans become so discontented?— is important, complex, and paradoxical. The question is important because how Americans feel about themselves and their country affects how they will think and act. The quality of the nation's future hangs in the balance. In the late twentieth century, the particularly American characteristics of that dilemma contain distinctive complexities.

As the twenty-first century approaches, most Americans enjoy a material standard of living that exceeds any in previous human history. No foreign foes seriously threaten us. Unprecedented advances in medical science provide health care and longevity that earlier societies could scarcely imagine. Unemployment figures and inflation rates are favorable. The programs are not perfect, but government safety nets help huge numbers of unfortunate people. More and more Americans are going to college and university. Although prejudice and racism have not been eliminated, opportunity keeps opening for minorities. The list of advances could go on and on. The United States is not utopia, far from it, but progress is one of our most important products. Yet uneasy Americans—the poll numbers hover around 60 percent—lament the quality of national life. We worry that the future will not be better than the past. We fear that our children's lives will be less desirable than our own. Uneasiness breeds uncertainty; uncertainty gives birth to the pessimism that stands knocking at American doors.

The paradox—"Americans," writes Samuelson, "are feeling bad about doing well"—is compounded by the immense irony that it includes. Americans are better off than they often think, he argues, but their glum attitudes are laced with irony because optimism has typically been the hallmark of American belief. According to traditional self-characterization, Americans—individually and collectively—are "can do," problem-solving folks who have the know-how and the gumption to make the American Dream, as President Bill Clinton has said, a reality for everyone who is willing to work for it.

The irony is that American optimism took us to considerable success and then left us discontented to such an extent that optimism itself has been called into question. This outcome, however, need not be the last word. Samuelson's point is that a wise awareness of this condition suggests a way out. The way out cannot be a return to misguided optimism, but it may be found in greater realism and responsibility.

Tantalizing, ambiguous, frustrating—the American Dream has a central part to play in Samuelson's outlook. As Samuelson acknowledges, pursuit of the American Dream has produced and expanded "the good life," whose priorities are largely materialistic and economic. Typically, those priorities start with possessing a nice house, a late model car, and a well-paying job to provide other creature comforts that are viewed increasingly as necessities. Yet the priorities are not exclusively materialistic and economic where the American Dream is concerned. That dream also involves ideals: liberty, for example, and justice for all. It inspires hopes: All problems have solutions, tomorrow will be better than today, and life will be better for our children than it was for us. In the fifty years from 1945 to 1995 that occupy Samuelson's attention, the American Dream increasingly has come to mean entitlement: Americans often believe that they have a right not only to pursue happiness but also to specific outcomes, including everything from ever-increasing wages to state-of-the-art health care and superior education.

Samuelson's point is not to bash the economic ambitions or the ideals and hopes that characterized the American Dream even before the historian James Truslow Adams popularized the literal concept in his 1931 book, *The Epic of America*, which was widely read during the Great Depression. What does trouble Samuelson is the "Age of Entitlement" mentality that the American Dream's success has produced. It is fraught with problems as serious as they were unintended. He illustrates this point by noting that Adams defined the American Dream as the dream

> of a land in which life should be better and richer and fuller for every man, with opportunity for each according to his ability or achievement. . . . It is not a dream of motor cars and high wages merely, but a dream of social order in which each man and each woman shall be able to attain to the fullest stature of which they are innately capable, and to be recognized by others for what they are, regardless of the fortuitous circumstances of birth or position.

More than in Adams' own day or in previous American history, the American people snatched this expansively optimistic version of the Dream in the years after World War II. Nothing about that was surprising. The United States had unprecedented economic and political power. Goods and services multiplied at affordable prices. American business offered secure and upwardly mobile employment. Where corporations faltered, government was ready and able to pick up the slack. Quite ready to accept ever-escalating promises about new frontiers, great societies, and mornings in America, the American people thought that a well-managed trinity of government initiatives, corporate management, and the free marketing of capitalism would lead onward and upward. They did, at least for a time, but then Americans got impatient and restless because progress was not fast enough or thorough enough.

Assuming that the huge postwar strides were just what one should expect, we took the gains for granted and began to dwell on the shortfalls and the shortcomings. There were plenty of those—racism, poverty, homelessness, crime, and drug addiction only begin the litany—and, quite rightly, any American Dream worth having could not be indifferent to them. Nevertheless, perspective, balance, and humility, Samuelson suggests, were what this mixture lacked. Their absence did not serve us well because it led to the deceptive belief that government should do more than it could, economic forces were more manageable than they are, and social conditions are more malleable than they turn out to be.

A key part of Samuelson's message is that Americans take too much for granted. So the chief problem with an unrevised American Dream is that it lacks sound senses of realism and responsibility. James Truslow Adams is not the culprit. When he defined the American Dream as pointing toward a life that would be better, richer, and fuller, a nation mired in the Great Depression probably needed to hear such words. When we keep hearing that siren call in the 1990's, when we embrace such language in the midst of an Age of Entitlement, then the dreaming is likely to lose prudent restraint. Better, richer, fuller—postwar American dreams embraced those inviting words. The invitation became an unrealistic and irresponsible "overpromise," because it pointed toward an ever-receding horizon that Americans, somehow, thought they were destined to reach.

The Dream's allure has always been in its power to expand and open up horizons of possibility. Not only did the horizons expand and open up but also many Americans took advantage of them and to a remarkable degree the good life became ours. Nationally as well as individually, Americans could get there if they tried, but the problem in postwar America turned out to be that "there" was not a real destination because "more" always seemed possible and then necessary—so much so that Americans began to feel entitled to personal and national "progress" only to find that they were frustrated, discontented, and eventually pessimistic about their society when progress did not take place on the schedule or to the degree that they expected.

Neither excessive optimism nor excessive pessimism serves America well, but where does Samuelson locate the middle way—the realistic and responsible path— that we need to take in the future? He starts with the conviction that people should do more for themselves and expect government to do less. More specifically, the federal budget should be balanced, a step that would require changes but not wrenching ones. Along with restricting health care costs, Samuelson estimates that raising retirement ages and reducing benefits for the well-off elderly would go a long way toward needed federal budget controls.

In addition, Samuelson believes that Americans should stop "catering to group needs," which he takes to be one of the tell-tale signs of the Age of Entitlement. Affirmative action programs are a particularly bad bargain in Samuelson's view because they produce "more ill will than social justice." Furthermore, we simply have to recognize that "there are no clear solutions for many of our most pressing social problems, especially those involving race and poverty."

Resting on the belief that individual freedom is of fundamental importance, American life can be resourceful, industrious, and fulfilling, but Samuelson also emphasizes that it can be "messy, violent and dissatisfied" as well. American commitment to freedom entails that our options for social control are limited and modest. Hence, an appeal to responsibility is all the more important, even though it cannot be a panacea in a society where not everyone is likely to be responsible and where "some economic, social, or personal conditions defeat the greatest individual exertions."

Revised to be responsible and realistic, the American Dream that Samuelson envisions would lead to a society that understands what cannot be done as well as what is possible, a nation in which our sense of what ought to happen is not controlled by expected entitlement but tempered by shared obligations. Leaner and better fitting, this version of the American Dream starts with the recognition that no individual or institution—government, corporations, schools, voluntary groups, families—can do everything. Then it moves to accept the challenge that all of these parts can and must do something to improve the quality of the whole society. Incrementally, some of the worst problems can diminish if Americans do the work for themselves.

Samuelson's prescription is conservative, unpretentious, and sketchy. He acknowledges that it may not be enough. He is also convinced that the Age of Entitlement cannot be sustained and that attempts to sustain it will do more harm than good. He sees Americans groping their way toward a more responsible society. As Americans move in that direction, he hopes that a revised American Dream can encourage us to meet our obligations to one another by laying the Age of Entitlement to rest.

John K. Roth

Sources for Further Study

Choice. XXXIII, May, 1996, p. 1527.
The Economist. CCCXXXVIII, January 20, 1996, p. 85.
Institutional Investor. XXX, May, 1996, p. 172.
Los Angeles Times. January 12, 1996, p. E6.
The Nation. CCLXII, March 18, 1996, p. 25.
The New York Times Book Review. CI, January 28, 1996, p. 25.
Publishers Weekly. CCXLII, November 13, 1995, p. 52.
The Virginia Quarterly Review. LXXII, Summer, 1996, p. 97.
The Wall Street Journal. January 16, 1996, p. A12.
The Washington Post Book World. XXVI, February 4, 1996, p. 5.

GOOD NATURED
The Origins of Right and Wrong in Humans and Other Animals

Author: Frans de Waal (1948-   )
Publisher: Harvard University Press (Cambridge, Massachusetts). Illustrated. 384 pp. $24.95
Type of work: Science

De Waal attempts to show that morality is fundamentally biological and that there is an essential connection between human morality and animals' communal behavior

Frans de Waal, a leading primatologist specializing in sociobiology, tries to solve the problem Charles Darwin once faced: If nature is amoral, how can humans be moral? All behaviors, many sociobiologists believe, can be explained by a so-called "selfish gene." De Waal, however, seeking biological and evolutionary roots of human behavior, believes morality can be accounted for in the same way as other human traits.

Through de Waal's eyes the reader sees all kinds of animals help each other, share food, resolve conflicts to mutual satisfaction, and even demonstrate a crude sense of justice. It seems as if chimpanzees in particular do most of the things that humans do in the moral realm, but without the trappings of culture and abstractions of religion. Animals may not have morality, or may not comprehend morality as humans do, but they exhibit the same fundamental tendencies and behaviors, such as altruism and kindness.

De Waal argues that animals possessed a natural sense of morality millions of years before humans even appeared on the evolutionary scene. He writes: "Humans and other animals have been endowed with a capacity for genuine love, sympathy and care." This fact "can and will one day be reconciled with the idea that genetic self-promotion drives the evolutionary process."

De Waal does not contend that animals have a morally conscious sense, the way humans do. For example, animals cannot have the concept of right and wrong in a human sense. He hesitates to call the members of any species other than our own "moral beings" but argues that, by observing certain behaviors in animals, humans can account for the genesis of their own moral sensibilities and practices.

Chimpanzees, the closest relatives of humans, exhibit reconciliation, sharing of food, and signs of distress over the suffering of their group members. They also show signs of guilt and shame when violating the social rules of the colony in which they live. De Waal presents numerous anecdotes to illustrate animal shame and guilt. These characteristics, he believes, antedate the appearance of humans. That is why he thinks the study of social behaviors among apes and other animals can establish the biological foundation of morality in humans.

In dealing with animal behavior, it seems as if de Waal has given voice to what animals would say if they could speak. In the last few decades animal behaviorists have attempted to show the correspondence of ape social life with that of humans. One popular example is the sense of kinship and reciprocity discovered by David

Attenborough in his encounters with gorillas. De Waal unabashedly claims that animals possess a kind of primitive moral faculty which is at root similar to human morality.

According to most religions, humans are stuck in a peculiar realm between the angels and apes, always striving heavenward but always being pulled downward by their base, animal nature. De Waal believes there is only the realm of nature which contains morality as a function of sociality. Humans have evolved to be morally more complex than other animals but still remain within the purview of evolutionary biology, not within a divine realm or a realm of Kantian Categorical Imperatives. Humans ought to be good simply because it makes sense within the sociobiological, evolutionary framework.

De Waal demystifies the humanocentric ownership of morality and extends humanism beyond the human species. The question of good and evil for some people is "a veneer beneath which we have remained as amoral or immoral as any other form of life." De Waal refutes this idea and instead gives an account of morality that includes both animals and humans. In short, humans are moral beings and there is no escaping the responsibility that comes with it. Primatologists often focus on the dark side of human and animal nature. Yet by uncovering some of the similar noble impulses in closely related species, such as apes and chimps, humans can recognize the nobility in their own nature. This result is a culmination of the thoughts lucidly expressed in de Waal's *Chimpanzee Politics* (1982) and *Peacemaking Among Primates* (1989).

How does de Waal come to such conclusions? He employs philosophy, anecdotal reports, and scientific data. It is this combination of sometimes incompatible methodologies that makes his explanations and claims interesting and dynamic. He uses philosophy to connect animal morality with human ethics. His approach is similar to that of Alan Gibbard, one of the leading philosophers of evolutionary ethics and author of *Wise Choices, Apt Feelings: A Theory of Normative Judgement* (1992).

De Waal employs anecdotal reports both as evidence and as a means of charming readers into accepting his metaphors and anthropomorphism. He admits that anthropomorphism cannot take the place of scientific data but thinks it can serve the same function as intuition does for scientific or mathematical discoveries and inventions. He warns against taking anecdotes and parallelisms between animals and human too seriously but is still able to combine science, personal experiences, and anecdotes in a coherent investigation.

De Waal also utilizes a huge amount of the latest data collected by himself and other scientists studying animals' social behaviors, such as careful counting of when and how frequently animals share food, groom and stroke one another, confront one another aggressively, or engage in significant behaviors such as sympathy, altruistic actions, and reciprocity.

When de Waal presents his delightful anecdotes, he is not looking for conclusive proofs. He is more interested in enticing the reader to share the intuitions behind his scientific theories. He has the same intuitive intentions when, in an interesting and persuasive manner, he freely brings in his own random observations, theories from neurobiology, comparative psychology, evolutionary science, and cognitive ethology.

De Waal's anecdotes and anthropomorphic metaphors make the book enjoyable for nonspecialists. In fact, the seduction of de Waal's book comes from his anecdotes, backed by scientific data and a combination of lucid writing and graceful arguments. He breathes moral life into animals he deals with, making the perplexing problem of human morality accessible to laypeople and manageable for investigation in a scientific setting. He also paints the grimmer views of human nature with a lighter and more positive brush.

Years of observation and personal contacts with apes have given de Waal a special perspective to express his impression with expertise and wisdom. He tells compelling stories of individual animals, mainly apes and monkeys, to support his conclusions. For example, Mazu, a wild Japanese monkey born without feet but surviving for twenty years in his colony, is a vivid example of supportive camaraderie.

In another story, a group of rhesus monkeys modify their behavior around Azalea, a mentally retarded member. In another story, de Waal describes a chimp named Atlanta who screams empathetically, identifying with his mate giving birth.

De Waal tells about whales risking their lives to stay with sick or injured members of their family, and how elephants try to care for the weak or sick family member and often return to the scene of a relative's death.

There are four sets of photographs, selected to demonstrate animals' anthropomorphic expressions. They visually chronicle humanlike behaviors displayed by apes and monkeys.

What de Waal wants to do in *Good Natured: The Origins of Right and Wrong in Humans and Other Animals* is to dismantle the notion prevalent among many scientists that Darwinian theory makes it certain that humans are genetically predisposed to seek their selfish interests which preclude any notion of altruism or moral explanation for animal behavior. These scientists emphasize that they accept the physical, not the moral, evolution of humans from apes.

De Waal argues, however, that natural selection is adaptive to pressures of communities as well. The adaptation of moral traits, such as altruism, would make the survival of a species more likely and more prosperous. Evolutionary moral development in animals and humans is not less significant than, say, intelligence in tool making in animals and use of language in humans. Natural selection, although seemingly harsh, has produced highly successful species, such as humans, that survive through cooperation and reciprocal coexistence. In fact, de Waal believes many species would have become extinct if they had not developed some fundamental moral sense of cooperation and mutual assistance.

In this sense, then, animals have a faculty of morality which can be considered the evolutionary predecessor of human morality. Similarities between animal and human moral behavior are striking. De Waal observes that chimps who help other chimps to win their quarrels later receive assistance in the same manner. He argues that humans can find the Golden Rule widely practiced among socially advanced animals such as monkeys, apes, dogs, whales, dolphins, and elephants. There are social rules and etiquettes among animals for interaction, for example, in courtship and sharing tools and food. He even argues that animals may have a crude sense of justice and fairness, as if they possessed a primitive form of conscience.

Incredible amenability to training among animals such as apes, dogs, and dolphins is another indication that they respond successfully to a rule-based life. De Waal in his research at Arnhem Zoo discovered a "Machiavellian" politics among the chimp colony. For example, alliances among the members would shift from one group to another based on the immediate social needs of members. He concludes that chimpanzees are fundamentally political animals.

"Social regularities" in chimpanzees have the same effect they do in human societies: they punish antisocial behaviors and reward prosocial ones. For example, Gwinnie, an Arnhem chimpanzee, did not share her food with beggars while Mai did. The result was that Mai was usually surrounded by beggars and they reciprocated when her turn came to beg. In contrast, Gwinnie was friendless and her begging was often futile. De Waal believes that higher apes can even remember the behavior of other apes in social interactions in the past and adjust their present behaviors accordingly.

There are, however, a few difficulties with de Waal's argumentation about animal morality. First, why can we not extend the same kind of account to other animals which, in de Waal's estimation, do not quite fit the moral picture he has painted? For example, how about fiercely social animals like ants, termites, and bees? It seems that some of the seemingly moral behaviors such as self-sacrifice, sharing, and communal rules apply quite well to these morally lower communal animals.

Second, how are we supposed to take de Waal's intensely anthropomorphic anecdotal insertions as part of his overall account of animal morality? After all is said and done, are we clear as to exactly what moves animals to engage in their "moral" behaviors? Is shame or guilt the motive that causes a dog's "guilty look"? What exactly is the motive behind a gorilla's "self-sacrifice" or an elephant herd's communal effort on behalf of a stranded calf?

Finally, are we fundamentally selfish beings using altruism to fulfill our sophisticated selfish desires? What does it mean to be "genuinely" or "truly" altruistic? What are the evolutionary-biological advantages of being genuinely altruistic? De Waal confidently assumes he has given a ground-breaking account in which "we seem to be reaching a point at which science can wrest morality from the hands of philosophers." Yet even if he succeeds in giving a conclusive neurobiological account of human morality, he still needs to deliberate about the nature of good and evil and respond to the question, "Ultimately, why do we have to be good rather than bad?" These and other problems related to morality cannot be resolved in biology or in natural selection. They remain, to de Waal's chagrin, in the purview of philosophy and even perhaps theology.

De Waal, however, believes that humans and animals are simultaneously noble and brutish. A single account from either brutishness or nobility would not explain the moral phenomenon. Humans are, in a sense, genetically predisposed to be moral creatures, even if they have to go against their natural or rational best interest. This is supposed to be the greatest truth emerging out of juxtaposing genetic self-interest with fierce sociality.

Good Natured is an important book full of fascinating implications. It can influence the way one thinks about what it means to be a human and humane, and about the nature of one's kinship with animals.

Chogollah Maroufi

Sources for Further Study

Library Journal. CXXI, February 15, 1996, p. 172.
Los Angeles Times Book Review. April 28, 1996, p. 3.
Nature. CCCLXXX, March 28, 1996, p. 301.
New Scientist. CLII, April 13, 1996, p. 40.
New Statesman and Society. IX, May 3, 1996, p. 39.
The New York Times. April 8, 1996, p. C14.
The New York Times Book Review. CI, March 24, 1996, p. 22.
Newsweek. CXXVII, February 26, 1996, p. 52.
Publishers Weekly. CCXLIII, January 22, 1996, p. 56.
Scientific American. CCLXXV, September, 1996, p. 176.
The Times Literary Supplement. September 6, 1996, p. 25.
The Washington Post Book World. XXVI, May 12, 1996, p. 5.

GRAND EXPECTATIONS
The United States, 1945-1974

Author: James T. Patterson (1935-   )
Publisher: Oxford University Press (New York). Illustrated. 829 pp. $35.00
Type of work: History
Time: 1945-1974
Locale: The United States

A brilliant narrative of American history from the close of World War II to the end of Richard M. Nixon's presidency

World War II transformed American life, and Americans knew it. The war brought suffering and sacrifice to untold thousands of homes. It also brought excitement and adventure. This war, no more than any other social phenomenon, could not bring complete harmony to the racially and ethnically divided American people. Yet it did seem to inspire more fellow feeling than Americans had known for many years. Before the war, the United States had been mired in a decade of economic depression. Millions of lives had been scarred by want and blighted opportunities. The war changed all that. Americans enjoyed full employment. Women flocked into jobs left vacant by men enrolled in the military. African Americans found doors beginning to open for them as well. People had money in their pockets, and not enough consumer goods to spend it on. The war also heralded the end of the American tradition of isolation from world affairs. The "mistakes" of 1919-1920 would not be repeated when this war ended. A people increasingly encouraged to think in terms of "one world" was prepared to embrace the new vision of collective security. The United States, the great "Arsenal of Democracy," the only power largely untouched by wartime destruction, seemed destined to play a leading role in the emerging world order. For most Americans, the dropping of the atomic bombs in August, 1945, confirmed rather than caused America's global dominance.

The potent social forces and human energies released by World War II raised Americans' expectations for the future. To a remarkable extent, these expectations would be met in the postwar years. For the quarter century following 1945, the United States would experience an extraordinary prosperity. At its height, Americans would produce 57 percent of the world's steel, 62 percent of the oil, and 80 percent of its automobiles. The United States would control three-fourths of the world's gold supply. At the same time, Americans grew accustomed to the responsibilities of international leadership and habituated to wielding their power in far corners of the earth.

James Patterson's *Grand Expectations: The United States, 1945-1974* is an illuminating exploration of the legacy of World War II. He traces the ways in which war-engendered confidence and optimism marked American life for decades. He provides a compelling account of an exuberant period in American history, when dreams of an "American Century" seemed quite tangible, and a "Great Society" appeared a project just within grasp.

Patterson's book is the third study to appear in a projected eleven-volume history of the United States published by Oxford University Press. This series will be a magisterial account of American history, summarizing the best of American historical scholarship at the end of the twentieth century. The two previously published volumes in the series have lived up to anticipations. Robert Middlekauff's *The Glorious Cause: The American Revolution, 1763-1789* (1982) won a number of prizes. James M. McPherson's *Battle Cry of Freedom: The Civil War Era* (1988) received a Pulitzer Prize for history. Patterson's *Grand Expectations* holds its own in such company.

Patterson's decision to make the heightened expectations of the American people in the postwar era the organizing theme of his work succeeds admirably. His invocation of *Grand Expectations* works on several levels. The simplicity bestows an enlightening clarity on a cacophonous period in American history. By eschewing the temptation of oversubtle or ingenious interpretations of his material, Patterson sacrifices some originality of presentation, but gains an impressive degree of explanatory force. This is possible because the theme of rising expectations genuinely fits the facts. A sense of possibility, and a high-spirited impatience with limits, lay near the heart of the great trends of the postwar years. As Patterson points out, the generous G.I. Bill passed during World War II to provide for the conflict's veterans set the stage for a "rights revolution" in the United States, in which the benefits of an affluent society blurred imperceptibly into entitlements. So profound a social movement as the civil rights struggle of the 1950's and 1960's was born of the gains made during the war, but fueled by an aching consciousness of the gap between practice and possibility for African Americans in the United States. The vaunting ambitions of American statesmen in these same years, both in domestic and foreign policy, was nourished by the conviction that the United States was wealthy enough to support any initiative, whether a "New Frontier" or a "Great Society."

Finally, Patterson's theme gives his narrative a powerful moral force, albeit of a peculiarly traditional sort. His tale of American presumption enables him to rework the conventions of classical Greek tragedy, in which the hero is laid low by hubris. Yet Patterson's is an American tragedy. For him it is innocence which is tainted by pride, and it is the "city upon a hill" which lies elusive, ultimately beyond the vision, if not the aspiration, of his flawed protagonists. Indeed, Patterson is haunted by what might have been, had not the bounty of the postwar era been betrayed by overreaching. As it is, he regards this period as one of the most progressive in the nation's history. The extension of economic and civil benefits to African Americans, women, and other groups was unprecedented. The struggle against Communist totalitarianism was a necessary and just cause. Had America's resources been husbanded more carefully, had America's leaders shown more restraint at home and abroad, what might have been? Patterson is wise enough not to speculate. It is enough for him to lament the errors and lost opportunities. As it was, the United States reaped the whirlwind. By 1974, the United States was bloodied by a lost war, wracked by dissension and scandal, and already caught up in the toils of the "stagflation" which brought to an end the postwar economic boom. The dreams of the previous decade were already becoming terms of reproach for the conservative prophets of a new era of limits.

Knowledge of what is to come lends a certain poignancy to Patterson's survey of the postwar era. Much more than time distances Americans of the 1990's from the world of Harry Truman, or even Lyndon Johnson. A mental and moral gulf separates them from the relentlessly optimistic America of those days. The great expectations of which Patterson writes so eloquently stand between that time and our own like a wall. The divide is not unlike that which stretched between the generations before and after the Great War of 1914-1918. F. Scott Fitzgerald explored this moral chasm in his novel *Tender Is the Night* (1934). His doomed hero Dick Diver revisits the scene of savage fighting during the war. Acting as a cicerone for a party of friends, he evokes a sense of loss, distance, and decline, mourning the abyss cutting off the prewar world from the world the war left them. He declares that such a war could not be fought again, that the young men of the 1920's lack the "sentimental equipment" which animated the soldiers of the Great War. For us, like the characters in Fitzgerald's novel, the "sentimental equipment" of post-1945 America is only a memory, growing increasingly mysterious, bound up somehow with crumbling Howdy Doody puppets, Davy Crockett hats, and John, Jean, and Judy readers. The bland assurance and easy idealism of the generation which was launched into the Vietnam War is unlikely to be recaptured. We who lack its confidence envy the postwar generation its hope, and even, to some extent, its blindness. We look back on that lost world with nostalgia. We relive it vicariously on television by watching Nickelodeon and speaking of "Happy Days." For a young person of the 1990's, the suburban milieu of *Leave It to Beaver* is as foreign and mannered as that of the English gentry captured in the novels of Jane Austen.

None of this is to deny the very real evils of postwar America, often conveniently elided from our nostalgic reminiscences. The United States in 1945 was a land torn by bitter racial injustice. Jim Crow still ruled in the South. Within a few years, the second Red Scare and McCarthyism would distort and limit American political life. The looming specter of the atomic bomb and nuclear destruction haunted the popular culture of the postwar period, surfacing in phenomena ranging from monsters in horror films to backyard bomb shelters. The ongoing Cold War engendered a disturbing extension of governmental power and led to two major wars. The domestic and foreign policies of the 1960's, launched with a spirit of dauntless resolution, would culminate within a very few years in frightening levels of social and political discord.

Yet it is equally undeniable that a catalog of the ills of this period is an inadequate refutation of the nostalgic impulse, much less the postwar era's more serious calls on our attention. As Patterson makes clear, great expectations could coexist with deprivation, inequality, and wrong. The postwar generation demanded progress, not perfection. Soldiers returned from World War II, and their wives, perhaps recently released from war production work, crammed their families into the tidy little houses of the first suburban Levittowns because these developments represented a measurable advance in housing from the straitened days of the Depression. Bigger and prettier houses would, if they came at all, come in the future. For the moment, however, the new tract housing was good enough. The privilege of sitting and receiving service at a Woolworth's lunch counter was bare at best, but signified a tangible advance in dignity for the youthful African American students who braved taunts and the wrath of southern police in 1960. The baby boom of the late 1940's to early 1960's defied demographic logic. The birthrate in the United States had been declining for decades, a trend accentuated by the Depression years of the 1930's. Yet the postwar period saw an explosion of fertility unprecedented in American history, creating the enormous "baby boom" generation. The prospective parents of this decade and a half could easily have limited the size of their families, maintaining the demographic pattern they had inherited. Presumably, they could have enjoyed the fruits of prosperity, indulging themselves with the money not spent on raising children. Instead came the boom. Patterson argues that the choice so many Americans made to have large families was a manifestation of their "grand expectations." They realized that they could support and educate more children than their parents, and believed that this would be a good thing for themselves and for their country. Thus millions of Americans willingly embraced the sacrifices and challenges of bringing up the baby boomers.

A crucial, and often unspoken, component of the high expectations of Americans in the years following World War II was a commitment to individual and social uplift which transcended idiosyncratic self-interest. The singular prosperity of the postwar era produced much waste, but no bacchanal. The generation tempered by World War II and the ensuing Cold War assumed that affluence came at a price, which if necessary must be paid. This spirit was best captured by John F. Kennedy's inaugural address, with its challenge to: "Ask not what your country can do for you; ask what you can do for your country." As late as 1966, Barry Sadler's "Ballad of the Green Berets" could become a smash hit on America's airwaves, celebrating struggle and heroic devotion, and ending with a dying Green Beret asking his wife to raise their son to wear, in his turn, the green beret.

Another product of the popular culture of the 1960's, and emblematic of the temper of the postwar generation, was the television series *Star Trek*. This landmark program, self-consciously modeled on popular Westerns, saw Captain James Kirk of the starship *Enterprise* lead his comrades to worlds where no humans had ventured before. Human society in Captain Kirk's world had attained a degree of order and justice longed for in the 1960's. Instead of resting on their laurels, however, the men and women of Star Fleet pushed on, accepting risk and loss to advance human knowledge and promote interstellar peace. Prosperity was not enough. Therein lies the triumph and dignity of the postwar period. The dreams of those days did not come to full fruition. Yet at least they were dreamed. Patterson's book reminds us that beneath the tumult of war and revolution, and the posturings of captains and kings, the most profound subject of history lies in the record of the vagaries of the human heart.

Daniel P. Murphy

Sources for Further Study

The Atlantic. CCLXXVIII, September, 1996, p. 107.
Booklist. XCII, January 1, 1996, p. 784.
The Economist. CCCXXXIX, April 20, 1996, p. 4.
The Guardian. July 12, 1996, II, p. 21.
Library Journal. CXXI, February 1, 1996, p. 87.
National Journal. XXVIII, March 30, 1996, p. 735.
The New Leader. LXXIX, August 12, 1996, p. 23.
The New York Times Book Review. CI, June 30, 1996, p. 13.
Publishers Weekly. CCXLIII, January 1, 1996, p. 64.
The Wall Street Journal. June 7, 1996, p. A10.
The Washington Post Book World. XXVI, May 26, 1996, p. 1.
The Weekly Standard. II, September 16, 1996, p. 33.

GREAT BOOKS
My Adventures with Homer, Rousseau, Woolf, and Other
Indestructible Writers of the Western World

Author: David Denby
Publisher: Simon & Schuster (New York). 492 pp. $30.00
Type of work: Education; social issues

A journalist and film critic returns to Columbia University to retake two "great books" courses and to write first-hand about the controversy over the canon of Western literature

In 1961, David Denby entered Columbia University as a first-year student and took two required "great books" courses: Literature Humanities (Lit Hum for short) and Contemporary Civilization (dubbed C.C.). Lit Hum centered on a collection of classic Western texts, from Homer's *Iliad* and *Odyssey* (ninth or eighth century B.C.) to Johann Wolfgang von Goethe's *Faust* (part I, 1808; part II, 1832); the basic list had changed little since its institution as a "core course" in 1937. C.C. featured bedrock political (and scientific) treatises such as the *Politics* of Aristotle (384-322 B.C.) and Niccolò Machiavelli's *The Prince* (*Il principe*, 1513), although the list over the years had been revised much more extensively than that of Lit Hum.

By 1978, Denby had become the regular film critic of *New York* magazine, and had mostly forgotten his freshman studies. Around 1990 or so, however, he developed an interest in the controversy surrounding the "canon"—a list of those books generally considered "great" and of enduring value—and its significance for a U.S. student population becoming increasingly diverse. Goaded by his wife, he resolved to return to his alma mater and enroll once again in the Lit Hum and C.C. courses. *Great Books: My Adventures with Homer, Rousseau, Woolf, and Other Indestructible Writers of the Western World* is, he writes, "An adventure book, then, and also a naïve book, an amateur's book—in other words, a folly. It could not have been anything else."

The book's twenty-eight chapters deal more or less chronologically with many of the "great authors" Denby read. One of the chapters gives a visceral account of examination jitters, and there are seven "interludes" dealing with Denby's increasingly hostile evaluation of those on the academic left who charge that such core courses as Columbia's perpetuate a dominant white male perspective.

On the contrary, he says, "the core reading list features many works that revise and even overturn the earlier works on the list. If this is hegemony, it is also self-contradictory. . . . Might not left-academic talk of hegemony and logocentrism really amount to a glib way of gaining control, and even precedence, over an immense legacy of fiercely oppositional thought?" The canon is not closed; Denby credits the feminist movement for the inclusion of Jane Austen's *Pride and Prejudice* (1813) and Virginia Woolf's *To the Lighthouse* (1927). His objection is to any effort, by the left or the right, to impede the process of "oppositional thought." Although Denby takes issue with traditionalists such as Allan Bloom, William Bennett, and Lynne V. Cheney, criticizing them for elevating the canon as if it were the depository of eternal verities, most of his verbal salvos are directed against Catharine MacKinnon, Ti-Grace Atkinson, Edward Said, Chinua Achebe, and other scholars of the academic left who describe the great surviving literature of the West as "*guilty* of something. This is no harmless truism (anything that becomes part of the dominant discourse must serve some need of the powerful). At its most severe, it's a moral attack on art itself."

Art brings pleasure, and the greatest art brings the most complex and hard-won pleasure. "Pleasure never lies," he writes, "though pleasure requires cultivation, and complex pleasures the greatest cultivation of all: education." Such pleasure is not an end in itself, however; the "right kind" of pleasure, the kind that arises from the intense struggle with another human mind through literature, serves to open the door to long-forgotten memories, building a kind of continuity between the person one once was and what one has become. The integrated self is formed out of that continuity, a self distinct from its connections with the mass media of the late twentieth century.

Such a self was what Denby yearned for. "Normally, when I tried to remember things from long ago, I came away with nothing and wandered off into daydreams or movie images—the flood of desire and trivia where memory should be. I had no story to tell." He describes his media-focused existence as blurring the boundary between self and image and writes that since his earlier student days:

> I had abandoned the pleasures of concentration to the pleasures of fantasy; that anguish of being *lost* in the media, a part of the swamp of representation, and therefore merely another producer and consumer of images and words without identity or form of my own.

According to Denby, this inner sense of being lost was mirrored in the "social demoralization" in the United States in the early 1990's, and Denby found that Lit Hum, addressing the nature of the human being, and C.C., addressing the nature of human society, were ideally suited to his inquiries.

Caution is in order, however, in Denby's instrumental view that the great works are a kind of therapy for the soul. If that is the case, the core works of the canon are not very efficacious. There seems to be little correlation between the studying of these books (even in later life) and the development of exemplary character. They do not appear to be sufficient, or, it might be argued, even necessary, to the formation of the kind of self Denby seeks. In some readers, the study of the great works may provide the occasion of such formation, or the stimulus for it, but any defense of the canon based on its therapeutic nature only provides ammunition to those who would propose alternative, more effective, therapies.

Instead, *Great Books* may be read, not so much as a defense of the Western core curriculum, but as a manifesto for traditional liberal humanism, an emphasis on the this-worldly nobility of the human enterprise which is sensitive to criticism but exuberant in the face of the possibilities of each human life. As the chapters make clear, many of the books in the core course, especially those arising in and after the European Renaissance, express this enthusiasm, although Denby's description of the pleasures of reading certain authors tends toward the florid. He enjoys *The Confessions*

(*Confessiones*, C. A.D. 400) of Augustine in its honest depiction of the frailties of human beings, but also for its portrayal of the possibilities of redemption. He almost weeps for joy as one of his professors expounds the political philosophy of John Locke. William Shakespeare in *King Lear* (1608) provides Denby with the greatest pain and pleasure of any of the readings. Denby voraciously consumes *Pride and Prejudice*, reading it straight through. Friedrich Nietzsche makes him giddy.

In reading Nietzsche, Denby realizes that "my taste in 'great books' had become clear: I was drawn to energy, play, vivacity, speed, perversity."

With Woolf's *To the Lighthouse*, discussed in his final chapter, Denby notices that the tendency to daydream, so vexing in his struggles with the Homeric tales, returned, transformed, in his encounter with the novel. He characterizes himself as giving "free rein to my wanderings, swinging across the vines of association and memory and judgment and desire." The experience at Columbia in "putting himself together again" had changed the content of his inner musings, mixing the film image of Tarzan swinging from vine to vine with the project of his most admired instructor, Professor Edward Tayler: to have students form themselves "around the structured response to literature. They would stretch and create themselves in order to read these complicated books."

There is a curious discontinuity in Denby's book, one relating to irony. The author finds in Michel Eyquem de Montaigne, especially in his essay "Of Repentance" (1585-1588), a kindred spirit, one who delights in irony, in seeing a human being not as a fixed essence (as had Aristotle and Plato in the fourth and fifth century B.C.), but as an ever-changing individual, self-contradictory at times, sometimes profound, sometimes banal. Montaigne focuses on becoming, not on being.

Yet the life-giving sense of irony in Montaigne does not seem to square with Denby's complaint about modern media society:

> Like my sons, Max and Tommy, they [the Columbia students in Denby's classes] were children of the media, and I got the sense that for them an identity was provisional; everything could be *taken back*. The media had tricked them out of facing what young people in all societies have not wanted to face—that you make certain choices that you can't go back on, that identity itself is a kind of fate.

For Denby, Lit Hum was

> a struggle with difficult and faraway texts, which forced, willy-nilly, the trying on of selves; and it ended in the uniqueness of the individual student that emerged from the many selves. That's why the students' lives were at stake when they read Montaigne, for Montaigne was the supreme example of the kind of becoming that Professor Edward Tayler believed in.

What is the difference between the young ironist of the 1990's, putting on and taking off selves at will, and the trying on of selves promoted by the core curriculum at Columbia? The answer for the author seems to lie in whether the irony comes in the context of the search for the higher pleasures. Although he feels destined to his own identity, that of a self-identified bourgeois, secular, Jewish, middle-aged heterosexual family man with certain values, Denby realizes that it has come not in a blinding flash but in the long, slow process of experience and choice. His studies of the great books help him recall earlier events, and he is able to trace in his responses the details of that process of becoming that led to the formation of his deepest self. In Denby's recounting of this process there is an underlying willingness to engage in self-evaluation. By contrast, the young ironist is not ironic enough, failing to see, as Denby says in his chapter on Sophocles (c. 495-406 B.C.) and *Oedipus the King*, that there is irony at the very center of life: What one seeks to avoid at all costs, that is what one becomes. Denby observes that the young Columbia students would not have understood.

Denby is grieved that in a meeting to discuss the core curriculum at Columbia, an African American student protests having to listen to some of the works of Wolfgang Amadeus Mozart; she characterizes the requirement as a kind of slavery. In his chapter on Plato's *Republic*, Denby notes that what made him sad is the student's rejection of a new, possibly transcendent, experience for the sake of ideology. The student was not ironic enough, took life too narrowly. As Denby notes in his chapter on Machiavelli, "Reality is in itself ironic; and Machiavelli's writing is an act of malice directed at the literal-minded, just as life is a condition of malice directed at the literal-minded." The point is that self-awareness of one's responses to the ironies of life—when one expects one thing and gets another—enables an individual to discern the lineaments of the self he or she has become, and is becoming, and provokes meditation on whether that is the self one truly desires to be. The 1990's-style irony aims for disengagement—the kind of irony the reader of the great books is confronted with demands earnest self-examination.

Great Books is above all the "recollection" of a self via an encounter with the Western canon. The less cynical among his readers may well discover Denby's enthusiasm to be infectious.

Dan Barnett

Sources for Further Study

Chicago Tribune. September 8, 1996, XIV, p. 1.
Education Week. XVI, November 6, 1996, p. 40.
First Things. January, 1997, p. 42.
Harper's Magazine. CCXCIV, January, 1997, p. 66.
Los Angeles Times Book Review. October 13, 1996, p. 8.
The New Republic. CCXV, October 7, 1996, p. 34.
The New York Review of Books. XLIII, September 19, 1996, p. 31.
The New York Times. September 16, 1996, p. B4.
The New York Times Book Review. CI, September 1, 1996, p. 10.
Publishers Weekly. CCXLIII, July 22, 1996, p. 219.
Time. CXLVIII, September 9, 1996, p. 68.
The Wall Street Journal. August 27, 1996, p. A10.
The Washington Post Book World. XXVI, September 29, 1996, p. 3.

HEARING VOICES

Author: A. N. Wilson (1950-   )
Publisher: W. W. Norton (New York). 214 pp. $22.50
Type of work: Novel
Time: 1966-2000
Locale: England and New York City

A vivid continuation of the Lampitt saga, the fourth novel in a series about an important British family and the attempts of their biographers to research and to publish books about them

> Principal characters:
> RAPHAEL HUNTER, the celebrated biographer of James Petworth Lampitt
> JAMES "JIMBO" PETWORTH LAMPITT, a belletrist historian, the subject of Raphael Hunter's two-volume biography
> SARGENT LAMPITT, a renowned political theorist and one of the family's more eccentric characters
> FERGUS NOLAN, a strict Catholic and distinguished scientist
> MARGARET MARY NOLAN, Fergus' very attractive wife
> JULIAN RAMSEY, the novel's narrator and biographer of the Lampitts
> PERSY NOLAN, Margaret Mary's sister and Julian's lover
> BONAVENTURE REILLY, Julian's friend who marries Persy Nolan
> VIRGIL D. EVERETT, an American businessman who purchased the Lampitt papers and was later murdered

A. N. Wilson is a prolific novelist and biographer. In addition to his Lampitt saga, he has published eleven other novels and seven biographies, including lives of Jesus and the Christian writers C. S. Lewis and Hilaire Belloc. Wilson's concern with Catholicism is pronounced in nearly all of his writing. The chapter headings in *Hearing Voices*, for example, are quotations from *A Catechism of Christian Doctrine, Approved by the Archbishops of England and Wales and Directed to Be Used in All Their Dioceses* (revised edition, 1985), published by the Catholic Truth Society. The novel's title, in fact, may be a sly reference to both religion and biography, for both the biographer and the believer claim, in some sense, to hear voices. The trouble is, of course, whether or not the voices are genuine. Fallible, sinful human beings can see only part of the truth.

The novel's narrator, Julian Ramsey, is a would-be biographer of the Lampitt family. Eventually he will come to New York City in a one-man show that is an impersonation of James Petworth Lampitt. An actor by profession, one of the stars of a soap opera, "The Mulberrys," Julian is used to performing roles and imitating other personalities. Yet he realizes that biography calls for something more. He wants his book to be based on data, on the Lampitt papers that have been sold to the American millionaire, Virgil D. Everett. This businessman has been evidently guided by another biographer, Raphael Hunter, who has made a career out of the Lampitts in spite of the fact that the family has shunned him. Julian suspects that Hunter has invented much of the "evidence" in his biography of James "Jimbo" Petworth, and to prove his case Julian visits the Everett archive in Manhattan.

Julian is frustrated, however, by the archive's rules, which dictate that the papers have to be consulted one leaf at a time—a task that prevents researchers from getting a sense of the collection's scope. Julian wants to rummage through the entire collection to see if the titillating sexual anecdotes with which Hunter studs his biography are really there. Julian solves his problem when he befriends the female librarian, who finds him sexually attractive. Between their intense lovemaking bouts on library tables, he scours the Everett collections, confirming his hunch that Hunter's view of Jimbo is largely a fiction.

Julian then considers what to do with his knowledge. The librarian vows that she will tell her employer that he has been "sold a pup"—in British parlance, the businessman has been had. Yet when she breaks off her brief affair with Julian, he is uncertain as to what she has actually said to Everett. For Julian to tell him is to virtually admit that he has somehow circumvented the archive's rules.

Before he can resolve his dilemma, Julian is called away to England to attend the funeral of his grandmother. Then his own personal crises get the better of him, and for a time he is hospitalized during a mental breakdown. In the meantime, Everett mysteriously falls from the balcony of his penthouse, and Hunter publishes the second volume of his acclaimed biography. Julian suspects that Hunter has murdered Everett, who has found out that his papers are largely autographs, unrevealing diaries, and letters from other people who shed little light on the Lampitts. At the end of the novel, not all the mysteries have been solved. Julian has not written his own book, and he is still trying to fathom the true history of the Lampitts. Unlike Hunter, he is close to the family, having an uncle who was best friends with Sargent Lampitt, the family's literary light, and finding himself an invitee at important family gatherings.

What to believe—in both the biographical and religious sense is really the subject of this novel. Ramsey is not a Catholic, but he is surrounded by Catholics, former Catholics, converts to Catholicism, and apostates. This commitment to and renunciation of belief pervades the novel. Julian's friend, Bonaventure Reilly, for example, is an ardent Dominican, but he also lusts after Margaret Mary Nolan (the target of Julian's desire as well) and renounces his religious life to marry Julian's former lover Persy Nolan, Margaret Mary's sister.

Margaret Mary is herself a conundrum in the belief/doubt nexus of the novel, apparently unaware of all the men whose passion she excites. Yet she is repeatedly referred to as M.M.—inevitably suggesting Marilyn Monroe. Julian suspects that she has had an affair with the rogue biographer Hunter (appropriately named as a predator of others' lives), and that her pregnancy, after years and years of trying for a child with her husband, Fergus, is the result of her liaison with Hunter.

The very process of researching a biography and thinking about the biographical form seems to have undone Julian. He compares biography unfavorably to fiction. A biography can never tell the whole truth, and it cannot penetrate to the core of character as novels do. In particular, detective novels offer the satisfaction of a solution that is denied to biographers. Ramsey contends that the mystery story is a religious form because it resolves doubts.

Julian is so bedeviled by the problematic nature of biography that he begins to fantasize himself into the roles of detectives. In a hilarious scene, he becomes Hercule Poirot, assembling the suspects and announcing in his inimitable Belgian construction of English that Everett has "purchased ze puppy," and Poirot has solved the crime. In Julian's fantasy, Hunter can be summoned, arraigned before the detective, and convicted as the murderer. In essence, Julian is driven mad by a reality that is so much more ambiguous than mystery stories suppose. As his publisher tells him, only in detective stories are human motives clear cut. Indeed, his publisher is not sure that people always act from motives or could explain their actions.

In this atmosphere of uncertainty, the chapter headings from the Catholic catechism reinforce the desire for authority, for an absolute, unquestionable source of truth. The catechism explains that those who commit mortal sins go to hell. In Julian's world, however, those who sin—like Hunter—are rewarded. The church, the catechism emphasizes, cannot err in regard to faith or morals. Julian himself, without a commitment to the church, agonizes over his sins and tortures himself when he realizes that his lover, Persy Nolan, has aborted their child without telling him. The church insists that there are mysteries that are above reason. Lacking the conviction to accept this teaching, Julian tears himself apart trying to solve secrets of the Lampitt family and its archive. In the church's teaching, Julian has sinned against hope because he has given way to despair and presumption. He has taken too much upon himself, the novel implies. He has heard too many voices, and they have confused him.

This novel has an intricate time scheme. It begins in October, 1968, with Everett's murder, then projects forward to October, 2000, and then back to April, 1966, Summer, 1966, Spring, 1968, Summer, 1968, and Christmas, 1969. This pattern conforms to Julian's way of piecing together his own story, but each section is not situated solely within his understanding of those periods. In other words, each section also carries with it Julian's consciousness of other times and the dated sections refer to the events covered rather than to what the narrator's consciousness encompasses. Moreover, part of each section seems given over to a third-person narrator, a sign that Julian is unable to comprehend fully even those parts of history that he is investigating. *Hearing Voices* does a splendid job of showing just how confusing and frustrating a biographer's work can be. Impatient readers may bridle at the host of minor characters and side issues that seem to get in the way of solving the mystery of what is in the Lampitt papers. Yet the novel is not merely about this plot. Rather, it is about the biographer and about the way his story is constantly interfering with the biography he is trying to write. All biography is, to an extent, autobiography, Julian concedes, and *Hearing Voices* is structured to make precisely that point.

An additional difficulty is that this novel is part of a series. It can be read without reference to its three predecessors, but Wilson does not quite allay the feeling that his characters have a history that this novel does not always clearly explain. To remedy this problem, "A List of Characters Mentioned in the Story," has been appended to the novel. While the list is useful, especially in drawing attention to which characters appear in earlier novels, it is also a confession that *Hearing Voices* does not completely stand on its own. The virtue of this defect is that it is rather like a real history or biography, in which it is always assumed that the biographer or historian cannot possibly give a sense of context for every personage and event.

Wilson's own practice as biographer and novelist obviously informs *Hearing Voices*. Biography gets the worst of it—as it usually does when novelists write about the form. Thus Julian opines: "The mercurial quality of human characters, and of their interactions, can more easily be captured by works of literature which do not proclaim themselves to be 'true.' Novels and plays tell us, in their darting and haphazard manner, more than the scientifically researched biographies with acknowledgements to all the big American libraries." Just so, but when Julian adds that there is no "one truth," he is actually favoring biographies, whose apparatus concedes the biographer's fallibility as much as it is a pretention to scientific accuracy. Few biographers would risk the wholesale inventions of a Raphael Hunter, which turn his subject, as Julian observes, into himself.

Biography has its origins in hagiography, in the desire to praise the saint whose life becomes an exemplary story. This religious origin of biography has in modern times been transferred to the profession of literary biography. Writers have become modern saints, often shown to be fallible, but nevertheless presented as representative of their times. Biographers struggle with what to believe about these figures; the shape biographies take is a revelation of the patterns biographers see not only in the evidence but in their own lives, their quests for belief, for solutions to the mysteries of life. If Julian Ramsey fails to complete his Lampitt biography, it is largely because he cannot overcome his doubts and release himself to the act of faith that is ultimately what biography is all about.

Carl Rollyson

Sources for Further Study

Booklist. XCII, February 15, 1996, p. 992.
Chicago Tribune. March 31, 1996, XIV, p. 6.
Kirkus Reviews. LXIII, December 15, 1995, p. 1729.
Library Journal. CXXI, February 15, 1996, p. 177.
The New York Times Book Review. CI, March 3, 1996, p. 30.
The Observer. December 24, 1995, p. 12.
Publishers Weekly. CCXLIII, January 8, 1996, p. 58.
The Spectator. CCLXXV, November 11, 1995, p. 47.
The Times Literary Supplement. November 10, 1995, p. 23.

HEAVEN'S COAST
A Memoir

Author: Mark Doty (1954-   )
Publisher: HarperCollins (New York). 305 pp. $24.00
Type of work: Memoir
Time: 1989-1995
Locale: New England

A harrowing yet luminous account of poet Mark Doty's surviving the death of his longtime partner

> *Principal personages:*
> MARK DOTY, an award-winning poet and teacher
> WALLY ROBERTS, his life partner
> BEAU and ARDEN, their two labrador retrievers
> LYNDA, Doty's friend, fellow poet, and relentlessly free spirit
> BOBBY, Wally's oldest gay friend

When a public health worker gave Mark Doty and his partner Wally Roberts the results of their AIDS test in May of 1989, the world cracked open for the couple. Although it was only Wally who tested positive for the human immunodeficiency virus (HIV), Doty registered it as a solvent that dissolved both of their lives, erasing their future together and thus signaling an end to Doty's life as well. They had built a solid and deeply satisfying relationship over the course of eight years, and would have another four years before Wally's death in January, 1994.

Heaven's Coast is an eloquent memoir of those last years and of the turbulent aftermath, Doty's year-long struggle with grief over so elemental a loss. It is by turns angry and tender, defiant and reverent; for all the pain, for all the physical and emotional difficulties it portrays, it is never less than clear-eyed and unflinching, always scrupulously descriptive and unashamed of its revelations. In the end, the account of Doty's spiritual journey—through suffering and separation to a cathartic acceptance of life's betrayals—achieves tragic dimensions. The transcendence he discovers and articulates by the memoir's last pages provides a fitting finale to an intensely moving story.

Doty's is one of several books to have been published in 1996 which recount the experience of being an AIDS survivor, building on a tradition first established in 1988 with Paul Monette's *Borrowed Time: An AIDS Memoir*. As powerful as Monette's book was, however, it was told from the point of view of a surviving partner who was himself HIV-positive. (After writing two more novels and an award-winning autobiography, Monette died in 1995.) These new memoirs, on the other hand, are written by men who have not acquired the virus and who are left to fashion a rather different and perhaps more complicated narrative of survival, a narrative encompassing guilt as well as grief and rage. Fenton Johnson's *Geography of the Heart* and Bernard Cooper's *Truth Serum* both explore this increasingly familiar landscape of disease and remembrance, but the fact that they are novelists gives their accounts a somewhat different shape. Their books are not any less effective as tributes to their lost lovers, but they are somehow less immediate, and finally less affecting than Doty's. They are the work of experienced practitioners of prose, whereas *Heaven's Coast* represents Doty's first foray outside of his usual field of poetry. Happily, his roots show: All the gifts he brings to bear in the poems are readily perceptible here—the uncanny ear, the discerning eye, the restless desire to understand the images that press themselves insistently upon him. As a result, the memoir has a richness, a sensuous finish to it, the feel of having been written by a man on whom nothing—no feeling, no experience, no sensory detail—is lost. The language has all the sheen of a newly burnished poem, the images shimmer and linger in the mind; yet it reads, amazingly, as naturally as conversational prose.

The author of four volumes of poetry and the winner of numerous awards, including the prestigious National Book Critics Circle Award for *My Alexandria* (1993), Doty has made a name for himself as a poet of almost Keatsian lusciousness, alert to the richness of human experience as well as to its evanescence, its awful fragility. His voice seems most naturally pitched in an elegiac key, and in his meticulous tracings of the clear beauties of the physical world, he never fails to remark the ambivalent quality of nature's offerings. His poems after Wally's HIV diagnosis are, not surprisingly, even more finely attuned to this doubleness, to the flux that underlies apparent stability, to the provisional nature of identity, to the contradictions that surround life and death. The poems collected in *Atlantis* (1995) cover much the same ground as *Heaven's Coast* though they do so in the more chiseled and concise manner of poetry. They document Doty's loss with the same grace and bravery, placing Wally's death in the larger context of nature and, more precisely, in the natural landscape of Provincetown, Massachusetts, their home, *their* Alexandria—a border town where various cultures mingle and remain separate at once, where a fascinating spectrum of relationships exists and where difference and surprise is the expected. Here is not only a welcoming human community but an unusual geographical configuration that seems to embody Doty's sense of existence. The narrow strip of land, the surrounding water, the ceaseless alteration of earth and shore—these images of transformation, of ebb and flood, of renegotiated boundaries accompany Doty's reflections throughout the poems and the prose and eventually suggest to him a means of coming to terms with Wally's death and his own ongoing life. Yet the passage toward accommodating so radical a change does not come easily; the vision of grace he finally embraces does not arrive without innumerable interruptions and regressions, yet the memoir traces these emotional fluctuations with a bracing candor.

Doty has solved the problem of how to structure such a challenging narrative by making *Heaven's Coast* a compendium—of journal entries (from a journal he kept for two years during Wally's final illness), letters to and from friends, vignettes from the couple's past, minihistories of various friends, accounts of Doty's serious and persistent back problems, short essays and extended meditations on memory, gardening, sex, animals, the sea, among many other things. It is an impressionistic collection, circling always, temporally and thematically, around the central figure of Wally and his slow decline from progressive multifocal leukoencephalopathy (PML), a brain infection that leads to gradual paralysis and death. Left emotionally paralyzed himself after Wally's death and in the grip of immobilizing back pain, Doty stopped writing for a month. Then, in February, he entered these questions in his journal: "How can I begin, how can I not begin?" The way back was through language. He had been asked to contribute to Brian Bouldrey's anthology about AIDS and religion, *Wrestling with the Angel* (1995), but very soon he found that he was writing about himself, writing to give shape to his experience, and discovering that in doing so he could inscribe his memory of Wally. In the process, he reanimates all of his love for his lost partner, getting inside their relationship in ways he had never felt before; and he learns the consoling lesson that we are not merely our bodies but are fluid, multiple, extended, that Wally is not entirely lost to him. It is Wally's presence he imagines encountering when he meets the depthless gaze of a coyote or watches the buoyant play of a coast seal. These totems come bearing signs of the otherness that is death, but intimations, too, of the connections that may exist between this living world and the shadowy one beyond us.

In a real sense, it was Doty's work that saved him, the effort of making, of writing—and becoming—a story. He remembers reading that when his wife Camille was on her deathbed, Claude Monet said, "I found myself, without being able to help it, in a study of my beloved wife's face, systematically noting the colors." In the same way, Doty cannot help but note the colors. "What does a writer do when the world collapses," he asks, "but write?" So he writes, at first about the immediate pain of absence, the deep and pervasive sorrow that seemed to him, in those initial months after Wally's death, to be a large and inhabitable space or a season that simply had to be endured, a winter without much promise of spring. He took endless walks out on the salt marsh and in the woods with the two dogs, Beau and Arden, who had lived through Wally's illness and been such responsive and loving companions to both men. In the dogs' natural insistence on living life now, in the moment, Doty found some power to attend to the hard but essential realities of his life in the present difficult moment. In their pure directness of being, he found the courage to examine his own identity and what it meant to have discovered that identity in his relationship with Wally over the course of a dozen years.

He writes of a trip taken back to their Boston neighborhood weeks after Wally's death, a visit full of Dantean echoes of an underworld journey since so many of the men who lived in the tall old Beacon Street brownstone were by now dead too, casualties of the AIDS epidemic. It was here that he and Wally had their first apartment, here as a twenty-eight-year-old man that Doty had plunged into his first passionate gay love affair. Before this, he had been married but had fled both the marriage and the Midwest when the reality of being gay became overwhelmingly clear to him. With six hundred dollars to his name, he packed up all he had in a little yellow Chevette and headed to Manhattan, living off his earnings as a temporary typist and a part-time job teaching in a summer writers program. Within months he had met Wally, and within another three months he had left New York for Boston and the promise of a life together—a life that would take them to Vermont when Doty got a teaching position at Goddard College, then to Provincetown when Wally's diagnosis made them feel that they needed a more supportive, less isolated community in which to deal with this crisis.

He writes of the death of a close friend and fellow poet, the beautiful, complicated, self-destructive, prodigiously talented Lynda. It was a rich and prickly friendship, professionally and personally nourishing though frustrating. Her alcoholism made her wildly unpredictable, while that very unpredictability made her a fascinating companion. She was a creature of style and charm, mercurial, adventurous, defiant. She shared Doty's allegiance to an aesthetic of "lush surfaces spread over difficult, edgy material, art full of anguish and pleasure in the racked beauty of the world." When she died in an automobile accident a mere three months after Doty lost Wally, the strain that had been building erupted in a lava flow of rage and pain, a feeling of dread, of helplessness in the face of the relentless grinding force of life. Hit with these two nearly unbearable losses, Doty could only rail savagely against a reality that seemed nothing but a fiendishly efficient system for carrying people and things away.

Yet he also writes about the moments when, in spite of these larger forces ineluctably drawing people toward separation and destruction, they erect something that gives them hope in a future. The house and garden that Doty and Wally took on in Vermont are emblems of this persistent desire to build, to create beauty and stability in a world of flux. The pages in which he talks about rescuing the sagging Victorian house, transforming it into a warm and shining refuge for themselves and their friends, are full of joy. Like the house finches he watches nesting in his eaves, these two gay men make a dwelling place for their spirits in those five Vermont years. Yet even the lovingly restored house and the luxuriant garden cannot finally protect them.

Running through the text as a kind of *idée fixe* are the dark and inevitable questions raised by the biblical book of Job. The great and seemingly motiveless losses, the arbitrary motions of the cosmos, the vulnerability, the diminishment, the disillusionment, the pain—all this prompts Job to cry out in his bitterness, Why me? Why do I suffer? What is the point of all this pain? His refusal to accept easily and silently the gnawing black vision of an incomprehensible world, his great defining "No!" leveled at a mysterious power, is a sign of his humanity. Doty feels a kinship with Job in his despair; he too cannot understand and will not be silent. He will write; he will descend into the very blackness of his grief. And he does. He comes through, however, ascends in fact, to an understanding of Job's condition that is quite different from where he began: He now finds consolation as well as desolation. There *is* design; there *is* a power that, while indifferent to his suffering and unprepared to intervene in it, is nevertheless holding it all together. Great grief, yes, but great intimacy and light and love as well.

This vision of a world caught in a paradox, wrapped in indissoluble contraries, appears in another literary voice that winds through the memoir, the voice of Rainer Maria Rilke from the *Duino Elegies* (1923; English translation, 1930). When Doty reads the line "for beauty is nothing but the beginning of terror, which we are still just able to endure," he cannot help asking if it may not also be true that terror is only the edge of a beauty we can hardly bear. The hint that grief and joy are embraced in a curious but beautiful dance, is a saving revelation. It accounts for the strange shine around Wally's dying, the feeling that Wally leapt up and soared out, free and graceful and whole. It accounts for the way gladness seeps under Doty's blanket of grief when, all unbidden, the fragrant glamour of an Italian spring pulls him into a joyous present, rich with possibilities yet tinged with past sorrows. It accounts for the poignant comfort of the body when we know that the body can comfort only so much. "Each thing disappears; everything goes on." Absence and presence. The now and the hereafter. The boundaries are fluid, uncertain. For Doty, "the whole world is heaven's coast." Thus it is not surprising that he ends the book with "the story I've been saving." A mere week or so after Wally died, Doty took the dogs for a walk across the salt marsh and found himself thinking of the lines from Whitman's "Song of Myself," the section in which the poet imagines, joyously, that grass is the beautiful uncut hair of graves, that it has its origins in the bodies of the dead. Crying and shakily feeling his way through the poem, he reaches the lines he has clearly been moving toward: "All goes onward and outward, nothing collapses,/ And to die is different from what anyone supposed, and luckier." That note of transformation and renewal, the refusal to see *only* death, *only* grief, resonates in Doty's poems as much as it does in this radiant work of remembering.

Thomas J. Campbell

Sources for Further Study

Chicago Tribune. May 5, 1996, XIV, p. 5.
Kirkus Reviews. LXIV, January 1, 1996, p. 37.
Library Journal. CXXI, February 15, 1996, p. 157.
Los Angeles Times Book Review. April 14, 1996, p. 2.
The Nation. CCLXIII, July 15, 1996, p. 33.
The New York Times Book Review. CI, March 10, 1996, p. 10.
The New Yorker. LXXII, May 13, 1996, p. 95.
Ploughshares. XXII, Spring, 1996, p. 203.
Publishers Weekly. CCXLIII, January 29, 1996, p. 91.
The Washington Post Book World. XXVI, April 7, 1996, p. 11.

HERMAN MELVILLE
A Biography
Volume I, 1819-1851

Author: Hershel Parker (1935-   )
Publisher: The Johns Hopkins University Press (Baltimore). 941 pp. $39.95
Type of work: Literary biography
Time: The first half of the nineteenth century
Locale: New York City; the Pacific; Pittsfield, Massachusetts

This first installment of a two-volume biography of Herman Melville provides the definitive account of the life from his birth in 1819 through the writing of his 1851 masterpiece Moby Dick

Principal personages:
HERMAN MELVILLE, a sailor and author
ALLAN MELVILL, his father
MARIA GANSEVOORT MELVILL, his mother
GANSEVOORT MELVILL, his elder brother
ELIZABETH KNAPP SHAW, his wife
LEMUEL SHAW, his father-in-law, the chief justice of the Massachusetts
    Supreme Court
EVERT A. DUYCKINCK, his American publisher
JOHN MURRAY, his British publisher
NATHANIEL HAWTHORNE, the American novelist

Hershel Parker's massive first volume of a proposed two-volume life of Herman Melville is an impressive and often daunting work. Straightforwardly titled, *Herman Melville: A Biography* is written with the assurance that comes from years of researching and studying and then intimately knowing the subject in question. The book, more than nine hundred pages in length, covers Melville's life from his birth in 1819 to the moment in November, 1851, when he triumphantly presents an early copy of his masterpiece *Moby Dick* to his fellow author and, at that time, close friend Nathaniel Hawthorne, to whom the book was dedicated. It was, according to Parker, the "happiest day of Melville's life," and thus a propitious point at which to pause. Indeed, despite its shares of disasters and deaths, Parker tells a happy story in this book. (The next volume, already drafted, will perforce be a darker work, given the tremendous disappointments and tragedies in the second half of Melville's life.)

Parker's biography of Melville has been eagerly anticipated by devotees of the great writer. Parker, who began his formal Melville studies as a student at Northwestern University in 1962, is acknowledged by most as the leading authority on Melville's life, and his reputation for exhaustive and precise scholarship is legendary within academia. He has long served as the associate general editor of the Northwestern-Newberry *The Writings of Herman Melville*, which has as its goal the establishment of authoritative texts for all Melville's books and other writings. This series has been both revered and (by some) derided for its extremely rigorous, detailed editorial approach and the numerous appendices, charts, and explanatory essays which sometimes seem to occupy more pages than the writings they supplement. Most textual scholars have held the series in high regard, but other readers and critics have criticized both the method and the almost obsessive attention to particulars.

The same praise and criticism will, no doubt, also be directed toward Parker's scholarly biography, which belongs to the "too many facts are never enough" school of such works. Parker is nothing if not passionate about Melville. "My life is too valuable for me to waste it on someone who's not majestic, who I don't love," he is quoted as saying in a profile by Philip Weiss in *The New York Times Magazine*. For such a scholar-biographer, each discovery is invaluable and therefore terribly difficult to omit. Yet when one considers how much Melville material has already been lost, one hesitates to criticize the monumental inclusiveness of this work. (In addition to the loss of *The Isle of the Cross*, which Melville wrote in 1853, after *Moby Dick* and *Pierre*, published in 1852, Melville documents and letters were still being destroyed as late as the 1950's.) Better to have this information provided and protected than to risk further loss to time, accident, or fate, even if the reading experience is sometimes made more difficult by the repetitions, side-trips, and cumulation of details. To be sure, this is not an easy book to read. It is doubtful that many readers outside of dedicated Melvilleans will follow, or be able to follow, every page of this work. Even with genealogical charts for guidance, it is almost impossible to keep straight the various members of Melville's immediate families, and the amount of historical and cultural data, the details of the contemporary political and literary worlds, sometimes threaten to overwhelm the narrative itself.

Which is not to say that Parker has written a stiff or pedantic work. He takes such joy in his subject, has such affection for Melville the man, that the book has a feel of play about it. The cover illustration by Maurice Sendak, also reprinted as frontispiece in the book, represents this spirit. (Sendak, best known for his children's books, is also a great admirer of Melville; he has also supplied intriguing illustrations for Parker's 1995 newly edited version of *Pierre: Or, The Ambiguities*.) In the drawing, Melville stands in profile before the rigging of a ship, a feather held in one hand, a flower stuck in the brim of his hat. He seems both an adventurer and a poser, a man of action and of romantic imagination. This is the Melville that Parker reveals in the pages of this book, a dreamer and an explorer and a thoroughly impractical and egotistical and self-destructive character. "More than once, I would have warned him away from a precipice," Parker notes in his preface, "but I depict him as I see him. In an era when to write a biography is to expose a pathology, I hope I have manifested toward Melville and his family a measure of his own magnanimity and pudency, even if not . . . his unapproachable 'greatness of gusto.'"

It is impossible, then, to read this biography without noting the biases of the biographer. Parker is exceedingly precise in all matters of historical and personal fact, and his scholarship is to all appearances impeccable, but he clearly intends the work as a celebration of Melville. It is so steeped in the era it represents that there is almost an anachronistic tone to the book, and it often reads like a nineteenth century romance, with Melville as hero. Since Melville used his early adventures as the basis of his first writings, and, mixing fact (both personal and that mined from other books) with fiction, created a public persona of "Herman Melville," the roguish sailor, perhaps it is appropriate that his biographer also take a seminovelistic approach to his subject, surmising unspoken or undocumented thought, creating dramatic scenes based on the best possible evidence, assuming motive as suggested by overall knowledge of the person. Parker is very forthright about his method, and he carefully distinguishes between what he absolutely knows and what is his best guess. In the dramatic opening episode, for example, in which Melville, age eleven, is fleeing with his father from New York City to Albany to escape the family's creditors, Parker writes, "Herman may not have known that his father, a former importer of French dry goods, was three months in arrears on house rent, that other debts were unpaid, and that [Allan] Melvill [Herman added the final *e* to his name years later] feared a creditor might have him arrested before he got away, but there had been no hiding from the boy the urgency of the family plight." Similarly, the very last scene in the book, which depicts Melville's semiprivate presentation of *Moby Dick* to Hawthorne in the dining room of a Lennox, Massachusetts, hotel, is also dramatically re-created:

> There were onlookers aplenty, but no eavesdroppers to record their conversation. . . . Here, in the dining room, Hawthorne for the first time saw the extraordinary dedication and tribute to his genius—the first book anyone had dedicated to him. Never demonstrative, he was profoundly moved. Alone with the author, he could open the book in his nervous way (more nervous even than normally), and get from his friend a guided tour of the organization of the thing now in print, and even sample a few paragraphs that caught his eye or that the author eagerly pointed out to him, perhaps even some passages he had seen in manuscript in Melville's study.

This is, as Parker explains in a footnote, an "imaginative reconstruction" of the scene, based on a letter later written by one of the onlookers, and on "other evidence." Some readers may fault Parker for such scenes, arguing that he has stepped beyond the role of impartial biographer. Given the subjective nature of the entire work and the kinship Parker obviously feels with Melville, this is a criticism that misses the point of what Parker is attempting to do. Any biography is a "dramatic reconstruction," and what Parker has undertaken is the recovery of not just one man, but of a time, a country, a historical era. Somehow it seems petty to complain about his methods, given the grand scope of his intentions.

So who is this protagonist of Parker's magnum opus? The basic facts of Melville's life are well enough known. Herman (Parker assumes a first-name relationship) was the second son in a large, once prominent family now living on the edge of poverty and disgrace. Allan Melvill, the father, was son to Thomas, a close friend to Samuel Adams and an actual member of the Boston Tea Party. The mother, Maria Gansevoort Melvill, came from an even more distinguished line; her father was Peter Gansevoort, the "Hero of Fort Stanwix" during the Revolutionary War, and she was also related to the Van Rensselaers, the greatest of the Dutch families settled in New York. Despite his patrician background, Allan Melvill was a poor businessman and quickly squandered both his and his wife's inheritances. When he died at age fifty, he left his family deeply in debt and at the mercy of his creditors. The burden to preserve the family fell first on his widow and eventually on his eldest son, the ambitious Gansevoort. Parker emphasizes Herman's relationship with his brother, whom he greatly admired. Since Gansevoort seemed destined to be a success—he was not a much better businessman than his father, but he was deeply interested in politics and developed a reputation as a fine orator—Herman stood in his shadow and found little direction in his own life. After trying his hand at clerking, farming, and schoolteaching, he shipped out, in 1839 at the age of nineteen, as a common sailor on the merchant ship *St. Lawrence* for a four-month excursion to Liverpool, England. In 1841, he signed on the whaler *Acushnet* for a three-year voyage. In the summer of the next year, he jumped ship with a companion at the Marquesas Islands and lived for a short time among the Typee natives in the interior. On another whaler, the *Lucy Ann*, he next became involved in a mutiny and was placed under a loose form of house arrest in Tahiti. From there he traveled to the Hawaiian islands, where he worked for several months, and in August, 1843, he became an ordinary seaman on the naval frigate the *United States*, on which he returned home to Boston, arriving in October, 1844. His adventures over these approximately five years provided the materials on which his first books, the ones through *Moby Dick*, were based.

The quality of Parker's research and scholarship is nowhere more evident than in his recounting of these early years, in which public knowledge of Melville is often sketchy indeed. Drawing on a vast array of sources, Parker attempts to document every movement, to prove or dispel every rumor, to correct every popular error. When there is little to say about Herman directly, he concentrates on creating the world in which Herman lived. As a result, the first half of this first volume sometimes seems to be more about other people than Herman; as with Ishmael in *Moby Dick*, the reader may sometimes wonder if the author has momentarily misplaced his protagonist, and some may also feel overwhelmed by the completeness of Parker's work. After quoting from a letter, for example, is it necessary to restate what has just been presented? Indeed, it often is, for Parker is able to give perspective, to explain or note items that might well slip by too many of his readers.

The second half of the volume concentrates on Melville as writer and as public personality—an international "sex symbol" according to Parker's account. Once again at loose ends after his return, he writes *Typee* (1846) and its sequel *Omoo* (1847) almost on a lark. The books were controversial, considered obscene for their portrayal of the Typee natives' sexual freedom, and blasphemous for Melville's attack on Christian missionaries and their hypocritical destruction of native culture. Herman's brother Gansevoort arranged the publication of *Typee* in England, where he was serving as secretary to the United States minister to Great Britain. Long the more respected and admired brother, Gansevoort proved invaluable in helping the younger Herman get his start. Gansevoort's unexpected death in 1846, just as Herman was becoming a celebrity, then shifted the family responsibility onto Herman's shoulders. Parker carefully explores both the financial and psychological burdens this death placed on Melville at this early stage in his literary career.

As Parker shows, Melville's writing genius developed with incredible rapidity. In his third novel, *Mardi* (1849), he attempted an extravagant allegory, an audacious philosophical experiment and one largely unpopular with the readers of his "adventure" stories. Heeding practical necessity (he had married Elizabeth Shaw, daughter of Massachusetts Supreme Court chief justice Lemuel Shaw in 1847), Melville returned to the more conventional fictions with *Redburn* (1849) and *White-Jacket* (1850), both books written within one year's time. It was during this period that Melville became a part of the New York literary world, and Parker is at his best in explaining Herman's place in that society, most important in his relationship with Evert Duyckinck, his publisher and friend.

The volume ends with Melville's meeting Nathaniel Hawthorne (Parker gives almost a comic portrait of the solemn, inward author) and the writing of *Moby Dick*. It is, as already noted, a triumphant conclusion, but one that anticipates the sadness to come. If one could reasonably ask for yet more material in what is already a monumental work, it would be to have greater attention on the actual writing itself, especially of this truly astonishing novel. Much of this information can be found in the Northwestern-Newberry editions, but a clearer picture of Melville as creator would certainly have added to Parker's final achievement.

Thus, this first volume must be seen as the definitive work. (A fine one-volume biography of the entire life by Laurie Robertson-Lorant, first published in Great Britain as *Herman Melville: A Biography* and reviewed elsewhere in this volume, was released in the United States only months before Parker's book, but it cannot compete in scope or thoroughness.) It is the kind of overreaching, audacious, eccentric, yet brilliant deed that Melville would surely have admired.

Edwin T. Arnold

Sources for Further Study

The Atlantic. CCLXXIX, January, 1997, p. 96.
Boston Globe. December 15, 1996, p. N16.
Library Journal. CXXI, September 15, 1996, p. 69.
Los Angeles Times Book Review. December 15, 1996, p. 8.
The New York Times Book Review. CI, December 22, 1996, p. 12.
The New York Times Magazine. December 15, 1996, p. 60.
Publishers Weekly. CCXLIII, October 14, 1996, p. 70.
The Spectator. CCLXXVIII, January 4, 1997, p. 32.
The Times Literary Supplement. January 10, 1997, p. 3.
The Wall Street Journal. November 22, 1996, p. A12.
The Washington Post Book World. XXVI, December 1, 1996, p. 8.

THE HIDE

Author: Barry Unsworth (1930-   )
First published: 1970, in Great Britain
Publisher: W. W. Norton (New York). 192 pp. $22.00
Type of work: Novel
Time: The late twentieth century
Locale: England

With its mythic undertones, this novel tells of a young man's initiation into evil as he comes under the diabolical influence of two men, older than he and from widely different social strata

Principal characters:
> JOSIAH (JOSH), an amusement park worker, and later a gardener on the Wilcox estate
> MORTIMER CADE, Josh's mentor and confidant from the park
> SIMON THEBUS, a middle-aged bachelor living at his sister's house
> AUDREY WILCOX, the widowed sister of Simon, and Josh's employer
> MARION, housekeeper for Audrey, and Josh's girlfriend

Barry Unsworth is generally thought of as a historical novelist, since he won Britain's prestigious Booker Prize for *Sacred Hunger* (1992), about the slave trade, and was shortlisted again for the award for *Morality Play* (1995), a tale of murder which takes place in medieval times. Yet *The Hide* is set firmly in contemporary England. Although it contains echoes of D. H. Lawrence and of the angry working-class fiction of post-World War II, it perhaps will remind readers most strongly of Graham Greene's *Brighton Rock* in its horrifying depiction of the corruption of innocence, not least of all because its action opens at a seaside pleasure palace.

Unsworth tells his story using two alternating first-person narrators—with uncannily accurate voices appropriate to their diverse backgrounds and socioeconomic classes—in sections that crosscut more feverishly as the story moves to its conclusion. The novel's interlocking structure comes to mirror the way in which the lives of these characters, who are initially so disparate both socially and spatially, impinge on and affect one another. Unsworth's two narrators are Simon Thebus, a man in his late forties who is living with (sponging off might be more accurate) his widowed sister, Audrey Wilcox, in her rural home; and Josiah, known as Josh, a twenty-year-old rifle range attendant at the amusement park whom Audrey hires as her gardener when her brother's inattention to the property threatens its reversion to some "primeval swamp."

Not that Simon has not been busy, for he has been excavating the vast network of "the hide" from which he can spy secretly on others, on the girls who ride by the property on their bicycles or, using his binoculars, on the woman across the way as she goes about her housework unaware of being watched by an audience. His voyeurism causes him both ecstasy and torment, pleasurable titillation, sometimes to climax, followed by "desolation" and "self-disgust" and "malaise." Although he has lived with his sister for fifteen years, he still feels isolated and excluded from the circle of her acquaintances, and so he sees Josh's arrival as gardener as a threat to a tidy, if strained, existence with Audrey. Widowed and recovered from a hysterectomy, Audrey displays an outer poise, making believe she is content now to live withdrawn and emotionally asleep. Yet her rejection by the local dramatic society, which refuses to cast her as Mrs. Alving in Ibsen's *Ghosts*, reduces her to frenzied tears, revealing how tenuous is her hold on her self-control and helping to propel her into a motherly but strangely seductive interest in Josh, with whom she shares her art books, many of them featuring pictures of nudes. When Audrey orders Simon to leave after he embarrasses her by plopping his false teeth into the mousse she has prepared for her guests, he retaliates by plotting the expulsion of Josh from the estate, so that at the end he will win back control of his territory and be alone with a dependent Audrey after she has attempted suicide by cutting her throat.

If Simon is a voyeur where sex is concerned, Mortimer Cade experiences sex only vicariously. Apparently physically impotent himself, his pandering and lechery take the form of insinuating himself into others' lives, longing to hear descriptions of a graphic nature and, in effect, possessing the woman through the other. This need may have its source in a denial of his own repressed homosexuality, for the bonds he forms with younger men—which are more nearly a kind of bondage—are clearly homosocial in nature. Both Mortimer and Simon turn the intimate friendships in which Josh is involved, with the older Audrey and his sexual liaison with the younger Marion, into *ménages à trois* of a kind, in which Mortimer and Simon actively observe rather than participate physically. Mortimer, indeed, is a frightening, almost Iago-like villain, who dissembles and tries to sully everything with which he comes into contact. The depths of his evil nature are suggested in the novel's first pages when he says that the immigrant Cypriot, the outsider who threatens to take the food from their mouths, should be "incarcinerated," a coined word that neatly calls up images both of political tyranny and of the gas chambers. Yet often Mortimer's language, though it exerts an undisputed power over Josh, seems divorced or disconnected from the reality, which renders it all that more treacherous for those he dominates. Obsessed with the dark side of life, Mortimer orders Josh to visualize the night world after the pubs close so vividly, with all the vomiting and urinating and fornicating that ensue, that Josh will become physically ill and believe that only Mortimer in all the world, and no woman like Marion, could ever be able to hold and comfort him.

Josh, the novel's other first-person narrator and really its focal character, is barely beyond his teen years; product of a family in which his father "took up" with his own half-sister, he is insecure and in need of approval, particularly from those older than himself. His burgeoning sexuality, including an adolescent need to lose his virginity, though earthy and crude and at times dishonestly boastful, is still—unlike that of either Simon or Mortimer—natural and healthy. Although a skilled artisan who carves a noticeably beautiful small horse that, acting on Simon's advice, he gives to Audrey after he fears Mortimer would only laugh derisively were he to receive such a present, Josh admits to being deficient in reading and expressing himself well in words. Afraid of losing Mortimer's friendship, Josh does not realize until too late the kind of hold the older man secures over him; occasionally, he will be deliberately circumspect and even deceitful to prevent Mortimer from knowing things that would lessen Josh in his eyes or threaten to sever their growing bond. When Mortimer, for instance, accuses Josh's new girlfriend Marion of being whorish, Josh determines to keep private and hidden the intensity of his growing feeling for her, afraid that he might be unable to justify his opinion of her in the face of Mortimer's denigration. He needs, in short, to ingratiate himself to maintain his position of approval in Mortimer's eyes, and, in his psychological dependency, will shy away from any attempt to articulate his true emotions in order to accomplish this. Yet Josh is much more mature in the ways of the heart than is Marion. A reader of romances, she comments dreamily that love always has the "color" of the loved one's eyes, whereas Josh understands that love, rather than have a color, is a deep feeling. Marion does, however, respond with genuine tenderness to Josh's plight over his premature ejaculation during their first lovemaking, reassuring him that he need never turn away from her in embarrassment again.

The Hide is rife with imagery of the garden, both literal and symbolic/archetypal. If Josh is literally the hired gardener, he is also a contemporary version of that first gardener, Adam, tempted to sin by the satanic Mortimer, the serpent of biblical myth, who insinuates his way into Josh's life. In this pattern, Simon becomes the garden's overseer, a kind of perverse demigod who blights the place he inhabits. The Wilcox property is already a post-lapsarian world, however, where nature is luxuriously overripe and where beetles attack the inviolate roses, butterflies are caught in the spider's web, and predatory insects devour one another. Simon's clothes and person smell of the clay from which, for the past two years, he has been creating the roofed, underground trench, with a circular pit that is somewhat womblike in nature, from which he adopts an all-seeing perspective on the rest of the world. Unsworth has Simon remark about the trench that, "like artistic conceptions, it grew magnified in the execution"; and one of the dinner guests at the house calls Simon "simply the agency of an impersonal force." If the first Creator brought the universe into existence out of chaos and the void, Simon himself complains of a "tiredness from striving always to fit everything that happened into a *design*"—something he says is "best left to the Supreme Author."

Josh's initiation into evil comes in two stages, the second more horrifying than the first. The first moment occurs when Mortimer takes a baby bird from its nest and orders Josh to poke its eye out with a thorn. Afterward, Josh knows that he has done something it was not in his nature to do, but that everything which came before in his relationship with Mortimer had almost inevitably led up to. Mortimer posits that this violation of Josh's "moral framework" was but a necessary test at a certain stage in Josh's development, springing from the "touch" of Original Sin inside each human being. Mortimer's argument, however, goes well beyond the Miltonic notion that goodness untried is not goodness at all, for he counsels that some "outrage" must actually be performed or committed, or all of life is simply habit.

The second moment in Josh's initiation, more premeditated than the first and an offense against a fellow human bring rather than an animal, occurs when Mortimer arranges with Josh to watch Marion's sexual violation at what Josh thinks will be his mentor's hands. Claiming to know that Marion has been a loose woman simply by the way she walks, Mortimer proposes that sexual intercourse is purely physical, a thing only of "organs and penetration," and therefore it is of absolutely no consequence who is performing the act. Mortimer never intends that he himself will abuse Marion (even if he were capable), but brings along Lionel, whom Josh sees as a threat to his position as Mortimer's closest friend. All along, Josh has seen Marion differently from Mortimer, as a "real person" rather than just an object for sexual satisfaction, so he understands sadly not only his failure to have convinced Mortimer of her intrinsic worth, but also that his desertion of her has been a "terrible thing." Unsworth specifies that the betrayal occurs at three o'clock on a Friday afternoon, the biblical moment at which the fall from grace in the garden was atoned for through the death of a savior, betrayed by one of his disciples, but at which darkness covered the face of the earth. Here, the Faustian pact is consummated: Josh has exorcised the presence of Lionel, his rival for Mortimer's attention, and he and Mortimer will "always be together now" in their own self-created and self-generating hell.

As might be expected of a novel in which one of the dual narrators is a voyeur and whose title denotes a hidden place from which to peer unbeknownst upon the world, Unsworth's *The Hide* is very centrally about the nature of seeing and the moral and ethical dimensions of perception. Simon himself, whose sole *raison d'être* is minute observation of and absorption in the details, particularly the forbidden ones, of existence, expresses annoyance over his human limitation or inability to freeze or stop time: Try though he might to turn movement into stasis and arrest perpetual disappearance, images continually dissolve into one another. Mortimer assumes what he himself would call a "realist" point of view, though it is more nearly the perspective of a rationalist; it pretends to be objective, factual, empirical, analytical, allowing no room for what he would see as the sentimental or romantic, for what Josh would call a more intuitive or creative understanding. In short, Mortimer's view discounts affective response, whereas Josh sees feelingly—as even Simon does momentarily when he breaks through the inhumanely distanced and objectifying gaze of the voyeur and responds, although with uncharacteristic empathy, to Marion's plight. In short, Josh's failure to believe in and act upon his higher level of perception, fearing that he is personally limited in what he could teach Mortimer, is what damns him irretrievably. Unsworth's *The Hide* makes the reader feel chillingly the absolute corruption of Josh's—and potentially all humankind's—capacity for good.

Thomas P. Adler

Sources for Further Study

Booklist. XCII, June 1, 1996, p. 1678.
Boston Globe. June 30, 1996, p. B37.
Kirkus Reviews. LXIV, April 1, 1996, p. 484.

Los Angeles Times Book Review. July 21, 1996, p. 10.
The New York Times Book Review. CI, August 5, 1996, p. 12.
Publishers Weekly. CCXLIII, April 8, 1996, p. 53.
San Francisco Chronicle. June 30, 1996, p. REV5.
The Virginia Quarterly Review. LXII, Autumn, 1996, p. 131.
The Washington Post Book World. XXVI, July 21, 1996, p. 7.

HIGH LATITUDES
A Romance

Author: James Buchan (1954-　　)
Publisher: Farrar Straus Giroux (New York). 192 pp. $22.00
Type of work: Novel
Time: Autumn, 1987
Locale: Great Britain, New York City, Alaska, and Antarctica

A highly paid, talented woman maneuvers in the world of London commerce in a year of disasters

> *Principal characters:*
> JANE HADDON (née JANET MCKAY), the managing director of
>   Associated British Textiles
> MOIRA and DENIS HADDON, her foster parents at Motherwell
> SISI LUSTGARTEN HERIOT and ANGUS HERIOT, heads of the Heriot
>   Clinic who rescued the young Jane
> STEPHEN COHEN, an investment banker with S. L. Brimberg
> ELIZABETH "LIZZIE" PINTO, Stephen's girlfriend
> ALAN NIXON, the chief executive officer of Reuben & Style, a premier
>   British textile firm
> JOHNNY BELLARMINE, Jane's first husband and friend of Stephen Cohen
> CANDIDA TURPE BELLARMINE, Johnny's second, somewhat
>   conventional, wife
> RODERICK "RODDIE" WYNYATES TURPE, Candida's uncle, an agent at
>   Lloyd's of London
> CECILIA TURPE, Roddie's wife
> MEG THOMKINS, Johnny Bellarmine's sister
> DEREK MAUGHAN, a worker at Lloyd's
> LORD DONCASTER, Jane's boss, the owner of the Doncaster group of
>   textiles factories in England, Scotland, and Northern Ireland
> CATHY MCKAY, Jane Haddon's half sister, a worker at the Queen
>   Elizabeth II Works at Motherwell
> SEAN MCVIE, the General Secretary of the Political Committee of the
>   Workers' Party
> TOM SALE, a writer for the *Workers Week*
> SHEILA WRIGHT, once the firebrand leader of the Young Socialists
> THOMAS WALDO BURKE, the minister of state at the Department of Trade
>   and Industry
> RICKY DE SOTO, a trader and gambler, sometime lover to Candida
>   Bellarmine
> CHARLOTTE MEREDITH, the owner of an airline flying out of Punta
>   Arenas in Chilean Patagonia for the Antarctic
> WALT and ANDY, pilots who fly Johnny Bellarmine around to Anarctica
> MADONNA CONSETT, a journalist for *The Sun*

Connecting commercial London with the icefields and icebergs of Antarctica may seem a reach, especially for a book that calls itself a "romance," but nodding to Nathaniel Hawthorne's idea that a romance frees the writer from "minute fidelity to the ordinary or probable," James Buchan invents a host of landed gentry, business tycoons, and working-class laborers to tell the story of Jane Haddon who, at the age of thirty, had become responsible for what was left of England's textile industry. Jane Haddon, as managing director of Associated British Textiles, is the highest paid woman in Great Britain—blessed with a brilliant mathematical mind and cursed with a terrible past that comes to light in a series of cleverly conceived and swiftly paced flashbacks woven into the main plot.

Centering in the autumn of 1987, the plot depicts the disastrous effects of the financial chaos that followed the market crash in 1987 on the lives of the characters who inhabit the London financial world and focuses on, among other things, Jane's attempts to save a manufacturing plant in Motherwell, Scotland, to save her former husband from bankruptcy induced by his (and many others') unwise investments in Lloyd's of London, and, indeed, to win him back after divorcing him eight years earlier. Lonely, driven, and a recovered heroin addict, Jane Haddon is a remarkably tough, yet sensitive young woman, who must face up to startling truths about her past, including an unknown half sister who happens to be a strike leader at Motherwell.

In contrast and opposition to Jane Haddon is Roddie Turpe, "that thug from Lloyd's." An important theme of the book emerges from its examination of the insurance business, the predacious vermin who run it and profit by it, and their victims, largely the old monied class who have little ready cash but have vast amounts of property which they seek, with the help of R. W. Turpe and others like him, to convert to money without actually selling it. Roddie, the stupidest of "all the Members Agents at Lloyd's at this period," and his wife, Cecilia, use their questionable riches to embed themselves into "that most transient of realities: society." The embedding is not without wider consequences, for, as Buchan notes, "A class in decline meets a class on the make; they combine; and detonate." In his brilliant analysis of the Turpes, Buchan creates his own Snopes, a vision of rapacity who "carted off" the possessions of the older, propertied class:

> not in body but in essence, as the phantom capital of his insurance ventures; and the squire or lady, rising each morning to see the Ferneley in its wonted place above the sideboard in the dining room, and the sideboard itself, forgot those objects were at risk of fire or shipwreck ten thousand miles away; forgot, indeed, that they no longer owned them. For money, which is perfectly mobile and utterly indifferent, is a terrible destroyer of social form.

The various scams by which Lloyd's of London operates until it all comes undone beneath the weight of the combined disasters, both natural and human-made, of 1987—chemical waste dumps, oil spills, hurricanes, the explosion of oil platforms in the North Sea, a fire in Malibu—are the subject of Buchan's mordant irony, expressed via a point of view that reminds one of a Conrad or a Hawthorne. Turpe is a splendidly crafted villain—"Was ever worldly ruin so plausibly impersonated?"—who despite his lack of intelligence saw that Lloyd's was not equal to the claims of five billion dollars likely to result from the oil spill disaster in Alaska. Even he, Buchan says, understood that "there is no such thing as insurance on the earth; that human activity leaves injuries that cannot be redeemed by money; that there is more to history than probability and compound interest."

Buchan connects his attack on the insurance business and specifically Lloyd's with other evils of modern-day business practices such as Shell Oil's decision between 1953 and 1968 to burn chemical waste in open drums at the Rocky Mountain Arsenal, a decision that resulted in horrific depredations not only against the immediate victims, agriculture and wildlife, and farm families in the United States but also "about thirty thousand families of the English and Scots gentry" and "the people of the United States, and their descendants, and the land, and even, who knows, God in his great patience." As a former writer for the *Financial Times* of London, Buchan commands a vast body of knowledge about the "sharp" practices of modern international business that convinces the reader always (even if bewildering at times).

Yet Jane Haddon is not an independent agent; her employer is the evil "Jimmy,"—James, Lord Doncaster, who has pillaged the Queen Elizabeth II Works at Motherwell, Scotland, a "rust-bucket" textiles factory, over the years by various financial schemes. Jane, under pressure to sell it, seeks instead to save it by a daring stock-sharing scheme that will make the workers part owners of the plant at the cost, however, of a reduction in their pay for a period of five years. The workers are not delighted with the prospect and vote to strike, an action which causes Jane to plan to lock out the workers, dismantle the plant and sell it to an Asian company, and sell the land to whoever wants it.

As Turpe is laid out in the first half of chapter 10, Jane Haddon is "laid out" in the second half, the exposure of her early life (including an early heroin addiction and an unacknowledged half sister, Cathy McKay, a strike leader at Motherwell) breaking about her head, the revealing of which brings the stock of Associated British Textiles down disastrously. Even in the midst of her personal pain, Jane seizes the opportunity to buy enough shares to cover a proposed employee stock-sharing plan with cash on hand at a good ratio. In a powerful scene of confrontation with Sean McVie, an evil and abusive leader of what is left of the British Workers' Party, she makes clear the consequences of the strike that McVie has fomented at Motherwell, the conflict between the two now taking on the dimensions of a morality play in which the good power of Jane Haddon, while not sufficient to save herself totally, is sufficient to destroy the evil dragon of a corrupt and morally bankrupt socialist labor movement. Perhaps this plot shape is one reason Buchan refers to the novel as a "romance."

Other actors in this morality play include Johnny Bellarmine, the handsome and enigmatic lord of Wexley Park in Northumberland, whom Jane meets while she is a student at Oxford. Persuaded to invite Jane to visit Wexley, Johnny's mother sees Jane's possibilities despite her birth, educates Jane in business practices and French, loves her, and leaves her two million pounds when she dies from a fall in her massive library. Jane marries Johnny, but her ambitions and a heroin habit drive her to divorce him, go to the United States to "dry out," and then to Harvard for a business education, and to talk her way into Doncaster's employment. Although he remarries and engages in a number of activities befitting a man of his pedigree, Johnny grows increasingly dissatisfied with his life because he is haunted, partly by the memory of Jane and partly by the historical presence of a dashing and illustrious ancestor who had sailed to the "high latitudes" off the Cape of Good Hope in a noble feat of eighteenth century navigation. Johnny flies himself to the Antarctic and nearly dies there but finally escapes with his pilots to return to England. Johnny's decision to go to the Antarctic in search of himself nearly costs him his life, but it does give him a sense of himself that will, readers are convinced, make up for the imminent loss of his estate owing to the financial collapse of Lloyd's with whom he had invested heavily at the insistence of Candida's uncle, the odious Roddie Turpe.

The past, the hold it has on various people and the collapse of old power and privilege, property and values, are figured in many ways in this short but complex and deftly constructed novel. In one scene, Stephen Cohen vows his love for Jane, asking her if he "might hope" to marry her. Her answer is: "I don't believe in these things. I believe that England is disintegrating and that quite soon no family will know the name of its grandparents. . . . The tragedy of history lies in that nobody understands the tiniest part of it as it is happening. We live through it without understanding a bloody thing." She chastises Stephen for living in the past: "Why do you live in this fraudulent old English past? You're Jewish, for God's sake. Your father was a grocer. . . ." He replies, "Pharmacist, actually, Jane." Woven throughout these reflections is the thread of "commercial parasitism, where business is mere handmaid to snobbery, . . . as if commerce and snobbery were so implicated that they couldn't be unraveled."

Another powerful theme connected with "commercial parasitism" focuses on the ecological disasters that commercial rapacity foists upon society, figured perhaps most powerfully in the scenes involving Stephen Cohen's trip to Alaska during the first week of November, 1987. Trying to get some handle on the financial extent of the disaster of the gigantic oil spill, which some figure at no less than five billion dollars, the probable hit on Lloyd's portending an absolute disaster for the insurance firm, Stephen hires a boat and travels up the Prince William Sound to the site of the spill, seeing at first hand the dead and dying wildlife and suffering a slashing (and symbolic) bite from an oil-covered sea otter.

At the end of the book, Buchan brings sisters Jane Haddon and Cathy McKay together for the first time in the ruined environs of the Motherwell factory destined now, because of the strike, to be dismantled. At this juncture, Buchan tells readers the story, in clinical language via a flashback, of Jane's early, seriously abused childhood. The daughter of a Glasgow prostitute, Jane at an age somewhere between four and six is rescued by officials of the Child Welfare Department when her mother is discovered dead. The story of Jane's rescue is quickly summarized as a result of the faith and work of Sisi Lustgarten, an extraordinary Viennese intellectual who had escaped Vienna just before the Nazi conquest and had been sheltered in Hampstead by the Freuds. Lustgarten is responsible for making Jane's life and development possible. The change from a drug-addicted, abused, injured child, "enuretic, encopretic, with very low speech skills," to a mathematical whiz, British countess, and business tycoon is, of course, the stuff of romance. Yet here is romance rendered in a crisp, densely allusive, scenic prose style so tempered and seasoned with irony and so informed with all of the inside and even arcane specialist knowledge of the worlds of high finance, manufacturing, arbitrage, and British politics that the result is a distinctly different sort of fairy tale. Even so, as the narrative voice informs readers:

> as you always knew, and in the manner of all true romance, my beggar-maid was a princess. For just as Johnny, and the Motherwell seamstresses and Sean McVie and R.W. Turpe, were the last flowers of long social traditions, so too was Jane: in the beauty and severity of her personality, created over years and years by this great doctor of sick children, she was a movement of Mahler, a thought of Wittgenstein, a sentence of Hayek or Popper or Gombrich, a theorem of Ludwig Boltzmann: the last gleaming of that Enlightenment that came down this century upon the Viennese.

Theodore C. Humphrey

Sources for Further Study

Boston Globe. November 24, 1996, p. N16.
The Guardian. April 12, 1996, p. 10.
Los Angeles Times Book Review. November 17, 1996, p. 2.
New Statesman and Society. IX, April 12, 1996, p. 40.
The New York Times Book Review. CI, November 17, 1996, p. 34.
Publishers Weekly. CCXLIII, September 16, 1996, p. 68.
The Spectator. CCLXXVI, April 13, 1996, p. 34.
The Times Literary Supplement. April 12, 1996, p. 23.

HIS HOLINESS
John Paul II and the Hidden History of Our Time

Authors: Carl Bernstein (1944-   ) and Marco Politi
Publisher: Doubleday (New York). 582 pp. $27.50
Type of work: Biography
Time: 1920-1996
Locale: Poland, Vatican City, the Soviet Union, the United States, and Latin America

Two investigative journalists chronicle the career of Pope John Paul II, focusing on his sometimes paradoxical role in bringing about the collapse of communist rule in Poland even as he struggled against liberation theology in Latin America

Principal personages:
POPE JOHN PAUL II (KAROL WOJTYLA), the first Polish pope in five
    hundred years, assumed the papal throne in 1978
STEFAN WYSZYNSKI, the archbishop of Warsaw and primate of the
    Polish Church during Nazi and Soviet occupations
LEONID BREZHNEV, the Soviet premier during the first three years of
    Wojtyla's papacy
MIKHAIL GORBACHEV, the Soviet premier who presided over the
    collapse of the Soviet Union
GENERAL WOJCIECH JARUZELSKI, the Polish head-of-state who
    attempted to crush the Solidarity trade union movement in 1981
LECH WALESA, the Polish shipyard worker who led the early Solidarity
    movement and became the first president of post-communist Poland
RONALD REAGAN, the fortieth president of the United States, 1981-1989,
    who collaborated with John Paul II in lending support to the
    Solidarity movement
WILLIAM CASEY, the director of the Central Intelligence Agency (CIA)
    under Reagan

Best known for his exposés of the Watergate scandal (*All the President's Men*, 1974; *The Final Days*, 1976), written in collaboration with fellow *Washington Post* journalist Bob Woodward, which brought the presidency of Richard Nixon to an ignominious end in 1973, Carl Bernstein is nothing if not ambitious. In *His Holiness: John Paul II and the Hidden History of Our Time*, Bernstein shifts his attention to the world stage, to the life of Pope John Paul II—the man who played a pivotal role, along with Ronald Reagan, in bringing an end to the Cold War—by any estimate the most important geopolitical event of the latter half of the twentieth century. Given the scope of this undertaking, Bernstein has wisely wedded his investigative skills with those of Italian journalist Marco Politi, a veteran correspondent who has covered Vatican politics for almost two decades. Politi brings to this project an astonishing array of Vatican sources, perhaps as many as one-quarter of the more than three hundred interviews conducted by the authors between 1993 and 1996 in preparation for this book. While Bernstein and Politi have, to judge by their bibliography, consulted most of the major and a good many minor works on the life and papacy of Karol Wojtyla, it is this formidable body of interviews which forms the primary source material. The result is a vivid if not always penetrating account of Wojtyla's career as Polish patriot, Catholic church leader, theologian, and global diplomat—an account which at times threatens to overspill the bounds of historical biography to become epic docudrama.

His Holiness is organized chronologically, though never rigidly so. Early chapters dwell at some length upon the young Wojtyla's childhood in provincial Wadowice; his studies at the Jagiellonian University in Krakow; his clandestine entry into the priesthood; his involvement in the underground Rapsodic Theater of Mieczyslaw Kotlarczyk and in dissident intellectual circles during the Nazi and, later, Soviet occupations; his rapid rise in the Polish church hierarchy; his introduction to church politics at the highest level as one of the Polish delegates to the Second Vatican Council; and his elevation to the papacy after the unexpected death of John Paul I in 1978.

While Bernstein and Politi's treatment of the pre-papal years of Wojtyla's life is full of fascinating anecdote and much high drama (especially in part 3, entitled "Conclave," which deals with all those behind-the-scenes machinations employed in the making of a pope), the only truly substantive addition involves Wojtyla's collaboration on the standard English edition of his most important, if not best known, philosophical work, *The Acting Person* (1979). Anna-Teresa Tymieniecka, a Polish American émigrée of aristocratic lineage, and a trained philosopher, ran across the original Polish edition of *The Acting Person* (*Osoba I Czyn*, 1967) in the course of her research in 1972. Thrilled to discover a philosopher whose work dovetailed in many respects with her own, she established contact with Cardinal Wojtyla in Krakow by the spring of 1973. Wojtyla appears to have been delighted to find that his work was not wholly ignored in the West, but he was well aware that the Polish edition of the book was seriously flawed. He himself had undertaken sole responsibility for the editing of the book, and the result was an "almost impenetrably dense" work of intimidating length. In Tymieniecka's view, the book was important in its ambitious attempt to develop a comprehensive philosophical-anthropology: a philosophy of the "person" which might stand against the predominant trend (then and now) toward Marxist, structuralist, and poststructuralist attacks upon the integrity of the acting subject.

Convinced that the book deserved a wider reading public in the West, Tymieniecka persuaded Wojtyla to revise the work for publication in an English-language edition. Wojtyla and Tymieniecka embarked upon a four-year period of intense philosophical dialogue that culminated in a global revision of the original work and, with Wojtyla's blessings, Tymieniecka was credited with coauthorship. Nevertheless, after Wojtyla was elevated to the papacy in 1978, according to Williams' testimony, the pope's Vatican handlers began to express their disapproval that this collaboration should become widely known and "sought to disavow [the book] in Catholic circles." The official reason given was that the shift toward phenomenology and away from orthodox Thomism (the traditional method of Catholic theology) was one which the Vatican did not wish to encourage. Yet could such a shift have been dangerous enough to require suppression of the book?

Such an attempt was apparently made, but Wojtyla had already signed over world rights to the English version to Tymieniecka and "proclaimed it the 'definitive' and authorized edition." Politi and Bernstein, following Williams' lead, suggest by implication that the real reason for the Vatican's disavowal of the book had less to do with philosophical issues than with the story behind the collaboration. For it seems that Wojtyla and Tymieniecka developed far more than a professional relationship; they established an enduring friendship. The authors document this friendship meticulously, and though the account has raised some eyebrows, it is difficult to see why. True, Wojtyla and Tymieniecka are said to have met frequently, both in the United States and in Poland, to have taken long philosophical walks together in the woods, and even to have gone swimming together in a lake near Tymieniecka's summer home in Vermont. Yet Politi and Bernstein are careful to show that these were always chaperoned outings with not even a hint of impropriety. Although such revelations are bound to disturb those who have sought to protect the pope from anything that could be used to cast aspersions upon his virtue, the Vatican clearly overreacted in this case.

The truth is that Bernstein and Politi have done Wojtyla a great service, for the story of his collaboration with Tymieniecka is the best proof on record of the pope's respect for women. That he was able to accept her as an intellectual equal, to learn from her and to publicly acknowledge his debt to her, demonstrates that he is far from being the reactionary antifeminist that he is often said to be. According to Tymieniecka, Wojtyla "was an incomparable philosophical partner."

The most important revelations in *His Holiness* appear in the latter half of the book dealing with John Paul's policy on Poland and with his efforts to thwart the advance of liberation theology in Latin America. Here Politi and Bernstein have benefited enormously by the recent release of Politburo documents unavailable prior to the collapse of the Soviet Union. They have supplemented the information gleaned from those documents with dozens of interviews with the key political players in Moscow, Warsaw, and Washington, D.C., as well as with Vatican insiders such as Secretary of State Cardinal Agostino Casaroli. The resulting scenario is quite dramatic.

During his tenure as the archbishop of Krakow, Wojtyla had walked a fine line between support for the dissident Committee for the Defense of the Workers (KOR) and a long established policy of *Ostpolitik*, that is, a willingness on the part of Catholic church officials to concede political authority to the Communist Party in exchange for a sphere of relative religious freedom for the church and some limited recognition of civil rights for the people. As pope, Wojtyla was for the first time in a position to take a more aggressive posture. Few inside the Vatican, and certainly no one in the communist sphere, were capable of seeing past a policy of accommodation that had lasted for decades. Political conditions in Poland had improved little in the wake of the 1970 workers' riots that had culminated in the so-called Gdansk Accords and Edward Gierek's assumption of Party leadership. If the influx of Western monetary credits had led to some temporary improvement in economic conditions, its most notable effect had been to contribute to an atmosphere of rising expectations on the part of workers. When those expectations were dashed by yet another plunge into scarcity in 1976, a holy alliance between the church and dissident forces led by the

KOR—forerunner of Solidarity—was born. Wojtyla had played a cautious but critical role in the formation of this alliance, one which drew deeply from the wellsprings of a resurgent Polish nationalism.

Among the Western heads-of-state, as in the Vatican, *Ostpolitik* had rested upon a grand misconception. Soviet-style communism, it was widely believed on both the left and the right, was a stable system of totalitarian control. On the right, this stability was believed to be the result of an essential stasis in the system itself: Nothing had really changed after Stalin. On the left, this supposed stability was said to be the result of incremental reforms within the system. Change was occurring, the left argued; the old Stalinist model was gradually evolving of its own initiative toward a more humane socialism—something like the Western model. As Andrzej Walicki has argued (*Marxism and the Leap to the Kingdom of Freedom*, 1995), neither side could see clearly that the Soviet system was radically unstable, was actually crumbling rapidly from within. This fact was nowhere more apparent than in Gierek's Poland. While Bernstein and Politi fail to cite Walicki, even in their bibliography, they have clearly taken up his line of argument.

Western leaders were taken by surprise, then, when the new pope threw down the gauntlet to the Soviet regime—though the Soviet leaders themselves were prepared. Internal Politburo documents produced by Bernstein and Politi illustrate clearly the repeated efforts of Leonid Brezhnev and other members of the inner circle to persuade Gierek of the danger in allowing the new pope to visit Poland. Gierek (and after him, Jaruzelski) understood that the Catholic church had become a power in Poland that could not be denied. If the proposed visit were refused, martial law would have to be imposed, and the Polish army could not be relied upon to shoot Poles in the streets. When John Paul II's visit became a reality, the Western world (and a good part of the Eastern bloc) watched with astonishment as millions of Poles filled the streets of Warsaw and other Polish cities to welcome him. These outsiders watched with incomprehension as the red Solidarity banners and wooden crosses were raised, side by side, by thousands of Polish youth—even as the army stood by and did nothing. The Polish pope's first visit to his native land, in commemoration of the martyrdom of St. Stanislaw, patron saint of Poland, was an unprecedented triumph of the spirit. In Moscow, this spectacle was alarming, to say the least; in the West, President Ronald Reagan was the only politician of significance to understand that a revolution had begun. To their credit (and probably against the grain of their own political biases), Bernstein and Politi do recognize the historic importance of Reagan's intuition.

Bernstein and Politi's most enduring contribution to readers' understanding of the papacy of John Paul II is the wealth of proof they have brought to light regarding the Reagan administration's involvement in the survival of the Solidarity movement, which began almost immediately after Reagan assumed office in January of 1981. The authors show that initial contacts were established with the Vatican (assumed correctly by Reagan and his advisers to be the ultimate force behind Solidarity) through Polish American John Cardinal Kroll, the archbishop of Philadelphia; Archbishop Pio Laghi, the Vatican's apostolic delegate to Washington, D.C.; and by the indefatigable efforts of William Casey, himself a pious Catholic. Eventually Reagan and Pope John Paul II met and, by all accounts, warmed to one another immediately in spite of a number of ideological differences (not the least being the pope's antipathy to the unbridled free-market faith which drove Reagan's domestic economic policy). Out of this relationship grew a plan that would seek to accelerate the process of disintegration which both Reagan and John Paul II were convinced was already occurring. If the two men first met resistance even within the circles of their own advisers, each managed by sheer force of will and personality to make the new policy prevail.

At Reagan's behest, the pope was given unprecedented access to American intelligence, including satellite photos detailing the shifting positions of the Red Army along the Polish border in 1980-1981 when the Soviets repeatedly threatened Polish leaders with invasion if they could not bring striking workers, led by Solidarity, under control. In return, the pope provided Casey and Reagan with reliable intelligence on the internal affairs of Poland (gathered through well-placed, sympathetic contacts inside the Gierek and Jaruzelski regimes), not to mention equally reliable information on Latin American affairs. At stake in Poland was the very survival of Solidarity, which the Communist Party saw as a dangerous threat to its monopoly of representation, and which Jaruzelski, especially, did everything in his power to undermine—especially with his declaration of martial law in December of 1981, followed by the imprisonment of hundreds of Solidarity leaders (Lech Walesa among them).

At this point, as Bernstein and Politi reveal, the Reagan Administration's support for the nascent underground movement of resistance went far beyond anything heretofore documented. With the pope's blessing and invaluable assistance, the CIA steadily increased American material support for the movement between 1981 and 1989. The authors claim that the "greatest secret" of the Cold War was the knowledge that during this period the U.S. government spent "more than $50 million to keep Solidarity alive." Perhaps even more important, the CIA set up a supply network to provide the underground movement with what it needed most desperately: tons of printing equipment which made possible the emergence of hundreds of covert publishing operations throughout Poland. Such activities were probably the most critical development in fanning the flames of resistance among the populace at large—resistance which, at the insistence of the pope (and Lech Walesa), remained for the most part nonviolent. The underground presses were instruments of that "truth speaking" which was the constant theme of John Paul II's public addresses on the Polish question and which was, in the last analysis, the weapon which brought about the collapse of the Jaruzelski regime, the one weapon missing in the Soviet arsenal, and the definitive answer to Nikita Khrushchev's old question: "How many armies has the Pope?"

If Bernstein and Politi have made a significant contribution to the world's understanding of the importance of the U.S.-Vatican alliance in bringing an end to communist rule in Poland (and, eventually, the Cold War), their treatment of the pope's struggle against political oppression in Latin America is less convincing. It is certainly true, as the authors suggest, that John Paul II was often less insistent in his demands for human rights in speeches delivered in Latin America than he had been during several visits to Poland. Yet their further suggestion that this apparent inconsistency was motivated by some secret agreement with the Reagan administration to deemphasize human rights themes in Latin America, remains largely speculative. Certainly, Reagan and the pope shared a concern that insurgent communist movements in countries such as El Salvador were a serious threat to stability throughout Latin America, and the authors do raise a legitimate issue when they imply that the pope may have been fed a distorted view of American covert operations in the region—a view which he may have been too willing to accept. Still, Bernstein and Politi appear to have their own agenda. In dealing with the communist Ortega regime in Nicaragua, for example, they imply that the pope was prevented by anticommunist zealotry from recognizing the essentially peaceful and democratic aims of the "popularly elected" Sandinistas and thus failed to support them with the same enthusiasm that he gave to Solidarity. The authors apparently have turned a blind eye to numerous, well-documented abuses by the Sandinistas against indigenous peoples within their own borders, not to mention their exportation of arms into El Salvador to foment an already bloody revolution and the presence of Cuban and Bulgarian agents in Nicaragua.

Similar biases—and perhaps a good deal of plain ignorance—are also evident in Bernstein and Politi's attempts to come to terms with the pope's attempts to discipline priests such as Leonardo Boff, Brazilian author of one of the most controversial works of liberation theology. Instead of making a serious effort to present the arguments for and against liberation theology, Bernstein and Politi choose instead (in a short chapter entitled "Repression") to focus primarily on the melodrama of Boff's summons to Rome by the German-born Cardinal Joseph Ratzinger, secretary of the Congregation for the Propagation of the Faith. This may be good docudrama, but it is not responsible journalism. Indeed, nowhere either in the text or in the notes do the authors cite the most devastating (and widely read) attack on liberation theology, John Milbank's *Theology and Social Theory* (1990), in which this so-called people's theology is clearly traced to its origins in an outmoded tradition of secular positivism. Moreover, although Bernstein and Politi are aware of the importance of George Williams' studies of the papal thinking which undergirds Cardinal Ratzinger's *Instruction on Certain Aspects of Liberation Theology* (1984), they fail to note Williams' detailed (and largely positive) examination of that document in his book *The Law of Nations and the Book of Nature* (1984).

Bernstein and Politi have written a book which makes a number of valuable contributions to a knowledge of the papacy of John Paul II. Their ultimate aim, however, seems to have been to reach a mass audience, which in turn resulted in a series of compromises which damage the integrity of the work as a whole.

Jack E. Trotter

Sources for Further Study

Boston Globe. October 6, 1996, p. N15.
The Christian Century. CXIII, October 23, 1996, p. 1007.
The Economist. CCCXLI, November 16, 1996, p. 5.
The Guardian. October 3, 1996, II, p. 10.
Los Angeles Times Book Review. October 13, 1996, p. 1.
The New York Review of Books. XLIII, October 31, 1996, p. 8.
The New York Times Book Review. CI, September 29, 1996, p. 10.
Newsweek. CXXVIII, September 30, 1996, p. 73.
Publishers Weekly. CCXLIII, September 23, 1996, p. 51.
The Washington Post Book World. XXVI, September 22, 1996, p. 1.

A HISTORY OF READING

Author: Alberto Manguel (1948-   )
Publisher: Viking (New York). Illustrated. 372 pp. $26.95
Type of work: History
Time: Approximately 3000 B.C. to the late twentieth century
Locale: The Orient, Europe, and the Americas

Through a compilation of anecdotes, Manguel offers a survey of reading from antiquity to the end of the twentieth century

> *Principal personages:*
> ARISTOTLE, the Greek philosopher and book collector
> RICHARD BANCROFT, the archbishop of Canterbury, 1604-1610, and one
>   of the translators of the King James Bible
> JORGE LUIS BORGES, the Argentinean author and librarian
> CALLIMACHUS OF CYRENE, a librarian at Alexandria in the third
>   century B.C.
> CICERO, the Roman rhetorician and philosopher
> ANTHONY COMSTOCK, the founder of the New York Society for the
>   Suppression of Vice
> JOHANNES GUTENBERG, an inventor of printing from movable type
> FRANCESCO PETRARCH, the fourteenth century Italian humanist
> PLINY THE YOUNGER, the Roman writer

In his *Confessions*, Augustine expresses surprise at the silent reading of Ambrose, Bishop of Milan. Throughout antiquity and the Middle Ages, reading meant reading aloud; such reading was probably the most common form of ancient publication. The phrase *scripta manet, verba volat*—the written word remains stationary, the spoken word travels—implied that only when the word was given a voice could it serve as a means of communication. Manguel notes that the Hebrew and Aramaic word for reading also means to call, again expressing this view that one should not read silently. In the twelfth century, Abu Hamid Muhammad al-Ghazali devised rules for studying the Koran. The ninth rule required reading the text aloud. Manguel suggests that the absence of spaces between words in classical and early medieval manuscripts reflects this practice of reciting; the ear would separate what the eye could not. Yet the eye must separate the words before the mouth can utter them. The lack of spaces more likely resulted from a desire to conserve papyrus or parchment. Further, those likely to own a manuscript probably knew the text pretty well by heart; the written word served as a reminder. Anyone familiar with a language will fairly readily separate words even without spaces (as evidenced in poems by E. E. Cummings or the prose of John Dos Passos). The introduction of spaces between words reflects not a moving away from reading aloud but rather a decline in familiarity with the language, particularly Latin, already a foreign language to most by the sixth century A.D.

In the classical and medieval world, literacy was uncommon; no more than twenty percent of those living in the Roman Empire could read. Reading aloud served to make texts available to the illiterate, though even the literate enjoyed these performances.

Pliny the Younger wrote that he liked to hear a book being read while he ate, and this practice of reading at meals was required by the Rule of St. Benedict. Jongleurs from the eleventh century onward imitated the ancient rhapsodes, reciting poetry they and their master troubadours had composed. The jongleurs performed rather than read, but their texts were written down. In 1309, Jean de Joinville addressed his *Life of St. Louis* to those who would hear the book. The fourteenth century historian Jean Froissart read his romance *Méliador* to the Count du Blois, and Geoffrey Chaucer almost certainly read his *Troilus and Criseyde* to the Ricardian court.

Family members also read aloud to each other for pleasure and instruction. Manguel quotes the Tuscan notary Ser Lapo Mazzei asking a friend for a copy of *The Little Flowers of St. Francis* to read aloud to his sons. An innkeeper in *Don Quixote* tells a priest how much the laborers enjoy hearing a chivalric romance. In the nineteenth century, the Scottish publisher William Chambers recalled a boy who traveled from house to house reading his copy of Josephus as if the Jewish historian were the latest news. Later in the 1800's cigar makers in Cuba and then in Florida hired a reader to entertain and instruct them while they worked. The nineteenth century was the golden age of public reading, with stars such as Charles Dickens and Alfred, Lord Tennyson. Dickens' reading texts included elaborate stage directions: "Beckon down . . . Point . . . Shudder . . . Look Round in Terror." The continuing popularity of public reading and the proliferation of books on tape reflect the power of the written word to please when spoken.

For others, being alone with the page is the greatest pleasure. As Thomas à Kempis remarked, "In omnibus requiem quaesivi, et nunquam inveni, nisi in angulo cum libro,"—I have sought peace everywhere and found it nowhere except in a corner with a book. Marcel Proust would sneak into the dining room to read when the rest of his family was away; for him the cook always appeared too early to set the table and so disturbed his isolation.

Manguel looks at how reading was taught in the Middle Ages. Among Jews the traditional time to begin this instruction was Shavuot, fifty days after Passover. On this holiday, which celebrates God's giving the Ten Commandments to Moses, Jewish children would be taken to their teacher, who showed them the alphabet written on a slate, together with a passage from the Torah and the inscription, "May the Torah be your occupation." After the teacher read the slate to the child and the child repeated the lesson, the slates were covered in honey, and each child licked his, so that he would learn how sweet learning is. Nurses and mothers often bore the responsibility for teaching the rudiments of reading to the young. Manguel reproduces two sculptures showing Mary teaching Jesus and St. Anne teaching Mary to read.

The Church used illustrations to reach those who could not read. As Pope Gregory the Great wrote,

> For that which writing makes present to the reader, pictures make present to the illiterate, to those who only perceive visually, because in pictures the ignorant see the story they ought to follow, and those who don't know their letters find that they can, after a fashion, read. Therefore, especially for the common folk, pictures are the equivalent of reading.

Just as the meaning of texts was controlled by scholasticism, which insisted on obedience to authority, so was the interpretation of pictures. The Seventh Church Council in Nicaea declared in 787, "The execution of pictures is not an invention of the painter but the recognized proclamation of the laws and tradition of the overall Church."

The Biblia Pauperum, or Bible of the poor, served as the textual equivalent of frescoes, carvings, and stained glass. Manguel links such pictorial representations with modern advertising, which also relies on images to convey meaning.

To find books to read or look at one needs some system of organization. The vast library of Alexandria supposedly contained half a million manuscripts. Callimachus of Cyrene began cataloging this collection, dividing the works under eight headings: drama, oratory, lyric poetry, legislation, medicine, history, philosophy, and miscellany. Under each heading Callimachus listed works alphabetically by author. The Alexandrian catalog eventually filled one hundred twenty scrolls. In the Middle Ages, other systems emerged, such as Hugh of St. Victor's 1120 tripartite division of books into the theoretical, the practical, and the mechanical. A century later, Richard de Fournival offered another three-part system consisting of philosophy, the "lucrative sciences" (medicine and law—how little some things have changed since 1250), and theology. Like older schemes, modern classification systems seek to situate each book in a particular niche in the world of learning, but in the process the system excludes that book from all other categories where it might also fit.

While people classify books, books also classify people. Manguel relates that one of his cousins carefully considered the image her choice of reading matter would convey, so that when she traveled she would not take Romain Rolland because she would seem too pretentious, and she would not take an Agatha Christie mystery because it was too lowbrow. The very presence of books confers a sophisticated image, as interior decorators know. A motivation for buying (or stealing) books is the sense of learning that ownership conveys. Satires on such an outlook are at least as old as Seneca, but the best known of these attacks is Sebastian Brant's *Büchernarr* or book fool depicted by Albrecht Dürer's woodcut in *Das Narrenschiff* (1494; ship of fools).

Manguel discusses various iconic uses of books. Rogier van der Weyden's *Virgin and Child* (c.1450) shows Christ tearing a page of his mother's book, indicating that he will replace the Old Testament with the New, and perhaps also demonstrating his intellectual superiority over his mother. After the fatwā was issued against Salman Rushdie for *The Satanic Verses*, the television reporter John Innes kept a copy of the book on his desk to show his support for the author. This iconic significance works in other ways also. Manguel relates that his heterosexual friends told him they would be embarrassed to display an anthology of gay literature that Manguel had edited.

The fatwā against Rushdie is but one example in a long line of efforts to limit reading. Theophrastus argued that women should not receive too much instruction because too much reading made a woman "a quarreling, lazy gossip." In Heian Japan, women were barred from reading serious writing, but they developed a literature of their own, most notably Lady Murasaki's *Tale of Genji* (c.1001-1010) and *The Pillow*

Book of Sei Shonagon (c.1000). The latter probably derives its name from its being concealed in the drawers of the author's wooden pillow. In the eighteenth century, South Carolina forbade teaching all blacks, slave or free, to read. Southern plantation owners would hang slaves who tried to teach other slaves to read, but slaves circumvented the restriction. In 213 B.C., the Chinese emperor Shih Huang-ti tried to eliminate literacy by burning every book he could find. Diocletian hoped to abolish Christianity by destroying all Christian books. Anthony Comstock, founder of the New York Society for the Suppression of Vice, wished that no one had ever learned to read, and he certainly did not want Americans to read novels from what he called the "lust-crazed nations" of France and Italy.

Some have been unable to read not because of censorship or illiteracy but because of poor vision. Until the thirteenth century no remedy was available except listening to others read. A plaque in the church of Santa Maria Maggiore in Florence credits the invention of eyeglasses to Salvino degli Armati (d. 1317). In 1268, Roger Bacon referred to using a crystal or glass to make letters larger and clearer, and in 1301 one of the rules of the Guild of Venetian Crystal workers explained the process of making reading glasses. By the mid-fourteenth century, glasses appear in a portrait of Cardinal Hugo de St. Cher by Tommaso da Modena. Glasses, like books, became a symbol of erudition. In the fifteenth century, someone added a pair of glasses to a figure in an eleventh century painting to suggest that character's learning, and sages from antiquity and the early Middle Ages, such as Cicero and St. Augustine, began to be depicted with glasses. This iconography persists in the design of Manguel's dust jacket, which shows a pair of reading glasses on the page of an open book.

Translators also make texts available to audiences who otherwise could not read a work, though the Italian adage warns *traduttore traditore*—translators are traitors. Such betrayal can take various forms. George Steiner claimed that Rainer Maria Rilke's translations of the sixteenth century French poet Louise Labé failed because their beauty surpasses the original. The most controversial translations have been of the Bible. In 1536, William Tyndale was executed for rendering the Bible into English, and virtually every subsequent translation has provoked argument.

At the end of his book, Manguel imagines an ideal history of reading. He acknowledges that he has not written the definitive account of the subject, which would explore such topics as private and public reading tastes, the invention of the reader and of the writer, the way one reads fiction and fact, how the reader's tone affects a text. Such a book would in fact be a collection of volumes not much smaller than the one Jorge Luis Borges imagines in "The Library of Babel," which is infinite. The book that Manguel has written leaves many topics unexamined, but its many anecdotes complemented by black-and-white illustrations provide much delight and instruction.

Joseph Rosenblum

Sources for Further Study

Booklist. XCIII, September 1, 1996, p. 34.
Boston Globe. September 15, 1996, p. N16.
Chicago Tribune. November 12, 1996, V, p. 3.
Library Journal. CXXI, July, 1996, p. 117.
Los Angeles Times. September 5, 1996, p. C1.
The New York Times Book Review. CI, November 17, 1996, p. 37.
Publishers Weekly. CCXLIII, July 8, 1996, p. 66.
Time. CXLVIII, September 9, 1996, p. 68.
The Times Literary Supplement. August 2, 1996, p. 8.
The Washington Post Book World. XXVI, September 29, 1996, p. 3.

HISTORY WARS
The *Enola Gay* and Other Battles for the American Past

Editors: Edward T. Linenthal (1947-   ) and Tom Engelhardt (1944-   )
Publisher: Metropolitan Books (New York). 295 pp. $30.00
Type of work: History; essays

Eight historians reflect on the cancellation of the original, controversial 1995 exhibition of the Enola Gay, *the plane that dropped the atomic bomb on Hiroshima*

Principal personages:
> MARTIN HARWIT, the former director of the Smithsonian Institution's
>   National Air and Space Museum who resigns because of the
>   controversy surrounding the *Enola Gay* exhibition
> COLONEL PAUL W. TIBBETS, JR., the pilot of the *Enola Gay* for the
>   Hiroshima mission, he is still alive in 1995
> JOHN T. CORRELL, the editor of *Air Force Magazine* who becomes an
>   influential critic of the tendentious, revisionist first draft of the
>   exhibition's display script
> HARRY S TRUMAN, the thirty-third president of the United States,
>   1945-1953, who ordered the use of the atomic bomb at Hiroshima
> I. MICHAEL HEYMAN, the new secretary of the Smithsonian Institution
>   who cancels the original exhibition
> MICHAEL NEUFELD, a controversial curator at the National Air and
>   Space Museum
> WILLIAM M. DETWEILER, the national commander of the American
>   Legion and a vociferous critic of the original exhibition
> RICHARD KOHN, the former chief of air force history for the U.S. Air
>   Force

Suddenly, in the fall of 1993, a major conflict erupted between ambitious historians and American veterans who had actually participated in the events the historians sought to scrutinize. As recounted in a series of eight related articles that compose *History Wars: The* Enola Gay *and Other Battles for the American Past*, the historians had been working on a controversial exhibit featuring the display of the *Enola Gay*, the B-29 Superfortress that dropped the atomic bomb on the Japanese city of Hiroshima on August 6, 1945.

Under the leadership of its forceful new director, Martin Harwit, the National Air and Space Museum of the Smithsonian Institution in Washington, D.C., planned to display the restored *Enola Gay* as centerpiece of an exhibition scheduled for 1995, coinciding with the fiftieth anniversary of the end of World War II in the Pacific. As originally planned, co-editor Edward T. Linenthal explains in the introductory chapter of *History Wars*, the historians working with Harwit went to great length "to ensure that the exhibit not be celebratory."

Instead, the clear focus and "didactic objective" of the exhibition was to present the Japanese of Hiroshima "as the first victims of the nuclear age." To deliver its "essentially antiwar and antinuclear" message, however, the historians had chosen an event in history which, to many people, also carried a very different message. The clash over the exact meaning of Hiroshima, and what should be remembered and displayed about it, is what *History Wars* sets out to analyze.

With historians working on their script for the planned exhibition, veterans of the Air Force Association began to voice their early criticism. What was missing from the script, critics believed, was a clear indication that Japan had initiated the war with the United States after embarking on an aggressive attack of other Asian nations such as China, which had been invaded in 1937.

Once the first version of Martin Harwit's exhibition script was completed in January of 1994, the project quickly became embroiled in controversy. At the museum, criticism had been relatively mild; only two historians on the advisory committee voiced some concerns that the script "did not do justice to 'Japanese brutality to subject peoples,'" since it failed to acknowledge the millions of Asian people who suffered from Japanese military action in and occupation of their countries. Even at the time of the Japanese surrender in August of 1945, millions of Asians were living still under Japanese military occupation in places such as northwestern China, Korea, and Vietnam.

The two internal critics also pointed their fingers at the issue which would soon explode on the opinion pages of all major American newspaper: The planned exhibition challenged the commonly held belief that President Harry Truman's decision to drop two atomic bombs avoided an invasion of Japan that would have resulted in huge casualties for the Americans and Japanese alike. Yet as Edward Linenthal documents in *History Wars*, this internal criticism was mild, and the dissident historians still congratulated curator Michael Neufeld for doing an "impressive" job.

Outside the museum, however, a public storm broke loose. Coordinated in part by John T. Correll, editor of the *Air Force Magazine*, veterans and some military historians voiced their increasingly vehement opposition to the museum's script. Newspapers in America picked up on some of the script's most egregious lines, which characterized America's military actions in the Pacific as "a war of vengeance" against the Japanese, who wanted "to defend their unique culture against Western imperialism." Clearly, whoever had written these words to be on display in the National Air and Space Museum in Washington succeeded only too well in creating "alternative readings of American history"—if not of world history itself.

Once veterans, journalists, and politicians spoke up and their chorus was joined by the *Enola Gay*'s former pilot, retired Colonel Paul W. Tibbets, Jr., many of the historians reacted with pique. As *History Wars* shows, they failed to understand how much they had misjudged the American public's tolerance for a major exhibition in the nation's capital which tried to push to the limit a "revisionist, countercultural, and condemnatory" view of America.

With a substantial number of the American populace outraged over the script, museum director Marvin Harwit still tried to save the exhibition. He invited a second team of historians to suggest revisions to the original script, which was altered so that some of the most inflammatory passages were toned down.

Such action came too late to effect a reconciliation. In spite of Marvin Harwit's good faith efforts to work with his critics, partisans on both sides turned up the heat. *History Wars* outlines how a group of radical scholars resigned from the advisory committee, denouncing the revisions to the script. On the other side, many implacable opponents began to lobby for the total cancellation of an exhibition which they believed was compromised beyond repair.

When I. Michael Heyman became new secretary of the Smithsonian Institution, he quickly moved to cancel the original exhibition on January 30, 1995. Instead, the museum settled on a minimalist display of the fuselage of the *Enola Gay*. Inside the restored body of the plane, which was shown without its wings attached, visitors saw a video of the explosion of the bomb. The exhibition provided no further explanation or context for that event. Under pressure, Martin Harwit resigned as director on May 2, 1995, saddened and embittered by his failure to reconcile his opponents.

One of the great accomplishments of *History Wars* is its clear display of how certain contemporary American historians have moved far beyond the mainstream understanding of American and world history. Moreover, in an era in which "oral history"—the use of eyewitness accounts and oral narratives—has become so important in writing, presenting, and interpreting history, it is ironic to read how historians clashed with the very people who have lived through the events, such as the bombing of Hiroshima, that are objects of new historical inquiry.

History Wars also demonstrates the difficulties of placing events into historical contexts, and the politics involved in such decisions. When critics complained about the original exhibition's relative inattention to the outbreak of hostilities in the Pacific Theater that culminated most spectacularly in the Japanese attack on Pearl Harbor, some curators defended their decision by loftily declaring "that their show was not meant to be a history of the war in the Pacific, but rather to 'freeze' a transformative moment in the twentieth century."

What appears to be a rather curious insistence on decontextualizing history—history as a sequence of freeze-frames exposed by the historian, is revealed to be patently false. As *History Wars* shows, the whole exhibit was planned to place Hiroshima in a particular context. Instead of considering Hiroshima as one of the final events of a war caused by Japanese military aggression against people of other Asian nations and the United States, "the war was but prelude to the bomb, which drew back the curtain on a new age," thus allowing the curators to convey their antinuclear message.

In his eloquent essay, "History at Risk," which forms a crucial centerpiece of *History Wars*, historian Richard H. Kohn differentiates himself from the revisionist historians who created the first script. Given the original motivation of these academics to create an exhibition which "was in fact unbalanced," it was clear that their agenda proved irreconcilable with the equally forceful desire of the American Legion under William M. Detweiler. Detweiler's veterans wanted an exhibit commemorating the dropping of the bomb. They wanted a clear focus on the heroism and professionalism of Colonel Tibbets' crew, and argued for the mainstream idea that the bombs ended the war and thus saved many American lives.

With positions hardening on both sides, the fall of director Harwit and the cancellation of the large exhibition appear almost inevitable. Kohn and the other contributors to *History Wars* clearly regret this outcome and view the cancellation of the original exhibition as a missed opportunity to come to terms with the conflict underlying the fight over the proper display of the *Enola Gay*. It is in part to fill this gap that *History Wars* has been written.

In "Three Narratives of Our Humanity," contributor John Dower does a nice job of outlining the way in which one historical event can have many interpretations and generate historical narratives that can be almost diametrically opposed. Dower demonstrates how Hiroshima can be seen as victimization, triumph, or tragedy. He reminds the reader that in the later stages of World War II, "combatants on all sides had identified civilian populations as legitimate and indeed primary targets," and the firebombing of enemy cities was practiced by Axis and Allies alike, differing only according to each side's waning or waxing military capacities.

Dower further rejects as impossible the idea of juxtaposing images of Japanese atrocities with those of Japanese bomb victims. Here, however, a reader may wonder if these jarring contrasts would not have come closer to reflecting a haunting inner reality about this war, than an exclusive focus on either victims or successful soldiers.

Paul Boyer similarly focusses on the different meaning of Hiroshima for different people. Michael Sherry and Mike Wallace, a historian who is editor of the *Radical History Review*, see the cancellation as the result of political pressure from the political right. Marilyn Young and co-editor Tom Engelhardt place the controversy over the *Enola Gay* in the context of America's reaction to the loss in Vietnam, and a general postwar uneasiness with Truman's decision to use atomic bombs.

It is Richard H. Kohn who points out how misleading is any debate about the exact number of envisioned American (and Japanese) casualties, had Japan been invaded. Similarly misleading appears historical speculation about what might have been if the bombs had not been dropped. In the absence of historical facts, each side can feel free to project their own ideas onto an imagined alternative future.

In the end, *History Wars* shows convincingly how each side implicitly and explicitly rejects the academic position of postmodernism, or the belief that all history is quintessentially fabrication, falsehood, and merely make-believe. Instead, both revisionist historians and indignant veterans express their firm belief in the truth of their view of history. While both sides in the history wars do not see eye to eye on the issues, the warring sides agree that historical truth exists. They also agree to fight over what is the correct remembrance of past events of momentous consequences. As a history lesson on the nature of a great cultural confrontation over the true meaning of the past, *History Wars* is invaluable.

R. C. Lutz

Sources for Further Study

Bulletin of the Atomic Scientists. LIII, January, 1997, p. 63.
Kirkus Reviews. LXIV, June 15, 1996, p. 879.
Los Angeles Times Book Review. August 4, 1996, p. 1.
Oregonian. August 11, 1996, p. F5.
Publishers Weekly. CCXLIII, June 10, 1996, p. 79.
Sacramento Bee. August 25, 1996, p. EN20.
San Francisco Chronicle. September 8, 1996, p. REV6.
The Washington Post Book World. XXVI, August 18, 1996, p. 13.

HITLER'S WILLING EXECUTIONERS
Ordinary Germans and the Holocaust

Author: Daniel Jonah Goldhagen
Publisher: Alfred A. Knopf (New York). 622 pp. $30.00
Type of work: History
Time: 1933-1945
Locale: Primarily Nazi Germany

Touting his book as a much-needed revision of Holocaust scholarship, Goldhagen argues that German antisemitism was the central cause that induced thousands of "ordinary Germans" to slaughter European Jewry while millions more of them actively collaborated in the Holocaust or at least gave their compliant approval for that genocide

Begin with a young Harvard professor of government who is as bright as he is brash and whose ways with words are as pretentious as they are perplexing. Take his doctoral dissertation and turn it into a book whose methodology, tone, and content intentionally collide with judgments of the major scholars in the field. Promote the book in ways that propel it to international best-seller status and hurl its largely unknown author into media spotlights. Such ingredients are bound to cause a stir. Focus them on a topic charged with intense feeling and profound implications—the Holocaust, the annihilation of the European Jews by Nazi Germany and its collaborators—and the resulting controversy will come to a boil. So it has been with Daniel Goldhagen and *Hitler's Willing Executioners: Ordinary Germans and the Holocaust.*

Even when they are about immensely important subjects such as the Holocaust, 600-page history books rarely get the attention that Goldhagen's has received. Repeatedly finding his research at odds with their own, most Holocaust scholars in the United States, Europe, and Israel do not give Goldhagen marks to match the high sales figures this his book has enjoyed. For mainly good reasons, the leading scholars whom Goldhagen vies to supplant take his methodology to be suspect, the tone of his writing to be arrogant and disdainful of even the best work in Holocaust studies, and his research results to be either far less original than Goldhagen claims or perniciously incorrect to the point of being destructive because they reignite undeserved prejudices against Germans and Jews alike.

What did Goldhagen say—and how did he say it—to provoke such critical reactions, which, ironically, call even greater attention to his book? Note, first, that *Hitler's Willing Executioners* was preceded, even scooped, by the work of Christopher Browning, a distinguished historian who published a 1992 work that has already achieved classic status in Holocaust studies. Browning called his book *Ordinary Men.* It analyzed the postwar judicial interrogations of 210 members of Reserve Police Battalion 101, a 500-man killing squadron of the German Order Police that was responsible for 83,000 Jewish deaths in Poland during the Final Solution.

Goldhagen targeted Browning's book when he chose *Ordinary Germans and the Holocaust* as the subtitle for *Hitler's Willing Executioners.* Having probed the same archival material about Reserve Police Battalion 101 that Browning had investigated,

Goldhagen believed that Browning mishandled and misinterpreted the data. Specifically, Goldhagen contended that Browning underestimated the extent and depth of antisemitism in Germany and played down its tenacious grip and deadly influence on the German people. Furthermore, Goldhagen charged that Browning wrongly advanced a universalistic perspective about the Holocaust. In Goldhagen's judgment, that outlook inadequately explained the killing behavior of the men in Reserve Police Battalion 101 by taking conformity to peer pressure, blind acceptance of current political norms, and careerism to be among its chief motivational causes.

Browning's interpretation did stress that the reserve policemen, German though they were and antisemitic though they may have been, were of special significance because they were also very ordinary human beings. He maintained that the story of Reserve Police Battalion 101 should cause, at the very least, discomfort for men and women everywhere. For as post-Holocaust history shows, people in other times and places—people like *us*—are also capable of complicity in genocide. Goldhagen was not impressed, let alone persuaded. He found fault with Browning's book because it missed what he regarded as the essential point about the Holocaust: Only the deep-seated racist antisemitism that infested the German people could motivate, and thus account for, the behavior of particular Germans who committed the atrocities that advanced the Final Solution.

Making his case, however, obliged Goldhagen to do more than disagree with Browning's interpretation of the archival records about Reserve Police Battalion 101. He would have to show, first, that "Germans' antisemitic beliefs about Jews were the central causal agent of the Holocaust," a claim that required him not only to trace the history of German antisemitism but also to document how that history involved authority and power fatal enough to account for the Holocaust's vast destruction. In addition, Goldhagen's case would hinge on demonstrating that "ordinary Germans"—not just rabidly antisemitic Nazis who had the political power to define social reality and to dominate a German population that might be more ambivalent about the so-called Jewish question—either willingly engaged in the slaughter or were so willing to let it go forward that they would have become active killers if called upon to do so. In short, Goldhagen had to show that the Holocaust, contrary to Browning's "ordinary men" hypothesis, was essentially the willful act of "ordinary Germans," who were much more lethally antisemitic than previous scholarship admitted.

To establish these positions, Goldhagen's book argues in two directions that govern its organization. Beginning with the history of German antisemitism, Goldhagen aims to show how, in particular, a potentially lethal anti-Jewish racism had a powerful influence in pre-Nazi Germany. Then he focuses on the actual German perpetrators of the Holocaust, studying specifically the personnel and work of killing squadrons such as Reserve Police Battalion 101 and the parts played by other "ordinary Germans" in the huge system of concentration, labor, and death camps that was, as he correctly puts it, "the emblematic institution of Germany during its Nazi period." To these perspectives, he adds detail, as hideous as it is valuable, about a lesser-known aspect of the Holocaust, namely, the brutal "death marches" that took place from late 1939 until the end of World War II.

As it moves in both of these directions—one looking toward a Holocaust that had not yet taken place, the other looking back from the Final Solution to determine how it happened—Goldhagen's basic argument can be summarized in two syllogisms. They reason as follows: First, ordinary Germans were antisemitic. Their antisemitism entailed elimination of the Jews. Therefore, ordinary Germans were prepared to be willing executioners. Second, far from being reluctant murderers, some Germans actually became willing executioners of the European Jews. Typically, those same Germans were a representative cross section of the German population. Therefore, with exceptions that only prove the rule, ordinary Germans stand indicted for the destruction of the European Jews.

Goldhagen's evidence for these claims derives initially from an appraisal of the history of antisemitism in Germany. According to his reading of that history, venomous forms of cultural and racist antisemitism became normative in Germany in the nineteenth and twentieth centuries, well before Hitler and the Nazi Party gained power in 1933. Such antisemitism called for the elimination of Jews and Jewish influence in Germany. In one way or another, then, the vast majority of the German populace was prepared to destroy Jews.

When the Nazis came to power, they advocated an overtly *exterminationist* antisemitism. Crucial to Goldhagen's argument is his claim that this exterminationist ideology was only a variation on the already *eliminationist* antisemitism that had existed in Germany for some time. During the Nazi period, 1933-1945, German perpetrators of the Holocaust willingly persecuted and destroyed Jews because they basically shared the Nazis' antisemitic perspective. This perspective held that the annihilation of the Jews was necessary and just because they were an unremitting pestilence threatening the racial superiority and political prerogatives that properly belonged to Germans.

Given legitimacy by the Nazi regime, the German killers, according to Goldhagen, were not an extraordinary minority. Instead they were representative of the German populace. Goldhagen's logic entails this relationship to mean that the vast majority of Germans were not only willing to let the Holocaust happen. Probably they would have participated directly in the killing if the need enjoined them to do so.

Goldhagen's reading of the pre-Holocaust history of German antisemitism musters his evidence that ordinary Germans were possible perpetrators and accomplices in a potential but not yet real Final Solution. This part of his account makes it no surprise, however, that the potential elimination of German Jews became the actual destruction of the European Jews. While recognizing that this movement from potential to actual annihilation has many dimensions and multiple causes, Goldhagen holds that too many scholars have agonized needlessly, often to the point of confusion, in their misguided efforts to show why and how the Holocaust happened.

Ever confident of the superiority of his own judgment, Goldhagen thinks that few puzzles remain about the Holocaust's causes. Although explaining how the Holocaust happened remains a long story, he believes that there is no need to dwell on most of the complexities that so much causal analysis of the Holocaust has produced. As Goldhagen sees it, the Holocaust had one cause that outweighed the others. Direct and straightforward, it involved the motivation without which the Holocaust was unthinkable, namely, the Germans' antisemitic beliefs about Jews. Remove that factor and the Holocaust that actually happened would not have taken place. On the other hand, to realize the Final Solution, the antisemitism of Goldhagen's ordinary Germans did need the catalyst that Hitler and the Nazi Party provided. Nevertheless, by themselves Hitler and the Nazi Party alone could not have made the Holocaust happen as it did. The actual Holocaust required willing, ordinary Germans to effect it.

Fanatically antisemitic as they were, Goldhagen suggests, Hitler and the Nazi Party had a reciprocal relationship with ordinary Germans when it came to the Jewish question. In Hitler and the Nazi Party, ordinary Germans got the organization, determination, and legitimation to carry out their latent, if not active, will to destroy European Jewry. In ordinary Germans, Hitler and the Nazi Party found a people who were well prepared to carry out the plan for a Third Reich that would be *judenrein* ("cleansed of Jews"). Thus, when Goldhagen reckons with the actuality of the Holocaust, his book becomes much more than an explanation of how he thinks the Holocaust took place. With his view that the Germans' antisemitic motivation was the most crucial condition—necessary though not alone sufficient—for the Holocaust, Goldhagen indicts "ordinary Germans," a category as broad as it is undiscriminating, and renders a sweeping verdict of collective German guilt.

Goldhagen's book has its merits. They exist primarily in his expansion of some details about the Final Solution, but not in the book's specious promise to achieve a groundbreaking analysis that meets a need—more imagined than real—for "radical revision" of nearly all previous scholarship on the Holocaust. Nowhere is this appraisal of his book more apt than in regard to his claim that "German's antisemitic beliefs about Jews were the central causal agent of the Holocaust."

Goldhagen is wrong when he implies that scholars such as Raul Hilberg, Yehuda Bauer, and Christopher Browning have "denied or obscured" the importance of German antisemitism. What they and other leading Holocaust scholars have done, however, is to avoid the oversimplifications that make and break Goldhagen's book. Antisemitism, for example, was a major current in pre-Nazi times. Nevertheless, while Goldhagen's work fills in empirical details about that ugly picture, pre-Nazi antisemitism in Germany was not primarily the essentially lethal variety that Goldhagen requires to make his claims hold. Conveniently dismissing any evidence to the contrary as insufficient or inadequate, failing to do the comparative work that ought to modify his extreme views about German antisemitism by placing it in a larger European context, Goldhagen relies too much on an assumed German uniformity to buttress his case.

At times Goldhagen emphasizes that his "ordinary Germans" must not be caricatured as a slavish, order-obeying people and that their freedom of choice should be recognized as crucial if they are to be held responsible for their Holocaust-related actions. To cite one of Christopher Browning's succinct rebuttals, however, Goldhagen ignores his own principles by describing ordinary Germans as basically "undifferentiated, unchanging, possessed by a single, monolithic cognitive outlook," especially as far as Jews were concerned before and during the Holocaust.

How will Goldhagen's work stand the test of time? Will it be more than a 1996 international book sensation? In deliberately provocative ways, Goldhagen has raised issues about Germans, Jews, antisemitism, and Holocaust scholarship that will not be taken lightly by any of the parties involved. At least for a time, his book will continue to be the subject of impassioned debate. In the long run, however, *Hitler's Willing Executioners* is likely to be much less than it was hyped to be. More than anything else, it will be remembered in the history of Holocaust studies as a phenomenon that did more harm than good.

John K. Roth

Sources for Further Study

The Economist. CCCXL, July 20, 1996, p. 45.
Foreign Affairs. LXXV, May, 1996, p. 144.
Los Angeles Times Book Review. March 24, 1996, p. 4.
The Nation. CCLXII, May 6, 1996, p. 50.
The New Republic. CCXIV, April 29, 1996, p. 32.
The New York Review of Books. XLIII, April 18, 1996, p. 4.
The New York Times Book Review. CI, April 14, 1996, p. 6.
The New Yorker. LXXI, April 22, 1996, p. 44.
Newsweek. CXXVII, April 29, 1996, p. 42.
Time. CXLVII, April 1, 1996, p. 73.
The Times Literary Supplement. June 7, 1996, p. 9.
The Virginia Quarterly Review. LXXII, Autumn, 1996, p. 738.
The Washington Post Book World. XXVI, March 24, 1996, p. 1.

HOOD

Author: Emma Donoghue (1969-   )
First published: 1995, in Great Britain
Publisher: HarperCollins (New York). 309 pp. $23.00
Type of work: Novel
Time: 1994
Locale: Dublin, Ireland

A critical week in the life of a young Dublin elementary school teacher trying to come to terms with her grief over the untimely death of the woman she loves

> *Principal characters:*
> PENELOPE (PEN) O'GRADY, a young lesbian schoolteacher narrating the novel in the first person
> CARA WALL, Pen's recently deceased lover who appears throughout the book in flashbacks representing Pen's memories of the past fourteen years
> MR. WALL, Cara's father, a quiet, introverted intellectual who works as a librarian
> KATE WALL, Cara's thoroughly Americanized older sister who now lives in Boston

Many homosexual novels deal with the complex problems connected with "coming out." The expression used to be a joking allusion to so-called closet queens who behaved like "straight" males in the workaday world but kept a wardrobe of glamorous feminine apparel to wear in secret after hours. This fragment from the idiom of the gay subculture has found a niche in the English language because no other suitable term previously existed to describe an important phenomenon. Coming out is no longer a joke but a very serious matter for both male and female homosexuals. It is felt to be a sort of moral and political duty as well as a necessity for psychological health. Homosexuals who refuse to come out of the closet are evading the demonstration of solidarity, leaving all homosexuals more vulnerable to legal and illegal aggression by default.

There are several stages that homosexuals tend to go through in the painful process of coming out. First, there is coming out to one's self, admitting one is really a homosexual. Then there is the stage of coming out to other homosexuals and entering into the demimonde still inhabited by most homosexuals. Next, there is the stage of coming out to one's friends and acquaintances. The biggest step, and the one that many homosexuals never dare to take, is coming out to their parents.

The effects of such a confession are unpredictable. Parents may feel guilty, or horrified. They may refuse to be introduced to the same-sex lover of their son or daughter. They may disown their homosexual offspring. Religious-minded parents may ask their homosexual child to receive unwanted prayers and spiritual counseling. Scientifically oriented parents may try to pressure the son or daughter into equally unwanted psychiatric treatment or even such drastic procedures as electric shock therapy. Parents may feel disgraced, even suicidal. In any case, the revelation usually cuts off their hopes of ever having grandchildren through that child, and this may become a source of guilt-inducing recriminations.

Hood is as much about coming out as about dealing with grief over the death of a loved one. Penelope "Pen" O'Grady discovers that the two problems are intricately intertwined. She cannot express her grief as long as she conceals the truth about her sexual orientation and her passionate love affair with Cara Wall, who was killed in a car crash after returning from a vacation trip to the Mediterranean. The enormity of death, especially the death of a loved one, has made everything else in Pen's life seem trivial.

Emma Donoghue's novel bears many resemblances to James Joyce's *Ulysses* (1922). Both novels are set in Dublin, although they are separated in time by most of the twentieth century. In both novels there is very little happening on the surface but a great deal going on inside the viewpoint characters' minds. Both stories take place during rigidly limited time periods. *Ulysses* covers exactly one day; *Hood* covers exactly one week during which the heroine (who has the same name as the classical Ulysses's wife) is teaching elementary school students (like Joyce's Stephen Dedalus). Just as Stephen Dedalus is haunted by his mother's death, Pen is haunted by Cara's. Through Pen's eyes, the reader gets the feeling of revisiting some parts of Dublin visited in Ulysses with Stephen Dedalus and Leopold Bloom. It is the same dear, dirty Dublin, with only a slightly faster pace and a slightly improved economy.

Much of Donoghue's story is told through flashbacks. Pen and Cara have been lovers ever since high school. In recent years, Pen has been sharing Cara's bedroom. Mr. Wall is appropriately named because he is as emotionally expressive as a wall and because his bedroom is only separated by a wall from the room where Pen and Cara have to shut each other's mouths with kisses to smother outcries during mutual orgasms. Cara's father may feel deep affection for his daughter but he has never been able to express it. Some readers will suspect that the absence of a strong love relationship between father and daughter may have been responsible for Cara's lesbianism in the first place. His daughter's death has made the bookish Mr. Wall withdraw even deeper into himself. He seems almost completely helpless. Pen has taken over the housekeeping and all the new and strange but terribly mundane matters involved with deaths, funerals, and interments. Although she and Cara had wild orgies in their bedroom and customarily took long, sensual baths together afterward, Pen has always believed that Mr. Wall was completely oblivious of what was really going on. She is to find out later that the mousy little librarian knew a great deal more than they realized. This discovery leads her to understand that it is not only wrong but nearly impossible to conceal the truth. It prompts her to take the final, most difficult and most dangerous step in the process of coming out, which is revealing the truth to a parent. Pen's father is dead; she feels a need to reveal her true identity to her surviving parent while her mother is still alive. Cara's death has made Pen realize how fragile and uncertain life really is.

Sophisticated, thoroughly Americanized Kate Wall returns to Dublin for her sister's funeral but is ill at ease in what now seems like a foreign land. She is obviously anxious to return to her business and social life in Boston. She regards Dublin as a quaint, archaic city, a good place to be *from*. It was Kate with whom Pen was initially in love as a schoolgirl fourteen years ago, just before the Walls were divorced and Kate went off to America with her mother. Pen still has sexual fantasies about Kate. Although nothing happens between the two women, the revival of her desire for the elder sister makes Pen realize that she is still alive inside even though she may appear emotionally dead. When Pen tells the urbane, cynically amused Kate the whole truth about her relationship with Cara, her confession is a crucial step in the process of coming out.

In addition to Pen's internal conflict, retrospective conflict is revealed in the flashbacks. Cara was not as committed to the love relationship as Pen. Cara was afraid of accepting her lesbianism and afraid of committing herself to a permanent relationship with one woman. She had several unsuccessful affairs with men and any number of furtive affairs with other women, but always came back to Pen. Cara was returning to Pen after a trip to Greece when she was killed in a traffic accident. The fact that Cara is returning to Penelope from Greece is an allusion to the Homeric epic which Joyce parodied in his own *Ulysses*.

The relationship that existed between Pen and Cara is reminiscent of the relationship between George and Ann Smiley in John le Carré's *Tinker, Tailor, Soldier, Spy* (1974) and *Smiley's People* (1980). Pen is like George, a long-suffering lover who provides Ann with the kind of emotional anchor she needs. Cara is like Ann, taking outrageous advantage of her lover while engaging in one affair after another without bothering to conceal her infidelity. Pen's unwavering devotion always draws Cara back to her like a moth to a flame. At times, Cara hates Pen for the very reason that she is unable to escape from her love.

There is apparently very little difference between the kind of English spoken in modern Ireland and that spoken in America. The reader might be momentarily puzzled by a word such as "binliner" until realizing that it refers to the familiar plastic garbage bag. The dialogue is chock-full of Americanisms picked up from books, films and such television serials as *Cagney and Lacey*. The term "coming out" itself is an Americanism, as are "gerrymandering," "fax," "gay," "wisecracking," "fast food," "ghetto-blaster," "guilt trip," "yuppie," and all the others that sprinkle the dialogue.

Although the American influence is obviously strong, Ireland is still like Joyce's Ireland in many ways and still dominated by the Roman Catholic church. Mr. Wall, for example, regularly attends mass although he no longer believes in any of the church's teachings. The same is true of Pen. Many Irish men and women are participating in church rituals on a regular basis while breaking the rules in such flagrant ways as using contraceptives and engaging in free homosexual and heterosexual behavior.

For better or for worse, Ireland is decades behind America in liberalizing its attitudes about sex. The only people with whom Pen feels free to acknowledge at least part of the truth about herself are a small circle of women who consider themselves crusaders for gay/lesbian liberation in a small, ultraconservative, priest-ridden island from which nonconformists such as James Joyce and his fictional hero Stephen Dedalus traditionally emigrate to foreign lands. This lesbian circle appears to contribute more lip-service than militant action to their cause. They make Pen realize that they have not really come out of the closet but are all hiding in the same closet together. She will not share her grief with them, nor will she believe in the grief they are displaying at the impromptu, segregated, and clandestine wake they hold for Pen's deceased lover. Instead, she gets drunk and wakes up with a terrible hangover.

On the last page of the novel, Pen experiences a Joycean epiphany as she begins to come out to her mother over tea. The flood of tears the young lesbian has been repressing for the entire week finally begin to flow.

Hood is Emma Donoghue's second novel. In addition to her first novel, *Stir-Fry* (1994), she published a nonfiction book entitled *Passions Between Women: British Lesbian Culture 1668-1801* in 1995. She lives in Cambridge, England, where she is completing a doctoral thesis on eighteenth century women novelists. Her novels have been well received. It remains to be seen whether she will emerge to prominence from among the legions of aspiring new novelists. She has a better chance than many because she has a penetrating intelligence as well as strong feelings and a subject in which she believes. Her intelligence can be seen in the insights and *aperçus* that enrich her story, as in the following striking example: "Then it occurred to me that maybe all the people we saw behaving oddly or madly were not a distinct type at all, they were just us on a very bad day." She also shows her courage by inviting comparison with the formidable James Joyce as well as the distinguished Christopher Isherwood, whose ground-breaking novel *A Single Man* (1964) likewise deals with a day in the life of a homosexual teacher trying to come to terms with grief over the recent death of his long-term live-in lover.

The title of Donoghue's *Bildungsroman* is intentionally ambiguous. The word "hood" appears in the story in many different contexts. It can refer to the hood of the clitoris. Author Donoghue's love scenes leave little to the imagination. In fact, it is the description of lesbian lovemaking rather than any compelling narrative that will keep most readers turning the pages. On the other hand, the word "hood" can suggest the hoods worn by the nuns with whom Pen works every day. These pious virgins would be horrified if they knew about Pen's sexual behavior. Pen would certainly lose her teaching job at the Convent of the Immaculate Conception if she told the truth about her homosexuality. At one point the heroine mentally plays with terms such as "lesbian-hood" and "maidenhood." Most important, "hood" symbolizes hiding one's true identity from the world and simultaneously having one's vision drastically circumscribed as an inescapable consequence. A lesbian who tries to hide the truth from the world is like a cloistered nun or, like Little Red Riding Hood in the Grimm brothers' fairy tale, a naïve, frightened little girl.

Bill Delaney

Sources for Further Study

Booklist. XCII, March 1, 1996, p. 1120.
Boston Globe. March 17, 1996, p. B43.
The Guardian. March 14, 1996, II, p. 4.
Kirkus Reviews. LXIV, January 15, 1996, p. 85.
The New York Times Book Review. CI, March 24, 1996, p. 12.
Publishers Weekly. CCXLIII, January 22, 1996, p. 59.
San Francisco Chronicle. May 19, 1996, p. REV6.
The Times Literary Supplement. April 21, 1995, p. 22.

HUGO L. BLACK
Cold Steel Warrior

Author: Howard Ball (1937-   )
Publisher: Oxford University Press (New York). 368 pp. $35.00
Type of work: Biography
Time: 1886-1971
Locale: Harlan, Ashland, and Birmingham, Alabama; Washington, D.C.

Ball's biography of the late Justice Black draws on interviews and Library of Congress files to tell the story of the former Ku Klux Klansman who went on to lead the Supreme Court's "due process revolution"

Principal personages:
> HUGO L. BLACK, the son of a poor Alabama farmer and shopkeeper,
> parlayed a successful law practice first into a U.S. Senate seat, then a
> place on the high bench of the Supreme Court, where he acted as one
> of the most influential jurists of the twentieth century
> WILLIAM O. DOUGLAS, Black's colleague on the Court, whose views
> were for many years so similar to Black's that when the Alabaman
> was asked to comment on Douglas' career, he declined, saying that to
> do so would be too much like self-analysis
> ROBERT H. JACKSON, another of Black's fellow justices, Jackson was
> perhaps Black's arch-antagonist, giving vent publicly to his
> frustration over what he believed to be Black's attempt to
> outmaneuver him in gaining the chief justiceship
> FELIX FRANKFURTER, the former law professor and New Dealer who,
> once he was appointed to the Court, failed to achieve his promise as
> jurist, while at the same time alienating Black and others of his
> Supreme Court brethren with his assumption of superiority

The story of Hugo Lafayette Black is an all-American story. Throughout his life Black referred to himself as a "backward county fellow," and although he frequently invested this description with a great deal of irony, in many senses it describes just what Black was. He was born in 1886 in rural Harlan, Alabama, the eighth and last child of a poor farmer and shopkeeper and his wife. The Blacks' prospects did improve in 1889, when William Black moved the family to Ashland, population 350, where he again set himself up as a merchant.

By the time Black was ready to attend college, his family was firmly established in the middle class, and Black decided to follow his brother Orlando into the medical profession. Despite his lack of a college education, Black was accepted into Birmingham Medical College. He stayed only a year, however, deciding that he was more suited to the study of law. In 1906, he graduated with honors from the University of Alabama Law School. Even in the face of this academic success, however, Black retained a strong sense of educational inferiority and embarked on a campaign of intellectual self-improvement, focusing on ancient Greek civilization. It was a campaign that would last for the rest of his life: Even after he reached the pinnacle of his profession as a U.S. Supreme Court justice, he continued to read economics, history, and the classics at the Library of Congress.

After graduating from law school, Black set himself up in private practice, first in Ashland, then in Birmingham. Almost immediately, however, he discovered his true vocation: politics. In 1910, he accepted an appointment to become the Birmingham police court judge. It was a thankless position, but his two-year tenure there filled Black with political ambition, and shortly thereafter he was elected county prosecutor, a position he held from 1914 to 1917. After a brief hiatus occasioned by World War I, during which Black trained soldiers in Tennessee, he returned to his legal practice—this time with an eye on the U.S. Senate.

Black's political skills and ambitions always proved to be his primary source of strength, but in 1923, they led him to make a nearly ruinous decision. Alabama politics was at the time largely controlled by moneyed, aristocratic downstate "Bourbon" Democrats. As an unpedigreed native of the northern part of the state, Black, like many of his peers, felt obliged to join the then powerful Klan in order to get the political backing he needed. It worked. Black's later protestations to the contrary, he was for several years an active Klan member, and in 1926—despite Black's quiet resignation from the group a year earlier—Klan backing helped send him to the U.S. Senate.

Once in Congress, however, Black established one of the most liberal voting records around; his advocacy of the thirty-hour workweek even led to accusations that the senator was a "Bolshevik." During his two terms, Black maintained a high profile serving as chairman on committees investigating the public utilities industry and lobbying practices. He was also an ardent New Dealer, even supporting President Franklin D. Roosevelt's questionable court-packing plan, which would have led to an undermining of Supreme Court power and therefore of the separation of powers. In 1937, Black was rewarded for his loyalty by a nomination to the Supreme Court.

Black had gained a reputation as the Senate's "Chief Inquisitor" and made a number of political enemies there, so when his name came before the same body for confirmation, it provoked a stormy response. For the first time in his public life, Black's onetime Klan membership became an issue, but the Judge, as he always preferred to be called, once again exercised his considerable political talents to diffuse the crisis. Confronting the problem head-on, Black went before the American public via radio and made a confession. The matter of his KKK membership would never again be the subject of public debate.

Black served for thirty-four years on the Court, and for at least the first twenty-five, he was one of the most liberal—and influential—justices on the high bench. He replaced Associate Justice Willis Van Devanter, one of the notorious "Four Horsemen" who were responsible for undermining nearly all of the initiatives that constituted FDR's "first" New Deal, and Black never forgot what he regarded as the evil of judicial interference with the legislative process. This attitude was responsible for some of the conservative attitudes he assumed in the later years of his High Court tenure, when he felt many of his brethren were taking too active a role in deciding public policy. More likely, though, Black's constitutional fundamentalism was responsible; throughout his life he took a literal approach to the nation's foundation document, a dogeared copy of which he always carried on his person.

Initially, however, Black's insistence on the letter of the law—and particularly the dictates of the First Amendment—helped to institute the Court's liberal reorientation, which lasted into the 1960's. His favorite decision remained *Chambers v. Florida* (1940), in which, writing for the majority, he helped to overturn the murder convictions of four unjustly accused African Americans; tears came to his eyes whenever he reread the opinion. Notwithstanding his opinion in *Korematsu v. United States* (1944), upholding U.S. internment of Japanese Americans during World War II, Black is best remembered for the constitutional revolution occasioned by his belief that the so-called due process clause of the Fourteenth Amendment made the guarantees of the Bill of Rights applicable at the state as well as the federal level.

Black's literalist interpretation of the Constitution led him, in 1951, to dissent vigorously from the majority's opinion in *Dennis v. United States* that suppression of political dissent by American Communist Party members was justified during the Cold War era. But in later years, this same philosophy led him to dissent, in *Griswold v. Connecticut* (1965), from the majority view that the Constitution protected a right to privacy, which he could locate nowhere in the document.

Appropriately, Black's last Supreme Court opinion—indeed, the last case he participated in—was the Pentagon Papers case, *New York Times Co. v. United States* (1971). Writing separately, Black was able, once again, to assert his First Amendment absolutism, insisting, with a majority of his brethren, that the government was obliged to adhere to the constitutional proscription that, "Congress shall make no law . . . abridging the freedom of speech, or of the press." Within three months of writing his opinion, Black was dead.

Hugo Black was such an influential force on the Court largely because of his political gifts. His energy and steely resolve were combined with an archetypal Southern graciousness that enabled him to persuade his brethren of the correctness of his views and build voting coalitions that would convert these views into law. He was helped in his crusade by a number of like-minded justices, particularly William O. Douglas, whose record, at least though the early 1960's, mirrored his own. Yet Black also had some formidable opponents, including the redoubtable Felix Frankfurter, the intellectual leader of the conservative wing of the Court during the 1940's and 1950's. Black's influence also engendered the antipathy of the politically ambitious Robert H. Jackson. When Chief Justice Harlan F. Stone died in 1946, Jackson was absent from the Court, serving as chief prosecutor at the Nuremberg war crimes trials. Before Stone's successor was confirmed, Black temporarily assumed the chief justice's duties, fueling Jackson's belief that Black intended to co-opt the position Jackson felt was rightfully his. When Jackson took his complaint to the press, his actions marked one of the few occasions that Supreme Court rivalries have been put on public display.

Howard Ball does a fine job of rehearsing both Hugo Black's jurisprudence and professional affiliations, but equally important aspects of Black's private life go unexplored or unexplained in *Hugo L. Black: Cold Steel Warrior*. The one real detour

Black ever took, leaving his position as county prosector and joining the army, allegedly because of an unsuccessful romance, obviously constitutes an important chapter in his life. Ball devotes only four brief paragraphs to this intriguing episode. Similarly, although Ball does explain that Black's first wife suffered from depression and eventually committed suicide, little time is devoted to examining the effect this traumatic event doubtless had on Black and his three children. Ball writes nothing at all about Black's courtship of and marriage to his second wife, who as Elizabeth Seay DeMeritte had initially worked as his secretary. As Elizabeth Black died several years before the appearance of *Hugo L. Black*, it is hard to explain such reticence.

Omissions such as these, together with too frequent editing errors, mar what is an otherwise engrossing tale of archetypal American accomplishment. *Hugo L. Black: Cold Steel Warrior* is not really a biography, but rather a review of the high points of Black's career. Our sense of his greatness would only have been enhanced by a more thorough inquiry into the adversities he overcame to achieve his place in the nation's history.

Lisa Paddock

Source for Further Study

Library Journal. CXXI, June 1, 1996, p. 118.

THE HUNTER GRACCHUS
And Other Papers on Literature and Art

Author: Guy Davenport (1927-   )
Publisher: Counterpoint (Washington, D.C.). 339 pp. $25.00
Type of work: Essays, lectures, and book reviews

A collection of pieces written by Guy Davenport during the 1980's and 1990's on literature and painting, poets, writers and painters, along with selections from the author's informal journals

The Hunter Gracchus: And Other Papers on Literature and Art is the third collection of essays by Guy Davenport, whose literary scholarship, fiction, translations, poetry and drawing have enriched American culture for more than four decades. Few of his essays, in the present volume or the two preceding—*The Geography of the Imagination* (1981) and *Every Force Evolves a Form* (1987)—require the reader to absorb as pedestrian an opening line as the one above.

Davenport's rich mind, attention to imagination's power, vast learning, and attractive style have combined with his dread of boredom to generate pieces a reader cannot stop reading. Open to almost any essay, lecture, or journal entry in *The Hunter Gracchus* and the first sentence engages the mind—and the second, and the third. "The Comic Muse," a review of *The Oxford Book of Comic Verse* (1994), begins: "We trust seriousness to be the firm ground beneath our feet while knowing full well that it is ultimately dull and probably inhuman." This statement works on a reader like a fast-acting drug. It says something one feels or wants to say but does not quite have the vision or courage to formulate. Vistas of experience, personal and social, open in sharp focus.

Many of the pieces are book reviews. Studded with arresting perceptions, a Davenport book review can make the book seem almost irrelevant. Typically, the title is not presented until well into the review. A subject sets Davenport's mind working, his sentences flowing, and a reader eagerly reading. Here is another sentence early in a review of a scholarly book on American Indians, collected in the first book of essays, *The Geography of the Imagination*:

Custer, who had watched Lee hand his sword to Grant at Appomattox, must have known that his opponent on this occasion, a sachem of sachems who seemed to be a cross between a Roman senator and an owl with all its feathers blown backward, would merely grunt with disgust if he offered him his sword, and get on with the ticklish business of scalping so bald a man as George Armstrong Custer.

The writer Davenport is more palpable than the reviewer Davenport. For him, book reviews are occasions for long rich sentences combining cultural commentary and humor and anything else driven by a fact-based flow of imaginative (not fantastical) dramatic projection. No wonder Professor Zolla, author of the book being reviewed, seems a trifle pale when his name arises a few paragraphs later.

The subjects in *The Hunter Gracchus*, whether books or people or observations from Davenport's journal, can include anything from the great writer Franz Kafka, author of the short story "The Hunter Gracchus," to the drunk redneck, detailed in a section of the "Micrographs" piece, who Davenport witnessed being tossed off a bus when the hillbilly would not stop messing around with a woman passenger's hair. Open to another piece at random, this one titled "On Reading." A sentence, near the end of the essay, proclaims "The mind is a self-consuming organ and preys on itself." One can read the paragraph before it to establish context, or simply quiver under the statement's implications without reading further. This is the domain of utterance common to Heraclitus, Jesus, Samuel Johnson, Ralph Waldo Emerson, and Lucretius, where common things are illuminated out of their ordinariness. Reading on in "On Reading," one discovers the theme of conventions tipped over (seriousness is "ultimately dull and inhuman") again being played: "We do not read enough to have seen that literature itself is not interested in the transcendental role society has assumed for it. The pleasure of reading has turned out not to be what our culture calls pleasure at all." Reading is not to inform, to keep people "up" on things or didactically inform them on how the American president makes his congressional appointments (what reading does in school) but to develop the imagination, the essential human organ. Davenport tells of meeting an illiterate man:

> The horror of his predicament struck me first of all because it prevents his getting a job, and secondly because of the blindness it imposes on his imagination. I also realized more fully than ever before what a text is and how it can only be realized in the imagination, how mere words used over and over for other purposes and in other contexts, can be so ordered by, say, Jules Verne, as to be deciphered as a narrative of intricate texture and splendid color, of precise meanings and values.

The mind, "that self-consuming organ" is freed from itself by reading.

In *The Hunter Gracchus*, the developed, curious, open eye which Davenport acknowledges reading fostered in him, from *Tarzan* in childhood to years of reading and rereading *Finnegan's Wake*, searches the works of writers, artists, and historians, with the same eagerness to discover and demonstrate what those minds have also read, found, and included in their story or painting. A work of art studied by Davenport is always shown to be something its creator made from other things, and then transmuted. Everywhere apparent in these essays is the awareness of the artist's place in a community. Artist and writer, consumers of art and writing that they are, take inspiration, sustenance, and teaching from the arts as much or more than anyone else. Davenport is an artist, poet, and fiction maker, and his writings about other makers have the authority of observations an NBA point guard will make about a player he admires. When Davenport speaks of a writer or painter finding a new form, readers know they are not hearing the theories of an academic but the recognitions of a doer.

Davenport's Kafka is not a shadowy figure composed of academic clichés about his obsessions. The title essay, "The Hunter Gracchus," uncovers the Kafka who read a novel, Wilkie Collins' *Armadale*, mixed its decaying protagonist with his own dreams (recorded in Kafka's notebook) and produced a story, "The Hunter Gracchus," which prophesies the calamities awaiting twentieth century humanity. The way Davenport writes his explication of this story, provocative subheads ("Death Ships," "Sind sie Tot?" "Raven and Blackbird") followed by short paragraphs or single sentences housing epigrams, allusions to history, and quotations, presents the subject to the reader in an alluring brickwork or set of stepping stones, and transforms scholarly exposition into reader response as art: the art of finding. The short story about Gracchus demands such reading. It is not really a story, but a sequence of images, as the sick "hunter" makes his way from a boat, through the town of Riva, and into a room where a conversation ensues and the story ends. If a story such as "The Hunter Gracchus" eschews the usual machinery of storytelling, this means the writer is usually a klutz or a genius—an overturner of conventions so new meanings can be forecast and new ways of feelings expressed. Kafka's genius receives persuasive confirmation through Davenport's reading.

Picasso's famous painting *Guernica*, discussed in an essay of the same name requires similar flexibility of its "reader." "*Guernica* may well not be a 'painting.' It is a Magdalenian glyph, a poster, a sign." When painting *Guernica*, Picasso resisted the dictates of making a painting just as Kafka resisted the conventions of storytelling. This is not being different for the sake of difference, but to get at truth: "Art all too often brings its subject into the domestic *hereness* of Art. The rarest success of the artist is to leave his subject where he found it (like Joyce, Goya, Van Gogh) and take us to it." In *Guernica*, "painting" is dumped for evocation of the bombing of helpless people in a Spanish town and all that this act suggests about what happens in so-called civilization. Kafka's stories are dreamlike, since he did in fact dream parts of them ("leave his subject where he found it"). The Davenport essays in *The Hunter Gracchus*, demonstrating the meanings in things written and painted, proceed in the sentence by sentence accretion which testify to a real meaning-hunter awake at the controls, following his nose and finding his way.

Finding is exhilarating and pleasureful but readers need the genius of wakefulness to be awake, the latter qualification possibly culturable but turning also on the luck of breeding and natural gifts. Charles Darwin "read the Galapagos finches . . . ; he read the fossil record, he brought all of creation into one grand plot of chance and adaptation. He must have known that he was changing the way every honest mind saw the world." Darwin "had the good luck to be born into a family whose traditions were scientific and technological." This excerpt is from the essay titled "Life, Chance and Charles Darwin." Like Picasso and Kafka, Darwin was utterly devoted to the given, the real. Elsewhere in "Thoreau and the Dispersion of Seeds," Davenport notes: "Thoreau's eye is as lively as a squirrel and his descriptions are beautiful not because he is out to write poetic prose but because they are accurate and meticulously responsible as to information."

Davenport's emphasis is always put on how the scientist (Thoreau, Darwin), poet (Walt Whitman, Jack Sharpless, Ronald Johnson), historian (Edward Gibbon), story-teller (Donald Barthelme, John Cheever), painter (Picasso, Stanley Spencer, Paul Cadmus) or author of a book under review sees what he or she is saying, as well as

what he or she is saying. Quality of attention guarantees content found and presented. Running through all the pieces is Davenport's constant assurance that modern
culture and life will not develop attention in the populace. Modern architecture is a
bad deal, typified by buildings made of windows that require unending washing
(possibly a good lifetime job for illiterates). The automobile has destroyed the once
great achievement-invention of humanity, the city:

> We are all owned by automobiles, creatures whom we must feed gas and oil (a necessity so
> transcending political rhetoric that we continued to buy oil from Iran while it held our citizens
> hostage, and from Libya while we bombed it), shoe with rubber, wash and lavish with other attentions
> not the least of which are lifelong car payments. It is the most successful of parasites, far beyond
> the wildest hopes of microbes or rats.

And television, that other signature twentieth century technology, dulls and spoils the
innate attentiveness of children.

Yet the sweeter theme that plays through *A Hunter Gracchus* is the availability of
the alternate worlds art and reading continue to offer. Reading is encouraged. One
need not be the creator of the work to be a creator, to be involved in mystery and
elevated out of solitude. "We can get out through the imaginative alchemy of reading,
a skill complementary to writing but psychologically more mysterious." Readers go
into new worlds, which are often the oldest world reimagined by the writer or invoked
by the painter. "The more diligent the writer, the deeper into the past he can reach."
Unlike the products of modern commerce, quickly consumed, reading offers a
permanent feast. "Neither Ruskin nor Proust can be read up; they are best when read
a second or third time, when the resonances become richer and richer."

The Hunter Gracchus points to many works, old and new, worthy of living with. It
is a tribute to genius, to makers of signs, to imaginers anchored in what is in front of
their noses. While the civilization gasps for breath as it drives cars and watches
television, the fluid interchange between mediums goes on, forms are found, other
worlds for minds to live in are made. Davenport blesses with all he can see, writes
with irresistible allure, and encourages his reader to do more and more with *their* minds
and attention. His writing can feel like the sweetest therapy as this mad century ends.

Bruce Wiebe

Sources for Further Study

Booklist. XCIII, December 1, 1996, p. 637.
Lexington-Herald Leader. January 5, 1997, p. E4.
Library Journal. CXXI, December, 1996, p. 93.
Publishers Weekly. CCXLIII, November 18, 1996, p. 58.
The Washington Post Book World. XXVI, p. 15.

I'M LOSING YOU

Author: Bruce Wagner (1954-   )
Publisher: Villard (New York). 319 pp. $23.00
Type of work: Novel
Time: 1996
Locale: Los Angeles

A satirical portrait of the powerful, the weak, and the depraved in contemporary Hollywood

Principal characters:
    DONNY RIBKIN, an agent
    BERNIE RIBKIN, his father, a washed-up producer
    SERENA RIBKIN, Bernie's former wife, an invalid
    KATHERINE GROSSECK, Donny's former wife, a screenwriter
    PHYLLISS WOLFE, a film producer
    SIMON KROHN, an aspiring screenwriter
    CALLIOPE KROHN-MARKOWITZ, Simon's mother, a psychiatrist
    RACHEL KROHN, Calliope's daughter, a producer's assistant
    PERRY NEEDHAM HOWE, Rachel's boss, a television producer
    JEREMY STEIN, a television producer
    SARA RADISSON-STEIN, Jeremy's wife, a casting director
    TOVAH BRUCHNER, Jeremy's mistress, an agent
    URSULA SEDGWICK, a waitress and stripper
    TAJ WIEDLIN, a producer's assistant
    ZEV TURTLETAUB, Taj's boss, a film producer
    LESLIE TROTT, a dermatologist
    OBERON MALL, a film star
    GINA TOLK, a masseuse
    KIM GIRARD (KIV GIRAUX), a star of pornographic films
    TROY CAPRA, a director of pornographic films
    CHET STODDARD, a washed-up talk-show host
    SEVERIN WELCH, a washed-up screenwriter
    PIERRE RUBIDOUX, a film producer

In *Force Majeure* (1991), Bruce Wagner presents contemporary Hollywood as an only slightly exaggerated version of hell on earth. While Wagner's first novel focuses on one character's slow descent into madness, his second, *I'm Losing You*, shows a cross-section of people connected directly or indirectly with the film and television business engulfed in varying degrees of decadence. Much like Nathanael West's *The Day of the Locust* (1939), invoked several times by Wagner, *I'm Losing You* uses the impersonality and desperation of Hollywood as metaphors for moral decline in general. Far from being didactic, however, the novel is satirical, often hilariously so, displaying as much glee as censure in the excesses of its characters.

Unlike with *Force Majeure*, because of the inevitable identification with its woebegone protagonist, Wagner achieves considerably greater ironic distance through having no main character and no conventional plot, the novel consisting of a series of vignettes. *I'm Losing You* is told from the points of view, sometimes first-person, usually omniscient, of about twenty characters, all despicable or pathetic in widely varying degrees, whose lives interact, often to the detriment of all concerned.

Wagner's subject and aggressively hip style recall such contemporary novelists as Martin Amis, T. Coraghessan Boyle, James Ellroy, and Thomas Pynchon, but his narrative strategy, with the alternating focuses, resembles that of another master satirist, Evelyn Waugh, whose *Vile Bodies* (1930) could easily be a model for *I'm Losing You.*

Donny Ribkin is a powerful agent whose father, Bernie, produced a series of popular horror films twenty-five years earlier but has gone downhill since. In a drunken-driving accident, Bernie killed the mother of Pierre Rubidoux who became an agent only to have Donny outshine him. Rubidoux plays a cruel trick on Bernie to get revenge on them all, leading to Bernie's death. Donny has never gotten over his former wife, Katherine Grosseck. Wagner fittingly describes this obsession in terms of decay, a central metaphorical conceit in the novel: "Their love continued to grow the way nails were said to grow on a corpse." Katherine is a screenwriter who expects to be nominated for an Academy Award for her film biography of the suicidal poet Anne Sexton. After Donny, Katherine turns to lesbianism, becoming the lover of the hot director Pargita Snow, stealing her from the producer Phylliss Wolfe. Katherine is much happier in her new life and is amused at news of Donny's homosexual activity.

Bernie has long been separated from his wife, Serena, now dying of cancer. (Most of the characters are physically or spiritually ill or both.) Years earlier, Bernie passed his syphilis on to Serena, who infected her lover, cantor Sy Krohn, whose wife also contracted the ailment, all becoming "characters in a Preston Sturges nightmare." (Wagner shares with his creations the cinema as a constant point of reference.) Sy's subsequent suicide was covered up as a random murder. Serena is befriended by Simon Krohn, not knowing he is Sy's son. Simon, a would-be screenwriter, meets her when he investigates a suspicious odor in her house. Calling himself "the Dead Animal Guy," Simon removes squirrels, raccoons, and other creatures he calls "Fluffy" that have died beneath houses or inside their walls. Simon's mother is psychiatrist Calliope Krohn-Markowitz, whose patients include Donny and several other characters. Calliope kicks Simon out of her house for trying to interest her famous clients in his script ideas.

Simon's sister, Rachel, is personal assistant to Perry Needham Howe, a successful television producer. Perry's young son has died of cancer, and now he has the disease himself. Seeing himself near the end, Perry becomes obsessed with intricate watches costing hundreds of thousands of dollars. Since some such timepieces are capable of registering the end of the millennium, Perry's concern with time becomes suggestive not only of approaching death but also of apocalypse. Perry is friends with Jeremy Stein, whose infant son is blind. Jeremy's wife, Sara, a casting director, knows he is having an affair, and becomes more and more wrapped up in her son. The letters in which she pours out her emotions to Samson are published and optioned for the big screen with Sara's dear friend Holly Hunter, with whom she and the baby move in after she leaves Jeremy, to play her. Perry's mistress Tovah Bruchner, an agent and Rachel's best friend, wants Perry to produce the film with Jane Campion to direct.

(Hunter and Campion are only two of dozens of real-life entertainment figures who become sidelights to the lives of Wagner's characters. Alec Baldwin, Laura Dern, Richard Dreyfuss, and Harry Dean Stanton are among those who make cameo appearances, and Steven Spielberg's mother is struck by Bernie's car.)

Donny takes in an attractive homeless woman, Ursula Sedgwick, and her daughter, Tiffany. Ursula drifts away from Donny, becoming a waitress and a stripper, and eventually rescues the homeless Taj Wiedlin. Taj has been assistant to the producer Zev Turtletaub but runs away after repeatedly being humiliated, including being forced to have sex with Zev and his friends. Taj beats Tiffany to death and later hangs himself in jail. The dazed, desperate Ursula, who has attempted to impose some order on her chaotic existence by following a New Age religion, kidnaps Samson.

The other main characters whose lives cross those of these figures include Leslie Trott, an overweight, homosexual dermatologist who supplies his patients with drugs. One of these, Oberon Mall, a major star, goes into a coma, ironically, after a root canal. Gina Tolk, a masseuse who has convinced herself she has created successful television series, impersonates Katherine when Calliope refuses to accept such an important person as a patient. Kim Girard is an innocent who comes to Hollywood hoping for stardom, changes her name to Kiv Giraux, and finds success in soft-core cable pornography directed by Troy Capra, a once-serious stage director who becomes her lover. Chet Stoddard is a briefly popular talk-show host reduced to participating in an insurance scam involving AIDS patients. This plotline recalls Nikolay Gogol's *Myortvye dushi* (*Dead Souls*, 1842), which several of the characters are trying to update as a film. Chet is redeemed somewhat through falling in love with Zev's sister, Aubrey, who is dying of AIDS. Chet's former father-in-law, Severin Welch, is perhaps the most pathetic character, waiting for years for Charles Bluhdorn, the late head of Paramount, to return his telephone calls. Severin and Bernie represent those who fall under Hollywood's spell, achieve some success, are unable to adjust to change, and hang on inexplicably hopeful of resurrection.

In his final, desperate stage, Severin uses a scanner to monitor car telephone transmissions and has his daughter type transcripts of the fragmented conversations of agents, producers, pimps, and drug dealers he intercepts: "Severin poured over them, ruminating, sonic editor on high, scaling heights of cellular Babel, ducking into rooms of verbiage, corroded, dank, dead end." He decides to incorporate this material into the screenplay that is his life's work, an adaptation of *Dead Souls*. Severin wants to "use it all to stitch one hell of an American Quilt. These were the voices of a dying world, no doubt."

This means of communication provides the novel with its heavily symbolic title since these conversations are subject to the vicissitudes of technological limitations that create "unnerving fast food airwave static." "I'm losing you" is the standard message when one communicator is about to travel beyond the range of another, leading to a "symphony of hungry ghosts begging to be let in." The crazed Severin imagines that when the call he has long been awaiting finally comes he is out of range. Both thinking that they have missed the call that would transform their lives and believing that such a call—such a change—could occur summarize the triviality of the characters. As with Simon and Serena never discovering their connection and Bernie actually believing that his greatest enemy would help him make a comeback, failures to communicate—to understand—undercut much of what they do. Sara writes her book to convey her love for her son only to care finally as much about how dramatizing it will glorify her supposed sainthood.

Wagner's characters are constantly punished in various ways for their failings, and Hollywood is the right place for such punishment. Taj's ambition to produce commercially successful films leads him to suffer Zev's tortures, even being tied up and vomited upon. Wagner's Hollywood is one that has progressed from that of Budd Schulberg's *What Makes Sammy Run?* (1941), in which someone ruthlessly ambitious will do anything to get to the top, to a world in which those already in power will do anything to those less powerful. These self-appointed victims allow themselves to become sideshow freaks who live for humiliation.

The insecurities of Wagner's characters also lead them to bitchy gossip about Hollywood legends and would-be legends and to put down celebrities. When Calliope's husband chastises Simon for harassing one of her patients, the star of a science-fiction series, Simon responds, "He's a f——ing *Vorbalid*, Mitch—we're not talking Anthony Hopkins here! We're not even talking Michael Douglas!" Phylliss Wolfe wonders what persona she should convey in her memoirs: "Am I supposed to be Jackie Mason or Oscar Wilde? Carrie Fisher? (She's kinda both)." Phyllis's observation that "sometimes the Wolfe sound-bites more than she can chew" is typical of the characters' wit. They each think they have an undeveloped or unrecognized talent, but they are capable only of glib sarcasm.

Even more than in *Force Majeure*, Wagner portrays this society as lacking in values. Bud Wiggins, the antihero of that novel, attempts vainly to find recompense in Judaism only to discover his rabbi-guru is a fraud. In *I'm Losing You*, Rachel tries to turn her back on decadence and thoughts of suicide by seeking refuge in traditional Jewish ceremonies and finds a degree of peace: "After twenty-five years, Rachel stopped training for the unnamed, unannounced event." Because of the sting of his satire, the gritty detail of his vision of a corrupt world, and the essentially conservative values that emerge from this morass, Wagner resembles a younger, hipper Saul Bellow.

Wagner, who has lived in Los Angeles since he was eight, knows his subject thoroughly. He has been a screenwriter on films such as *A Nightmare on Elm Street 3: Dream Warriors* (1987) and *Scenes from the Class Struggle in Beverly Hills* (1989), and is best known for writing the cult television miniseries *Wild Palms* (1993). While these credits indicate a certain facile glibness and a talent for the offbeat, they give little indication of Wagner's worth as a novelist. While his novels are frequently funny, especially in the early going, both eventually become painful journeys into despair, but they are the work of a potentially major artist with a distinctive, hallucinatory style, a Louis-Ferdinand Céline for our time.

Michael Adams

Sources for Further Study

The Advocate. July 23, 1996, p. 55.
Booklist. XCII, July, 1996, p. 1805.
Chicago Tribune. September 5, 1996, V, p. 3.
Entertainment Weekly. July 26, 1996, p. 49.
Library Journal. CXXI, June 15, 1996, p. 94.
Los Angeles Times Book Review. August 4, 1996, p. 6.
The New York Times. July 30, 1996, p. C15.
The New York Times Book Review. CI, August 18, 1996, p. 11.
The New Yorker. LXXII, August 5, 1996, p. 74.
Publishers Weekly. CCXLIII, May 6, 1996, p. 67.
San Francisco Chronicle. August 14, 1996, p. E5.
Time. CXLVIII, October 7, 1996, p. 96.
Variety. CCCLXIV, September 16, 1996, p. 8.
The Washington Post Book World. XXVI, December 1, 1996, p. 6.

IN SEARCH OF NATURE

Author: Edward O. Wilson (1929-   )
Publisher: Island Press (Washington, D.C.). 214 pp. $19.95
Type of work: Essays; science

A *collection of twelve recent essays that explores Edward Wilson's biophilia hypothesis*

Edward O. Wilson has been hailed as one of America's most distinguished scientists. The author of major works on *The Insect Societies* (1971), *Sociobiology: The New Synthesis* (1975), *On Human Nature* (1978), *Biophilia* (1984), *The Ants* (1991) with Bert Hölldobler, *The Diversity of Life* (1992), and *Naturalist* (1994), Wilson has been an articulate proponent for his innovative theories of sociobiology and biophilia. Beginning with his authoritative study of ants, Wilson has emerged as a major theoretical ecologist and advocate for the diversity of life. His concept of biophilia offers an ethical and spiritual foundation for the preservation of all living forms.

In Search of Nature presents a selection of twelve of Wilson's essays, written between 1975 and 1993, that explore his major ideas of biophilia, sociobiology, and biodiversity. The first section, "Animal Nature, Human Nature," examines the concept of biophilia, or humanity's innate tendency to affiliate with nature, through an exploration of human attitudes toward snakes, sharks, and ants. The second section, "The Patterns of Nature," examines the foundations of sociobiology, exploring the underlying genetic basis of social behavior and its implications for humanity's future. The third section, "Nature's Abundance," studies biodiversity and explains why it is essential to human survival. Each section is beautifully illustrated with sketches by noted artist Laura Southworth.

Perhaps none of Wilson's ideas is more far-reaching in its implications than his concept of biophilia. Our tendency to focus on life and lifelike processes, he argues, might express a biologically based need, integral to our development as individuals and as a species. Biophilia and its opposite, biophobia, are linked reactions expressing a biological predisposition for strong positive or negative orientations toward living things, a kind of prepared or genetically conditioned learning. Psychological, cultural, symbolic-linguistic, and aesthetic implications follow from Wilson's biophilia hypothesis.

Some examples Wilson cites to support his thesis are that people fear objects in nature—storms, snakes, sharks, or spiders—more than they do manufactured weapons or technological objects that may pose a much greater threat to us today than does nature. People are preconditioned to fear poisonous snakes or spiders because of the survival benefit such behavior conferred during our evolutionary history, but we have not yet had time to evolve a comparable fear of guns or weapons. Given their choice of a landscape, people would rather look at grass, water, trees, or flowers, Wilson observes, than steel or concrete. He speculates that this may be an innate preference related to our evolutionary past as savanna dwellers. Moreover, the development of language, myth, and thought appears to be largely dependent upon the use of natural symbols, particularly animals. Wilson's biophilia hypothesis, if substantiated, provides a powerful argument for the preservation of biological diversity. What are the evolutionary and spiritual consequences for us of our wholesale dismantling, within a few decades, of the biological inheritance of the planet?

Wilson's key conceptual essay is "Biophilia and the Environmental Ethic." Here he attempts to apply sociobiological concepts to the environmental ethic. According to Wilson, biophilia is "not a single instinct but a complex of learning rules that can be teased apart and analyzed individually." The emotions aroused by nature can range from awe and attraction to fear and aversion, and these emotions then become rooted in language and culture. For most of our evolutionary history, humans have lived in small hunter-gatherer bands in close contact with the natural world. Human survival depended upon an intimate knowledge of nature. As humans gradually acquired language and culture, living organisms became sources of metaphor and myth. The human brain evolved in a biocentric world, not an urban-industrial society of the past two hundred years. As human culture has become increasingly alienated from the natural world, we have become divorced from our cultural roots, and our emotional and spiritual lives have atrophied from the lack of stimulation and reinforcement in nature. The potential significance of biophilia for human well-being invites us to take a pragmatic view of environmental ethics. Protecting biodiversity may well prove to be in our long-term self-interest.

If biophilia is so significant to humans, how could it have evolved? Wilson thinks that gene-culture coevolution offers a plausible explanation. He uses the human-snake relationship as an illustration of his hypothesis. Why has the serpent been so significant as a universal human cultural symbol? As Wilson argues in "The Serpent," snake and serpent, reptile and dream image, reveal the complexity of our relationship with nature. The serpent image appears in cultures as diverse as the Hopi and Australian aboriginal, Zulus and Aztecs. To explain this connection, Wilson evokes the biophilia hypothesis, using an inferential chain of connections: Because poisonous snakes cause sickness and death to primates, old world primates, in particular, show a combined fear and fascination for them; this genetic propensity is inherited and expanded by humans, whose cultural ambivalence is reflected in stories, myths, and religious symbols. Constant exposure to the malign influence of snakes, Wilson argues, has been expanded by natural selection to a hereditary fear and attraction, expressed in dreams and cultural symbols. Few modern technological artifacts, with the possible exception of the automobile, elicit such strong human responses. Comparable arguments based upon the biophilia hypothesis may be made to explain the human preference for savanna-like environments; the propensity to use natural images in human language and art; and the almost universal desire to keep pets, even in the most confined urban settings.

Yet even if the biophilia hypothesis seems plausible, how can it be tested? Wilson proposes a variety of methods. Psychologists might devise a correlation analysis of human knowledge of and attitudes toward nature in diverse cultures. Cognitive linguists could explore the comparative metaphoric and linguistic influence of natural images. Scholars such as Carl Jung and Joseph Campbell have assembled rich archives of universal human archetypes and symbols drawn from nature. The pastoral context of world religions could be explored as yet another area of support for the biophilia hypothesis. Another avenue of research might be to design a scale of human physiological responses to attractive and unattractive natural phenomena. Through such interdisciplinary research, the natural world may emerge as the most significant influence on the formation of human culture.

If this is the case, Wilson ponders, then what are the implications of our contemporary global loss of biodiversity? What will be the cultural implications of television and advertising replacing nature as the primary sources of cultural symbols and as the cultural context for childhood education? What will be the long-term effects on the human psyche of this replacement of the natural world with an artificial urban-technological culture? Can we long survive, divorced from the natural world, in an increasingly artificial world of our own making? These questions provide the ethical and moral context for Wilson's arguments for the protection of biodiversity.

Wilson's biophilia hypothesis implies biodiversity. The natural world is not merely an empty void to be developed, a place of recreation and renewal, or a source of new pharmaceuticals and wonder drugs, but the context of our evolution and the source of our psychic health and well-being. Yet even these are self-serving arguments that beg the question of the right of the natural world to exist of and for itself. Can the philosophical foundation of human rights, itself barely two hundred years old, be extended to encompass the nonhuman world as well? As Aldo Leopold has pointed out, even our organization of knowledge reflects an anthropocentric bias, with separate "ecologies" of human and natural communities, when in reality they are inextricably fused. Even worse, our assumptions and measurements of economic growth show no awareness of the economy of nature, in which continual unrestricted growth is impossible. Having taken over the life-sustaining processes of the planet without yet having evolved an ecological awareness of our sustainable place in the larger scheme of things, we threaten the life-support systems upon which we and other forms of life depend. An ethic of biodiversity must, it seems, evolve in the broader context of a sustainable planetary economics. Ecosystems function in the context of biological laws, not human economic systems. How can we reconcile our own economic well-being with the larger health and well-being of the planet?

One of Wilson's most controversial areas of study has been sociobiology, which he defines as the "systematic study of the biological basis of social behavior." Some social scientists have objected to the deterministic implications of a sociobiological study of human nature, implications which Wilson denies. Sociobiology is a comparative science that studies patterns of behavior in terms of their genetic, ecological, or ethological implications. As Wilson explains in his essay "Altruism and Aggression," sociobiology tries to find the "underlying hereditary basis of social behavior." If humans share altruistic or aggressive tendencies with other creatures, it is because there is some genetic advantage in doing so, but this does not imply genetic determinism because of the role of culture in shaping human behavior. As Wilson emphasizes,

"What the genes prescribe is not necessarily a particular behavior but the capacity to develop certain behaviors and, more than that, the tendency to develop them in various specified environments."

What does sociobiology tell us about human nature? There are some common patterns in hunter-gatherer societies: The groups generally number one hundred or less; some aggressive and territorial behavior is manifest; adult males are the most aggressive and dominant; societies are organized around extended maternal care and parent-child bonding; and play is common. Beyond these few generalizations, Wilson cautions about the dangers of a naturalistic ethics that assumes that what is must be. Human nature is remarkably plastic and to a large degree culturally determined. Moreover, one must factor in gene-culture coevolution and the possibility of genetic drift among populations. Genetic change may have resulted in the rapid emergence of the human brain, but cultural evolution largely shapes our social behavior.

One of the most difficult theoretical problems for sociobiologists is to distinguish between genetic and social coevolution. Wilson suggests that the interactive process may occur as follows: Genes prescribe the growth of the human brain, which grows by absorbing cultural units; culture in turn is renewed by each generation, in which some individuals are better adapted than others to survive.

In his essay on "Culture as a Biological Product," Wilson speculates on the crucial role of language in cultural transmission. The human brain is clearly "wired" in some way to learn rules of language—grammar and syntax—at an early age, but are there cultural universals such as geometric shapes, basic emotions, or primary colors that are shared across cultures? Or does human cultural diversity suggest a "tabula rasa" theory of cultural development? Wilson believes that culture is deeply rooted in biology, even if we have not yet discovered the underlying mechanisms of causation.

In his last essay, "Is Humanity Suicidal?," Wilson speculates on how the human evolutionary impact on the planet might appear to alien observers. Are we a kind of planetary "cancer" that is increasingly multiplying our species and devouring the biomass at the expense of the rest of life? Are we so species-centered that a sense of global responsibility will emerge too late? Do we have the flexibility to adapt to global crises emerging within a lifetime? Can we adopt an environmentalist worldview that links the future well-being of our species to the overall health of planetary ecosystems? Wilson is cautiously optimistic, although he does not believe in the feasibility of planetary management. There will be some loss of planetary diversity that cannot be replaced in any human timespan but, given a shift in our species' outlook from exceptionalism to environmentalism, planetary stability is possible.

In Search of Nature presents an E. O. Wilson primer with twelve selected essays that introduce the key ideas—sociobiology, biophilia, and biodiversity—of one of the major twentieth century biologists. Wilson demonstrates how inextricably linked are humans and nature in the great web of life. Our task is to find our place in the proper order of things.

Andrew J. Angyal

Sources for Further Study

Booklist. XCIII, September 1, 1996, p. 35.
Boston Globe. September 10, 1996, p. D3.
Kirkus Reviews. LXIV, July 1, 1996, p. 959.
Library Journal. CXXI, September 1, 1996, p. 206.
Los Angeles Times Book Review. September 22, 1996, p. 3.
Natural History. CV, September, 1996, p. 11.
The New York Times Book Review. September 22, 1996, p. 24.
Publishers Weekly. CCXLIII, June 10, 1996, p. 77.

IN THE BEAUTY OF THE LILIES

Author: John Updike (1932-   )
Publisher: Alfred A. Knopf (New York). 491 pp. $25.95
Type of work: Novel
Time: 1910-1990
Locale: New Jersey, Delaware, California, and Colorado

> *Updike presents a panoramic view of the growth of American popular culture in the twentieth century through the chronicle of an American family over four generations*

> *Principal characters:*
> CLARENCE WILMOT, a Presbyterian minister who loses his faith and
>   must give up his ministry
> STELLA WILMOT, his wife
> TEDDY WILMOT, their youngest child, who becomes a postal carrier in
>   Basingstoke, Delaware
> EMILY WILMOT, Teddy's wife
> ESTHER "ESSIE" WILMOT, Teddy and Emily's daughter, who becomes a
>   Hollywood star under the name Alma DeMott
> CLARK, Esther's son, who abandons the California lifestyle to join a
>   commune in the Colorado mountains

The American writer Henry David Thoreau once observed that most men lead lives of quiet desperation. In many ways, the heroes and heroines of John Updike's novels are dramatizations of that maxim. Although there are exceptions—the ruler of the African country who emerges as the hero in *The Coup* comes immediately to mind—the majority of the figures who have populated his fiction are ordinary folk. On occasion, some have extraordinary sensibility, but almost without variation they are much like one's next-door neighbors. Their range of occupations has been wide; his most famous character, Harry "Rabbit" Angstrom, makes his living as a car salesman, while others are ministers, teachers, businessmen, artists, or housewives. Only rarely does he introduce larger-than-life figures into his stories; characters such as Darryl Van Horne, the mysterious and diabolical tempter in *The Witches of Eastwick,* seldom have center stage in any of his tales.

Hence, the challenge of making the everyday interesting is one that Updike accepts repeatedly, and at which he has excelled. In his seventeenth novel, *In the Beauty of the Lilies*, he takes up the gauntlet once again, focusing his attention on the lives of an American family whose only brush with notoriety comes when one of its members leaves her small-town surroundings to become a Hollywood star. Through nearly five hundred pages, Updike tells the story of four generations of the Wilmots, tracing the histories of Clarence, a minister in Paterson, New Jersey; Teddy, his third child; Esther, Teddy's daughter; and Clark, Esther's son. Each is the subject of a major section of the work, and the four divisions read almost like small novellas. Nevertheless, the simple construction belies a complex and compelling rendition of the novelist's vision of a century of American social history.

The first section of the novel gives Updike space to declaim again upon one of his perennial favorite themes: the disappearance of traditional religious faith in America. Clarence Wilmot is a good man who can no longer accept without question the tenets of received doctrine. Trained in the rigorous historical, "higher criticism" of nineteenth century theology, he finds that he cannot continue preaching from the pulpit a creed he no longer holds in his heart. What readers quickly learn is that the decision has economic as well as personal consequences. The Wilmots are removed from their home at the rectory and forced to find more modest circumstances; sadly, Clarence discovers that a man trained for the clergy is ill-prepared by skill or temperament for the world of commerce, and he spends years eking out a meager living as a salesman. Ultimately, he is overcome by tuberculosis, and the family is forced to subsist on the income of mother and children.

A minor figure in the first section, Clarence's youngest child Theodore is the subject of the second part of the novel. Forced to move with his mother and sister from Paterson to Basingstoke, Delaware, so the family can save on expenses, Teddy becomes withdrawn and somewhat embittered. While his brother Jared has gone to New York and become involved in the exciting life of the city (including involvement with the city's gangster population), Teddy remains reclusive even in this backwater community. At every opportunity for advancement, he seems to balk. A brief stint in New York working for his brother Jared and Jared's shady boss proves unsuccessful. Returning to Basingstoke, Teddy takes up one menial occupation after another. He finally marries a girl whom most others shun, the clubfooted Emily Sifford. The decision proves to be fortuitous, however, since the Siffords have some money, and the newlyweds receive some assistance in setting up house. Nevertheless, even with these new responsibilities, Teddy is hesitant to take risks with his life, instead becoming content as a postal carrier—a job where everyone knows him but no one is close to him. He is certainly not unhappy, but there is a sense that he has traded his chances for commercial success and personal fame for the contentment which comes from having personal and family security.

Teddy and Emily's daughter Esther—Essie, as she is known in the family—is the subject of the third section of the novel. A beautiful child who grows into a beautiful woman, she is doted on by her parents and her aunt Esther, Teddy's older sister. Unlike her father, she is adventuresome, and is quick to seize the opportunity to enter the world of modeling and show business. Aided in New York by her cousin Patrick, the son of her Uncle Jared, she makes the connections she needs to land contracts in magazine advertisements, on television, and eventually in films. Her successful career as the starlet Alma DeMott leads to roles opposite all the major male stars of the 1940's and 1950's, but she pays a price in her personal life: constant besiegement by fans, a string of lovers and husbands, and demeaning treatment by agents, directors, and producers who want her for her image, not herself. The contrast between the Hollywood life and that of small-town America is brought into sharp relief on the occasions when Updike shows Essie visiting family in Basingstoke.

The final section focuses on Essie's son Clark. The offspring of one of her marriages, he grows up in the Hollywood environment of the 1960's and 1970's. Frequently neglected by his hardworking mother, he drifts into the company of people often older than himself but with little sense of direction in their lives. As a young man, Clark ends up working at a Colorado ski resort for his great-uncle Jared, who, after moving from New York to avoid criminal prosecution, has landed in the Centennial State, where he has made a fortune through a series of fortuitous land deals and a generous share of plain luck. Clark's chance encounter at the resort with a young woman he mistakes for a free-spirited ski enthusiast leads him to the mountain retreat of a religious sect headed up by a charismatic figure modeled on the real-life cult leader David Koresh. The group openly defies state and federal law, and as a result becomes involved in a bloody stand off with authorities. Clark, renamed Esau by the leader, serves as spokesperson for the group with outside agencies. Although he is not able to avert a tragic ending for his fellow cultists, when federal agents storm the group's compound, Clark exhibits personal heroism in saving some of the women and children from being murdered by the more extreme members of the sect.

Updike manages to hold together these disparate strands in a single novel by highlighting overt links among family members, and by providing a subtext that unites all four generations of the Wilmots: their relationship to motion pictures. Clarence finds solace in films when his faith is gone. Teddy also finds escape in the dark houses where fantasies are played out on the silver screen. Essie becomes involved directly in the industry, making her life a living fantasy as she interacts with screen stars such as Clark Gable, Gary Cooper, and Bing Crosby. Clark serves as a living reminder of the dark side of the motion picture industry, which uses up people and discards them without regard to their needs or their personal dignity. As more than one reviewer has suggested, Updike is fascinated with the way the films have replaced religion as both the symbol of hope for many Americans and as an object of worship in the society.

What also unites the Wilmots is the similarity of their desires. Despite the generational gaps, despite the widely disparate professions in which they engage, and despite the changing social climate which influences their actions and colors their perceptions, their life stories strike a chord of recognition in every man and woman. Clarence, Teddy, Essie, and Clark are all concerned with those basic personal and social issues that characterize all humanity: discovering oneself, falling in love, choosing one's life work, finding God. No doubt some readers will find most of the Wilmots rather ordinary people, and even the exciting Hollywood life which Essie leads is given short shrift in the novel. Instead, Updike is content to focus on the commonplace to highlight the universality of human desires exhibited over four generations in this typical American family.

The supporting cast of characters, however, is far from banal. Updike provides readers a number of sketches of men and women whose lives intersect those of the major figures in his tale. A number of these are quite tantalizing: Mr. Dearholt, the chief elder in Clarence's church, who is reminiscent of Mr. Bounderby in Charles Dickens' *Hard Times* (1854), but who provides quiet assistance to the Wilmots long after Clarence has left his ministry; Clarence's brother Jared, the rebel of the family who marries into a gangster family in New York, flees to Colorado to escape prosecution, and ends up prosperous as much through good fortune as through foresight; Clarence's sister Esther, who defies the moral code in Basingstoke by taking up with a married man who is also her boss, and who encourages both her brother and niece to flaunt convention in the pursuit of happiness; Jared's son Patrick, openly gay and deeply involved in the New York social and entertainment scene; and Jesse, the Vietnam War veteran who drops out of the mainstream to found the cult where conservatism on many educational and political issues is united easily with liberal sexual mores. Any one of these might have made a more "interesting" subject for a novelist bent on entertainment, but Updike sticks to his self-appointed task of presenting figures who (with the exception of Essie) remain out of the spotlight.

There are also pages and pages of descriptive detail: items in the local drugstore, people wandering the streets of small towns and large ones, buildings and landscapes that make up small towns and great cities, events momentous and trivial which form the backdrop against which the lives of the Wilmots are played out. Updike wants readers to get a sense of the American scene, variegated and changing; his work is a paean of praise for the commonplace in the life of the country. For every notation of a change in presidents or an announcement of war, there is some mention (frequently rendered with more lavish attention) on the everyday events in the United States during the twentieth century.

Laurence W. Mazzeno

Sources for Further Study

The Christian Century. CXIII, April 24, 1996, p. 452.
Commentary. CI, April, 1996, p. 64.
The Economist. CCCXXXVIII, February 24, 1996, p. 89.
London Review of Books. XVIII, March 21, 1996, p. 23.
Los Angeles Times Book Review. January 28, 1996, p. 3.
Maclean's. CIX, February 26, 1996, p. 70.
The Nation. CCLXII, February 12, 1996, p. 25.
National Review. XLVIII, February 26, 1996, p. 63.
New Leader. LXXVIII, December 18, 1995, p. 27.
The New Republic. CCXIV, May 27, 1996, p. 29.
New Statesman and Society. IX, May 3, 1996, p. 37.
New York. XXIX, January 15, 1996, p. 52.
The New York Review of Books. XLIII, February 29, 1996, p. 4.
The New York Times Book Review. CI, January 28, 1996, p. 9.
The New Yorker. LXXII, March 11, 1996, p. 105.
Time. CXLVII, January 29, 1996, p. 78.
The Wall Street Journal. January 17, 1996, p. A12.
The Washington Post Book World. XXVI, February 4, 1996, p. 1.

INCIDENTS IN THE RUE LAUGIER

Author: Anita Brookner (1938-   )
First published: 1995, in Great Britain
Publisher: Random House (New York). 233 pp. $23.00
Type of work: Novel
Time: 1971 to the 1990's
Locale: Paris and London

A young woman invents her version of her mother's life

> *Principal characters:*
> MAUD GONTHIER HARRISON, the narrator's mother, whose life revolves
>   around memory
> EDWARD HARRISON, Maud's husband, who agrees to marry Maud though
>   she never loves him
> DAVID TYLER, Maud's first lover, whose memory occupies Maud for
>   most of her life
> NADINE DEBUREAU GONTHIER, Maud's mother, who contributes to
>   Maud's haughty manner
> MARY FRANÇOISE HARRISON, the narrator, who invents her mother's life
>   to understand her own

Anita Brookner has written many novels, including *Hotel du Lac* (1984), winner of that year's prestigious Booker Prize. Her works are frequently populated with men and women whose familial obligations and societal demands freeze them into making choices, often against their will. Although many of her characters isolate themselves from society by choice, many become desirous to be part of some society, often at a more respectable level. Brookner's focus, however, is not only limited to these issues; rather, she doggedly focuses on the complex psychological lives of her characters, these people who are forced to deal with outward and internal pressures. Although often quite ordinary people, Brookner's characters resonate; their inner searches and attempts to understand their precarious existences become our own. Although stylistically lush with detail, Brookner's worlds are cold, often harsh backdrops for these characters, places abounding in complicated affairs, marriages without love, disastrous familial relationships, and often early deaths. Although *Incidents in the Rue Laugier*, Brookner's fifteenth novel, contains this basic interest of creating characters in crisis, she also explores the notion of fiction-making, an extraliterary effort on her part which broadens the scope of the linear story line, a plot which threatens at times to become too conventional. Certainly, her effort at showing the importance of memory to storytelling, as well as her allusions to Marcel Proust, aid in making this novel more complex than the rather simplistic plot of "boy meets girl; boy marries girl" might suggest. Brookner succeeds in this novel almost in spite of herself.

Incidents in the Rue Laugier is narrated in the present by Mary Francoise Harrison, a self-proclaimed unreliable narrator, who happens upon her mother's journal after her mother Maud Gonthier, the main character of the novel, dies. Rather than finding a full-blown account of her mother's life in this journal, however, the narrator finds only the opening line, in French, to Proust's *Remembrance of Things Past* (1913), some cryptic words, mostly place names, and a recipe. From these findings, the narrator, then, feels compelled to reconstruct her mother's life, a life her mother kept guarded from her daughter and everyone else.

Brookner's opening conceit of reconstructing a life from found evidence forces the reader into collusion with the narrator and calls into question the notion of fictionality and its importance to Brookner's narrator and to us as modern readers. Rather than belabor this metafictional point as a postmodernist writer might do, Brookner shows how fiction-making occurs naturally in human lives, and how those self-created fictions inform the larger arena of novelists creating their own fictional worlds. Brookner showcases this conceit in chapters 1 and 15, creating a frame for the narrator's imagined life of her mother. Yet, Brookner also shows how these framing chapters contain elements of the rest of the novel. For the narrator, the need to "create" her own version of her mother mirrors both the reader's desire to "read" another's life, as well as the main character Maud's need to fictionalize certain events in her life. As the narrator closes the first chapter, she rather succinctly sums up this theme which permeates the rest of the novel: "It [this story] is a fabrication, one of those by which each of us lives, and as such an enormity, nothing to do with the truth. But perhaps the truth we tell ourselves is worth any number of facts, verifiable or not."

The story within the story opens when Maud Gonthier is eighteen, near the age of making important decisions about her future. Because of the early death of her father and her mother's inability and disinclination to work, the family can afford only a good education for Maud, education being a calculated maneuver so she can be introduced properly to society, and thus make a good marriage. Her mother Nadine, the first of a successive line of haughty, aloof women which will include Maud, as well as her daughter, the narrator, spends most of her life preparing Maud for this marriage without considering her daughter's wishes. Maud is ill-prepared for the awakening passions which lead her to believe in the romantic notion that a man will come and, essentially, sweep her off her proverbial feet. Here, Brookner's women become almost cartoonishly nineteenth century, though the time period when Maud comes of age, the early 1970's, might suggest that these women would have had some knowledge of broadening possibilities for women. Certainly, life in and around Paris would prepare Maud for something beyond attachment to the most promising suitor. Brookner comes dangerously close to losing the tight realism which her novels depend upon by closeting these characters in this patriarchal milieu. Yet, because these women have a heritage of depending on men, the reader is able to pull back and recognize this as a construct which others in the novel will also find demeaning. (Indeed, later in the novel, one of Maud's friends will comment on her lack of motivation, her inability to do anything with her life.) As such, readers are able to suspend the outrage readers might otherwise feel concerning Nadine's attempts to limit her daughter's choices to marriage only. Furthermore, because of Maud's youth, readers are also able to forgive her her romantic ideals of being captured by a man. Although Maud threatens this status quo at one point by vocalizing a desire to live alone in Paris and study languages, her romantic idealizations generally tie in with her mother's rather archaic expectations of a woman's destiny. Like a Jane Austen heroine, Maud Gonthier seems destined to marry.

Yet Nadine's desires for her daughter get thwarted somewhat when Maud becomes enamored of and the subsequent lover of David Tyler, the rogue friend of her cousin Xavier. David impregnates her and leaves her waiting for him at a house on the Rue Laugier where he has taken her with his friend, Edward Harrison. Brookner adeptly poses the inexperienced, yet passionate Maud as one end of a triangle which contains David, her romantic, but unprincipled equal, and Edward Harrison, unromantic, yet steady and reliable. After David leaves Maud, alone, penniless, and pregnant, Edward suggests marriage to Maud as a way for her to regain her respectability.

If Brookner had stopped here, the novel would have had the "happy," highly conventional ending which the loosely sketched plot suggests—Maud marries the respectable boy and lives happily ever after. Yet Maud does not forget or forgive Tyler and fall earnestly in love with Edward. Rather, after Maud agrees to marry Edward, the novel begins to leave behind Maud's romantic idealizations and concentrate more entirely on how Maud, and Edward, to a lesser extent, survive the loss of their dreams which this hasty marriage precipitates. For them, marriage closes off hoped for independence and the possibility of "real" love, and this loss of innocence threatens to destroy their ability to love anything until each learns how to remember.

Brookner's frequent references to Proust, both in the narrator's discovery of the Proust line in her mother's journal and in her imagined reverie as to its significance, suggest the importance of memory to the creation of this fiction, as well as to the survival of persons within these created fictions. Unlike David Tyler, who lives for "the moment, of the here and now," both Edward and Maud begin to exist in dream worlds, created almost entirely of memory. Edward recalls over and over again an unfallen state of childhood, a picturesque scene of sunlight which he occupies with his younger sister. This reconstructed image comes to him throughout the novel, and he calls it up as solace when his real world falls apart. His dream represents his need to have a separate life, as if a different sphere could create the illusion of loneliness, a necessity for him to gain this memory. Although these childhood memories initially provide Edward with comforting thoughts of an idyllic childhood, as he grows older and gets further from the actuality of these memories, he cannot use them as comfort measures. Indeed, these remembrances of wholeness as a child become nightmarish rather than protective, probably because Edward begins to realize the inadequacy of his childhood to the maintenance of his own adult home he shares with Maud, and eventually their daughter. As he resorts more to memory, and as he grows sicker with an undiagnosed brain tumor, he finds himself disconnected from his family and this dream state, tortured by half-formed memory. Clearly, Edward needs the solace which memory can provide since he has been thrown into a loveless marriage.

Brookner, however, focuses most prominently on Maud's use of remembering, particularly because her use of memory more clearly represents the restructuring which the narrator and author are doing in various ways in the novel itself. Although Maud spends essentially only two weeks with David Tyler, she finds that the "episode was to her an experience so seamless that she might well spend the rest of her life contemplating the memory of it." That is essentially what Maud does. For the first part of her married life, she spends each day practically in a vacuum, with nothing but the memory of her supposed love with David to sustain her.

This memory remains pure until she is given the chance to see David again. Rather than speak to him about the events which have been reappearing daily in her solitary world, however, Maud decides, much as Newland Archer does in Edith Wharton's *The Age of Innocence* (1921), not to see the beloved one of memory in order to preserve the fiction of a more positive memory. As Maud concludes, "Reality was an insufficient record." For Maud, the fictionalized past becomes more true than the truth for sustaining her life.

Maud's retreat after this realization into reading and re-reading Proust and her study there of memory aides her in recovering her sense of self. Although to modern readers she appears adrift and lonely, particularly following the birth of her daughter, her husband with his ability to live in memory subject to problems, envies her her apparent wholeness, wholeness which her all-inclusive need for memory harbors.

The novel concludes with the narrator's summation of the relevance of memory and fiction-making, particularly as it often discloses not the happy moments of lives, but the bleak life which she fears her mother must have lived. What the narrator, and Brookner as well, makes clear at the novel's end is the unreliability of any one truth about a life or the events which occur within a life. One also feels that both are hinting at the individual's need for fiction. Maud needs the fiction of remembered love and passion with David as she enters into and stays within a loveless marriage. Maud's daughter needs her mother's life created so she can begin to understand her own past. Brookner's fiction, then, also becomes one of necessity for its reader. One gets the feeling that Brookner's narrator could not have told a truer story had she had her mother's extensively penned journal. By extension, then, Brookner poses the same notion about fiction as a reliable recorder of human existence—a novel is perhaps truer than life.

Incidents in the Rue Laugier, like many of Brookner's works, presents the reader with a painful look at relationships gone awry. In this case, she also explores what happens when two people make a wrong decision, but more important, perhaps, how these persons can gain some consolation from using memory to sustain them beyond their mistakes. Although Brookner occasionally runs the risk in this novel of presenting the reader with a highly conventional plot and unrealistic expectations, of women in particular, she uses her incisive look at these people's crushed lives to force the reader away from any easy assumptions about the character's actions, creating a fictionalized account of one woman's failed expectations and commenting on the nature of fiction-making in the process.

Rebecca Hendrick Flannagan

Sources for Further Study

Booklist. XCII, November 1, 1995, p. 434.
Library Journal. CXX, November 15, 1995, p. 98.
Los Angeles Times. January 2, 1996, p. E5.
The New York Times Book Review. CI, January 14, 1996, p. 13.
The Observer. June 11, 1995, p. 14.
Publishers Weekly. CCXLII, November 20, 1995, p. 66.
The Spectator. CCLXXIV, June 17, 1995, p. 43.
The Times Literary Supplement. June 2, 1995, p. 21.
The Virginia Quarterly Review. LXXII, Summer, 1996, p. 92.
The Wall Street Journal. January 12, 1996, p. A9.

INDIAN KILLER

Author: Sherman Alexie (1966-   )
Publisher: Atlantic Monthly Press (New York). 420 pp. $22.00
Type of work: Novel
Time: The late 1960's to the 1990's
Locale: Seattle, Washington; the Tulalip Indian Reservation

Alexie's novel recounts how difficult it is for Native Americans to retain a sense of their own identity as they attempt to survive in an alien, hostile society

> *Principal characters:*
> JOHN SMITH, a young Native American
> OLIVIA SMITH, his adoptive mother
> DANIEL SMITH, his adoptive father
> MARIE POLATKIN, a Spokane Indian, a student at the University of Washington and an activist
> REGGIE POLATKIN, her cousin, the offspring of a Native American mother and a white father
> DR. CLARENCE MATHER, a white professor at the University of Washington
> JACK WILSON, a writer, supposedly of Shilshomish descent
> TRUCK SCHULTZ, a talk-show host
> DAVID ROGERS, a student in Mather's class

As a full-blooded Native American, born and reared in Wellpinit on the Spokane Indian Reservation in Washington, Sherman Alexie is well aware of his people's problems in contemporary, white-dominated society. Since 1992, when as a college student he published his first book, a collection of poems entitled *I Would Steal Horses*, he has voiced his concerns about Native Americans in several genres, including fiction. There were five short stories in *The Business of Fancydancing* (1992), as well as a number of poems and vignettes, while *The Lone Ranger and Tonto Fistfight in Heaven* (1993) was devoted entirely to short fiction. A number of the characters from that collection reappeared in Alexie's first novel, *Reservation Blues* (1995). Like his other works, *Reservation Blues* told the stories of people who, having lost the traditions which once sustained them, live desperate lives, bereft of hope and of significance.

Indian Killer has the same subject and the same settings as that novel and Alexie's earlier short stories. Like *Reservation Blues*, it is also complex in structure, using various points of view in order to illuminate the lives of not just one protagonist, but a number of characters. While the earlier works were brightened by flashes of humor, however, the tone of *Indian Killer* is quite different. Even though Alexie presents some scenes in which a group of Indians fall into uncontrollable laughter, which the author says is their way of driving away the devils that haunt them, he does not join the fun. Instead, he maintains a tone of righteous indignation, stressing the tragic consequences of prejudice and discrimination.

The protagonist of *Indian Killer* is John Smith, who is first shown at the time of his birth to a fourteen-year-old Indian girl. Despite the young mother's heartrending cries for her baby, a nurse bundles him up immediately after the delivery and rushes him out to a helicopter. Soon he is in the arms of Olivia Smith, a well-to-do, childless white woman, and her architect husband Daniel. A kindly, well-meaning couple, they adopt him and rear him as lovingly as if he were of their own blood, never realizing that the fact John is cut off from his heritage will eventually drive him mad. While Olivia does her best to inform John about his people and frequently takes him to functions where other Native Americans are present, all of her efforts fail to give John a sense of his own identity. Without knowing the name of his mother or even of her tribe, he will never feel a part of the Indian community.

Meanwhile, John is also coming to realize that he has no place in the white world. As a young child, he is troubled by the fact that his skin color is so different from that of his parents. Because they show John so much affection, however, it is not until he is old enough to date that he really becomes aware of prejudice or how he will be isolated as an Indian in a white society. Although the parents of the white girls he likes are invariably polite when John comes to pick up their daughters, his request for the second date is always met with some excuse. By the time he has finished high school, John is convinced that he must find his identity among his own people, rather than among the whites, who have so clearly rejected him.

Turning down his parents' offer of a college education, John goes to Seattle and becomes a construction worker, primarily because he has read that other Native Americans can be found building skyscrapers. His coworkers, however, are white, and although they are friendly enough, John will have nothing to do with them. He also avoids his parents. Increasingly concerned about their only son, Olivia and Daniel besiege him with letters. When he does not respond, they take turns coming to Seattle, hoping to find him and win him back, but John evades them. Throughout this period of self-imposed seclusion, he broods about the wrongs that have been done to him and to all Native Americans. Eventually, he begins to believe that only by killing a white man will he become a part of his community. After that initial murder, for the first time John feels that his life has a purpose and he has a real identity. Thereafter, he is an Indian warrior, who stalks his victims, scalps and mutilates them, then disappears into the darkness, leaving two white owl feathers as his signature.

One must assume that the author is presenting Smith's activities as a result of injustice, not as an appropriate means of redressing past grievances. The tragic life and death of his emotionally fragile protagonist, however, illustrate how difficult it is for even a Native American who has close ties with his culture, like Alexie himself, to find a place in the contemporary world. Although these murders are obviously the work of a single unbalanced person, the public's reaction reveals the extent of prejudice against Native Americans which can be found even in the most enlightened community. For that reason, it is not difficult for one of the most obnoxious characters in the novel, the conservative talk-show host Truck Schultz, to influence his audience. The killings are a boon for him; they boost his ratings and increase his popularity. If, as a result of his broadcasts, some innocent Indians are attacked by racists, Schultz believes the victims are getting no more than they deserve. Ironically, however, Alexie and the characters who clearly serve as his spokespersons, such as the activist Marie Polatkin, are as infuriated by the whites they call "wannabe" Indians as by those who make no secret of their racial prejudice. It might be assumed that such characters as Dr. Clarence Mather are honestly sympathetic with Native Americans. Despite his Irish and British ancestry, this white professor classifies himself as an Indian by adoption. Nevertheless, he is in a sense the enemy of the very people he pretends to admire. Like Schultz, Mather profits from the Indians. He has based his entire academic career on what is actually a very superficial knowledge of Native American culture. Therefore he is threatened by Marie Polatkin's presence in his class. As a full-blooded, reservation-reared Indian of considerable intelligence, Marie had much she could have taught Mather if he had been willing to admit his own limitations. Instead, in his arrogance, he has Marie expelled from his class so that, unchallenged, he can continue transmitting his stock of misinformation to gullible students and drawing his high salary from an administration which is just as easily fooled.

Another character who makes a good living from Native American culture is Jack Wilson, a former policeman who found writing about Indians more profitable than arresting them. When Marie learns that one of Wilson's books is an assigned text in Mather's course, she explodes. As she points out, although he claims to be a member of the Shilshomish tribe, Wilson has never been able to produce any proof of his ancestry. When there are so many fine writers who are real Native Americans, not just pretenders for profit, Marie asks, why are their works not incorporated into the course? She further infuriates Mather by adding that his use of Wilson's work in a class on Native American culture constitutes an insult to the people they are supposed to be studying. Of course, Marie loses this battle; she is ousted, and Wilson's book stays in the curriculum.

There are, however, some sympathetic white characters in *Indian Killers*, particularly Olivia and Daniel Smith, whose initial sin must be attributed to a flaw in the adoption process rather than any evil intent on their part. To their credit, they do try to put their son in touch with his heritage. Even if the Smiths are not totally innocent, the nightmares that disturb Daniel's rest, the terrors that haunt Olivia, and the anguish one knows they will experience after they learn about their son all appear to place them among the victims in this novel.

Another victim, and in this case a wholly innocent one, is David Rogers. Rejecting the family prejudices, David enrolls in Mather's class and falls under Marie's spell. His unfeigned interest in Native Americans sends him to one of the Indian-owned gambling casinos, where he wins a considerable sum. On his way to his truck, however, he is attacked and robbed, then disappears. It is assumed that David is another victim of the Indian Killer. Prompted by their father, as well as by the rabble-rousing broadcasts of Truck Schultz, David's brother Aaron assembles some friends and goes forth to avenge his brother's death. Thus the violence escalates, and more innocent people become victims of racial hatred.

Another victim is Marie Polatkin's cousin Reggie, a man of mixed blood who wants to be white as badly as Wilson wants to be an Indian. Reggie's mother is a Native

American, his father, a white man who hates Indians so much that he denies Reggie his surname until he can prove that he has eradicated his maternal heritage. It is evident, however, that Reggie still has some feeling for his mother's people; he cannot stomach Mather's using tapes on which elderly Native Americans talked about their people's traditions. As a result of the ensuing fight, Reggie is expelled from college. Like John, Reggie is shown as being in an untenable position, but unlike John, he does not even know whom to attack, the white backpacker, who in skin color resembles his abusive father, or John himself, who represents the side of himself that Reggie is attempting to forget.

The use of Reggie, the would-be white, as a foil for John, the would-be Indian, is just one instance of the intricate patterning which makes *Indian Killer* so complex and sometimes so puzzling a novel. Alexie penetrates the mind of Aaron the Indian-hater, as well as that of the generous-spirited David; he records the thoughts of Schultz, Mather, and Wilson, permitting them to reveal themselves as essentially similar. Character balances character, and similarly, situation balances situation. Thus the Indian girl grieves for her lost baby, Olivia yearns for her grown son, and the mother of six-year-old Mark Jones agonizes over the fate of her little boy, who has been kidnapped by the notorious serial killer.

It is somewhat disturbing that Alexie exhibits so little sympathy for most of the killer's victims, who are chosen at random merely because they are white, and that he ends the novel, not with an explicit condemnation of violence as a solution to frustration, but with the prediction that more Native American warriors will arise to take revenge on the white community. Perhaps readers are expected to take comfort in the fact that Mark Jones is returned unharmed to his family. In this single act of compassion on the part of a man who has devoted his life to killing people of another race, Alexie may intend to indicate that there is a glimmer of hope.

Rosemary M. Canfield Reisman

Sources for Further Study

Boston Globe. November 10, 1996, p. E16.
Chicago Tribune. November 17, 1996, XIV, p. 3.
The Christian Science Monitor. January 6, 1997, p. 13.
Kirkus Reviews. LXIV, August 1, 1996, p. 1064.
Library Journal. CXXI, August, 1996, p. 109.
The New York Times Book Review. CI, November 24, 1996, p. 34.
Publishers Weekly. CCXLIII, September 16, 1996, p. 39.
San Francisco Chronicle. September 29, 1996, p. REV3.
Time. CXLVIII, October 21, 1996, p. 90.
The Washington Post. October 18, 1996, p. D3.

INFINITE JEST

Author: David Foster Wallace (1963-   )
Publisher: Little, Brown (Boston). 1097 pp. $29.95
Type of work: Novel
Time: Early in the twenty-first century
Locale: New England, Arizona, and Washington, D.C.; Quebec, Canada

*In a nonlinear vision of a terrible future which provides a language map into the imagination,
an artist engages in a soul-searching exploration of addiction, obsession, and the tendency of
Americans to pleasure themselves to death*

> *Principal characters:*
> HAL INCANDENZA, the principal narrator, a tennis prodigy at Enfield
>   Tennis Academy
> DON GATELY, a former burglar and Demerol addict who is a live-in staff
>   member at Ennet House, a drug rehabilitation center
> MARATHE, a fanatical Quebeçois terrorist whose cynical love of irony
>   overwhelms his many philosophical reasons for not being a terrorist
> ORIN INCANDENZA, a punter for the Phoenix Cardinals who has a nearly
>   normal life
> PEMULIS, a tennis player who supplies drug-free urine needed when the
>   academy players undergo drug-testing by the Junior Tennis
>   Association
> CHARLOTTE TREAT, a former prostitute who is an inmate at Ennet House
> SCHTITT, the philosophical head tennis coach at Enfield Academy
> MARIO INCANDENZA, the middle brother of the Incandenza family

In *Infinite Jest*, main character Hal Incandenza recalls his own father telling him
that:

> talent is sort of a dark gift, that talent is its own expectation; it is there from the start and either lived
> up to or lost . . . leaving you yourself in a kind of feral and flux-ridden state with respect to talent . . .
> avoid thinking about any of this by practicing and playing until everything runs on autopilot and
> talent's unconscious exercise becomes a way to escape yourself, a long waking dream of pure
> play. . . . The irony is . . . you . . . become regarded as having a prodigious talent to live up to.

In writing *Infinite Jest*, author David Foster must "live up to" his own prodigious talent
and expectations as a writer. His artistry with the English language is a "feral" talent
that makes *Infinite Jest* a "long waking dream of pure play."

The story takes place during the twenty-first century. New England is so polluted
that President Johnny Gentle wants to cede it to Canada. The book's title is taken from
that of a film made by Hal Incandenza's father, James O. Incandenza. *Infinite Jest:
The Film* is so entertaining, addicting, and lethal that viewers are unable to stop
watching it and literally die from an overdose of pleasure. It is no surprise that the film
is fanatically pursued by Quebeçois terrorists who plan to use it to kill all Americans
and thus avoid the acquisition of New England.

In the chaotic and episodic storytelling of *Infinite Jest*, environment is a key
element, as reflected by the expression "if the walls could talk." The major environ-

ments in *Infinite Jest* are the Enfield Tennis Academy and Ennet House, a drug rehabilitation center. They exist down the road from each other in Enfield, Massachusetts, a community located within commuting distance of Boston and Cambridge.

A storyteller usually wishes to convey an idea to an audience. When there is no clear purpose or function in telling a story, the writer becomes a language artist. The story is then experienced as art for art's sake, with the artist as explorer. Writers who follow this path are often linguistic pioneers or revolutionaries who seek to shake things up, change the way people think, and question the fundamental laws governing their chosen art form.

David Foster Wallace's "long waking dream of pure play" lapses frequently into levels of artistic exploration which generously contribute to *Infinite Jest's* one-thousand-plus pages. His mad, rambling, drug-addled descriptions postulate the double-bind of a writer who is both shaping and reflecting his culture. Wallace's art-for-art's-sake approach is his escape from the very vision he shapes and reflects, his prose reading as if it were the rant of a madman.

Infinite Jest follows the three basic functions of storytelling: "autopoiesis" or "self making," the process by which storytellers produce, transform, or regulate themselves; "dissipation," in which the story journeys through an environment while refraining from disturbing the environment's organization; and the "cognitive" criteria, which effects closure in the mind of the reader and presupposes both acquired and intuitive knowledge on the part of the observer. The cognitive function answers the questions "Where do we come from?," "How are we are adding to the confusion in the world?," and "Where we are going?" *Infinite Jest* is a clear example of how humans add to the confusion of the world.

In nonlinear structures, idiom follows form. Hal Incandenza, a tennis prodigy (and drug user as a result of discovering his father's suicide) provides the voice of the rigidly coached, driven to excel, live-up-to-your-seed tennis academy environment where much of the story takes place. Hal is contrapuntally echoed by the narrative voice of Don Gately, a resident staff counselor at Ennet House. Yet so many other voices abound in the novel that it is easy to lose track of everyone. They each tell stories within stories like Russian nesting dolls, ad infinitum. Ultimately, the author's omniscient viewpoint and visionary environment becomes the story's decisive narrator.

Structure follows idiom, and in *Infinite Jest*, the structure is multilevel and sequence-spaced. Environments that tell stories should provide metaphorical openings or cues and artificial finish lines as closure clues. They should take journeys that are both literal, linear, and logical as well as allegorical, circular, and cultural. Tension thus comes from contrast not necessarily conflict.

Time is subsidized in Wallace's word sculpture. Each year is named after a consumer product. Each chapter is headed by one of the years, such as "Year of the Depend Adult Undergarment" or "Year of the Perdue Wonder Chicken." The story opens during the "Year of Glad," which is significantly the twelfth and final year in Wallace's pantheon.

Environments that tell a story through space and time cycles need to communicate "where we are" to the readers and ultimately "take us where we want to be." The cues and clues to effect this are sorely lacking in Wallace's phenomenal ordering of his creative chaos. The reader is rarely told what is happening. None of Wallace's numerous stories seem to converge, and readers can only imagine they do in the minds of the story's literally crazy characters. While Wallace is an unparalleled wordsmith, there is an obsessive quality to his language artistry that unfortunately begs the question: "Who cares?" Begging this question is a legitimate story purpose, but the answer is certainly not found in any of his characters.

Wallace's prose is understandable if confusing. His considerable craft gives meaning and order to what seems like utter chaos. He is painfully accurate about his fantastic and nightmarish landscape as he makes the strange familiar and the familiar strange. The three-dimensional quality in his wordcraft is evident as he steps out of what readers will perceive as endless and pointless misdirections rather than away from them. He literally talks until he is speechless. He has a distinct point of view, but his characters are so noncommittal, even spineless, that—with the exception of Marathe—all of them are always ready to acknowledge any other point of view than their own.

Wallace deserves credit for knowing "where to open" and "when to close" the story, which are critical concepts to crafting nonlinear word-art. This epic opens with a stymied, babbling, and out of control Hal, who is unable to communicate his inner thoughts to the panel interviewing him for acceptance in the Enfield Tennis Academy. Wallace closes his fiction with hundreds of footnotes, addenda, and desiderata, which attest to the nonlinear need for closure rather than ending. The final ten footnotes are descriptions of real and fictional drugs, categorized either by their initials or the slang of a street-vending drug culture.

Surface follows craft, and the mask or final image (which often works out to be a story's title) of *Infinite Jest* is a giant three-dimensional written animation placed in a futuristic, visionary, polluted, and hopeless landscape. Its only escape is addiction or a literal "giving oneself away to something else." By this point, however, this is no great surprise or revelation.

David Foster Wallace has chosen to disconnect from the exhausted plot lines of everyday storytellers. *Infinite Jest* actually follows two very simple strategies. One is a no-pain, no-gain coach's strategy, which provides the cognitive inner structure. The other is a twelve-step strategy that structures the verbal rant of the entire book as Hal opens by acknowledging he is "out of control." The answer to "Who cares" is handled by Wallace when Hal says, "It seemed like some kind of black miracle to me that people could actually care deeply about a subject or a pursuit." Through the obsessive use of language for art's sake, Wallace dumps his all-for-naught vision of life as he sees it into *Infinite Jest* as his narrator Hal steps into the Year of Glad as a babbling, raging, mutant idiot. Wallace apparently intends this characterization to be a sly commentary on his readers as well.

Environments that tell stories usually have cognition as their goal, otherwise they are simply an exercise in art appreciation. With cognition as the story's goal, the inner structure has a capacity to reflect upon itself. A necessary condition for self-reflection is that the mind runs unimpeded by rigid and accepted learning, which is certainly true for this author. Yet Wallace's feral long-waking dream organizes chaos with no apparent regard for his readers. Readers have no sense, therefore, that Wallace cares about them, much less the world he has created.

Grotesque and bizarre lives are rendered with brilliant humor or depressing sadness through Wallace's linguistic genius. There are few "normal" moments or people in his world. Yet if the writer of nonlinear word sculptures wants his readers to have an emotional response or reach a cathartic place within his chaotic structure, the story's linear journey must be enfolding and autopoetic to show readers who "we" are and who "we" would want to resemble. Unfortunately, there is not one character in Wallace's vision of the future that any reader might want to resemble. Readers can enter the landscape and enjoy the artistry of Wallace's use of language tools, but they will find themselves wondering: "If the characters and the author do not care, why should I?"

David Foster Wallace is a genius as a language artist, as an imagineer, and as a world-maker. His characters constantly express sorrow and joy, but Wallace relates this expression through his own unique filter rather than that of his readers. As a guide to the human soul, Wallace ultimately fails his readers. The most powerful sanctuary of the human soul is language which instructs, heals, provides meaning, sustains, responds, imagines, sings, paints, or sculpts. For Wallace, language is a hammer and a buzzsaw on the one hand, a map to self-indulgence and escape on the other. He adapts language to his own symmetry with every combination of variation, harmonic, interval, or phrase he can muster. It is as if he is telling his story to other obsessive-compulsives in a meeting room of addicts, letting them know without question that he is the master. Wallace considers his readers as observers in that room, obsessive codependents who might be willing to explore his grotesque sculpture until they are exhausted. Those readers whose ghetto nightmares and urban decaying visions echo Wallace's will be able to answer in the affirmative to "Who cares?"

The book's message is that people either reflect their culture or shape it. To this end, Wallace demonstrates a brilliant ability to merge the two streams of reflecting and shaping in his narration, seemingly turning information into story as it is occurring. The relationship between cause and effect is radically different in Wallace's mind as Wallace's characters not only handle information, but information handles them.

Another critically important positive about the work is that none of Wallace's character's "know" anything and are all unconscious of their ignorance. It is the source of their madnesses, fanaticisms, and addictions. It is also a slogan at Ennet House: "I didn't know I didn't know." In creating this monumental world of pollution, ignorance, and addiction, Wallace is coincidentally ridding himself of his own ignorance and opening himself to create a vacuum for new experiences and better visions. In creating a monstrously sick version of the future, Wallace shapes this future by instructing us how not to be—how not to add to the confusion of the world as we know it.

The last good word about a novel that is so abundant with words is that *Infinite Jest* reads aloud better than it does silently. Wallace truly has an "if the walls could talk" talent with language that deserves to be heard, if not read.

Barbara Elman Schiffman

Sources for Further Study

The Atlantic. CCLXXVII, February, 1996, p. 106
Esquire. CXXIV, December, 1995, p. 60
Hungry Mind Review. XXVI, Spring, 1996, p. 46.
Library Journal. CXXI, January, 1996, p. 146
Los Angeles Times Book Review. February 11, 1996, p. 1.
The Nation. CCLXII, March 4, 1996, p. 27.
The New York Times. February 13, 1996, p. B2
The New York Times Book Review. CI, March 3, 1996, p. 8.
New York. XXIX, February 12, 1996, p. 54
Newsweek. CXXVII, February 12, 1996, p. 80.
Publishers Weekly. CCXLII, November 27, 1995, p. 50.
The Review of Contemporary Fiction. XVI, Spring, 1996, p. 141.
Time. CXLVII, February 19, 1996, p. 70.
The Times Literary Supplement. June 28, 1996, p. 22.
The Washington Post Book World. XXVI, March 24, 1996, p. 5.

THE INHERITANCE
How Three Families and America Moved from Roosevelt to Reagan and Beyond

Author: Samuel G. Freedman (1955-   )
Publisher: Simon & Schuster (New York). 464 pp. $27.50
Type of work: History
Time: The 1890's to the 1990's
Locale: England, Italy, Poland, and the United States

The political evolution of America is traced through three families, from their immigrant roots and New Deal Democratic allegiance to their involvement in conservative Republican Party politics

> *Principal personages:*
> MARY ELIZABETH SANFORD, an Irish Catholic immigrant from Liverpool, England
> LIZZIE SANFORD GARRETT, her daughter, a domestic worker
> RICHIE GARRETT, Lizzie's son, a gravedigger and environmental activist
> EDITH GARRETT CAREY, Lizzie's daughter, a waitress
> TIM CAREY, Edith's son, a Republican campaign strategist
> MARTIN BURIGO, an Italian Catholic immigrant to New York
> SILVIO BURIGO, Martin's son, a plumber and loyal union member
> LORRAINE BURIGO, Silvio's daughter, a telephone operator
> FRANK TROTTA, SR., Lorraine's husband, janitor for a public housing project
> FRANK TROTTA, JR., Frank and Lorraine's son, a lawyer active in Republican politics
> ALEKSANDER OBRYCKI, a Polish immigrant to Baltimore
> JOSEPH OBRYCKI, Aleksander's son, a gambler involved in Baltimore Democratic machine politics
> VILMA OBRYCKI MAEBY, Joseph's daughter, a housewife
> JACK MAEBY, Vilma's husband, manager of a Montgomery Ward warehouse
> LESLIE MAEBY, Vilma and Jack's daughter, a Republican Party official

In *The Inheritance: How Three Families and America Moved from Roosevelt to Reagan and Beyond*, Samuel G. Freedman attempts to understand and explain America's turn toward the political right in the 1980's and 1990's by focusing on the history of three particular families, from their immigrant roots to their struggle to achieve middle-class status. Although each has its own fascinating history, these families have much in common. With Irish, Polish, and Italian roots, all arrived in this country around the turn of the century, are Catholic, working-class individuals, and were involved in Democratic politics from 1932 to 1968, remaining loyal to the party during the New Deal, World War II, and the postwar boom years. By the 1960's and 1970's, however, the third generation changed this pattern as a backlash against the antiwar movement, race riots, black power, welfare, affirmative action, and busing formed, and these children of the Democratic working class—Frank Trotta, Jr., Tim Carey, and Leslie Maeby—became Republican Party activists.

Frank Trotta, Jr.'s great-grandfather, Martin Burigo, left Italy for America in 1890, and within ten years owned his own construction company and a home in the suburb of New Rochelle, New York. His luck changed, however, when his wife fell ill, his youngest son drowned, his business failed, and he lost his home. After Martin hanged himself in 1910, his wife distributed the older children among various relatives in America and returned to Italy to die.

One of these children, Silvio Burigo, left school at the age of fifteen to apprentice as a plumber. His life soon became defined by his membership in the plumbers' union; he prided himself on not missing a union meeting or dues payment and never accepted a nonunion job, even while his family went hungry. His loyalty to the union was accompanied by an unquestioning allegiance to the Democratic Party—an allegiance he passed on to his daughter, Lorraine.

Lorraine found a job as a telephone operator right out of high school and worked for the telephone company for thirty-eight years. She married Frank Trotta, also a Democrat, who worked as a janitor at the Robert R. Hartley public housing project until his retirement at age seventy. Frank had an intimate view of the gradual deterioration of the once immaculate and hopeful housing project, as the working-poor tenants gave way to welfare recipients who not only took less pride in their surroundings but also considered the public housing to be a permanent residence rather than a step on the way to self-sufficiency. Although he never gave up his membership in the Democratic Party, Frank Trotta became disheartened by the fact that he and his family scrimped and sacrificed their entire lives to purchase a house much more modest than public housing, and that his own children often needed the free lunches thrown away by the project residents.

Frank Trotta, Jr., was politically active in high school, but his working-class background, rather than drawing him to the Democratic Party of his parents, led him to join the Teen Age Republicans and support Richard Nixon and the Vietnam War. Young Frank campaigned for local Republican politicians even in high school, and when he attended the State University of New York at Albany, he found himself politically out of step with the majority of his classmates. Gravitating toward his conservative classmates, he met Tim Carey and Leslie Maeby for the first time. Trotta graduated from law school, entered a large Manhattan law firm, and remained active in the world of Republican politics, working alongside Carey and Maeby on Lewis Lehrman's campaign for governor of New York in 1982.

Trotta's political colleague, Leslie Maeby, also had a great-grandfather who arrived in the United States at the turn of the century. Aleksander Obrycki was forced to leave Poland for political reasons, settled in Baltimore, Maryland, and became a U.S. citizen in 1907. Obrycki worked for a Democratic ward boss, escorting new immigrants to the polling place on election day. He opened a bar and allowed the local numbers boss to run an operation there, initiating Obrycki's son Joe into the business at age fifteen by using him as a numbers runner. Joe thrived in the illegal gambling business, even during the Depression, and maintained close ties to the corrupt Democratic political machine that dominated Baltimore politics. Joe eventually became a renowned restaurateur and owner of Obrycki's Olde Crab House in Baltimore.

Joe's daughter, Vilma, married Jack Maeby in 1951. Maeby, who also grew up in heavily Democratic Baltimore, began to question his political assumptions in the army and as a student at Bucknell University, which he attended on a football scholarship. After being exposed to new ideas, Jack Maeby rejected the Democratic assumptions he had grown up with and began thinking like a Republican. After his marriage to Vilma (who was still a loyal Democrat), Jack Maeby worked his way up the socioeconomic ladder and eventually moved to the Albany suburb of Colonie, a community as solidly Republican as Baltimore had been Democratic. Despite the influence of their mother, Leslie and Jack Maeby, Jr., grew up favoring the Republican politics of their neighbors.

Leslie Maeby began her political career early, volunteering for a local Republican candidate while still in high school. Like her grandfather Joe, she absorbed her party affiliation initially through her surroundings more than any conscious choice. Like Frank Trotta, Jr., she attended college at Albany, becoming involved in Republican politics through her sorority. She eventually joined the group of young politicos who referred to themselves as the State Street Gang.

Maeby joined Trotta and Tim Carey to work on the 1982 Lehrman gubernatorial campaign before serving as finance director for the state Republican Party in 1989. She then retired from politics for a time in order to direct public relations for the New York Institute for Special Education. Urged on by Tim Carey, Maeby returned to politics to work on George Pataki's 1992 campaign for New York State Senate.

Tim Carey, like Trotta and Maeby, was also descended from immigrant stock. His great-grandmother, Mary Elizabeth Sanford, was a poor, Irish Catholic widow living in Liverpool, England, in 1905. In desperation, she sent her oldest child to New York that same year and followed with her other two children in 1907. Sanford supported her family by working as a chambermaid, and her daughters left school at age fourteen to work as well. Sanford died at age forty-five and her daughter Susan died during childbirth three years later, leaving twenty-one-year-old Lizzie Sanford to care for her younger brother.

Lizzie married Edward Garrett in 1917 and gave birth to three children: Edith, Jack, and Richie. The family lived in the San Juan Hill neighborhood of New York City, but moved to Crotonville, New York, during the Depression. Struggling to survive, the family was barely able to put food on the table until Franklin Roosevelt's Work Progress Administration hired Edward for construction and road building. An avid Democrat and grateful Roosevelt supporter, Lizzie volunteered to work for the Democratic Party, as did her children Edith and Jack.

Richie Carey played football in high school, entered the Marine Corps Reserve, worked for a Buick dealership and later as a construction laborer before finally taking over his father's job as a gravedigger when Edward retired. Richie kept the family interest in Democratic politics alive through his concern about the environment. An avid fisherman concerned about the state of the Hudson River, Richie became a vocal and active proponent of the environmental movement almost in spite of himself.

Yet Richie's nephew, Tim Carey (Edith's son), ended the Democratic family tradition. Growing up working-class poor in Crotonville, Tim Carey was originally initiated into politics by his Democratic grandmother, Lizzie. Although Tim was bright, his working-class origins caused him to be tracked in high school to study shop and auto mechanics rather than college-preparatory academics. Unprotected by student deferment, he was drafted into the army and found himself guarding the Pentagon against antiwar demonstrators during the 1967 peace march on Washington, D.C. This event marked a turning point in his life, as he realized that money and privilege, not ability, intellect, or hard work, separated him from the antiwar college students. He understood the term "liberal elite" for the first time.

After being discharged from the army, Carey attended community college and, proving his high school counselors wrong, was accepted to the State University of New York at Albany in 1971. Different from most of his fellow students as a result of his experiences as well as his temperament, Carey gravitated toward the company of other veterans. Through them, he became involved in Republican Party politics. Carey campaigned for Nixon in 1972, worked for various New York politicians, including Lehrman and George Pataki, and went on to make a career as a party campaigner.

Samuel Freedman's approach of tracking a national tendency through the personal stories of three families proves both entertaining and enlightening. Although each family's ethnicity and personal circumstances are quite different, the similarity in their political evolution is remarkable. When personalized, the drift of the working class from Democrat to Republican becomes not only much clearer but also quite understandable. These children of Democratic working-class parents felt caught in the middle between privileges of money and class unavailable to them on the one hand, and allowances made for minorities and welfare recipients on the other hand. The values of hard work and sacrifice they had grown up with somehow seemed not to matter anymore, and they found a sympathetic ear for these concerns with the conservative Republicans rather than with the liberal Democrats.

Although the second half of his book is too heavy on detailed descriptions of New York State political campaigns for the average, nonpolitical reader, Freedman does an admirable job of making the minutiae of obscure political campaigns engrossing reading. The heart of the book, however, lies in the telling of these three average, yet remarkable, American stories. The format of skipping back and forth between families can occasionally make the narrative difficult to follow, but the overall impact of these tales is thought-provoking and cuts through the usual political verbiage to reach closer to America's political heart than other more conventional works.

Mary Virginia Davis

Sources for Further Study

Business Week. September 30, 1996, p. 13.
Campaigns and Elections. XVII, October, 1996, p. 59.
Chicago Tribune. September 22, 1996, XIV, p. 1.
Commonweal. CXXIII, September 27, 1996, p. 17.
Los Angeles Times Book Review. September 29, 1996, p. 6.
The Nation. CCLXIII, October 28, 1996, p. 11.
The New York Times Book Review. CI, September 22, 1996, p. 15.
Publishers Weekly. CCXLIII, July 8, 1996, p. 66.
The Wall Street Journal. August 26, 1996, p. A8.
Washington Monthly. XXVIII, September, 1996, p. 40.
The Washington Post Book World. XXVI, October 20, 1996, p. 1.

INTEGRITY

Author: Stephen L. Carter (1954-   )
Publisher: BasicBooks (New York). 277 pp. $24.00
Type of work: Ethics; political philosophy

An inquiry into the qualities that make up the virtue of integrity, stressing the role of discernment, forthrightness, demonstrative action, the reliability of commitment, and respect for rules

Stephen Carter is rapidly emerging as one of this country's premier public intellectuals. Applied in the past to such luminaries as Walter Lippmann, Reinhold Niebuhr, and Eric Hoffer, "public intellectual" is an unofficial title earned by one possessing both specialized knowledge and an unmistakable sagacity about the affairs of the republic. A teacher of constitutional law at Yale Law School since 1983, Carter has clearly demonstrated his capacity for technical legal argumentation in law journals. *The Confirmation Mess* (1994) and *The Dissent of the Governed* (1996) speak to readers with a background in legal theory, ethics, and political philosophy. In *Reflections of an Affirmative Action Baby* (1991) and *The Culture of Disbelief: How American Law and Politics Trivialize Religious Devotion* (1993), however, Carter manifested a remarkable broadness of reach, depth of concern, and popular appeal. Indeed, the latter work received the enthusiastic endorsement of President Bill Clinton, who recommended that it be widely discussed. In *The Culture of Disbelief*, Carter argues that in recent decades, such powerful institutions as the courts, universities, media, and government have trivialized religion, making it a matter of private taste.

Integrity will advance Carter's reputation as an author who is able to instruct the nation's conscience and make its dialogue more profound. Significantly, the book is meant to be the first in a three part series. Designed for a general audience, the works will all explore "pre-political" virtues: "elements of good character that cross the political spectrum and, indeed, without which other political views and values are useless." The next book to appear will be on the subject of civility.

In turning his attention to integrity, Carter obviously responds to a distinct *Zeitgeist*. The Clinton presidency has seemed to many plagued by periodic revelations which suggest that moral principles have too often lost out to political expediency. The Iran-Contra scandal was a disquieting feature of the Bush and Reagan years. Indictments of high officials, sudden resignations, the calling of special prosecutors, "tell-all" best-sellers, sensational confirmation hearings, the addition of the suffix "gate" to a variety of "cases"—all have become far too familiar features of the political landscape. As if in reaction, professional ethics has sought to clarify and refurbish the ideal of integrity. Thus, scholar Nancy Schauber argues that integrity concerns the underlying or "passive" commitments that help constitute moral selfhood. Stan van Hooft defines integrity as a psychological property of the inner self, one which "makes certain actions impossible to the caring person." Jeffrey Blustein, Gabriele Taylor,

Bernard Williams, and Lynne McFall have produced substantial writings on this topic, the latter two having the most influence on Carter.

In the short "Explanations" section of *Integrity*, Carter lucidly sets forth his view that integrity is a moral virtue, "perhaps the first among the virtues that make for good character." In the much longer "Applications" portion (120 pages), Carter tries to show how this account allows one to describe how a person of integrity thinks and acts in a variety of contexts. Interestingly various, these contexts or problem areas include: letters of recommendation, grade inflation, exaggeration and distortion in advertisement, lying by journalists in order to acquire a story, zealotry in a lawyer's defense of her client, making marriage vows, living with integrity in a nearly failed marriage, the Pete Rose gambling case, the emphasis on winning in sports, and civil disobedience. The book contains a brief concluding section entitled "Ruminations." Here, Carter inquires into the question of whether integrity can be legislated, what principles might be followed in giving American politics a more "integral" shape, and what the greatest evils are which a nation with integrity must avoid.

An extraordinarily gifted writer, Carter creates a conversational and personal authorial presence. In a profile published in *U.S. News and World Report*, Paul Parshall called Carter "Yale's Doctor of Dialogue," emphasizing the exploratory, dialectical back-and-forth of his classrooms. Not surprisingly then, *Integrity* clearly displays the starting points for Carter's analytic work: He is a Christian, an admirer of the Constitution and fundamental American institutions to a degree that many consider him a neoconservative, and an adherent of the classical tradition in ethics, especially as represented by Aristotle and Aquinas. That Carter is an African American is evident mostly by some of the examples treated: the Clarence Thomas hearings, the O. J. Simpson trial, and the negative impact of grade inflation and hyperbole in letters of recommendation on black advancement. It is perhaps also revealed in the way he identifies the most profound evils facing America: "racial hatred; violence based on difference; and violence resulting from a closed mind." Carter agrees with Malcolm X that racism is "the earth's most explosive and pernicious evil," warning that "the racist impulse can explode in the racist . . . , so that suddenly, with little warning, individual mobs may carry out acts of violence against the despised, or, worse, the state may adopt policies of oppression or even destruction."

What do these starting points mean for the way Carter develops his understanding of integrity? One suspects that this question will be much debated as the book works its way into academic and popular discussion. Carter certainly uses ideas from such Christian writers as Lewis Smedes, Margaret Farley, Jean Bethke Elshtain, Stanley Hauerwas, Philip Edgcumbe Hughes, Karl Rahner, and Paul Jersild. He frequently invokes Roman Catholic moral and sacramental theology, Augustine, Thomas Aquinas, the Bible, and Jewish legal ideas. Yet one senses that his own long wrestle with the concerns of American jurisprudence as well as his natively shrewd readings of recent history play a more important part in the shaping of his account of integrity. For example, an advocate of moral education and community-resident virtue such as Stanley Hauerwas would not say, as Carter does: "A person of integrity lurks somewhere inside each of us: a person we feel we can trust to do right, to play by the rules, to keep commitments." Hauerwas, like the Catholic legal theorist Thomas Shaffer, would doubtless deny this implicit appeal to a universal humanity, arguing that what constitutes "integrity" may differ radically depending on the communities in which moral formation takes place. Convinced that Christians are "resident aliens" in an American culture that has been thoroughly pluralized and secularized, Hauerwas and Shaffer deny that Christian categories and references can be very persuasive in a "neutral" and "public" context. To be understood fully, they must be uttered in the common life of actual living traditions.

Yet Carter is confident that readers of all persuasions can find insight in his argument. This is clearly evident in his treatment of integrity and marriage in the chapter "Until We Are Parted." The extremely high divorce rate in the United States raises the question of whether Americans practice much integrity when undertaking such vows and such a commitment. Carter's first mark of "living the integral life" is that of reflection: "doing the hard work of discerning right from wrong." He therefore commends those religious and secular practices which "require couples consider-ing marriage to attend counseling sessions, to prepare them of the many realities—spiritual, emotional, even economic—of the choice they are in the process of exercis-ing." For the same reason, he praises the fact that even secular ceremonies are surrounded by ritual, causing participants to take seriously their action and ponder "its uniqueness among promises." In a distinctively Christian way, he offers these words of witness: "But even if, as society grows sadly more secularized, vows in other forms are used, their genesis, their unspoken model, remains the oath in the name of God."

Integrity also involves "acting on what one discerns, even at personal cost." If two individuals who are married become radically different persons from the ones they were a quarter of a century ago, staying married—continuing to honor their vows—may prove very costly. Must they remain married "at all costs"? Carter allows for divorce in cases of severe spousal abuse and flagrant infidelity, and he does not embrace the Roman Catholic position that civilly divorced persons cannot be remar-ried in the church. Nevertheless, his position will strike many readers as austere. Carter begins with the Christian view that marriage is a sacramental undertaking that imitates and therefore reproduces the promise of undying fidelity that God made to Moses and the Hebrew people. Furthermore, Carter agrees with Karl Rahner that marriage is an event in church history, not just in the lives of the couple. It is a moment of "self-actualization" for "the church as such." These interpretations produce the view, enunciated by the theologian and preacher Lewis Smedes, that although the married partners may change and grow (apart), "the person who makes and keeps the promise is always 'the one who will be there' with the other." The purpose of the vow, claims Carter, is self-limitation: "By limiting our freedom to answer the call to love other people, we free ourselves to be better and truer people for our spouses."

That Carter considers divorce a deeply serious matter—and a profound compromise of integrity—is obvious. For him, at the time of making a marriage vow, one assumes a huge liability to incur great costs. So if the price of remaining married seems terribly high, then one begins to take a truer measure of what "integrity" means. At the same time, there must be some proportionality between the price being paid and the value of maintaining the commitment, so "there will be times when what seems at first to be obviously right turns out not to be worth the cost." What must above all be guarded against is "divorce driven by self-indulgence."

Stephen Carter believes that this fundamentally theological treatment of "integral marriage" will be widely appealing. Secular Americans presently resort to a bewildering variety of interpretations of marriage vows—utilitarian/contractual; pragmatic arguments based on notions of the state's interest in good childrearing; highly romantic views of love. It is therefore somewhat hard to believe that they will attend carefully to this part of Carter's argument. They may instead be drawn to other sections of the book where theological perspectives are less in evidence. These are quite numerous. For example, in "The Integrity of Fun and Games," Carter takes a careful look at the American obsession with winning, something that contradicts older traditions of sportsmanship and honor in competitive play. A passionate football fan, Carter considers such issues as Proposition 48, the NCAA rule that stipulates minimum academic standards for admitting athletes to college; professional players salaries; and whether, when officials err in a team's favor, that team should refuse to accept its advantage. The thesis he defends in this chapter is the same as that developed throughout: "Integrity . . . usually means following the rules, even when following the rules costs victory. Sometimes integrity means breaking the rules, but only with a good and clear and openly articulated reason that appeals to a superior moral virtue. 'Otherwise I would lose' is not one."

How might integrity be restored to the common life? Carter's book has many suggestions, including "Eight Principles in Search of a Democracy." Here he offers guiding ideas for healing the body politic. The first of these is that the public in America is too often regarded as something to be manipulated: through advertising or through being represented by interest groups. Thus, "The nation exists for its people" is far from an empty slogan for Carter. Other principles include the following: "Consistency matters," "Everybody gets to play," "We must be willing to talk about right and wrong without mentioning the Constitution," "Our politics must call us to our higher selves," and "Sometimes the other side wins." While these sound a touch platitudinous, Carter elaborates his principles in ways that most readers will find fresh, specific, and all too relevant.

Leslie E. Gerber

Sources for Further Study

America. CLXXIV, April 27, 1996, p. 22.
Chicago Tribune. April 7, 1996, XIV, p. 3.
Los Angeles Times Book Review. March 17, 1996, p. 4.

National Review. XLVII, December 25, 1995, p. 54.
The New Republic. CCXIV, March 18, 1996, p. 34.
The New York Times Book Review. CI, March 3, 1996, p. 12.
Publishers Weekly. CCXLII, December 11, 1995, p. 61.
Time. CXLVII, March 25, 1996, p. 73.
U.S. News and World Report. CXX, March 18, 1996, p. 75.
The Washington Post Book World. XXVI, March 10, 1996, p. 5.

INVENTING IRELAND
The Literature of the Modern Nation

Author: Declan Kiberd
First published: 1995, in Great Britain
Publisher: Harvard University Press (Cambridge, Massachusetts). 719 pp. $35.00
Type of work: Literary history

An important new critical history of postcolonial Irish literature that describes how major twentieth century Irish writers created their own version of reality and culture

The first thing readers will notice about this new literary history of modern Irish literature is the seven-hundred-plus-page heft of the book; it is indeed a major tome. The second thing they will notice when they begin to read it is that it is *not* a routine literary history filled simply with facts, titles, dates, and anecdotes, and fit only for future reference. For this is a history with a critical thesis—suggested by the title—that Irish literature, and indeed Irish culture, in the modern world is a creative invention of Irish writers disengaging themselves from their European-dominated colonial past.

Kiberd, a lecturer at University College, Dublin, who has published previous books on major Irish writers and on modern literature and culture, announces in his introduction that he wishes to examine a number of central works in Irish literature of the last hundred years in terms of their social context. The result is a book that is half detailed analysis of the great masterpieces of modern Irish literature and half discussion of the considerable political and cultural history that has impinged on Irish literature. As Kiberd notes, "If there is no nationality without literature, there is no great literature without nationality." Kiberd insists, however, that whereas he does not intend to view works of art in "splendid isolation," at the same time he is not wiling to give in completely to current critical fashions, for he reminds readers that "certain masterpieces do float free of their enabling conditions to make their home in the world."

Inventing Ireland is divided into ten major sections that focus on the great writers of modern Ireland, separated by ten short inter-chapters that establish social and political frameworks for those works. Writing a history of modern Irish literature is no small task, for although Ireland has often been seen by its European neighbors as a tiny backward country, it has given birth to, arguably of course, the modern world's greatest dramatist (George Bernard Shaw), greatest poet (William Butler Yeats), and greatest novelist and short-story writer (James Joyce). The task is further complicated by the fact that there is no way to talk about Irish literature without talking about the long and complex history of Irish political conflict.

It is inevitable that a book about Ireland's invention of itself should begin with a writer whose main claim to fame is the theatrical invention of himself—Oscar Wilde. Kiberd makes the case that Wilde fought against Anglo-Saxon prejudice by becoming more English than the English themselves and thus challenging the old stereotypes about the Irish. Kiberd also argues that, like Wilde, Shaw used England as a sort of laboratory in which he redefined what it meant to be Irish. Although Kiberd's argument that Wilde and Shaw exploited stereotypes as a way of exposing them as such sometimes seems sophistical and strained, overall he makes a vigorous case that even those writers who turned to England did so as a way to better redefine Ireland.

Arguing that personal autobiography by Irish writers becomes the autobiography of Ireland, Kiberd attributes the emphasis on style in Irish writing from Yeats onward to the fact that if people create a world that exists by virtue of style, then language becomes extremely important. Yeats, Kiberd says, agreed with Wilde that the self was a creation and that when a self is confronted as if it were external, it leads to a discovery of an answering self within. Thus, Kiberd argues, Yeats, much like the American poet Walt Whitman, created a mask or series of masks that served to mythologize the self, reinforcing his conviction that a poet is not so much the man who goes about everyday activities as one who always speaks through a self-consciously created persona.

Although most of the chapters in *Inventing Ireland* focus on masterpieces of modern Irish literature, such as John Millington Synge's *The Playboy of the Western World* (1907) and Joyce's *Ulysses* (1922), Kiberd devotes other chapters to political and social issues that have affected, and been affected by, Irish writing, such as Douglas Hyde's arguments for "The Necessity of Deanglicizing Ireland," the resultant development of the Gaelic League at the end of the nineteenth century, and the 1916 Easter Rebellion (which Kiberd says was staged as street theater.)

In spite of Kiberd's early disclaimer of not giving in to current Marxist trends in literary criticism, *Inventing Ireland* is peppered with the paraphernalia and terminology of that approach to the literature and culture of the postcolonial world. For example, in his discussion of *The Playboy of the Western World*, Kiberd attributes the "exoticism" of Synge's language to the remoteness of his characters and discusses the "marginalization" of the women in a play that he says is filled with Synge's "gender-benders." Moreover, he compares the poetic self-justification of the women in Synge's play to the "black-is-beautiful" poetry of Martinique in the 1940's. Kiberd argues that Synge is the most gifted exponent of artistic decolonization in Irish literature, effortlessly assimilating the culture of the English occupation and then immersing himself in the native culture of Ireland.

Sean O'Casey's play *The Shadow of a Gunman*, staged at the famous Abbey Theater in the spring of 1923, is discussed by Kiberd from within the inescapable context of the Irish Civil War. In keeping with his theme of self-invention, however, he focuses more on such O'Casey plays as *Juno and the Paycock* (pr. 1924) and *The Plough and the Stars* (1926), in which O'Casey's characters attempt, by the very language put in their mouths, to create a more spacious imaginative world than the drab world in which they live.

In a central chapter entitled "Writing Ireland, Reading England," Kiberd makes explicit one of his central metaphors—that every Anglo-Irish relationship involves four persons: "the two actual persons and the two fictions, each one a concoction of the other's imagination." The result of this Prospero-Caliban relationship is that Irish writers inevitably attempt to connect romanticism and realism in a single moment. By this critical stroke, Kiberd argues that Joyce's epiphanies have inevitably lead to the Magic Realism of postmodernism.

When he begins to discuss the heart of modern Irish literature—the so-called Irish Renaissance—Kiberd seems to be caught in a common trap of modern criticism. For even as he tries to follow the current trend of cultural materialism, for which the basis is Marxist and the vehicle is the postcolonial world of minority cultures, Kiberd falls back on the aestheticism of his kinsman Oscar Wilde. Many of Synge's finest ideas, says Kiberd, spring from the idea that one must lie to create anything new and that realism is a failure; the artist is one who proceeds from form to thought, not from feeling to form.

When Kiberd discusses those two great modernist literary giants, Joyce and Yeats, he examines how they repudiate the realism characteristic of the European bourgeoisie and instead invent forms that, as Salman Rushdie (a favorite literary touchstone for Kiberd) says, allows the "miraculous and the mundane to coexist at the same level—as the same order of event." Thus, *Ulysses*, triumphantly claims Kiberd, is a truly multicultural text that establishes not a European modernism, but a postcolonial modernism seen more recently in such works as Gabriel García Márquez's *Cien años de soledad* (1967; *One Hundred Years of Solitude*, 1970).

Kiberd makes use of the current links established between Marxist criticism and radical Freudian criticism in two matching chapters entitled "Fathers and Sons" and "Mothers and Daughters." In his discussion of male identity, the focus is on how sons, faced with inadequate fathers, must engage in the reinvention of their parents. In Joyce's *Ulysses*, Stephen Daedalus becomes his own father; in *The Playboy of the Western World*, Christy Mahon must destroy the father in order to be able to conceive the self. This very process is, Kiberd argues, to use a well-known text of modern criticism, an *Anti-Oedipus*, in which the death of the father is not a tragedy, but a comedy. All children in the colonies, says Salman Rushdie, possess this power to destroy the parents in order to reinvent them whenever that is necessary.

There is no way to discuss Irish culture without discussing religion, and Kiberd focuses on Shaw's play *Saint Joan* (pr. 1923), Yeats's collection of poetry, *The Winding Stair and Other Poems* (1933), and Samuel Beckett's novels *Murphy* (1938) and *Molloy* (1951) in terms of their Protestant-Catholic interrelationships. Kiberd is particularly interested in those writers who wanted a fusion of the two religious traditions, who dreamed of a hybrid nicknamed a *Protholic* or a *Cathestant*—a image of the Catholicized Protestant or Protestantized Catholic that Kiberd says was implicit in the Irish Revival from its beginning. Shaw's vision of Saint Joan is discussed as the central characterization of this combination, but Yeats's poems in *The Winding Stair* are explicated as Yeats's effort to Catholicize the Protestant Ireland of his youth and then to Protestantize the Catholic Ireland of his age.

Kiberd discusses the central tension in Irish literature between the country and the city in the chapter entitled "The Periphery and the Centre." Tackling the common myth—that rural Ireland is the real Ireland, Kiberd looks at Dublin in the early years of the twentieth century as a classic example of a "periphery-dominated-centre," in which the city was dominated by the surrounding countryside. One result of this phenomenon in literature, Kiberd, says is the Irish mastery of the short story. Not only can this mastery be seen in the groundbreaking modernist text, Joyce's *Dubliners* (1914) and later in the works of Sean O'Faolain, Frank O'Connor, Mary Lavin, and others, but also in such modernist novels as Flann O'Brien's *At Swim-Two-Birds* (1939), Joyce's *Ulysses*, and Beckett's trilogy—all of which Kiberd says are thinly disguised collections of short stories. The form seems so amenable to Irish writers both because it is an oral/rural genre, a form that focuses on the lives of the marginalized, or as Frank O'Connor has called them "submerged population groups," and because it is a genre that has always been supremely aware of its form and style and thus unwilling to give into the naïvete of realism.

The last section of *Inventing Ireland* focuses on Irish culture and literature since the 1960's—an era in which Ireland has been transformed by modernism, an era symbolically initiated by the famous visit of President John F. Kennedy, who embodied, Kiberd says, and appealed to a national self-deception—playing, as he did, the rebel, when he was secretly a "superstraight." With the rapid liberalization of the Catholic church, however, and the increasing modernization of Ireland brought on by technology giants establishing factories there, the question has increasing become, says Kiberd, "what kind of society was to replace the pious, mainly rural and Catholic community of an earlier period?"

The answer would seem to lie in what Kiberd thinks may be a new revival at the end of the century, comparable to the Irish Renaissance near its beginning. To support such a claim, he discusses a number of contemporary writers, such as Thomas Kinsella and Seamus Heaney who in their poetry have tried to "translate the violence of the past into the culture of the future." He also focuses on the best-known contemporary novelist in Ireland, Roddy Doyle, whose *The Commitments* (1987) dealt with the differences between Dublin social classes, as well as one of the best-known Irish dramatists, Brian Friel, whose 1990 theatrical hit, *Dancing at Lughnasa*, dealt with similarities between seemingly disparate cultural traditions.

Although Kiberd says there has been a proliferation of courses in Irish Studies in Britain, Canada, and the United States, which has encouraged many nationalists to maintain the narcissistic notion that the Irish are exceptional, it has not led Irish intellectuals to study the ways that outsiders see Ireland. The central moral of the Irish experience, Kiberd concludes, is this: "If the native culture of a people is devalued and destroyed for the sake of material progress, what follows may not be material progress of the kind hoped for, but cultural confusion and a diminished sense of enterprise." Kiberd concludes *Inventing Ireland* by arguing that if the task of the Irish Renaissance was to shape and reshape an ancient past, the task of the current generation is, if less heroic, more complex—to translate the recent past of the Irish Renaissance into the terms of the twenty-first century. It is obvious that Kiberd intends *Inventing Ireland* to be part of that effort.

Charles E. May

Sources for Further Study

Boston Globe. April 2, 1996, p. 57.
The Chronicle of Higher Education. XLII, March 15, 1996, p. A16.
The Guardian. February 16, 1996, II, p. 21.
Library Journal. CXXI, May 15, 1996, p. 62.
London Review of Books. XVIII, April 18, 1996, p.14.
New Statesman and Society. VIII, November 24, 1995, p. 40.
The New York Times Book Review. CI, March 17, 1996, p. 6.
The Observer. January 7, 1996, p. 15.
The Times Literary Supplement. May 31, 1996, p. 32.
The Washington Post Book World. XXVI, March 17, 1996, p. 8.

ISAIAH BERLIN

Author: John Gray (1948-   )
First published: 1995, in Great Britain
Publisher: Princeton University Press (Princeton, New Jersey). 189 pp. $19.95
Type of work: Biography; philosophy
Time: 1939-1995
Locale: Latvia, the Soviet Union, the United States, and Great Britain

A close look at the intricate and often contradictory ideas of one of the most influential public philosophers of modern time

> *Principal personage:*
> ISAIAH BERLIN, the Russian-born philosopher, educator, and intellectual historian

Sir Isaiah Berlin, born in Riga in 1909, was in Petrograd in 1917 where, at the age of eight, he witnessed the first Russian Revolution and the Bolshevik coup later in the same year. In 1921 his parents moved to England. He had been brought up in Riga speaking Russian and German, and by the time he reached his teens as a schoolboy at St. Paul's, he was not only trilingual but so polished in learning and language that his acceptance at Oxford was a foregone conclusion.

Except for the three years when he lived first in New York, then in Washington, D.C., working for the British government, and briefly in Moscow in 1945, Berlin has spent his life at Oxford. He completed his university education at Corpus Christi College and remains, to this day, a Fellow of All Souls College, having also held the Chichele Chair in Social and Political Theory there (1957-1967). The first president of Wolfson College (1966-1975), he was also president of the British Academy from 1974-1978.

The pluralism of Isaiah Berlin's cultural background is, says John Gray, an important source of the unique liberalism at the core of his thought. That liberalism is "agonistic," according to Gray—"a liberalism of conflict and unavoidable loss among rivalrous goods and evils."

Berlin's Jewish and Russian heritage gave him a passion for ideas and a tragic sense of life whereas the standards of rigor and clarity exemplified in his writing and thinking distinguish British empiricism at its best. His dedication to seeing life as a whole, unflinchingly aware of its tragic dimension, has prevented him from settling for abstractions or rational systems that ignore the complexity of experience.

Human beings cannot rely on absolute rational standards for determining moral action. It is true of many goods, according to Berlin, that they are "rivalrous and conflictual." We live in a world of "value-pluralism." Berlin insists that this idea must not be confused with moral relativism. What is foolish is to hold moral behavior to an idea of a perfection that encompasses all the rivalries among the virtues. Reasoning cannot provide such a standard; it cannot resolve all the rivalries under one principle. Although Berlin accepts the idealism of Kant, he is obviously not persuaded that a rationally grounded categorical imperative for moral action is a possibility. Indeed, it is one of Berlin's principal contentions that many of the dilemmas of practical life, political or moral, are, at bottom, insoluble, radical and tragic, and undecidable by rational reflection.

How does Berlin's tragic sense of moral action prevent him from despairing of the possibility of a viable human ethics? The answer lies in his belief in the necessity of radical choice. Human beings must make choices, and they must be persuaded of the moral rectitude of the choices they make even if they cannot be guided by universally determined principles. In Berlin's "agonistic liberalism" the value of freedom derives from the *limits* of rational choice. His liberalism of conflict among inherently rivalrous goods "grounds itself on the radical choices we must make among incommensurables, not upon rational choice." Berlin is not, Gray hastens to add, an irrationalist. Although heavily committed to the ideal of rational inquiry, Berlin is nevertheless convinced that the Enlightenment concept of human nature as a constant to be perceived in universalist terms has little to do with the actual dilemmas of moral practice in the real world of experience.

Berlin rejects the view of "man" as a natural object in a natural order subject to natural laws and intelligible in his behavior and nature by reference to those laws. As anyone who knows his famous essays on Leo Tolstoy, Johann Gottfried von Herder, Giambattista Vico, and dozens of other historical figures, Berlin is convinced that "man" is inherently unfinished and incomplete, essentially self-transforming and only partly determinate, at least partly the author of himself and not subject comprehensively to any natural order. These ideas put Berlin closer to the Romantics and to the "Counter-Enlightenment" than to the Enlightenment, whose values of intellectual emancipation and rational self-criticism, according to Gray, "he nevertheless steadfastly defends."

Berlin's rational-romanticism thrives on its oxymoronic contradiction. Negative freedom—the right *not* to do things—is a supreme good for Berlin because it is expressive of choice and promotes self-creation. Self-creation cannot be reduced to the absolute principle of autonomy. Berlin does not subscribe to the essentialism of an idea of the individual self. Here, we can say, his rational empiricism holds his romanticism in check. What Berlin does believe is that there are many excellent lives that are not especially autonomous, for example, the lives of the nun, professional soldier, or passionately devoted artist. In other words, moral freedom must include the opportunities for all kinds of choices to be made that may not necessarily increase the autonomous freedom of the individual person. This is at the heart of Berlin's differences with John Stuart Mill, one of his most important precursors. Mill's utilitarian ideas commit his ethical system to the creation of human happiness, and this for Mill is largely the result of a liberal society's giving the freedom of the individual the widest possible scope. Mill's liberalism precludes the idea of radical choice—choice without criteria, grounds, or principles—that, says Gray, "is at the heart of Berlin's liberalism."

The choices individuals make are grounded in more than their individual self assertion; for Berlin, and for his most important mentor, the late eighteenth century

German thinker, Johann Gottfried von Herder, history is conceived as the "exfoliation of incommensurable cultures." Unlike David Hume and Niccolò Machiavelli, who saw nothing of true novelty in history—merely the rise and fall of civilizations— Herder believed that cultures, rather than individuals, were the precious repositories of human choices. Like Hegel, Herder also believed that the historical working out of a culture's destiny involved a *telos* or goal in time. Berlin, however, rejects any idea of teleology in the historical experience of cultures because it simply brings back abstract concepts of humanity and rationalizes the pluralism of choices (that actually constitute cultural reality) under a totalizing idea or principle.

For Berlin, cultures are tragic; they can be obliterated—and with them all of the freedom that went into the choices that gave them life, choices that were incommensurable, contradictory, and beyond rational tracing. The Enlightenment ideal of a cosmopolitan civilization in which particularistic attachments have been transcended or marginalized is rejected by Berlin. He sees in this ideal an impoverishment of the cultural diversity in which the incommensurable possibilities of human nature best find their expression. So adamant is he in this belief that he comes dangerously close to questioning the validity of the principle of individual freedom itself. His insistence that a "sane nationalism" is the best hope that free human beings have moves Berlin to a pronouncement on human happiness too patronizing for comfort: " In the last analysis, a sane nationalism is to be justified by a utilitarian argument—that most men and women are happy only when their way of life prolongs customs and habits which are familiar to them." This kind of thinking risks validating poverty, ignorance, and tribal exclusiveness in the name of cultural affirmation.

The utilitarianism of the nineteenth century never overcame the taunt, "Is it better to be a pig satisfied or Socrates dissatisfied?" Berlin's repeated rejection of universals makes him vulnerable to the same attack. Berlin's distrust in assimilation as a solution to persecution makes him a strong supporter of Zionism, but it is revealing that his support of Jewish statism is contingent on Israel's avoidance of the "pathologies" of nationalism: "It is as the embodiment of the ideals of its founders, as a state committed to the ideals of the Enlightenment, that Berlin remains a (far from uncritical) supporter of the state of Israel." Isaiah Berlin has never deserted the ideal at the very heart of the Enlightenment, an idea which remains at the heart of Judaism as well—the rational and moral unity of all humankind. His brilliant intellectual dance on the margins between the universals of the Enlightenment and the particularist and culturally national emphases of the Romantic reaction to eighteenth century rationalism and universalism continues to fascinate and puzzle his admirers. His critics have suggested that one of the reasons Berlin has written historical and/or biographical essays rather than full-length books is his not wishing to be committed to any synthesis or unified view of "liberalism" or the "problems of the modern world."

Professor John Gray, a Fellow in Jesus College, Oxford University, is a longtime colleague and admirer of Isaiah Berlin. He has done his subject justice and clarified the issues, but he has not resolved the contradictions at the heart of Isaiah Berlin's work. Berlin's ideas seem burdened with a strange combination of contradiction and suggestive paradox; nevertheless, the clarity and revelatory power of his political and historical observations and reflections promises to be one of the great achievements of British political thought in the twentieth century. This in itself is a paradox and suggests that we are too close to Isaiah Berlin to assess him adequately. He is definitely a subject for the next century's thinkers. Gray has attached a useful primary and secondary bibliography on Berlin and his critics that readers of all sorts will find helpful.

Peter Brier

Sources for Further Study

AB Bookman's Weekly. XCVII, June 24, 1996, p. 2520.
Choice. XXXIV, October, 1996, p. 293.
The Guardian. November 4, 1996, II, p. 29.
National Review. XLVIII, November 25, 1996, p. 69.
The New York Review of Books. XLII, October 19, 1995, p. 28.
The New York Times Book Review. CI, July 7, 1996, p. 7.
Publishers Weekly. CCXLIII, March 11, 1996, p. 47.
The Times Literary Supplement. February 10, 1995, p. 4.
The Wilson Quarterly. XX, Spring, 1996, p. 72.

JERZY KOSINSKI
A Biography

Author: James Park Sloan (1944-   )
Publisher: Dutton (New York). 506 pp. $27.95
Type of work: Literary biography
Time: 1933-1991
Locale: Poland and New York City

James Park Sloan carefully analyzes the life and death of the Polish-born writer Jerzy Kosinski, whose account of a childhood under Nazi persecution proved as shocking as his suicide

> *Principal personages:*
> JERZY KOSINSKI, the Jewish immigrant author whose semi-autobiographical book on his survival in Nazi-occupied Poland made him famous
> MIECZYSLAW "MOSES" (LEWINKOPF) KOSINSKI, his father
> ELZBIETA KOSINSKI, his mother
> KATHERINA "KIKI" VON FRAUNHOFER, his second wife
> MARY HAYWARD WEIR, his first wife, a socialite eighteen years his senior whose wealth changed his lifestyle
> URSZULA "ULA" DUDZIAK, his last love, a Polish jazz singer
> LILLA VAN SAHER, an older Hungarian American woman who shared Kosinski's taste for literature and kinky sex
> DR. KRYSTYNA IWASKIEWICZ RYTEL, Kosinski's early Polish American lover
> PETER SKINNER, a British teacher whose assistance with Kosinski's written English became the subject of controversy
> GEOFFREY STOKES and ELIOT FREMONT-SMITH, two journalists whose 1982 article charged Kosinski with falsifications and plagiarism

For many readers, the story of Jerzy Kosinski has all the ingredients of a classic tragedy, and James Park Sloan's *Jerzy Kosinski: A Biography* will not disappoint them. Here was a young Jewish immigrant from Poland who could speak very little English when he escaped to America from behind the Iron Curtain in 1957. In a few years, however, his best-selling account of his survival of the Holocaust came out in perfect English; he married an American heiress and published first-rate fiction in his new language.

Then, suddenly, fate struck him down in the person of two hostile New York journalists who claimed others had written his works. Many of Kosinski's readers deserted him, and his last novel was a colossal failure. Finally, his suicide, on May 2, 1991, was executed with the stoic precision of one of his literary protagonists. Without disturbing his wife, who slept in their bed next door, Kosinski took an overdose of barbiturates and alcohol. Lying down in his bathtub, he put a plastic bag over his head to make sure he would suffocate while drowsing toward death.

Jerzy Kosinski treats its fascinating subject in an inquisitive, informed, and finally sympathetic manner. Sloan does not downplay Kosinski's tendency to embellish his life's story and to shock his audience. After all, it was exactly this shock value that propelled his first novel, *The Painted Bird* (1965), to the international best-sellers lists.

Marketed as thinly veiled autobiography, *The Painted Bird*'s harrowing tale of a young Jewish or Gypsy boy's six-year odyssey through the horrors of Nazi-occupied Poland stunned its readers. People were shocked by episodes describing the boy's first sexual encounters, the acts of cruelty he suffers at the hands of Polish peasants, and his ultimate acts of revenge such as the derailment of a passenger train.

When doubts emerged about the veracity of the book's autobiographical elements and it became clear to most people that Kosinski's book was a special form of fiction, quite a few of his readers and critics were shocked again, although for a different reason. Now, as Sloan shows, they felt bewildered and betrayed by an author whom they soon came to consider the ultimate literary trickster.

According to James Sloan, however, the roots for Kosinski's lifelong desire to surprise and startle, to trick other people, lay deep in his past. Sloan clearly forgives Kosinski for the sake of the real ordeals he lived through in his youth. As Jews living in Nazi-occupied Poland, the Kosinski family had to survive by deceiving their Nazi enemies about their real identity. Jerzy Kosinski documents how Moses Lewinkopf wisely changed his Jewish last name to the Polish "Kosinski" in the spring of 1941, and how his eight-year-old son Jerzy lived up to his father's plans for survival.

Thus, Sloan is not surprised by the likely discrepancies between Kosinski's actual youth and that of the boy in *The Painted Bird*. In the crucial case of the boy's separation from his parents, Sloan's research reveals how neighbors and relatives remember that, unlike his protagonist, Kosinski was never separated from his family.

When the Nazi horror ended, the Kosinskis eventually settled back in the Polish city of Lodz. Here, Sloan's research shows how hard the biographer had to work to establish a historically accurate picture of Jerzy Kosinski's young life. Pursuing photography and women while studying social sciences, for example, Kosinski would later claim to have studied seriously in Moscow; yet while he did independent research in the city, there are no surviving records of his ever having been an enrolled student there. Thus, since Kosinski proved himself so notoriously unreliable about the events of his life, most of Sloan's findings are based on interviews with people who have known Kosinski or on secondary materials, such as official documents and the printed recollections of others who had contact with Kosinski.

This method succeeds well in giving the reader a good sense not only of the facts of Kosinski's life but also of the ways in which his mind creatively embellished and altered factual episodes. While his actual departure for the United States was suffi- ciently dramatic with missed deadlines and special intervention by friendly professors to allow him to leave Poland on a student exchange program in late 1957, Kosinski would rewrite the episode in his novel *Cockpit* (1975). There, the protagonist invents a whole university department of his own to escape with forged documents to enroll in a fictitious program in the United States.

As with *The Painted Bird*, Kosinski again would not dispel the false idea that his fiction corresponded exactly to his real experiences. Again, Sloan forgives these alterations and stays with his central argument that, even when "the public record says otherwise . . . [Kosinski's] melodramatic claims no doubt embody an inner truth." While Sloan's book thoughtfully argues its points, it remains somewhat ironic, however, that Kosinski the charming storyteller has still triumphed over Kosinski the real person. Thus, his "auto-fictions," as he would call them later, have made their way into even such supposedly well-researched reference works as *Merriam-Webster's Encyclopedia of Literature* (1995), which prints as facts parts of the self-invented Kosinski legend.

Coming to America, Sloan shows, provided Kosinski with a major step towards his goal of self-realization, and continuous reinvention. Instead of academic work, Kosinski soon focused on writing, a talent that suited his creative personality. His first two books were nonfiction reflections on life in the Soviet Union. The fact that he published them under a pen name, "Joseph Novak," and that *The Future Is Ours, Comrade* (1960) was published in condensed form by *Reader's Digest* (a rare occurrence for an unknown author), gave rise to the idea that Kosinski may have enjoyed the help of the Central Intelligence Agency. Here, James Sloan concedes that it was impossible for him to discover the truth.

Sloan discovered, however, that Kosinski's problems with the English language led him to employ a translator at the Radio Free Europe. This incident foreshadows how his lifelong problems with idiomatic English would eventually land the author in hot water when hostile critics took a less benevolent stance on his continuous use of native speakers, such as his friend Peter Skinner, to help with the language of his books.

Apart from gaining its author international fame, *The Future Is Ours, Comrade* also brought Kosinski in touch with his first wife, Mary Weir. According to their story, which Sloan accepts as "more or less, the truth," Kosinski at first mistook the vibrant, vivacious forty-five-year-old widow for her own secretary.

Sloan nicely introduces the reader to Mary and Jerzy's whirlwind romance. Initially, in spite of the eighteen-year age difference between them, the lovers gave each other exactly what they wanted. Mary received Jerzy's undivided attention, while her money made the American Dream come alive for him.

In a move which Sloan calls characteristic, Kosinski also used Mary's Lincoln Continental to drive around with his Polish American girlfriend Krystyna Iwaskiewicz, foreshadowing his absolute inability to be monogamous. At times, his unconventional lifestyle worked, but often his behavior demanded a steep price. Shortly before her death from what was likely an overdose, Mary Weir was divorced from Kosinski.

Throughout his life, Kosinski would form elaborate romantic triangles. When he met Lilla van Saher, he quickly acquired a taste for sexual appetites many of his friends termed bizarre. While married to Katherina "Kiki" von Fraunhofer, he fell deeply in love with another Polish American woman, Urszula "Ula" Dudziak, the last friend to see him alive.

As Kosinski's literary career took off in the late 1960's and his third novel, *Being There* (1971) was made into a successful motion picture, the author found himself at the center of literary America. His imaginative and creative works were celebrated as major achievements, and his enigmatic personality fascinated readers and critics alike. James Sloan gives Kosinski great credit for his artistic achievements, and feels that books like *Cockpit* have made a lasting impact on the American cultural landscape.

Yet with fame there also came danger, and Kosinski found himself in the midst of a literary scandal from which he never fully recovered. When Geoffrey Stokes and Eliot Fremont-Smith published their piece, "Jerzy Kosinski's Tainted Words," in *The Village Voice* of June 22, 1982, their charges that Kosinski's words were not his own hit literary New York like a bombshell.

Unfortunately, Kosinski had never acknowledged any help and again went on the offensive. As James Sloan's balanced account shows, Kosinski definitely had assistance with the English phrasing of his works. Yet unlike Stokes and Fremont-Smith, Sloan and others insist that the creative ownership of Kosinski's books is his alone.

Reeling from the attacks on his status as a genuine author, Kosinski retreated into the world of his many Polish and Jewish friends. The damage was done, however, and Kosinski's next novel, *Pinball* (1982), met with lukewarm critical responses.

Working on many extraliterary projects and traveling widely abroad, Kosinski's final work, *The Hermit of 69th Street: The Working Papers of Norbert Kosky* (1988; revised, 1991) became an unwieldy defense of himself. Created with the aid of his second wife Kiki, whom he married in 1987 after a long relationship, the novel failed to elicit much critical interest.

When Jerzy Kosinski committed suicide on May 2, 1991, the event shocked the literary world. To his friends, he had not appeared that desperate. Yet as James Sloan shows, the public had broken through the many masks that the author had created for himself, and the master of disguise had been tragically confronted with facts he could not reasonably refute.

In the end, Sloan's balanced biography succeeds in telling readers why Jerzy Kosinski may have been such a trickster in the game of literary fame and accomplishment. Sloan argues that in Jerzy Kosinski, the reading public has lost an author whose work provided a fascinating glimpse at a world in which the self is alone, and creativity and imagination are all that separates the survivors from those who fall prey to the evils of the twentieth century.

R. C. Lutz

Sources for Further Study

The Atlantic. CCLXXVII, April, 1996, p. 124.
Chicago Tribune. March 24, 1996, XIV, p. 4.
First Things. October, 1996, p. 58.
Los Angeles Times Book Review. May 12, 1996, p. 3.
The Nation. CCLXII, March 11, 1996, p. 28.
The New York Times Book Review. CI, April 21, 1996, p. 16.
The Washington Post Book World. XXVI, March 3, 1996, p. 3.

JESSE
The Life and Pilgrimage of Jesse Jackson

Author: Marshall Frady
Publisher: Random House (New York). 552 pp. $28.50
Type of work: Biography
Time: 1941-1995
Locale: Greenville, South Carolina; Chicago, Washington, D.C., and the Middle East

A biography of Jesse Jackson, one of America's best known yet possibly most misunderstood civil rights leaders, from his early childhood in the South through the tumultuous civil rights years to his quest for the presidency of the United States

> *Principal personages:*
> JESSE JACKSON, the African American religious and civil rights leader who sought the U.S. presidency in 1984 and 1988
> JACKIE JACKSON, his wife
> HELEN BURNS, his mother
> NOAH ROBINSON, his father
> CHARLES JACKSON, his stepfather
> MARTIN LUTHER KING, Jr., the famous civil rights leader whom Jackson served as an aide in the 1960's
> RALPH ABERNATHY, King's successor as leader of the Southern Christian Leadership Conference (SCLC)
> WALTER MONDALE, the Democratic Party's presidential candidate in 1984
> MICHAEL DUKAKIS, the Democratic Party's presidential candidate in 1988
> BERT LANCE, a Georgia banker who served in the Carter administration and became a Jackson confidant

Just who is Jesse Jackson? Preacher, politician, civil rights leader, unabashed opportunist and publicity-seeker—he has been characterized as all of these things and more. One thing is certain, however, when one is finished reading this remarkable biography: Jesse Jackson is an American phenomenon.

Jackson was born poor and illegitimate in Greenville, South Carolina, in 1941. Even as a youth, people seemed to notice something special about him—most notably his confident bearing in public and sharp intellect. He was also a gifted athlete, becoming a star player for Greenville High School, winning a football scholarship to the University of Illinois.

Racial discrimination was a fact of life in Greenville, and upon entering college, Jackson soon realized that racism was endemic in the rest of the nation as well. Only a few months into his freshman year, his feelings of disillusionment and isolation caused his grades to slip, and he decided to drop out and return home. Subsequently enrolling at North Carolina Agricultural and Technical College in Greensboro, he quickly became an honor student and star quarterback. He also fell in love, meeting his future wife, Jackie, there. They married in 1962, and in the midst of his whirlwind life they raised five children.

As the rising moral tide of the Civil Rights movement began to spread throughout the South, Jackson decided, with some reluctance at first, to join in the great crusade. He soon became involved in the early demonstrations in Greensboro, and proved to be a courageous, passionate, and inspirational leader in the campaign to integrate the city. Upon his graduation from college, he cast about for a stage upon which he could play out the script of his life. He thought about possibly following in the footsteps of Thurgood Marshall and pursuing a career in law, but his close friends convinced him that the seminary, and from there the pulpit, was the place from which he could best work for social change. He decided to return to Chicago, this time at the Chicago Theological Seminary. Only six months after his arrival at the seminary, however, he saw the civil rights demonstrations in Selma, Alabama, on television and decided to pack his bags and travel there to work alongside Martin Luther King, Jr.

Jackson joined King's Southern Christian Leadership Conference (SCLC), and later returned to Chicago to continue his theological studies. At age twenty-four, he was the youngest of King's aides. He was assigned to develop "Operation Breadbasket" in Chicago, an economic campaign which used boycott threats and intense negotiation to achieve integration among local businesses. Jackson's spectacular successes in Chicago eventually gained him national attention.

As the Civil Rights movement gained momentum in the late 1960's, Martin Luther King became a national figure. Jackson saw himself as King's protégé, destined to assume a national role as well. Soon, however, these two mammoth personalities began to clash. In the last years of his life, especially after his controversial opposition to the Vietnam War, King was becoming more subdued and cautious, even doubting the effectiveness of his nonviolent social philosophy. Jackson, meanwhile, was becoming more bold and ambitious; he seemed to thrive on the media attention. Many compared the relationship between King and Jackson to that of an aging father grooming and counseling his ambitious and energetic son.

All of this would change with the crack of a rifle shot on the evening of April 4, 1968, in Memphis, Tennessee. King died that night, and the chaos that followed the assassination resulted in one of the most controversial chapters of Jesse Jackson's life. Many who were there that night later claimed that Jackson used the incident for his own self-aggrandizement by playing to the cameras, and were especially offended when Jackson appeared on television the next morning still wearing his blood-spattered shirt. In spite of the controversy, the media was already describing Jackson as King's heir apparent on the national civil rights scene. He continued to work for SCLC and to preach at a Chicago church, but it became clear that neither the structure of the SCLC nor a local pulpit could contain his enormous ego; he was convinced, by 1968, that the entire world must be his parish. Many within the SCLC, including the Reverend Ralph Abernathy, King's hand-picked successor, were convinced that Jackson should move on.

In spite of the animosity between Jackson and Abernathy after King's death, Jackson stayed on at SCLC for almost four more years, the increasing leadership rift between the two men eventually forcing him out. Jackson decided to start his own organization,

Operation PUSH—"People United to Save Humanity" (the "Save" later changed to "Serve"). As the decade of the seventies opened, Jackson envisioned his new enterprise as propelling the Civil Rights movement, and his own public career, to new heights. The organization soon found itself in severe financial difficulty, but not before Jackson would succeed, by the end of the decade, in emerging as virtually the sole national voice of the black community in America. All that was lacking was a defining event, a national cause, to set things in motion. By the summer of 1983, he had his vision: a run for the presidency of the United States in 1984. With millions of blacks registering to vote, especially in the South, the cry of "Run, Jesse, run" began to be heard.

Jackson would soon be subjected, like all national candidates, to the blazing lights and microscopic examination of his personal character. As it turned out, there were some ghosts in Jackson's past—first, the story that while working as a waiter as a youth he had spit in some white customers' food, and then the recurring rumors of romantic encounters with various women. Author Frady recounts that this love-hate relationship with the media was always a central paradox of the Jackson persona: just when it seemed that the press was on his side, stories of such incidents would suddenly surface. No other incident better illustrates this than the infamous "Hymie town" remark which first appeared in *The Washington Post*. The remark was made public just three weeks after Jackson's remarkable triumph of personally securing the release of Navy aviator Robert Goodman from a Syrian jail in 1983. Even this successful rescue mission was pilloried by the press; Jackson was accused of staging a "publicity stunt" and shamelessly promoting himself. Perhaps even more damaging was his newly formed alliance with Nation of Islam leader Louis Farrakhan, a relationship that would for many place Jackson far to the left of the American mainstream.

In spite of these setbacks, Jackson was determined to make a serious run for the Democratic presidential nomination in 1984. He called on Bert Lance, then Georgia's Democratic state chairman, to advise him. He would not be a serious contender that year, but his electrifying speech to the convention in San Francisco that summer was proof that he had finally arrived on the national political scene. Four years later, in 1988, Jackson showed just how much political strength he possessed, with strong showings in the opening contests in Iowa and New Hampshire. On "Super Tuesday," March 8, Jackson ran first or second in sixteen out of twenty-one state caucuses, and later on in Michigan, he won a stunning fifty-five percent of the vote, which included twenty percent of the white vote. This, however, would prove to be the high-water mark of his campaign. While campaigning in New York, a crucial state, the old allegations of his anti-Semitism, his "Hymie-town" remark, and his embrace of Yasir Arafat, leader of the Palestinian Libertarian Organization—all came back to haunt him. After New York, there seemed to be little likelihood that Jackson would be able to wrest the nomination away from Michael Dukakis at the Atlanta convention. Nevertheless, Jackson still held out hope that his strong showing in the primaries might at least secure for him a spot as Dukakis's running mate, but even this was not to be.

Perhaps no major political party was ready to take the bold step of placing an African American on their presidential ticket. In any case, when looking back at the slow and difficult road that American blacks have had to travel to gain equality and legitimacy, Jackson's 1988 presidential run must be viewed as a remarkable achievement. For the first time in history, an African American demonstrated that Americans could look past the race barrier and judge candidates by the "content of their character."

The years following the 1988 race were difficult ones for Jackson, as he struggled to once again redefine himself and to find a cause to which he could devote his energies. He still endeavored to become the prophet-hero of his time, but seemed to have somehow lost his way. This overwhelming desire to "belong," to be taken seriously, has always been one of the driving forces of Jackson's life. The last chapter of the book dramatically sums up the paradoxes of Jackson's public life. During the early weeks of the Persian Gulf crisis in August of 1990, he journeyed to Iraq to try to persuade Saddam Hussein to release the foreign nationals he was holding hostage. His trip to Baghdad set in motion the beginning of a wholesale release of hostages, but his diplomatic skill and courage received little attention from the press, many of whom felt that Jackson was again merely grandstanding.

Frady ends the book by remarking that perhaps this has always been Jackson's most damaging weakness. His tremendous desire to be recognized, to be quoted and consulted, had perhaps been overplayed, bringing many to think that he was simply a shallow publicity hound, eager to see his name in print and his face on television. There is considerable truth to this charge, but the larger truth is that despite his faults and his propensity for self-aggrandizement at every opportunity, there lies beneath a man deeply committed to the plight of the oppressed throughout the world. After reading this remarkable biography, however, there is little doubt that there is much more to Jesse Jackson than the image we see. When looking at his life, one can only be awed by his incredible journey from humble beginnings in Greenville, South Carolina, through the flames of the civil rights struggle, to the courts of kings, presidents, and popes. All this he accomplished through the sheer force of his will and an overwhelming desire to make something of his life. Frady's portrait of Jackson illuminates for the reader the inner workings of this remarkable man, and is as much a study in leadership as it is an intimate and balanced portrait of a fascinating and complex individual.

Raymond Frey

Sources for Further Study

Los Angeles Times Book Review. June 23, 1996, p. 1.
The Nation. CCLXIII, July 8, 1996, p. 25.
The New Republic. CCXV, July 15, 1996, p. 29.
The New York Review of Books. XLIII, September 19, 1996, p. 61.
The New York Times Book Review. CI, June 9, 1996, p. 12.
Washington Monthly. XXVIII, July-August 1996, p. 46.
The Washington Post Book World. XXVI, June 2, 1996, p. 1.

THE LAST OF THE SAVAGES

Author: Jay McInerney (1956-   )
Publisher: Alfred A. Knopf (New York). 271 pp. $24.00
Type of work: Novel
Time: 1965-1995
Locale: Connecticut, Tennessee, Massachusetts, the Himalayas, Ecuador, Greece, New York, and London

Two young men from vastly different backgrounds form a friendship at prep school that endures in spite of the opposite directions their lives subsequently take

> *Principal characters:*
> PATRICK KEANE, a young man from a lower-middle-class background eager to enter the Ivy League and the world of wealth and privilege
> WILL SAVAGE, unwilling scion of an aristocratic Southern family impatient to leave his heritage far behind
> TALEESHA JOHNSON SAVAGE, Will's African American wife
> LOLLIE BAKER, occasional girlfriend of both Will and Patrick
> CORDELL SAVAGE, Will's powerful, strong-willed father
> ELBRIDGE SAVAGE, Will's wild older brother, killed in a car crash
> CHERYL DOBBS, Elbridge's fiancée, and later Cordell's wife

The Last of the Savages is an ambitious novel of historical sweep and manifold themes, suggestive of both F. Scott Fitzgerald and William Faulkner, which addresses issues as diverse as racial guilt, class differences, sexual repression, the 1960's, and the inescapability of the past. While greatly different in theme and scope from McInerney's first and best-known novel, *Bright Lights, Big City*, his fifth novel, like the first, explores the heart and soul of a young man striving to come to terms with his place in the world.

The novel flashes between past and present as Patrick Keane narrates the history of his friendship with prep school roommate Will Savage, which begins with their meeting in 1965 and extends over thirty years. United by their shared desire to put as much distance between themselves and their family heritage as possible, the two forge an unlikely alliance. Although their time together at school spans less than two years, the attachment proves intense enough to connect their lives in most intimate ways for years to come.

Patrick almost immediately becomes entranced with Will, who so carelessly embodies all the traits he has worked so hard to try to achieve, and fascinated by his family, whom he meets on visits to Bear Track, the Savages' Tennessee estate. Patrick even uses the diary of a Savage ancestor, which chronicles a supposed slave uprising on the family plantation, as the basis for his Ph.D. dissertation. He also develops a close relationship with Will's father, Cordell, filling in as the "good" son that Cordell never had.

Although Patrick and Will share a desire to flee their origins and fashion lives based on a denial of their history, the past they are escaping and the visions they are pursuing are altogether different. Patrick, the overachieving son of a New England appliance salesman, is running from a middle-class background, embarrassed by the same parents who have made it possible for him to aspire to the upper echelons of society. Striving to be accepted as an authentic "preppie," aping the dress and characteristics of those "to the manor born" in the hope that his humble origins will not betray him, Patrick desperately hopes he can avoid introducing his parents to his Ivy League classmates.

Will, on the other hand, was born into the aristocracy to which Patrick aspires, but has no interest in the traditional Ivy League education his family insists upon, reserving his passion for rhythm and blues music, and for running a "numbers" racket from their dorm room. Will goes out of his way to fly in the face of everything his family represents, cruising the Tennessee countryside in a cement mixer wearing a British soldier's uniform, and hanging out in black "juke joints." Harboring not only guilt for his slave-owning ancestors' lives and his own father's racist beliefs, he also feels responsible for the death of the younger brother who took his place at the last minute on a hunting trip that cost him his life, and later for the death of his brother Elbridge, who was driving Will's car when local authorities ran him off the road.

Will not only endeavors to disown and escape his history, however, he engages in a vendetta against his father, who, while repudiating Will, still understands this compulsion, as he explains to Patrick, "Didn't you sit down one day when you were a boy and disown your father in your heart?" Will entertains wild theories about Cordell's nefarious plots and business dealings, some of which may be true, while seeking ways to wound and destroy him, including sleeping with his second wife, Cheryl. This episode, however, precipitates a reevaluation of Will's motives and feelings toward his father, and he never reveals this betrayal, and even comes to Cordell's aid when his empire is being threatened.

Patrick sacrifices not only his family in pursuit of his vision, but his sexuality as well. His lackluster pursuit of women, lukewarm or confused response to their advances, and continued fascination with Will all point toward a dearth of heterosexual fervor and stronger sexual feelings submerged. When Will informs Patrick that he has lost his virginity to Lollie Baker, with whom Patrick has had some abortive romantic liaisons, he "was in no way prepared to entertain the possibility that it wasn't Will Savage I was jealous of, but Lollie Baker." Somewhat belatedly Patrick comes to recognize his sexual leanings, long after others have understood what he has been denying, but, except for three isolated instances, he suppresses these desires.

When Lollie Baker, who at the time is Patrick's date, is discovered in their dorm room near the end of their senior year at prep school, Will shoulders the blame while Patrick hides (both literally and symbolically) in the closet. This incident, which results in Will's expulsion, marks a turning point in their friendship. Although from this juncture their lives take decidedly divergent paths, their relationship has been cemented, and they will continue to turn to one another at crucial times in their lives. Will has demonstrated the depth of his feeling for Patrick (although he relishes the idea of getting kicked out of school) while Patrick feels forever indebted to, and connected with, Will.

Graduating with honors and advancing to Yale, Patrick continues to pursue his goal of being the perfect "preppie," even as this icon becomes an anachronism in the turbulent 1960's. Following a path that his contemporaries are beginning to desert in record numbers, Patrick realizes the world of convention and privilege he lusts after is becoming daily more irrelevant: "even I was beginning to suspect that the old order to which I wanted to pledge allegiance was crumbling." Even so, he attains all the trappings of success as he has always measured it: marriage to the daughter of a prominent judge, two beautiful children, and a flourishing and lucrative career in corporate law.

While Patrick pursues his predictable goals at Yale and Harvard Law, Will follows what Patrick refers to as the "greatest-hits-of-the-hippie-trail, " trekking to the Himalayas, Ecuador, and a remote Greek island. Upon his return to Tennessee, he forms his own talent management and production company, settling in Memphis and scouring the South for rhythm and blues acts to book. He falls in love with and marries Taleesha Johnson, a black singer, and begins a wildly successful career, during which he mingles with the aristocracy of rock and roll, appears in *Rolling Stone*, and is inducted into the Rock and Roll Hall of Fame. Eventually his out-of-control lifestyle, fueled by drugs and lavish spending, imperils both his business and his marriage, but with some help from Patrick, he ultimately salvages both.

Having finally achieved a rapprochement with Cordell, Will's major disappointment remains his inability to father a child. After Taleesha suffers three miscarriages, he becomes convinced that his excessive drug use has damaged his genes in some way, and asks Patrick to be the biological father of his child, thus "consummating" their lifelong relationship. As Patrick ponders their history, and the unborn child's future he wonders, "whether a child of two races might redeem the original sin of our heritage. Or whether, at least, he might be happier with who he is than we were."

Despite the diametrically opposed paths followed by each, in their forties Will and Patrick arrive at remarkably similar destinations. His drug problems behind him and his business on fairly solid ground, an overweight and balding Will has settled into middle age with Taleesha. Patrick, enjoying the social position and material success he worked and sacrificed for, is usually content, except in the spring, when "The fecund and portentous air . . . makes me restless and sad, germinating a sensation of regret, stirring an awareness of all the roads not taken and all the desires stifled as if under perpetual winter woolens."

Molding a life out of denial, Patrick philosophizes that "desires are infinite and insatiable; it is only by mastering them that we stand a chance at happiness," while Will, who pursued every urge and surrendered to every desire, winds up possibly no happier than Patrick. As Will suggests to Patrick, "Hell, maybe repression and conformity've made you happier than me. . . . Maybe I was wrong all along."

The key to the strength and endurance of Patrick and Will's unlikely friendship perhaps lies in the fact that each embodies qualities that the other lacks or gave up. As Patrick admits, his attachment to Will is the one eccentricity he allowed himself in an otherwise repressive existence: "Passing the midpoint of a lifetime of small triumphs and failures, of pursuing false idols and common virtues, I see that cleaving to Will was the single daring and unpredictable choice I allowed myself along the way. If this has been the story of Will's life, more than my own, that is because he has lived." Will, on the other hand, relies on more than one occasion upon Patrick's stability and responsibility to provide an anchor in his often chaotic and undisciplined life. Patrick not only bails him out of financial, legal and business difficulties, but even provides him with the means for obtaining a child, which his permissive and uncontrolled lifestyle has denied him.

The Last of the Savages is a characteristically American novel, reminiscent especially of *The Great Gatsby*, with Patrick playing Nick to Will's Gatsby, but also suggestive, in its Southern Gothic undertones, of William Faulkner. Overly ambitious, the novel tackles more themes than it can successfully handle, but is nevertheless entertaining and satisfying in the effort. Although occasionally straining credulity, the friendship between Patrick and Will provides a revealing mirror for the generation that came of age during the 1960's. Ironically, these two men, whose chosen paths through life could not be more different, discover that their midlife destinations are remarkably similar.

Despite the great sweep of the novel, its most memorable moments reside in its details. For example, McInerney's account of Cheryl Dobbs, the new Mrs. Cordell Savage, performing her baton twirling routine as after-dinner entertainment at her husband's elegant London dinner party, is both touching and hilarious, and the anecdote of Patrick inadvertently caught in a Gay Freedom Day parade on the way to discuss wedding plans with his fiancée is equally poignant. Replete with such moments, *The Last of the Savages*, while neither a great book, nor even McInerney's best, is nevertheless an engrossing, and often moving, novel.

Mary Virginia Davis

Sources for Further Study

The Atlantic. CCLXXVIII, July, 1996, p. 106.
Library Journal. CXXI, April 15, 1996, p. 123.
Los Angeles Times Book Review. June 9, 1996, p. 10.
The Nation. CCLXII, June 10, 1996, p. 30.
New Statesman and Society. IX, June 28, 1996, p. 45.
The New York Review of Books. XLIII, May 23, 1996, p. 28.
The New York Times Book Review. CI, May 26, 1996, p. 11.
Publishers Weekly. CCXLIII, April 8, 1996, p. 54.
Time. CXLVII, May 20, 1996, p. 76.
The Times Literary Supplement. June 14, 1996, p. 24.
The Wall Street Journal. May 9, 1996, p. A16.

LAST ORDERS

Author: Graham Swift (1949-   )
Publisher: Alfred A. Knopf (New York). 295 pp. $23.00
Type of work: Novel
Time: April 2, 1990, with numerous flashbacks over the last three generations
Locale: London and the county of Kent, England

A day trip by four drinking buddies to honor Jack Dodds's last request that his ashes be dumped off the Margate pier occasions a review of all their lives and reflections on the meaning of life and death generally

Principal characters:
JACK DODDS, a London butcher who dies of stomach cancer
AMY DODDS, his wife of fifty years
JUNE DODDS, their severely retarded daughter who is institutionalized
VINCE DODDS, their adoptive son, a slick auto dealer
MANDY DODDS, Vince's sexy wife
KATHY DODDS, Vince and Mandy's daughter
RAY JOHNSON, the Dodds' best friend, an insurance man
CAROL JOHNSON, Ray's wife who leaves him for another man
SUE JOHNSON, their daughter who leaves for Australia
LENNY TATE, another friend, a fruit-and-vegetable man
JOAN TATE, Lenny's wife
SALLY TATE, their daughter who is unlucky with men
VIC TUCKER, another friend, an undertaker
BERNIE SKINNER, the owner of the Coach and Horses pub

At first glance, Graham Swift's Booker Award-winning *Last Orders* seems a rather slight novel built around a plot gimmick: "four blokes on a special delivery." Their mission—to deliver Jack Dodds's ashes approximately seventy-five miles from London to Margate pier for disposal—is interrupted by "two detours, one fight, a piss-up and a near-wetting." The story sounds like good British fun, maybe material for a light made-for-television film, as the characters and setting tend to suggest. The characters are small shopkeepers from Bermondsey, a section of Southwark between London Bridge and Tower Bridge. These small shopkeepers hardly rank with the likes of Hamlet or James Bond, but they do promise some local color, particularly with their colloquial language (apparently a dressed-up relation of Cockney).

Readers get a taste of the Bermondsey patois in the novel's complex narration. The story is told from the first-person points of view of seven characters (mainly five, since two speak only once), in numerous segments varying in length from two words to a dozen pages, with many segments flashing back over time. The segments ranging over time are titled after the character speaking, while most segments in the present are titled after points along the route between Bermondsey and Margate, a faded seaside resort. The segments in the present and titled after locations are all narrated by Ray Johnson, an insurance man nicknamed "Lucky" and the closest to a central consciousness in the novel.

The narrators are characterized more by their individual obsessions and life histories than by their separate voices, though they do seem to differ in the extent to which they utilize the Bermondsey patois. The patois seems to come out most in Lenny Tate, the fruit-and-vegetable man, and least in the women, Amy Dodds and Mandy Dodds (originally from Lancashire), with Ray Johnson somewhere around the middle. The patois is distinguished not so much by occasional bad grammar as by vocabulary, slang terms such as "berk" (girl), "nosh" (food), and "piss-up" (pub stop). In any event, Swift seems to throw just enough of these in to give a local flavor rather than interfere with the reader's understanding. His balancing of concerns here—patois, individual voices, reader's understanding—requires a great deal of literary virtuosity, and the degree of his success could become a hot topic for endless literary debate.

Like the language, the many place names underscore the novel's local color angle. Some readers will enjoy this aspect of the novel, which evokes nostalgia for scenes of merry old England, such as hop-picking in Kent and pub-hopping all over. Tourists and geography buffs can savor the author's loving descriptions of such landmarks as Smithfield Market, the Sailors' Memorial at Chatham, and Canterbury Cathedral, and they can chart the progress of the journey with a detailed map. Yet fortunately for other readers, *Last Orders* is more than a novel with a plot gimmick and some local color. What it is, in fact, is a splendid example of the postmodern novel.

Like any good postmodern novel, *Last Orders* presents something of a minimalist surface, but its heart beats with the anxiety of influences. For this mode, Swift might be indebted to his compatriots, the playwrights Harold Pinter and Tom Stoppard. Yet the debts do not stop there. The most obvious model for *Last Orders*, both in subject and form, is William Faulkner's novel *As I Lay Dying* (1930). The punning title, referring to the last orders in a pub before closing time, recalls a similar motif in T. S. Eliot's definitive poem *The Waste Land* (1922): "HURRY UP PLEASE ITS TIME." Another influence might be James Joyce: A drinking song supplies the title for his novel *Finnegan's Wake* (1939), his masterpiece *Ulysses* (1922) takes place in one day, and everywhere Joyce celebrates the universal in the local (for Joyce, always Dublin).

For perhaps the most important literary echo in *Last Orders*, one has to dig back much further, to the father of English literature. The parallels between *Last Orders* and Geoffrey Chaucer's *The Canterbury Tales* (c. 1386-1400) are muted but nevertheless striking: both begin at an inn or pub in Southwark, involve a motley group of characters identified mainly by their occupations, and utilize the narrative framework of a pilgrimage into Kent, with individual tales and byplay inserted therein. But the huge difference between the two works, aside from time, is likewise striking. Chaucer's characters are on a religious pilgrimage to seek spiritual renewal at the shrine of St. Thomas à Becket in Canterbury. They are gathered together in a sacramental context that gives some of their tales the appearance of confessions. Swift's postmodern pilgrims also have a lot to confess, but no one seems to be listening (except the reader). They pass a lot of shrines and monuments along their way, but these have lost most of their meaning, except as landmarks or tourist meccas. The postmodern pilgrims are not too sure about the meaning of the pilgrimage itself, which has become only a day trip, a "turn-up," with the main no-show being the wife of fifty years. As in the work of the late British poet Philip Larkin, the sense of postmodern loss in *Last Orders* is both farcical and depressing.

Besides religion, another area of loss in *Last Orders* is personal relationships, where the affective content of marital and family ties has shrunk or dried up. For example, the marriage of Amy and Jack Dodds, begun with an exciting tumble in the hops and a resultant shotgun wedding, settles down into a dull and predictable fifty-year stand. He ought to know that women should be cultivated like gardens, but he turns out to be a real dud, despite his big jolly Englishman exterior. His severely limited philosophy, handed down from his butcher father, is shockingly revealed in a mere half-page segment toward the novel's end where he, the dead man, makes his only appearance as narrator: Avoid "wastage." Yet he is the one who, for fifty years, would not go and see his severely retarded, institutionalized daughter, and he is the one that all the other characters are making so much fuss about. As far as Amy is concerned, Jack was the no-show.

Other characters show similar results in their personal relationships. Ray Johnson's nickname "Lucky" is ironic, since his luck betting on the horses does not carry over to women: His wife left him for another man, and his daughter, who ran off to Sydney with an Australian, never writes him. Conversely, the daughters in the various families have troubles with men: They live in a diminished world where men really have only one thing on their minds. Vince, the only son shown, is one of those men; his values center around a glitzy life of sex, fancy cars, flashy clothes, and money. Ironically, however, his marriage to Mandy seems relatively happy, maybe because they are two of a kind. Their personal relationships suffer more in other directions: Mandy was a teenage runaway from home, Vince could never accept his role as an adoptive son, and he seems willing to pander his daughter for the sake of a big sale to rich Hussein, very likely a former British subject.

Yet if religion and relationships have shrunk like the empire, one thing in postmodern Britain still has the power to command attention, still has its sting: death. In Bermondsey, as elsewhere, the death of someone close inspires not only postmortems but also taking stock and reflection. As the characters in *Last Orders* look back over their lives, they mirror the universal human experience. Their lives are marked, inevitably, by failure, disappointment, and missed opportunities: Jack had ambitions to be a doctor, Lenny to be a prizefighter; Amy was seeking romance, Mandy the bright lights of London. They all had to settle for less, but, as Amy reflects, their missed opportunities are nothing compared to those of aborted fetuses or her severely retarded daughter June. Other characters recall the lives of soldiers and civilians snuffed out in World War II: Vic, who was in the Royal Navy, can remember the oily faces of whole shiploads of men floating in the ocean. Now, as an undertaker, he understands that death still has meaning in the postmodern world.

Gradually the other characters come to their understandings. Musing on Jack's death, they become more aware of the possibilities remaining in their own lives: Vince seems to reject pandering his daughter, Ray contemplates visiting his in Australia, and

Amy decides to leave hers and become her own woman. They also move closer together as family and friends. When Jack was alive, Vince was always breaking away from him; now that Jack is dead, Vince acknowledges their ties and is even emotional about them. Vince and Ray both look out after Amy. Despite their bickering and fighting on the trip to Margate, Ray, Vic, Lenny, and Vince still unite to get the job done. All of the men once served in the military—Jack, Ray, and Lenny against Rommel in North Africa, and Vince in colonial Aden—and this background helps to bond them ("last orders" can also refer to military orders). For the older men, especially, service in World War II was the one big event in their lives. Now as they march down the Margate pier, led by Vic, they adopt a military bearing. The final tableau of the four men standing against the raging sea to fling Jack's ashes to the wind pretty much sums up the novel.

Readers will also be impelled to reflect on the meaning of *Last Orders*. For example, the novel's emphasis on the local draws attention to the fact that, even in a world of mobility and mass communications, most people's lives are still defined by local circumstances. People tend to relate to a locality and their circle of family and friends in it. In Britain, the local pub, like the Coach and Horses in *Last Orders* (which "makes you think of a church"), still seems to be a powerful institution even in these postmodern times. Like all the monuments and literary works, the pub is a reminder of the continuity of British history stretching back some fifteen hundred years. Religion and relationships might be in decline and Britannia no longer rule the waves, but cries of "Carry on!" still ring through the meadhall.

Harold Branam

Sources for Further Study

The Economist. CCCXXXVIII, March 16, 1996, p. 14.
London Review of Books. XVIII, February 8, 1996, p. 20.
Los Angeles Times Book Review. July 7, 1996, p. 6.
New Statesman and Society. IX, January 19, 1996, p. 37.
The New York Review of Books. XLIII, April 4, 1996, p. 8.
The New York Times Book Review. CI, May 5, 1996, p. 13.
Publishers Weekly. CCXLIII, March 4, 1996, p. 53.
The Spectator. CCLXXV, January 27, 1996, p. 33.
The Times Literary Supplement. January 19, 1996, p. 25.
The Washington Post Book World. XXVI, April 7, 1996, p. 1.

THE LAST THING HE WANTED

Author: Joan Didion (1934-   )
Publisher: Alfred A. Knopf (New York). 227 pp. $23.00
Type of work: Novel
Time: 1984
Locale: The United States, Costa Rica, and an unidentified Caribbean island

A journalist covering the 1984 presidential campaign abruptly quits her assignment and visits her ill father in Florida, takes his place in running guns to the Nicaraguan contras, and inadvertently finds herself enmeshed in an international conspiracy from which she cannot escape

> *Principal characters:*
> ELENA MCMAHON, a reporter for *The Washington Post* who attempts to help her father retrieve payment for a lucrative munitions contract
> DICK MCMAHON, her father, who does business deals that remain vague to his family and who is most likely a CIA operative
> TREAT MORRISON, an ambassador-at-large for the United States who is sent to a Caribbean island to investigate Elena McMahon, with whom he has a relationship
> THE ANONYMOUS NARRATOR, who distantly knows Elena, interviews Treat Morrison, and researches Elena's demise
> MAX EPPERSON (alias BOB WEIR), Dick McMahon's business partner and sinister manipulator of people and events
> WYNN JANKLOW, Elena's former husband, a wealthy oil magnate and Hollywood power broker

The novel opens with the unnamed narrator attempting to recall the events of 1984 and introduces the reader to Elena McMahon, a middle-aged woman who has a history of abrupt career changes and personal redefinitions. This pattern first becomes evident in 1964 when McMahon loses her scholarship to the University of Nevada "and within a week invented herself as a reporter for the Los Angeles *Herald Examiner*." When she meets her future husband four years later, she reinvents herself into his wife.

Soon she becomes one of the pampered, beautiful Los Angelenos, giving and attending parties, being seen by the right people, and raising her only child. After cancer surgery, Elena reinvents herself again, leaving her husband and taking their daughter east. She later secures a job with *The Washington Post* covering the 1984 presidential campaign, only to drop that job abruptly and search out her estranged father in Florida. The common thread in each of these personal shifts is the absence of cause and effect logic; whim and capriciousness move Elena among the various stages of her life.

Her father assures Elena that his big score is imminent, and when he falls ill she takes his place accompanying a shipment of arms to Costa Rica and then relocates to a Caribbean island in hopes of collecting her father's fee, Soon she fears she is involved in something sinister, learns her father has died, and warns her former husband that he must take their daughter and hide in California. With an altered passport she cannot return home easily; she takes a job as a social director in a hotel meets Treat Morrison, and is eventually assassinated on the beach.

In this novel, Didion explores the hidden world behind the political looking-glass, the world of conspiracies, assassinations, and quasi-military operations. The immediate context is the Iran-Contra arms affair, but Didion takes aim at a larger target. In the broadest sense, she attempts to uncover the clandestine machinations of governments and their agents who speak the language of liberation but operate for dollars and power and at the expense of average citizens such as Elena McMahon, who in spite of her intelligence is overwhelmed by forces she should have recognized as threatening from the beginning.

Readers of Didion's four earlier novels will recognize distinct similarities between Elena McMahon and the protagonists of those works. In many ways, she is the typical Didion heroine—edgy, spontaneous, and emotionally bruised. Like Maria Wyeth in *Play It As It Lays* (1970), Elena McMahon has seen into the heart of her own darkness and struggles to find some meaning in her life. Both women are accused of being selfish and willful by those closest to them, and both are deeply alienated from everything and everyone, especially their families and their past.

In *The Last Thing He Wanted*, however, this sense of alienation has been transformed into an anomie induced by a crumbling social facade. In all of Didion's books, there is an exacting anatomization of the unravelings of the social tapestry. This novel illustrates an important change that began with *A Book of Common Prayer* (1977) and continued with *Democracy* (1984)—the nexus between the private and the political experiences. In her earlier novels, Didion's concern was with the personal and how an individual survived humiliation and a callous world, but the later works have another focus—how the personal slides into or is absorbed by political machinations.

The Last Thing He Wanted reveals an unfortunate change in Didion's treatment of characters. The supporting cast is uniformly two-dimensional; these are less personages than personality types, and their colors bleed into one another and become indistinguishable. Indeed, the villains—Bob Weir, a nameless Salvadoran, and Wynn Janklow—are threatening or despicable to one degree or another, but they are not memorable. They are simply stock figures marched out to add variety and atmosphere.

Didion has often been praised as a writer keenly attuned to the sound of an individual voice, and her renderings of dialogue are typically precise and telling. Once again, *Play It As It Lays* is an illustrative case in point, with its multiple narrators telling that story. Maria's voice is separate from those of Carter, BZ, and Helene, and the reader cannot mistake one for another. In *The Last Thing He Wanted*, figures from various walks of life are given their moments in the narrative—ambassadors, smugglers, journalists, teenagers, and deal makers, among others—and each is presented in the idiom of his or her occupation or station. Initially it appears that distinct linguistic patterns will distinguish, identify, and define personality, but they do not. Instead, the voices blend, the argots lose their distinct textures, and each begins to sound like an outsider trying to imitate a voice that is simply not convincing. Perhaps the point that Didion wishes to demonstrate is the ways in which the rhetoric of political evasion and dissimulation invade everyday lives so thoroughly as to corrupt the ability to find and maintain originality. Yet if this is the novel's objective, then the narrator must possess a compelling individual voice to reveal the ways in which the language and thinking of others have become coopted by political double-talk.

The narrator is also a curious figure, a strong presence who announces herself frequently and shifts attention from the protagonist to the consciousness through which the novel's events are filtered. The narrator is a casual acquaintance of Elena McMahon's from their California days, and like Elena, she, too, is a journalist, engaged in interviewing Treat Morrison when she happens on the story behind the story and searches through public documents to unravel Elena's fate. The impression is that the reader stands at only a slight remove from actual historical events, events that one has heard and read about but until now only dimly understood. In effect, the journalist-narrator gives readers a glimpse not of President Ronald Reagan or Oliver North but of the secret players behind those notorious public events.

The self-consciousness of the narrator is overwhelming—she literally labors over every narrative decision, weighing possibilities, rejecting alternatives, and selecting judiciously. Her opening remarks of the second chapter are particularly telling:

> For the record this is me talking. You know me, or think you do.
> The not quite omniscient author.
> No longer moving fast,
> No longer traveling light.
> When I resolved in 1994 to finally tell this story, register the clues I had missed ten years before, process the information before it vanished altogether, I considered reinventing myself as PAO at the embassy in question, a career foreign service officer operating under the USICA umbrella. "Lilianne Owen" was my name in that construct, a strategy I ultimately jettisoned as limiting, small-scale, an artifice to no point. *She told me later*, Lilianne Owen would have had to keep saying, and I *learned this after the fact*. As Lilianne Owen I was unconvincing even to myself. As Lilianne Owen I could not have told you half of what I knew.
> I wanted to come at this straight,
> I wanted to bring my own baggage and unpack it in front of you.

The passage works in complex, even contradictory ways. On the one hand, it is an undeniably ironic remark from author to reader, in which Didion responds to the complaint that it is she speaking in each of her novels and not a narrative invention. The audience may *think* it knows the narrator (as a thinly veiled version of the author), but it does not. One the other hand, the narrator informs the audience that she is anything other than omniscient, but instead is someone who is searching for the truth.

Later, when trying to locate the exact event that triggered the unlikely events that follow, the narrator announces a series of beginnings for her story, each plausible and each revealing. The effect of all the self-scrutiny of method and approach, the role of the narrator as purveyor and arranger of information, and the constant asides and direct invocations of the audience is to give a distinctly postmodern veneer to the narrative. This is as much a story about Elena McMahon and, to a lesser extent, Treat Morrison, as it is a story about fictions themselves and the craft of fiction-making.

When reading anything by Didion, one can never forget that she is a consummate stylist, a writer who has crafted not only a distinct vision but also a style that is taut and highly distinctive. Once again the minimalist approach that one associates with *Play It As It Lays* characterizes this novel. There are numerous brief chapters, elliptical passages and scenes, and a prose that is sparse and tense. In one of her essays, Didion comments that in writing *Play It As It Lays* she wanted to create "a novel so fast that it would scarcely exist on the page at all." It would be a novel as much about characters, as about images and the most compelling of these was "Empty space. This was clearly the picture that dictated the narrative intention of the book—a book in which anything that happened would happen off the page, a 'white' book to which the reader would have to bring his or her own bad dreams."

There is, then, a nervous energy to that novel the sense that vacancy on the page reflects the sense of vacancy in the protagonist, an emptiness she tries desperately to fill with only the fragments of an existence. In *The Last Thing He Wanted*, however, the thematic connection between narrative gaps and holes in the personalities of the characters is replaced by purely self-conscious prose, what one reviewer aptly described as an "anxious discipline of style" for its own sake. The rich intricacies of exposition are often replaced with annoying mannerisms, such as the frequent use of repetitions that draw more attention to their repetitiveness than to the circularity of event that they presumably are meant to evince.

Didion is working in the fictional territory often associated with Graham Greene. While *The Last Thing He Wanted* has moments of tension and drama, it lacks the probing moral questioning of Greene's work and the sense of truly hidden dangers that huddle behind the appearances of things. With *The Last Thing He Wanted*, there is little genuine suspense, and besides some obvious political adventures, the novel seems in search of a compelling human center.

David W. Madden

Sources for Further Study

Commentary. CII, October, 1996, p. 70.
Los Angeles Times Book Review. August 25, 1996, p. 2.
The Nation. CCLXIII, September 30, 1996, p. 23.
National Review. XLVIII, November 11, 1996, p. 57.
The New Republic. CCXV, October 14, 1996, p. 44.
New York. XXIX, September 2, 1996, p. 28.
The New York Review of Books. XLIII, October 31, 1996, p. 4.
The New York Times Book Review. CI, September 8, 1996, p. 10.
The New Yorker. LXXII, June 24, 1996, p. 118.
Time. CXLVIII, September 9, 1996, p. 69.
The Wall Street Journal. August 29, 1996, p. A8.

THE LAWS OF OUR FATHERS

Author: Scott Turow (1949-   )
Publisher: Farrar Straus Giroux (New York). 534 pp. $26.95
Type of work: Novel
Time: 1969-1970 and September 7, 1995-September 7, 1996
Locale: Kindle County, a fictional location

A murder trial in the 1990's reawakens relationships and conflicts from the 1960's

Principal characters:
SONIA "SONNY" KLONSKY, a judge
SETH WEISSMAN, a journalist and Sonny's sometime lover
HOBIE TUTTLE, a lawyer
LOYELL EDDGAR, a 1960's activist turned 1990's politician
JUNE EDDGAR, Loyell's wife, ultimately his former wife
NILE EDDGAR, their son, on trial for the murder of his mother
LUCY, Seth's wife, formerly Hobie's lover
HARDCORE, a top-ranking member of a street gang
LOVINIA, a gang member also known by the nickname "Bug"
TOMMY MOLTO, a prosecutor

A practicing attorney and former federal prosecutor, Scott Turow made his debut as a writer of fiction in 1987, and established himself at once on the best-seller list, with *Presumed Innocent*, as slick and stylish a suspense novel as any published in the 1980's. His second novel, *Burden of Proof* (1990) confirmed its author's status as a writer of best-sellers, while marking a slight but discernible change in direction. Compared to the earlier novel, *Burden of Proof* was less ingeniously plotted and, for better or worse, more concerned with the emotional lives of its principal characters. Some critics felt that this change did not exploit Turow's most impressive gifts and that the characters did not justify in vitality or complexity the attention Turow devoted to them. Still, the novel enjoyed brisk sales and seemed, whatever its shortcomings, to confirm Turow's place as one of the preeminent practitioners of the legal thriller, itself a genre of growing popularity in the 1980's and 1990's.

The Laws of Our Fathers will certainly not dislodge Turow from that place. Almost from the moment of its publication, it appeared on the nation's best-seller lists; it was for the most part favorably, in some cases enthusiastically, reviewed; and, at least in its subject matter, it seems clearly an example of the genre with which Turow has become associated. Yet, once again, Turow seems unwilling to settle for repeating past accomplishments. Even more than in *Burden of Proof*, Turow seems determined in *The Laws of Our Fathers* to transcend the genre to which his book at one level clearly belongs and to narrow if not obliterate the gap commonly supposed to exist between genre fiction and serious literature. The effort may be applauded or deplored in itself. The immediate critical question must be whether the author has succeeded in it, and, regrettably, the answer must be negative. If the question becomes whether the author has written a best-seller, on the other hand, the answer is quite different.

The organizing action of *The Laws of Our Fathers* is, as in most legal thrillers, a trial. June Eddgar, a middle-class white woman of about sixty, has been shot to death in an overwhelmingly black housing project, which is also notoriously a center of gang activity and of drug dealing. The first mystery is what she was doing there. She was, it turns out, the former wife of Loyell Eddgar, a state senator known for his avowal of liberal causes. As the case unfolds, it begins to seem that she was the victim by accident. It was Eddgar himself who was supposed to die on the morning of September 7, 1996. According to the theory developed by the prosecutors assigned to the case, the murder was planned by Nile Eddgar, the son of the intended and of the actual victim.

Presiding in the case is Judge Sonia "Sonny" Klonsky. (Readers of *Burden of Proof* will recognize her as a character first encountered in that novel.) Her situation is complicated by the knowledge that in the late 1960's, Sonny was acquainted with all three of the Eddgars. At that time, Nile was a child, while his parents were committed activists in the cause of revolution. Sonny recognizes that this may indicate she ought to recuse herself, but neither the prosecution nor the defense seems to have any problems with it, and Sonny's own scruples are not strong enough to compel her to act on them.

Further complications for Sonny arise when she realizes she recognizes the attorney for the defense. He is Hobie Tuttle, another acquaintance from Sonny's past life as some kind of 1960's radical, the kind whose radicalism seems curiously wanting in specific content. Hobie, a black man, went through a black separatist phase in those days and was somehow involved in far left political activities. Once again, however, Sonny finds in this situation no adequate reason for withdrawing from the case.

Seth Weissman is not a principal in the case before her, but he too represents problems for Sonny. He is in regular attendance at the trial, and he seems connected, in ways that Sonny tries to figure out, with Hobie. Seth and Hobie, Sonny knows, have been friends since boyhood, but she is not quite sure how Seth fits into the present set of circumstances. It is true that, as Nile's former babysitter, Seth would take an interest in the trial, but what most concerns Sonny is that Seth is not merely Nile's former babysitter; he is also Sonny's former lover. Sonny has a few bad moments with this, but they are not enough to force her off the case, even though she more than once suspects that Hobie and Seth are somehow in league against her.

Seth is on Sonny's mind, not only because of their past relationship but also because, with the kind of sappy single-mindedness usually associated with hormonally driven adolescents, her middle-aged and balding former lover insists on forcing his attentions on her. His marriage to Lucy, another survivor of the old days and the former lover of Hobie, is on the rocks, he tells Sonny. Sonny realizes that, given what is fast becoming a ludicrous network of old acquaintances, she, as the judge in Nile's murder trial, should have little to do with Seth, at least while the trial is underway. Again, however, Sonny finds that such considerations need not be taken too seriously. She is soon inviting Seth to her home to meet the daughter she had with a husband who is now out of the picture, and, not long after, she is joining Seth in his bed. This last event occurs when Sonny, disturbed after an encounter in a hotel dining room with some unsavory politicians, feels the need for someone to talk to and remembers that, by the happiest and most amusing of coincidences, Seth is staying in that very hotel. The marijuana they smoke no doubt contributes to the outcome.

Keeping all this straight might be difficult for Judge Klonsky under any circumstances, but she needs to keep her wits about her even more than usually in this case. Pretrial publicity has made it unlikely that a jury could give Nile a fair trial. As a result, judge and counsel have agreed to a bench trial, that is, a trial in which the judge will assume the responsibility of reaching a verdict of guilty or not guilty. To be sure, Sonny suspects that she may have been tricked into this position, perhaps by Hobie, possibly with an assist from Seth, but she goes ahead anyway.

This may read like the summary of a comic novel about the misadventures of a singularly clueless judge, but the sad truth is that, for all the virtues that have led to his popular success, Turow has nowhere in his fiction revealed the slightest trace of a comic sense. Not only does the novel seem to take Judge Sonny seriously, readers must regard her with respect if the story at whose center she has been placed is to engage their intellectual interest, emotional involvement, or imaginative commitment.

Of course, readers looking for a lively potboiler may not be disturbed by any of this. Absurd as it all may be, anything that sets the pot to boiling may be deemed acceptable. Unfortunately, this pot never boils, because the author seems to have higher things on his mind. Through the central situation of the novel and the tangled relationships that situation entails, Turow embarks on an exploration of the 1960's as perceived from the perspective of the 1990's. Chapters set in the present are juxtaposed with chapters set in the past. This arrangement virtually rules out anything in the way of the kind of narrative momentum that might encourage a reader to overlook the shakiness of the novel's premises. It does not help that the shifts from present to past and back again are never more than mechanically motivated. The author's way is to bring the narrative to some sort of climactic moment, rendered for the most part in painfully melodramatic writing, and then to jump to another time frame. It is all supposed to keep the reader in a state of excruciating suspense, but what it amounts to is sliced narrative.

The portrayal of the 1960's includes most of the expected ingredients: demonstrations, drugs, bombs, orgies. There are a few references, also expected, to actual events such as the Kent State killings and, slightly disguised, the kidnapping of Patty Hearst. Each character is placed in a prefabricated slot and made to say pretty much what the slot demands. Beyond this, whatever insight into the period one might have hoped for is sacrificed to plot. On the other hand, it must be admitted that, whatever its unfortunate consequences for the author's more high-minded ambitions, the central plot device in this portion of the novel, an elaborate kidnapping scam, provides the book with some of its liveliest moments and reminds the reader in its controlled twistiness of Turow in better days.

The juxtaposition of past and present serves yet another thematic function, as it foregrounds not only the contrast between periods but also the conflict between generations. If Sonny is the protagonist of those segments of the novel set in the 1990's, Seth assumes that role for the segments set in the 1960's. He is at the center of the kidnapping scheme, and, as that scheme unfolds, it throws into sharp relief Seth's troubled relationship with his parents, both survivors of the Holocaust. Yet this is only one instance of generational conflict. Both in the 1960's and in the 1990's, Sonny is trying to come to terms with her radical and erratic mother, Zora. At the same time, the struggle between parents and children is at the heart of the case being tried in Sonny's courtroom.

Unfortunately, this thematic thread never achieves full narrative realization. A number of elements contribute to this failure, but the principal one is the novel's descent into sentimentality. Ultimately, things must be made right between the generations, at least for those principal characters whose side the novel is on. Father and mother must finally be honored. First, parenthood itself must be reaffirmed. Sonny becomes aware that the greatest tragedy is that of Hardcore and Lovinia, ghetto dwellers who do not know what it is to have parents. She also recognizes the gap in her life that has resulted from her never having known her father; she is, in one of the last of her self-definitions, half an orphan. Having mourned his mother, Seth must, before this novel is through with him, eulogize his father. Finally, the relationship between Sonny and her daughter Nikki is sentimentalized, while that between Seth and his daughter Sarah is idealized. The novel ends with an affirmation of continuity and tradition, of the laws of our fathers, that remains unearned.

There are thrillers. There are novels. There are best-sellers. The three categories obviously overlap, but they suggest possibly useful distinctions. *The Law of Our Fathers* is too sluggish in its narrative to succeed as a thriller. It never makes the serious commitment to an honest exploration of the human condition that marks the authentic novel. Yet it cannily combines sprawl and neatness, offering a large cast of characters, a generous sampling of big issues, and what publishers' blurbs like to call a sweeping historical panorama, then meticulously and mechanically making everything fit together. The result is history without mystery. The book's ultimate capitulation to received values, moreover, guarantees that it will not disturb the middlebrow reader for whom it seems to be aiming. There is no doubt about it. Scott Turow has written another best-seller.

W. P. Kenney

Sources for Further Study

Chicago Daily Law Bulletin. October 8, 1996, p. 2.
Chicago Tribune. October 13, 1996, XIV, p. 1.
Legal Times. November 4, 1996, p. 66.
Los Angeles Times Book Review. October 20, 1996, p. 1.
The National Law Journal. September 9, 1996, p. A1.
The New York Times Book Review. CI, October 13, 1996, p. 10.
The Wall Street Journal. October 15, 1996, p. A20.
The Washington Post Book World. XXVI, October 13, 1996, p. 3.

LEAVING A DOLL'S HOUSE
A Memoir

Author: Claire Bloom (1931-   )
Publisher: Little Brown (New York). 251 pp. $23.95
Type of work: Memoir
Time: 1931 to 1996
Locale: London and New York City

Bloom writes a searing and self-critical account of her life and career, surely one of the most candid and painful revelations of an ambitious, needy, and sensitive artist

Principal personages:
CLAIRE BLOOM, the British-born stage and film actress
EDWARD BLOOM, her father
ELIZABETH BLOOM, her mother
CHARLIE CHAPLIN, the world-renowned comic genius who made
    Bloom's film debut possible
RICHARD BURTON, her first lover
ROD STEIGER, her first husband
HILLARD ELKINS, her second husband
PHILIP ROTH, her third husband
ANNA JUSTINE STEIGER, her daughter

In film history, Claire Bloom will be remembered as the vibrant young star of one of Charlie Chaplin's greatest works, *Limelight* (1952). On the stage, she appeared in historic revivals of Henrik Ibsen's *A Doll's House* and Tennessee Williams' *A Streetcar Named Desire*. In television, she scored a brilliant success in the adaptation of Evelyn Waugh's masterpiece, *Brideshead Revisited*. Although she acknowledges that her career has had its ups and downs—an unevenness that plagues most actors and actresses who are at the mercy of fashion, producers, and a range of factors beyond their control—Bloom has had an extraordinary success in London and in New York, the two cities where she has spent most of her life. Her triumphs, however, have been darkened by a personality that is both vulnerable and tenacious. She has been willing to sacrifice nearly everything—including her daughter—to please a man, yet she seems never to have stopped working, and never to have stopped trying to reconcile her personal needs with her obligations as a mother and wife. Bloom calls herself a passive personality, yet she also recognizes the strength of her resilience and her desire to break out of self-destructive patterns.

Bloom has written a book that is remarkably without vanity, the common evil in autobiographical accounts of artist's lives. Her writing seems an effort to take control of her life by admitting her weaknesses as well as assessing the power that has pulled her through innumerable crises. As her title suggests, she is rather like Nora, the character she played in an important revival of Ibsen's classic play. At the beginning of that drama, Nora seems passive, childish, and all too willing to please and appease her dictatorial and pompous husband. She allows herself to become a plaything of the male sex—a walking and talking doll. Yet her husband's need for such an infantile mate eventually suggests to Nora that she has been stronger than she realized. It has been her job to maintain her husband's fantasy of a what a woman, a wife, and a mother should be. When Nora realizes how much cunning it has taken to live this "role," she is released to lead her own. She walks out of the doll's house determined to live her own life, which is exactly where Bloom leaves her readers at the end of her book—a woman in her mid-sixties determined to take possession of her own life.

Yet what made Bloom a Nora for so many years? She explains in ruthless chronological fashion, starting in her first sentence with the announcement that she was born on February 15, 1931. This simple declaration is a dramatic one for an actress, since aging is exactly what most actresses still worry about, dreading the onset of their middle years when a career usually sags, if it is not ended because of the scarcity of roles for women who are neither young nor yet old.

By announcing the year of her birth, Bloom is implying she was a child of the worldwide economic depression and of World War II. Both of those events instilled great fear and courage in people of her generation. Like many others, Bloom endured but was scarred by traumatic family and world history. In her case, she grew up in an Eastern European Jewish family that grimly but triumphantly adapted to the rigid English class system. She had a supportive mother and aunt who recognized early that Bloom had extraordinary talent. At the same time, Bloom saw herself and her mother at the mercy of a wayward, feckless father, who never could seem to make a living and who deserted the family for another life abroad. Bloom suggests that much of her later experience with men has to do with her father and her fear of abandonment. During the war, she was separated from her father and her native land and lived, like many other British children, in the United States. It was a bitter experience, for her American relatives treated her and her mother as ungrateful burdens.

Although a strong woman, Bloom's mother, Elizabeth (called Alice by her family,) put up with her errant husband and hectoring American relatives, desperately clinging to the semblance of a family life and stability for her talented daughter. Bloom herself sublimated much of her grief and insecurity in acting, finding that fashioning roles gave her confidence and put her in touch with herself in a way that her family and society could not provide.

Yet the terrifying lesson that Bloom seemed to learn was that no matter how strong she might be, the world—and specifically men—could undermine, if not destroy, her sense of security and accomplishment. In what amounts to a classically Freudian story, Bloom turned again and again to powerful men who became substitute father figures, often lovers, and then destroyers of her peace of mind—as if she wanted to reenact the truths of her childhood.

Bloom has nothing but praise for Charlie Chaplin, who always behaved like a gentleman but who worked her to the bone to produce her riveting performance as a young dancer in *Limelight*. Although Chaplin was notorious for seducing young girls, Bloom met him when he was happily married to his young wife, Oona O'Neill. As a result, Chaplin felt free to father Bloom's talent in a strictly fatherly way. Bloom reciprocated by idolizing Chaplin and aping every gesture he provided for her role.

He was, in essence, her ventriloquist. Bloom is proud of her performance, but as a mature woman she recognizes it came at the price of an almost total compliance to her director's wishes.

Bloom's first lover, Richard Burton, had the talent that Bloom's father lacked, but otherwise offered another version of the unpredictable males who would rule her life. Burton was married and a father. He never led Bloom to believe that he would divorce his wife. On one remarkable train journey, he left his wife's compartment and went to an adjoining one to make love to Bloom. Captivated by a man who was the most exciting and accomplished actor of his generation, Bloom also had a need to abase herself and to again select a man, like her father, who would prove ultimately unavailable and abandon her. Abandonment, Blooms confesses, has always been her worst fear, and yet she has pursued precisely those men who have confirmed it.

Rod Steiger seemed an antidote to Bloom's self-destructive pattern. Although he specialized in intense roles in films such as *On the Waterfront* (1954) and *The Pawnbroker* (1965), he was a gentle, caring man. Bloom experienced considerable calm and stability during their marriage. After she became a mother, however, he wanted her to subordinate her ambition, to turn down roles that would mean she would travel and be absent from home. When he left home to star in a film abroad, he left her in the hands of Hillard Elkins, a womanizing producer. Steiger seemed to invite his wife to have an affair, and she complied, attracted to a man who glorified her talent and later, as her husband/producer, got her the role of Nora. Elkins succeeded where other producers had failed. He also took Bloom to the very edge of sexual experimentation—a thrilling but dangerous period for Bloom that caused her to neglect her precocious, talented daughter.

Again, fulfilling the pattern, Elkins left Bloom just as she was becoming interested in the writer Philip Roth. Roth seemed to offer everything—genius, sensitivity, and a powerful sexual attractiveness. From the beginning, however, he scared Bloom. His critical eye was unnerving. He took the measure of people mercilessly. He told the dying writer Bernard Malamud that his last work was no good. He told Bloom she felt guilty about her daughter and that her efforts to appease Anna were destroying their romantic life. Then Roth went through a harrowing series of mental breakdowns— some of them perhaps induced by the medication used to control his depression. According to Bloom, Roth eventually came to demonize her, making her responsible for his increasing paranoia. He also hid from her his involvements with other women, and then blatantly confronted her with them when he gave her the manuscript of *Deception* (1990), in which the boring wife of the main character (based on Roth himself) is called Claire.

Bloom finally drew the line, making Roth omit her name. Yet because of his mental breakdowns she felt unable to stand up to him. Her fatal passivity, however, only made Roth more contemptuous and manipulative, proving in Bloom's view, that he had an overwhelming fear of being dominated by women, of loving them and allowing them to take over his life. Roth even confesses, at his lowest point, to suicidal feelings and his fear that Bloom will abandon him. Yet it is this fear that makes him hostile to her, because he hates to acknowledge that he is so needy. In Roth, Bloom found her ultimate male counterpart.

Bloom has been criticized for these revelations about Roth, and her memoir has been taken as a vendetta against him. Bloom does not hide her anger and disappointment. She and Roth shared a life for eighteen years, and she believes that most of it was lived on his terms. Yet she is honest enough to reveal what the relationship must have seemed like to Roth, a man of fixed, even rigid habits, who had to write every day and who was upset by any variation in routine. He hated Bloom's worries about her daughter, and he was upset because he realized his stepdaughter criticized him. Like many writers, he was incredibly selfish. Nothing ultimately mattered except his work. This should not have surprised Bloom—nor did it really, except that she kept hoping he could be just a little more flexible.

It is hard to see how the Bloom-Roth marriage could have survived. Had Bloom been more independent, Roth would have left her anyway. Her passivity and caving into his demands did not work either, because it undoubtedly created guilt in Roth, a guilt that made him mad, even though she was giving him exactly what he said he wanted. Naturally Roth appears as a monster in Bloom's account. He felt cornered by his need for her; as she fed that need, he became more upset. She did everything to please him, and he was not pleased. Like Nora, she had to belittle herself, but by belittling herself she earned her husband's contempt.

What saves Bloom's book from being a diatribe against Roth and the other men in her life is her self-scrutiny. She realizes that she brought much of her suffering upon herself. She also acknowledges that all of the men in her life gave her much joy and often advanced her career. Roth, for example, helped her hone dramatic readings and gave her a feeling for character development that enhanced her performances.

Like all retrospective accounts, Bloom's can seem wise after the fact. She analyzes her mistakes, sees the pattern of error, and strives to overcome it. What makes her writing most effective, however, is the way she ends her book. In a final meeting with Roth, she has him offer a reconciliation, a chance to start all over again. She leaps at it, then confesses that she has written a fantasy. There was no offer of reconciliation, no chance to begin again. Yet that fantasy, Bloom grimly admits, is still a part of her. She has not left the doll's house: rather, she is leaving it, and as with Nora, Bloom's audience wonders, as she does, what the rest of her life will become.

Carl Rollyson

Sources for Further Study

Boston Globe. October 22, 1996, p. D1.
Chicago Tribune. October 20, 1996, XIV, p. 3.
Los Angeles Times Book Review. October 13, 1996, p. 3.
The New York Times Book Review. CI, October 13, 1996, p. 7.
The Times Literary Supplement. October 25, 1996, p. 31.
The Washington Post Book World. XXVI, October 20, 1996, p. 3.

LIFE AS WE KNOW IT
A Father, a Family, and an Exceptional Child

Author: Michael Bérubé (1961-   )
Publisher: Pantheon Books (New York). 284 pp. $24.00
Type of work: Memoir

The birth of his son Jamie in 1991 caused Bérubé to write this compelling and detailed account of rearing a Down syndrome child

Principal personages:
JAMES LYON "JAMIE" BÉRUBÉ, a Down syndrome child
MICHAEL BÉRUBÉ, his father, a professor of English
JANET LYON, his mother, a registered nurse and professor of English
NICHOLAS "NICK" BÉRUBÉ, his brother, some five years Jamie's senior
ANNE and MAURICE BÉRUBÉ, Jamie's paternal grandparents
BUD and SARAH LYON, Janet Lyon's brother and his wife

Virtually every page of *Life as We Know It: A Father, a Family, and an Exceptional Child* resonates with love as a brilliant, sensitive, well-educated father of a Down syndrome child writes a book for the express purpose of representing the interests of a child who cannot, and perhaps never will be able to, represent himself adequately. The ethical base from which Michael Bérubé, a celebrated figure in critical theory and a political activist in much of his writing, works will be immediately apparent to anyone who reads this admirable account of coping with heartbreak and conquering it through love.

A great deal of the book is a personal memoir about the aftermath of James Lyon Bérubé's birth in September, 1991. The delivery was difficult. The newborn, its umbilical cord wrapped around its neck, was purple from oxygen deprivation. A nurse attending the birth remarked that the baby looked "downsy" around the eyes.

Once the umbilical cord was cut and oxygen administered, the baby's color improved. Jamie came back to life, but he did not cry. Both parents instantly faced the possibility of losing the child, whose heart was defective and who had no sucking reflex, making it impossible for him to nurse. This difficulty was exacerbated by a twenty-degree bend in the baby's neck.

Michael and Janet's older son, Nick, at five was a uniquely gifted child who had followed the course of his mother's pregnancy with considerable interest. When the sonogram revealed that the fetus was a boy, Nick was excited at the prospect of having a brother. He had awaited the day of his brother's birth with happy anticipation. Now Michael, still reverberating from the shock of becoming the father of a Down syndrome baby, had to fetch Nick from a friend's house and tell him that his brother was not quite what Nick had anticipated.

Sandwiched into the poignant but never sentimental details of Bérubé's personal memoir is considerable information about the causes and history of Down syndrome, chromosomal information to which the parents of most Down syndrome babies are exposed almost immediately after the birth of a child with this condition. Bérubé also intermixes considerable literary reference and philosophical insight with the purely personal parts of his narrative.

Trained in English, it is not surprising that Bérubé addresses some linguistic concerns relevant to Down syndrome. He writes, "words and phrases are the devices by which we beings signify what homosexuality, or Down syndrome, or anything else, will mean. There surely were, and are, the most intimate possible relationships between the language in which we spoke of Down syndrome and the social practices by which we understood it—and refused to understand it." That this condition was for years called "mongoloid idiocy" bestowed an immediate, and quite unfair, stigma upon the condition.

What followed from such a designation was draconian medical advice given gratuitously and universally to the parents of Down babies. Most of them were told that there was little hope for their child and that institutionalization was the most sensible course to follow. Parents were also advised not to grow too attached to their Down babies, whose life expectancy was extremely limited.

As Bérubé points out, the predictions traditionally given to parents of Down babies, themselves severely stressed at the shock of having a newborn with this condition, were self-fulfilling. If a Down baby—or, for that matter, any baby—is isolated from its parents and put into a facility ill-equipped to give it either the care or intellectual stimulation it should be receiving, the result will be a child whose development is severely limited. If medical intervention is not available when sleep apnea or other emergencies threaten such children's lives, obviously their life spans will be abbreviated considerably.

Michael Bérubé and Janet Lyon never considered committing Jamie to an institution, although, because of the specialized care he needed initially, they did have to leave him in the hospital's intensive care unit (ICU) for three weeks after his birth. This was a considerable deprivation.

Because the baby was hooked up to tubes through which he was nourished and given oxygen, neither parent could hold him and nurture him in the way the parents of newborns usually do. Bonding in the traditional sense was delayed. The parents and Nick had to settle for visiting Jamie regularly, talking to him, and hoping that the outflowing of love they felt for him would in some way be communicated to a child whose life support system was more mechanical than human.

Besides dealing with their own adjustments to living with and caring for a Down child, Michael and Janet had to deal with how Nick, sensitive and superintelligent, would react to the situation. Hospital rules forbade Nick from seeing his brother in the ICU, a rule his parents succeeded in having waived because they realized it was necessary for Nick to grow used to Jamie. Ultimately, with the promise that Nick would scrub before his visits, as his parents and other visitors were required to do, hospital personnel permitted Nick to join his parents in their frequent visits to Jamie's temporary home.

Nick began the bonding process by drawing endless pictures of automobiles to scotch tape to his brother's high-tech bassinet. When he expressed some doubts about having his brother come home, his father told him that such feelings are usual when a new baby arrives because the new baby will receive more attention for a while than an older child or children. Certainly Jamie's presence in the house would require considerably more attention than a more typical newborn would demand.

The three weeks Jamie spent in the ICU, as difficult as the separation was, afforded his parents and Nick a brief reprieve, time to learn more about Down syndrome and about caring for a Down baby, time to rent the specialized equipment they would need once Jamie came home, time to settle into the realization that their lives would be forever changed by the birth of this child.

On the day of Jamie's birth, Janet courageously announced to Michael, "This is not a stopper. We can handle this." Her attitude all along was that if a Down baby had to be born to someone, it was fortunate Jamie had been born to them. She enumerated the advantages they could offer him as parents: Janet was a registered nurse; having just completed her doctorate in English, she had been hired to teach at the University of Illinois, where her husband also taught, giving them excellent health insurance coverage; the two of them could arrange their schedules so that someone would always be at home with Jamie. Janet's optimism in the face of crushing disappointment buoyed Michael's spirits when things looked darkest to him. Their relationship deepened through their shared adversity.

Janet and Michael were, however, realistically aware of the commitment that would be required of them. The night before Jamie was scheduled to be released from the hospital and brought home, they went to the best French restaurant in town for a dinner they could ill afford, knowing that such evenings out would likely be extremely rare in their immediate future. On that evening, they also arranged to rent a summer place at Old Orchard Beach, Maine, where Janet had summered as a child. They could ill afford that extravagance, but they had to afford it to give their drastically altered lives—and Nick's young life—some semblance of normalcy.

The parts of the book that detail how these two parents coped initially with Jamie's return to their home will probably be the most instructive and encouraging to readers who themselves have a Down syndrome baby. The course of treatment they needed to follow scrupulously involved considerable lack of sleep and much uncertainty, but they survived it and, most important, Jamie lived and developed and grew into his own being. As a personality emerged from the tiny being who had lived his first weeks in a web of tubes, his parents gained hope and were thankful for his life.

Jamie's condition would have been detected had Janet undergone amniocentesis as well as having a sonogram. The prospective parents discussed the possibility of Janet's undergoing this invasive procedure but rejected the possibility, reasoning that the likelihood of having a Down syndrome baby is slight. All the other pertinent information they needed was provided by the sonogram, which is not invasive and therefore unlikely to cause a miscarriage.

Also, had Janet undergone amniocentesis, which would have revealed Jamie's condition, she and Michael would have gained little. They would not have aborted the fetus. The only difference would have been that they might have gained a little time that they could have used to teach themselves more about Down syndrome and to prepare for their baby's impending arrival.

Much of Michael Bérubé's past writing has been political. His frequent articles in *The Village Voice* have politically with pressing social issues, as have his earlier books, *Marginal Forces/Cultural Centers* (1992), *Public Access* (1994), and *Higher Education Under Fire* (1995). It is, therefore, not surprising that *Life as We Know It* is at times stridently political, focusing particularly upon governmental inaction and cutbacks in aid for handicapped people.

Bérubé points out the considerable expense involved just in the first few weeks of life for a child in Jamie's situation. His twenty-one days in the ICU, covered quite well by his parents' combined insurance benefits, cost upward of thirty thousand dollars. Such charges are not extraordinary in situations like this one and, as Bérubé notes, not many people have the combined insurance benefits that he and his wife have.

Bérubé also comments on the discomfort that medical people have in dealing with situations such as the one his family faced. The obstetrician who delivered Jamie never again visited with the parents. Bérubé speculates that she felt somehow responsible for Jamie's condition or feared that the parents might blame—perhaps even sue—her.

In situations like this there is more than enough guilt to go around. Bérubé tells of how Janet, during one dark moment, feared that she was somehow responsible for Jamie's condition because she bent over a computer for hours during her pregnancy, rushing to complete her doctoral dissertation before she had to face the demands of mothering a new baby. Rock-solid emotionally, Janet enjoyed no exemption from dark moments, from bleak periods about facing the future with Jamie.

Despite its subject, *Life as We Know It* is an upbeat book written by a man of admirable strength, courage, and compassion. In a way, the book was co-written by Janet Lyon because, although Michael did the actual composing, everything the book touches on was a joint effort. Janet and Michael are both pillars of strength supporting a temple of love. Within that temple dwells a child who, but for having parents like them, might have landed on humanity's trash heap.

R. Baird Shuman

Sources for Further Study

Boston Globe. October 13, 1996, p. N16.
Kirkus Reviews. LXIV, August 1, 1996, p. 1112.
Library Journal. CXXI, August, 1996, p. 100.
Los Angeles Times Book Review. October 27, 1996, p. 10.
The Nation. CCLXIII, October 28, 1996, p. 30.
The New York Times Book Review. CI, October 27, 1996, p. 22.
Publishers Weekly. CCXLIII, August 26, 1996, p. 82.
The Washington Post. October 14, 1996, p. D2.

LIFE OF A POET
Rainer Maria Rilke

Author: Ralph Freedman (1920-   )
Publisher: Farrar Straus Giroux (New York). Illustrated. 640 pp. $35.00
Type of work: Literary biography
Time: 1875-1926
Locale: Europe

Freedman combines a detailed narrative of the great German poet's life with an intimate reading of his work

> *Principal personages:*
> RAINER MARIA RILKE, a German poet
> LOU ANDREAS-SALOMÉ, a writer, his Russian-born lover and lifelong friend
> CLARA WESTHOFF, the sculptor who became his wife
> PAULA MODERSOHN-BECKER, an artist and close friend
> PRINCESS MARIE VON THURN UND TAXIS, his patron
> AUGUSTE RODIN, a famous French sculptor
> BALADINE (ELISABETH KLOSSOWSKA), an artist and Rilke's lover

The reader seeking a brief overview of Rilke's life or a succinct evaluation of his work will be disappointed. *Life of a Poet: Rainer Maria Rilke* is a ponderous book, but for the scholar or student of this acclaimed poet, well worth the reading. Ralph Freedman fleshes out his portrait of Rilke by a steady accretion of details, resulting in a remarkably dispassionate view of this complex man.

Freedman, professor emeritus of Comparative Literature at Princeton University, is an obvious admirer of Rilke's work. This book, a labor of love, was initiated by a 1980 Guggenheim Fellowship and took more than fifteen years to complete. The synthesis that Freedman employs is impressive, interweaving events of the poet's life with excerpts from his letters, poetry, and prose.

Translating Rilke seems to be an industry in itself; there is no standard English version of his work. Freedman offers his own translation of the prose and adds a striking new verse translation by Helen Sword, "There stands death, a bluish residue/ in a teacup without a saucer." The book contains a number of portraits by Rilke's artist friends, as well as photographs of family, friends, and places he lived.

Rilke was a man of contradictions. He was largely anti-Semitic, yet he had Jewish friends and was attracted to Jewish women. He felt the need to travel, yet once at his destination he longed to return. He acquired friends and lovers when convenient and dropped them when he had no further use for them. He visited wealthy patrons and charmed their guests. Many were faithful to his needs, opened their homes to him, and gave him money, yet he demanded more.

Some details of his life are familiar. In a world where one's nationality was determined by heritage, not by birthplace, he was a German, although born in Prague, Czechoslovakia, which in 1875 was part of the Austro-Hungarian Empire. Christened

René Karl Wilhelm Johann Josef Maria Rilke, he was dressed in girls' clothing by his mother until he was ready to go to school. At ten, in accordance with his father's wishes, he was sent to a military academy near Vienna, where he was thoroughly miserable. During this time he developed migraine headaches, unexplained fevers, and depression, all of which would recur throughout his life. A victim of mood swings, he may well have suffered from a form of bipolar disorder.

Rilke left military school under questionable circumstances, having made clear that military life was not for him. Financed by a well-to-do uncle (basically for the rest of his life), he made a pretense of studying but had really decided, encouraged by his mother, to become a poet. He was not particularly adept to start with, but he made connections in the literary world and shamelessly sought support for his work. His writing was sporadic, with long dry spells.

Rilke envisioned himself as a footloose poet, a wanderer who always had difficulty remaining in one place. "For staying is nowhere," he wrote, expressing his fear of being trapped by love or commitment. Freedman attributes Rilke's attitude in part to a statement made by his mentor, French sculptor Auguste Rodin: "One must work, only work." Everything must be sacrificed for the sake of art.

Freedman believes that Rodin and the Russian writer Leo Tolstoy served as Rilke's surrogate fathers. Tolstoy disappointed Rilke by largely ignoring him in favor of his companion, Lou Andreas-Salomé; Rodin alternately inspired and rejected him in a long and sometimes troubled relationship. Freedman also views Lou—fourteen years Rilke's senior, married, and a former lover of philosopher Friedrich Nietzsche—and his patron Princess Marie von Thurn und Taxis as surrogate mothers. It was Lou who convinced him to change his name from René to the German form, Rainer. Although most other biographers discount the story, Freedman also suggests that Lou became pregnant by Rilke in 1898, with a resultant abortion, although she later denied it. Together with her and her husband, Rilke visited Russia, a land that inspired much of his early writing, including the three-part *Das Stundenbuch* (1905; *The Book of Hours*, 1941). Rilke always insisted that Lou was the only person who understood him, and even after they had ceased being lovers, she remained his friend until his death.

Freedman also suggests a more significant relationship between Rilke and the painter Paula Modersohn-Becker than is generally accepted. Paula was a close friend of Rilke's future wife, Clara Westhoff, at the artists' colony of Worpswede in northern Germany, but he seemed to make little distinction between them, courting them both. Apparently Clara became pregnant; the die was cast, and Rilke married her in 1901. He distanced himself from Paula as she prepared for marriage with artist Otto Modersohn. The Rilkes lived together less than a year and then engaged in what Freedman calls a "marriage by correspondence" when he moved alone to Paris to meet Rodin, the sculptor with whom Clara had studied. Rilke's subsequent monograph and lectures on Rodin would make him famous.

Yet his uneasy relationship with Paula continued. In 1903, Paula left her husband to pursue her career in Paris. She hoped to make this separation permanent; it gave her freedom to paint. She was alone, largely destitute, and very happy. Her relationship with Rilke was friendly and helpful to both; during her most fruitful period in 1906, Paula began the unfinished portrait of him that appears on the book's dust jacket. Only when friends convinced her she could not support herself did she reconcile unwillingly with her husband and yield to his demand for a child.

Rilke originally intended his "Requiem für eine Freundin" (1909; "Requiem for a Friend," 1935) to mark her symbolic death as an artist, but his poem gained new significance after Paula's actual death of a childbirth-related embolism. He was stunned by the unforgiving link between sexuality and death epitomized by Paula's life. At the same time, he appeared to have little concern for the fate of his sculptor-wife or their baby daughter. Religious considerations prevented the divorce they both sought.

Princess Marie von Thurn und Taxis, though not his only patron, was one of the most significant. She not only offered him money and a place to stay but also put her ancestral Duino Castle at his disposal, the site where, in 1912, he began his mature work, the great *Duineser Elegien* (1923; *Duino Elegies*, 1930).

Drafted briefly during World War I, Rilke found himself attracted to left-wing causes in postwar Munich. For his own safety, he was urged to leave Germany by his publisher. He settled in Switzerland, where he continued to write. Germany's inflation lessened his income from publishing, and he had to depend even more on the kindness of wealthy admirers.

The artist Baladine encouraged him to remain in Switzerland and inspired him to write the French poems of *Les Fenêtres* (*Windows*), published posthumously in 1927, along with her drawings. In 1920, Rilke found himself, as always, torn between physical love and the need to write. As he had with Clara, he announced that he preferred the "nonpossessive love" of separation, but he could not give up Baladine completely. Over the next six years, they were together at Rilke's country home of Muzot and apart, depending on his whims. Often she was relegated to the status of his cook and housekeeper. In his letters, he still refused to address her with the familiar French *tu*.

Eventually Rilke developed mouth ulcers and abscesses, the unrecognized symptoms of leukemia. As his health declined, he began a series of cures at various sanitoriums. His death was hastened when, after he had picked roses to impress a beautiful woman, a wound from a thorn became severely infected. His illness was correctly diagnosed shortly after his fifty-first birthday, and he died two and a half weeks later, his skin covered with black blisters, on December 29, 1926. As Rilke once said on learning of a friend's death, "How dangerous life is and how pitiless up to the last moment."

A major problem with this fine biography is that Freedman assumes a great deal on the part of the reader. To someone who has no prior knowledge of Rilke or other names in European arts and letters, *Life of a Poet* is difficult to read. Too many scholarly details tend to obscure the man himself. One may see the trees but not the surrounding forest.

Rilke knew literally hundreds of people; he had many patrons and an inordinate number of lovers. An initial reading does not suggest who will prove to be of major significance in his life and who will disappear after a page. Some names are mentioned once and never repeated, or a reference is made to someone who will not be heard of again for a hundred pages. For the reader new to this milieu, the book is rather like a Russian novel, involving a desperate memorization of names.

Place names can also create problems. For example, Worpswede and Westerwede are easily confused by one unfamiliar with the German landscape. Definitions can be delayed. When Freedman first refers to the Angel of the *Duino Elegies,* he does not identify this figure for six pages. There are occasional lapses of syntax "The elegy became the form to adapt this view of women as bearers of an inevitable fate to an increasingly cosmic vision"—a difficult sentence to untangle even in context. If this book was a labor of love for the author, it may be a labor of love for the reader as well.

On the other hand, and most important for a biographer, Freedman is unerringly fair in his treatment of Rilke, presenting his life objectively. To thus present a man whose personal relationships were largely self-serving, whose manipulation of others was continuous and obvious, is the epitome of restraint. Rilke was indeed a great poet, as his work testifies, but he was a sad excuse for a human being, a charming hypochondriac with no concept of the value of money, dependent on others to furnish it for him. He adopted a fatherly interest in attractive young women but was a wretched father to his own daughter, admitting to a friend that he was more comfortable around dogs. Freedman's only judgment on the man appears on the book's final page "His life was no model."

Joanne McCarthy

Sources for Further Study

The Atlantic. CCLXXVII, April, 1996, p. 112.
Booklist. XCII, January 1, 1996, p. 777.
Chicago Tribune. May 5, 1996, XIV, p. 6.
Library Journal. CXX, December, 1995, p. 108.
The Nation. CCLXII, April 1, 1996, p. 27.
The New Republic. CCXV, July 1, 1996, p. 32.
The New York Times Book Review. CI, April 28, 1996, p. 16.
Publishers Weekly. CCXLIII, January 8, 1996, p. 51.
The Wall Street Journal. March 19, 1996, p. A16.
The Washington Post Book World. XXVI, March 31, 1996, p. 5.

THE LIFE OF NELSON A. ROCKEFELLER
Worlds to Conquer, 1908-1958

Author: Cary Reich
Publisher: Doubleday (New York). Illustrated. 875 pp. $35.00
Type of work: Biography
Time: 1908-1958
Locale: Primarily the United States

An engaging account of the early career of a major American political figure

> *Principal personages:*
> NELSON A. ROCKEFELLER, businessman and public servant
> JOHN D. ROCKEFELLER, Jr., his father
> ABBY ALDRICH ROCKEFELLER, his mother
> MARY TODHUNTER CLARK ROCKEFELLER, his wife

The first volume in a projected two-volume series, Cary Reich's *The Life of Nelson Rockefeller: Worlds to Conquer, 1908-1958* is a splendid account of the early career of one of the most colorful figures in American history. Although memories of Rockefeller are dimming in the 1990's, he was once a fixture on the political landscape. Rockefeller was elected governor of New York for four consecutive terms in an era in which governors of the Empire State were routinely considered contenders for the presidency. Yet Rockefeller did not need the shades of Franklin Delano Roosevelt and Thomas Dewey to urge him forward. His ambitions, like his appetites, were legendary. He sought the Republican presidential nomination three times—in 1960, 1964, and 1968—only to be denied each time. Ironically, given the range of his aspirations, Rockefeller's career culminated in a two-year stint as vice president in Gerald Ford's lame duck administration.

It was Nelson Rockefeller's misfortune to become the standard bearer of liberal Republicanism at a time when the Republican Party was embracing an increasing conservatism. As governor of New York, Rockefeller compiled a record that many Democrats would have envied. He self-consciously set out to change the face of his state and instigated an enormous amount of construction, building more than forty university campuses, dozens of medical facilities, and thousands of miles of highways. No governor of New York ever built as much or on such a scale as "Rocky." He was equally expansive in granting entitlements. At one point, forty-five percent of New York residents were covered by Medicaid. Yet Rockefeller's imperial style, at once grand and generous, came at a steep price. Soon after he left Albany, the state of New York was facing a credit crisis and New York City was on the brink of bankruptcy. Although he was a sincere Republican, socially conservative and resolute in his insistence on law and order, Rockefeller nevertheless embodied the faith in big government and social intervention which infuriated the rising right wing of the GOP. A man of Rockefeller's instincts could only be confounded by the fervor of the Goldwater crusade of 1964 and Richard Nixon's shrewd and cynical crusade of the "silent majority." The man of the future in the Republican Party of the 1960's was not to be Nelson Rockefeller, but another governor on the opposite coast—Ronald Reagan of California.

Nelson Rockefeller was not fated to lead his country into the last quarter of the twentieth century. Perhaps that was just as well. He was not a man suited to deal with a time of limits, of economic dislocation and moral confusion. Rockefeller was too quintessentially a product of an earlier, more ebullient era. Some men are said to be born ahead of their time. A few are thought to have been born too late to flourish fully. The younger Nelson Rockefeller was perfectly adapted to his era, the middle decades of the century. He was perfectly suited to the rhythms of an industrialized and urbanizing America. His was a streamlined spirit made for a streamlined age. Rockefeller loved speed, and he loved machines. He also wanted his machines to move fast, whether they were automobiles, boats, or planes. He enthusiastically embraced modernism in the arts, building a world-class collection of modern art and helping found New York's Museum of Modern Art (MOMA). As impresario of Rockefeller Center in New York City, he made his contribution to the skyscraper landscape of modern America. Although Rockefeller owned the rich man's obligatory rural retreats, it was in the city, especially New York City, that he was truly at home.

From first to last, Nelson Rockefeller was a New Yorker, and he prospered in the years when New York City stood closer to the heart of American life, symbol in stone and steel of the "American Century." Both privately and publicly, Rockefeller represented the self-confident ethos of the United States during World War II and its aftermath, when America first assumed the mantle of "leader of the free world" and commentators invoked visions of a "Pax Americana." Throughout his career, Nelson Rockefeller refused to recognize bounds. He sincerely believed that any challenge could be surmounted, and in this he mirrored the expectations of a people buoyed by unparalleled power and affluence. His reckless expenditures on bricks and mortar in New York State was at one with such contemporary endeavors as the War on Poverty and the race to put a man on the moon. Indeed, Johann Wolfgang von Goethe's generous biographical maxim could be applied to Nelson Rockefeller—his virtues were his own; his sins were those of his age.

Rockefeller's affinity for his times is not surprising. He was born into a cradle of the historical forces shaping modern America. His mother, Abby Aldrich Rockefeller, was the daughter of Senator Nelson Aldrich of Rhode Island, the czar of the U.S. Senate in the first decade of the twentieth century and a staunch defender of the great trusts and industrial combines that were reshaping America's economic and social landscape. His father, John D. Rockefeller, Jr., was the son and namesake of John D. Rockefeller who founded Standard Oil and had been one of the most infamous "robber barons" of the Gilded Age. Nelson Rockefeller thus inherited a legacy, memorialized through both his names, at once potent and ambiguous. Throughout his life, he would enjoy the multitudinous advantages available to a scion of one of the first families of the nation. At the same time, he would have to wrestle with the American public's jaundiced impression that of the origins of that fortune as well as their suspicions that he was simply the pampered product of luxury, rather than a man worthy of respect in his own right.

Rockefeller's parents, and especially his father, were anxious that their progeny not be spoiled by the wealth that surrounded them. The children were given small allowances and had to work for any extra spending money. They were expected to keep detailed records of their expenditures, and these were examined by their father every Sunday morning. The Rockefeller household was governed by a strict sense of Baptist rectitude. Such pastimes as card-playing, dancing, and attending the theater were prohibited. Nelson Rockefeller's upbringing was distinctive in other ways as well. He missed the usual male aristocrat's educational path of boarding school followed by attendance at Harvard or Yale. Instead, his father sent him to an experimental school in New York and then on to Dartmouth College, a school in those days better known for its athletic bonhomie than its intellectual force. Rockefeller's educational accomplishments were limited by his high spirits and a severe dyslexia, which would make reading difficult for him for his entire life.

Upon graduation from Dartmouth in 1930, Nelson Rockefeller faced a decision about what to do with his life. The Rockefeller family no longer ran Standard Oil. In fact, his father had been working for years to refashion the image of the family by directing the mighty Rockefeller Foundation and other philanthropic institutions. His father expected Nelson to join him in administering the family's far-flung benevolent empire. Nelson, however, did not want simply to follow in his father's footsteps. He set his sights on Rockefeller Center, the huge complex of office towers and theaters the Rockefeller family was building in midtown Manhattan. He embraced the project with a will and began by attracting tenants to the center at the height of the Great Depression. Once he had learned what he needed to know, he maneuvered himself into control of the project. Yet Rockefeller Center, vast as it was, could not contain his energies and ambitions. Possessed of unusual dynamism and blessed with the quality of staff ample money could buy, Nelson Rockefeller always involved himself in more than one activity at a time. Even as he was winning command of Rockefeller Center, he was, among other things, involved in the fledgling Museum of Modern Art and waging a bitter political struggle at his children's school.

Rockefeller had long been fascinated by Latin America, and traveled there extensively in the late 1930's. He began to see the southern hemisphere as a fertile field for Rockefeller philanthropy. Possibilities for stimulating economic development in the region excited him. Rockefeller launched his first Latin American project in 1939, investing heavily in Venezuela. Rockefeller's interest in South and Central America came at a crucial juncture. World War II was underway, and officials in Franklin Roosevelt's administration were deeply concerned about German and Italian activities in a number of Latin American states. Aware of these concerns and increasingly intrigued by the idea of entering government service, Rockefeller began cultivating well-placed contacts in Washington and offered a series of suggestions for countering Axis influence in Latin America. The upshot of Rockefeller's labors came in 1940, with an appointment by Franklin Roosevelt to head a new agency, that of the

Coordinator of Inter American Affairs, charged with choreographing American initiatives to woo Latin American support. Here Nelson Rockefeller would spend most of the war years, breathing life into Franklin Roosevelt's Good Neighbor policy, carrying on the struggle against the Axis through a variety of means, ranging from economic deals to a massive propaganda campaign, which deluged Latin America with American magazines and motion pictures. His effort won him intense support from Latin American leaders, who appreciated his enthusiasm and understanding. His work as coordinator also earned him appointment as assistant secretary of state for Latin American affairs in December, 1944. As assistant secretary, Rockefeller played a key role at the founding of the United Nations in May, 1945. Effectively controlling the Latin American vote, he caused controversy and threatened to wreck the conference over his support for the inclusion of Axis-leaning Argentina. Anxious to promote inter-American unity, he also insisted on a clause allowing regional security pacts. Disputed at the time, Article 51 of the United Nations Charter would later make possible the international recognition of such institutions as the North Atlantic Treaty Organization (NATO).

Soon after this, Rockefeller was asked to resign, as President Harry Truman reorganized the State Department. Several frustrating years out of government ensued. Rockefeller busied himself with various projects, including new development ventures in Brazil and Venezuela. He became an enthusiastic and vocal backer of President Truman's Point Four plan, which called for the United States to aid the developing world with scientific and technical assistance. Rockefeller even rejoined the administration in 1950 as an adviser to the president on implementing the plan, but he left in frustration the next year when he realized that a combination of congressional and bureaucratic opposition would prevent the plan from living up to its potential.

Rockefeller early on supported Dwight D. Eisenhower's bid for the presidency, and was rewarded for his services in the 1952 campaign by being named undersecretary of the Department of Health, Education, and Welfare (HEW). Rockefeller loyally worked for the new HEW Secretary Oveta Culp Hobby, but he was only waiting for a chance at a job dealing with international relations. He got his opportunity in late 1954, when he secured an appointment as the special assistant to the president for psychological warfare. In this position, Rockefeller pondered the complexities of the Cold War and mulled over ways to counteract Soviet propaganda. His great moment came at the 1955 Geneva Summit, when he persuaded President Eisenhower to make his famous "open skies" proposal, which confounded the Soviets with a plan for mutual aerial inspections of nuclear weapons sites. Yet Rockefeller's glory was short-lived. Bureaucratic jealousies, centered especially in the State Department, drove him from the government by the end of the year.

Rockefeller would continue to do odd jobs for Eisenhower, including sponsoring a study on American nuclear strategy which would begin an important association with Henry Kissinger. At this point, however, his career took a different direction. Having been rebuffed again in Washington, Rockefeller began listening to the blandishments of friends in New York State, who saw him as an excellent candidate for governor. He threw his hat into the ring, and proved himself a formidable campaigner, displaying a common touch with voters that was unexpected from a multimillionaire. In 1958, he bucked a general Democratic trend and carried the New York gubernatorial race by a healthy majority.

Reich's book ends on that election night, with Nelson Rockefeller triumphant, the grandson of the old robber baron vindicated by popular vote. Superbly researched and elegantly written, this biography when completed will be a major contribution to modern American political history. It is also a fitting monument to a man who accomplished much, and dreamed of doing more.

Daniel P. Murphy

Sources for Further Study

Booklist. XCIII, October 1, 1996, p. 320.
Boston Globe. November 5, 1996, p. C3.
Houston Chronicle. December 8, 1996, p. Z29.
Library Journal. CXXI, October 1, 1996, p. 92.
The New York Times Book Review. CI, November 3, 1996, p. 10.
Publishers Weekly. CCXLIII, September 2, 1996, p. 99.
San Francisco Chronicle. November 17, 1996, p. REV1.
The Wall Street Journal. October 31, 1996, p. A21.
The Washington Post Book World. XXVI, December 1, 1996, p. 1.